The Definitive History of World Championship Boxing
Super Middleweight to Heavyweight
By Barry J. Hugman

Published by G2 Entertainment Ltd
© Barry J. Hugman 2016

All rights reserved. No part of this publication may be reproduced, stored in a retrieval system, or transmitted in any form by any means, electronic, mechanical, photocopying, recording or otherwise, without the prior permission of the publishers.

Every effort has been made to ensure the accuracy of the information within this publication but the publishers cannot be held responsible for any errors or omissions. Views expressed are those of the author and do not necessarily represent those of the publishers.

Author: Barry J. Hugman
http://tiny.cc/2r16gy
Editor: Sean Willis
Cover Design: Paul Briggs (twocan.co.uk)
Publishers: Edward Adams and Jules Gammond
Printed in the UK & USA

Contents

4	Acknowledgements
6	Introduction
12	Super Middleweight – Fight Summaries
63	Super Middleweight – Boxers' Index
66	Light Heavyweight – Fight Summaries
171	Light Heavyweight – Boxers' Index
177	Cruiserweight – Fight Summaries
221	Cruiserweight – Boxers' Index
224	Heavyweight – Fight Summaries
345	Heavyweight – Boxers' Index

Acknowledgements

I dedicate this work to my Mother and Father who gave me an excellent start in life. It was this that enabled me to pursue my dreams, one of them being boxing, both inside and outside the ring.

After working on this project since the late 1980s and having quickly realised that listings of world title fights did not add up in many cases, I have decided to go into print and set the record straight. It has been a mammoth task, and one which I couldn't have achieved on my own.

Once I had analysed the work of Harold Alderman MBE, who has made a 60-year study of British boxing and had recorded much of what he found, I realised that this was the missing piece of the jigsaw. Harold is *the* foremost expert on English championship boxing which took place between 1870 and 1909. He is also a walking mine of boxing information, having been involved in the sport for as long as he can remember. As a young schoolboy boxer he had aspirations of eventually turning pro, but unfortunately poor eyesight meant that he had to give the game up. A longstanding member of London Ex-Boxers' Association and other ex-boxers' associations, as well as being a member of the American-based International Boxing Records Organisation, over the years he has also helped family members with information relating to their boxing fathers.

I first met Sean Willis, a passionate editor of sports books as well as occasional author, towards the end of 2015 at which point I shared the outline of this labour of love with him. He embraced my vision and has worked alongside myself, tirelessly and enthusiastically for many months in editing this unique and comprehensive boxing tome, without once throwing the towel in.

Tracy Callis, of the International Boxing Record Organisation, has helped no end with information on the heavyweight and middleweight divisions, especially 'black titles', and is a hugely valued researcher.

Luckett Davis, who is recognised as one of the leading record compilers and co-ordinators in America, gave me much help in having a greater understanding of how boxing was in the early days in America providing key data prior to my many visits to American libraries in the 1990s.

John Sheppard, of BoxRec (boxrec.com), also deserves a big thank you for setting up a website totally immersed in boxers' records, both past and present. With it expanding by the minute it has become the largest boxing website in the world and is used by all involved in the sport as well as those who have an interest. In short, anyone who reads this must make a point of visiting it.

Other people who have helped in no small way include those listed below:

Mike Attree	Charles Johnston	David Roake
Paul Baumgartner	Ove Jonassen	Hy Rosenberg
Joseph Brower	Ric Kilmer	John Sheppard
Les Clark	Jack Kincaid	Ron Silverberg
Mike Delisa	Joe Koizumi	Kevin Smith
Mike Featherstone	Tim Leone	Bob Soderman
Christer Franzen	Ruth Lewis	Mike Sweeney
Tony Gee	Arne Leyenberg	Matt Tegan
Herb Goldman	Andrew Lindsay	Miles Templeton
Jose Luis Gomez Camarillo	Bill Matthews	Daniel Van de Wiele
Elio Guzman	Derek O'Dell	Bob Yalen
Peter Hatton	Perry Palumbo	Robert Young
John Hogg	Jeffrey Pamungkas	Paul Zabala
Jennifer Hugman	Gary Phillips	
Raymond Hugman	John Redfern	

Acknowledgements

Jean Adkins & Sherie Brown (Massillon Public Library)
Mary Beveridge (Missouri Valley Special Collections)
Don Bonsteel (Enoch Pratt Free Library, Baltimore)
Mary Piero Carey (Stark County District Library, Canton, Ohio)
Linda Chapman (Allen County Public Library, Indiana)
Janice Collins (West Palm Beach Public Library)
Marc D'Houre/Wim De Troyer (Bibliotheque Royal de Belgique)
Debra Dixon (San Diego LB, California)
Terri Dood (Bozeman Public Library)
Anna Fahey-Flynn and Patricia Feeley (Boston Public Library)
Wendy Flourno (Library of Michigan)
Natalie Fritz (Clark County Historical Society)
Ellen Gamache, Katie Quinn, Virginia Marcellus (Albany Public Library)
Michael Gillman (Sacramento Public Library)
Varney Greene (Buffalo & Erie County Public Library)
Cathy Hackett (Clark County Public Library, Springfield, Ohio)
Richard Hill (State Library of Pennsylvania)
Lynn Humphries (Sheffield Central Library, UK)
Judy James (Akron Public Library)
Cara Janowski (New York State Library)
Paula Kepich (Carnegie Library)
June Kofi (Brooklyn Public Library)
Katherine LaBarbera & Gayle Camarda (St Louis Public Library)
Ronald Lee (Tennessee State Library)
Lauren Leeman (State Historical Society of Missouri)
Bonnie Linck & Marcia Matika (Connecticut State Library)
Margot McCain (Portland Public Library)
Sara McKinley (Muncie Public Library)
Bill Markley (Georgia Historical Society)
Janet Meek (Indiana State Library)
Michelle Mellor (Youngstown Public Library)
David Mook (Sioux City Public Library)
Karen Myers (Mullins Library)
Phil Panum (Denver Public Library)
Gloriane Peck (Library of Michigan)
Ann Poulos & Mark Sweberg (Providence Public Library)
Janice Prater (Denver Public Library)
Marianne Reynolds & Arlene Belletire (Cincinnati Public Library)
Hope Rider (Arkansas State Library)
Jeanne Sanchez (Wyoming State Public Library)
John Sheppard (BoxRec.com)
Dr Skelton-Foord & Brian Hough (British Newspaper Library)
David Smith (New York Public Library)
Hampton Smith (Minnesota Historical Society)
Sarah Striner, Georgie Higley & Frank Carroll (Library of Congress, Washington DC)
Louise Talbott (Akron-Summit County Public Library)
Pat Watson (New Britain Public Library)
Melissa Williams & Sally Freaney (Public Library of Youngstown & Mahoning County)
Melissa Whitesell (Terre Haute Public Library)
Julie Zachau (Superior Public Library)

Introduction

Having spent many years researching the history of world championship boxing from the start of gloves (1871 to date), I am delighted to present my extensive findings in the shape of these four volumes.

The Definitive History of World Championship Boxing - Mini Fly to Bantam.
The Definitive History of World Championship Boxing - Junior Feather to Light.
The Definitive History of World Championship Boxing - Junior Welter to Middle.
The Definitive History of World Championship Boxing - Super Middle to Heavy.

This work came about due to limited information on world title fights being available when I was growing up, it becoming clearer to me each year that the record books of the day were merely scratching the surface. After discovering that boxing with gloves had started in Britain I could not understand why the majority of fights happened in America according to the record books, especially as some of the great fighters of the 1880s fighting in America were born in Britain, such as Nonpareil Jack Dempsey and Jack McAuliffe. I was already convinced that many of the contests recorded in the listings prior to the early 1900s were American title bouts only. Thus I began my research.

Years later, as the editor of the British Boxing Board of Control (BBBoC) British Boxing Yearbook, I was introduced to Harold Alderman MBE who told me that, starting in the 1960s, he had documented all of the contests of note that had taken place in Britain since the early 1870s. I had already done much research of my own on boxing in Britain, Europe, the Commonwealth and America, visiting many libraries around the world, and Harold's input was the missing link. Once the British (then known as the English) championship contests, winners and claimants at every two pounds had been built in everything came together.

Wherever possible, all of the leading fighters down the years since the early 1870s have had their known records analysed and cross referenced against thousands of newspapers and magazines in order to find the weight that their prime contests were made at. This exercise also led to many more claimants and contests being discovered.

There is a fight summary for all of the championship contests that are listed within these pages. All are shown in chronological order within their respective weight divisions by date, weight, result, scheduled rounds, venue, recognition, referee (if known) and scorecards. In the days leading up to 'modern day' boxing, when there were fewer recognised weight divisions and therefore a wider range of weights within each division, I have detailed the stipulated fight weight (shown in brackets) after the fight date. Therefore there are many 'claimants' at varying weights within each division at any given time. From thereon in use 'Recognition' to follow the body in question's champions, as well as relative information. Because the term 'Junior' was the original name used to determine recently added weight divisions, I have continued in that vein rather than using the term 'Super'.

Historical Background

After going from 'bare-knuckle fighting' under London Prize Ring Rules to 'boxing with gloves' under Marquess of Queensberry Rules (MoQ Rules), the sport of boxing gradually found its way to North America and Australia by the 1880s. The Marquess of Queensberry Rules had been established in 1867, whilst London Prize Ring Rules were developed in 1838 by the London-based Pugilistic Society, being revised in 1853 and 1866. They had replaced the Broughton's Rules of 1743.

While hard and skin-tight gloves were more often than not used in America prior to the 1890s, in Britain it was far more acceptable, especially in clubs, to use gloves weighing no less than two ounces and up to eight ounces right from the beginning. Bare-knuckle fights are not covered within these pages.

Some of the men who were classified as champions in the days before proper regulation are now viewed as 'claimants', unless stated otherwise, as they were not officially recognised and gained their reputation purely through newspaper support. You only have to view the number of men claiming a title at the same weight at the same time to see the chaos. Even in America it was difficult to decide on a champion, and much of what has been printed in the following years has been selective to make things look black and white. On top of that the main men in Britain, who rarely met their American counterparts due to the amount of travelling required, had as much right to claim the British version of the world title if the fights could not be made. Because of this I have shown many of the English championship winners and claimants as having a share of the world title prior to the National Sporting Club (NSC) introducing the eight named weight divisions on 11 February 1909. With the English championships being phased out from that date, from thereon in only men recognised throughout Britain as having a strong claim to the world title are recorded.

In the early part of the 20th Century in much of America, when no-decision and short distance bouts kept boxing alive due to those of endurance being banned, because it was impossible to know whether a title claimant was contractually protected or not I have gone with the weights shown in the press. In those days contractual conditions would barely have mattered if a claimant was beaten inside the distance. A good example of this came when George Chip claimed the American version of the world middleweight title in 1913 after twice stopping Frank Klaus in six-round no-decision contests, despite neither man weighing inside the generally accepted American middleweight limit of 158lbs.

At the start of gloved fighting although certain named weight classes were already recognised, such as bantam, feather, light, middle and heavy, men in Britain generally claimed what was then known as the English title at every two pounds within those loosely defined weight bands. Welter (1887) was the next to arrive followed by light heavy (1899) and fly (1909), prior to junior light (1921), junior welter (1923), junior middle (1962), junior fly (1975), junior feather (1976), cruiser (1979), junior bantam (1980), super middle (1984) and mini fly (1987) becoming established at later dates.

Because there were many variations in the weight limits between Britain and America in the early days, I have gone with what was generally perceived by those running the sport in Britain at the start of boxing - bantam (116lbs), Feather (126lbs), Light (140lbs), Middle (166lbs) and Heavy (166lbs+). The middleweight limit of 166lbs includes those fighting at catchweights between 160 and 166lbs who were too small for the heavyweights. With the advent of new weight classes, and in certain cases where great fighters moved up in weight and were seen by the majority of the press to have taken their named title with them, as in the case of Young Corbett at featherweight, I have massaged the weight divisions accordingly until we enter the modern era.

In hastening the demise of the every two-pounds English championships, on 11 February 1909 the NSC in London stipulated that there should be eight named weight classes governing British boxing - Fly (112lbs), Bantam (118lbs), Feather (126lbs), Light (135lbs), Welter (147lbs), Middle (160lbs), Light heavy (175lbs) and Heavy (175lbs+). With fights held in Britain, the British Empire and Europe, I have gone with those weights from that date. For the same period, and falling in line with those running boxing in America, I have taken the American weight classes to be 116lbs for Bantam, 122lbs for Feather, 133lbs for Light, 142/145lbs for Welter and 158lbs for Middle. By 1920 all the weight class limits had been standardised and are reflected as such within the listings.

With regard to weights in the days before tighter regulation, without contractual knowledge I have gone with what was reported in newspapers. In many cases I discovered that fighters weighed-in according to contract and that the weights announced were those at ringside, which would, in most cases, have been heavier. This has made it extremely difficult to ascertain whether title claims were on the line or not. However, when in doubt I have built those fights into the text. In America at the early part of the 20th Century, especially in New York, weights reported were nearly always those taken at ringside immediately prior to the fight. I have ignored those weights if contracts called for a stipulated weigh-in time.

Fight Summary and General Text

Reports on all selected fights are given, using at least two different newspapers in order to eradicate inaccuracies. I have used many miscellaneous worldwide newspapers since 1871, including Britain's *Sporting Life* and *Mirror of Life*, and more recently *Boxing News* and *The Ring* magazine. The internet's *YouTube* was more than useful when trying to find better information, even for some fights that took place years ago. Using a précis format I have tried to give one a general idea of how any fight in question went in general, as well as mentioning cut eyes, knockdowns and stance, if a southpaw. I have also tried to produce it in a way that fight fans readily understand.

All title fights involving 'second tier' (called 'regular' champions by commissions who have got a 'super' champion in place) and 'interim' champions are shown within the text. For my purposes, 'super' champions take precedence over 'second tier' champions for obvious reasons. Details regarding those handed 'emeritus' status, which is a lifetime award issued by the WBC to top-class champions who are retiring or cannot defend their title for whatever reason, are also shown in the text. If such a champion returns to the ring he may request an immediate challenge to a WBC world champion without first boxing in an elimination contest. The WBA's term 'champion in recess' effectively serves the same purpose. Where an 'interim' champion moves on to contest the main title the 'interim' title is automatically declared vacant.

If the IBF, WBA, WBC or WBO fail to accept a title fight for whatever reason but continue to recognise the champion involved, I have left the general status intact while making note of their reasoning within the text. This tends to happen when a challenger is not seen as a worthy opponent. If a title changes hands under these circumstances the body concerned would either recognise the winner or declare their portion of the title vacant.

Fights of less than ten rounds duration, including no-decision affairs, are not included as championship contests, other than when a title claim changed hands. They are, however, shown within the text where a risk is involved, which would have come about when a claimant allowed his opponent to make the weight that he was claiming a title at, whether he did so or not. Also shown in the text, are 'black title' fights, politics, fights leading to championship bouts where applicable, eliminators, and information for all champions who forfeited or relinquished their titles or claims.

The term 'modern day boxing' used within these pages relates to when weights in all weight divisions other than heavyweight were standardised, ie 1920. Regarding the heavyweight division, I have taken the Jack Johnson v Tommy Burns fight in 1908 to be the first of the modern era, as it was the first time a black man fought for what was generally recognised by the great majority as the World title.

'Black title' bouts are shown specifically because of the 'Colour Bar' being in place in America at the start of boxing. Not only did many States ban mixed matches, but many 'white champions' used it as an excuse to avoid meeting top black fighters. However, despite black champions and their 'title fights' not being officially recognised in the United States I have included instances of fights and boxers that warrant mention on the grounds of the undoubted abilities of the black boxers concerned, who were never given the chance to officially prove their skills and prowess in the ring against white opponents. A great number of black men suffered, which was exacerbated during and after Jack Johnson's title reign, and it was not until Joe Louis became heavyweight champion that things began to settle down and laws changed. Even in the 1940s there were 'black title' fights, but these champions were not ignored as in the past.

English championship tournaments, normally contested between three and six rounds, along with other tournaments where a title claim emanated from the winner are spelt out within the text. It was boxing in this format that allowed matches to take place in Britain prior to the 1900s when finish fights were deemed to be illegal. Many of these tournaments were governed by Amateur Boxing Association (ABA) rules, and because there were so many contests involved I have selected those that backed up leading fighters' claims.

Additional contests and other data, including dates by day/month, that have been built into the text of a title fight belong to the same year and the same weight unless stated otherwise.

Also built into the text are all the top-five rated fighters according to *The Ring* magazine rankings between May 1928 and March 1989 who do not show up in championship contests. I have not gone beyond that date due to there being four world organisations in operation from that time onwards, thus giving more opportunities to fighters.

Because I have built all ongoing information appertaining to the champion and body/bodies concerned into the text, follow the applicable 'Recognition' for continuity.

Weights

The weight at which fights were contracted at fall into two categories within these pages, those that were contested prior to what I classify modern day boxing and those that followed. Within each weight division the weight that the contest was made at is shown in brackets immediately following the date, and when the modern day era is reached there is an explanatory note.

Individual weights for both fighters are given, if published, and are shown (in pounds) alongside the fighter's name. Where the figure is the same as the limit it could be that the men in question came in exactly on the weight or that the officials declared that both men were inside, but failed to announce the exact individual weights. Also, on occasion, the weights were reported in the press to the nearest pound and that is what we have shown.

In the no-decision era of boxing in America many of the weights reported were those taken at ringside immediately prior to the contest taking place, but in some cases those weights have been ignored if contractual conditions called for an earlier weigh-in that both fighters adhered to. Where known weighing-in times are reported.

Results

Here are the abbreviations used within these pages to describe results of contests:

CO - Count Out. Often given as a knockout, it involves a fighter being counted over up to 'ten' seconds before getting into a standing position. Over the years many record books have listed stoppages, retirements and knockouts under the heading of KO. All results within these pages are broken down separately.

DISQ - Disqualification.

DREW - In the early days of boxing, especially in America, it was agreed in some fights that if both men were still standing at the end of the contest a draw should be given, regardless. Draws were also given on occasion after the police stopped a contest. In more recent times draws have given either by a sole arbiter or by three judges, which is the current situation.

NC - No Contest. It includes contests that were stopped due to neither man giving of his best, police interference, and if both men are fighting outside the rules. Such a decision can also be made at a later stage if a fighter fails a drugs test, etc.

ND - No Decision. For the first 30 odd years of the 1900s many States in America allowed no-decision contests to take place, enabling boxing to carry on by bending the rules after government officials had decided that only exhibition bouts were legal. Although a referee was in place to make sure that the rules were not broken, he could not give a decision apart from counting out, disqualifying, or stopping a fighter from carrying on. For betting purposes, one of the ways of getting around the situation when a fight went the full distance was by allowing pressmen representing three named local newspapers to give a decision that would be reported the next day. For example, nd-w pts 10 would determine a press win for one of the fighters if at least two of the selected papers had him winning. Because this was not a perfect system as one does not know which three papers were selected at the time, I have gone with three different local newspaper reports. This, at least, gives one an idea of who was the better man on the night even if it does not always agree with what others might have recorded.

PTS - Points. Fights can won on points unanimously (all three judges in favour of one man), by a majority (two judges for one man and the other calling a draw) or on a split decision (two judges for one man and one against).

RSC - Referee Stopped Contest. Sometimes recorded elsewhere as referee stopped fight, the term also includes a situation where one of the fighters is probably going to be counted out but the referee discards or discontinues the count as to allow treatment to be given. Unfortunately, many stoppages came about when a fighter's injuries were too bad for him to continue even if he was ahead on points at the time. This has been partly rectified by the use of technical decisions. Another way a fighter can be stopped from continuing is if he is knocked down three times in a round and the 'Three Knockdown' rule is in place.

RTD - Retired. A retirement is recorded when the decision is made by his corner rather than by the referee, during the interval between rounds. Retirements also used to take place if the corner threw the towel or sponge into the ring while the contest was ongoing, but more recently stoppages in mid-round can only be made by the referee. Because it is too difficult to know which countries/states allowed mid-round retirements to take place I have gone with the term 'referee stopped contest' (rsc) from 1920 onwards after the New York State Athletic Commission (NY/NYSAC) was restructured and the National Boxing Association (NBA) was formed. If a towel was thrown in prior to the stoppage it will be reported in the text.

TDEC - Technical Decision. Where a contest goes beyond four rounds - previously three and six, dependent on the body - and is stopped due to an accidental injury to one of the fighters.

TDRAW - Technical Draw. The term denotes that a contest has been stopped due to an accidental injury in a round deemed to be too early in the contest to go to the scorecards. At present all the main bodies agree on it being prior to the fifth round.

Scheduled Rounds

Shown after the result in brackets, it includes all fights that were contested above ten rounds and those where a claimant lost his title claim in a six or eight round no-decision contest. When the scheduled rounds become standardised across the world of boxing in the late 1980s the brackets disappear. At the beginning of boxing many contests were made to a finish, and are shown as such, but as boxing progressed the rounds decreased in line with common sense and safety. In the early part of the 20th Century it was commonplace to have 45 rounds for a championship fight, but gradually 20 rounds, then 15, and now 12 became the standard.

Venues

In earlier times many fights were not reported locally due to the fact that they were illegal, and because of this we have limited details. However, where known, the venues are spelt out in English. This has been standardised because a high percentage of foreign venues are more often than not reported in English.

AC - Athletic Club
SC - Sporting Club

Recognition

Prior to boxers receiving general recognition from established bodies within the sport, those shown within these pages without it should be seen as claimants. Things really got going in America when the New York State Athletic Commission (NY/NYSAC) legalised boxing in New York with the passing of Walker Law in 1920 and the National Boxing Association (NBA) was set up in 1921, the latter body being formed to protect States who were not aligned to the NYSAC or were not independent, such as California. In Europe the International Boxing Union (IBU) had been formed in 1911 to bond European nations together, while after the Great War those involved in boxing in Britain had a working agreement that would eventually see all parties concerned signing up to form the British Boxing Board of Control (BBBoC) in 1929. Although there was an on-off relationship between the IBU and the BBBoC during the early days, in 1946 all countries in Europe, including Britain, became members of the newly formed European Boxing Union (EBU). Recognition from Great Britain alone is shown as GB, while Hawaiian recognition comes under Territorial Boxing Commission (TBC).

Despite there being several attempts to create a workable World Boxing Commission it never properly came to fruition due to the stance taken by the NYSAC, who deemed that they were only empowered to deal with boxing in New York. Eventually, after many attempts to set up one body the NBA reorganised themselves in August 1962 and were renamed as the World Boxing Association (WBA), while in February 1963 the World Boxing Council (WBC) was formed, with the NYSAC still isolating themselves. In 1983 a breakaway group from the WBA set themselves up, initially as the United States Boxing Association/International (USBA/I) and then as the International Boxing Federation (IBF). Then, in 1989, the World Boxing Organisation (WBO) was formed by another group of disaffected former WBA members. Although there are several other organisations purporting to be world bodies, the above mentioned groups are the only ones given credit within these pages other than *The Ring* magazine champions since December 2001. Men holding *The Ring* Championship Belt should be considered as the most worthy of champions, whilst men shown with World recognition are those who are supported by all the main bodies.

Scorecards

Where known, scores listed only apply to fights going the full distance or those that require a technical decision. Many early contests and some more recently used a referee only to decide a winner. Not only that, but they did not make their scorecards available to the outside world. Prior to the current 'ten-point must' ruling, other scoring methods that have also been used at various times include the 'five-point must', the 'one-point' system, and by rounds. The 'five-point must' ruling allowed for the winning fighter to be given five points and the loser four or less, while the 'one-point' system saw the winning fighter awarded one or more points and the losing fighter zero. The most simple way of scoring was the one in which the round was awarded to the winning fighter. More recently, judges have used the 'ten-point' must system, which assigns ten points to the winner of each round, whilst the loser receives nine. When a fighter is knocked down (or in some cases outclassed) he will receive eight points or seven if he is floored twice. On occasion both men can receive ten points if they are deemed equal, and if and when both are knocked down the same amount of times during the round the knockdowns are disregarded. At the end of the contest, the boxer with the most accumulated points is the winner as long as two of the three judges are in agreement.

Boxers' Index

At the end of each weight division is an alphabetical listing of boxers mentioned within that section. Boxers belonging to a different weight division are shown elsewhere. They are all shown by: country of birth (where known)/Domicile. Other than some of those boxing in America prior to the modern era birthplace and domicile are the same unless stated. If the names of countries have changed, the modern adaptation is used. Although Hawaii and Alaska became American States in 1959 they are shown among the listings as separate countries. Out of interest, Ireland was part of the United Kingdom until 1922. Also, where two fighters' names are the same, I have shown career dates in order to distinguish them. If by chance a boxer is not in the specific index you are looking at he will certainly be found in one of the other weight indexes.

Super Middleweight Division

One of the most recent divisions, and also known as the junior light heavyweight class, it took a while in coming, probably due to the highly prestigious middleweight division being established over a long period. Introduced as we know it by the International Boxing Federation (IBF) in 1984 as a means of furthering fighters' opportunities, it was, in truth, sorely needed, with a 15lb weight differential holding many good men back.

Although the IBF are to be given credit for developing it to full international status, 'world' titles at 168lbs, even if little known, had been in existence previously in America. On 3 April 1967, at the Valley Music Hall, Salt Lake City, Utah, Don Fullmer won an advertised version of the 12 stone title, beating Joe Hopkins by a knockout in the sixth of a scheduled 12 rounds. There is no evidence that Fullmer ever saw his new title as more than a stepping-stone for a crack at the middleweight crown.

Five years later, Billy Douglas, the father of Buster, knocked out Danny Brewer in the second round of another advertised 12-stone title fight at the Ohio State Fairground, Columbus, Ohio on 27 November 1974, but had no interest in the artificial title whatsoever and moved on immediately.

Apart from the World Athletic Association, a minority group who named Jerry Halstead as champion in 1982, it was left to the recently formed IBF to announce Murray Sutherland and Ernie Singletary as the nominations for their first ever championship contest.

Weight Band
160lbs to 168lbs

Super Middleweight World Championship Fights:

28 March 1984. Murray Sutherland w pts 15 Ernie Singletary.
Venue: Harrah's Hotel, Atlantic City, New Jersey, USA. **Recognition:** IBF. **Referee:** Larry Hazzard.
Scorecards: 146-139, 147-140, 146-139.
Fight Summary: Battling for the inaugural IBF super middleweight title and boxing to orders, Sutherland (167¼) kept Singletary (167¾) at bay with the left jab for round after round as the latter continually plodded forward. They were not solid jabs but they were effective, and with Sutherland's side-to-side movement making him a difficult target Singletary found it hard to get inside where he could get to work. There were no knockdowns, but the harder punches came from Sutherland, right crosses and left hooks to the body being his speciality.

22 July 1984. Chong-Pal Park w co 11 (15) Murray Sutherland.
Venue: Changchung Gym, Seoul, South Korea. **Recognition:** IBF. **Referee:** Tom Evaristo.
Fight Summary: In what was a hard fight, Park (167½), who was dropped by a left to the temple in the second round, came roaring back to knock the champion over in the fifth following several heavy blows to the body. Even though Sutherland (167¼) boxed well on the back foot Park caught up with him again in the eighth, decking him with left hooks and right crosses to the head, and despite the Scottish-born fighter coming back well with jabs and right hands he was put under more pressure in the 11th. Beaten down by combination punches, although Sutherland fought back with more rights and lefts he was eventually put down with body shots and counted out on the 1.12 mark.

2 January 1985. Chong-Pal Park w co 2 (15) Roy Gumbs.
Venue: Munhwa Gym, Seoul, South Korea. **Recognition:** IBF. **Referee:** Abraham Pacheco.
Fight Summary: Although Gumbs (165½) made a bright start, hurting the champion with a left hook in the opening round, he was quickly under pressure in the second, being dropped early in the session by a right to the jaw. Back

on his feet and looking to put the knockdown behind him, Gumbs took the fight to Park (167½) before being counted out on the 1.42 mark after a left hook to the body had taken all the wind out of his sails.

30 June 1985. Chong-Pal Park w pts 15 Vinnie Curto.
Venue: Munhwa Gym, Seoul, South Korea. **Recognition:** IBF. **Referee:** Yasujiro Fujimoto.
Scorecards: 146-139, 144-142, 146-141.
Fight Summary: Despite the decision being unanimous the clever challenger made life extremely difficult for Park (168), who used fast footwork and landed the more effective punches after both men had made a cautious start. There was no doubting the quality of Curto (168), especially with his ability to evade punches and respond, and it came as no surprise when he was given chance of revenge in a return match the following year.

11 April 1986. Chong-Pal Park w co 15 (15) Vinnie Curto.
Venue: Sports Arena, Los Angeles, California, USA. **Recognition:** IBF. **Referee:** Henry Elesperu.
Fight Summary: After boxing well in the opening couple of rounds, Curto (166¾), moving well and making the champion miss, was dropped by a right to the head in the third and never really showed again despite getting up. From there onwards, Park (168) controlled the fight, and in the eighth and again in the tenth he battered Curto unmercifully with both hands. With both men tiring in the latter stages it was Park who had more left in the tank. Having hurt Curto with a big right in the 15th another right to the head dropped the American for the full count, the finish being timed at 2.15.

6 July 1986. Chong-Pal Park tdraw 2 (15) Lindell Holmes.
Venue: Sports Arena, Chungju, South Korea. **Recognition:** IBF. **Referee:** James Reilly.
Fight Summary: Classified as a technical draw by the IBF, the fight came to an abrupt end at 1.17 of the second round after Park (168) was accidentally cut over the left eye following a clash of heads. At that point the ringside doctor advised the referee to stop the fight as the cut was too dangerous for the champion to continue. Both men had got the fight underway with left hand leads as they looked to find openings, and although there was no real action to speak of it looked like Holmes (166) was going to make it an interesting evening.

With this being the first world title contest that was decided in this fashion I have followed it as an example wherever a fight, caused by an accident, ends too early for the scorecards to be of use, which is normally prior to three or four completed rounds.

14 September 1986. Chong-Pal Park w pts 15 Marvin Mack.
Venue: Kudok Gym, Busan, South Korea. **Recognition:** IBF. **Referee:** Frank Cappuccino.
Scorecards: 145-142, 146-144, 145-141.
Fight Summary: Defending his title for the fifth time Park (167¾) continually went forward as the clever Mack (167½) boxed on the back foot, scoring as he went and showing good movement. There was never a great deal between them, but it was Park (167¾) who made all of the running, catching the American with left and right hooks and almost closing his left eye by the final bell. Showing little ambition and lacking power, Mack was never in with a shout.

25 January 1987. Chong-Pal Park w rsc 15 (15) Doug Sam.
Venue: Hilton Hotel, Seoul, South Korea. **Recognition:** IBF. **Referee:** Herbert Minn.
Fight Summary: The opening nine rounds saw Sam (166¼) on the back foot, counter-punching as the aggressive champion tried to get his punches off while using the left lead well along with solid rights over the top. From the 11th on, however, it was all Park (167½) as he looked to take the fight by the scruff of the neck with strong rights hurting Sam, who was desperately tired at this stage of the fight. In the 14th, when Sam's left eye was almost closed, although the referee let the fight continue he stopped it at 1.55 of the 15th when judging the Australian unfit to continue after shipping lefts and rights to the head and not fighting back. Even though Sam protested bitterly at the stoppage, the judges overall had Park in front at that point with scores of 138-129, 135-132, 134-134.

3 May 1987. Chong-Pal Park w pts 15 Lindell Holmes.
Venue: Sunin Gym, Incheon, South Korea. **Recognition:** IBF. **Referee:** Abraham Pacheco.
Scorecards: 143-142, 144-143, 139-145.
Fight Summary: Getting a second chance to win the title after their previous encounter ended in a second-round technical draw, Holmes (165¼) started strongly to have the champion down in the fifth from a right to the head. However, from thereon in Park (168) increased his work-rate, coming on strongly in what had been a gruelling battle to take the last three sessions as Holmes ran out of steam.

26 July 1987. Chong-Pal Park w co 4 (15) Emmanuel Otti.
Venue: The Coliseum, Kwangju, South Korea. **Recognition:** IBF. **Referee:** Bill Connors.
Fight Summary: South Korea's Park (168) yet again proved that despite being wild on occasion he had the power to finish opponents off in what was a fairly lively scrap while it lasted. Catching up with Otti (167¾) in the fourth round, the champion eventually dropped his man with solid body shots that sent the Ugandan down to be counted out eight seconds after the bell had gone to end the session.

Park relinquished the IBF version of the title in December, immediately prior to meeting Jesus Gallardo for the inaugural WBA crown. That was followed by Graciano Rocchigiani and Vincent Boulware being matched to decide the vacant IBF title.

6 December 1987. Chong-Pal Park w rsc 2 (12) Jesus Gallardo.
Venue: Sajik Gym, Seoul, South Korea. **Recognition:** WBA. **Referee:** Carlos Berrocal.
Fight Summary: In a contest that was the first WBA championship fight at the weight, Park (168), who had given up the IBF version of the title to take on Gallardo (165), came out firing in the opening round only to be floored by a southpaw left. Back on his feet Park immediately retaliated when putting Gallardo down twice before the first round was over, and after just 27 seconds of the second had elapsed the contest was over when the referee held the latter up following a cracking straight right that had threatened to put him down.

1 March 1988. Chong-Pal Park w co 5 (12) Polly Pasireron.
Venue: Indoor Gym, Chungju, South Korea. **Recognition:** WBA. **Referee:** Isidro Rodriguez.
Fight Summary: Making the first defence of his new WBA title, Park (167½) kept on top of the relatively inexperienced Pasireron (168) right from the start before getting down to business in the fifth round. By now dominating the exchanges, Park eventually sent the Indonesian down to be counted out on the 2.25 mark following a barrage of head and body shots.

12 March 1988. Graciano Rocchigiani w rsc 8 (15) Vincent Boulware.
Venue: Philips Hall, Dusseldorf, Germany. **Recognition:** IBF. **Referee:** Joe Santarpia.
Fight Summary: Contested for the vacant title, Rocchigiani (166½) had Boulware (168) in real trouble in the third, slowing him down with southpaw left hooks to the body, and although the American came back well in the fifth and sixth he was soon up against it in the seventh. Badly hurt but refusing to go down Boulware made it into the eighth, but after twice being on the verge of a knockdown he was rescued by the referee at 2.11 of the session, his right eye almost closed and totally out of steam.

23 May 1988. Fulgencio Obelmejias w pts 12 Chong-Pal Park.
Venue: Waikiki Arena, Suanbo, South Korea. **Recognition:** WBA. **Referee:** Sean Curtin.
Scorecards: 114-110, 115-110, 117-109.
Fight Summary: Using his extra reach to good effect and scoring well Obelmejias (166) made life difficult for Park (167), who concentrated on the body and was in contention up until the seventh. In that session Park was badly cut over the right eye by an accidental butt, losing ground thereafter as Obelmejias stepped up the pace. The recess after the eighth saw Park's eye damage being inspected by the ringside doctor, but having been allowed to carry on he was sent down by a heavy left hook. From there on it was all one-way traffic, with Park being knocked down twice more before bravely staying the course to lose heavily on points.

Following a walkout by 27 delegates at the WBA convention, held in Venezuela during October, the World Boxing Organisation (WBO) was immediately formed, naming Thomas Hearns as its first champion at the weight.

3 June 1988. Graciano Rocchigiani w pts 15 Nicky Walker.
Venue: Deutschland Hall, Berlin, Germany. **Recognition:** IBF. **Referee:** Waldemar Schmidt.
Scorecards: 146-137, 148-140, 147-137.
Fight Summary: Rocchigiani (167½) dominated his first defence of the title from the second round through to the tenth, and although shaking Walker (167¾) up on occasion he was never able to drop him. Realising he needed a kayo the last five sessions saw Walker picking up the pace, but unable to stop Rocchigiani from advancing the latter easily took the 14th and 15th with constant use of the southpaw jab. Both men finished with cut eyes, Rocchigiani over the right optic and Walker over the left, the champion's damage being the worst.

This would be the last 15-round contest for the weight class, following the announcement that, as from 1 September, all world title contests held under the auspices of the IBF would be restricted to 12 rounds, thus falling into line with the WBA and WBC.

7 October 1988. Graciano Rocchigiani w rsc 11 (12) Chris Reid.
Venue: Deutschland Hall, Berlin, Germany. **Recognition:** IBF. **Referee:** Frank Cappuccino.
Fight Summary: Although Reid (165½) made an aggressive start he was soon finding the champion's southpaw stance difficult to handle. Round by round Rocchigiani (166¼) moved ahead as his jab continued to pick up the points, and in the seventh Reid was under severe pressure and fortunate to last out the session. Cut over the left eye in the eighth and then dropped, even though it was classified as a slip it did not do much for Reid's chances, especially as he was unable to hurt Rocchigiani at any stage. The finish, timed at 2.39 of the 11th, came when the referee stopped the contest in Rocchigiani's favour after Reid had taken several heavy blows to the head and his corner had thrown the towel in.

4 November 1988. Thomas Hearns w pts 12 James Kinchen.
Venue: Hilton Hotel, Las Vegas, Nevada, USA. **Recognition:** WBO. **Referee:** Mills Lane.
Scorecards: 115-112, 114-112, 113-114.
Fight Summary: Having appointed Hearns (165½) as their champion when the organisation was formed, his defence against Kinchen (166) would be the first championship fight at the weight for the WBO. Hearns started as he said he would, throwing big punches, but when Kinchen took them and started hitting back with some of his own a heavy right-left hook had the 'Hitman' over in the fourth round. Somehow beating the count, Hearns looked to be all over the place. However, after holding on for dear life to get through the rest of the session, for which he was deducted a point, he began to jab and move. Hearns was still at risk though, and after being hurt in the sixth, seventh and eighth by big rights to the head he boxed cagily before giving Kinchen a bit of a hammering towards the end of the eighth. From there onwards, despite carrying a swollen eye and always having to be continually on his guard against Kinchen's right hand, Hearns took the last four rounds to make sure of the win. Following the contest, Hearns claimed that as his right hand had gone early on he had been unable land power punches after that.

7 November 1988. Sugar Ray Leonard w rsc 9 Donny Lalonde.
Venue: Caesar's Palace, Las Vegas, Nevada, USA. **Recognition:** WBC. **Referee:** Richard Steele.
Fight Summary: In a contest for the inaugural WBC title, and with Lalonde's light heavyweight title also on the line, most of the money was on Leonard (165). But after four rounds he was behind on all the scorecards, having been knocked down by a right in that session. From there on, however, Leonard made it his fight when gradually cutting Lalonde (167) down to size, his combination punching being the main difference between them. Eventually, in the ninth, Leonard backed Lalonde up on the ropes and hammered him with lefts and rights before a left hook sent the latter down, blood coming from his mouth, bringing about an immediate stoppage with 30 seconds of the session remaining. Lalonde, who entered the ring one pound inside the limit, should not have been forced to put his 175lbs crown on the line at the same time.

Leonard relinquished the WBC light heavyweight title following the fight in order to concentrate on defending his lighter belt. Further to that, a match was made between Dennis Andries and Tony Willis, the North American Boxing Federation (NABF) champion, to find a successor.

27 January 1989. Graciano Rocchigiani w pts 12 Thulani Malinga.
Venue: Deutschland Hall, Berlin, Germany. **Recognition:** IBF. **Referee:** Sam Williams.
Scorecards: 117-111, 119-113, 119-112.
Fight Summary: With Malinga (165½) ducking low and keeping out of range throughout the contest, the southpaw champion, continually frustrated, failed to find a way of dealing with it. There was very little action and what there was turned out to be messy. After the contest Rocchigiani (167¾) apologised to his fans for his poor display.

Rocchigiani handed in his IBF Championship Belt in September due to continuing weight problems. That announcement was followed by the IBF matching Lindell Holmes, the United States Boxing Association (USBA) champion, against Frank Tate to decide the vacancy.

28 May 1989. In-Chul Baek w rsc 11 Fulgencio Obelmejias.
Venue: Hongkuk Gym, Seoul, South Korea. **Recognition:** WBA. **Referee:** Bernie Soto.
Fight Summary: Starting well by using his reach advantage to fire in left jabs the champion kept it tight until the eighth round when, after trading punches, Baek (167½) turned it around with a couple of hooks that floored Obelmejias (167). Although Obelmejias survived he was badly wobbled in both the ninth and tenth sessions, repeatedly holding on in order to survive. The end was now in sight, and in the 11th Obelmejias was down from a flurry of blows before getting up and immediately being sent crashing flat on his back from an explosive right hand. There was no way he was going to be able to recover from that, the referee calling the fight off there and then. The official time of the stoppage was given as 2.21.

12 June 1989. Sugar Ray Leonard drew 12 Thomas Hearns.
Venue: Caesar's Palace, Las Vegas, Nevada, USA. **Recognition:** WBC/WBO. **Referee:** Richard Steele.
Scorecards: 113-112, 112-113, 112-112.
Fight Summary: Despite being badly hurt himself at times during the contest Hearns (162½) had Leonard (160) down twice, in the third and 11th, before the latter came back to snatch a draw after making a big last-round effort. Following the first knockdown Leonard seemed to be in good working order by the fifth, shaking Hearns up several times in that session. The next five rounds were almost uneventful, but after the 11th, in which Leonard showed his courage to survive, the final round saw Hearns struggling under a barrage of blows, being almost spent at the bell. The result saw both men retain their respective titles, even though the WBO Championship Belt was not officially up for grabs.

8 October 1989. In-Chul Baek w co 11 Ron Essett.
Venue: Inter-Continental Hotel, Seoul, South Korea. **Recognition:** WBA. **Referee:** Julio Alvarado.
Fight Summary: Making his first defence Baek (167½) showed plenty of aggression, but by the third round Essett (167½) had warmed to the task before coming with a big attack in the fifth when penetrating the champion's guard throughout the session. However, the sixth saw Baek starting to turn things around as left and right hooks put Essett under pressure, and after concentrating on the body thereafter by the end of the tenth the latter was fast fading. Coming out quickly in the 11th, when Baek picked up where he had left off in the previous session a flurry of clubbing blows to the head sent Essett down to be counted out after 29 seconds.

7 December 1989. Sugar Ray Leonard w pts 12 Roberto Duran.
Venue: Mirage Hotel & Casino, Las Vegas, Nevada, USA. **Recognition:** WBC. **Referee:** Richard Steele.
Scorecards: 119-109, 116-111, 120-110.
Fight Summary: This had to be one of the most disappointing contests between once great fighters, with Leonard (160) content to stay on the outside, scoring whenever he could, while the ponderous Duran (158) followed after him. Several times Leonard had Duran on the verge of defeat, remaining contented on the outside, and it was not until the 11th that the action heated up. That was when Leonard finally moved in on Duran before a heavy right from the Panamanian inflicted a bad cut on his left eye. With Leonard's corner unable to stem the flow of blood it

was surprising that Duran failed to take advantage of the situation, seemingly happy to plod along to the final bell. Afterwards, Leonard's cut and other facial injuries would eventually require a total of 60 micro stitches to repair.

When Leonard relinquished the WBC version of the title in September 1990, saying he was too light to defend, a short while later Mauro Galvano, the European champion, and Dario Matteoni, the South American champion, were matched to decide the vacancy.

13 January 1990. In-Chul Baek w rtd 7 Yoshiaki Tajima.
Venue: Hyundai Indoor Gym, Seoul, South Korea. **Recognition:** WBA. **Referee:** Pinit Prayadsab.
Fight Summary: Proving far too strong for Tajima (166½) the champion put him down in the second round with a countering right uppercut before gradually working him over with punches that came from all angles. By the fourth the Japanese southpaw was carrying a swollen right eye, testament to the pounding he had received, and after Baek (168) had continued to batter him right through to the end of the seventh he was retired during the interval.

27 January 1990. Lindell Holmes w pts 12 Frank Tate.
Venue: Municipal Auditorium, New Orleans, Louisiana, USA. **Recognition:** IBF. **Referee:** Lucien Joubert.
Scorecards: 116-112, 119-112, 114-114.
Fight Summary: In a battle for the vacant title Holmes (168) got away well in the early rounds when outscoring Tate (166), who had a four-inch-reach advantage, while using his jab to set up the right hand and attacking both the head and body. Although Tate had not really impressed prior to the tenth he was not out of it and during the next two sessions he scored with several solid combinations before Holmes came back with good jabs and rights to the body to well-deserve the points decision in his favour. A big underdog, Holmes had silenced his critics, and how one of the judges had both men on level terms at the final bell was surprising to say the least.

30 March 1990. Christophe Tiozzo w rsc 6 In-Chul Baek.
Venue: Gerland Sports Palace, Lyon, France. **Recognition:** WBA. **Referee:** Carlos Berrocal.
Fight Summary: Giving the best performance of his career Tiozzo (166½) was too good for the champion, who was outscored right from the start as the left jab found its mark unerringly. Dropped by a right hook in the second, Baek was then given a standing count in the third after being caught again. Although the tough Baek (168) tried to fight back in the fourth and fifth he was still shipping too much punishment, and having been allowed to carry on with a cut left eye once it had closed completely the referee stopped the fight with six seconds left of the sixth.

28 April 1990. Thomas Hearns w pts 12 Michael Olajide.
Venue: Taj Mahal Hotel & Casino, Atlantic City, New Jersey, USA. **Recognition:** WBO. **Referee:** Tony Orlando.
Scorecards: 119-107, 120-107, 119-110.
Fight Summary: Despite picking his shots well the champion was no longer the great fighter of the recent past, and had Olajide (166½) gone looking for him the result could well have been different. Prior to the ninth Hearns (168) had done the better work, being ahead in an absorbing if not exciting contest, but in that session he finally had Olajide over from a whistling right to the jaw. After Olajide got up at 'six' Hearns put everything into a finish but having exhausted himself he spent the remainder of the contest on the defensive to make sure of the win. Olajide, who had a point deducted in the fourth for going low, would never again have a better chance to become champion and retired just one fight later.

Hearns relinquished his WBO version of the title in April 1991 to concentrate on his WBA light heavyweight challenge against Virgil Hill, which was followed by Michael Watson and Chris Eubank being matched to decide the vacancy.

19 July 1990. Lindell Holmes w rsc 9 Carl Sullivan.
Venue: The Kingdome, Seattle, Washington, USA. **Recognition:** IBF. **Referee:** James Reilly.
Fight Summary: Making his first defence Holmes (167) started emphatically when having Sullivan (166½) down in the third, wobbling badly in the fourth and staggering all over in the seventh. Despite being hurt in the seventh, especially by a blow to the jaw that threatened a knockout, Sullivan came back strongly in the eighth when catching Holmes with lefts and rights. However, following that Holmes was in total control, and when Sullivan was

flattened face down after being hit by four smashing rights to the head the referee stopped the fight immediately, the finish being timed at 45 seconds of the ninth round.

20 July 1990. Christophe Tiozzo w rsc 8 Paul Whittaker.
Venue: The Bullring, Arles, France. **Recognition:** WBA. **Referee:** Julio Alvarado.
Fight Summary: On top right from the beginning the champion was soon putting lefts and rights into the face of Whittaker (167¾), having far too much skill for the American, and by the third round he was looking to counter with solid rights as the latter came in to the attack. Although Whittaker was getting closer by the sixth, unable to pin Tiozzo (168) down, he was still being outpunched and losing ground. Finally, Tiozzo made his punches count in the eighth when sending Whittaker down from two solid left hooks, and when the latter was back on his feet and being blitzed from both hands the referee called it off with 22 seconds of the session remaining.

23 November 1990. Christophe Tiozzo w rsc 2 Dan Morgan.
Venue: Cergy Hall, Cergy-Pontoise, Val d'Oise, France. **Recognition:** WBA. **Referee:** Franco Priami.
Fight Summary: Although dominating Morgan (168) with accurate left jabs and right crosses the champion picked up a bad cut over the nose and left eye before the opening session came to a close. Roaring out for the second, both hands blazing away, Tiozzo (167¾) soon had Morgan in difficulty before a cracking left hook put the American down. Having got up at 'eight', Morgan was blasted by lefts and rights to head and body before the referee stopped the contest on the 2.38 mark.

15 December 1990. Mauro Galvano w pts 12 Dario Matteoni.
Venue: Star Concert Hall, Monte Carlo, Monaco. **Recognition:** WBC. **Referee:** Vince Delgado.
Scorecards: 114-113, 114-113, 117-113.
Fight Summary: Fighting for the title vacated by Sugar Ray Leonard, Galvano (166) boxed cleverly on the back foot and scored well with the left jab to keep the tough Matteoni (167) at bay over the opening seven rounds before the latter began to chase him down. After the crude Matteoni was cut over the left eye in the sixth and Galvano was docked a point in the seventh for holding and hitting, the Argentine began to put his punches together better, almost having Galvano over from right hooks and uppercuts in the 11th. When Galvano fell to the floor, following the referee ordering the men to break, he was told to box on before being given the unanimous decision if not the plaudits at the final bell.

16 December 1990. Lindell Holmes w pts 12 Thulani Malinga.
Venue: Ice Palace, Marino, Italy. **Recognition:** IBF. **Referee:** Rudy Battle.
Scorecards: 116-112, 116-112, 117-113.
Fight Summary: The contest was fairly even during the opening five rounds as Malinga (166¼) walked into the champion, forcing him to fight his fight and making things difficult in general. From the sixth onwards the fight belonged to Holmes (165½) as he slipped inside Malinga's wild punches to land solid lefts and rights, and in the 12th he nearly had the South African over with a terrific right to the head. Holding on whenever he could as Holmes attacked non-stop, Malinga made it to the final bell. Although he was clearly beaten he had at least preserved his record of never having been knocked out in 38 fights.

7 March 1991. Lindell Holmes w pts 12 Antoine Byrd.
Venue: Sports Palace, Madrid, Spain. **Recognition:** IBF. **Referee:** Waldemar Schmidt.
Scorecards: 115-113, 117-111, 113-115.
Fight Summary: Up against a clever southpaw opponent in Byrd (164½), although the champion seemed to be in charge for long periods he was never able to set his man up for a stoppage. Byrd, to his credit, always seemed to be able to finish strongly in the last part of each round, but coming into the tenth when it really mattered he was too tired to make a final effort to turn the fight around. Following that, Holmes (165½) stepped up the pace to make sure that the decision went in his favour.

5 April 1991. Victor Cordoba w rsc 9 Christophe Tiozzo.
Venue: Sports Palace, Marseille, France. **Recognition:** WBA. **Referee:** Enzo Montero.

Fight Summary: Even though both men got off to a good start, as early as the opening round the champion had felt the weight of Cordoba's punches, saying afterwards that he had boxed on in a fog from there onwards. But Tiozzo (167¾), not a champion for nothing, continued to take the fight to the taller Cordoba (167¼) despite being hurt by solid southpaw lefts on the way in. The sixth was the best of the fight as both men gave it everything, but by the eighth Tiozzo was weakening. That became clear when he was rocked by a right-left at the end of the session. Realising he had Tiozzo in real trouble Cordoba came out strongly in the ninth, and after landing hooks from both hands and dropping the Frenchman with a heavy left the referee stepped in. The finish was timed at 53 seconds.

18 May 1991. Darrin Van Horn w co 11 Lindell Holmes.
Venue: Sports Palace, Verbania, Italy. **Recognition:** IBF. **Referee:** Robert Byrd.
Fight Summary: Having gone well for the opening three rounds the champion was knocked down by a right over the top from Van Horn (165½), and although the referee did not start a count it was the first significant punch of the fight. Shaken up again in the sixth from a right to the head, when Holmes (166½) was cut over the left eye in the seventh from there onwards Van Horn pegged back any deficit with short bursts of punches in virtually every session. Coming out for the 11th on tired legs, following a series of vicious blows, Holmes was dropped by a left hook under the ribs and counted out on the 1.49 mark.

27 July 1991. Mauro Galvano w pts 12 Ron Essett.
Venue: Sports Palace, Capo d'Orlando, Italy. **Recognition:** WBC. **Referee:** Franz Marti.
Scorecards: 116-114, 117-115, 118-115.
Fight Summary: Fairly even for the first seven rounds, the champion then picked up the pace in the eighth, hurting Essett (167¼) in that session, before pushing on over the last four rounds. Superbly conditioned, Galvano (166½) took no chances when boxing behind the left jab and banging in rights whenever the opportunity arose. Afterwards, Galvano admitted that he had been hurt by body shots and that had influenced his decision to box on the outside.

17 August 1991. Darrin Van Horn w co 3 John Jarvis.
Venue: Bren Events Centre, Irvine, California, USA. **Recognition:** IBF. **Referee:** Lou Moret.
Fight Summary: Making the first defence of his title, the confident champion was soon landing solid hooks to the body with Jarvis (168) content to keep his distance. Coming out fast in the second Van Horn (168) hurt Jarvis with heavy lefts and rights, and although the latter hit back hard it did not dissuade his opponent who started the third in the same vein. After a bout of heavy hitting, when Van Horn beat Jarvis to the punch the challenger was counted out at 1.11 having been dropped by a left hook to the body followed by a right cross to the jaw.

21 September 1991. Chris Eubank w rsc 12 Michael Watson.
Venue: White Hart Lane, Tottenham, London, England. **Recognition:** WBO. **Referee:** Roy Francis.
Fight Summary: Determined to avenge a defeat at the hands of Eubank (167) three months earlier, Watson (166) had got himself into great condition for this battle that was billed for the vacant title after Thomas Hearns had moved up a weight class. Driving on for round after round Watson walked through Eubank's heavy counter punches to get his own off, and at the end of the tenth there was little between them. In the 11th it was Eubank's turn to mount a big attack, but after surviving the assault Watson, having sensed tiredness in his foe, floored the man from Brighton with a left-right combination that was followed by a cracking right to the head. As Watson moved in for the kill, after Eubank had scrambled up, he walked straight into a terrific right uppercut that dropped him in a heap. Saved by the bell, in hindsight Watson should not have been allowed out for the 12th, and with Eubank all over him the referee stopped the fight 29 seconds into the session. At the time of the stoppage Watson was ahead on all three cards, but moments later he had slumped into unconsciousness and was on his way to hospital to have a blood clot removed from his brain. Having survived, after being given little chance at one stage, Watson would eventually sue the British Boxing Board of Control in a landmark case.

13 December 1991. Victor Cordoba w rsc 11 Vincenzo Nardiello.
Venue: Bercy Sports Palace, Paris, France. **Recognition:** WBA. **Referee:** Stan Christodoulou.

Fight Summary: In a battle of southpaws the champion started the better of the two when dropping Nardiello (165½) with a straight left in the second round, but by the sixth it was the Italian who was ignoring the jab to apply steady pressure. While Cordoba (168) looked for one big left to finish the fight it was the aggressive Nardiello who had boxed his way into the lead by the end of the tenth. The previous two sessions had seen Cordoba getting back into the fight, and in the 11th he soon had Nardiello in trouble when smashing in a heavy left. Never properly recovering from that punch, after Nardiello had been dropped with a similar blow the referee brought the fight to a halt on the 1.44 mark without even bothering to take up the count.

10 January 1992. Iran Barkley w rsc 2 Darrin Van Horn.
Venue: MSG Theatre, Manhattan, NYC, New York, USA. **Recognition:** IBF. **Referee:** Arthur Mercante Jnr.
Fight Summary: Right from the opening bell Barkley (168) went after the champion, nearly having him over with a left hook as the two men went toe-to-toe in the opening round. With there being no let-up in the second Van Horn (167) was soon down after taking another cracking left hook. Back on his feet at 'six', Van Horn was knocked down again, a left uppercut-short right to the jaw doing the damage, and after taking another battering before dropping to the floor in a groggy state the referee stopped the contest with 1.27 of the session remaining.

1 February 1992. Chris Eubank w pts 12 Thulani Malinga.
Venue: National Indoor Centre, Birmingham, England. **Recognition:** WBO. **Referee:** Steve Smoger.
Scorecards: 116-112, 115-113, 112-115.
Fight Summary: Fighting for the first time since the Michael Watson tragedy it was unclear as to how Eubank (168) would react in this title defence, but after a round or so he was back in the groove before sending Malinga (167) crashing down from a terrific right to the head in the fifth. Although Malinga made it up, still shaky he was taking some heavy blows when the bell came to his rescue. However, from there on as both men tired there little action worthwhile to mention.

6 February 1992. Mauro Galvano w pts 12 Juan Carlos Gimenez.
Venue: Ice Palace, Marino, Italy. **Recognition:** WBC. **Referee:** Larry O'Connell.
Scorecards: 115-114, 119-115, 116-114.
Fight Summary: After three close rounds the champion began to find the range with the jab before settling down into a monotonous rhythm, beating a steady tattoo on the plodding Gimenez's features. Gimenez (167½) tried hard to get to close quarters, but to no avail, being tied up by Galvano (167) again and again. From the middle rounds onwards the fight had turned into a dull, mauling affair with Galvano deciding to concentrate on nullifying the Paraguayan's work rather than keeping him at distance with the jab which had been so effective earlier on.

25 April 1992. Chris Eubank w co 3 John Jarvis.
Venue: G-Mex Leisure Centre, Manchester, England. **Recognition:** WBO. **Referee:** Stan Christodoulou.
Fight Summary: With just one fight to his name in the last 20 months, Jarvis (168) should not have been challenging Eubank (168) for his title, but when Juan Carlos Gimenez and then Ron Essett pulled out he stepped in to save the show. After controlling the opening two rounds and expected to up the pace in the third, Eubank continued to strut his stuff before landing a tremendous right flush on Jarvis' jaw, the American going down heavily to be counted out on the 1.50 mark.

27 June 1992. Chris Eubank w pts 12 Ron Essett.
Venue: Quinto Do Lago Hotel, Quinta Do Lago, Portugal. **Recognition:** WBO. **Referee:** Roberto Ramirez.
Scorecards: 117-112, 117-113, 118-110.
Fight Summary: Once again the champion was unable to close down a negative opponent, allowing the light-hitting Essett (166) to score with flicking jabs and remain in the fight when boxing in a haphazard fashion. Even though Eubank (168) occasionally scored heavily he was unable to set the American up for a finishing blow. By the seventh session, when it was clear that Eubank needed to up the pace he began to put in more effort, hurting Essett and flooring him in the eighth. It should have incurred a count, but after the referee ruled it a slip Eubank was unable to improve on that despite having his man in trouble up against the ropes in the ninth. Although Eubank won by a unanimous decision there were many who thought that the contest was closer than scored.

12 September 1992. Michael Nunn w pts 12 Victor Cordoba.
Venue: Thomas & Mack Centre, Las Vegas, Nevada, USA. **Recognition:** WBA. **Referee:** Mills Lane.
Scorecards: 114-112, 114-113, 112-114.
Fight Summary: Making his first defence Cordoba (168) appeared unlucky to have lost his title to fellow southpaw Nunn (168), especially after hurting the latter throughout the contest and knocking him down in the tenth with a solid left to the head. Several times earlier in the contest Nunn looked to be in trouble from body shots, but he continued to fight back even if his punches did lack power. By the ninth Cordoba seemed to be out of steam while Nunn was beginning to put his punches together. In that session, however, Cordoba was deducted a point for a questionable low blow, an action that would ultimately cost him the title. Thereafter it was Nunn who was the busier, and despite the knockdown he did the better work in the last two sessions as Cordoba slowed.

19 September 1992. Chris Eubank w pts 12 Tony Thornton.
Venue: Scottish Exhibition Centre, Glasgow, Scotland. **Recognition:** WBO. **Referee:** Roberto Ramirez.
Scorecards: 114-112, 114-113, 112-114.
Fight Summary: Having coasted through the opening four rounds the champion then surprisingly gave up several sessions due to lack of effort and was outworked by Thornton (168). Shaken up several times during the contest occasionally Eubank (168) looked like he might go down, but he always fought back strongly when hurt. In the ninth and tenth it was Eubank who had his man groggy, and although he tried his utmost to finish the American off he was unsuccessful. The last two sessions saw Eubank, now throwing arm punches and looking tired, content to allow Thornton to make the running. At the final bell it was a close call with many believing a draw to have been a fairer result.

3 October 1992. Nigel Benn w rtd 3 Mauro Galvano.
Venue: Ice Palace, Marino, Italy. **Recognition:** WBC. **Referee:** Joe Cortez.
Fight Summary: In action straight from the opening bell, having realised that it might be fatal going to the scorecards in Italy, Benn (167½) caught the champion with several cracking rights to the head to have the latter holding on at the end of the session. Picking it up again in the second Benn landed several hard rights, one of them opening a cut on Galvano's left eye, and although being consistently held he continued to stalk the Italian. The third round was much the same, with Benn landing solidly before he was bundled through the ropes more by pushing than being hurt by lefts and rights thrown by Galvano (168). At the end of the third, with Galvano's eye damage having worsened, his corner pulled him out of the fight and tried to claim that the cut had been caused by a head butt and not a punch. Overruled by the referee, who saw it as a third-round retirement, even if it had gone to the cards Benn would have won the title on a technical decision as all three judges had him in front at the time.

28 November 1992. Chris Eubank w pts 12 Juan Carlos Gimenez.
Venue: G-Mex Leisure Centre, Manchester, England. **Recognition:** WBO. **Referee:** Steve Smoger.
Scorecards: 119-109, 118-110, 118-110.
Fight Summary: Although Gimenez (168) absorbed the champion's best punches, remaining upright throughout, he was never in a fight that often appeared to be no more than a sparring session. Round after round Eubank (168) sent in powerful blows from either hand, and even when he had Gimenez over in the fifth from a left hook it was ruled a slip. By the eighth Gimenez was carrying a bad cut on the bridge of his nose, but he continued to assimilate Eubank's best efforts, including several crunching right uppercuts to the jaw, right through to the end.

12 December 1992. Nigel Benn w rsc 11 Nicky Piper.
Venue: Alexandra Pavilion, Muswell Hill, London, England. **Recognition:** WBC. **Referee:** Larry O'Connell.
Fight Summary: Putting up a tremendous display of guts and boxing ability Piper (167) took the champion into the final stages of the contest, even being ahead on one of the judge's cards when the referee stopped the fight at 1.44 of the 11th round to save him from taking further punishment. Stalking his man throughout, while landing the heavier punches Benn (167) was often picked off by the jab when standing back to admire his work. Finally, in the 11th, Benn made his harder punching pay off when a wide left hook dropped Piper for 'nine', and after the latter had been subjected a series of left hooks and right uppercuts without fighting back the referee had seen enough.

30 January 1993. Michael Nunn w pts 12 Victor Cordoba.
Venue: The Pyramid, Memphis, Tennessee, USA. **Recognition:** WBA. **Referee:** Ernesto Magana.
Scorecards: 115-107, 120-106, 117-106.
Fight Summary: After losing his title unluckily to Nunn (168) last time out Cordoba (168) was expected to regain it in many quarters, but having been dropped twice in the second round and then having four points deducted for low blows he was eventually beaten out of sight by his fellow southpaw. Allowed to take a bad beating in the second and constantly fouling, Cordoba should never have made it to the final bell, especially after putting Nunn down four times from low blows and continuing to go low right up to the end.

13 February 1993. James Toney w rsc 9 Iran Barkley.
Venue: Caesar's Palace, Las Vegas, Nevada, USA. **Recognition:** IBF. **Referee:** Richard Steele.
Fight Summary: Challenging for the IBF super middleweight title, the IBF middleweight champion, Toney (167), made a good start, being well in control by the fifth, having landed the better punches and closing Barkley's left eye. Although Barkley (168) came back strongly he was still being picked off and rocked by solid blows to head and body. By the eighth Barkley was fighting a totally uphill battle and after being under constant pressure in the ninth, when bleeding badly from the nose and walking into solid shots, the doctor advised the referee to stop the fight at the end of the session.

20 February 1993. Chris Eubank w pts 12 Lindell Holmes.
Venue: Olympia National Hall, Kensington, London, England. **Recognition:** WBO. **Referee:** Stan Christodoulou.
Scorecards: 116-114, 120-109, 117-112.
Fight Summary: Getting away fast the champion had Holmes (167) over from a slip in the first session, and after slamming in a big right to the head in the fourth he saw his rival saved by the bell. Holmes, scoring well at times with left hooks, showed his grit throughout the 12 gruelling rounds by continuing to be a nuisance up until the ninth when he was cut over the left eye. From thereon in, Eubank (168), despite carrying a swelling under the left eye took complete control. However, he was unable to stop the stubborn Holmes who deserved to last the course even if he did resort to going low on the blind side of the referee several times.

20 February 1993. Michael Nunn w co 1 Dan Morgan.
Venue: Aztec Stadium, Mexico City, Mexico. **Recognition:** WBA. **Referee:** Enzo Montero.
Fight Summary: This was a mismatch from the start with Morgan (167¾), lacking the tools to keep the strong southpaw champion away from him, soon in difficulty. After trying to walk through the punches without success Morgan was sent down for 'eight' from heavy blows to the head, and upon getting to his feet he was soon in trouble again. Dropped by a cracking left as Nunn (168) went all out for the finish, Morgan was counted out at 2.59 of the opening session in the act of rising.

6 March 1993. Nigel Benn w pts 12 Mauro Galvano.
Venue: Scottish Exhibition Centre, Glasgow, Scotland. **Recognition:** WBC. **Referee:** Tony Perez.
Scorecards: 118-114, 117-113, 118-112.
Fight Summary: Happy to put his title up against the man he won it from Benn (167¾) was given a much harder time than he might have anticipated, being forced to travel the full distance and having to shake off a tremendous short right to the head immediately prior to the final bell. If the punch had landed a minute or so earlier the result could have been very different. The fight had begun with the referee calling 'break' 20 times in the opening three minutes, making it clear that Galvano (167¾) had come to survive, his clutching tactics throughout making it difficult for Benn to attain any kind of rhythm. It was not one of Benn's better performances, his punching often being ineffectual, but he was the one making the fight even if he could not find a way through the Italian's defences for much of the time.

23 April 1993. Michael Nunn w rsc 6 Crawford Ashley.
Venue: The Pyramid, Memphis, Tennessee, USA. **Recognition:** WBA. **Referee:** Julio Alvarado.
Fight Summary: Making his third defence inside four months Nunn (167½) ultimately punched too hard for Ashley (163), who for four rounds was in with a chance against the champion. However, by the fifth it was clear that Ashley was beginning to be ground down, especially after sustaining cracked ribs as Nunn concentrated on the

body, and he was floored twice in that session before being dropped three more times in the sixth. The finish came with just one second remaining of the sixth after the referee was forced to call the fight off on the WBA's 'three knockdowns in a round' ruling.

15 May 1993. Chris Eubank drew 12 Ray Close.
Venue: Scottish Exhibition Centre, Glasgow, Scotland. **Recognition:** WBO. **Referee:** Paul Thomas.
Scorecards: 116-112, 113-116, 115-115.
Fight Summary: Having beaten Vincenzo Nardiello in Italy Close (168) had certainly earned his crack at the champion, but regardless of that the Irishman was not really expected to pose too many problems. Setting a fast pace from the opening bell Close worked away with both hands, and even when occasionally hurt by right uppercuts he kept it together to match Eubank (168) blow for blow. Cut by the left eye in the eighth, after Eubank began to put more urgency into his work he found a gap in Close's defences in the 11th to fire in a right uppercut to the jaw that dropped the latter heavily. Although it seemed to be all over, Close amazingly got up at 'eight' before taking the fight to the fast-tiring Eubank who appeared lucky to retain his title at the final bell.

26 June 1993. Nigel Benn w rsc 4 Lou Gent.
Venue: Olympia Grand Hall, Kensington, London, England. **Recognition:** WBC. **Referee:** Larry O'Connell.
Fight Summary: Although Gent (167) got through the first two rounds without too much damage he was soon put under pressure in the third as Benn (167) looked to finish the fight as soon as possible. Driving Gent into a neutral corner, a cracking right-left quickly had the challenger over for 'six'. Surprisingly, Gent went straight into Benn, only to be dropped twice more and cut over the left eye before the session was over. With Benn menacing, after Gent had got up from being floored by a right to the head he was put down by right to the ribs. At that point the referee stopped the fight 35 seconds into the fourth.

9 October 1993. Nigel Benn drew 12 Chris Eubank.
Venue: Old Trafford, Manchester, England. **Recognition:** WBC/WBO. **Referee:** Larry O'Connell.
Scorecards: 115-113, 113-115, 114-114.
Fight Summary: Even though Benn had been beaten inside the distance at the middleweight limit by Eubank, now as the 168lbs WBO champion, he was happy to put his WBC super middleweight title on the line in a rematch. Always intense, despite there being no knockdowns both men had their successes and neither man ever set up a good lead although Benn (167) appeared to land the heavier blows. However, Eubank (168) was always solid, and in the fifth he hurt Benn before the sixth saw the latter deducted a point for going low having been warned previously to keep his punches up. At the final bell the majority thought that Benn had got home, but under scrutiny it was clear that neither deserved to lose, the decision eventually being seen as a fair one.

29 October 1993. James Toney w pts 12 Tony Thornton.
Venue: Civic Centre, Tulsa, Oklahoma, USA. **Recognition:** IBF. **Referee:** Sam Williams.
Scorecards: 118-110, 118-110, 116-112.
Fight Summary: In a contest that saw each and every round go virtually the same way the champion appeared happy to let Thornton (167) stalk him for much of the time, responding with countering blows and good movement. The opening two sessions saw Thornton concentrating on the body and having some success before deciding on a more predictable plan of campaign when coming forward in a straight line, throwing hooks, uppercuts and combinations. From thereon in Toney (168) was always one step ahead, Thornton having little success other than to make the champion work hard for the decision while winning three rounds at most.

18 December 1993. Michael Nunn w pts 12 Merqui Sosa.
Venue: Cuauhtemoc Stadium, Puebla, Mexico. **Recognition:** WBA. **Referee:** Julio Alvarado.
Scorecards: 116-113, 116-112, 116-112.
Fight Summary: Unable to initially make the weight, and fighting at altitude, the southpaw champion was thought to have a hard fight on his hands against the hard-hitting Sosa (165½). Prior to the contest the Dominican was seen as a danger man but after the opening six rounds, when Sosa got through with body punches, Nunn (168) dominated the action. Docked a point for carrying on after the bell to end the tenth, with Sosa fighting desperately

in the last two sessions, swinging wildly with both hands, he was beaten to the punch with sharp jabs and good movement as Nunn fully justified the verdict.

5 February 1994. Chris Eubank w pts 12 Graciano Rocchigiani.
Venue: Deutschland Hall, Berlin, Germany. **Recognition:** WBO. **Referee:** Genaro Rodriguez.
Scorecards: 115-113, 118-109, 114-113.
Fight Summary: Retaining the WBO title for the tenth time, Eubank (168) was well on his way after three rounds due to Rocchigiani (163¾) scarcely throwing a punch. However, the southpaw challenger made up for that when hitting back strongly in the fifth through to the eighth. During that spell Eubank appeared negative, but after Rocchigiani was cut on the right eye in the ninth he reasserted himself. Although the German's cut worsened in the 11th he came back strongly to force Eubank to hold on grimly, an action which brought him a point deduction. Having been outworked in the last round Eubank just about scraped home on two of the cards, the scoring being marred by the judge who gave the champion 11 rounds making a mockery of Rocchigiani's fine effort.

26 February 1994. Nigel Benn w pts 12 Henry Wharton.
Venue: Exhibition Centre, Earls Court, London, England. **Recognition:** WBC. **Referee:** Tony Perez.
Scorecards: 115-113, 116-114, 117-112.
Fight Summary: After doing little work during the opening three rounds the unbeaten challenger gave himself a mountain to climb, but by the fifth he was back in the fight when handed a disputed knockdown decision over Benn (168) despite it looking more like a push following a left hook. Taking confidence from that Wharton (167½) came right back at Benn, forcing him to bob and weave to avoid hooks from both hands. By now boxing an intelligent fight, when Benn landed a right hook in the eighth, the heaviest punch of the contest thus far, Wharton almost went down. With Benn conserving his energy the last four sessions saw him drop the pace as Wharton tried in vain to find a winning punch. Although the margins were close Benn was a clear winner, while Wharton could take heart from his worthy performance.

26 February 1994. Steve Little w pts 12 Michael Nunn.
Venue: Exhibition Centre, Earls Court, London, England. **Recognition:** WBA. **Referee:** John Coyle.
Scorecards: 115-112, 116-114, 113-115.
Fight Summary: Giving his former sparring partner a crack at his title despite him not having had a fight for 15 months, Nunn (167) was on his back after just 30 seconds following a wide left hook to the jaw. Although the squat Little (168) rushed in to finish the job he was unable to do any further damage to the 6'2" Nunn, who tied his man up effectively before getting back to work. However, after the fourth round it was clear that the southpaw champion was taking it far too easy, while Little continued to throw sweeping punches in from both hands without ever looking convincing. Round after round followed with the lethargic Nunn, who had trouble making the weight, unable to up his work-rate while thinking that the decision was his for the taking, only to lose his title to the unheralded Little who worked that much harder. Most onlookers felt that despite being unimpressive Nunn had won, but two of the judges saw it differently and they were the men that counted.

5 March 1994. James Toney w rsc 4 Tim Littles.
Venue: Olympic Auditorium, Los Angeles, California, US. **Recognition:** IBF. **Referee:** Pat Russell.
Fight Summary: It had been fairly even up until the third round, but when an unintentional head butt opened up a bad cut over the champion's left eye and Littles (166½) tried to take advantage of the situation he almost immediately paid the price. Realising that the fight might be stopped, Toney (167¾) hurt Littles with a solid left hook before dropping him with an overarm right close to the end of the session. Racing out of his corner at the start of the fourth Toney soon had Littles in trouble, and after dropping him three times with heavy rights to the head the referee called the fight off on the 1.03 mark.

21 May 1994. Chris Eubank w pts 12 Ray Close.
Venue: King's Hall, Belfast, Northern Ireland. **Recognition:** WBO. **Referee:** Paul Thomas.
Scorecards: 115-114, 118-112, 114-117.
Fight Summary: Yet again Close (168) gave the champion a run for his money, once more appearing slightly unlucky not to receive the decision. Defending himself well against the right uppercut Close matched jabs with

Eubank (167¾) in the early stages, using in-and-out tactics. Even when the Irishman was cut on the forehead in the sixth Eubank failed to take advantage. Realising that the fight might be slipping away from him Eubank started to pick the pace up in the eighth, and from the tenth right through to the final bell he stormed into Close, who despite tiring badly kept his defences in place to deny the champion a stoppage victory.

9 July 1994. Chris Eubank w pts 12 Mauricio Amaral.
Venue: Olympia Grand Hall, Kensington, London, England. **Recognition:** WBO. **Referee:** Steve Smoger.
Scorecards: 116-114, 115-113, 116-113.
Fight Summary: Although Amaral (166) started well, the champion began to match him with jabs from the second round while taking the judges' eyes with bursts of hard punches prior to the end of each session. Despite this Amaral was still going well, especially when driving Eubank (168) back across the ring and opening a cut on his left eye in the seventh. Continuing to press forward Amaral was still in the fight at this stage, but following a couple of messy rounds Eubank came back to dominate the last three sessions as the Brazilian tired.

29 July 1994. James Toney w co 12 Charles Williams.
Venue: MGM Grand, Las Vegas, Nevada, USA. **Recognition:** IBF. **Referee:** Joe Cortez.
Fight Summary: Despite having height and reach advantages, Williams (167½), the former IBF light heavyweight kingpin, was happy to work at close quarters where he could close down the champion and take the sting out of his punches. Closely contested, by the end of the seventh both fighters had their left eyes closed and swollen, and in the eighth Toney (168) had a point deducted for hitting and nearly flooring Williams after the bell. With Toney coming on stronger in the latter stages Williams began to tire, being all but done for in the 11th. The final session saw both men tired, but it was Toney who got his second wind before sending Williams down with a right to the jaw to be counted out on the 2.45 mark.

12 August 1994. Frankie Liles w pts 12 Steve Little.
Venue: Villa Lujan Defenders Football Ground, Tucuman, Argentina. **Recognition:** WBA. **Referee:** Steve Smoger.
Scorecards: 118-112, 116-114, 118-113.
Fight Summary: In one of the poorest fights ever seen in Argentina, Little (166¾) lost his title first time round when being well outpointed by Liles (164¾). Scoring with good jabs and right crosses the tall southpaw was always going too well for the champion, who found it difficult to get inside and was consistently wrong-footed. Whatever Little tried he was thwarted, the only real surprise coming when one judge had him just two points down.

27 August 1994. Chris Eubank w rsc 7 Sam Storey.
Venue: International Arena, Cardiff, Wales. **Recognition:** WBO. **Referee:** Dave Parris.
Fight Summary: Jabbing away with the southpaw right, despite having been forced to take heavy blows when the champion occasionally opened up, Storey (168) was well in the fight up until the fifth round when badly cut on the right cheek. Knocked over from a right to the head in the sixth it was clear that Storey was having trouble with his left ankle when he got up, and early in the seventh he went down on one knee without taking a punch. Although Storey got to his feet, after quickly being put under a two-fisted attack by Eubank (168) and floored again, the referee stopped the contest when the Irishman's corner tossed in the towel. The finish came one minute into the session.

10 September 1994. Nigel Benn w pts 12 Juan Carlos Gimenez.
Venue: National Exhibition Centre, Birmingham, England. **Recognition:** WBC. **Referee:** Luis Guzman.
Scorecards: 119-115, 117-112, 118-112.
Fight Summary: Taking part in his third championship fight Gimenez (167½) once again proved to be a game, durable performer as he soaked up all the champion could throw at him. Occasionally working away well with both hands, Gimenez was almost dropped in the eighth by a crashing right to the head as Benn (167¼) looked to finish early. Amazingly, after the tough Paraguayan recovered almost immediately, in the tenth he was landing solid rights to the body before bundling Benn to the floor. In the 11th Benn tried again with lefts and rights to the head, but on failing to drop his man he got behind the jab right through to the final bell.

15 October 1994. Chris Eubank w pts 12 Dan Schommer.
Venue: Superbowl, Sun City, South Africa. **Recognition:** WBO. **Referee:** Stan Christodoulou.
Scorecards: 116-113, 116-114, 117-113.
Fight Summary: This was yet another fight for Eubank (168) in which the pundits disagreed with the judges' scorecards. Starting brightly the southpaw Schommer (167½) was soon on the back foot, banging out jabs and crosses, and despite not working flat out for several rounds he was able to evade the champion's best punches with good movement. In the seventh Eubank finally had some success when a right to the jaw hurt the American, but unable to capitalise it was only in the ninth that he began to take over. Even then Schommer, who had only boxed twice in three years, had his moments as Eubank continued to miss with wild punches. Regardless of that, the fact that Schommer very rarely came forward would have counted against him.

18 November 1994. Roy Jones w pts 12 James Toney.
Venue: MGM Grand, Las Vegas, Nevada, USA. **Recognition:** IBF. **Referee:** Richard Steele.
Scorecards: 119-108, 118-109, 117-110.
Fight Summary: Defending his title against the IBF middleweight titleholder, Toney (167) was comprehensively outboxed by a man who would glide away from punches while scoring at the same time, especially with left hooks. In the third round Jones (168), who was posing at the time, suddenly produced a right cross that caught Toney off balance and sent him down for the mandatory 'eight'. More embarrassed than hurt Toney tried hard to corner Jones, but the latter, showing great movement and footwork, was never in one place for long until tiring towards the end. Even in the last four rounds when Jones slowed Toney was still unable to take advantage, continuing to be second best.

10 December 1994. Chris Eubank w pts 12 Henry Wharton.
Venue: G-Mex Leisure Centre, Manchester, England. **Recognition:** WBO. **Referee:** Steve Smoger.
Scorecards: 115-113, 118-112, 116-112.
Fight Summary: On top from start to finish the champion answered his many critics when convincingly outscoring the tough Wharton (167¾) in all but the fifth and the final two sessions. Showing greater work-rate than he had for some time Eubank (168) continually stung Wharton with cracking counters, and in the ninth lefts and rights had the latter's head snapping back and forth. Refusing to quit, although Wharton's left eye was swollen shut, he still pushed on regardless before receiving much acclaim at the finish for his display of courage.

17 December 1994. Frankie Liles w pts 12 Michael Nunn.
Venue: Ruminahui Coliseum, Quito, Ecuador. **Recognition:** WBA. **Referee:** Rafael Ramos.
Scorecards: 114-113, 115-112, 117-111.
Fight Summary: Starting well when staggering Nunn (168) with a southpaw straight left in the first round the champion continued to be busy during the opening six sessions, landing solidly with short right and left hook counters. After Nunn, who worked the body from the third onwards, was docked a point in the fifth for going low he continued to sail close to the wind before Liles (167) got his jab going again in the eighth. In the last three rounds both men did some good work, but it was Liles who impressed the judges the most to take the decision.

25 February 1995. Nigel Benn w co 10 Gerald McClellan.
Venue: Docklands Arena, Millwall, London, England. **Recognition:** WBC. **Referee:** Alfred Asaro.
Fight Summary: This was one of the great fight nights in Britain, but it also turned out to be one of the saddest when McClellan (165) finished up being taken to hospital to remove a blood clot from the brain. As a fight it had everything. The hard-hitting McClellan, who had recently vacated the WBC middleweight title, set about the champion with gusto when knocking him out of the ring and cutting his right cheek in the opening session. Almost miraculously Benn (168) came right back in the second with heavy blows to head and body, and although McClellan was still landing the harder single shots neither gave ground. With round after round following the same pattern when a badly tiring Benn was dropped in the eighth it looked to be the end for him. But when he came back with big punches of his own it was McClellan who was down in the ninth, claiming a foul to which the referee told him to box on. Benn, whose face was badly swollen as was McClellan's, came out at the start of the tenth, and following a right to the head the latter took a count of 'six' before being dropped to his knees for the full count at

1.46 of the round. Having walked unaided back to his corner, shortly afterwards McClellan slumped into unconsciousness and was rushed immediately to hospital.

18 March 1995. Roy Jones w rsc 1 Antoine Byrd.
Venue: Civic Centre, Pensacola, Florida, USA. **Recognition:** IBF. **Referee:** Bill Connors.
Fight Summary: Making his first defence, and fighting a southpaw for the first time in his career, Jones (167½) quickly got down to business when landing bunches of blows before smashing in big rights to the head followed by a left hook to floor Byrd (167½). Back on his feet Byrd was immediately dropped again, and after rising and being hit without reply the referee called the fight off on the 2.06 mark.

18 March 1995. Steve Collins w pts 12 Chris Eubank.
Venue: Green Glens Arena, Millstreet, Ireland. **Recognition:** WBO. **Referee:** Ron Lipton.
Scorecards: 117-113, 114-112, 114-112.
Fight Summary: Taking six of the first eight rounds Collins (167¾) outworked and outhustled the champion, knocking him down in the eighth and generally staying on top of him. As the rounds passed by Eubank (167¾) became aware that the fight was slipping away from him as Collins worked well with both hands. And although he was on the floor again in the ninth no count was given. In the tenth Eubank finally caught up with Collins, dropping him with a right to the temple, but when the Irishman got up on shaky legs he was surprisingly left alone. The last two sessions saw Eubank desperately trying to save the day, and although he jarred Collins up a couple of times and cut his left eye the latter spent the final 30 seconds of the fight dancing his way out of trouble to make sure of the decision. Having lost his 43-fight unbeaten record, it was clear that Eubank would welcome the return match eventually set for September.

27 May 1995. Frankie Liles w rsc 6 Frederic Seillier.
Venue: Broward County Convention Centre, Fort Lauderdale, Florida, USA. **Recognition:** WBA. **Referee:** Bill Connors.
Fight Summary: Almost put down in the opening session by the southpaw champion Seillier (167) kept ploughing forward despite taking a battering. Even then it was clear that he had little or no chance of winning. In fact, the only punches that bothered Liles (166¼) were those below the belt, for which Seillier was continually warned. In the fourth round Seillier was stunned on more than one occasion as Liles began to pick up the pace, and in the fifth the Frenchman looked a sorry sight as blood poured from a cut on the left eye. Rarely missing, after Liles crashed in a batch of combination punches a short right to the head floored Seillier. Although the challenger got up and was allowed to continue he was barely able to stand, eating up punch upon punch before the referee finally stopped the one-sided affair with 16 seconds of the sixth remaining.

24 June 1995. Roy Jones w rsc 6 Vinny Pazienza.
Venue: Convention Centre, Atlantic City, New Jersey, USA. **Recognition:** IBF. **Referee:** Tony Orlando.
Fight Summary: After seeing what Pazienza (168) could do in the opening two rounds the champion went after his challenger from the third onwards, having cut him under the left eye and bloodied his nose by the end of the fourth. Continuing to come off worse in the exchanges Pazienza could not cope with the speed of Jones (168), and after being cut on the right eye in the fifth he tore into the latter in the sixth only to be dropped by a left hook. Up at around 'four', Pazienza was soon down for the second time, courtesy of a cracking right, but after getting up again and being sent crashing after a lightning fast six-punch combination the referee called it off with two seconds of the session remaining.

22 July 1995. Nigel Benn w rtd 8 Vincenzo Nardiello.
Venue: Docklands Arena, Millwall, London, England. **Recognition:** WBC. **Referee:** Larry O'Connell.
Fight Summary: Retaining his title for the eighth time Benn (168) was just too heavy-handed for Italy's Nardiello (167), who was retired by his corner at 1.43 of the eighth round after being down five times. Strangely, although being floored three times in the seventh and twice in the eighth, only two of them were counted as knockdowns. Having won the opening three rounds Benn became ragged in the fourth and fifth, which allowed Nardiello, boxing behind the southpaw lead, back in to the fight. After Nardiello dropped to his knees towards the end of the fifth, complaining that he had been butted, from there on the result was never in doubt.

Super Middleweight Division

2 September 1995. Nigel Benn w co 7 Danny Perez.
Venue: The Stadium, Wembley, London, England. **Recognition:** WBC. **Referee:** Mickey Vann.
Fight Summary: From the second round Perez (167) had begun to feel the champion's power, especially from the right uppercut, and in the fifth a cracking right dropped the American for the mandatory 'eight' count. Back in the fight Perez gave it a go, surprising Benn (166¼) with combinations, but by the sixth he was on the back foot and fast running out of steam. Sensing a stoppage win in the seventh, when Benn finally caught up with Perez after bludgeoning him to the canvas with another heavy right the latter was counted out on one knee at 2.23 of the session.

9 September 1995. Steve Collins w pts 12 Chris Eubank.
Venue: Padraig Ó Caoimh Gaelic Football Stadium, Cork, Ireland. **Recognition:** WBO. **Referee:** Ismael Fernandez.
Scorecards: 115-113, 115-113, 114-115.
Fight Summary: As in their previous contest the new champion made a solid start to take the play away from Eubank (167½), the latter only getting into the fight for the first time in the sixth after the pace slowed. Up until then Eubank had found it difficult to get set, but after a nasty head clash left Collins (167) with a badly cut right eye in the seventh he began landing more right hands. Although Collins was slowing down he was still marching forward, and it was only in the last three sessions when Eubank began to let the punches go that he clawed back much of the points' deficit. Certainly close, had one of the judges not given Collins the last round it would have been scored a draw.

30 September 1995. Roy Jones w rsc 3 Tony Thornton.
Venue: Civic Centre, Pensacola, Florida, USA. **Recognition:** IBF. **Referee:** Brian Garry.
Fight Summary: Right from the opening bell Thornton (165¾) was befuddled by the speed of the champion, and towards the end of the second round a big left hook put him down on his back. Although Thornton got up and made it back to his corner, it was only 45 seconds into the third that the referee brought an end to the contest after Jones (167½) had battered away with punch after punch without anything coming back.

25 November 1995. Steve Collins w pts 12 Cornelius Carr.
Venue: The Point, Dublin, Ireland. **Recognition:** WBO. **Referee:** Ismael Fernandez.
Scorecards: 116-112, 116-112, 117-111.
Fight Summary: Although he never looked like beating the champion Carr (167½) showed great determination and durability in going the full distance. For his part, Collins (167¾) made an aggressive start, opening up a bad cut on the side of Carr's left eye in the third round. However, he lacked the spark to finish his rival off despite working hard. There was no doubting that Collins, who picked up a cut left eye in the ninth, was landing the better punches, but Carr, who showed an accurate jab and solid countering at times, won the sixth, eighth and ninth before finishing strongly in the 12th.

9 December 1995. Frankie Liles w pts 12 Mauricio Amaral.
Venue: Hanns Martin Schleyer Hall, Stuttgart, Germany. **Recognition:** WBA. **Referee:** Hubert Earle.
Scorecards: 119-108, 118-110, 118-111.
Fight Summary: Winning virtually every round bar the sixth, despite Amaral (165¾) hammering in rights to the body the champion continued to score well with solid southpaw jabs throughout, barely raising his game. Strong and durable, even if somewhat easy to work out, with Amaral always going to be a hard man to stop the nearest Liles (168) came to achieving that was when he dropped him in the last ten seconds of the fight. Needless to say, the Brazilian was on his feet at the final bell.

2 March 1996. Thulani Malinga w pts 12 Nigel Benn.
Venue: International Arena, Newcastle, England. **Recognition:** WBC. **Referee:** Richard Steele.
Scorecards: 118-109, 115-111, 112-114.
Fight Summary: For round after round Malinga (165¾) kept the champion on the end of his left jab and follow-up rights, apart from in the fifth when he was floored by a big right to the head, and either kept out of range or closed the space down. Despite Benn (166½) looking in great condition he never really got to grips with Malinga, having struggled to beat the South African almost four years earlier. By the end of the fourth, with Benn's right eye fast

closing it looked as though he was having great difficulty timing his punches thereafter. Towards the end, as Malinga tired, Benn tried to take advantage but was unable to do so. And when he was forced to take a count from what looked to be just a slip in the last session it merely highlighted the end of his reign.

9 March 1996. Steve Collins w rsc 11 Neville Brown.
Venue: Green Glens Arena, Millstreet, Ireland. **Recognition:** WBO. **Referee:** Ismael Fernandez.
Fight Summary: Making an excellent start after a poor performance last time out the champion charged into Brown (167), punching away at the body, before dropping the latter for the mandatory count with a heavy right to the head. After Brown touched down again in the second it looked all over, but showing great resilience he came back to take the fourth as Collins (167¾) tired from his earlier exertions. Having been cut on the right eye in the fifth Brown was under big pressure from there onwards as Collins attacked him with venom, and with his face a mass of lumps and bumps he somehow kept going until the 11th when dropped by a solid right to the head. Although Brown was up at the count of 'six' the referee had seen enough, stopping the fight 54 seconds into the session.

8 June 1996. Frankie Liles w rsc 3 Tim Littles.
Venue: International Arena, Newcastle, England. **Recognition:** WBA. **Referee:** Mitch Halpern.
Fight Summary: With both men going for an early finish it was Littles (167) who came off worse, being dumped heavily by a right-left to the head from the champion after he was set up by a right uppercut that left him dazed on the ropes. When the bell to end the session went a minute early, Littles was so confused that he went to the wrong corner. Taking the fight to Liles (167¼) in the second, Littles hurt his man with a cracking right to the jaw before sending him down with a swinging right to the body that looked to be low. Not scored as a knockdown, Littles, now cut over the left eye, followed it up with blows to the back of the head that put Liles on his knees. This time the referee deducted a point for excessive fouling from Littles, who moments later was smashed down by a right hook and saved by the bell. The third round saw Liles knocked out of the ring from a series of rights to the head and then bundled to the floor. Coming back strongly, Liles put Littles down with a right hook to the jaw before forcing the referee to come to the latter's aid when he was staggering around with just two seconds of the round remaining.

15 June 1996. Roy Jones w rtd 11 Eric Lucas.
Venue: Veterans Memorial Coliseum, Jacksonville, Florida, USA. **Recognition:** IBF. **Referee:** Brian Garry.
Fight Summary: Taking every round at a canter, the champion, hands held low, battered away at Lucas (165¾) whilst hardly taking a blow in return. Showing remarkable durability Lucas withstood the hammering, and even when he was sent to the floor in the tenth it was ruled a slip. Desperately trying to put Lucas away, whatever Jones (166) produced was met by solid resistance from the French-Canadian. It was only when the bad cut over his right eye worsened that he was pulled out by his corner after the 11th.

6 July 1996. Steve Collins w rsc 4 Nigel Benn.
Venue: Nynex Arena, Manchester, England. **Recognition:** WBO. **Referee:** Genaro Rodriguez.
Fight Summary: The champion started the better of the two, firing in uppercuts and blows to the body, with Benn (167½) having problems finding the range and being forced to back up. It was not until the third round that Benn began to get going, trading heavy punches with Collins (165¾) on equal terms, but in the fourth it suddenly went sour for him when he missed with a big right and fell to the canvas, suffering a twisted right ankle in the process. On getting up it was clear that Benn was not in a position to mount any kind of a challenge, and after Collins had pounced on him with a two-fisted attack the referee called the fight off with 20 seconds of the session remaining.

6 July 1996. Vincenzo Nardiello w pts 12 Thulani Malinga.
Venue: Nynex Arena, Manchester, England. **Recognition:** WBC. **Referee:** Mickey Vann.
Scorecards: 116-112, 114-112, 111-116.
Fight Summary: Defending his title for the first time Malinga (165¾) fought in an uninspiring fashion against an opponent who was so negative himself that he hardly deserved to win the title. Even so, Nardiello (167) took the opening three rounds as the South African struggled to find any rhythm against his southpaw opponent. It was only in the ninth that the fight sprang into action. After Nardiello went to the floor claiming that he had been hit

low, when asked to box on Malinga immediately tossed in another low one that this time brought about a point deduction. Although they both gave it a go in the last session, Nardiello sustaining a cut on the left eye, the decision was received almost in silence.

4 October 1996. Roy Jones w rsc 2 Bryant Brannon.
Venue: MSG Theatre, Manhattan, NYC, New York, USA. **Recognition:** IBF. **Referee:** Ron Lipton.
Fight Summary: Up against a brilliant champion the unbeaten Brannon (168) at least had a go, tearing in to get his punches off before being dropped by a left hook. Although he was on his feet at 'five' the referee completed the mandatory count before allowing Brannon back into the fight, and despite taking some heavy shots from Jones (168) he made it to the bell. Putting on a brave show, Brannon was soon down again, this time for 'two' after taking hooks and uppercuts to the jaw. Back in action, after two rights and a left hook sent Brannon down face first the fight was stopped at 2.23 of the second.

When Jones relinquished the IBF version of the title in March 1997 on being recognised as the WBC light heavyweight champion, Charles Brewer, the USBA champion, was matched against Gary Ballard to decide the vacancy.

12 October 1996. Robin Reid w co 7 Vincenzo Nardiello.
Venue: Assago Forum, Milan, Italy. **Recognition:** WBC. **Referee:** Frank Cappuccino.
Fight Summary: Going forward right from the opening bell Reid (167¼) began well, looking to get inside to work the body, and had a fair amount of success before flooring the southpaw champion in the second. It should have brought about a count, but Nardiello (168) got away with it by claiming a foul and being told to box on. From the third through to the fourth Nardiello's better boxing had taken him into the lead as he controlled the pace while putting his punches together better. However, that all changed in the fifth when Reid dropped him with a left hook and two rights to the head. Up at 'six' but cut over the left eye, Nardiello made it to the end of the session. Even though Nardiello got through the sixth he was counted out with just two seconds of the seventh remaining after being dropped by a left hook to the ribs.

9 November 1996. Steve Collins w rtd 6 Nigel Benn.
Venue: Nynex Arena, Manchester, England. **Recognition:** WBO. **Referee:** Paul Thomas.
Fight Summary: Having been forced out of their previous match with an injured ankle Benn (167) was looking to turn things around this time, and although he went well for the opening three rounds the champion picked it up in the fourth, especially with long rights to the head. After being penalised a point in the fifth for rubbing his head in Benn's face, Collins (168) really went to town, walking through his opponent's punches and landing heavily himself. Even then it was a surprise when Benn was retired by his corner at the end of the sixth, but with his best punches bouncing off Collins to no effect he had nothing left. Following the fight Benn announced his retirement from the ring.

8 February 1997. Robin Reid w rsc 7 Giovanni Pretorius.
Venue: Docklands Arena, Millwall, London, England. **Recognition:** WBC. **Referee:** Lou Filippo.
Fight Summary: Threatening to win early the champion raced into Pretorius (166), switching from head to body with powerful blows, and hammered away until the South African was forced to touch down for 'eight'. Having put everything into the first round, Reid (166½) took so much out of himself that he did not start to control the fight again until the fifth when he dropped Pretorius and cut him over both eyes. After taking time out in the sixth Reid came again in the seventh, and following a tremendous right to the head he floored Pretorius so emphatically that the referee did not even bother to count, calling it off on the 2.10 mark to allow the latter to be treated.

8 February 1997. Steve Collins w rsc 5 Frederic Seillier.
Venue: Docklands Arena, Millwall, London, England. **Recognition:** WBO. **Referee:** Joe Cortez.
Fight Summary: Taking over from the opening bell the champion found Seillier (167½) an easy target, and in the second round, having felt the power of the Frenchman's right hand, he smashed open a cut over his left eye with a heavy right. Thereafter, Collins (167½) took his time, knowing he had the beating of Seillier. With Collins controlling the fight with solid lefts and rights another right sliced open a further bad cut in the fifth, this time on the bridge of

the nose. Following on from that, after a cracking left hook had knocked Seillier back a few paces the referee led him back to his corner where the doctor advised an immediate stoppage, timed at 2.20.

19 April 1997. Frankie Liles w rsc 5 Segundo Mercado.
Venue: Memorial Auditorium, Shreveport, Louisiana, USA. **Recognition:** WBA. **Referee:** Terry Woods.
Fight Summary: Fighting a southpaw for the first time, when Mercado (166¾) was put down within 30 seconds by the hard-hitting champion he never looked like coming to terms with the style. With poor balance and much smaller than Liles (168) the Ecuadorian took a terrible beating for the next three rounds, being hammered by lefts and rights without too much response. In the fifth it was obvious that Mercado could not be allowed to carry on much longer, and at 1.37 of the session he was pulled out of the fight by the referee when shipping lefts and rights.

3 May 1997. Robin Reid w pts 12 Henry Wharton.
Venue: Nynex Arena, Manchester, England. **Recognition:** WBC. **Referee:** Larry O'Connell.
Scorecards: 118-111, 117-113, 114-114.
Fight Summary: A little slow to get going Wharton (168) lost the first two sessions before coming back well to edge the next three. Subsequently, however, Wharton failed to take a round on at least two of the judges' cards, and by the ninth his face was badly swollen, testament to the champion's more accurate punches. In the next round a big right also opened up a cut on the bridge of his nose. Boxing on the back foot Reid (166¼) scored well with accurate left jabs and rights as Wharton followed him around, but he was never able to relax against an opponent who punched his weight and was always dangerous, especially with the left hook. How one of the judges managed to call it a draw was certainly a puzzle as one could not have been anything but impressed with Reid's performance.

21 June 1997. Charles Brewer w rsc 5 Gary Ballard.
Venue: University of South Florida Sun Dome, Tampa, Florida, USA. **Recognition:** IBF. **Referee:** Max Parker Jnr.
Fight Summary: Contesting the vacant IBF title Brewer (165) proved far too good for Ballard (167¼), knocking him down with a solid right to the jaw after 30 seconds and dropping him twice more in the fifth with left hooks and heavy rights before the referee rescued the game South African at 1.40 of the session. In between, Brewer hit Ballard with everything going. Although Ballard showed great resilience he was hurt in every round, his left cheek bleeding badly from the third round before being despatched.

5 July 1997. Steve Collins w rsc 3 Craig Cummings.
Venue: Kelvin Hall, Glasgow, Scotland. **Recognition:** WBO. **Referee:** Roy Francis.
Fight Summary: On the floor in the opening ten seconds after being caught by a right-left to the temple the champion returned the favour when a thumping right put Cummings (161½) down for the mandatory count not long after. Pushed over at the end of the second and cut below the left eye in the third, Cummings was then put under a constant battering as Collins (167¾) looked to finish the fight. Clearly under the cosh, with the American not fighting back the referee rescued him at 1.17 of the session.

Due to make a defence against Joe Calzaghe on 11 October, when Collins was forced to relinquish the WBO version of the title at the end of September after sustaining a foot injury in training Chris Eubank was quickly drafted in to meet the Welshman. Collins announced his retirement on 2 October, his failure to force a championship match against Roy Jones being the main reason.

19 July 1997. Frankie Liles w pts 12 Jaffa Ballogou.
Venue: The Arena, Nashville, Tennessee, USA. **Recognition:** WBA. **Referee:** Anthony Bryant.
Scorecards: 117-111, 118-109, 115-110.
Fight Summary: In a match between southpaws the champion had a fair amount of trouble with the big-punching Ballogou (167½), both men being docked points as the contest degenerated. Ballogou, the biggest offender, really should have been disqualified for countless transgressions, but all the while he was in the ring he remained dangerous despite being outboxed by Liles (166½). After being pounded for much of the ninth, Ballogou put Liles down with a wide right to the jaw, and in the 12th the latter was in a bad way following a similar punch that sent him staggering around the ring and slipping down with 40 seconds on the clock. However, Liles hung on for the win.

Super Middleweight Division

11 September 1997. Robin Reid w pts 12 Hacine Cherifi.
Venue: Kingsway Leisure Centre, Widnes, England. **Recognition:** WBC. **Referee:** Tony Perez.
Scorecards: 117-111, 116-113, 113-115.
Fight Summary: After having problems making the weight the champion was not at the top of his game, but he just about held on for the split decision in his favour against the tough Cherifi (165¼) who had made life extremely difficult for him. For several rounds it was a battle of jabs, and even when Reid (166) stepped it up to bang in rights over the top and left hooks to the body the tough Frenchman stood his ground and came back firing. The last three sessions were extremely hard for the fast-tiring Reid, now fighting open mouthed, and the 11th was Cherifi's best round to date as he hammered in lefts and rights despite being badly cut on the bridge of his nose. With Reid coming back well in the 12th, although Cherifi thought that he had done enough it was not to be.

11 October 1997. Joe Calzaghe w pts 12 Chris Eubank.
Venue: The Arena, Sheffield, England. **Recognition:** WBO. **Referee:** Joe Cortez.
Scorecards: 116-111, 118-110, 118-109.
Fight Summary: Fighting for the belt vacated by Steve Collins, Calzaghe (167¼) clearly beat the former champion. Eubank (167¾) was down twice from left hands, inside the opening 15 seconds and again in the tenth, before coming back to make Calzaghe work hard for his win. While Eubank showed that he was as game as a pebble in defeat, it was Calzaghe's hand-speed that was too much for him, and even when he hit back hard the latter proved that he had a chin to match his southpaw boxing skills.

2 December 1997. Charles Brewer w pts 12 Joey DeGrandis.
Venue: Blue Horizon, Philadelphia, Pennsylvania, USA. **Recognition:** IBF. **Referee:** Rudy Battle.
Scorecards: 119-109, 117-111, 120-108.
Fight Summary: Making the first defence of his title, despite being unable to stow away his rock-hard opponent Brewer (166½) dominated the proceedings with his ten-inch-reach advantage keeping DeGrandis (168) at bay for much of the time. When DeGrandis did occasionally manage to close the champion down he was able to land heavy overarm rights, but in the main he was the one taking the shots while showing plenty of grit to make it to the final bell.

19 December 1997. Thulani Malinga w pts 12 Robin Reid.
Venue: Docklands Arena, Millwall, London, England. **Recognition:** WBC. **Referee:** John Keane.
Scorecards: 117-113, 115-114, 117-112.
Fight Summary: Putting his title on the line for the fourth time Reid (167½) blew his chances of a unification opportunity when losing to the 42-year-old Malinga (166), who hardly deserved to get his championship honours back. Even switching to southpaw for a few rounds failed to bring any improvement in Reid's work, it only being in the final session that he came to life. Unbeaten after 25 fights and one draw Reid rarely landed solidly, and even when forcing Malinga down in the ninth he failed to follow up.

24 January 1998. Joe Calzaghe w rsc 3 Branko Sobot.
Venue: International Arena, Cardiff, Wales. **Recognition:** WBO. **Referee:** Paul Thomas.
Fight Summary: Coming in as a replacement for Tarick Salmaci, and soon under fire from the champion's educated fists, despite showing a good defence Sobot (166½) was put down for a count of 'three' in the third round. Back in action, Sobot was hit with all manner of blows as Calzaghe (167¾) went into overdrive before the referee stopped the fight on the 1.35 mark after a cracking left to the head had left the Croatian shaken and bewildered. Both men were southpaws.

27 March 1998. Richie Woodhall w pts 12 Thulani Malinga.
Venue: Ice Rink, Telford, England. **Recognition:** WBC. **Referee:** Bob Logist.
Scorecards: 118-110, 117-111, 118-109.
Fight Summary: Taking the fight to his challenger from the off Malinga (167¾) gave it his best shot before being comprehensively outboxed. Not interested in getting into a war Woodhall (166¼) stayed cool throughout, sticking the left jab out time and again while refusing to let solid body blows deter him from the task ahead. Dropped in the third round by more of a push than a punch Malinga never took a backward step, and when Woodhall was cut

over the left eye in the fourth he battled on with renewed confidence. It was only in the eighth that Woodhall began to outpunch the South African, but unable to find a winning blow he had to be satisfied with the points win.

28 March 1998. Charles Brewer w rsc 10 Herol Graham.
Venue: Convention Centre, Atlantic City, New Jersey, USA. **Recognition:** IBF. **Referee:** Earl Morton.
Fight Summary: Given another opportunity to win a world title Graham (167) appeared to be on well on his way to victory after six rounds, having dropped the champion twice in the third with solid southpaw lefts to the head and generally outboxing him. From the seventh onwards, however, Brewer (168) finally got himself going, and although Graham scored well in the ninth he was beginning to show signs of tiredness. Dead level on the cards coming into the tenth despite being kept at bay in the early stages of the session, after Brewer finally began to land with heavy shots from both hands when Graham slumped to the floor he was rescued by the referee on the 1.34 mark.

3 April 1998. Frankie Liles w pts 12 Andrey Shkalikov.
Venue: Ruben Rodriguez Coliseum, Bayamon, Puerto Rico. **Recognition:** WBA. **Referee:** Waldemar Schmidt.
Scorecards: 115-114, 115-112, 118-110.
Fight Summary: Looking a poor imitation of a champion, having been out of the ring since the previous July, Liles (168) was almost dropped by a long right in the third and struggled to find any rhythm. Cut on the forehead after a head clash in the second round Shkalikov (168) rarely looked like winning, remaining almost pedestrian for much of the time. However, the southpaw champion seemed unable to take advantage, even being deducted a point for throwing the Russian to the floor in the ninth. After losing the tenth due to lack of work, Liles finally got his jab working to take the last two sessions despite being almost doubled over by a body shot in the 11th. Regardless of Liles' poor showing he rarely looked like losing.

25 April 1998. Joe Calzaghe w rtd 9 Juan Carlos Gimenez.
Venue: Ice Rink, Cardiff, Wales. **Recognition:** WBO. **Referee:** Michael Ortega.
Fight Summary: Seemingly impervious to punishment, Gimenez (166½) failed to win a round from Calzaghe (166½) before retiring on his stool at the end of the ninth round. In fact, Gimenez seemed quite happy to take everything thrown at him as if it was just another day at the office. Having failed to drop the Paraguayan with head shots the southpaw champion eventually went downstairs and it was suspected that the enforced retirement was due to Gimenez possibly suffering a punctured lung from a broken rib.

22 August 1998. Charles Brewer w rsc 3 Antoine Byrd.
Venue: Stadium Hall, Leipzig, Germany. **Recognition:** IBF. **Referee:** Denny Nelson.
Fight Summary: In what was an all-action affair, Brewer (167¾) took the fight to his southpaw challenger from the opening bell, almost paying for his over-confident approach when he was badly hurt by a big right hook to the head in the second round. Brewer eventually found a cracking left uppercut in the third, and after Byrd (167¾) had been down twice the referee called the fight off at 1.11 of the session.

5 September 1998. Richie Woodhall w pts 12 Glenn Catley.
Venue: Ice Rink, Telford, England. **Recognition:** WBC. **Referee:** Richie Davies.
Scorecards: 116-113, 115-113, 114-114.
Fight Summary: Having trained to meet the southpaw Vincenzo Nardiello the champion found himself making his first defence against the British middleweight title holder, Catley (167¾), who came in at short notice. Clearly out of sorts, Woodhall (166¾), who was cut over both eyes in the latter stages, admitted afterwards that he felt that Catley had won the fight, a statement that was supported by the British press. Boxing on the back foot almost throughout Woodhall was certainly active, but while many of his blows appeared not to land correctly it was clear that Catley, who threw less, hit the target more often and with greater force. The last third saw Catley gaining in confidence, especially when scoring well to the body, and after winning the final two sessions the vast majority, other than the judges, thought the title was about to change hands.

24 October 1998. Sven Ottke w pts 12 Charles Brewer.
Venue: Philips Arena, Dusseldorf, Germany. **Recognition:** IBF. **Referee:** Randy Neumann.
Scorecards: 115-113, 116-112, 111-117.

Fight Summary: Unbeaten in 12 contests Ottke (166¾) started well, sending in rapid combinations before moving away and making the champion miss. Eventually, when Brewer (168) stepped it up he had difficulty in catching the fast-moving German with solid punches before becoming more and more frustrated when finding his extra power being negated. It was always close, and if Brewer had won the final session instead of coasting he would have retained his title on the basis of a drawn verdict.

13 February 1999. Joe Calzaghe w pts 12 Robin Reid.
Venue: Telewest Arena, Newcastle, England. **Recognition:** WBO. **Referee:** Roy Francis.
Scorecards: 116-111, 116-111, 111-116.
Fight Summary: Boxing way below his best, no doubt due to an injured left hand suffered in the fifth, the champion found Reid (167¾) right in his face throughout the duration of the contest. The harder blows, especially right hands, were delivered by Reid, and one of them that went low in the eighth saw him deducted a point. With Calzaghe (167) having the hand-speed it was that which kept him in front during the last few sessions as both men tired from their exertions.

13 February 1999. Richie Woodhall w rsc 6 Vincenzo Nardiello.
Venue: Telewest Arena, Newcastle, England. **Recognition:** WBC. **Referee:** Lupe Garcia.
Fight Summary: Coming right back to form after his previous disappointing defence, Woodhall (167) took the fight to Nardiello (168) from the start with sharp jabs and rights to both head and body. Despite being outboxed Nardiello came on with solid southpaw lefts that forced Woodhall to cover up in the third round, and in the fifth he put the latter down for 'three' with another big left. Woodhall was soon back on top, dropping his man with a right to the body for 'nine' immediately prior to the Italian throwing himself down after the bell when looking for a foul. It did not work. Then, in the sixth, Nardiello took several rights to the body before being dropped for 'eight' from a right to the head. With Nardiello wanting out, when Woodhall opened up with both hands, the referee made a timely intervention on the 1.44 mark.

27 February 1999. Sven Ottke w co 3 Giovanni Nardiello.
Venue: Max Schmeling Arena, Berlin, Germany. **Recognition:** IBF. **Referee:** Bobby Ferrara.
Fight Summary: Defending his title for the first time, Ottke (167¼), normally a slow starter, soon got down to business in the second round when he realised that Nardiello's southpaw jabs were falling short and his defence was lacking. Coming out confidently in the third to send Nardiello (168) staggering into the ropes, for which the latter appeared to take longer than ten seconds to recover, Ottke eventually crashed in another heavy right to the jaw that saw the Italian counted out with 30 seconds of the session remaining.

8 May 1999. Sven Ottke w pts 12 Gabriel Hernandez.
Venue: Philips Arena, Dusseldorf, Germany. **Recognition:** IBF. **Referee:** Sam Williams.
Scorecards: 118-110, 118-110, 119-109.
Fight Summary: Despite Hernandez (165¼) bringing a sharp left jab to the proceedings he was too one-dimensional and lacked the power to hurt the champion. For round after round Ottke (167½) built up a good lead, shooting in jabs and fast combinations, but at no time did he ever look like winning inside the distance before having to settle for a wide points victory. At this stage of his career, Hernandez, with just 15 bouts under his belt, lacked the know-how required to succeed at championship level.

5 June 1999. Joe Calzaghe w pts 12 Rick Thornberry.
Venue: International Arena, Cardiff, Wales. **Recognition:** WBO. **Referee:** Rudy Battle.
Scorecards: 120-107, 119-108, 119-109.
Fight Summary: Expected to despatch his challenger early, Calzaghe (167) was unable to do so despite having the Australian down in the second round for the mandatory 'eight' count and cut over the right eye. Even though Calzaghe toyed with Thornberry (167) at times he failed to floor his rival again, possibly due to suffering an injury to his left hand early on, and had to be content with a landslide points win. Coming to the ring with 23 wins from 25 contests Thornberry had no answer to the southpaw skills of the champion, having little to offer other than courage and pride.

12 June 1999. Byron Mitchell w rsc 11 Frankie Liles.
Venue: Shriners Auditorium, Wilmington, Massachusetts, USA. **Recognition:** WBA. **Referee:** Gerry Leone.
Fight Summary: Back in action after a torn rotator cuff injury to his right shoulder, the southpaw champion looked as though he would suffer an early defeat when he was dropped by a sweeping right uppercut to the temple in the second round. However, on getting up at 'eight' Liles (168) began to outbox and hurt Mitchell (168), who was unable to respond in kind until late in the ninth when lashing in heavy blows of his own. Regardless of that, with Liles sticking to his boxing, by the end of the tenth he had won all but one session, the second, on the judges' cards. Finally, in the 11th, Mitchell found the punches that he had been looking for. After forcing two counts he blasted Liles to the floor with a big right to the chin, and when the latter got to his feet, his right eye bleeding badly, the referee called the fight off at 1.17 under the 'three knockdowns in a round' ruling.

4 September 1999. Sven Ottke w tdec 11 Thomas Tate.
Venue: Borderland Hall, Magdeburg, Germany. **Recognition:** IBF. **Referee:** Raffaele Argiolas.
Scorecards: 97-93, 97-93, 96-94.
Fight Summary: Although Tate (165½) had a good opening round he was soon under pressure from the champion, rarely showing until the fifth when he shook his man up with solid blows to the head. From the sixth through to the ninth it was virtually all Ottke (167½), scoring well with fast jabs and punches from both hands which forced Tate on the back foot. With swellings over both eyes, the ninth round saw Tate deducted a point after the referee claimed that he had butted Ottke and cut his left eye when most ringsiders felt that damage had been done by a heavy right. Having been given time out the dazed Ottke went on the back foot, and after Tate had continued to work on the damaged eye the referee called the fight off 25 seconds into the 11th, stating that the scorecards should determine the outcome.

23 October 1999. Markus Beyer w pts 12 Richie Woodhall.
Venue: Ice Rink, Telford, England. **Recognition:** WBC. **Referee:** Laurence Cole.
Scorecards: 115-113, 115-111, 114-113.
Fight Summary: Floored three times, once in the opening round and twice in the third, the champion appeared to have nowhere to go. However, after winning the sixth and seventh and the last three sessions he closed the gap before going down on a unanimous decision. Even though Woodhall (167¾), carrying a broken nose and cut over both eyes, tried to box his way out of trouble the German southpaw continued to be dangerous with heavy left hooks. The last two sessions saw Woodhall fighting like a man possessed, and although the rapidly tiring Beyer (166¾) held on for all his worth had the referee taken a point away from him in the 12th for continuously clinching the contest would have been ruled a draw.

27 November 1999. Sven Ottke w pts 12 Glen Johnson.
Venue: Philips Arena, Dusseldorf, Germany. **Recognition:** IBF. **Referee:** Randy Neumann.
Scorecards: 115-113, 115-113, 115-112.
Fight Summary: Showing great technique the champion unanimously outscored the tough Johnson (166¾) in a very close fight, even though the latter was dangerous with solid blows to head and body. Although Johnson picked the pace up in the last two sessions, throwing punches almost in desperation, Ottke (168) remained cool under pressure to box his way to the final bell. However, it had been a close call.

11 December 1999. Byron Mitchell drew 12 Bruno Girard.
Venue: Grand Hotel, Tunica, Mississippi, USA. **Recognition:** WBA. **Referee:** Elmo Adolph.
Scorecards: 116-114, 113-115, 114-114.
Fight Summary: After recovering from a bad start Girard (166) had found his rhythm by the fourth round, and left-right combinations began to worry the champion who was continually being forced back. By the tenth it was anybody's fight, but when Mitchell (167) began to get through with hard rights the last two sessions saw both men going toe-to-toe in an effort to swing the fight in their direction. With Girard, his nose pouring blood from the second onwards, showing great resolve he signed for a return match shortly afterwards.

29 January 2000. Joe Calzaghe w pts 12 David Starie.
Venue: MEN Arena, Manchester, England. **Recognition:** WBO. **Referee:** John Coyle.

Scorecards: 120-108, 116-113, 118-110.
Fight Summary: Despite being second best in most sessions Starie (167½) made it to the final bell as the southpaw champion failed to find the punch that would ensure an early finish. It was a clear win for Calzaghe (167¾), but once again he failed to show his best form against a man who was cut over the right eye in the sixth and one who was unable to exert any real influence over the proceedings. Afterwards, Calzaghe admitted that having been out of action for over six months due to surgery had affected him.

29 January 2000. Markus Beyer w co 7 Leif Keiski.
Venue: Sachsen Arena, Riesa, Germany. **Recognition:** WBC. **Referee:** Jay Nady.
Fight Summary: Regardless that Keiski (166¼) made a reasonable start he was soon under pressure in the second round before being dropped by a southpaw left as the champion began to find his way. The next two sessions saw much of the same as Beyer (167¼) pushed on, and in the fourth he again floored Keiski with a solid left to the jaw. Showing he had something left Keiski came back well to take the fifth but, after Beyer had worked him around in the seventh, he was sent down and counted out on the 1.47 mark having taken a heavy left to the body.

11 March 2000. Sven Ottke w pts 12 Lloyd Bryan.
Venue: Borderland Hall, Magdeburg, Germany. **Recognition:** IBF. **Referee:** Denny Nelson.
Scorecards: 117-109, 118-108, 120-106.
Fight Summary: Having shared the opening session Bryan (168) found himself in trouble in the second round as the champion opened up. He was then badly hurt by a left hook in the fifth and docked a point in the eighth when going low. Continuing to pile on the pressure Ottke (168) went after Bryan in the tenth, and after dropping him with a right to the jaw he cruised through to the final bell.

8 April 2000. Bruno Girard w pts 12 Byron Mitchell.
Venue: Bercy Sports Palace, Paris, France. **Recognition:** WBA. **Referee:** John Coyle.
Scorecards: 117-114, 116-113, 116-113.
Fight Summary: Making good his return with Mitchell (167½) on home ground, Girard (168) lifted the title after coming on strongly to take three of the last four rounds as the champion tired. There was no doubt that Mitchell was the harder puncher of the two, boxing well behind the jab in the early stages, but had he paced himself better it could have been a different story.

6 May 2000. Glenn Catley w rsc 12 Markus Beyer.
Venue: Hoechst Ball Sports Hall, Frankfurt, Germany. **Recognition:** WBC. **Referee:** Bob Logist.
Fight Summary: Shaken up by a heavy southpaw left in the second round as the champion looked to assert himself, Catley (167) saved his best work for the latter stages. Having nicked many of the rounds with Catley seemingly content to box on the outside, Beyer (167¼) possibly thought that he had the fight already won when he stepped out for the final session. However, Catley had different ideas. Dropping Beyer for 'five' with a left-right-left combination he tore in, belting away with both hands, before the referee rescued the latter after 53 seconds of the session had elapsed.

3 June 2000. Sven Ottke w pts 12 Tocker Pudwill.
Venue: Europa Hall, Karlsruhe, Germany. **Recognition:** IBF. **Referee:** Raffaele Argiolas.
Scorecards: 119-107, 118-107, 119-106.
Fight Summary: Although the opening six rounds were relatively even it was more to do with the champion not working to his maximum ability rather than Pudwill (167) extending him. Pudwill, who survived a badly cut scalp following an accidental clash of heads in the first session and had been shaken up by a left-right to the jaw in the fifth, was still there in the seventh when being deducted a point for illegal use of the head. It was totally one-sided thereafter, with Pudwill being forced to endure counts in the ninth and tenth after Ottke (166½) landed heavily with lefts and rights before making it to the final bell.

12 August 2000. Joe Calzaghe w rsc 5 Omar Sheika.
Venue: Conference Centre, Wembley, London, England. **Recognition:** WBO. **Referee:** Genaro Rodriguez.

Fight Summary: Following three disappointing title defences Calzaghe (168) finally got his act together when taking Sheika (167) apart and battering him to defeat at 2.08 of the fifth. Making a confident start Calzaghe soon had the southpaw jab in and out of Sheika's face as the latter looked to work the body. Cut over the left eye towards the end of the fourth Sheika came out fast for the fifth, but within moments he was also cut on the other eye. And, with Calzaghe punching him without response and the blood flowing, the referee decided that he had seen enough.

1 September 2000. Dingaan Thobela w co 12 Glenn Catley.
Venue: Carnival City Arena, Brakpan, South Africa. **Recognition:** WBC. **Referee:** Eddie Cotton.
Fight Summary: With Catley (167¼) ahead on the cards coming into the eighth, in what had been a tough fight, he was hurt by solid combinations and under constant pressure from there onwards. Deducted a point for illegal use of an elbow in the tenth Catley was still in front, but Thobela (167) was coming on strong. Giving it everything in the final session, after having the champion down from a heavy left-right combination Thobela was only moments away from victory. Although Catley made it to his feet in time he was immediately in trouble as crashing punches to head and body took their toll, and it was no surprise when another volley of blows sent him to the floor again. Counted out with just seven seconds left on the clock, Catley complained that Thobela's bandages had been tampered with, thus giving him greater hitting power. Following an inquiry, despite no concrete evidence of wrong doing, the WBC ordered the winner of Thobela's defence against Dave Hilton to meet the winner of Eric Lucas v Catley.

2 September 2000. Sven Ottke w pts 12 Charles Brewer.
Venue: Borderland Hall, Magdeburg, Germany. **Recognition:** IBF. **Referee:** Brian Garry.
Scorecards: 116-111, 116-112, 113-116.
Fight Summary: In what was a return match, Ottke (167½) having earlier taken the title from Brewer (167), the champion was far more aggressive than in their previous fight. This time there were far more infringements, Ottke given time out after a low blow in the sixth. Also, both men were careless with their heads throughout, Brewer being cut over the left eye in the eighth. Eventually, in the tenth, the American was deducted a point for a head butt, and in the 11th he showed a distinct lack of interest in the proceedings before coming back to take the final session. Despite damaging his left hand Ottke fully deserved the win, showing excellent sharpness and accuracy throughout.

16 September 2000. Bruno Girard w pts 12 Manny Siaca.
Venue: Circus Tent, Chateauroux, France. **Recognition:** WBA. **Referee:** John Coyle.
Scorecards: 117-111, 116-113, 113-117.
Fight Summary: It was the champion's aggression and work-rate against the classier boxing skills of Siaca (167½). Although Siaca scored well with left jabs, especially in the middle rounds, Girard (167½) barely gave him time to think as he bored in looking to get inside. The last two sessions were somewhat frenetic, and while Siaca won them on the cards he failed to make up the leeway despite one of the judges having him the winner by seven rounds to three with two even.

Further to Girard forfeiting the WBA version of the title in February 2001 after refusing a rematch against Siaca due to contractual problems, the latter was matched against Byron Mitchell to find a new champion.

15 December 2000. Dave Hilton w pts 12 Dingaan Thobela.
Venue: Molson Centre, Montreal, Canada. **Recognition:** WBC. **Referee:** Elmo Adolph.
Scorecards: 115-113, 117-111, 113-115.
Fight Summary: After nearly 20 years in the ring, Hilton (160½), eight pounds inside the weight limit, finally won a world title when taking a split decision over Thobela (166½). The contest had been extremely close, with no knockdowns, and had the referee taken a point from Hilton for low blows in the tenth the champion would have retained his title. With Hilton going from head to body in short bursts against Thobela's better boxing, it was only when the latter began to tire that the Canadian got his nose in front.

When Hilton forfeited the WBC title in April 2001 on being jailed for sex crimes, Eric Lucas and Glenn Catley were matched to find a new champion.

16 December 2000. Joe Calzaghe w rsc 10 Richie Woodhall.
Venue: The Arena, Sheffield, England. **Recognition:** WBO. **Referee:** Roy Francis.
Fight Summary: Making his seventh title defence Calzaghe (167¾) proved too strong and durable for Woodhall (167½), winning five of the first eight rounds before opening up in the ninth and forcing a stoppage after 28 seconds of the tenth. Prior to the finish Woodhall had boxed well, shooting in good lefts and straight rights, but towards the end of the ninth, his right eye swelling badly, he was put down from southpaw lead right and lefts for a count of 'four'. At the start of the tenth Woodhall had nowhere to go, and after Calzaghe picked it up where he left off in the ninth, slamming in rights and lefts, the referee had seen enough.

16 December 2000. Sven Ottke w pts 12 Silvio Branco.
Venue: Europa Hall, Karlsruhe, Germany. **Recognition:** IBF. **Referee:** Arno Pokrandt.
Scorecards: 117-111, 117-111, 116-112.
Fight Summary: Despite not boxing at his best the champion worked much harder than Branco (167¾), who was out of sorts for much of the time and unable to take advantage of opportunities that presented themselves. Even then the scores did Branco a disservice according to *Boxing News*. The trade paper made the point that if Ottke's pushing, pulling and hitting with the inside of the glove had been cut out the scoreline would have been much closer. In his last contest Branco had beaten England's Robin Reid, but he failed to use his left hand enough while ultimately allowing Ottke (168) to steal rounds as he did in the first, third, seventh and eighth.

3 March 2001. Byron Mitchell w rsc 12 Manny Siaca.
Venue: Mandalay Bay Resort & Casino, Las Vegas, Nevada, USA. **Recognition:** WBA. **Referee:** Jay Nady.
Fight Summary: Contesting the title vacated by Bruno Girard, Mitchell (168) overcame a points deficit to stop Siaca (168) with just 28 seconds of the fight remaining. Siaca had made a good start, scoring well with long lefts and rights over the top as Mitchell came onto him while firing in solid right uppercuts at close range. Mitchell was also busy, and by the end of the seventh there was significant damage to Siaca's left eye. Things turned in Mitchell's favour in the ninth when he dropped Siaca with a cracking right, but after the latter was back in action both men had a point deducted for carrying the fight on after the bell. Although Siaca came back strongly in the next two sessions, looking to be well on his way to victory in the 12th, disaster struck when he missed with a right and walked on to a tremendous left hook to the jaw that sent him down to be counted out.

24 March 2001. Sven Ottke w co 8 James Crawford.
Venue: Borderland Hall, Magdeburg, Germany. **Recognition:** IBF. **Referee:** Robert Byrd.
Fight Summary: Taking more risks than usual the champion set about the limited Crawford (167¼) right from the opening bell, dictating every round on his way to a relatively easy victory. Having thrown 165 blows at Ottke (167¾), landing with only seven, the American did not have the technical defensive ability to avoid punches coming his way, his demise being just a matter of time. Badly cut on the nose in the sixth Crawford tried his best to stay in the fight, but all that came to nought when a series of left-rights to the head followed by a cracking right to the body sent him down to be counted out with eight seconds of the eighth remaining.

28 April 2001. Joe Calzaghe w rsc 1 Mario Veit.
Venue: The International Arena, Cardiff, Wales. **Recognition:** WBO. **Referee:** Mark Nelson.
Fight Summary: Showing all the form expected of him the southpaw champion tore into Veit (167), his 6'4" challenger, and within 30 seconds he had dropped the German for 'three' with a left over the top. Having taken the mandatory 'eight' count Veit was immediately put under further pressure before being floored again after a crunching left from Calzaghe (167¾) detonated on his jaw. Although Veit got to his feet he was quickly in trouble, being rescued by the referee when taking a battering against the ropes. The finish was timed at 1.52 of the opening session.

9 June 2001. Sven Ottke w rsc 11 Ali Ennebati.
Venue: Frankenland Hall, Nuremberg, Germany. **Recognition:** IBF. **Referee:** Arno Pokrandt.

Fight Summary: Successfully defending his title for the tenth time Ottke (166½) won virtually every round before the fight was stopped in his favour at 2.28 of the 11th, despite being up against a hard puncher who hurt him on several occasions, especially with rights to the head. By the end of the eighth it was clear that Ottke was lining himself up for the finish, and in the ninth a terrific right to the body had Ennebati (165½) doubled up in pain. Having dominated the tenth with Ottke going all out in the 11th, after he had dropped Ennebati twice with heavy rights to the head, the referee brought matters to a close.

10 July 2001. Eric Lucas w rsc 7 Glenn Catley.
Venue: Molson Centre, Montreal, Canada. **Recognition:** WBC. **Referee:** Lupe Garcia.
Fight Summary: Battling for the vacant title, Lucas (167¾) ultimately avenged a previous defeat at the hands of Catley (167¼) when he stopped his old rival at 2.04 of the seventh round. The contest had been relatively close up until the fifth even though Catley was falling short with the jab and being countered heavily for his pains, and in the sixth the writing was on the wall for him when he was twice dropped by heavy rights. Still dazed at the start of the seventh Catley continued bravely, but after a crashing right to the jaw sent him to the floor with no chance of beating the count the referee immediately brought the contest to an end.

1 September 2001. Sven Ottke w pts 12 James Butler.
Venue: Borderland Hall, Magdeburg, Germany. **Recognition:** IBF. **Referee:** Randy Neumann.
Scorecards: 118-109, 118-109, 119-108.
Fight Summary: Even though he posed a threat throughout the fight with big rights to the head Butler (167½) was unable to get going until the sixth round against a champion who knew too much for him and gave him little opportunity. Although still being outmanoeuvred by Ottke (167½), Butler finally threw caution to the wind in the last three sessions in an effort to turn things around, only to have a point docked from his total for rabbit punching in the 12th. A worthy winner, Ottke's speed was supplemented with good footwork, accurate jabs and solid combinations.

29 September 2001. Byron Mitchell w pts 12 Manny Siaca.
Venue: Madison Square Garden, Manhattan, NYC, New York, USA. **Recognition:** WBA. **Referee:** Arthur Mercante Jnr.
Scorecards: 114-112, 114-112, 112-115.
Fight Summary: In what was a third title challenge for Siaca (167½) he fell short yet again in a difficult fight to score, the judges only agreeing on three rounds. The champion made a good start when dropping Siaca in the opening session, a right to the head doing the trick, and then dominated the second before the latter came back well in the third. Thereafter, both men had their moments, but by the fifth Siaca was on the back foot, landing good counters as Mitchell (168) tried to close him down. With Siaca tiring Mitchell went all out for the stoppage in the ninth, but after failing to put his man down he himself was floored in the 12th when caught by a left hook to the jaw. Although Siaca seemed to have Mitchell at his mercy when the American got to his feet, he let the opportunity slip and ultimately paid for it.

13 October 2001. Joe Calzaghe w rsc 4 Will McIntyre.
Venue: Parken Stadium, Copenhagen, Denmark. **Recognition:** WBO. **Referee:** Rudy Battle.
Fight Summary: Looking badly out of his depth, McIntyre (167½), who had substituted for Antwun Echols, was picked apart and dissected by the champion's southpaw jab right from the opening bell. And by the third round Calzaghe (167½) was winding up jabs, uppercuts and heavy lefts that eventually left McIntyre totally exposed, at which point the referee exacted a standing 'eight' count before the bell came to the latter's rescue. Still shaky at the start of the fourth McIntyre should have been retired by his corner, but after being dropped following a steady barrage of blows from Calzaghe and getting to his feet the referee stopped the fight 45 seconds into the session.

30 November 2001. Eric Lucas w rsc 8 Dingaan Thobela.
Venue: Molson Centre, Montreal, Canada. **Recognition:** WBC. **Referee:** Laurence Cole.
Fight Summary: Boxing in a defensive mode with little on offer other than durability, Thobela (168), looking even older than his 35 years of age and performing more like a sparring partner, rarely gave the champion a problem and was nearly out of wind by the fifth. The sixth saw Lucas (167¾) ramping up the pace, but having hurt Thobela

by the ropes there was a clash of heads that saw him pick up a badly cut left eye. Deducted a point for what was termed an accidental head butt Thobela was almost through for the night, and after taking heavy punishment from there onwards he was finally rescued by the referee at 2.15 of the eighth following a two-fisted hammering that left him in a dazed state on the ropes.

1 December 2001. Sven Ottke w co 10 Anthony Mundine.
Venue: Westphalia Hall, Dortmund, Germany. **Recognition:** IBF. **Referee:** Wayne Kelly.
Fight Summary: Working well from the outside Mundine (166½) set the champion several problems for a few rounds, even having his man over in the eighth although the count was never picked up. In the ninth, however, Ottke (167), beginning to put his punches together better, had to weather a bit of a storm as Mundine looked for an early finish. Initially, the tenth session saw Mundine having an edge and scoring well with fast lefts, but after a couple of body shots had lowered his guard Ottke hammered home a tremendous right hook to the jaw that sent him down to be counted out on the 2.40 mark. At the time of the finish Ottke was ahead on all three cards by a reasonable margin, which would have been a lot closer had Mundine not been deducted two points in the fourth for intentional butts.

1 March 2002. Eric Lucas w pts 12 Vinny Pazienza.
Venue: Foxwoods Resort Casino, Ledyard, Connecticut, USA. **Recognition:** WBC. **Referee:** Eddie Cotton.
Scorecards: 117-111, 117-112, 119-110.
Fight Summary: Although well on top of the 39-year-old Pazienza (168), who hardly deserved a crack at the title, Lucas (167¾) was unable to drop the former IBF lightweight and WBA junior middleweight champion before having to settle for the wide points decision. Pazienza had promised his fans that he would brawl his way to victory, but it was only in the final session that he gave them a glimpse of what he used to be. Being cut over the right eye in the second merely added to Pazienza's woes.

16 March 2002. Sven Ottke w pts 12 Rick Thornberry.
Venue: Borderland Hall, Magdeburg, Germany. **Recognition:** IBF. **Referee:** Denny Nelson.
Scorecards: 120-108, 120-108, 120-108.
Fight Summary: Despite securing a shut-out points win Ottke (168) failed to come close to dropping an extremely competitive challenger who was always in front of him. It was clear right from the opening bell that Thornberry (167½) was not at the same level as Ottke, but that did not stop him from trying at every opportunity. Defending his title for the 13th time Ottke consistently got through with solid left jabs and combinations, and once again delighted the crowd with his consummate boxing skills.

20 April 2002. Joe Calzaghe w pts 12 Charles Brewer.
Venue: International Arena, Cardiff, Wales. **Recognition:** WBO. **Referee:** Mark Nelson.
Scorecards: 117-112, 119-109, 118-111.
Fight Summary: While the scorecards tell you that it was a relatively easy win for Calzaghe (167¾) it was certainly not, especially in the seventh round when Brewer (167¾) tested his chin and body when hammering in heavy punches from both hands. Ultimately it was the southpaw champion's speed of hand and foot that was the main difference between him and Brewer, and that allowed him to move in and out of range without having to take more than he had to. Afterwards, Calzaghe admitted that the hard-hitting American had given him one of his hardest fights.

1 June 2002. Sven Ottke w pts 12 Thomas Tate.
Venue: Frankenland Hall, Nuremburg, Germany. **Recognition:** IBF. **Referee:** Randy Neumann.
Scorecards: 119-108, 118-109, 116-111.
Fight Summary: The champion proved to be far too quick and accurate for Tate (168), in what was a return match, scoring a second-round knockdown following a sharp left-right. Ottke (168) also kept the latter on the end of the jab for much of the time. In the fourth Tate's left eye began to swell following the constant attention paid to it by the jab, and by the eighth it was bleeding. Towards the end Tate began to come on strong, but by that time Ottke knew that he only had to avoid trouble to make sure of a 14th successful title defence.

27 July 2002. Byron Mitchell w rsc 4 Julio Cesar Green.
Venue: Mandalay Bay Resort & Casino, Las Vegas, Nevada, USA. **Recognition:** WBA. **Referee:** Vic Drakulich.
Fight Summary: In what started as a brawl the champion was soon on the end of things in the opening round when downed twice, firstly by a cracking left hook and secondly following a flurry of blows as the unfancied Green (168) looked for the finish. Although suffering the after-effects in the second, by the third Mitchell (167½) was beginning to put his punches together prior to sending in a solid short right that opened up a gash over Green's left eye in the fourth. At this point Mitchell went for broke, and after hammering Green around the ring and the eye damage worsening the referee stopped the fight on the 1.55 mark.

17 August 2002. Joe Calzaghe w pts 12 Miguel Angel Jimenez.
Venue: Cardiff Castle, Cardiff, Wales. **Recognition:** WBO. **Referee:** Dave Parris.
Scorecards: 120-107, 120-107, 120-107.
Fight Summary: Up against a challenger who was intent on survival, although Calzaghe (167¾) won every round the fight was made more difficult for him after he damaged the knuckles on his left hand as early as the second. Jimenez (168), who certainly proved his durability, offered up little and immediately covered up when under attack. By the latter stages it had become monotonous, with Calzaghe going for the body more in order to preserve his hands. At the final bell it was difficult to understand quite why Jimenez, who had a point deducted in the tenth for head butts, was given a title shot when there was only one recognised name on his record.

24 August 2002. Sven Ottke w rsc 9 Joe Gatti.
Venue: The Arena, Leipzig, Germany. **Recognition:** IBF. **Referee:** Raffaele Argiolas.
Fight Summary: Gatti (168), the elder brother of Arturo, started well when taking the opening session, but from there onwards he was always running second best despite making the champion work hard for the points. After being cut over the right eye in the seventh Gatti found it difficult to stay with Ottke (167½), and in the ninth after being dropped twice he was rescued by the referee with 17 seconds of the round remaining. Following the contest, when Gatti was found to have a minor bleed to the brain he never boxed again.

6 September 2002. Eric Lucas w pts 12 Omar Sheika.
Venue: Bell Centre, Montreal, Canada, USA. **Recognition:** WBC. **Referee:** Lupe Garcia.
Scorecards: 117-111, 117-111, 119-109.
Fight Summary: After dropping two of the opening three rounds and being badly hurt in the third the champion picked up the pace to go clear as Sheika (167) appeared happy to box on the back foot. By the fifth, although Sheika was boxing a clever fight Lucas (166¾) was one step ahead of him, scoring well with left-right-lefts. Cut over the left eye in the seventh Sheika tried to force Lucas on the back foot in the latter rounds, but unable to get past the jab he was well beaten at the finish.

16 November 2002. Sven Ottke w pts 12 Rudy Markussen.
Venue: Frankenland Hall, Nuremburg, Germany. **Recognition:** IBF. **Referee:** Robert Byrd.
Scorecards: 116-112, 116-112, 116-112.
Fight Summary: Although the unbeaten Markussen (166) made the early running, using his strength to push Ottke (167½) back, once the champion had got his left hand working by the fourth round there was only going to be one winner. Markussen, who had never been beyond eight rounds before, continued to be picked off in the latter sessions by jabs and rights over the top as Ottke upped the pace. Giving it one last effort in the 11th Markussen pressed for all he was worth before fading as Ottke coasted home for his 16th successful defence.

14 December 2002. Joe Calzaghe w rsc 2 Tocker Pudwill.
Venue: Telewest Arena, Newcastle, England. **Recognition:** WBO. **Referee:** Dave Parris.
Fight Summary: Despite the American, who came in at short notice, lasting 12 rounds with the IBF champion, Sven Ottke, this was a mismatch. Dumped three times by the southpaw champion in the opener, his right eye a mess, Pudwill (167½) came out for the second round only to be stopped with 39 seconds on the clock when he was rescued by the referee after being floored with a body punch. Angry at not being able to meet Thomas Tate, who pulled out earlier with a burst eardrum, Calzaghe (167¼) took his frustration out on the limited Pudwill.

15 March 2003. Sven Ottke w pts 12 Byron Mitchell.
Venue: Max Schmeling Arena, Berlin, Germany. **Recognition:** IBF/WBA. **Referee:** Stan Christodoulou.
Scorecards: 115-113, 116-114, 112-116.
Fight Summary: In a fight to unify the IBF and WBA titles, it was Ottke (167) who ultimately came out on top after surviving a tough last round when he was shaken up by heavy left and rights as Mitchell (167¼) tried to turn the fight his way. Ottke, who started as he meant to carry on, jumping in with jabs and straight rights before moving away and denying Mitchell openings, always appeared to be one step ahead. With four rounds to go Mitchell moved in, looking to land heavily, but was thwarted more often than not as Ottke, now cut by the side of the left eye, made him miss again and again. At the final bell most good judges had Ottke further ahead than the officials, and how one of them had the American in front beggared belief.

5 April 2003. Markus Beyer w pts 12 Eric Lucas.
Venue: The Arena, Leipzig, Germany. **Recognition:** WBC. **Referee:** Laurence Cole.
Scorecards: 116-113, 116-113, 114-115.
Fight Summary: Making a fast start the champion won the opening sessions, shaking Beyer (167¼) up with a big right in the third before the latter settled in what became a difficult fight to score. There was no doubt that the German southpaw took most of the middle rounds, but Lucas (166¼), always in contention, tried to finish strongly in every one of them. However, it was Beyer who came through in the 11th and 12th when standing his ground and throwing combinations to swing the fight his way.

14 June 2003. Sven Ottke w pts 12 David Starie.
Venue: Borderland Hall, Magdeburg, Germany. **Recognition:** IBF/WBA. **Referee:** Randy Neumann.
Scorecards: 116-112, 116-113, 115-113.
Fight Summary: Even though the decision was unanimous in the champion's favour had Starie (168) upped his work-rate, especially in the middle rounds, the result could have been very different. Once again Ottke (167½) boxed in a conservative fashion, doing what he had to in order to keep ahead when picking his punches and using the left hook well on the inside. The last three sessions saw Starie finally take more risks, outpunching Ottke three to one in the 11th, but the German continued to work on the outside as if he knew the fight was already his.

With Ottke continuing as a double champion, Anthony Mundine outscored Antwun Echols over 12 rounds on 3 September, at the Entertainment Centre, Sydney, Australia to win the vacant WBA 'second tier' title.

28 June 2003. Joe Calzaghe w rsc 2 Byron Mitchell.
Venue: The International Arena, Cardiff, Wales. **Recognition:** WBO. **Referee:** Dave Parris.
Fight Summary: Knocked down for the first time in his career when nailed by a short right hook in the second, Calzaghe (167) was up at 'eight' and came back swiftly to belt Mitchell (168) to the canvas with a big left. Having also taken the 'eight' count, the challenger was immediately set about and driven to the ropes where the referee rescued him after 2.36 of the round had elapsed. This was a good win for the Welshman against a former champion and a man who gave it a real go while it lasted.

16 August 2003. Markus Beyer w disq 5 Danny Green.
Venue: Nurburgring Formula One Racetrack, Nurburg, Germany. **Recognition:** WBC. **Referee:** Bill Clancy.
Fight Summary: Green (167½) made a great start when having the southpaw champion over in the opening two sessions from big right hooks. However, he also had a point deducted in the second when an accidental butt left Beyer (167½) badly cut over the right eye. Although Beyer came back refreshed in the third he was still being outworked by Green, but by the fourth he finally won a round when holding his boxing together. At this stage the hard-punching Green was still ahead, almost throwing Beyer to the floor in the fifth as he looked for a finish. By now Beyer was bleeding heavily, and following another butt from Green that opened up a further cut on the champion's right eye the referee was advised by the ringside doctor to stop the fight. At that point, with the butt deemed to be intentional, instead of being handed the win Green found himself on the end of a disqualification defeat, timed at 2.15 of the fifth.

On 20 December, at the Bell Centre, Montreal, Canada, when Green stopped Eric Lucas in the sixth round he won the WBC 'interim' title in doing so. Regardless, he would have to wait some 15 months before being given another crack at the title.

6 September 2003. Sven Ottke w pts 12 Mads Larsen.
Venue: Fair Hall, Erfurt, Germany. **Recognition:** IBF/WBA. **Referee:** Pete Podgorski.
Scorecards: 115-113, 115-113, 114-114.
Fight Summary: Facing a southpaw for the first time the champion had some difficulty in fathoming Larsen (167½) out initially, but with good footwork and classy countering, especially with rights to the body, he began to get on top. Although it had been expected that the hard-hitting Larsen would show more in the middle sessions he continued to miss wildly at times, there being only one winner at the final bell. Once again Ottke (168) had proved to be the master of just doing enough to win.

13 December 2003. Sven Ottke w pts 12 Robin Reid.
Venue: The Arena, Nuremburg, Germany. **Recognition:** IBF/WBA. **Referee:** Roger Tilleman.
Scorecards: 115-112, 115-112, 117-111.
Fight Summary: Yet again Ottke (168) successfully defended his title on home turf when all seemed lost, this time against the unlucky Reid (168). With the referee taking centre stage virtually throughout, warning Reid continuously and ignoring what seemed to be a perfectly good knockdown when Ottke was floored in the sixth, it turned into an untidy affair. The sixth also saw Reid deducted a point for an accidental head butt after Ottke had theatrically dropped to the ground. From the seventh through to the 12th the action became more and more untidy, which suited Ottke more than it did Reid, and the German just about got his nose in front.

Anthony Mundine retained the WBA 'second tier' title with a fifth-round stoppage win over Yoshinori Nishizawa at the Entertainment Centre, Wollongong, Australia on 19 January 2004.

21 February 2004. Joe Calzaghe w rsc 7 Mger Mkrtchyan.
Venue: Ice Rink, Cardiff, Wales. **Recognition:** WBO. **Referee:** Paul Thomas.
Fight Summary: Defending for the 14th time Calzaghe (167¾) took his time to deal with the tough Mkrtchyan (167), who was not overawed in the least, but by the fifth it was clear that the challenger was gradually being worn down. Although the brave Armenian was still willing to trade the seventh saw him hit with a barrage of punches, the last two being heavy lefts which sent him down. Up before being counted out, and not looking like a man who could last much longer, the referee rescued Mkrtchyan on the 1.05 mark.

At the Westphalia Hall, Dortmund, Germany, on 8 May, Mario Veit outpointed Kabary Salem over 12 rounds to win the vacant WBO 'interim' title. However, it was Salem who got first crack at Calzaghe.

28 February 2004. Markus Beyer w pts 12 Andre Thysse.
Venue: Mehrzweck Hall, Dresden, Germany. **Recognition:** WBC. **Referee:** Larry O'Connell.
Scorecards: 119-109, 117-111, 117-112.
Fight Summary: Giving away six inches in height to the tough challenger, also a southpaw, was not a problem for Beyer (166¾) and he was soon landing with accurate rights and lefts from range to avoid any repetition of his last contest. In the third round Thysse (167¼) did manage to hurt Beyer with a right hook to the jaw, but thereafter rarely threatened as the latter boxed his way to a comprehensive points win.

27 March 2004. Sven Ottke w pts 12 Armand Krajnc.
Venue: Borderland Hall, Magdeburg, Germany. **Recognition:** IBF/WBA. **Referee:** Armando Garcia.
Scorecards: 120-108, 120-110, 119-109.
Fight Summary: Putting on his best performance for some time the champion, Ottke (167½), was soon threading in the jabs to head and body, with Krajnc (166½) having great difficulty in keeping up with his speed. Although Krajnc had little joy, being outboxed round after round, he gave it a real go over the final three sessions to no avail.

Super Middleweight Division

Ottke announced his retirement from boxing immediately following the contest, and while the IBF title remained vacant Anthony Mundine took over full recognition as the WBA champion.

Meantime, the IBF set up two eliminating bouts between Syd Vanderpool v Tito Mendoza and Jeff Lacy v Vitaliy Tsypko. While Vanderpool outpointed Mendoza over 12 rounds on 17 April, the Lacy v Tsypko fight on 5 June was stopped at the end of the second round and declared a technical draw after the latter received a badly cut forehead. To allow the IBF title fight to go ahead it was Lacy who was selected to take on Vanderpool.

5 May 2004. Manny Siaca w pts 12 Anthony Mundine.
Venue: Entertainment Centre, Sydney, Australia. **Recognition:** WBA. **Referee:** Raul Caiz Jnr.
Scorecards: 115-113, 115-113, 113-114.
Fight Summary: Making his first title defence since taking over from Sven Ottke, Mundine (167¼) made a bad start when dropped in the second round by a left hook to the jaw. Although Mundine was up at 'four' he did little to show himself as championship material during the rest of the contest. Having entered the ring after turning an ankle a week earlier Mundine was on the back foot from thereon in as Siaca (167½) went after him, and in the tenth he twice went to the floor due to his injury. Occasionally, Mundine landed good combinations, but Siaca was always the master of the situation.

5 June 2004. Cristian Sanavia w pts 12 Markus Beyer.
Venue: The Arena, Chemnitz, Germany. **Recognition:** WBC. **Referee:** Mark Green.
Scorecards: 116-113, 116-115, 114-115.
Fight Summary: In a battle of southpaws, Sanavia (166½) started the better when scoring well with the right jab while the champion found it difficult to find any rhythm. And when Sanavia began to get his hooks and uppercuts going it became even more difficult for Beyer (167½) to raise his game. However, there was never that much between them and by the tenth it looked as though Beyer might have found the answer, hammering home lefts and rights, before the final two sessions saw him hand the initiative back to Sanavia and, at the same time, relinquish his title.

2 October 2004. Jeff Lacy w rsc 8 Syd Vanderpool.
Venue: Caesar's Palace, Las Vegas, Nevada, USA. **Recognition:** IBF. **Referee:** Robert Byrd.
Fight Summary: Fighting to decide who should wear the IBF Championship Belt after Sven Ottke's retirement, Vanderpool (167), a crafty southpaw, began well with the jab before Lacy (168) picked up the pace in the fourth when landing heavily with rights and lefts. By the sixth Lacy was into his stride, shaking Vanderpool up with left hooks, and he built on that in the eighth before hurting the latter badly enough in the eighth with solid uppercuts to force the referee to stop the fight in his favour. Timed at 1.37 of the eighth, the finish saved the brave Canadian from taking more than he had to.

9 October 2004. Markus Beyer w rsc 6 Cristian Sanavia.
Venue: Fair Hall, Erfurt, Germany. **Recognition:** WBC. **Referee:** Ian-John Lewis.
Fight Summary: Defending the title against the man he won it from Sanavia (165¾) started slowly in the opening session before taking the next four rounds. At that stage of the proceedings he looked the more likely winner. However, boxing coolly, Beyer (167¼) had begun to show signs of his form late on in the fifth, and in the sixth he turned the fight on its head when smashing Sanavia to the floor with a right and two lefts to the jaw. Although Sanavia was up at 'eight', because he was sagging badly the referee continued to count to 'ten'. The finish came after 54 seconds of the session had elapsed.

22 October 2004. Joe Calzaghe w pts 12 Kabary Salem.
Venue: Royal Highland Showground, Edinburgh, Scotland. **Recognition:** WBO. **Referee:** Paul Thomas.
Scorecards: 117-109, 118-107, 116-109.
Fight Summary: Calzaghe (168) was possibly the best super middle around, but unfortunately this was not a good day for him. However, because Salem (167¾) had come to spoil there was no way he was ever going to win the title despite putting the southpaw champion down in the fourth after cutting him on the head in round two following a coming together. It was a big right-hand counter that had put Calzaghe on his pants for 'four', and

although he looked shaken he was soon back in the action. Eventually rising above the lethargy Calzaghe got himself going to cut Salem over the right eye in the seventh before nearly putting him away in the final session after a solid straight left had dropped the Egyptian for 'eight'. Both men had points deducted for butting, Salem in the third and Calzaghe in the 11th.

On 6 November, at the Erdgas Arena, Riesa, Germany, Mario Veit successfully defended the 'interim' title when stopping Charles Brewer in the ninth round.

12 November 2004. Mikkel Kessler w rtd 7 Manny Siaca.
Venue: Brondby Hall, Copenhagen, Denmark. **Recognition:** WBA. **Referee:** Stan Christodoulou.
Fight Summary: By the end of round two the champion was already under pressure, and by the fourth Kessler (168) was well in control as he pushed his man back with solid blows from both hands. Although Siaca (168) was dropped by a right to the jaw in the seventh it was not ruled as a count, but thereafter he had little chance of retaining his title as Kessler battered him throughout the session. It was no surprise when Siaca was retired by his corner at the end of the seventh after he had been taken apart by cracking combinations before slumping on to his stool.

4 December 2004. Jeff Lacy w pts 12 Omar Sheika.
Venue: Mandalay Bay Resort & Casino, Las Vegas, Nevada, USA. **Recognition:** IBF. **Referee:** Tony Weeks.
Scorecards: 115-113, 117-111, 115-113.
Fight Summary: In his first defence, Lacy (168) was shocked in the opening two sessions being staggered by lefts and rights before getting back on course. For several rounds the crafty Sheika (166) made life difficult for Lacy, who was trying to overpower his rival without success. Lacy always had his nose in front, but it was not easy as Sheika took his best punches before coming back with some of his own. By the ninth, however, Lacy's extra power was beginning to tell, and he continued to land thudding blows that would have dropped a lot of other fighters.

18 December 2004. Markus Beyer w pts 12 Yoshinori Nishizawa.
Venue: Upper Franconian Arena, Bayreuth, Germany. **Recognition:** WBC. **Referee:** John Keane.
Scorecards: 116-111, 117-111, 118-109.
Fight Summary: Having put the 38-year-old Nishizawa (167) down in the opening round, even though it was not counted as a knockdown, the southpaw champion was forced to take the mandatory 'eight' count himself after being dropped by a solid right in the second. It was more surprise than hurt, and Beyer (166¾) was soon dictating matters even though he could not find the punch to finish Nishizawa off. Afterwards, Beyer stated that he was amazed that his brave opponent was able to take so many heavy shots without crumbling, testament to the man from Japan's durability.

5 March 2005. Jeff Lacy w rsc 7 Rubin Williams.
Venue: Mandalay Bay Resort & Casino, Las Vegas, Nevada, USA. **Recognition:** IBF. **Referee:** Tony Weeks.
Fight Summary: Williams (167) surprised all by attacking the champion with solid long jabs and taking the best he could muster before being stopped after 47 seconds of the seventh round. All three judges gave Williams the fourth when he went punch for punch against the tank-like Lacy (167), the former continuing to show resolve even when bombarded by vicious left hooks in every session. The fight ended when Lacy, punching away for all his worth, was using Williams' head as target practice with the latter trapped and unable to get off the ropes.

12 March 2005. Markus Beyer w pts 12 Danny Green.
Venue: Stadium Hall, Zwickau, Germany. **Recognition:** WBC. **Referee:** Laurence Cole.
Scorecards: 114-113, 115-112, 114-114.
Fight Summary: Finally getting his return against the champion Green (166) was expected by many to take over the title, and although it was always close the verdict was a fair reflection as to how the fight went. This time round, with much of Green's aggression ineffective he was occasionally hurt by southpaw lefts to the body as Beyer (167) looked to find a weakness. However, in the tenth Green came on strongly, smashing in lefts and rights before having Beyer counted on in the 12th following a big right to the head. Although the ropes stopped Beyer

from hitting the floor, when the German was allowed to box on Green jumped all over him until running out of time.

7 May 2005. Joe Calzaghe w rsc 6 Mario Veit.
Venue: Volkswagen Hall, Braunschweig, Germany. **Recognition:** WBO. **Referee:** Genaro Rodriguez.
Fight Summary: Although Calzaghe (167¾) had beaten Veit (167¾) inside two minutes previously the German was a much improved fighter, while the champion was looking to put the Kabary Salem fight behind him. It was soon apparent that the challenger's best chance of winning lay in keeping his distance as he stuck to the task well, his left jab popping out consistently. However, once Calzaghe began to work the body, his hand-speed blistering, to the initiated it seemed to be just a matter of time. And so it proved when Calzaghe dropped Veit with a smashing left at the end of the fifth. Storming out for the sixth the champion soon had Veit down again following a barrage of heavy shots, and although the German got his feet he was rescued by the referee with just 42 seconds of the session gone.

8 June 2005. Mikkel Kessler w pts 12 Anthony Mundine.
Venue: Entertainment Centre, Sydney, Australia. **Recognition:** WBA. **Referee:** Luis Pabon.
Scorecards: 116-112, 120-108, 117-113.
Fight Summary: Starting fast, Mundine (166¾) traded with the champion in the opening session before going on the back foot and making himself a difficult target. However, in the fourth Kessler (167½) finally made his mark, punching away with both hands before increasing the tempo in the middle rounds with stiff jabs and solid right crosses. Mundine was still boxing well though, especially when coming on strongly in the ninth with combinations and right crosses that shook Kessler. The last three sessions saw both men looking to make a point, but it was Kessler who impressed most when going for the body and landing heavily to make sure of the win.

6 August 2005. Jeff Lacy w rtd 7 Robin Reid.
Venue: St Petersburg Times Forum, Tampa, Florida, USA. **Recognition:** IBF. **Referee:** Jorge Alonso.
Fight Summary: In control right from the start the champion was soon banging in big punches, and in the third a low left hook dropped Reid (167½) for which the latter was given valuable seconds to recover. Lacy (167) really picked it up in the fourth, but after being butted in the fifth he dropped Reid with a right to the jaw on the referee's call of 'break'. Not only was it the first time in his career that Reid had been dropped he also had a point deducted for the head work before being floored again by a terrific left uppercut to the jaw. Although saved by the bell, Reid was down again in the sixth. Docked another point for holding in the seventh, Reid was then smashed to the floor by a right uppercut to the jaw following a series of heavy blows. It was no surprise when Reid was retired in his corner at the end of the session, having taken far more than was good for him.

3 September 2005. Markus Beyer w pts 12 Omar Sheika.
Venue: ICC Centre, Berlin, Germany. **Recognition:** WBC. **Referee:** Massimo Barrovecchio.
Scorecards: 118-110, 116-112, 116-112.
Fight Summary: Clearly at his best the champion cut Sheika (167¼) on the right eye in the opening session before settling down to outbox the American, mainly by the use of a southpaw straight left. It was not until the fifth that Sheika landed a meaningful blow, a right to the jaw that shook Beyer (167¼), but he was unable to follow it up. While almost putting Sheika away in the eighth with a solid left, as in most of Beyer's fights he seemed content to sit back and box his way to a comprehensive points victory.

10 September 2005. Joe Calzaghe w pts 12 Evans Ashira.
Venue: International Arena, Cardiff, Wales. **Recognition:** WBO. **Referee:** Mark Nelson.
Scorecards: 120-107, 120-108, 120-108.
Fight Summary: Dominating from the opening bell the champion swarmed all over Ashira (168) with southpaw rights and lefts, and following an accidental clash of heads in the second round the latter was cut over the left eye. Although Calzaghe (167½) continued to throw plenty of leather at Ashira, from thereon in it was clear that something was up with the Welshman's left hand as he stopped throwing it after the fourth and relied on his lead right to get him through the contest. Afterwards, it transpired that as Calzaghe had broken a metacarpal he would be unable to fight Jeff Lacy, regardless of the ongoing negotiations, in the immediate future.

5 November 2005. Jeff Lacy w rsc 2 Scott Pemberton.
Venue: Caesar's Palace, Lake Tahoe, Stateline, Nevada, USA. **Recognition:** IBF. **Referee:** Vic Drakulich.
Fight Summary: Even though a good fighter, Pemberton (168) was several levels below the champion, and right from the opening bell he was forced to use every part of the ring to survive the heavy bombs being thrown at him. Eventually, in the second round, Lacy (168) caught up with his rival when a big right put Pemberton down for 'nine'. Back on his feet, despite ducking low and moving away Pemberton was sent crashing in his own corner following a right hook that hit him flush. Without bothering to take up the count the referee stopped the fight with one second of the session remaining.

14 January 2006. Mikkel Kessler w rsc 10 Eric Lucas.
Venue: Brondby Hall, Copenhagen, Denmark. **Recognition:** WBA. **Referee:** Luis Pabon.
Fight Summary: Although there were no knockdowns the champion outclassed the hardy Lucas (167), winning all nine completed rounds before the latter's corner threw the towel in to enforce the referee's stoppage on the 1.51 mark. With Kessler (165) in total control, dominating behind the jab and still strong, it was clear that Lucas would struggle the longer the fight went on. Cut over both eyes with his face a bloody mess at the end, the corner saved him to fight another day.

28 January 2006. Markus Beyer w rsc 12 Alberto Colajanni.
Venue: Tempodrom Arena, Berlin, Germany. **Recognition:** WBC. **Referee:** Larry O'Connell.
Fight Summary: Hardly concerned that this was a boring affair, the southpaw champion appeared content at times to let the outclassed Colajanni (164) remain in the fight. Throwing few punches, Colajanni had been floored in the fourth by a right-left combination before being badly hurt in the 12th when dropped for 'eight' by a heavy left. With Colajanni unsteady on his legs, when Beyer (167) smashed him down again the referee called matters off at 2.25 just as the towel was thrown in.

4 March 2006. Joe Calzaghe w pts 12 Jeff Lacy.
Venue: MEN Arena, Manchester, England. **Recognition:** IBF/WBO/The Ring. **Referee:** Raul Caiz.
Scorecards: 119-105, 119-107, 119-107.
Fight Summary: In what was a unification contest between Calzaghe (168), the WBO representative, and the IBF champion, Lacy (167), the former put in one of his best ever displays to outclass the American danger man. Pounded for round after round by southpaw lefts and rights and cut over both eyes, Lacy showed his mettle as he continually looked for a winning blow. Calzaghe, who was deducted a point in the 11th for an illegal punch, had been at his best, ripping in speedy punches from all angles, and in the final session he finally had Lacy down. Getting up at 'four' Lacy looked to have a breather until almost being taken out by a clutch of uppercuts and being saved by the bell. *The Ring* Championship Belt was also up for grabs in this one.

13 May 2006. Markus Beyer tdraw 4 Sakio Bika.
Venue: The Stadium, Zwickau, Germany. **Recognition:** WBC. **Referee:** Joe Cortez.
Fight Summary: Cut under the right eye in the second by a left hook, the southpaw champion was under pressure in the third when a left uppercut put him on the back foot. Although finishing the round strongly with several hard lefts that backed Bika (168) up, at 1.45 of the fourth Beyer (167¾) was ruled out of the contest when a nasty clash of heads left him with a cut on the right eye. Following an inspection by the doctor the referee ruled it a technical draw under the WBC ruling that a contest has to go beyond four completed rounds for a decision to be given.

14 October 2006. Joe Calzaghe w pts 12 Sakio Bika.
Venue: MEN Arena, Manchester, England. **Recognition:** IBF/WBO/The Ring. **Referee:** Mickey Vann.
Scorecards: 116-111, 117-110, 117-110.
Fight Summary: With his three championship belts on the line it was not one of Calzaghe's better nights, but he still boxed well enough to win clearly over the tough Bika (168). In the fifth round Bika had a point deducted for repeated head butts, and at the end of the contest Calzaghe (168) finished with a vertical cut over the left eye and a badly swollen jaw, testament to the former's rough, tough tactics. Boxing well on the counter Bika had occasionally hurt his southpaw opponent, especially in the ninth, but the Welshman continually threw more punches than his rival, something that was reflected on the scorecards.

On 27 November, it was reported that Calzaghe had relinquished the IBF version of the title in order to defend his WBO crown against Peter Manfredo rather than face Robert Stieglitz, the IBF's mandatory challenger. Following that, the latter was matched against Alejandro Berrio for the vacant title. Despite losing to Stieglitz in an earlier contest, Berrio had earned his opportunity when defeating Yusaf Mack (w rsc 6 at the Club Cinema, Pompano Beach, Florida, USA on 19 May 2005) in an eliminator.

14 October 2006. Mikkel Kessler w co 3 Markus Beyer.
Venue: Parken Stadium, Copenhagen, Denmark. **Recognition:** WBA/WBC. **Referee:** Guido Cavalleri.
Fight Summary: Looking to unify two titles, when the WBA champion, Kessler (167¾), met the WBC's Beyer (168) it was the former who came out on top by a third-round kayo win after starting well with the jab to unsettle his southpaw opponent. Marked over the right eye, coming into the third Beyer was quickly under pressure as Kessler stepped it up, and at 2.58 of the session he was counted out after being caught heavily by a right cross to the jaw.

Now that Kessler was recognised as the WBA 'super' champion, Anthony Mundine stopped fellow Australian, Sam Soliman, at the Entertainment Centre, Sydney, Australia on 7 March 2007 to win the vacant WBA 'second tier' title.

3 March 2007. Alejandro Berrio w rsc 3 Robert Stieglitz.
Venue: Town Hall, Rostock, Germany. **Recognition:** IBF. **Referee:** Remigio Ruggeri.
Fight Summary: Contested for the vacant title after Joe Calzaghe handed in his belt, it was Berrio (168) who came home the winner when he stopped Stieglitz (167¼) at 2.37 of the third. Having already beaten his opponent Stieglitz was favoured, but he failed to find the range and in the third was dropped by a combination of blows. Back on his feet, Stieglitz was then put down again by a right hand, and although allowed to continue he was almost out on his feet when the referee brought the fight to a halt.

24 March 2007. Mikkel Kessler w pts 12 Librado Andrade.
Venue: Parken Stadium, Copenhagen, Denmark. **Recognition:** WBA/WBC. **Referee:** Laurence Cole.
Scorecards: 120-108, 120-108, 120-108.
Fight Summary: Despite it being one-sided, the champion winning every round, the tough Andrade (168) made it an absorbing contest right up to the final bell. There were no knockdowns, but that was due to Andrade's ability to take excessive punishment as Kessler (168) hit him with every punch in the book and more. How Andrade, remaining virtually unmarked, took everything thrown at him and came back with heavy shots of his own was amazing and marked him out a real 'Iron Man'.

Anthony Mundine outpointed Pablo Daniel Zamora Nievas over 12 rounds at the Leisure Centre, Broadbeach, Queensland, Australia on 27 June to retain his WBA 'second tier' title.

7 April 2007. Joe Calzaghe w rsc 3 Peter Manfredo.
Venue: Millennium Stadium, Cardiff, Wales. **Recognition:** WBO/The Ring. **Referee:** Terry O'Connor.
Fight Summary: Far below the level to be fighting for two world championship belts, especially when up against an unbeaten champion who was looking to make it 20 defences, the game Manfredo (166) was stopped at 1.30 of the third round, a decision that was thought by many to be premature. Regardless of that, Manfredo was on his way to a beating and was not fighting back against the fast-handed southpaw when the decision was made. After the contest Calzaghe (167¾) stated that he had fractured his left hand again, which probably explained why he looked for the early win and went downstairs more often than not.

19 October 2007. Lucian Bute w rsc 11 Alejandro Berrio.
Venue: Bell Centre, Montreal, Canada. **Recognition:** IBF. **Referee:** Marlon Wright.
Fight Summary: On the back foot from the bell, the southpaw challenger found the hard-hitting Berrio (167¾) not too willing to accommodate him, and although the former always appeared in control he had to take more blows than he would have cared. Several times Bute (167) stunned Berrio, but was unable to finish him off. Having taken the ninth and tenth sessions, coming into the 11th Bute finally found the punches he had been looking for; a right hook to the head sending Berrio crashing back before he was left slumped in a corner, eyes glazed, following

further heavy blows. With 1.27 on the clock the referee stopped the fight, leaving Bute, his right eye badly swollen, the winner.

3 November 2007. Joe Calzaghe w pts 12 Mikkel Kessler.
Venue: Millennium Stadium, Cardiff, Wales. **Recognition:** WBA/WBC/WBO/The Ring. **Referee:** Michael Ortega.
Scorecards: 117-111, 116-112, 116-112.
Fight Summary: With Kessler (168) putting his WBA and WBC titles on the line while Calzaghe (167½) had his WBO crown and *Ring* Championship Belt up for grabs, it was the latter who came home by a unanimous decision. Although Kessler fought at the top of his game he could never close down the Welsh southpaw, who continually went up the gears and took over completely in the second half when winning five of the last six rounds. Always dangerous, Kessler proved to be a very good fighter, but in Calzaghe he was up against a great one.

At the Entertainment Centre, Sydney, Australia on 10 December, Anthony Mundine knocked out Jose Alberto Clavero inside four rounds to retain the WBA 'second tier' title, prior to outpointing Nader Hamdan over 12 rounds on 27 February 2008 at the same venue in another defence. The day after Mundine made a further successful defence, when outpointing fellow Australian Sam Soliman over 12 rounds at the Vodafone Arena, Melbourne, Australia on 28 May 2008, he relinquished the title in order to drop down a weight division.

Following that, Kessler knocked out Dimitri Sartison inside 12 rounds at the Brondby Hall, Copenhagen, Denmark on 21 June 2008 to capture the WBA 'second tier' title, bearing in mind that Calzaghe continued to be recognised as the 'super' champion.

Towards the end of June 2008, Calzaghe relinquished the WBC title to pursue a fight at the light heavyweight limit against Roy Jones, and Carl Froch was eventually selected to meet Jean Pascal to decide the vacant crown. Initially, it had been reported that Froch would be taking on Jermain Taylor, but with the latter's planned contest against Jeff Lacy virtually signed and sealed Pascal turned down the chance of a WBO 'interim' title fight to meet Froch. Meantime, Taylor beat Lacy (w pts 12 at the Vanderbilt University Memorial Gym, Nashville, Tennessee on 15 November 2008) in what was billed as an official WBC eliminator and would meet the winner of Froch versus Pascal.

Now that a match against Jones at 175lbs was signed and sealed, Calzaghe relinquished his WBO and WBA titles as well as handing in *The Ring* Championship Belt on 26 September 2008 as he felt that regardless of his forthcoming contest he would find it too difficult to make 168lbs again. That decision allowed the WBO 'interim' title fight scheduled for the next day between Denis Inkin and Fulgencio Zuniga to go ahead for the full title, and saw Kessler promoted to full WBA championship status.

29 February 2008. Lucian Bute w rsc 10 William Joppy.
Venue: Bell Centre, Montreal, Canada. **Recognition:** IBF. **Referee:** Marlon Wright.
Fight Summary: Having failed to win a round on the cards coming into the ninth, and having taken some solid left hands from the southpaw champion, the 37-year-old Joppy (167¾), both eyes swelling, was up against it. The first knockdown of the fight came in the ninth, Joppy being put down after Bute (167½) dug in several left hooks to the body, and in the tenth he was dropped twice more before the referee came to his rescue at 1.08 of the session.

27 September 2008. Denis Inkin w pts 12 Fulgencio Zuniga.
Venue: Color Line Arena, Hamburg, Germany. **Recognition:** WBO. **Referee:** Mark Nelson.
Scorecards: 117-111, 116-112, 118-110.
Fight Summary: Contested for the vacant title after Joe Calzaghe decided he could not make 168lbs again, it was Inkin (167¼) who took control early on. Although Zuniga (166¼) tried hard his punches were ineffective and failed to stop Inkin's march to the title, one of the judges giving him just one round. There were no knockdowns.

24 October 2008. Lucian Bute w pts 12 Librado Andrade.
Venue: Bell Centre, Montreal, Quebec, Canada. **Recognition:** IBF. **Referee:** Marion Wright.
Scorecards: 117-109, 115-111, 115-110.

Fight Summary: For round after round the champion circled the ring, picking off the tough Andrade (167¾) with southpaw jabs and solid combinations without ever being able to feel secure as the latter merely walked through the punches. In the tenth Andrade was put down when off balance, but was soon up and running as Bute (168) tired rapidly, and from the tenth onwards he surged all over his man. The final session saw Bute staggering around the ring as Andrade looked to finish, and with ten seconds remaining he smashed the champion to the floor. When Andrade failed to get back to a neutral corner quickly enough, by the time the referee took up the count his opportunity had gone.

25 October 2008. Mikkel Kessler w co 3 Danilo Haussler.
Venue: Weser-Ems Hall, Oldenburg, Germany. **Recognition:** WBA. **Referee:** Stan Christodoulou.
Fight Summary: Defending the title that had been handed to him after it was relinquished by Joe Calzaghe, Kessler (167¼) was far too good for the brave Haussler (167¼), who was polished off inside three rounds. Right from the start Kessler made it his fight, stunning Haussler with right hands to the head and solid body shots in the second before going to work in the third. The fight came to an end at 1.08 of the session after Haussler had been dropped by a right, left combination and counted out.

6 December 2008. Carl Froch w pts 12 Jean Pascal.
Venue: Trent FM Arena, Nottingham, England. **Recognition:** WBC. **Referee:** Guido Cavalleri.
Scorecards: 116-112, 117-111, 118-110.
Fight Summary: In a battle for the vacant title after Joe Calzaghe decided to move up a division, it was Froch (166½) who came home the winner after 12 rounds of pulsating action. Both fighters gave it everything, giving and taking, but it was Froch who was doing the most damage, Pascal (167¾) ending up with his right eye almost closed. It was hard to believe that there were no knockdowns, such was the ferocious power of Froch, and although he carried a cut left eye from the seventh and hurt his right hand he was never going to lose his grip on the fight in front of his home fans.

10 January 2009. Karoly Balzsay w pts 12 Denis Inkin.
Venue: Borderland Hall, Magdeburg, Germany. **Recognition:** WBO. **Referee:** Jose Rivera.
Scorecards: 115-113, 116-112, 116-112.
Fight Summary: Fairly even after four rounds, it was Balzsay (167¼) who picked up the pace in the fifth with fast southpaw jabs beginning to find their mark. In the sixth and seventh Inkin (167¼) was forced to take some heavy left hands as Balzsay caught up with him, but instead of taking the fight to his challenger he failed to take advantage of several openings and lost four of the last five rounds when being outworked.

13 March 2009. Lucian Bute w rsc 4 Fulgencio Zuniga.
Venue: Bell Centre, Montreal, Quebec, Canada. **Recognition:** IBF. **Referee:** Lindsay Page.
Fight Summary: Putting his previous defence behind him Bute (167½) began to make progress in the second, and in the third he took complete control of Zuniga (167¾) when hammering home solid blows from both hands. The fight came to an end at 2.25 of the fourth after Zuniga had been dropped by a southpaw right uppercut to the body before somehow managing to continue and then being battered by a whole clutch of punches without return. The referee would have been fully justified to have intervened earlier.

25 April 2009. Carl Froch w rsc 12 Jermain Taylor.
Venue: Foxwoods Resort & Casino, Mashantucket, Connecticut, USA. **Recognition:** WBC. **Referee:** Michael Ortega.
Fight Summary: Making his first defence, Froch (167) came back from the brink of defeat to score a terrific win over Taylor (166), who was four rounds ahead according to two judges at the end of the 11th. Having taken some heavy shots in the opening two rounds, Froch was dropped by a hard right to the head in the third. It was the first time he had ever taken a count, amateur or pro, but not panicking he was up at 'seven' and back in the contest. With Taylor's left jab being his key punch it was not until the ninth that Froch began making him miss as he began to tire after taking some heavy blows to the body. Although Taylor was definitely slowing by the 11th, it was only in the final session that Froch managed to catch up with him. In what was a race against the clock Froch finally put Taylor down for 'nine' with a couple of smashing right hands, and after belting away at his almost defenceless challenger the referee made the stoppage with just 14 seconds of the fight remaining.

25 April 2009. Karoly Balzsay w rsc 11 Maselino Masoe.
Venue: Konig Sports Palace, Krefeld, Germany. **Recognition:** WBO. **Referee:** Mark Nelson.
Fight Summary: Although Masoe (167¼) made the opening moves the southpaw champion held him at bay with solid combinations before suffering a cut right eye when heads collided. Keeping calm and collected, Balzsay (196½) used speed and timing to make sure that his right leads found the target on a regular basis. Balzsay finally caught up with Masoe in the 11th, a tremendous right-left sending him crashing, and although he beat the count the referee waved it off on the 2.07 mark, realising that the latter was in no position to defend himself.

22 August 2009. Robert Stieglitz w rsc 11 Karoly Balzsay.
Venue: SYMA Sport & Leisure Centre, Budapest, Hungary. **Recognition:** WBO. **Referee:** Joe Cortez.
Fight Summary: After winning the opening six rounds when boxing well behind the southpaw jab, the champion appeared to go to pieces in the ninth after an old wound on his forehead opened and blood began running into his eyes. It had been a fast-paced contest, and although both men were tiring it was Stieglitz (167¼) who found the extra energy to pound away at Balzsay (166¾), who merely covered up. In the tenth it was more of the same and before the 11th could get underway, with Balzsay still slumped on his stool, his corner informed the referee that their man could not continue. When Balzsay ignored his corner's decision and tried to fight on it was the referee who brought matters to halt after 12 seconds of the 11th.

12 September 2009. Mikkel Kessler w rsc 4 Gusmyr Perdomo.
Venue: MCH Exhibition Centre, Herning, Denmark. **Recognition:** WBA. **Referee:** Russell Mora.
Fight Summary: Suffering from ring rust after being out of action for ten months, the champion seemed bothered by the taller Perdomo (167¼), a southpaw, at first but soon got his measure. Opening up in the third, Kessler (167¾) began to put his punches together and had Perdomo over in what was described as a flash knockdown. Out quickly in the fourth, Kessler went after Perdomo with a vengeance, and after being hurt by a couple of cracking left-rights the latter was rescued by the referee as he began falling to the floor, eyes glazed. The finish was timed at 51 seconds.

17 October 2009. Carl Froch w pts 12 Andre Dirrell.
Venue: Trent FM Arena, Nottingham, England. **Recognition:** WBC. **Referee:** Hector Afu.
Scorecards: 115-112, 115-112, 113-114.
Fight Summary: In what was part of the 'Super Six Tournament', by the champion's standards it was a bore as both men boxed cagey fights, Dirrell (167½), who had a point deducted in the tenth for holding, being deemed too negative to win the title. It was only in the last two rounds that Dirrell, a southpaw, came to life when showing that his speed of both punch and foot should have made more of his opportunity. Froch (167½), who described Dirrell as a 'nightmare', felt that as he had forced the fight he had deserved the win, while his trainer implied that if you want to win a title in someone else's country you should be more positive and not leave things to chance.

21 November 2009. Andre Ward w tdec 11 Mikkel Kessler.
Venue: Oracle Arena, Oakland, California, USA. **Recognition:** WBA. **Referee:** Jack Reiss.
Scorecards: 97-93, 98-92, 98-92.
Fight Summary: Defending his title in another 'Super Six Tournament' pairing, Kessler (167) came unstuck against the extremely gifted Ward (166½), who proved a difficult man to tag with speed to burn, fast hands and the ability to rough an opponent up. Guilty of head butts, Ward should have been deducted points on at least two occasions, but escaped bar a single caution. The head butts certainly played a big part in the fight and led to Kessler being unable to see out of his left eye by the end of the seventh. This worsened in the eighth when Ward's head did further damage, but by this time the challenger was virtually in an unassailable lead. After Ward's head caused a large bump under Kessler's left eye in the tenth, the referee eventually asked the ringside doctor to take look, which led to the fight being stopped at 1.42 of the 11th. Because the second of Kessler's two cuts was ruled to have been caused by an accidental butt the cards were called for. According to *Boxing News*, the British trade paper, "the referee later stated that the severity of Ward's butts were more apparent when watching them on replay than at first hand."

On the same night at the Sparkassen Arena, Kiel, Germany, Dimitri Sartison forced Stjepan Bozic to retire at the end of the fifth round to win the WBA 'second tier' title.

28 November 2009. Lucian Bute w co 4 Librado Andrade.
Venue: Pepsi Coliseum, Quebec City, Quebec, Canada. **Recognition:** IBF. **Referee:** Benjy Esteves Jnr.
Fight Summary: Having been under intense pressure in their previous bout the champion left nothing to chance this time round, even though he was forced to fight hard in the third round as Andrade (166½) closed the ring down while looking for a quick win. In the fourth, however, Bute (167) stepped up a gear, dropping Andrade with a short southpaw right for 'eight'. Although back on his feet there would be no let-up for Andrade, and he was counted out at 2.57 of the session after being sent crashing from a left uppercut to the solar plexus.

9 January 2010. Robert Stieglitz w rsc 5 Ruben Eduardo Acosta.
Venue: Borderland Hall, Magdeburg, Germany. **Recognition:** WBO. **Referee:** Jose Rivera.
Fight Summary: It was the challenger who started the better, despite having come in at short notice, when catching Stieglitz (168) with some big hooks in the opening session. However, Stieglitz soon got his act together, dropping Acosta (167½) with a solid left hook in the third. Clearly hurt, Acosta got through the fourth before being set upon in the fifth. Dropped by a right hook to the body Acosta got up shakily, but with Stieglitz pouring in punches with nothing coming back the referee rescued the Argentine at 1.48 of the round.

17 April 2010. Lucian Bute w rsc 3 Edison Miranda.
Venue: Bell Centre, Montreal, Canada. **Recognition:** IBF. **Referee:** Ernest Sharif.
Fight Summary: With Bute (167¼) taking the opening two rounds by negating the challenger's power punches, it was only in the third that the fight got going. Although starting the session aggressively Miranda (167) was soon under pressure after taking a cracking left hook to the body, and after shipping heavy southpaw lefts he was sent crashing to the deck by a left uppercut. Getting to his feet after a few seconds, Miranda was rescued by the referee on the 1.20 mark when it was clear that he had been badly hurt.

17 April 2010. Robert Stieglitz w pts 12 Eduard Gutknecht.
Venue: Borderland Hall, Magdeburg, Germany. **Recognition:** WBO. **Referee:** Manfred Kuchler
Scorecards: 117-111, 119-108, 117-110.
Fight Summary: While showing good hand-speed, the champion was matched by Gutknecht (168) in the opening session, the latter finishing strongly. Stieglitz (167) then started to get into a rhythm, working well with the jab to head and body before being stunned when hit on the back of the head in the fifth. With Gutknecht deducted a point and Stieglitz given time out to recover when the fight got going again it had lost momentum, and despite Stieglitz winning six of the last eight rounds and having his man going at times he was unable to force a stoppage.

24 April 2010. Mikkel Kessler w pts 12 Carl Froch.
Venue: MCH Exhibition Centre, Herning, Denmark. **Recognition:** WBC. **Referee:** Michael Griffin.
Scorecards: 115-113, 117-111, 116-112.
Fight Summary: In what was termed by some as a barbaric 'tear up', Froch (167¼) not only lost his title but his unbeaten record as well. The men proved their toughness with no knockdowns scored despite the heavy hitting, although Froch, for whatever reason, failed to follow up several times when he apparently had Kessler (167) going, especially in the sixth. There was never more than a round or two between them regardless of what one of the cards showed, and on another night it could have been different. This night, however, belonged to Kessler, who took advantage of the room he was given early on, made excellent use of his jab and took some heavy shots that would have knocked many men out. Not surprisingly, both finished with cuts over their left eyes and plenty of respect for each other. By the way, the contest belonged to the 'Super Six Tournament'.

Due to fight Allan Green in the next leg of the 'Super Six Tournament', Kessler was forced to withdraw from the contest at the end of August due to an eye injury which affected his vision. Vacating his WBC title at the same time and given 'emeritus' status, he was told that he would be given the opportunity of regaining his belt when fully fit again. Following that, the WBC announced that Andre Ward and Andre Dirrell would meet for the vacant title, but after much protest Froch, who had beaten the latter, was matched against Arthur Abraham to find a successor.

19 June 2010. Andre Ward w pts 12 Allan Green.
Venue: Oracle Arena, Oakland, California, USA. **Recognition:** WBA. **Referee:** Raul Caiz.
Scorecards: 120-108, 120-108, 120-108.
Fight Summary: Dominating Green (166) both on the inside and outside, the champion raced to a shut-out points win against this recent addition to the 'Super Six Tournament'. There were no knockdowns, mainly due to Green's toughness, but Ward (167¾) was always looking to work, occasionally switch-hitting while using his fast left jab to home in on the Australian. He also proved he could take a punch, shrugging off an uppercut to the jaw that hurt him in the eighth before going back to work as if nothing had occurred.

On 31 July, Dimitri Sartison successfully defended the 'second tier' title when outpointing Khoren Gevor over 12 rounds at the O2 World Arena, Hamburg, Germany.

Sartison relinquished the 'second tier' title on 15 July 2011 after not recovering sufficiently from a bad knee injury in time for a defence against Stanislav Kashtanov.

15 October 2010. Lucian Bute w co 9 Jesse Brinkley.
Venue: Bell Centre, Montreal, Quebec, Canada. **Recognition:** IBF. **Referee:** Sam Williams.
Fight Summary: There was no doubting that Brinkley (167¾) came to fight, and he certainly provided Bute (167½) with some problems, but ultimately it was the champion's superior hitting power that undid him. Dropped heavily in the fifth by a cracking southpaw left to the body, Brinkley somehow made it up in time courtesy of a slow count to survive into the eighth round. Cut over the left eye in that session, Brinkley was then dropped for 'eight' by a right uppercut to the jaw before being knocked out in the ninth after a left uppercut had flattened him. The finish was timed at 2.48.

20 November 2010. Robert Stieglitz w pts 12 Enrique Ornelas.
Venue: Freiberger Arena, Dresden, Germany. **Recognition:** WBO. **Referee:** Joe Cortez.
Scorecards: 117-111, 117-111, 117-111.
Fight Summary: Although a clear winner the champion was forced to fight back at times as Ornelas (167¾) began to pick holes in his defence with hard punches finding their mark, especially during the last half of the contest. It was during the seventh and eighth that Stieglitz (168) was forced to endure head punches that saw his eyes become swollen, but he showed his mettle when coming back with heavy blows of his own to take the play away from Ornelas, winning four of the last five rounds. Giving it all he had in the 12th, Ornelas won the session but was unable to turn the fight his way.

27 November 2010. Andre Ward w pts 12 Sakio Bika.
Venue: Oracle Arena, Oakland, California, USA. **Recognition:** WBA. **Referee:** Dan Stell.
Scorecards: 120-108, 118-110, 118-110.
Fight Summary: Making the second defence of his title Ward (168) did not have matters all his own way, being forced to battle hard as a determined Bika (168) gave him no respite. Bika may have lost most of the rounds, but he was always in Ward's face when clubbing in punches from both hands and leaving the champion with cuts over both eyes. No respecter of reputations, Bika's stock went up in this one.

27 November 2010. Carl Froch w pts 12 Arthur Abraham.
Venue: Hartwall Arena, Helsinki, Finland. **Recognition:** WBC. **Referee:** Frank Garza.
Scorecards: 120-108, 120-108, 119-109.
Fight Summary: Contested for the vacant title after Mikkel Kessler handed in his belt on being given 'emeritus' status, Froch (166¾) scored a virtual shut-out win over the tough Abraham (167¼), who had run out of ideas by the midway stage but continued trying. Keeping Abraham at bay by dint of stiff rights and lefts to head and body Froch produced a master-class performance, later claiming that he never had to get out of second gear. While Froch finished the contest with a swollen left eye, which was a small price to pay for the win, the shell-shocked Abraham knew that he would have to do better when facing up to Andre Ward for the latter's WBA title in the very near future.

19 March 2011. Lucian Bute w rsc 10 Brian Magee.
Venue: Bell Centre, Montreal, Canada. **Recognition:** IBF. **Referee:** Pete Podgorski.
Fight Summary: In a match between southpaws, Magee (167¾) made a decent start in the opening five rounds as he marched through the champion's defences, taking some hard head shots to land solid body blows of his own. Regardless of all that he was well down on the cards. Then, in the sixth and seventh he was dropped three times from lefts to the body, one of them being palpably low, before recovering well. Moving up a gear in the tenth, Bute (167¾) finally saw Magee off when a body blow that turned into a left uppercut floored the tough Irishman, who was rescued by the referee at 2.04 of the session.

9 April 2011. Robert Stieglitz w disq 10 Khoren Gevor.
Venue: Borderland Hall, Magdeburg, Germany. **Recognition:** WBO. **Referee:** Manfred Kuchler.
Fight Summary: Stieglitz (168) had been due to defend his title against Dimitri Sartison, but when the latter injured a knee a week before the fight he was replaced by Gevor (168). After making a slow start, Stieglitz began to get going in the third, landing solid lefts and rights on his southpaw opponent for round after round. Gevor had already shown his frustration in the sixth following a clash of heads that went unpunished, and in the ninth he threw Stieglitz to the floor. Fortunate not to have points deducted, he was less lucky in the tenth when he was disqualified on the 2.45 mark, having already lost a point for hitting behind the head. The final transgression saw him push Stieglitz to the floor before jumping on top of him and cutting his right eye in the process.

14 May 2011. Andre Ward w pts 12 Arthur Abraham.
Venue: Home Depot Centre, Carson, California. **Recognition:** WBA. **Referee:** Luis Pabon.
Scorecards: 120-108, 118-110, 118-111.
Fight Summary: Defending his title in the 'Super Six Tournament' Ward (168) had things almost all his own way, especially after he found that the jab was the best way forward. Unfortunately, Abraham (167), who finished with a badly swollen right eye, was too slow to get to Ward, although he did catch the latter with a couple of cracking hooks in the final session. Ward was just too fast for Abraham, often doubling up the jab to push him back, a tactic that stopped the German from getting set.

On 30 July, Brian Magee outpointed Jaime Barboza over 12 rounds at the National Gym, San Jose, Costa Rica, to win the vacant WBA 'interim' title.

Karoly Balzsay won the vacant WBA 'second tier' title on 26 August, at the Donbass Arena, Donetsk, Ukraine, when outpointing Stanislav Kashtanov over 12 rounds.

4 June 2011. Carl Froch w pts 12 Glen Johnson.
Venue: Boardwalk Hall, Atlantic City, New Jersey, USA. **Recognition:** WBC. **Referee:** Earl Brown.
Scorecards: 116-112, 117-111, 114-114.
Fight Summary: Taking time to settle, with Johnson (167½) winning the opening two sessions, Froch (167½) was up and running by the third before having to play second fiddle in rounds six through to seven. From there on, however, the champion was in control, scoring well with bursts of heavy blows from either hand as his veteran opponent began to fade. Following the fight, which had been a semi-final leg of the 'Super Six Tournament', Froch explained that he had never had to get out of second or third gear and had taken no risks in order to reach the final.

9 July 2011. Lucian Bute w co 4 Jean-Paul Mendy.
Venue: Romexpo Arena, Bucharest, Romania. **Recognition:** IBF. **Referee:** Marlon Wright.
Fight Summary: Yet again meeting a fellow southpaw, the champion took his time before finishing Mendy (166) off. It was quickly apparent that the veteran Mendy had little to offer, other than pushing out lefts and rights, and Bute (167¾), moving in behind the jab in the fourth, smashed home a heavy straight left that sent the Frenchman down to be counted out. The finish was timed at 2.48.

5 November 2011. Lucian Bute w pts 12 Glen Johnson.
Venue: Pepsi Coliseum, Quebec City, Quebec, Canada. **Recognition:** IBF. **Referee:** Mark Nelson.

Scorecards: 120-108, 119-109, 120-108.
Fight Summary: Having sparred many rounds together made for a poor fight, the champion deciding early on that he would not take any chances with the 42-year-old Johnson (166½), who defended well with a high guard. Happy to outspeed and outwork his opponent, Bute (167½), cruised to a near shut-out win in a contest that was remarkable for the fact that there were virtually no signs of the body attacks that had he had built his reputation on.

17 December 2011. Andre Ward w pts 12 Carl Froch.
Venue: Boardwalk Hall, Atlantic City, New Jersey, USA. **Recognition:** WBA/WBC/The Ring. **Referee:** Steve Smoger.
Scorecards: 115-113, 115-113, 118-110.
Fight Summary: The final of the 'Super Six Tournament' saw the WBA and WBC titles at stake as well as the vacant *Ring* Championship Belt. In unifying two belts, Ward (168), the WBA titleholder, showed genuine ringcraft when beating the WBC's Froch (167½), his ability to get off punches and move out of range showed him to be one of the best in a long line of champions. Froch was never out of the fight but was unable to find any rhythm, and in order to land he was often prepared to throw many wasteful punches. In the last two sessions as Ward tired Froch gave it everything he had, but was unable to find the finishing blow he so desperately required that would turn certain defeat into victory.

Brian Magee successfully defended his WBA 'interim' title with a fifth-round stoppage win over Rudy Markussen at the Brondby Hall Arena, Copenhagen, Denmark on 18 February 2012.

Karoly Balzsay made a successful defence of the WBA 'second tier' title when stopping Dimitri Sartison in the 12th round at the Sport & Congress Centre, Schwerin, Germany on 21 April 2012.

It was announced by the WBC on 27 April 2012 that they were giving Ward 'champion in recess' status on the grounds that he had broken his hand last time out and it needed time to heal. Although there had been rumours that Ward was considering giving up the WBA and WBC Championship Belts, believing that *The Ring* Championship Belt was far more prestigious and he was not really interested in defending against Anthony Dirrell, with two months left to make a defence the WBC's actions were surprising to say the least. All of that was forgotten when he signed up to defend all three belts against Chad Dawson in September 2012.

14 January 2012. Robert Stieglitz w pts 12 Henry Weber.
Venue: Baden Arena, Offenburg, Germany. **Recognition:** WBO. **Referee:** Andre Van Grootenbruel.
Scorecards: 119-109, 118-110, 116-112.
Fight Summary: Starting fast, throwing accurate left jabs and combinations, the champion maintained the pace throughout to romp off with the decision over Weber (166¾), a man who had never gone beyond eight rounds. The outclassed Weber, boxing behind a high guard, occasionally got through with stiff punches, but there were never enough of them to unduly worry Stieglitz (167½), who marched on to a prospective defence against Arthur Abraham.

5 May 2012. Robert Stieglitz w pts 12 Nader Hamdan.
Venue: Fair Hall, Erfurt, Germany. **Recognition:** WBO. **Referee:** Dave Parris.
Scorecards: 117-111, 117-111, 120-108.
Fight Summary: A late substitute for the injured George Groves, Hamdan (167) found it hard going against the fast-moving champion and went down by a wide points margin. Showing his customary stiff left jab Stieglitz (166¾) dominated his opponent, who made life easier for him by attacking in straight lines and was made to take heavy combinations as a consequence. For Stieglitz it was little more than a routine defence, while the 38-year-old Hamdan proved yet again that he was a difficult man to stop inside the distance.

26 May 2012. Carl Froch w rsc 5 Lucian Bute.
Venue: The Arena, Nottingham, England. **Recognition:** IBF. **Referee:** Earl Brown.
Fight Summary: Taking on a champion with a hard-hitting reputation did not bother Froch (167½), who went for his man with heavy hands right from the start. Despite Bute (167¾) scoring well with southpaw lefts in the third

Froch walked straight through them, and until the bell rang to end the session Bute had been on the verge of being stopped, one of the judges making it a 10-8 round. By the end of the fourth Bute looked all-in and it was a surprise that he came out for the fifth. Realising it was his for the taking Froch unleashed punch after punch on the unfortunate Bute, who was being belted along the ropes when the referee decided to give him an 'eight' count. However, when it became clear that Bute was unable to defend himself properly the referee called it off at 1.05 of the session.

25 August 2012. Arthur Abraham w pts 12 Robert Stieglitz.
Venue: O2 World Arena, Berlin, Germany. **Recognition:** WBO. **Referee:** Joe Cortez.
Scorecards: 116-112, 116-112, 115-113.
Fight Summary: Normally a slow starter Abraham (167¾) got away well when scoring with solid punches, and although the champion came back strongly in the next two sessions he was shaken up in the fourth as well as finishing with a cut over the left eye. With Abraham dominating the next five sessions it was clear that Stieglitz (167¾) had to find a way to turn the tide, but by the tenth his job became even more difficult when cut over and under the right eye. Ultimately Abraham's strength and power proved to be too much for Stieglitz.

8 September 2012. Andre Ward w rsc 10 Chad Dawson.
Venue: Oracle Arena, Oakland, California, USA. **Recognition:** WBA/WBC/The Ring. **Referee:** Steve Smoger.
Fight Summary: Although he started the better of the pair, his extra height and reach to the fore, Dawson (168) soon found himself on the receiving end, being dropped in the third after taking a solid right to the body followed by a left hook to the head. There would be no let-up for Dawson in the fourth, and he was put down again after Ward (168) had lined him up with another left hook to the head. Despite the three-belt champion being just too fast for Dawson, who had come down from light heavy, the latter gamely plugged away, always looking for a punch that would get him out of trouble. However, after going down on one knee following a thumping five-punch combination in the tenth, the referee stopped the contest at 2.45 of the session when it was clear that Dawson had little left.

On 10 November, Stanislav Kashtanov outpointed Server Yemurlayev over 12 rounds at the Druzhba Sports Palace, Donetsk, Ukraine, to win the WBA 'interim' title, which had been vacated by Brian Magee in October when he was given the opportunity to challenge Karoly Balzsay for the latter's 'second tier' belt. Unfortunately for Magee the fight was called off twice due to the latter suffering a back injury.

In early November, Magee was awarded the WBA 'second tier' title, having already been booked to fight Mikkel Kessler on 8 December at the MCH Fair Centre Arena, Herning, Denmark. The fight duly took place, Kessler winning by a third-round stoppage to capture the belt.

Due to Ward's long-term shoulder injury, the WBC vacated the title on 11 April 2013. Following that, Ward was named as their 'emeritus' champion and told that he would be the prime challenger when fully fit again. However, once the WBC decided that Sakio Bika would be meeting Marco Antonio Periban for the vacant title on 22 June 2013, Ward effectively discarded the 'emeritus' tag on a matter of principle. Bika had beaten Nikola Sjekloca (w pts 12 at the Boardwalk Hall, Atlantic City, New Jersey on 16 February 2013) in a final eliminator, while Periban had knocked out Samuel Miller (w co 2 at the Grand Oasis Resort, Cancun, Mexico on 16 March 2013) to win the vacant NABF title.

When Carl Froch successfully defended his IBF title against Kessler (w pts 12 at the O2 Arena, Greenwich, London on 25 May 2013) he also took over the latter's WBA 'second tier' title.

Kashtanov made a successful defence of his WBA 'interim' title when knocking out Jaime Barboza inside ten rounds at the Donbass Arena, Donetsk, Ukraine on 24 August 2013, prior to announcing his retirement on 2 September 2014 due to health problems.

In a fight in which Ward was down to defend *The Ring* and WBA belts against Edwin Rodriguez at the Citizens Business Bank Arena, Ontario, California on 16 November 2013, when the latter came in two pounds over the weight it lost its title status. With Rodriguez unable to win the title, Ward cantered to 12-round points win.

A week later, on 23 November 2013, Froch made a successful defence of the WBA 'second tier' title when defeating George Groves (w rsc 9 at the Phones 4u Arena, Manchester, England), and followed that up with another win over Groves (w rsc 8 at The Stadium, Wembley, London, England on 31 May 2014). On both occasions, Froch's IBF title was also on the line.

Following Kashtanov's temporary retirement, Fedor Chudinov won the vacant WBA 'interim' title when knocking out Ben McCulloch in the second round at the Dynamo Sports Palace, Moscow, Russia on 11 December 2014.

The Ring Championship Belt was vacated in February 2015 due to Ward not making a defence against a top-five man for over two years.

On 9 May 2015, Chudinov outpointed Felix Sturm over 12 rounds at the Festival Hall, Frankfurt, Germany. The contest was originally billed as a defence of Chudinov's WBA 'interim' crown, but after Froch had been stripped two days earlier for not defending the WBA 'second tier' title for almost a year it was the latter belt that was on the line.

Further to that, Vincent Feigenbutz captured the vacant WBA 'interim' crown when stopping Mauricio Reynoso inside three rounds at the Gerry Weber Stadium, Halle, Germany on 18 July 2015. Feigenbutz then defended his new belt, outpointing Giovanni De Carolis over 12 rounds at the DM Arena, Karlsruhe, Germany on 17 October 2015.

Chudinov made another successfully defence of the WBA 'second tier' title when outpointing Frank Buglioni over 12 rounds at the Wembley Arena, London, England on 26 September 2015. Several weeks later, on 12 November 2015, Chudinov was handed full title status by the WBA after Ward had decided to move up a weight division.

Meanwhile, on 9 January 2016, De Carolis stopped Feigenbutz inside 11 rounds of a return match at the Baden Arena, Offenburg, Germany to win the vacant 'second tier' title.

17 November 2012. Carl Froch w co 3 Yusaf Mack.
Venue: Capital FM Arena, Nottingham, England. **Recognition:** IBF. **Referee:** Phil Edwards.
Fight Summary: Dropped in the first by a left-right the challenger gamely tried to keep going, but it was patently clear that Froch (167½) was never going to let him off the hook, it being merely a matter of time. Having battered his man throughout the second, at 2.30 of the third the luckless Mack (168) was counted out on his knees after taking four hefty blows to head and body.

15 December 2012. Arthur Abraham w rsc 8 Mehdi Bouadla.
Venue: Nurnberger Insurance Arena, Bayern, Germany. **Recognition:** WBO. **Referee:** Mark Nelson.
Fight Summary: Making his first defence Abraham (168) soon got down to business, using his left jab and left hook to stop Bouadla (164¾) in his tracks. A tough, walk-forward fighter, Bouadla was dangerous, especially with the left hook, but Abraham always held the upper hand with his extra power and know-how. In round seven Abraham picked it up, terrific right and left uppercuts leaving Bouadla cut over the right eye, and although the referee let things continue at 2.11 of the eighth he brought matters to a halt having seen enough.

23 March 2013. Robert Stieglitz w rsc 4 Arthur Abraham.
Venue: GETEC Arena, Magdeburg, Germany. **Recognition:** WBO. **Referee:** Mike Ortega.
Fight Summary: Seen as a huge upset, Stieglitz (168) regained his old title from the man he lost it to when Abraham (167½) was stopped at the end of the third on the ringside doctor's advice. This time round Stieglitz made a confident start, and although Abraham came back to some degree in the second by the end of the round his left eye was beginning to swell after the challenger had landed a cracking straight right. It became even worse

in the third for Abraham, being deducted a point for hitting and holding as Stieglitz gave him a rare pounding as lefts and rights found their mark.

25 May 2013. Carl Froch w pts 12 Mikkel Kessler.
Venue: O2 Arena, Greenwich, London, England. **Recognition:** IBF. **Referee:** Pete Podgorski.
Scorecards: 118-110, 116-112, 115-113.
Fight Summary: Gaining revenge for a previous loss at the hands of Kessler (166½), the champion punched his way to a unanimous decision in what was an exciting all-out war with no quarter asked for or given. Both men had come to fight, but it was the power of Froch (167¾) that saw him go to the front, terrific jabs and crunching rights keeping Kessler at bay for much of the time. Kessler, however, threw plenty of solid blows, his best rounds coming in the fourth, sixth, ninth and 11th when he forced Froch into defensive mode on occasion. At the final bell, although the vast majority felt that Froch had won there had never been more than three or four rounds between them, the 118-110 card being way out. Froch took over Kessler's WBA 'second tier' title on his victory.

22 June 2013. Sakio Bika w pts 12 Marco Antonio Periban.
Venue: Barclays Centre, Brooklyn, NYC, New York, USA. **Recognition:** WBC. **Referee:** Harvey Dock.
Scorecards: 115-113, 116-112, 114-114.
Fight Summary: Contested for the vacant title after Andre Ward was forced to give it up due to injury, Bika (167¼) became the new champion after being handed a majority decision over Periban (167¼). In what was Bika's fourth attempt to win a world title, he showed his power from the start, firing in overarm rights and pushing Periban back. However, Periban came back with some good punches of his own in the latter stages, and in the final session he battered away at the tiring Bika who probably saved his bacon when coming back strongly before the final bell. Both men received cuts, Bika on the forehead in the third and on the left eye in the eighth, while the previously unbeaten Periban was also cut in the eighth.

13 July 2013. Robert Stieglitz w tdec 10 Yuzo Kiyota.
Venue: Energy Composite Arena, Dresden, Germany. **Recognition:** WBO. **Referee:** Celestino Ruiz.
Scorecards: 100-89, 99-90, 99-90.
Fight Summary: Once the champion had found the range for solid lefts and rights he had settled by the third, despite the hard-hitting Kiyota (167¼) catching him with countering blows. The fourth round saw Kiyota stunned by a series of punches as Stieglitz (168) loaded up before he was deducted a point in the fifth for hitting on the break. Always dangerous when charging in head down, Kiyota was gashed above the left eye in the eighth from one such foray and was eventually pulled out of the fight after 40 seconds of the tenth when blood was restricting his vision. As it had been an accidental clash of heads that had caused the injury the referee went to the cards, the result being in favour of Stieglitz.

19 October 2013. Robert Stieglitz w pts 12 Isaac Ekpo.
Venue: Trade Fair Main Hall, Leipzig, Germany. **Recognition:** WBO. **Referee:** Eddie Cotton.
Scorecards: 118-110, 118-110, 119-109.
Fight Summary: Regardless of the fact that Ekpo (164½) made life difficult for the champion by ducking low, his negative tactics were ultimately futile. Controlling the fight from the centre of the ring, Stieglitz (167¾) was well on top by the fourth, his left jab and straight right ripping through Ekpo's defences. Although Ekpo remained dangerous with countering right hands, in the main Stieglitz ignored them to get off his own shots. Under pressure during the last three rounds, Ekpo weathered the storm to hear the final bell.

23 November 2013. Carl Froch w rsc 9 George Groves.
Venue: Phones 4u Arena, Manchester, England. **Recognition:** IBF. **Referee:** Howard Foster.
Fight Summary: In a contest that also involved Froch's WBA 'second-tier' title, Groves (166¾) gave a great display against the teak-tough champion before he was rescued by the referee in the ninth in what was thought by some to be a premature stoppage. Groves made a fast start, just as he said he would, and when Froch (167¾) tried to step in he was caught flush by a cracking right hand to the jaw that deposited him on the floor. Making it to the bell, Froch was more cautious when coming out for the second as Groves boxed sensibly and seemingly in control. Froch came back with some heavy shots of his own in the fifth before Groves matched the champion punch for

punch in the next three sessions, both men sending in hard blows. With Groves ahead on all three scorecards, it was in the ninth that Froch finally got to his man after catching him on the temple. Tearing after the challenger, when Froch nailed him with a left hook sandwiched between two heavy rights Groves fell into the arms of the referee who made the decision to stop it. Regardless of the finish, Groves had shown that he belonged at this level and would be back.

7 December 2013. Sakio Bika drew 12 Anthony Dirrell.
Venue: Barclays Centre, Brooklyn, NYC, New York, USA. **Recognition:** WBC. **Referee:** David Fields.
Scorecards: 114-112, 110-116, 113-113.
Fight Summary: With his back to the wall for much of the time, the champion retained his title even though he was dropped by Dirrell (167½) in the fifth by a right hook and then having a point deducted in the 11th for going low. Showing great durability and mental toughness, Bika (166½) continued to walk through the punches to get his own off, and in the sixth a terrific uppercut saw the challenger hurt and then pinned on the ropes before coming back. At the finish a crestfallen Dirrell felt that he had deserved the verdict, having controlled much of the action with heavy right hands and countering blows.

1 March 2014. Arthur Abraham w pts 12 Robert Stieglitz.
Venue: GETEC Arena, Magdeburg, Germany. **Recognition:** WBO. **Referee:** Genaro Rodriguez.
Scorecards: 114-111, 115-112, 112-113.
Fight Summary: Meeting Stieglitz (168) for the third time, the aggressive champion won three of the four opening sessions before having his best round in the fifth when taking Abraham (168) to the ropes and pounding him with hard lefts. The sixth, however, saw a resurgence in Abraham, who came right back into the fight with solid counters, and with neither man sure of victory the final round was a slugging match with Stieglitz being forced to the floor and barely able to make it to the bell. Both men were docked a point, Abraham in the eighth for rabbit punching and Stieglitz a round later for holding.

3 May 2014. Arthur Abraham w pts 12 Nikola Sjekloca.
Venue: Prenzlauer Berg Velodrome, Berlin, Germany. **Recognition:** WBO. **Referee:** Mark Nelson.
Scorecards: 116-112, 119-110, 116-113.
Fight Summary: Sjekloca (168) made a good start when winning the opening two rounds with the jab as the champion looked to settle. Abraham (167¾) began to get his punches off in the third and dropped two rounds at most from thereon in as Sjekloca was cut under the right eye and took more stick the longer the contest went on. Although Sjekloca gave it his best shot in the 11th and 12th it was never going to be enough, Abraham being happy to cruise to the win. It was stated afterwards that Abraham had badly injured his right hand in the eighth, which would probably explain the reason for his predominant use of the left from that point onwards.

31 May 2014. Carl Froch w rsc 8 George Groves.
Venue: The Stadium, Wembley, London, England. **Recognition:** IBF. **Referee:** Charlie Fitch.
Fight Summary: Fighting in front of an 80,000 strong crowd, the champion finally settled the argument between him and Groves (166¼) when the referee stopped the contest at 2.43 of the eighth having dispensed with the count with the latter on the floor. The contest had certainly lived up to expectations with both men landing good punches as the action swung to and fro. Coming into the eighth, with Froch (167¾) a round up according to two of the cards, the intensity moved up a gear as the men appeared happy to trade. At this point Groves was showing good footwork when moving out of range at the sign of danger, but when Froch followed him to the ropes, feinting to throw the left hook before landing one, a follow-up howitzer of a right hand landed flush and that was that.

Froch relinquished the IBF title in early February 2015 in order to pursue a career-defining fight before retiring, thus clearing the way for a James DeGale v Andre Dirrell meeting to decide a new champion.

16 August 2014. Anthony Dirrell w pts 12 Sakio Bika.
Venue: StubHub Centre, Carson, California, USA. **Recognition:** WBC. **Referee:** Jack Reiss.
Scorecards: 117-110, 114-113, 116-111.

Super Middleweight Division

Fight Summary: A much needed return saw Dirrell (168) finally get his hands on the title when taking the unanimous decision in yet another rough, tough brawl that left a lot to be desired. It was Dirrell's better boxing that won the day, and he also produced the punch of the fight when shaking Bika (167¾) up in the fifth with a terrific uppercut. While Dirrell was given time out after a punch landed on the top of his head, Bika further upset the referee when having a point deducted in the eighth for low blows.

27 September 2014. Arthur Abraham w pts 12 Paul Smith.
Venue: Sparkassen Arena, Kiel, Germany. **Recognition:** WBO. **Referee:** Robert Byrd.
Scorecards: 117-110, 117-111, 119-108.
Fight Summary: Unfortunately the judging left a lot to be desired in this one, Smith (167¼) being much better than the scores suggested with the majority of analysts believing that there was no more than two or three points between them. Abraham (168) did his best work early on when using good jabs and solid right hands as the challenger came onto him, but for several rounds he did little but cover up on the ropes behind a high guard. Smith, who boxed well behind the jab while applying continuous pressure, felt that he was the one making the fight at that stage and should have been rewarded as such.

21 February 2015. Arthur Abraham w pts 12 Paul Smith.
Venue: 02 World Arena, Kreuzberg, Berlin, Germany. **Recognition:** WBO. **Referee:** Raul Caiz.
Scorecards: 116-112, 117-111, 118-110.
Fight Summary: Winning just three rounds, the third, sixth and 11th, Smith (165½) never came close to dethroning Abraham (167¾) in what was a rematch, and although often matching the champion's aggression he lacked the power to make it pay off. From the fourth onwards Abraham was generally pushing Smith back with two-fisted rushes while looking to unload heavy right hands. Always trying to fight back when he had to, ultimately the brave Smith was unable to turn the fight his way and went down by a wide margin.

24 April 2015. Badou Jack w pts 12 Anthony Dirrell.
Venue: UIC Pavilion, Chicago, Illinois, USA. **Recognition:** WBC. **Referee:** Celestino Ruiz.
Scorecards: 116-112, 115-113, 114-114.
Fight Summary: Having dealt with the champion's early rushes, Jack (167½) gradually eased his way into the fight when trying to take over the inside ground. From the sixth onwards, as Dirrell (167¼) began to tire, it was Jack who started to edge the rounds as he pushed his man back. Having fallen behind it was clear that Dirrell needed a big finish, and although he came on strong Jack matched him punch for punch to walk off with the majority decision.

23 May 2015. James DeGale w pts 12 Andre Dirrell.
Venue: Agganis Arena, Boston, Massachusetts, USA. **Recognition:** IBF. **Referee:** Leo Gerstel.
Scorecards: 114-112, 117-109, 115-112.
Fight Summary: Contested for the vacant title after Carl Froch handed in his belt, DeGale (167¼) became the second British-born Olympic champion to win a version of the world title when he outscored Dirrell (167¾). He would be the first if Lennox Lewis, who won his Olympic gold while boxing for Canada, was not included. Making a great start against his fellow southpaw, DeGale, already cut over the right eye, had his man over twice in the second round following two cracking left hands as he looked for an early stoppage. Having won five of the opening six rounds, for whatever reason DeGale began to ease off, happy to land single punches, and for the next few rounds it was nearly all Dirrell. However, realising he had to do more, DeGale came back strongly in the last two or three sessions to make sure of the win.

18 July 2015. Arthur Abraham w rsc 6 Robert Stieglitz.
Venue: Gerry Weber Stadium, Halle, Germany. **Recognition:** WBO. **Referee:** Earle Brown.
Fight Summary: Despite suffering a broken jaw early on the champion made all the running against Stieglitz (167¼), in what was their fourth meeting, finding the latter with heavy rights and not allowing him room to work. Having gone down in the fourth from what seemed to be more of a slip than a punch as Abraham (167½) moved in aggressively, in the sixth Stieglitz eventually went to the floor after being struck on the temple following several combinations. With Stieglitz's corner asking for a stoppage the referee called the action off at 1.16 of the session.

12 September 2015. Badou Jack w pts 12 George Groves.
Venue: MGM Grand, Las Vegas, Nevada, USA. **Recognition:** WBC. **Referee:** Robert Byrd.
Scorecards: 116-111, 115-112, 113-114.
Fight Summary: Not making the best of starts, the challenger, having his third crack at a world title, was dropped in the opening session when a Jack (167½) overarm right connected heavily. Despite Groves (168) coming back well with the left jab to put himself in a good position at the halfway stage he started to tire from thereon in, his work becoming ragged. Taking advantage, Jack began to push Groves to the ropes, scoring with more than he took, and although there was never a great deal between them it was Jack who took the split decision. *Boxing News*, the British trade paper, stated that the punch stats showed Jack to have landed with 210 punches as opposed to Groves' 154.

21 November 2015. Arthur Abraham w pts 12 Martin Murray.
Venue: TUI Arena, Hannover, Germany. **Recognition:** WBO. **Referee:** Benjy Esteves Jnr.
Scorecards: 116-111, 115-112, 112-115.
Fight Summary: Hoping for fourth time lucky, having lost three times in world title bouts, Murray (166¼) came up short again despite giving it his best shot. Murray had started well when keeping Abraham (168) on the ropes while firing in lefts and rights, but at the finish it appeared that Abraham's short bursts of punches in each round had impressed two of the judges more than the Englishman's all-round work. Murray also delivered the punch of the night, a cracking right to the head that hurt Abraham in the eighth before he was deducted a point in the 11th for use of the shoulder.

28 November 2015. James DeGale w pts 12 Lucian Bute.
Venue: Videotron Centre, Quebec City, Quebec, Canada. **Recognition:** IBF. **Referee:** Marlon Wright.
Scorecards: 117-111, 117-111, 116-111.
Fight Summary: Making his first defence, and in a battle of southpaws, DeGale (167½) came out fast and took the opening three rounds to make sure that he had a good lead. While Bute (167¼) was always dangerous with his power punches the champion was controlling the pace of the fight, often switching to orthodox in an effort to bamboozle his opponent. Sustaining a bad cut over the left eye in the fifth from an accidental clash of heads did not further DeGale's cause, but he put it behind him to concentrate on the job in hand even though Vaseline obstructed his vision for a while. Once he put that behind him, DeGale took the last three sessions, even trading with Bute to make sure of the win.

20 February 2016. Felix Sturm w pts 12 Fedor Chudinov.
Venue: Koenig Pilsener Arena, Oberhausen, Germany. **Recognition:** WBA. **Referee:** Luis Pabon.
Scorecards: 115-113, 115-113, 114-114.
Fight Summary: Putting his title on the line for the first time since he was handed it after Andre Ward moved on, Chudinov (168) was the victim of what most ringsiders thought was poor judging when Sturm (167) won the fight by a majority decision. Gaining revenge for a previous defeat at the hands of Chudinov, the German fighter was certainly better than in their previous contest but was hardly convincing, especially when landing only 143 punches to his opponent's 297. Although Sturm was well in the fight up to the sixth, when he began to tire Chudinov appeared to take over, his body assaults beginning to take effect. Despite Sturm coming with a rush in the final session he appeared not to have done enough.

It was reported in April that Sturm had failed the post-fight drugs test and would be asking for sample 'B' to be tested.

Giovanni De Carolis held on to his WBA 'second tier' title by the skin of his teeth when drawing over 12 rounds with Tyron Zeuge at the Max Schmeling Hall, Berlin, Germany on 16 July 2016.

With no further news on the drugs testing front, Sturm, who had relocated from Germany to Bosnia in the interim, informed the WBA on 5 October that he was relinquishing his title as he was due to undergo elbow surgery and would be out of action for some time. As the 'second tier' champion, De Carolis would have automatically been granted full title status on that date.

9 April 2016. Gilberto Ramirez w pts 12 Arthur Abraham.
Venue: MGM Grand, Las Vegas, Nevada, USA. **Recognition:** WBO. **Referee:** Kenny Bayless.
Scorecards: 120-108, 120-108, 120-108.
Fight Summary: Making a fast start against Abraham (168), a man known for taking his time to get going, the southpaw challenger was soon picking up points with a sound jab and follow-up punches. Normally, Abraham catches up with opponents, but this time round he found Ramirez (168) just too fast and accurate for him. There were early warning signs that Ramirez could punch hard as well as box, and as much as the 36-year-old Abraham tried he could not get to grips with Mexican. With it going Ramirez's way for round after round it came as no surprise when the shut-out points tally in his favour on all three cards was announced.

30 April 2016. Badou Jack drew 12 Lucian Bute.
Venue: The Armory, Washington DC, USA. **Recognition:** WBC. **Referee:** Lupe Garcia.
Scorecards: 117-111, 114-114, 114-114.
Fight Summary: Pitted against a former 36-year-old champion in Bute (167), Jack (167½) was expected to be too much of a handful for his challenger regardless that he was only four years younger. Although Bute, who was cut over the right eye in the third, came forward for much of the time he often failed to pick up on openings and was forced to take jabs and point-scoring blows in return. Winning the last three rounds on the cards certainly brought Bute back into the fight, but Jack appeared to have done enough prior to that to warrant more than a majority draw.

30 April 2016. James DeGale w pts 12 Rogelio Medina.
Venue: The Armory, Washington DC, USA. **Recognition:** IBF. **Referee:** Malik Waleed.
Scorecards: 116-112, 115-113, 117-111.
Fight Summary: Up against a tough Mexican challenger, despite taking time out in a few rounds DeGale (167½) did plenty enough to earn the unanimous decision in a contest where he could have had even more control. Switching from his normal southpaw stance on several occasions, DeGale impressed with his work to the body as well as dishing out some hefty right uppercuts to the head, one such blow in the ninth stunning Medina (167¾). Not daunted, Medina kept on going forward, especially in the last two sessions when he worked hard enough to win them. However, it was too late to change matters, DeGale having already made sure of the win.

Super Middleweight Boxers' Index:
(Country of birth where known/Domicile - birthplace and domicile are the same unless stated)

A
Arthur Abraham (Armenia/Germany)
Ruben Eduardo Acosta (Argentina)
Mauricio Amaral (Brazil)
Librado Andrade (Mexico/USA)
Evans Ashira (Kenya/Denmark)
Crawford Ashley (England)

B
In-Chul Baek (South Korea)
Gary Ballard (South Africa)
Jaffa Ballogou (Togo/USA)
Karoly Balzsay (Hungary)
Jaime Barboza (Costa Rica)
Iran Barkley (USA)
Nigel Benn (England)
Alejandro Berrio (Colombia/USA)
Markus Beyer (Germany)
Sakio Bika (Cameroon/Australia)
Mehdi Bouadla (France)
Vincent Boulware (USA)
Stjepan Bozic (Slovenia/Croatia)
Silvio Branco (Italy)
Bryant Brannon (USA)
Charles Brewer (USA)
Danny Brewer (USA)
Jesse Brinkley (USA)
Neville Brown (England)
Lloyd Bryan (Jamaica/USA)
Frank Buglioni (England)
Lucian Bute (Romania/Canada)
James Butler (USA)
Antoine Byrd (USA)

C
Joe Calzaghe (England/Wales)
Cornelius Carr (England)
Glenn Catley (England)
Hacine Cherifi (France)
Fedor Chudinov (Russia)
Jose Alberto Clavero (Argentina)
Ray Close (Northern Ireland)
Alberto Colajanni (Italy)
Steve Collins (Ireland)
Victor Cordoba (Panama)
James Crawford (USA)
Craig Cummings (USA)
Vinnie Curto (USA)

D
Chad Dawson (USA)
Giovanni De Carolis (Italy)
James DeGale (England)
Joey DeGrandis (USA)
Andre Dirrell (USA)
Anthony Dirrell (USA)
Billy Douglas (USA)
Roberto Duran (Panama)

E
Antwun Echols (USA)
Isaac Ekpo (Nigeria)
Ali Ennebati (Algeria/France)
Ron Essett (USA)
Chris Eubank (England)

F
Vincent Feigenbutz (Germany)
Carl Froch (England)
Don Fullmer (USA)

G
Jesus Gallardo (Mexico)
Mauro Galvano (Italy)
Joe Gatti (Canada/USA)
Lou Gent (England)
Khoren Gevor (Armenia/Germany)
Juan Carlos Gimenez (Paraguay)
Bruno Girard (France)
Herol Graham (England)
Allan Green (USA)
Danny Green (Australia)
Julio Cesar Green (Dominican Republic/USA)
George Groves (England)
Roy Gumbs (St Kitts/England)
Eduard Gutknecht (Kazakhstan/Germany)

H
Jerry Halstead (USA)
Nader Hamdan (Morocco/Australia)
Danilo Haussler (Germany)
Thomas Hearns (USA)
Gabriel Hernandez (Dominican Republic/USA)
Virgil Hill (USA)
Dave Hilton (Canada)
Lindell Holmes (USA)
Joe Hopkins (USA)

Super Middleweight Division

I
Denis Inkin (Russia/Germany)

J
Badou Jack (Sweden/USA)
John Jarvis (USA)
Miguel Angel Jimenez (USA)
Glen Johnson (Jamaica/USA)
Roy Jones (USA)
William Joppy (USA)

K
Stanislav Kashtanov (Ukraine/Russia)
Leif Keiski (Finland/USA)
Mikkel Kessler (Denmark)
James Kinchen (USA)
Yuzo Kiyota (Japan)
Armand Krajnc (Sweden)

L
Jeff Lacy (USA)
Donny Lalonde (Canada)
Mads Larsen (Denmark/Germany)
Sugar Ray Leonard (USA)
Frankie Liles (USA)
Steve Little (USA)
Tim Littles (USA)
Eric Lucas (Canada)

M
Marvin Mack (USA)
Yusaf Mack (USA)
Brian Magee (USA)
Thulani Malinga (South Africa)
Peter Manfredo (USA)
Rudy Markussen (Denmark)
Maselino Masoe (Samoa/New Zealand)
Dario Matteoni (Argentina)
Gerald McClellan (USA)
Ben McCulloch (Australia)
Will McIntyre (USA)
Rogelio Medina (Mexico)
Tito Mendoza (Panama)
Jean-Paul Mendy (France)
Segundo Mercado (Ecuador/USA)
Samuel Miller (Colombia/USA)
Edison Miranda (Colombia/Puerto Rico)
Byron Mitchell (USA)
Mger Mkrtchyan (Armenia/Russia)
Dan Morgan (USA)
Anthony Mundine (Australia)

N
Giovanni Nardiello (Italy)
Vincenzo Nardiello (Germany/Italy)
Yoshinori Nishizawa (Japan)
Michael Nunn (USA)

O
Fulgencio Obelmejias (Venezuela)
Michael Olajide (England/Canada)
Enrique Ornelas (Mexico/USA)
Emmanuel Otti (Uganda/Australia)
Sven Ottke (Germany)

P
Chong-Pal Park (South Korea)
Jean Pascal (Haiti/Canada)
Polly Pasireron (Indonesia)
Vinny Pazienza (USA)
Scott Pemberton USA)
Gusmyr Perdomo (Venezuela)
Danny Perez (USA)
Marco Antonio Periban (Mexico)
Nicky Piper (Wales)
Giovanni Pretorius (South Africa)
Tocker Pudwill (USA)

R
Gilberto Ramirez (Mexico)
Chris Reid (USA)
Robin Reid (England)
Mauricio Reynoso (Peru)
Graciano Rocchigiani (Germany)
Edwin Rodriguez (Dominican Republic/USA)

S
Kabary Salem (Egypt/USA)
Tarick Salmaci (Lebanon/USA)
Doug Sam (Australia)
Cristian Sanavia (Italy)
Dimitri Sartison (Kazakhstan/Germany)
Dan Schommer (USA)
Frederic Seillier (France)
Omar Sheika (USA)
Andrey Shkalikov (Russia)
Manny Siaca (Puerto Rico)
Ernie Singletary (USA)
Nikola Sjekloca (Serbia/Montenegro)
Paul Smith (England)
Branko Sobot (Croatia/Germany)
Sam Soliman (Australia)
Merqui Sosa (Dominican Republic/USA)
David Starie (England)
Robert Stieglitz (Russia/Germany)

Sam Storey (Northern Ireland)
Felix Sturm (Germany)
Carl Sullivan (USA)
Murray Sutherland (Scotland/USA)

T
Yoshiaki Tajima (Japan)
Frank Tate (USA)
Thomas Tate (USA)
Jermain Taylor (USA)
Dingaan Thobela (South Africa)
Rick Thornberry (Australia)
Tony Thornton (USA)
Andre Thysse (South Africa)
Christophe Tiozzo (Italy)
James Toney (USA)
Vitaliy Tsypko (Ukraine)

V
Darrin Van Horn (USA)
Syd Vanderpool (Canada)

Mario Veit (Germany)

W
Nicky Walker (USA)
Andre Ward (USA)
Michael Watson (England)
Henry Weber (Germany)
Henry Wharton (England)
Paul Whittaker (USA)
Charles Williams (USA)
Rubin Williams (USA)
Richie Woodhall (England)

Y
Server Yemurlayev (Uzbekistan/Ukraine)

Z
Pablo Daniel Zamora Nievas (Argentina)
Tyron Zeuge (Germany)
Fulgencio Zuniga (Colombia)

Light Heavyweight Division

Originated in America following a series of articles written by Lou Houseman, a newspaperman based in Chicago who also managed a stable of fighters, the division was first 'thought up' in 1899. Although Houseman is mainly remembered for steering Jack Root to the 'title', he first promoted a fight in Dubuque in 1899 between Joe Choynski and Australian Jim Ryan as being for the vacant light heavyweight championship. According to the *Dubuque Herald*, Choynski was already claiming to be the champion. There were quite a few men who would have benefited from an interim weight class, but because the middleweight and heavyweight divisions were so prestigious it took many years before the light heavies were taken seriously.

Weight Band/Amendments

160lbs to 170lbs (29 August 1899 to 22 April 1903)
160lbs to 175lbs (With the weights for the 22 April 1903 Jack Root v Charles Kid McCoy fight set at 175lbs, the weight class would be contested at varying poundage within those limits until standardised. That came about on 11 February 1909 when The National Sporting Club (NSC) formally introduced their eight named weight classes, with the middleweight limit staying at 160lbs and the new light heavyweight class set at 175lbs)
168lbs to 175lbs (On 28 March 1984, the International Boxing Federation (IBF) launched the super middleweight division for all men between 160 and 168lbs)

Light Heavyweight World Championship Fights and Title Claims:

29 August 1899. (165lbs) Joe Choynski w pts 20 Australian Jim Ryan.
Venue: Athletic Club, The Auditorium, Dubuque, Iowa, USA. **Referee:** George Siler.
Fight Summary: Advertised as a 165lbs world title fight, the clever Choynski (158) soon got the measure of Ryan (162) and pushed ahead in virtually every round from the mid-point onwards as the latter got more and more ragged. Having campaigned among the heavyweights Choynski was also very strong at the weight, mixing his punches up well to stagger Ryan on several occasions. The last third of the contest was all one way as Choynski continued to outbox the Australian, the decision in his favour being a formality. There were no knockdowns.

25 September 1899. (170lbs) Joe Choynski w co 3 (20) Jim Hall.
Venue: Nonpareil AC, Music Hall, Louisville, Kentucky, USA. **Referee:** Ed Rucker.
Fight Summary: Again advertised for the title, this time at 170lbs, Choynski (160) allowed Hall (168) to take the first two rounds before opening up in the third. Scoring with accurate lefts and rights Choynski soon had the measure of Hall, and with about half a minute of the session remaining the Australian was sent to the boards to be counted out.

On 6 October, at the Fort Dearborn AC, Chicago, Illinois, Choynski drew over six rounds with Charles Kid McCoy, who was said to weigh in the region of 170lbs. Not known if Choynski's title claim was at risk, the contest was called a draw due to a pre-fight agreement.

20 October 1899. (170lbs) Joe Choynski w co 7 (20) Australian Jim Ryan.
Venue: Broadway AC, Manhattan, NYC, New York, USA. **Referee:** Johnny White.
Fight Summary: Made at 170lbs, and a return match between the pair, Choynski (168) was outscoring Ryan (165) right from the opening bell before getting down to business in the seventh. Having smashed Ryan to the floor with a solid right to the jaw, when the latter somehow regained his feet Choynski sent in another right to the chin that saw the Australian counted out.

Choynski next went on to kayo Dick Moore inside three rounds of a catchweight contest at the Athletic Club, St Louis, Missouri on 23 October. The report made no mention of any title, although one can safely assume that Moore was inside 170lbs.

12 January 1900. (165lbs) Charles Kid McCoy w rsc 4 (25) Joe Choynski.
Venue: Broadway AC, Manhattan, NYC, New York, USA. **Referee:** Johnny White.
Fight Summary: Not billed for the title, but with both men announced as being inside 165lbs Choynski's title claim was at risk. The fight itself was quite extraordinary, McCoy being put down three times in the second and looking as though he was finished for the night, only for the bell to go on the 2.20 mark. The timekeeper later explained that he had rung the bell to end the fight after the referee had missed the count, the gong having reached 12, and as far as he was concerned McCoy had lost. Adding insult to injury, in the following discussions between the referee and the timekeeper another two minutes, 30 seconds elapsed before the third round got underway. After McCoy had been dropped by another heavy right and got to his feet both men went crashing having landed simultaneously. On the gong to end the third, when Choynski dropped his arms and headed for his corner he was caught fully on the jaw by a short left hook and went down like a log. Dragged back to his seat after the bell went to end the round with the count not completed, when the gong to start the fourth clanged the referee awarded the fight to McCoy after Choynski, unable to stand up, fell on his face. According to many of the press and enraged fans McCoy lost twice, by a kayo and a foul, but according to a club official the latter had been in the process of throwing the winning blow as Choynski relaxed, thus making it legal. Some newspapers reported this as a retirement.

With McCoy concentrating on defending his middleweight claim and looking to get among the heavies there would be no more activity for him in the new weight class until he was selected to settle the title against Jack Root.

24 May 1901. (170lbs) Marvin Hart w co 6 (25) Dan Creedon.
Venue: Southern AC, The Auditorium, Louisville, Kentucky, USA. **Referee:** Ed McBride.
Fight Summary: In a contest made at catchweights, the unbeaten Hart (170) had closed Creedon's left eye by the end of the second round and was already looking to take his man out. Tearing into Creedon (169) in the third Hart had the New Zealander over for 'eight', a left hook doing the damage, but in the next session both were groggy at the bell after vicious lefts and rights to head and body had been exchanged. The fifth saw Hart piling on the pressure as Creedon began to capsize, and in the sixth the latter was counted out after a tremendous left hook to the jaw had sent him crashing.

Now claiming the American 170lbs title, Hart challenged the world at the weight on 6 October.

Having beaten Dan Creedon (w co 1 at the Convention Hall, Kansas City, Missouri on 4 October 1900) and George Byers (w co 9 at the National AC, San Francisco on 18 January), the *San Francisco Chronicle* reported that Jack Root should be recognised as the American 165lbs light heavyweight champion. This statement came immediately prior to his contest against Kid Carter.

28 June 1901. (165lbs) Jack Root w disq 15 (20) Kid Carter.
Venue: Mechanics' Pavilion, San Francisco, California, USA. **Referee:** Phil Wand.
Fight Summary: Made at 165lbs, Root was in the ascendancy after dropping Carter three times in the 13th, the last occasion being from a palpably low blow. With both men remaining strong it was anybody's fight up until the 15th round when Carter, after landing a hard left to the body, rushed Root to the ropes and pushed him down. Although the crowd had failed to spot a foul blow, Root, who was on his back grimacing in pain, was given the decision when the referee decided that he had been fouled.

30 October 1901. (165lbs) Jack Root w co 2 (20) Australian Jim Ryan.
Venue: Music Hall, Louisville, Kentucky, USA. **Referee:** Bat Masterson.
Fight Summary: Regardless of the fact that it was advertised as being for the middleweight championship of the West according to the *Chicago Tribune*, with neither man able to get below 158lbs at this stage of their careers, and reportedly weighing between 162 and 165lbs, this has to be seen as another defence of Root's 165lbs title claim. Ryan, who was blind in one eye, forced the fight from the opening bell before being staggered by a heavy blow to the jaw in the second round. Moments later, Root struck again when a big left swing to Ryan's jaw saw the latter floored and counted out.

1 November 1901. (170lbs) Marvin Hart w co 10 (20) Jack Beauscholte.
Venue: Empire AC, Music Hall, Louisville, Kentucky, USA. **Referee:** George Siler.
Fight Summary: Although articled at catchweights both men were said to be inside 170lbs, thus putting Hart's claim at risk, and after five rounds Beauscholte had given such a great showing that even money was being offered on him scoring a knockout win. It had been hammer and tongs all the way, but by the seventh Hart was beginning to force matters. In the eighth Beauscholte was being pummelled in his own corner before sinking to the boards with Hart on top of him. When the action continued, with both men fighting like madmen, Beauscholte stood his ground and partly closed Hart's left eye before a short hook to the point of his jaw in the tenth sent him down to be counted out. At that stage of the fight both fighters were so weak they could barely stand up.

17 December 1901. (170lbs) Wild Bill Hanrahan w co 1 (25) Marvin Hart.
Venue: Southern AC, The Auditorium, Louisville, Kentucky, USA. **Referee:** Tim Hurst.
Fight Summary: Reportedly carrying the American 170lbs championship, Hanrahan, who was out of the blocks quicker than Hart, soon had the latter on the floor from a right-hand smash to the back of the neck. Getting up in a dazed condition Hart took another hurtful blow to the body before Hanrahan sent in a left to the same region, following it up with a right hook to the jaw that sent the American to the floor to be counted out. All over after about one and a half minutes, the winner claimed the title on the result.

Hanrahan's claim gained support in the 16 January 1902 edition of the *Sporting Life* when he was recognised as the world champion at the weight.

31 January 1902. (165lbs) Jack Root w disq 7 (20) George Gardner.
Venue: Mechanics' Pavilion, San Francisco, California, USA. **Referee:** Phil Wand.
Fight Summary: Advertised for the middleweight title despite it being articled at catchweights according to the *Chicago Tribune*, what was really at stake was Root's light heavyweight (often reported as middleweight) title claim at 165lbs. Unfortunately for Gardner he suffered the misfortune of having his left eye practically closed in the second round after Root had got home with a solid right, not being himself thereafter. Regardless of that Gardner had Root on the floor from a right to the side of the head in the fourth, but the latter got up and cleverly clinched and stalled to get through to the bell. From there onwards it was all Root, and by the sixth Gardner had resorted to going low with claims of a foul being made on at least two occasions. With Root boring in methodically in the seventh after sending his rival to the floor groaning in pain, following a hefty blow to the groin Gardner was disqualified at 1.46 of the session.

7 March 1902. (170lbs) Joe Choynski w co 5 (25) Wild Bill Hanrahan.
Venue: Empire AC, Music Hall, Louisville, Kentucky, USA. **Referee:** George Siler.
Fight Summary: Defending his 170lbs title claim in this one, Hanrahan (169) started well when having Choynski (169) over in the first following a solid right swing to the neck. Regardless, after Choynski got to his feet apparently unhurt he quickly regained his composure. Although Choynski was picking his punches well in the next couple of sessions, in the fourth he was forced to take several blows to the jaw without return and appeared tired at the bell. The fifth began with a heavy exchange of blows before Hanrahan became wild and inaccurate as Choynski found him with hurtful right hands. With both men tiring it was ultimately Choynski who found the right punches at the right time, culminating in a left-right to the jaw that sent Hanrahan down to be counted out. While Choynski picked up his old 170lbs title claim as a result of the fight, shortly afterwards, on 18 April, his rival sadly passed away following a bout of pneumonia. Hanrahan had been ready to enter the ring when the doctor discovered he was running a temperature of 104, which hospitalised him for several days prior to his death.

24 March 1902. (165lbs) Kid Carter w co 1 (6) Joe Choynski.
Venue: American AC, Chicago, Illinois, USA. **Referee:** Malachy Hogan.
Fight Summary: Down three times and receiving a terrible battering, somehow Carter, still groggy, found the strength to land a mighty right to Choynski's jaw which saw the latter counted out inside the first three minutes. Despite it being a mere six rounder, Carter took over Choynski's claim at 170lbs on the result. George Siler was also reported to have refereed this contest.

3 May 1902. (170lbs) Marvin Hart w co 9 (20) Kid Carter.
Venue: Southern AC, The Auditorium, Louisville, Kentucky, USA. **Referee:** Tim Hurst.
Fight Summary: Reporting on this one, a catchweight contest with both men thought to be inside 170lbs, George Siler, the famous referee, stated in the *Chicago Tribune* that Hart should now meet the winner of Jack Root v George Gardner to settle the light heavyweights, a relatively new weight class. It had been a slugging match right up to the end of the fifth round before both men ran out of steam, staggering around the ring hardly able to stand and seemingly unable to land an effective blow. With the contest developing into one of endurance, just when Hart seemed ready to fall in the ninth he found a left hook to the jaw that sent Carter crashing. Both men showed the signs of battle, with Carter's right eye closed as was Hart's, and both were exhausted as well as bloody. Meanwhile, Hart's manager, H. C. Dickens, was telling the world that he had a coming heavyweight champion on his hands.

In his next 20 rounder, on 2 April 1903, an over-the-weight Hart beat Jack Bonner on a fourth-round disqualification at the Empire AC prior to meeting George Gardner. Bonner was thought to be inside 170lbs.

18 August 1902. (165lbs) George Gardner w rtd 17 (20) Jack Root.
Venue: Salt Palace Saucer Track, Salt Lake City, Utah, USA. **Referee:** Harry Hynds.
Fight Summary: Made at 165lbs, with both men inside, whatever claim at the weight Root had should have passed to Gardner on the result. Ignoring solid jabs to his cut-up face Gardner continued to pound the body, having Root in serious bother in the seventh round. Thereafter, with Gardner on top, Root was again belted to the deck in the 16th. Down again three more times in the 17th after taking more terrific punishment, Root was finally put out of his misery when his corner threw in the towel with their man still on the canvas.

Not really considering himself to be a champion of the new weight class, Gardner continued to fight among the heavyweights before being matched with Marvin Hart.

22 April 1903. (175lbs) Jack Root w pts 10 Charles Kid McCoy.
Venue: Light Guard Armoury, Detroit, Michigan, USA. **Referee:** Bat Masterson.
Fight Summary: Previously considered to be the division's first title fight, even if it was only billed for the American 175lbs championship, Root (168) started fast, landing lefts and rights to the head without return. Dropped in the second round by a body punch and saved by the bell McCoy (173) was again put down in the third (twice), seventh, eighth and ninth prior to desperately holding on to the end of the tenth. The famous referee, George Siler, writing in the *Chicago Tribune*, said "There was really no necessity to advertise the fight as a championship bout as the new light heavyweight class should only be seen as a maverick, and as such has no standing."

13 May 1903. (170lbs) George Gardner w rtd 12 (20) Marvin Hart.
Venue: Southern AC, The Auditorium, Louisville, Kentucky, USA. **Referee:** Tim Hurst.
Fight Summary: It was certainly a fierce contest, with Hart carrying a punch like a mule and as strong as an ox, while Gardner had the edge in speed and landed more often. Both men had their chances to win despite a lack of knockdowns, but by the 12th round they were so badly worn out from their exertions that it was impossible to call at that point. Although the 12th saw Gardner hitting Hart almost as he liked it was still a major surprise when the latter was pulled out by his corner at the end of the session, claiming a broken right hand. For the record, the *Chicago Tribune* stated that Hart, who was unable to get below 170lbs, had no realistic claim to the title when scaling 176lbs to Gardner's 168.

4 July 1903. (165lbs) George Gardner w co 12 (20) Jack Root.
Venue: International AC, Fort Erie, Ontario, Canada. **Referee:** Ed McBride.
Fight Summary: With the previous two so-called championship contests decided at 175 and 170lbs, respectively, this one was made at 165lbs. The *Chicago Tribune* claimed that with three days to go both men were already down to the weight, give or take a couple of pounds. Starting well, especially when banging in left hooks to the body, with Gardner well on top in the ninth round incessant pressure saw Root floored by a clip to the jaw. Back on his feet Root was in serious trouble before being saved by the bell. Down again in the 11th and twice in the 12th from

crashing body shots and swings to the jaw, the last knockdown saw Root unable to make it to his feet and counted out.

25 November 1903. (168lbs) Bob Fitzsimmons w pts 20 George Gardner.
Venue: Mechanics' Pavilion, San Francisco, California, USA. **Referee:** Ed Graney.
Fight Summary: Although the Articles of Agreement called for the men to make 168lbs, according to the *San Francisco Chronicle* Gardner came in at 170lbs while Fitzsimmons was spot on. Gardner was a good fighter, but had hardly set the world on fire, whereas the 40-year-old Fitzsimmons, who became the first man to win three titles at different weights, gave the light heavyweight division a certain air of respectability. Despite conserving his energy Fitzsimmons outboxed and outfought Gardner throughout, while the latter was unable to catch him often enough with any real force. There was no doubting that Fitzsimmons still had punching ability, Gardner being dropped in the fourth (twice), fifth, tenth, 13th, 14th and 17th. Afterwards, Fitzsimmons stated that he had been unable to kayo Gardner, who finished with cuts and abrasions over both eyes and a broken nose, due to him breaking the knuckles on both hands early in the contest. The referee claimed that the fight was as poor as he had handled, but had given the fight to Fitzsimmons due to the knockdowns.

Fitzsimmons retained his title claim after a six-round contest made at 165lbs against Philadelphia Jack O'Brien (nd-l rsc 6 at the National League Baseball Ground, Philadelphia, Pennsylvania on 23 July 1904).

20 December 1905. (175lbs) Philadelphia Jack O'Brien w rtd 13 (20) Bob Fitzsimmons.
Venue: Mechanics' Pavilion, San Francisco, California, USA. **Referee:** Ed Graney.
Fight Summary: Seen by some as one of a series of eliminators to decide the heavyweight title, the *Boston Daily Globe* and others reported it to involve both the world light heavyweight and heavyweight championships. O'Brien was already claiming the heavyweight title, while Fitzsimmons' light heavyweight crown was on the line at the same time. Once the fight got underway it was clear that O'Brien (164) was the faster, using good footwork to get away from trouble, while Fitzsimmons (165) looked for the punch to finish it. Throughout, O'Brien showed his ability to hit and shift, hurting Fitzsimmons badly in the fourth and flooring his rival in the eighth with a stiff right to the jaw. Although Fitzsimmons continued to come forward he was taking more and more punishment, and at the end of the 13th he collapsed in his corner with blood pouring from his nose and mouth, whereupon the referee awarded the fight to O'Brien after the towel was thrown into the ring. Fortunately, Fitzsimmons quickly recovered and left the ring unassisted.

Taking on two men on the same night, at the Naud Junction Pavilion, Los Angeles, California on 16 October 1906, O'Brien knocked out the 168lbs Jim Tremble inside nine rounds before taking out the 171lbs Fred Cooley in the third. Both contests were scheduled for ten rounds.

28 November 1906. (175lbs) Philadelphia Jack O'Brien drew 20 Tommy Burns.
Venue: Naud Junction Pavilion, Los Angeles, California, USA. **Referee:** James J. Jeffries.
Fight Summary: Fighting like a bulldog from beginning to end Burns (172) just about deserved to win the decision from O'Brien (163½), who was never far behind in the scoring. With both fighters' title claims at stake, despite there being no knockdowns the fight was unrelenting and there was plenty of hard hitting. Both men were damaged; O'Brien's right eye being cut early on and Burns' left optic closed shut at the final bell. According to O'Brien the fight was pre-arranged with Burns to be drawn. He explained "The promoter, 'Uncle' Tom McCarey, had figured it out that if we fought a spirited draw he could bill the return match during fiesta week and make a small fortune by charging top prices." Despite being billed as deciding the heavyweight championship, because both men were inside 175lbs record compilers who saw O'Brien as the light heavyweight boss logged it as a title defence.

8 May 1907. (175lbs) Tommy Burns w pts 20 Philadelphia Jack O'Brien.
Venue: Naud Junction Pavilion, Los Angeles, California, USA. **Referee:** Charles Eyton.
Fight Summary: In a return bout between the two claimants which was nothing like their previous set-to, each and every round became repetitive as Burns (175) chased after O'Brien (167). Although Burns came the closest to ending the fight with the occasional wild swing, O'Brien was too clever to be caught napping, being more

interested in getting to the final bell in one piece. Clearly, O'Brien was not up to the task, especially following revelations afterwards that he had offered Burns the winner's end of the purse to take a dive in the 11th round. Fearing that O'Brien would not accept the fight under any other circumstances, although Burns agreed to his terms he had no intention whatsoever of complying with them. According to Burns, having made up his mind to double-cross his opponent at the onset he immediately reported the matter to the promoter. The decision was then made to get both men into the ring before all bets were called off. Billed for the heavyweight title there were papers such as the *Albany Evening Journal* and others who reported it to also involve O'Brien's light heavyweight championship claim. Burns had also been reported as weighing 180lbs, while more recent research shows his weight to have been 175lbs.

Although Tom Andrews, of the *TS Andrews Annual*, and others recognised Burns as the champion following this contest there is no evidence that the heavyweight champion was interested in what was, in the main, seen as a synthetic title at that moment in time. Despite that, Burns' heavyweight defence against Jack Palmer on 10 February 1908 at 175lbs would automatically have been recognised by Andrews as a defence of Burns' light heavyweight title also.

10 February 1908. (175lbs) Tommy Burns w co 4 (20) Jack Palmer.
Venue: Wonderland, Mile End, London, England. **Referee:** Robert Watson.
Fight Summary: On the attack right from the start as Palmer (168) froze, Burns (175), who had the Englishman down twice in the first round, continued to batter away at him during the next two sessions. Finally, in the fourth, after Burns put Palmer down several more times the latter was counted out on his knees.

Regardless of Burns having no further contests at 175lbs, Tom Andrews continued to recognise him as a leading title claimant until early in 1912 following inactivity and being on the verge of retirement.

26 March 1909. (175lbs) Philadelphia Jack O'Brien nd-l pts 10 Stanley Ketchel.
Venue: National AC, Manhattan, NYC, New York, USA. **Referee:** Tim Hurst.
Fight Summary: Although the contest was made at 160lbs, which was inside the American light heavyweight poundage at that time, it appears that O'Brien had reclaimed the 175lbs title seeing that Tommy Burns was no longer interested. The fight itself was fairly even up until the sixth when O'Brien was dropped by a heavy right to the solar plexus. The last round was dramatic in the extreme as Ketchel drove in punch after punch on the weakened O'Brien, dropping him four times in all, the last occasion seeing the latter saved by the bell. Both men finished with badly cut eyes and swollen lips.

On 9 June, in a return no-decision match made at 160lbs and scheduled for six rounds at the National AC, Philadelphia, Pennsylvania, O'Brien was dropped twice in the second and again in the third before being rescued by the referee who did not even bother to count him out. And while there is nothing to suggest that Ketchel was the least bit interested in the light heavyweight title, any further claim by O'Brien would surely have been unfounded. Despite that, the *Mount Carmel Item* was still referring to him as the light heavyweight champion in November.

17 March 1910. (175lbs) Sam Langford w co 8 (45) Fireman Jim Flynn.
Venue: Vernon Arena, Los Angeles, California, USA. **Referee:** Charles Eyton.
Fight Summary: Up until the seventh Flynn was still in the fight despite being battered, bruised and cut, but towards the end of that session Langford was letting the punches go after deciding that he was going to finish it. In the eighth, having lulled Flynn into a head-down charge Langford took a step back before crashing in a heavy right uppercut that landed flush on the jaw and sent the man from Pueblo flat on his face to be counted out. Despite a lack of billing, with both men inside 175lbs Tom Andrews, of the *TS Andrews Annual*, claimed that Langford, along with Tommy Burns, should be recognised as the two leading light heavyweight title claimants.

One man who could have put a dampener on any claim that Langford may or may not have had at the time was Stanley Ketchel. When meeting Ketchel at the National AC, Philadelphia, Pennsylvania on 27 April, Langford was deemed to have won the six-round press decision in what was a tough fight. Newspaper reports of the day stated that both men would be inside 170lbs on the night.

Another contest for Langford where he supposedly boxed below 175lbs came against Tony Caponi at the Auditorium Ice Rink, Winnipeg, Manitoba, Canada on 16 June 1911. Originally booked for 15 rounds with a 168lbs weigh-in at 3pm, it ended up as a no-decision ten-rounder that was stopped by the police in the seventh round after Caponi was hurt and then allowed to continue after he'd had a good rest. Langford sauntered through the last three rounds so as to not antagonise the police, duly picking up the press verdict.

I have not included a ten-round contest against Jim Smith (nd-w rsc 5 at the Atlantic Garden AC, Manhattan, NYC, New York on 9 August 1911) as a mainliner, as I am unsure of the weights. It was reported that Langford was at least 20lbs heavier than Smith, who could have been inside the middleweight limit on the day.

15 August 1911. (175lbs) Sam Langford nd-w rsc 5 (10) Philadelphia Jack O'Brien.
Venue: Twentieth Century AC, St Nicholas Arena, Manhattan, NYC, New York, USA. **Referee:** Charlie White.
Fight Summary: Having won the opening two rounds by dint of his boxing skills it was already apparent that O'Brien (166) was going to struggle against the hard-hitting Langford (173), regardless of his cleverness. After going to the floor from a right to the head in the third O'Brien was quickly back on his feet, but before the end of the session he took a count of 'nine' following two heavy rights to the head. Saved by the bell at the end of the fourth having received a terrific pounding to the body, it came as no surprise when a smashing left hook to the jaw saw O'Brien rescued by the referee in the fifth. Although this one carried no title billing and was held at catchweights, O'Brien stated that if Langford made 168lbs the latter's recent championship claim would be on the line. Announced as being inside 175lbs, other reports gave Langford to weigh as much as 180lbs.

By this time most of the boxing world recognised 175lbs to be the limit for the weight class so when O'Brien was well and truly licked by Langford, *Boxing*, Britain's trade paper, reported that he should now be considered as the world champion. That statement was echoed by the *Buffalo Courier* and other papers of the day. Despite being recognised along with Tommy Burns by Tom Andrews as having the best claims, there is no record of him taking it any further.

On 22 December 1912, the newly formed New York State Athletic Commission (NYSAC) stated that they would now be recognising a new 'commission' weight class for men between 160 and 175lbs. Two days after the announcement Fireman Jim Flynn promptly laid claim to the 'commission' title, stating that he was through as a heavyweight and thought himself eligible to be placed at the head of the new weight class. It was no surprise that Flynn was not taken seriously by the NYSAC as he had been fighting well above the weight since taking on Langford in 1910.

Even when Langford was recognised by the recently formed International Boxing Union (IBU) as the world light heavyweight champion, when they first published their ratings in June 1913, he continued amongst the heavyweights.

12 February 1913. (175lbs) Georges Carpentier w co 2 (20) Bandsman Dick Rice.
Venue: The Circus, Paris, France.
Fight Summary: In a match made at 175lbs for the European title, Rice (164¾) held his own in the opening session before launching himself at Carpentier (166) in the second. Unfortunately for the Englishman, after missing with a mighty right hand and being countered by a lightning right hook to the jaw it was all over after one minute of the session. According to the 1914 *TS Andrews' Annual*, Carpentier carried off the world title following his win over Rice.

Having won the European heavyweight championship on defeating Bombardier Billy Wells just three contests later, Carpentier would then fight among the heavies before being inactive between July 1914 and July 1919 after answering the call to arms at the outbreak of World War One.

17 February 1913. (175lbs) Bob Moha nd-w pts 10 Cyclone Johnny Thompson.
Venue: Southside AC, Hippodrome Arena, Milwaukee, Wisconsin, USA. **Referee:** John McIntosh.
Fight Summary: Made at 175lbs in response to the NYSAC recognising a 'commission' weight class for men weighing between 160 and 175lbs, the *Fort Wayne Sentinel* stated that the winner would claim the title. Ultimately, Moha proved much too strong for Thompson despite the latter fighting on gamely to the final bell. According to press reports every round was full of action and hard hitting, with Moha landing heavily throughout and hurting Thompson on many occasions, especially with body blows.

Both the *Indianapolis Star* and *La Crosse Tribune* reported that Moha would now be claiming the 175lbs title, regardless of the fact that he could make the middleweight limit, which he did in three of his next four outings, against Eddie McGoorty (nd-drew 10 the Southside AC, Milwaukee on 24 March), Jack Dillon (nd-l pts 10 at the same venue on 28 April) and Johnny Howard (nd-drew 10 at the Irving AC, NYC, New York on 20 December). Had Moha lost any of these fights inside the distance, his 'commission' title claim would have been extinct. As it was, it was barely recognised.

1 January 1914. (165lbs) Bob Moha nd-w co 5 (10) Freddie Hicks.
Venue: Irving AC, Brooklyn, NYC, New York, USA. **Referee:** Patsy Haley.
Fight Summary: Articled at 165lbs, Moha (163½) put his claim on the line against Hicks (165) who hardly got a look in. Having got well on top by the fifth round Moha showered Hicks with lefts and rights to the head that ended with the latter taking a count of 'nine'. Back on his feet, but in a dazed condition, Hicks was taken out completely following a terrific right to the jaw.

Moha's next contest was against Jack Fitzgerald (w pts 15 at the Marieville AC, Providence, Rhode Island on 7 January), but with limited information it is difficult to assess whether his claim was at stake.

23 March 1914. (170lbs) Bob Moha nd-w pts 10 Battling Levinsky.
Venue: South Side AC, The Hippodrome, Milwaukee, Wisconsin, USA.
Fight Summary: With Levinsky beginning to make waves at weights between 165 and 175lbs, and Jack Dillon struggling to stay under 160lbs, the pair had already been brought together by an enterprising promoter to contest the vacant title the following month. Despite that, with Moha having plans of his own, first and foremost was to maintain his own claim at the weight. Tearing in with solid body shots throughout, Moha (170) almost put an end to Levinsky's plans there and then. Although Levinsky (165), who won no more than two rounds at best, defended obdurately he was badly hurt at times and finished the contest severely cut up.

In the aftermath Moha stated that he was still keen on the middleweight title, and to that end his next contest was at the same venue against Frank Mantell (nd-w pts 10 on 11 May) at 158lbs.

From here on in all title bouts would be contested at 175lbs after Jack Dillon and Battling Levinsky signed up to decide the American version of the world title at that weight.

14 April 1914. Jack Dillon w pts 12 Battling Levinsky.
Venue: Holland Arena, Butte, Montana, USA. **Referee:** Harry Stout.
Fight Summary: The *Anaconda Standard* reported this as being billed for the vacant 175lbs world title, with Dillon (164½) being too good for the clever Levinsky (170½). Stung in the fifth round by the hardest punch that Levinsky threw all night Dillon tore into his opponent from thereon in, building up a solid lead before having the Battler down in the penultimate session. Although Levinsky was quickly on his feet he was groggy at the bell and unable to put up much resistance in the 12th. It was a relatively easy win for Dillon, who was both the harder and faster puncher of the two.

Regardless that Dillon received scant support, he was recognised as such in the *TS Andrews' Annual* of the day. Interestingly, many latter-day historians thought that Dillon's claim emanated from his three-round kayo win over Hugo Kelly in a no-decision middleweight contest at the Empire Theatre, Indianapolis, Indiana on 28 May 1912, but this was the first time that he received any recognition as a light heavyweight title claimant. The confusion had been created by Dillon's manager making little sense at the time.

28 April 1914. Jack Dillon w pts 10 Al Norton.
Venue: 15th Street Garage Building, Kansas City, Missouri, USA. **Referee:** Walter Bates.
Fight Summary: Billed as a title bout, the *Kansas City Star* reported that Norton, inside 175lbs, excelled at long range with the left jab while Dillon (168) was at his best on the inside. The inexperienced Norton fought a cool fight throughout, and it was only in the ninth that Dillon was able to carry all before him, dropping his rival from more of a push than a punch and fighting flat out until the final bell.

15 May 1914. Bob Moha nd-drew 10 Al Norton.
Venue: 15th Street Garage Building, Milwaukee, Wisconsin, USA.
Fight Summary: Defending his 'commission' title claim against Norton, Moha was held up during the opening four rounds as the Californian forced the fight with a good left hand. However, Moha got more and more into it, having much success when getting to close quarters, and at the final bell had made up most of the leeway.

A few days later Moha was signed up to meet Jack Dillon in an effort to sort out the best man at the weight. Despite taking a bit of a beating at the middleweight limit when losing on points over 12 rounds to George KO Brown at the Atlas AC, Boston, Massachusetts on 27 May, Moha immediately started to get himself into condition for Dillon. Meanwhile, if Brown had any claim to the title he would have certainly lost it when beaten by Mike Gibbons next time out.

29 May 1914. Jack Dillon nd-w pts 10 Battling Levinsky.
Venue: Federal Park, Indianapolis, Indiana, USA. **Referee:** Edward W. Smith.
Fight Summary: Made at 175lbs, the *Indianapolis Star* reported that Dillon (162) made a fast start when driving Levinsky (170) around the ring in the opening four sessions before the latter settled down. At the start of the seventh there was no question as to Dillon's advantage, Levinsky being content to dance away with the left jab while showing what a good defensive boxer he was prior to coming right back into the contest. The last two rounds saw Levinsky battling like a wild man as he brought the crowd to its feet with sensational rallies, and although he was adjudged to have lost the press decision he showed a marked improvement from his earlier contests against Dillon.

15 June 1914. Jack Dillon w pts 12 Bob Moha.
Venue: Convention Hall, Butte, Montana, USA. **Recognition:** USA. **Referee:** John McIntosh.
Fight Summary: According to the *Anaconda Standard* this was a light heavyweight title battle at 175lbs, both men to scale inside 165lbs, with Moha (163½) and Dillon (163) looking strong at the weight. In what was a terrible contest, Moha covered up and stalled continuously as the aggressive Dillon made all of the running. The fight was so suspicious that Moha, who lost any claim he may have had to the title, was forced to settle for only part of his promised purse.

During the rest of 1914, often weighing in way above the middleweight limit, Dillon also risked losing his light heavyweight claim when defending his right to be recognised as the 160lbs middleweight champion. This applied in contests against Sailor Ed Petroskey (w pts 10 at Ascot Park, Kansas City, Missouri on 3 July), George KO Brown (nd-w pts 10 at the Baseball Park, Terre Haute, Indiana on 21 July), Howard Morrow (nd-w pts 6 at the Fuller Theatre, Kalamazoo, Michigan on 12 August) and Sailor Einert (nd-w pts 10 at the Baseball Park, Terre Haute on 7 September). Dillon again took on Brown (nd-drew 10 at the Knox County Fairgrounds, Vincennes, Indiana on 15 September) before coming to the ring at 183½lbs for a match against the 172lbs Frank Mantell (nd-w pts 12 at Goodale Aerodrome, Columbus, Ohio on 28 September). Then, for the third time in two months Dillon met up with Brown (nd-nc 3 at The Coliseum, St Louis, Missouri on 14 October). A few weeks later, Dillon (174¼) stopped Charley Weinert (173¾) inside two rounds of a six-round no-decision contest at the Olympia AC, Philadelphia, Pennsylvania on 9 November, further to meeting Young Ahearn (156½) at the same venue on 1 January 1915 in a no-decision six-round draw, weighing 164lbs.

Another occasion where there was possibly a risk of sorts came on 25 January 1915 at the Phoenix AC, Memphis, Tennessee when Dillon stopped Larry English in the fourth of an eight-round no-decision contest. Reporting on the fight, the *Memphis Daily Appeal* stated that although both men weighed about 170lbs they were almost certainly inside 175lbs.

20 February 1915. Jack Dillon nd-w pts 10 Frank Mantell.
Venue: Federal AC, Manhattan, NYC, New York, USA. **Recognition:** USA. **Referee:** William McPartland.
Fight Summary: After both men made 175lbs, Dillon's title claim was at stake in what turned out to be a poor fight with very little action involved. For the first two rounds the combatants clinched non-stop with the referee using all of his strength to break them apart. Coming to life in the third, Dillon (173) slammed in several left hooks to the body that had Mantell (171) hanging on before going back into his shell. Although Dillon tried hard to put Mantell out in the seventh and ninth it was to no avail, the fight drawing to an end almost as it had started. Throughout the action, or lack of it, with Dillon appearing to be holding back it came as no surprise when it was learnt that he had suffered an injury to his right arm in the third.

23 February 1915. Jack Dillon nd-w pts 10 Johnny Howard.
Venue: Broadway SC, Brooklyn, NYC, New York, USA. **Recognition:** USA.
Fight Summary: Putting his title claim up for grabs, Dillon (175) was forced to make a strong run for home after Howard (162½) had taken the opening five rounds, scoring at the rate of two to one. Having dropped Howard with a right to the jaw in the seventh Dillon continued to pound his man incessantly until the final bell. Had the fight lasted any longer it is doubtful as to whether Howard would have remained upright, so badly was he being beaten.

On 6 April, Dillon took on Billy Murray (nd-w pts 10 at The Arena, Hudson, Wisconsin), and with both men inside 160lbs once again this would have involved both of Dillon's title claims.

7 June 1915. Jack Dillon nd-l pts 10 Tom McMahon.
Venue: Airdome AC, Rochester, New York, USA. **Recognition:** USA. **Referee:** Harry Pollock.
Fight Summary: This should be considered a defence of Dillon's claim at the weight despite a lack of billing, as both men were inside 175lbs. Initially, it looked as though Dillon (170) was looking to get rid of McMahon (175) early as he bored in with two-handed assaults. Having had little success with that tactic, Dillon settled down to block all that McMahon could toss at him in what had become a pretty tame fight in the words of the local papers. The last two rounds saw McMahon swinging in punches from distance as Dillon eased his way through to the final bell.

11 June 1915. Jack Dillon nd-w pts 10 Frank Mantell.
Venue: Harlem AC, Baseball Park, Cincinnati, Ohio, USA. **Recognition:** USA. **Referee:** Lou Bauman.
Fight Summary: Risking his crown against his old rival once again Dillon (169) won at a canter, being the master of the situation at all stages of the contest. The only time Dillon, who fought in a cool and deliberate manner, raised his game was when Mantell (168½) caught him with right swings to the jaw that stung him into action. There were no knockdowns despite Dillon's superiority.

With the men inside 158lbs, both of Dillon's title claims were risk against George Chip (drew 10 at Association Park, Kansas City, Missouri on 5 July), and even though Dillon weighed 170lbs for a contest against Johnny Howard (nd-w pts 10 at Brown's Gym, Rockaway, Queens, NYC, New York on 12 July), with the latter weighing in at 160lbs his title claims were again on the line.

16 June 1915. Jack Dillon nd-w pts 10 Zulu Kid.
Venue: Bill Brown's Club, Far Rockaway, New York, USA. **Recognition:** USA. **Referee:** Bill Brown.
Fight Summary: In what was a hard, tough contest, the Kid (165) gave Dillon (169) all the trouble he could handle as the pair punched it out for the full ten rounds. While there were no knockdowns, both men proved their durability. The *Brooklyn Daily Eagle* reported that whatever blows Dillon threw, and from any angle, the Kid shrugged them off.

On 30 August, Dillon (171) was given the six-round press decision following a contest against Sailor Grande (165) at the Olympia AC, Philadelphia, Pennsylvania. It is not clear whether Dillon's contest against Tom McMahon (nd-drew 6 at the Duquesne Gardens, Pittsburgh, Pennsylvania on 25 September) carried his title claim, although the pair had boxed at 175lbs a short while earlier.

18 November 1915. Jack Dillon nd-w co 4 (10) Frank Farmer.
Venue: Armoury B, Oshkosh, Wisconsin, USA. **Recognition:** USA. **Referee:** Harry Stout.
Fight Summary: According to the wired news, Dillon (173) had matters all his own way for the opening three rounds before knocking Farmer (167) out in the fourth with a right-hand blow under the heart.

Towards the end of November, the newly formed American Boxing Association stated that they would be recognising Dillon as the 175lbs champion.

A contest for Dillon thought to have been made below 175lbs came against Al Norton (w rsc 4 at the Phoenix AC, Memphis, Tennessee on 20 December), a previous opponent, in what was an eight-round affair.

28 January 1916. Jack Dillon nd-l pts 10 Billy Miske.
Venue: Grand Opera House, Superior, Wisconsin, USA. **Recognition:** USA. **Referee:** Harry Stout.
Fight Summary: Billed for the 175lbs championship, the *Superior Telegram* reported that both men weighed in at 170lbs and that the contest was fiercely fought. Although Dillon, relying on body blows, was the more aggressive, Miske proved a tough nut to crack, catching the champion time and again with straight punches from both hands. In summing up, the general feeling was that Miske had won by two rounds to Dillon's one, with the remainder even.

Now that Battling Levinsky was fast becoming Dillon's number one challenger they met for the fifth time at the Broadway SC, Brooklyn, NYC, New York on 8 February. Weighing 175¼lbs, Levinsky made things tough for Dillon (168½) before being on the wrong end of the ten-round press decision. When Dillon fought Vic Hansen at the Phoenix AC, Memphis, Tennessee on 14 February, despite it being a mere eight-rounder the *Memphis Daily Appeal* reported it to be an advertised championship fight with the ringside weigh-in set at 170lbs. Whether or not either man was inside 175lbs barely mattered after Dillon was awarded the verdict in what was an easy victory. Another fight between Dillon (169) and Levinsky (177) at the Broadway SC, Brooklyn, NYC, on 28 March, saw the latter coming in two pounds over the limit, presumably to protect his opponent's title claim. However, once again Dillon prevailed, the press feeling that he deserved the decision.

14 April 1916. Jack Dillon nd-w pts 10 Billy Miske.
Venue: The Armoury, Minneapolis, Minnesota, USA. **Recognition:** USA.
Fight Summary: Both men were announced as being inside 175lbs, with Dillon thought to weigh 165lbs to Miske's 167. This was an easy win for Dillon, who was more aggressive and landed the cleaner punches in what was a tame bout characterised by too much holding.

25 April 1916. Jack Dillon w pts 15 Battling Levinsky.
Venue: Convention Hall, Kansas City, Missouri, USA. **Recognition:** USA. **Referee:** Edward W. Smith.
Fight Summary: Meeting for the sixth time, it was a hard, fast fight with Dillon (168) showing much speed and Levinsky (174) doing his best work at distance. There was no doubt that Dillon packed the heavier blows, Levinsky being in some distress on a number of occasions, and at the final bell he was handed the verdict. The general feeling was that Dillon had won six rounds to Levinsky's four, with five even. Afterwards, the *Chicago Tribune* reported "If there was any question as to where the light heavyweight title should be it was settled tonight."

Another fight between the pair, at Oriole Park, Baltimore, Maryland on 13 July, was originally scheduled for 15 rounds to a decision, but in the event it was changed to that of a ten-round no-decision contest due to a poor turnout. With Levinsky (175¼) coming in fractionally over the limit (due to contractual terms) there was no risk to Dillon (186½), but that did not stop the former handing out a beating when taking the press decision.

It was now quite clear that the rivalry between Dillon and Levinsky was not going to disappear, and on 12 September they met again, this time over eight rounds at the Phoenix AC Arena, Memphis, Tennessee. Reported as a press draw, although it was of limited duration there was obviously a risk attached to Dillon (169) had Levinsky (175) been able to find a winning blow.

10 October 1916. Jack Dillon nd-w co 2 Sailor Grande.
Venue: Broadway SC, Brooklyn, NYC, New York, USA. **Recognition:** USA.
Fight Summary: Making all of the running from the opening bell, Dillon (172) clearly showed his intent when forcing Grande (172½) to the ropes with solid lefts and rights. In the second round it was much of the same, and after attacking Grande with vicious body shots he put his man down for the full count following a left uppercut to the body and an overarm right to the jaw.

17 October 1916. Jack Dillon nd-w pts 10 Tim O'Neil.
Venue: Broadway SC, Brooklyn, NYC, New York, USA. **Recognition:** USA.
Fight Summary: Sticking to the task at hand O'Neil (172) was still there at the final bell, having shown the ability to take a lot of punishment without folding. Although Dillon (173) repeatedly attempted to knock O'Neil out he ultimately had to be satisfied with the press verdict of eight rounds to two in his favour. O'Neil, who gained many friends despite hanging on for dear life at times, finished the contest bleeding profusely from a cut left eye. Prior to the start O'Neil had been confident of taking over Dillon's claim at 175lbs but lacked a finishing punch.

24 October 1916. Battling Levinsky w pts 12 Jack Dillon.
Venue: Armoury AA, Boston, Massachusetts, USA. **Recognition:** USA. **Referee:** Larry Conley.
Fight Summary: The fight saw Levinsky have every advantage in all rounds bar the fifth, with Dillon lacking his normal aggression and speed. Rushing in wildly, Dillon was generally stopped in his tracks as Levinsky jabbed to the head and moved. On other occasions Dillon was rocked heavily by lefts and rights, while the challenger showed that he could take whatever was thrown at him before hitting back accurately. The *Boston Daily Globe* report of the fight said Dillon lost because his hands were in bad shape from fighting too frequently. In summing up, Luckett Davis makes the valid point that Dillon certainly did not behave like a champion defending a valuable title. Following Dillon's first loss for over four years, Levinsky, who had begun his professional career as Barney Williams, claimed the title. Although neither man seemingly weighed in, according to the *TS Andrews' Record Book* Levinsky was conveniently considered to have made the stipulated 175lbs despite some newspaper reports stating that he looked at least ten pounds heavier than Dillon.

At the Clermont Rink, Brooklyn, NYC, New York, on 30 October, Levinsky (181lbs) risked his newly won title when allowing Billy Miske (170½lbs) to make the weight for their ten rounder. Miske received the press decision but not the championship.

Then, on 8 December, Levinsky met Gus Christie at the Wayne Avenue Gymnastic Club, Dayton, Ohio. According to the *Dayton Daily News* the fight was made for 15 rounds, Lou Bauman, the referee, giving it as a draw, while *The Ring Record Book* showed it to be a ten-round no-decision bout. Regardless, it was made at catchweights with the southpaw Christie around the 170lbs mark and Levinsky a good 20lbs heavier. The paper reported that it did not involve the 'big title', but then went on to say that the light heavyweight championship was at stake. They also stated that for Christie to win the title he would have to beat Levinsky inside the distance. However, at no time did Christie look likely to score an early win despite him having the better of things up to the tenth round, and when Levinsky came on strongly over the last five sessions the press generally saw it too close to call.

On 10 January 1917, the *Indiana Weekly Messenger* reported that Dillon was still the recognised champion, but I have found nothing to support that and nothing to suggest that the latter was continuing to claim the title. In the meantime, with Levinsky hardly perceived to be a world champion the light heavyweight division remained away from the public eye.

Another fight which was billed for the title, involving Levinsky at catchweights, was held at the Grand Opera House, Youngstown, Ohio on 17 January 1917 when he met Bob Moha over 12 rounds with no referee's decision in prospect. Despite the fight being disqualified from having title status when Levinsky failed to weigh in, had Moha, who was reported to be comfortably inside 175lbs, won inside the distance there is no doubt that he would have laid claim to the title. For the record, Levinsky received the press decision. When Levinsky took on Billy Miske (nd-w pts 10 at the Auditorium, St Paul, Minnesota on 27 February 1917), the *St Paul Pioneer Express* reported that by his showing, Levinsky is the actual as well as the technical light heavyweight champion. While the paper went on to say that the fighters were due to make 175lbs, elsewhere it was reported that the men weighed in wearing their street clothes, Levinsky scaling 185½lbs to Miske's 182½. Sometimes referred to as a world title fight, when Levinsky met Jack Moran (w pts 12 at The Coliseum, St Louis, Missouri on 6 March 1917) the local papers reported both fighters to be in excess of 175lbs.

In the build-up, Levinsky's fight against Tommy Gibbons (nd-l pts 10 at the Auditorium, St Paul, Minnesota on 23 March 1917) was reported by the *St Paul Pioneer Express* to be a billed title contest with the champion hoping to make 175lbs. Regardless of billing the official weights reported in the press showed that while Levinsky came in at 176½lbs, Gibbons, at 161½lbs, was easily inside the championship weight. Another fight where an over-the-weight Levinsky (180) risked his title came at the Fairmont AC, Bronx, NYC on 9 May 1917 against Bob McAllister (164), the press giving both men a share of the spoils after ten rounds. Two more fights for Levinsky that carried a risk for the title claimant even though he was over the weight came against Leo Houck (nd-w pts 6 at the Athletic Club, York, Pennsylvania on 16 May 1917) and Bert Kenny (nd-w pts 10 at the Fairmont AC, Bronx, NYC, New York on 26 May 1917).

When Levinsky met Johnny Howard (w pts 12 at the National AC, Marieville Gardens, Providence, Rhode Island on 20 June 1917) in a contest billed for the 175lbs title, the *Providence Journal* reported that the latter was handicapped in height, weight and reach, and while Levinsky did not make the weight for Jack London (nd-w rsc 4 at the Military AC, Brooklyn, NYC, New York on 6 August 1917), the latter was inside 175lbs. London weighed 171lbs to Levinsky's 177.

It was now quite clear that Levinsky did not mind risking his title claim in catchweight fights. When he took on Harry Greb on 6 September 1917, losing the ten-round press decision at Forbes Field, Pittsburgh, Pennsylvania, the *Pittsburgh Gazette* reported Greb to be 162lbs with Levinsky possibly outside the weight class. On 15 October 1917, Levinsky outpointed Tom McMahon at the Amphitheatre Rink, Winnipeg, Canada, and although it was billed as a title fight it was announced that Levinsky scaled 178¾lbs to McMahon's 180.

On the same date at The Arena, Boston, Massachusetts, Billy Miske was outpointed over 12 rounds by Kid Norfolk, but while the latter claimed the title there was no tangible support forthcoming. With the *Boston Globe* reporting them to weigh at least 175lbs, there was never any real proof that either man was inside the limit anyway.

A further instance of Levinsky not bothering to make the weight came at Sohmer Park, Montreal, Canada on 31 October 1917 when he landed the ten-round press decision over the Zulu Kid. The *Montreal Herald* poured scorn on Levinsky's title claim when reporting that the Kid, really a middleweight, would have surely won the title had he carried a punch.

Throughout 1918 Levinsky's claim was mainly sidelined as he continued to fight above the weight, but he managed to give further opportunities to Greb (nd-l pts 6 at Shibe Park, Philadelphia, Pennsylvania on 6 August) and Houck (nd-w pts 6 at the Athletic Club, Lancaster, Pennsylvania on 25 December). Whether Levinsky made 175lbs for those two fights is not known.

17 February 1919. Battling Levinsky nd-l pts 10 Harry Greb.
Venue: Broadway Auditorium, Buffalo, New York, USA. **Recognition:** USA. **Referee:** Dick Nugent.
Fight Summary: The *Bridgeport Standard Telegram* reported that Levinsky's claim was at risk in this one, with both men inside 175lbs. After Levinsky (175) made a solid start, winning the opening three rounds, by the fourth Greb (164½) was punching him all round the ring, and during the last couple of sessions the champion was forced to hang on for dear life.

Next time out Levinsky met Ed Kinley (nd-w pts 8 at McGuigan's Arena, Harrison, New Jersey on 14 April). Although it is not clear whether Kinley was inside 175lbs he could have made that weight with ease. Levinsky took on Greb again, losing the press decision at the Auditorium, Canton, Ohio on 28 April over 12 rounds. This time around Levinsky did not even bother to make the weight, but allowed Greb to be inside 175lbs. Following the Greb fight, Levinsky met Johnny Howard (nd-l pts 8 at The Pavilion, Bayonne, New Jersey on 2 May), it being reported that the latter needed a kayo if he wanted to claim the title.

On 3 July, Levinsky was credited with a 12-round newspaper verdict over Billy Miske at the Rossford Arena, near Toledo, Ohio in what was, according to the *Toledo Blade*, an advertised title fight. However, no weights were given. The fight report described the proceedings as a joke so often perpetrated on an unsuspecting public, and should be viewed as merely an afterthought to the heavyweight title fight between Jess Willard and Jack Dempsey that took place the following day.

Given another crack at Levinsky, Greb was again unable to apply a finisher despite winning the six-round press verdict in decisive fashion, according to the *Pittsburgh Post*, at Shibe Park, Philadelphia, Pennsylvania on 14 July. Two more fights for Levinsky, contested in New Jersey over eight rounds, have to be seen as involving a risk to his title claim. Both went the distance, and on both occasions Levinsky was awarded the press decision. On 25 July, at the DeForest Gym, Long Branch, New Jersey, Kinley weighed 175lbs while there was no mention of Levinsky's weight, and on 11 August at the Armoury AA, Jersey City, New Jersey, Levinsky scaled 173lbs to Clay Turner's 170. A few weeks later, at the Baseball Park, Wheeling, West Virginia, on 3 September, an over-the-weight Levinsky yet again took on Greb in a no-decision fight, and one in which the press decided that he had lost the ten-round decision. The *Wheeling Register* reported that Greb, inside 175lbs, would have won the title had he possessed a kayo wallop. When Levinsky met Turner (nd-drew 10 at the Roller Palace Rink, Detroit, Michigan on 24 November), according to the *Detroit News* with both men down to weight the fight could justifiably be billed for the title. While Turner was well inside 175lbs, it is uncertain as to whether Levinsky was.

Kicking off 1920 with an eighth-round stoppage win over Bert Kenny at the Arena Gardens, Toronto, Canada on 1 January, it is not clear whether Levinsky risked his title claim in this one. Another no-decision contest, albeit only of eight rounds duration, saw Levinsky (178lbs) gain a press verdict over the 163lbs Johnny Howard at the Lotus AC, Perth Amboy, New Jersey on 23 January. Three more no-decision bouts between Levinsky and Turner in 1920 saw the title claimant fighting in the heavyweight class, while it was unclear whether Turner was inside 175lbs or not. Fighting over ten rounds at the City Boxing Club, Detroit on 16 February, the press verdict was in favour of Levinsky, as was the ten rounder between the men at the Church Street Auditorium, Hartford, Connecticut on 26 March. On 3 May, at the Exposition Hall, Portland, Maine, the match was made up of two six-round contests with a slight break between to get around the regulations. Again Levinsky was seen by the press to have won. Continuing to scale above the weight class limit Levinsky then drew over 12 rounds with Chuck Wiggins, who was thought to be inside 175lbs, at the Gymnastic Club, Dayton, Ohio on 21 May to set himself up for a meeting with Georges Carpentier.

Carpentier (171½) had re-won the European title on 19 July 1919 when knocking out Dick Smith (174) inside eight rounds at The Circus, Paris, France. Despite Carpentier's victory, on 5 February 1920 the International Boxing Union (IBU) stated that, although they recognised the weight class, as far as they were concerned the title was vacant. With the promoter, Tex Rickard, looking for a way to build Carpentier into a main-line heavyweight attraction and a worthy opponent for Dempsey he hit upon the idea of reviving the light heavyweight class, which was in fact, the ideal weight division for the Frenchman. Although Levinsky had been claiming the title for several years, with the fans never really taking to him this was an ideal opportunity for both men.

12 October 1920. Georges Carpentier nd-w co 4 (12) Battling Levinsky.
Venue: International League Park, Jersey City, New Jersey, USA. **Recognition:** World. **Referee:** Harry Ertle.
Fight Summary: Although a points decision could not be rendered it was advertised as a championship battle, thus giving the 175lbs title international status, with Carpentier (170½) being acknowledged as champion after defeating Levinsky (175) conclusively. The fight itself saw the Frenchman darting around Levinsky, stinging him with smart left leads before dropping him with a sizzling right to the jaw in the second round. Mistakenly given 15

seconds to recover, Levinsky was soon down again. Somehow getting through the third session and making Carpentier miss consistently, eventually a series of rapid-fire head shots dropped Levinsky in a heap to be counted out at 1.07 of the fourth.

With Carpentier being given a crack at Jack Dempsey's heavyweight title, Levinsky, who continued to bill himself as the holder of the American light heavyweight crown, made a successful defence when outpointing Dan O'Dowd over 12 rounds at The Arena, Syracuse, New York on 15 April 1921. Meanwhile, after being knocked out by Dempsey in the fourth round at Boyle's Thirty Acres, Jersey City on 2 July 1921, it came as no surprise that Carpentier decided to remain among the light heavies.

Later, on 13 January 1922, Gene Tunney, the future heavyweight champion, picked up the American mantle when beating Levinsky on points over 12 rounds at Madison Square Garden, Manhattan, NYC, New York. Regardless of billing, Tunney effectively risked his American 175lbs title a few weeks later when taking on Whitey Wenzel (nd-w rsc 4 at the Ice Palace, Philadelphia, Pennsylvania on 14 February 1922) and Fay Keiser (nd-w pts 10 at The Armoury, Grand Rapids, Michigan on 3 March 1922).

Throughout this period Kid Norfolk clearly saw himself as being the leading black fighter in the division although it is difficult to trace any legitimate championship bouts for him because most of his opponents were natural heavyweights. Prior to him fighting the Jamaica Kid at The Casino, Manhattan, NYC, New York on 3 May 1921 the *New York Times* had quoted Norfolk as saying he would claim the 'black title' if he won. Winning on points over 15 rounds, Norfolk was reported to weigh 181½lbs to the Kid's 175 at ringside, which placed him above the limit. However, if you accept that the two men weighed in earlier subject to contract Norfolk could well have been inside 175lbs. Not long after, on 30 May 1921, Norfolk was stopped in nine rounds at the Arizona AC, Phoenix, Arizona by Lee Anderson in what was a billed title bout. While this defeat failed to stop Norfolk from claiming the title, Anderson made defences against Rough House Ware (w pts 10 at the Arizona AC, Phoenix on 4 July 1921) and Tiger Flowers (w co 7 in Ciudad Juarez, Chihuahua, Mexico on 9 May 1922). Meanwhile, Norfolk, recognised by Tex Rickard as the 'black champion', had been presented with a diamond studded belt which he defended against the Jamaica Kid (w pts 8 at Madison Square Garden, Manhattan, NYC, New York on 30 December 1921). He also put his claim on the line against Jim Green, known as Young Jack Johnson (w rsc 8 at the Broadway Auditorium, Buffalo, New York on 20 February 1922).

11 May 1922. Georges Carpentier w co 1 (20) Ted Kid Lewis.
Venue: Olympia, Kensington, London, England. **Recognition:** World. **Referee:** Joe Palmer.
Fight Summary: Being no respecter of reputations Lewis (157) immediately went to work on the body, while Carpentier (175), who was soon cut on the mouth, clinched and looked to find a way to keep the English boy at bay. Still Lewis continued to charge in with both hands pumping out, and Carpentier, looking pained, again sought respite by holding on like a limpet. Following flagrant headwork inside the referee tried to part the men physically, but when Lewis stepped back to complain, with his hands at his side, Carpentier drove in a smashing right to the jaw that sent him to the floor to be counted out on the 2.15 mark. For some considerable time afterwards the subject of whether the winning punch had been legal or not in the light of the referee's instruction to break brought about much discussion.

Twelve days after the Frenchman's victory, Gene Tunney was parted from the American title when Harry Greb outpointed him over 15 rounds at Madison Square Garden, Manhattan, NYC, New York on 23 May. Regardless of billing, Greb (167) was happy to risk his title against Tommy Loughran (163½) at Shibe Park, Philadelphia, Pennsylvania on 10 July, before taking the eight-round press decision.

On the 'black title' front, after Lee Anderson had successfully defended his version of the championship against Gorilla Jones (w co 3 at the City Auditorium, Galveston, Texas on 15 August), he was outpointed over ten rounds by Kid Norfolk at the Arena AC, Boston, Massachusetts on 11 September. At that moment, the Kid was almost certainly the top black man at the weight.

24 September 1922. Battling Siki w co 6 (20) Georges Carpentier.
Venue: Buffalo Velodrome, Paris, France. **Recognition:** World. **Referee:** Henri Bernstein.
Fight Summary: With a supposedly poor opponent in front of him Carpentier (173½) was expected to win without raising a sweat, and after two rounds of outboxing Siki (174) he dropped his man in the third following a cracking right to the jaw. Getting up at 'seven', Siki surprised all in attendance when he immediately went for Carpentier, having the champion down for a short count from a wild swing. Although Carpentier looked weakened he again had Siki down in the fourth, but back came the man from Senegal, throwing all manner of punches. From that moment there was only going to be one winner, even though Carpentier somehow managed to make it through to the end of the fifth. Coming out for the sixth with both eyes almost closed, after Carpentier had been bundled to the floor with obvious damage to his left leg, the fight was halted at 1.10 of the session. Having called for Carpentier's corner to help their man back to the corner, the referee then announced that he had disqualified Siki for tripping. However, this action caused such uproar among the crowd that the decision was overturned by the judges within the hour on the grounds that the timekeeper had already counted Carpentier out before the contest was stopped.

The French Federation stripped Siki of the world title on 10 November due to him assaulting Francis Descamps, Carpentier's manager, a few days earlier. The Federation claimed that they were forced to take that action so as not to allow boxing to be dragged through the mud. Following that, the IBU took similar action against Siki on 12 January 1923, only to rescind the decision on 18 February when naming him among their list of world champions. Outside the ring, with Siki's behaviour eccentric to say the least, there was even more emphasis placed on the American title.

While Kid Norfolk had successfully defended his 'black title' claim when beating Lee Anderson (w pts 10 at the Mechanics Building, Boston, Massachusetts on 22 December), two 15-round fights that took place at Madison Square Garden, Manhattan, NYC, New York saw Harry Greb outscore Tommy Loughran on 30 January 1923 before losing the American title in reverse fashion to Gene Tunney on 23 February 1923. Prior to losing to Tunney, other fights in which Greb risked losing recognition came against Loughran (nd-w pts 10 at the Motor Square Garden, Pittsburgh, Pennsylvania on 15 January 1923), Billy Shade (nd-w pts 12 at the 4th Regiment Armoury, Jersey City, New Jersey on 22 January 1923), Pal Reed (nd-w pts 12 at the Broad AC, Newark, New Jersey on 5 February 1923) and Young Fisher (w pts 12 at The Arena, Syracuse, New York on 16 February 1923).

17 March 1923. Mike McTigue w pts 20 Battling Siki.
Venue: Scala Opera House, Dublin, Ireland. **Recognition:** NY/NBA/GB. **Referee:** Jack Smith.
Fight Summary: Siki, the recipient of a 'dodgy' decision, should have lost his title on the scales when refusing to weigh in, with McTigue (159lbs) knowing full well he was over the limit. However, the fight went ahead with McTigue content to keep Siki off him by dint of a solid left lead, and apart from the 11th round when the Irishman was cut over the right eye he was in well in command. By the 16th, with Siki extremely tired, McTigue took full advantage when swarming all over the champion, smashing in blow after blow while trying for the knockout. The last three sessions saw McTigue belting Siki all over the ring, and when the referee's decision in his favour was announced the roof nearly came off.

Following the fight the IBU stripped Siki of his European title, despite continuing to recognise him as the world champion until early 1924 and failing to credit McTigue who was seen as the titleholder in America and Britain. The IBU, who made the decision to continue to recognise Siki as the world champion because he had not made 175lbs for McTigue, finally ran out of patience with him after he moved to America having failed to defend their version of the championship. Once that decision had been made on 19 November, the IBU stated that they would not accept an American designated world light heavyweight champion until the leading European representative was given a fair crack at the title.

Kid Norfolk, who was still generally recognised as the 'black champion', successfully defended his title laurels against Tiger Flowers (w co 1 at the Coliseum, Springfield, Ohio on 8 May) and the Jamaica Kid (w co 2 at the Commonwealth SC, Manhattan, NYC, New York on 17 July) before going on to meet Siki.

On 25 June, in albeit just an eight-rounder at Shetzline Ballpark, Philadelphia, Pennsylvania, McTigue (164½) lost the press decision to Tommy Loughran (161), while a little later, on 31 July, Gene Tunney successfully defended the American title following a 12-round points win over Dan O'Dowd at Queensboro Stadium, Queens, NYC, New York.

2 August 1923. Mike McTigue nd-w pts 12 Tommy Loughran.
Venue: Playground Baseball Park, West New York, New Jersey, USA. **Recognition:** NY/NBA/GB. **Referee:** Eddie Dugan.
Fight Summary: In what turned out to be a tame affair McTigue (163½) forced the action almost all of the way, having the best of at least ten rounds, his destructive lefts and rights under the heart being particularly effective. Early on, Loughran (166) appeared content to rely on the left jab and an occasional right cross, but from the fourth onwards he was forced to clinch in order to avoid the knockout that the champion was hell-bent on delivering.

Towards the end of August, Tex Rickard announced that he had agreed terms with McTigue to defend against the American champion, Gene Tunney, at the Polo Grounds, Manhattan, NYC, New York on 25 September. However, for whatever reason the articles were never signed.

4 October 1923. Mike McTigue drew 10 Young Stribling.
Venue: The Auditorium, Columbus, Georgia, USA. **Recognition:** NY/NBA/GB. **Referee:** Harry Ertle.
Fight Summary: Following the fight, in which Stribling (165lbs) had appeared to win eight of the ten rounds and had battered and knocked McTigue (162lbs) down in the tenth round, it was claimed that the latter was forced at gunpoint to fight on even though he had suffered a broken hand. Another bone of contention came when the imported referee first called a draw before changing it to a win for Stribling when intimidated by the crowd, which included hooded Ku Klux Klansmen. Afterwards, when safely back home, the referee's explanation of events saw the fight remaining on record as a draw.

Some two months later at Madison Square Garden, Manhattan, NYC, New York on 10 December Gene Tunney retained his American title when outpointing Harry Greb over 15 rounds, and although fighting regularly among the heavyweights he looked forward to a crack against McTigue.

Earlier, on 20 November, Kid Norfolk had successfully defended his 'black title' when outpointing Battling Siki over 15 rounds at Madison Square Garden. He then went on to put his claim up for grabs against Lee Anderson (w pts 12 at the Commonwealth SC, Manhattan, NYC, New York on 23 February 1924).

31 March 1924. Mike McTigue nd-l pts 12 Young Stribling.
Venue: 113th Regiment Armoury, Newark, New Jersey, USA. **Recognition:** NY/NBA/GB. **Referee:** Hank Lewis.
Fight Summary: After their previous fiasco Stribling (165) was looking to set the record straight this time around, but although he decked McTigue (166½) with a terrific right cross to the jaw in the tenth round he was unable to keep the champion down. McTigue had been clearly outpointed in every round according to Nat Fleischer, of *The Ring* magazine, who went on to say "It was a travesty that the champion was able to keep his title as Stribling had been superior in every aspect." The general feeling was that champions should only be defending their titles in States where decisions could be given.

In early October McTigue was suspended by the New York State Athletic Commission (NYSAC) for repeatedly ignoring its requests to defend against a legitimate challenger, namely Gene Tunney, having demanded fabulous sums and evaded one issue after another. The Commission stipulated that McTigue, who was thinking of taking on the inexperienced Paul Berlenbach, would have to defend against Tunney first before he could fight in New York again.

Meantime, Tunney met Georges Carpentier in what some papers called a defence of the former's American title. With Carpentier being a Frenchman it was hardly that, although it was certainly seen as an eliminator for McTigue's title. In a contest where Carpentier seemed to have been struck in the groin, Tunney stopped his rival in the 15th round at the Polo Grounds, Manhattan, NYC, New York on 24 July. Prior to stepping up to heavyweight Tunney took on the middleweight champion, Harry Greb (nd-drew 10 at the Olympic Arena, Cleveland, Ohio on 17

September) and Harry Foley (w rsc 1 at The Auditorium, Memphis, Tennessee on 27 October). Both matches were contested inside 175lbs and appear to be the last at the weight for Tunney.

Earlier, on 12 May, Bob Lawson took over Kid Norfolk's 'black title' claim when beating the latter, albeit by a second-round disqualification verdict at the Broadway Auditorium, Buffalo, New York in a six-round contest. A growing fighter, Lawson (179) was soon up among the heavyweights, but not before knocking Norfolk (180) out inside a round at the Commonwealth SC, Manhattan, NYC, New York on 14 March 1925.

29 October 1924. Mike McTigue w rtd 6 (12) Frank Carpenter.
Venue: Marieville AC, Providence, Rhode Island, USA. **Recognition:** NBA/GB. **Referee:** Mike Broderick.
Fight Summary: The *Providence Evening Bulletin* carried adverts showing this to be a billed title bout at 175lbs, with Carpenter in the role of challenger. The paper went on to report that the latter would strive hard to gain the honours. However, it was soon clear that the Freeport man had no right to be in the same ring as McTigue, who did very much as he pleased with him, especially at close quarters. After taking some heavy jolts from the champion's educated fists Carpenter decided to call it a day at the end of the sixth round.

26 December 1924. Mike McTigue nd-w rsc 4 (10) Jimmy King.
Venue: City Auditorium, Atlanta, Georgia, USA. **Recognition:** NBA/GB. **Referee:** Jake Abel.
Fight Summary: Billed as a budding young puncher, King (162) was no match for the experienced champion who felt his way around in the first session before letting the punches go in the second, sending in left jabs, right crosses and wicked blows to the ribs. Down twice for counts of 'nine' in the third, hooks and uppercuts doing the damage, King was again at the mercy of McTigue (162) in the fourth as the slaughter continued. He was eventually rescued by the referee on the 1.26 mark after being dropped from a barrage of hooks. With McTigue well inside 175lbs, the *Atlanta Constitution* reported that the champion was not figuring on losing his title in this one. The paper went on to say that it was common practice for a champion to protect his title by contractually agreeing in advance that if both men were standing at the final bell a draw would be announced.

7 January 1925. Mike McTigue nd-l pts 12 Mickey Walker.
Venue: 113th Regiment Armoury, Newark, NJ, USA. **Recognition:** NBA/GB. **Referee:** Hank Lewis.
Fight Summary: After hurting both hands early in the fight, McTigue (160), who outweighed the challenger by a whopping 11¼lbs, was content to assume a defensive role in order to hold on to his title. Although Walker (149¾) carried off at least eight of the 12 rounds, despite shaking McTigue up on a number of occasions, he ultimately had to be satisfied with the newspaper verdict.

Having been reinstated by the NYSAC on 7 April and with Gene Tunney preparing for an assault on the heavyweights, McTigue's first defence in the Empire State would be against Paul Berlenbach. Known as 'Paralysing Paul' due to his tremendous punching power, Berlenbach was an open, walk-in fighter who had got his opportunity to challenge for the title after beating the former champion, Battling Siki (w rsc 10 at Madison Square Garden, Manhattan, NYC, New York on 13 March), in what was an eliminating contest. An interesting character who had become deaf-mute when contracting scarlet fever as a youngster, Berlenbach had also been a double Amateur Athletic Union (AAU) champion wrestler before turning to boxing. For Siki it was almost the end of the road. Just eight fights later, on 15 December, the former champion, who had the habit of walking his pet lion through the streets of New York City, was found shot to death in the gutter.

30 May 1925. Paul Berlenbach w pts 15 Mike McTigue.
Venue: Yankee Stadium, Bronx, NYC, New York, USA. **Recognition:** NY/NBA/GB. **Referee:** Ed Purdy.
Fight Summary: Defending his title for only the third time in a decision fight, McTigue (170½) disappointed against the crude Berlenbach (170½) when allowing the ex-wrestler too much room. Despite hurting Berlenbach with trip-hammer rights to the jaw in the sixth and seventh rounds McTigue was strangely lethargic, while his opponent, with just 27 contests under his belt, came through strongly to land the unanimous decision. From round three through to the fifth McTigue boxed cannily as Berlenbach threatened with heavy blows from both hands, but from the eighth onwards he was unable to muster an offensive, spending much of his time avoiding punches coming his way. The ex-champion finished with a badly cut left eye and the knowledge that he could have done better.

Although the winner of McTigue v Berlenbach was initially committed to defending against Gene Tunney, the American champion, following a brilliant win over Tommy Gibbons (w co 12 at the Polo Grounds, Manhattan, NYC on 5 June) Tunney relinquished his title to concentrate on winning the heavyweight crown, having become Jack Dempsey's leading challenger after Harry Wills.

At its conference in early July, the membership of the IBU continued to boycott an American designated world light heavyweight champion until the given boxer deigned to defend against the European titleholder, Louis Clement.

13 July 1925. Paul Berlenbach nd-nc 9 (12) Tony Marullo.
Venue: Dreamland Park, Newark, New Jersey, USA. **Recognition:** NY/NBA/GB. **Referee:** Harry Lewis.
Fight Summary: Advertised for the championship with no decision to be given if the fighters were still there at the final bell, both men were thrown out of the ring after 53 seconds of the ninth had elapsed. They had been warned several times by the referee that this was a title fight and should be treated as such. The Chief Deputy Boxing Commissioner had also twice spoken to the third man about it but to no avail. That Marullo (166½) was just about leading on points did not count for much, especially as he was unable to take advantage of the crude, lumbering champion constantly falling about on the ropes in front of him. The official line was that Berlenbach (173½) was carrying his rival. Although Berlenbach pointed out that he had broken his right hand in the fourth round he was told in no uncertain terms that there had been nothing going on even prior to that.

11 September 1925. Paul Berlenbach w rsc 11 (15) Jimmy Slattery.
Venue: Yankee Stadium, Bronx, NYC, New York, USA. **Recognition:** NY/NBA/GB. **Referee:** Patsy Haley.
Fight Summary: Never having gone more than ten rounds previously and having been stopped in the third round by Dave Shade three fights earlier was not the best preparation for the 21-year-old Slattery (161½), despite him being a skilful fighter with a good knockout ratio. However, for nine rounds the young challenger drifted around the ring, hands by his side, seemingly boxing his way to the title against the hard-hitting but sluggish Berlenbach (172), who up until that time had not had much success. Then it happened. In the tenth, Slattery, chinned by a series of heavy lefts, was put down for 'eight' and twice for 'nine' before being saved by the bell. Although coming out for the 11th it was obvious to all that Slattery was a beaten fighter, and after being smashed to the canvas on three more occasions for counts of 'nine' the referee rescued him with 92 seconds of the session remaining.

11 December 1925. Paul Berlenbach w pts 15 Jack Delaney.
Venue: Madison Square Garden, Manhattan, NYC, New York, USA. **Recognition:** NY/NBA/GB. **Referee:** Ed Purdy.
Fight Summary: Having already beaten Berlenbach (173½) inside four rounds, Delaney (166) made a solid start before dropping his former victim in the fourth following a crashing right-hand to the jaw. Up at 'three', Berlenbach fell over again, obviously dazed, before taking an 'eight' count. Strangely, Delaney let the beaten champion off the hook as he failed to go in to finish the job, and from the eighth onwards Berlenbach steadily gained ground to win the majority decision.

Despite losing to Berlenbach, following wins over Mike McTigue (w co 4 at Madison Square Garden on 15 March 1926) and Maxie Rosenbloom (w pts 10 at The Arena, Philadelphia, Pennsylvania on 22 March 1926), Delaney quickly earned himself a return.

10 June 1926. Paul Berlenbach w pts 15 Young Stribling.
Venue: Yankee Stadium, Bronx, NYC, New York, USA. **Recognition:** NY/NBA/GB. **Referee:** Jim Crowley.
Fight Summary: A disappointing fight saw a listless Berlenbach (174½) hold on to his title by a unanimous decision, mainly because Stribling (171) did not wish to mix it at close quarters and made very little effort to win, being content to escape unscathed. Before the final bell Stribling's father pleaded with his son to give it one last go, but even that could not goad him into action.

Although failing to recognise a world light heavyweight champion since stripping Battling Siki, the members of the IBU voted at their conference in July to accept the winner of the forthcoming Berlenbach v Jack Delaney contest as the titleholder.

16 July 1926. Jack Delaney w pts 15 Paul Berlenbach.
Venue: Ebbets Field, Brooklyn, NYC, New York, USA. **Recognition:** World. **Referee:** Jim Crowley.
Fight Summary: Fighting with a broken left thumb from the second round onwards, Delaney (166½) gained ample revenge for his earlier defeat at the hands of Berlenbach (174½) when being awarded the unanimous decision at the end of a hard-fought contest. Up to the 11th there had been little to choose between them, especially after the challenger had lost the previous four sessions, but from thereon in it was all Delaney as he outscored and outpunched the champion to walk off with the title. In the 13th round it looked as though Berlenbach would be stopped as Delaney cut loose, ripping in vicious uppercuts to the head and solid lefts to head and body, but he kept in the contest by holding on for all he was worth. Although dazed and staggered at times, Berlenbach, by now cut on the left eye, somehow kept going despite taking a constant battering, being almost out on his feet at the final bell.

10 December 1926. Jack Delaney w rsc 3 (15) Jamaica Kid.
Venue: State Armoury, Waterbury, Connecticut, USA. **Recognition:** World. **Referee:** Young McAuliffe.
Fight Summary: Having initially weighed in at 180lbs the Jamaica Kid (175) was given nearly three hours to take off five pounds before making the weight, but then failed to land a punch of any significance before being floored six times in the third and stopped at 1.13 of the session. Delaney (172½), on top all the way against the crude Kid, showed himself to be fast on his feet, fast with his hands and deadly accurate with left hooks and solid rights to both head and body.

Later, with Delaney due to defend his title in June 1927 against Mike McTigue, who had beaten Paul Berlenbach (w rsc 4 at Madison Square Garden, Manhattan, NYC, New York on 28 January 1927), the fight was moved to 11 August 1927 because the champion was obviously struggling to make the weight. Delaney was also thinking about a move into the heavyweight division.

Although the *Ring Record Book* shows Delaney as having relinquished the title in June 1927, the 9 August edition of *Boxing* (normally three weeks out of date) reported that Delaney would be relinquishing the championship sometime during the following week in order to fight the Spanish heavyweight, Paulino Uzcudun. Following that, on 27 July 1927 McTigue put in a claim for the title and was accepted by the NYSAC. Finally, on 10 August, Delaney confirmed that he was relinquishing the title forthwith in a letter to the NYSAC.

Meanwhile, the NBA, unhappy that McTigue had been handed the title on a plate, announced that they would be setting up an eliminating tournament involving Tommy Loughran, former middleweight champion Tiger Flowers, Jimmy Slattery, Maxie Rosenbloom and McTigue to determine Delaney's successor.

However, further to the news that McTigue was already booked to defend the NYSAC version of the title against Loughran, who was fresh from victories over Young Stribling and Tony Marullo, and that Flowers was contracted elsewhere, on 12 August 1927 the NBA announced that they had matched Slattery and Rosenbloom for their version of the championship.

30 August 1927. Jimmy Slattery w pts 10 Maxie Rosenbloom.
Venue: The Velodrome, Hartford, Connecticut, USA. **Recognition:** NBA. **Referee:** Young McAuliffe.
Fight Summary: Having beaten Rosenbloom (168½) twice previously, Slattery (169½) made it a hat-trick of wins when he was awarded the referee's decision in a contest to decide the NBA version of the title after Jack Delaney had moved up in weight. In a battle of wits and contrasting styles both boys showed clever ring-craft, and ultimately it was Slattery's speed and accurate hitting that caught the referee's eye rather than the open-gloved efforts of Rosenbloom. There were no knockdowns.

7 October 1927. Tommy Loughran w pts 15 Mike McTigue.
Venue: Madison Square Garden, Manhattan, NYC, New York, USA. **Recognition:** NY. **Referee:** Lou Magnolia.
Fight Summary: Throughout the entire fight the veteran McTigue (174½), who had been handed the title by the NYSAC and was making his first defence, carried the fight to Loughran (175), only to be picked off and rocked by the younger man. McTigue was always dangerous, but he was unable to pin down the challenger long enough to

do any real damage. By the 13th both men were tiring, and although McTigue had a bad swelling over his left eye he bored in continuously during the last two sessions in an effort to swing things his way. Even though he was hurt at times, Loughran was well worth the unanimous decision that went his way.

12 December 1927. Tommy Loughran w pts 15 Jimmy Slattery.
Venue: Madison Square Garden, Manhattan, NYC, New York, USA. **Recognition:** World. **Referee:** Lou Magnolia.
Fight Summary: In a battle to unify the title both men proved to be top class, and it was probably the eight-pound weight advantage that helped to swing the fight Loughran's way towards the finishing line. While Slattery (165½) showed great speed, making Loughran (173½) look pedestrian at times, when he was eventually forced to trade as he slowed it was then that the latter came into his own. Although Slattery had outboxed his man at the start, with snapping left hands scoring points, once Loughran's body shots began to take effect everything changed. Making his run for home Loughran continuously worked the body and smashed in overarm rights to the head, while Slattery tried his best to fight back but was too tired to make an impression. Press reports suggested that Loughran had won eight rounds to Slattery's five, with two even, on his way to the unanimous decision.

6 January 1928. Tommy Loughran w pts 15 Leo Lomski.
Venue: Madison Square Garden, Manhattan, NYC, New York, USA. **Recognition:** World. **Referee:** Jack Denning.
Fight Summary: The challenger, who was known as the 'Aberdeen Assassin', quickly proved the moniker was deserved when he smashed Loughran (174½) to the floor with a terrific right to the jaw moments after the fight had started. Somehow Loughran got to his feet at the count of 'nine' before being forced to defend as the non-stop Lomski (171) threw leather for fun. As much as Loughran tried to stop all the punches from hitting the target it was impossible, and eventually another right to the jaw sent him down and out in the eyes of most of those in attendance. Luckily for Loughran the bell came to his rescue. Thereafter, Lomski was never given another opportunity as the champion ran for the next few rounds prior to taking up the initiative with accurately placed lefts and rights to well-deserve the unanimous decision in his favour.

1 June 1928. Tommy Loughran w pts 15 Pete Latzo.
Venue: Ebbets Field, Brooklyn, NYC, New York, USA. **Recognition:** World. **Referee:** Jed Gahan.
Fight Summary: Boxing in front of a 20,000 crowd the champion's mastery and ring wizardry were too much for Latzo (168), who despite making himself a difficult target as he found a way of sliding under the left lead to score with short-arm blows and roundhouse swings, lacked the ability to make it pay. Although Latzo had a good tenth round, class ultimately told as Loughran (173¾) sailed home to receive the unanimous decision.

Having just defeated Mike McTigue to become Loughran's leading challenger, and unbeaten in 29 contests, Armand Emanuel met the champion in a non-title contest at Madison Square Garden, Manhattan, NYC on 28 June, impressing despite losing the ten-round points decision. At that point Emanuel seemed to be on his way to a title shot, but in his very next contest he was knocked out inside seven rounds by Mickey Walker (at the Recreation Ground, San Francisco, California on 27 August). Following that, it was Walker who went on to meet Loughran.

16 July 1928. Tommy Loughran w pts 10 Pete Latzo.
Venue: Abertillery Park, Wilkes Barre, Pennsylvania, USA. **Recognition:** World. **Referee:** Leo Houck.
Fight Summary: On a rain-soaked evening in front of 18,000 people Latzo (167½) plunged in recklessly time and again only to be picked off by the champion's immaculate left hand. While there was a brief success for Latzo in round four when he connected with a heavy left hook that brought blood from his rival's right eye, an injury that bled for the remainder of the fight, there was no joy for him when he tried to claim a disqualification in the seventh after being hit on the belt line. Loughran (172½), who had Latzo bleeding from the nose and mouth, landed at will with left jabs, left hooks and right uppercuts to run out an easy winner according to all three judges' cards.

With Loughran taking on four heavyweights between October and February 1929 the NYSAC grew impatient with him, banning him from fighting above the weight in New York until he had once again defended the 175lbs title.

28 March 1929. Tommy Loughran w pts 10 Mickey Walker.
Venue: The Stadium, Chicago, Illinois, USA. **Recognition:** World. **Referee:** Dave Miller.
Scorecards: 8-1-1, 6-2-2, 4-5-1.
Fight Summary: One newspaper report stated that Loughran (173¼) easily thwarted the challenger's efforts to land a heavy wallop, either by picking off his blows or by clever evasive tactics, to run out a decisive winner after ten rounds. Realistically, it was much closer than that with Walker (165) starting fast and attacking the body, while the champion surprised him with lightning fast left hands to the head. Although Walker's pressure began to tell in the middle rounds, Loughran came back with fast one-twos as he began to take control of the contest, nailing his hardy rival with sharp right uppercut counters before jabbing his way to the split decision.

Loughran's next challenger would be Jim Braddock, who had stopped Jimmy Slattery inside nine rounds of a scheduled ten at Madison Square Garden, Manhattan, NYC, New York on 11 March. Normally an out-and-out counter puncher, Braddock turned aggressor against the clever Slattery, forcing the fight throughout while showing good variety allied to heavy punching from both hands.

18 July 1929. Tommy Loughran w pts 15 Jim Braddock.
Venue: Yankee Stadium, Bronx, NYC, New York, USA. **Recognition:** World. **Referee:** Eddie Forbes.
Fight Summary: Giving a master class of boxing at its best, Loughran (174) left no room for doubt as to his superiority over Braddock (170) when winning all but one of the 15 rounds contested. The fight had only just begun when Loughran was gashed over the left eye, but he kept the jab going and boxed his way out of trouble. Although Braddock forced the fight throughout he got nowhere, even with his pet right hand, as Loughran moved first one way and then the other, constantly spearing him with the left while making a difficult target. In the sixth Braddock was cut over the right eye, while Loughran also received a gashed forehead. To be fair to Braddock he never gave up trying, but with Loughran giving him few chances the unanimous decision in his favour was a formality.

When Loughran relinquished his title in September in order to campaign as a heavyweight, the New York State Athletic Commission announced that Maxie Rosenbloom, Yale Okun, Lou Scozza and George Courtney would meet in two semi-final legs to find a new champion. However, after Slattery had outpointed Rosenbloom over ten rounds (at the Broadway Auditorium, Buffalo, New York on 25 November) he took over the loser's place in the tournament. Despite that, Rosenbloom was not finished, going on to outscore Okun over 12 rounds at Madison Square Garden, Manhattan, NYC on 9 December. Okun, who received quite a bad beating, was subsequently dropped from the tournament, while Scozza eliminated Courtney (w disq 5 at the Olympia Stadium, Detroit, Michigan on 13 December) to reach the final. Following his win over Okun, Rosenbloom was supported by the NBA in his quest for a return with Slattery.

10 February 1930. Jimmy Slattery w pts 15 Lou Scozza.
Venue: Broadway Auditorium, Buffalo, New York, USA. **Recognition:** NY. **Referee:** Jim Crowley.
Fight Summary: Meeting to decide the NYSAC version of the title vacated by Tommy Loughran when he moved up a weight, Slattery (166¾) outgeneralled Scozza (169½) for the opening eight rounds before the latter's persistence and aggression finally paid off from the ninth onwards. With Slattery tiring and Scozza coming on strong the fight took on a different ring to it, and in the 13th the former champion was almost knocked out as he hung on to the ropes in a helpless state following a heavy battering after a knockdown. Saved by the gong all Slattery could hope for from there on was survival as Scozza tore into him looking for a finisher, but luckily for him when his rival tired from his exertions he made it to the final bell. The majority decision in Slattery's favour was hardly convincing, many believing there should be a rematch, especially after Arthur Donovan, one of the most experienced officials in the game, called it a draw.

Following the contest, after the NYSAC ordered Slattery to defend against Maxie Rosenbloom within 60 days the latter baulked at meeting the champion in Buffalo, wanting 25% of the gate if he went ahead.

Meanwhile, the NYSAC decided that Rosenbloom must beat the winner of Pete Latzo and Larry Johnson at Madison Square Garden, NYC, New York on 21 February if he wanted to progress. Latzo duly beat Johnson, but the decision was deemed so poor that it was Johnson who was matched against Rosenbloom in the Garden on 30 March. When that contest was settled by a sixth-round disqualification win for the latter the NYSAC were still not satisfied, asking Rosenbloom to meet Harry Fuller at the Broadway Auditorium on 7 April, the date that had originally been put aside for his crack at Slattery. After outpointing Fuller over ten rounds most observers thought that Rosenbloom would be in a position to agree terms for Slattery, but with the NYSAC still not satisfied they asked him to meet Johnson in a return as their earlier contest had been controversial. On 30 April, Rosenbloom outpointed Johnson at Madison Square Garden to finally convince the NYSAC that he was a worthy challenger, and with a date of 25 June finally agreed and supported by the NBA contracts were eventually signed. All of the above contests, which should be considered as eliminators, were contested over ten rounds at 175lbs.

25 June 1930. Maxie Rosenbloom w pts 15 Jimmy Slattery.
Venue: Bison Stadium, Buffalo, New York, USA. **Recognition:** World. **Referee:** Patsy Haley.
Fight Summary: In this, the sixth meeting between the pair, and a contest that would unify the title, Rosenbloom (170½) was wise to his rival's moves as he slapped and cuffed Slattery (166½) around for the full 15 rounds, his speed being a deciding factor. However, although the verdict was split the fact that Rosenbloom barely landed with the knuckle part of the glove caused much dissent among the 15,000 crowd. Interestingly, while two judges voted for Rosenbloom, the referee, who had almost been knocked out by one of the latter's wild swings, voted for Slattery.

Despite losing twice to both Pete Latzo and Rosenbloom in successive fights, Larry Johnson came back strongly to take over *The Ring* magazine's number one spot in the ratings when defeating Fred Lenhart in September, maintaining that position until beaten by Lou Scozza in January 1931. Scozza would eventually get a crack at Rosenbloom some 13 fights later.

22 October 1930. Maxie Rosenbloom w rsc 11 (15) Abie Bain.
Venue: Madison Square Garden, Manhattan, NYC, New York, USA. **Recognition:** World. **Referee:** Lou Magnolia.
Fight Summary: Defending his title against the promising Bain (171½), the first round saw Rosenbloom (174½) reeling around the ring after being hit by a big left hook to the jaw. Rosenbloom then grabbed hold of his rival and hung on for dear life despite the referee's efforts to break them. Having made it to the bell, Rosenbloom completely outboxed and outpunched Bain from thereon in before the third man stepped in to rescue the latter, bleeding from a deep cut, at 1.47 of the 11th.

On 28 April 1931, the NYSAC ordered Rosenbloom to defend his title against the number one rated Billy Jones, Joe Banovic or Jimmy Slattery, who had placed their challenges on file, or face the consequences. Rosenbloom's response was to outpoint Jones on 29 June 1931 at The Arena, Philadelphia, and then Banovic at the Armoury, Scranton on 9 July 1931 in ten-round non-title bouts in Pennsylvania before signing up to meet Slattery in August 1931. Earlier, on 6 June 1931, the NBA also issued a stern warning to Rosenbloom, stating that he must defend his title at least every six months.

5 August 1931. Maxie Rosenbloom w pts 15 Jimmy Slattery.
Venue: Ebbets Field, Brooklyn, NYC, New York, USA. **Recognition:** World. **Referee:** William McPartland.
Fight Summary: Slapping and cuffing his way through the bout Rosenbloom (171½) met with little resistance from Slattery (170½) despite his title being on the line. He even landed the better quality punches. The longer the contest went the more boring it became, and the unanimous decision in Rosenbloom's favour was a formality. With four victories over Rosenbloom from a possible six Slattery was expected to do a lot better, but having failed to produce he retired five fights later.

At The Coliseum, Des Moines, Iowa on 14 September, Rosenbloom gained a ten-round press decision over Owen Phelps in a fight that was listed in *The Ring* magazine as a title bout, but was reported by the *Des Moines Register* to be a catchweight contest with both men weighing in above 175lbs.

A few hours later at the NBA convention held on 14-16 September, the Association withdrew recognition from Rosenbloom and set up an eliminating series in Chicago, Illinois to find a new champion. The move, generally felt to have been a political one, saw the NBA suffer much ridicule at the hands of *The Ring* magazine and the press, especially as Rosenbloom had defended against Slattery just six weeks earlier. However, in defence of the NBA, Rosenbloom appeared to be ignoring the top-rated George Manley, who had twice outpointed him on 30 April and 22 July in ten-round non-title bouts at Stockyards Stadium, Denver, Colorado. Thus, it was strange that Manley's name was not among the applications that were eventually received and accepted, namely Phelps, Bob Olin, George Nichols, Lou Scozza, Abie Bain, Dave Maier, Harry Ebbets, Willie Oster, Billy Jones, Baxter Calmes, Mario Campi, Tiger Roy Williams, Clyde Chastain, Humberto Curi, Larry Johnson, Rosy Rosales, Russ Rowsey, Harry Fuller, Tait Littman, Battling Bozo, Pret Ferrar, Roscoe Manning, Buddy McArthur, Willie Bush, Don Petrin and Charley Belanger.

Nevertheless, with 26 men entered the first series started at The Stadium on 11 December with five contests scheduled for eight rounds apiece, resulting in Ebbets (w pts 8 Oster), Jones (w pts 8 Phelps), Calmes (w co 3 Campi), Maier (w pts 8 Williams) and Chastain (w pts 8 Curi), making it into the next round. Next came six further first-round contests on 18 December that saw Johnson (w rsc 2 Rosales), Olin (w co 4 Littman), Bain (w pts 8 Fuller), Scozza (w co 2 Rowsey), Bozo (w pts 8 Ferrar) and Manning (w co 1 McArthur) all winning through.

It is difficult to know exactly how the NBA arrived at the last eight, but I have made certain assumptions based on the remaining contests. To finalise the first series, Nichols (w rsc 5 Petrin) and Belanger (w pts 8 Bush) won through on 30 December. Then, with Ebbets withdrawing injured, Jones (w pts 10 Johnson), Calmes (w pts 10 Manning) and Olin (w pts 10 Chastain) made it through the second series on the same date while Nichols (w pts 10 Belanger) joined them on 15 January 1932, along with Scozza, Bozo, Maier and Bain, who received byes. Having drawn a bye at this stage of the tournament, allowed Maier to take time out to record a ten-round non-title points win over Rosenbloom at the Auditorium, Milwaukee, Wisconsin on 1 January 1932, prior to coming back into the quarter-final action on 15 January 1932 and eliminating Bain (w co 1). On the same day Calmes beat Olin (w pts 10), before Jones (w rsc 9 Bozo) and Nichols (w pts 10 Scozza) came through unscathed on 28 January 1932 to join him and Maier in the last four.

With Calmes seeking a match against Rosenbloom on 12 February 1932 he was released from the competition, leaving Maier with a bye, while Nichols outpointed Jones over ten rounds on 18 February 1932 to reach the final. Strangely, the *Chicago Tribune* reported that Calmes was due to meet Ebbets in the semi-final leg when it had to be Maier, although the statement could have meant the pair meeting for the right to fight the latter.

18 March 1932. George Nichols w pts 10 Dave Maier.
Venue: The Stadium, Chicago, Illinois, USA. **Recognition:** NBA. **Referee:** Phil Collins.
Scorecards: 57-43, 51-49, 49-51.
Fight Summary: Billed for the vacant NBA title, and a battle between southpaws, the *Chicago Tribune* reported that at the final bell the three judges barely knew how to score a fight that had been a vicious, hard-punching, devil-may-care affair. Both Nichols (163) and Maier (173½) had whaled away at each other with so much force that one or the other might have been knocked all the way home and back again. Giving away over ten pounds in weight Nichols won the split decision, and Maier, who rallied in the closing sessions with left hooks and right-hand counters, would recall "I think I was robbed, but what could I do about it."

On the same bill Baxter Calmes and Harry Ebbets outpointed Jim Braddock and Roscoe Manning respectively over ten rounds. Although Manning had lost a disputed decision to Calmes in the elimination series, a meeting between the winners of these two contests was seen as a way of finding Nichols' first challenger. However, Ebbets and Calmes, by now fighting as a heavyweight, were never matched.

Meanwhile, Maxie Rosenbloom remained active, but having failed to make a further defence for nine months he was advised by the NYSAC on 4 May to meet Nichols within 30 days to unify the title or risk being stripped. Those plans were scuppered when Nichols was beaten by Scozza. Incorrectly recorded as a title fight in the *Boxing News Annual*, Scozza's ten-round points win over Nichols at the Broadway Auditorium, Buffalo, New York on 31 May was merely a non-title fight, the victor going on to challenge Rosenbloom for the NYSAC version of the title.

Regardless of being recognised as the champion by the IBU at their May convention, after losing three of his next four fights the NBA stripped Nichols of the title in December, ahead of announcing the following month that if a promoter matched any two men from their top five - Rosenbloom, Billy Jones, Mickey Walker, Bob Godwin and Joe Knight - they would recognise the winner as the new champion.

Ultimately, a match was made between Knight, who was unbeaten in his last 19 fights and had wins over Rosenbloom, Godwin, Nichols and Battling Bozo during that time, and Godwin, with two draws and a points loss against Rosenbloom in the same period. Interestingly, pre-fight articles in both the *Palm Beach Post* and *Miami Herald* suggested that as Knight was already considered by the NBA, a body which governed ring activities in 33 States, as their champion he would thus be defending the title.

14 July 1932. Maxie Rosenbloom w pts 15 Lou Scozza.
Venue: Bison Stadium, Buffalo, New York, USA. **Recognition:** NY. **Referee:** Gunboat Smith.
Fight Summary: Piling on the pressure in the first half of the fight Rosenbloom (175) had too much of everything for the plodding Scozza (173), who despite being cuffed and slapped tried his utmost to get to close quarters where he would be more effective. Often Scozza was left floundering as the champion used the ring, and in the seventh he was floored by a looping right to the jaw before jumping up without a count. However, from the 11th Rosenbloom was in trouble as Scozza began to find his mark, the former eventually being dropped by a heavy right to the jaw for 'nine' in the 14th. Although shaken up the champion weathered the storm to win by a majority.

With pressure mounting on Rosenbloom to make another defence of his title, Frank Bachman, his manager, notified the NYSAC on 26 January 1933 that he had agreed to fight against the sixth-ranked Billy Jones and had asked the promoters to put it on as soon as possible. With little interest in the fight two weeks later it was reported that Rosenbloom would be defending his title against the winner of a contest at Madison Square Garden, NYC, New York on 10 February 1933, between Adolf Heuser, making his debut in the States, and Harry Ebbets. After Heuser won on points over ten rounds the date was set for 10 March 1933.

According to the 1934 *Post Record Book*, a 15-round points win for Rosenbloom over Al Stillman at The Arena, St Louis, Missouri on 22 February 1933 was a title bout, but with the winner weighing 180lbs to his rival's 176 it should be seen as a catchweight contest.

1 March 1933. Bob Godwin w pts 10 Joe Knight.
Venue: Dixie Arena, West Palm Beach, Florida, USA. **Recognition:** NBA. **Referee:** Phil O'Connell.
Fight Summary: Billed for the championship of the Southern States as well as involving the NBA crown, the *Palm Beach Post* reported that the southpaw Knight (173) took the first round, with the second and third even, before knocking Godwin (164) down in the fourth and cutting his right eye in a free-swinging session. Godwin, weaving in with rights and lefts, began to rally in the fifth through to the tenth, while Knight, despite being hurt on occasion, continued to throw terrific left hooks. The final round saw both men going toe-to-toe, but Godwin, with both eyes nearly closed, did just enough to deserve the referee's decision. Surprisingly, bearing in mind what a tough fight it had been and the amount of damage done to his eyes, Godwin would meet Maxie Rosenbloom little more than three weeks later.

10 March 1933. Maxie Rosenbloom w pts 15 Adolf Heuser.
Venue: Madison Square Garden, Manhattan, NYC, New York, USA. **Recognition:** NY. **Referee:** Jed Gahan.
Fight Summary: Making an excellent start the challenger battered Rosenbloom (174) almost groggy in the second when landing a series of left and right hooks to the jaw, and in the sixth he buckled the latter's knees following a savage left hook to the body. Unfortunately for the stubborn Heuser (172), who had won all but one session prior to the seventh, he began to tire. The tide then turned in the eighth, Rosenbloom slapping in blows at the rate of ten to one as he moved on to take the next five rounds with ease. Although the German rallied to even the last two frames it came as no surprise that Rosenbloom took the unanimous verdict. Bloody but unbowed, Heuser finished with his left eye almost closed, damage to nose and mouth and covered in welts, while Rosenbloom was unmarked.

24 March 1933. Maxie Rosenbloom w rsc 4 (15) Bob Godwin.
Venue: Madison Square Garden, Manhattan, NYC, New York, USA. **Recognition:** NY. **Referee:** Pete Hartley.
Fight Summary: Having received a badly gashed right eye in his fight with Joe Knight that was further damaged in training, necessitating five stitches, Godwin (167¼) was a beaten man from the start. It was soon clear that he should never have been allowed to fight Rosenbloom (174¾). Dropped twice by the champion in the first, after the wound re-opened in the second the referee called it off at 1.16 of the fourth. Nat Fleischer, writing in *The Ring* magazine, stated that Godwin should never have been passed by the doctors, especially as he had appeared at the weigh-in with plaster dressing over both eyes.

Further to the NBA title being vacated on the result the Association sent out a questionnaire to its members asking whether Rosenbloom should be recognised, and on receiving an insufficient number of favourable replies decided not to give him their blessing. The British Boxing Board of Control (BBBoC) were among those who felt that Rosenbloom was an unworthy champion, saying that they would not recognise him until he met Jack Petersen. Then, on 22 June, in a further response, the BBBoC wrote to the NBA stating that as Len Harvey was the new British champion, having beaten Eddie Phillips (w pts 15 at Olympia, London on 13 June), he should be seen as a logical challenger instead of Petersen. It is thought that neither the BBBoC nor the IBU, who were removed from the NBA at their September convention, recognised Rosenbloom as champion from here on in.

Despite all the misgivings, the NBA announced at their convention that they would finally recognise Rosenbloom as champion, regardless of the fact that he had twice been beaten by John Henry Lewis on points over ten rounds at the Civic Auditorium, San Francisco, California in non-title contests on 10 and 31 July and did not have the full support of their membership.

Earlier, Rosenbloom had been contracted to defend the New York portion of the title against Mickey Walker, but when the latter was beaten by Lou Brouillard on points over ten rounds at The Garden, Boston, Massachusetts on 6 July, in a battle between former champions at two weights, it went off the boil as well as contractual differences getting in the way. Eventually, with Rosenbloom unable to fight in New York until after the contest had taken place the differences were sorted out on 27 September.

In a fight that was billed for the 'black title', Billy Jones (175) outpointed Harry English (173) at the Culver Park Arena, Ludington, Michigan on 24 August. The papers reported it as the first fight of its kind to be recognised by the State Boxing Commission, but Jones appears to have made no defences as such.

3 November 1933. Maxie Rosenbloom w pts 15 Mickey Walker.
Venue: Madison Square Garden, Manhattan, NYC, New York, USA. **Recognition:** NBA/NBA. **Referee:** Eddie Forbes.
Scorecards: 11-3-1, 9-6, 4-9-2.
Fight Summary: Even though the *New York Times* reported earlier that Rosenbloom (173¾) had been warned by the NYSAC that he must discard his open-glove style of slapping, cuffing and mauling he still managed to give one of his unorthodox displays when holding and hitting Walker (173½) on the break, for which he was repeatedly warned by the referee. With respect to the closed glove situation Rosenbloom did at least do his best on that score despite never really hurting Walker, and at times he wound up the right hand rather like a baseball pitcher. Regardless, apart from the ninth round when Walker hurt him with lusty two-fisted blows through to the bell, the cagey Rosenbloom, who finished carrying a cut over the right eye, was generally much too clever for his rival, keeping him off balance and at arm's length for most of the time.

5 February 1934. Maxie Rosenbloom drew 15 Joe Knight.
Venue: MSG Stadium, Miami, Florida, USA. **Recognition:** NBA/NY. **Referee:** Harry Graham.
Scorecards: 74-76, 75-75, 75-75.
Fight Summary: Although only ten-rounders were allowed in Florida at the time, the contest went ahead as a billed title fight over 15 rounds after the political 'okay' was received. Finding the going tough, as Knight (173), a southpaw forced the fight, Rosenbloom (174) soon resorted to his well-known back-hand slapping and open glove slashing before the referee deducted a point from him in eighth. Despite the champion continuing to crouch low and hit with the open glove he received no further warnings, whereas Knight, who was the cleaner puncher of the

pair, appeared to have won at the final bell, especially when Rosenbloom congratulated him on winning the title before a drawn verdict was announced. Following an investigation by the Miami Boxing Commission the referee was suspended for 30 days, having allowed the champion to continually use illegal blows.

Meantime, taking part in non-title fights Rosenbloom was beaten on points over ten rounds by both Clyde Chastain (at the City Coliseum, Oklahoma City, Oklahoma on 16 April) and Mickey Walker (at the Olympic Auditorium, Los Angeles on 8 May). Both men, however, lost their top rankings almost immediately, Chastain losing three of his next four fights while Walker was beaten next time out.

On 19 July, after Rosenbloom had been instructed by the NYSAC to sign for a defence against either Knight or Bob Olin within 30 days, it was announced that he would meet the latter in New York on 16 August. However, on 2 August it was learned that contracts of the prospective contest had not even been submitted to the NYSAC due to an enquiry in progress which was looking into whether Frank Bachman, Rosenbloom's manager, was also involved with Olin in a financial capacity.

Regardless of that situation, after the Miami Boxing Commission stripped Rosenbloom on 12 September for not being able to make a match with Knight they handed the title to the latter, a decision which was rubber-stamped by the authorities representing North Carolina and Georgia. A few days later, on 16 September, Rosenbloom was stripped by the NBA, who announced that they wanted to set up a tournament that included Knight, Tony Shucco (*The Ring* magazine's number one), John Henry Lewis, Al Gainer, Lou Brouillard, Len Harvey and Ambrose Palmer in order to find a more 'satisfactory' champion. They had finally lost patience with a man whom they felt had brought the sport into disrepute with his clowning antics and so-called illegal tactics, despite the fact that he had defended the title successfully many times.

It soon became clear that things were not as straightforward as the NBA would have wished, and when Knight pulled out of their prospective tournament following the decision not to recognise a coming fight (later cancelled) between him and Shucco as being for the vacant title they decided to wait and see how Rosenbloom's defence against Olin panned out before they made any further decisions on how to proceed. Rosenbloom v Olin was finally given the all-clear by the NYSAC on 5 October when it was announced that it would take place on 16 November.

Knight went on to stop Al Rodrigues in seven rounds at The Coliseum, Coral Gables, Florida on 15 October, knock out Wilson Dunn in the third at the City Auditorium, Galveston, Texas on 22 October and to find another one-punch finish to see off Mickey Dugan in the fifth at the Beach Arena, Miami, Florida on 1 July 1935. These were all ten-round contests set at 175lbs. While there must have been some risk attached to Knight's recognition in Florida, Georgia and North Carolina, as the fights were not billed as involving any titles, it can only be assumed that Knight continued to be seen as champion in those States up until he met Al McCoy on 5 September 1935.

16 November 1934. Bob Olin w pts 15 Maxie Rosenbloom.
Venue: Madison Square Garden, Manhattan, NYC, New York, USA. **Recognition:** NY. **Referee:** Arthur Donovan.
Scorecards: 5-8-2, 9-5-1, 8-6-1.
Fight Summary: In what was deemed by most of the press and audience present as a huge miscarriage of justice, Olin (173) took the title from Rosenbloom (173½) after the two men outside the ring decided in his favour. Prior to the fight Rosenbloom was told that unless he hit with the knuckle part of the glove throughout he would be penalised, and to all intents and purposes the champion did just that. By rights Rosenbloom should have won the decision when picking up at least ten rounds with much superior boxing to that of his foe, who had connected with far fewer blows and was generally outpunched and certainly outmanoeuvred. Although Olin was the aggressor during the first 11 rounds he was well outboxed in at least seven of them, while Rosenbloom swarmed all over his rival in the last four to win going away according to the unbiased Nat Fleischer, writing in *The Ring* magazine. Fleischer stated that unless the NYSAC acted quickly over the quality of some of their judges there would be no more title fights held in the State as they would have become the laughing stock of boxing.

Within a few weeks of the contest the NBA stated that they would be happy to recognise Olin as the champion, but would look to him to meet the winner of a fight between John Henry Lewis and Tony Shucco, won by the former on points over ten rounds at Madison Square Garden on 14 December.

Unfortunately, showing in-and-out form following his title win Olin took quite a beating at the hands of Lewis (l pts 10 at Dreamland Park, San Francisco, California on 12 April 1935) in an overweight contest. Following that he was out of the ring for five months with various illnesses keeping him away from the gym. Coming back, and having turned down an offer to defend against Jack Petersen in England, it was reported in New York boxing circles that if Olin did not sign for a defence soon he could well be stripped. Having already forfeited Canadian recognition in August 1935 when ignoring the claims of Al McCoy, who had beaten Bob Godwin, Al Gainer and Billy Jones earlier in 1935, Olin signed up to defend against Lewis.

5 September 1935. Al McCoy w pts 15 Joe Knight.
Venue: Mount Royal Arena, Montreal, Canada. **Recognition:** Montreal. **Referee:** Mickey McGowan.
Fight Summary: Fighting to decide the Montreal version of the world title, with just two rounds to go it appeared that either man could win it inside the distance despite Knight (171½) being the wearier. From there onwards though, McCoy (174¼), consistently pressing forward, blasted away with both hands to keep his southpaw opponent on the defensive right to the final bell, where the latter finished with cuts over the right eye and further damage to lips and nose. Although the judges gave Knight only three rounds it had been a close and gruelling struggle.

Further to the Knight fight, McCoy surprisingly met Lou Brouillard just 15 days later, at The Garden, Boston, Massachusetts on 20 September, in a fight the *Boston Post* viewed as a final eliminator for the world title. Regardless that McCoy won on points over ten rounds, with both men inside 175lbs there was obviously some risk attached to his Canadian recognition.

Following this, the hustling young Montreal promoter, Jules Racicot, lined up a defence for McCoy when matching him against Mickey Walker but, after the latter pulled out and the Montreal Boxing Commission failed to sanction Larry Johnson as a worthy foe, Abie Bain was brought in.

23 October 1935. Al McCoy w co 2 (12) Abie Bain.
Venue: The Forum, Montreal, Canada. **Recognition:** Montreal. **Referee:** Joe Glickman.
Fight Summary: Billed as a world title fight under the auspices of the Montreal Boxing Commission, McCoy (174¾) lost little time in finding his distance, larruping Bain (172¾) incessantly from the start before polishing his man off with a terrific short right hook to the jaw in the second. Bain, who never had a chance, was counted out on the 1.38 mark.

Just over a month later, after being outpointed over ten rounds by Jock McAvoy in a match made at 171lbs on 29 November, at Madison Square Garden, Manhattan, NYC, New York, McCoy moved up to heavyweight.

31 October 1935. John Henry Lewis w pts 15 Bob Olin.
Venue: The Arena, St Louis, Missouri, USA. **Recognition:** NBA/NY. **Referee:** Walter Heisner.
Fight Summary: In his first defence Olin (175) was unlucky to come up against an outstanding challenger in Lewis (174½), but in losing by a unanimous decision he went down in glorious fashion when fighting against the odds. Taking a severe beating in most of the rounds, Olin manfully stuck to his guns despite being battered from pillar to post at times. Olin's bravery had the crowd on his side as Lewis eventually grew weary of hitting him, and he even blasted back in the 13th before staggering through the next two sessions to make it to the final bell. Never one to set the pulses racing when winning, in defeat Olin finally got the kudos he deserved.

Lewis's first challenger would be Jock McAvoy, the reigning British and British Empire middleweight champion. McAvoy had gone to America with the sole purpose of getting a title shot at the weight, but after beating Al McCoy and then Babe Risko, the current NYSAC middleweight champion, by a first-round kayo there were no takers.

When two more wins followed, the hard-hitting McAvoy was more than happy to challenge Lewis, who since beating Olin had taken in nine non-title contests, losing to Emilio Martinez and Maxie Rosenbloom.

13 March 1936. John Henry Lewis w pts 15 Jock McAvoy.
Venue: Madison Square Garden, Manhattan, NYC, New York, USA. **Recognition:** GB/NBA/NY. **Referee:** Arthur Donovan.
Fight Summary: Outreached and carrying a badly injured right hand into the fight, McAvoy (168¼) was well in the running before the novocaine wore off in the middle rounds and forced him to concentrate on defence. Lewis (172¼) was a master at long range, but once the problems of the challenger surfaced he hit his man with all the punches in the book. From thereon in it was only the bobbing and weaving style of the Englishman, coupled with his toughness that kept him upright. Even though the decision was unanimous in favour of Lewis the crowd booed vociferously.

For some reason known only to themselves the IBU announced at their congress on 8 August that they would recognise the winner of the forthcoming European title fight between Heinz Lazek and Gustave Roth as world champion.

1 September 1936. Gustave Roth w pts 15 Heinz Lazek.
Venue: Engelmann Arena, Vienna, Austria. **Recognition:** IBU.
Fight Summary: Billed for the IBU version of the world championship, with Lazek defending his European title at the same time, the latter disappointed his fans when unable to use his greater power and longer reach effectively against the clever and experienced Roth. Not only having the speed of a middleweight, Roth was a revelation as he also showed power, toughness and great fighting spirit to dictate the fight almost from start to finish. It appeared that Lazek was not in the best of shape, being stiff and hesitant for too long. The press report of the fight stated that Roth won at least eight of the 15 rounds clearly, with Lazek possibly taking three, the rest being even. Time and again the audience waited for a decisive attack from Lazek, only for him to be thwarted as Roth held on when necessary and while the Belgian looked as fresh at the final bell as when he had started Lazek was heavily marked.

29 October 1936. Gustave Roth w pts 15 Adolf Witt.
Venue: Sports Palace, Berlin, Germany. **Recognition:** IBU. **Referee:** Roger Nicod.
Fight Summary: Making his first defence of the IBU version of the world title the clever Roth (165¼), despite being put down in the fifth, generally knew too much for the hard-punching Witt (172). Although he continuously looked to get his big punches off Witt had little joy. Once the champion had taken the steam out of Witt, mainly by excellent use of the left jab and good footwork, he set about the latter with well-placed rights to the jaw, which produced knockdowns in rounds ten and 15 before he landed the unanimous decision of the judges.

9 November 1936. John Henry Lewis w pts 15 Len Harvey.
Venue: The Arena, Wembley, London, England. **Recognition:** GB/NBA/NY. **Referee:** Jack Smith.
Fight Summary: For the whole 15 rounds the pair entertained the big crowd with their quality, although it was noticeable that the champion's fists carried more authority, especially after the Englishman's right hand went in the third. However, Harvey (172), carrying a damaged left eye, put on a tremendous display of ring-craft to make things difficult for Lewis (173½). And in the last three rounds, fighting as if his life depended on it, he came with a rush in a desperate effort to swing the referee's decision.

12 January 1937. Gustave Roth drew 15 Antonio Rodrigues.
Venue: Fluminense Football Ground, Rio De Janeiro, Brazil. **Recognition:** IBU. **Referee:** Rodrigo Jurado.
Fight Summary: In a fight that was too close to find a winner according to the referee, Roth (165½) held on to his title claim via a drawn decision. Newspaper reports of the contest state that while Roth showed excellent defensive ability and worked well on the inside, his Portuguese opponent made him fight every inch of the way. There was no mention of any knockdowns. With the partisan crowd solidly behind Rodrigues (167½), every time Roth took command of the situation the Portuguese man would come right back at him. Despite Rodrigues finishing strongly he was unable to find the punch to end matters, and on winning just one of his next six contests he retired.

24 March 1937. Gustave Roth w pts 15 Preciso Merlo.
Venue: Sports Palace, Brussels, Belgium. **Recognition:** IBU. **Referee:** Francois Vaisberg.
Fight Summary: According to the *L'independance* the fight was extremely one-sided with Roth landing the better punches throughout while Merlo merely received them. Within a round or so from the start Merlo's face began to show signs of wear, the damage continuing to worsen due to the flow of leather coming his way. The former European champion, who had come into the contest following just one win in his last five outings, proved to be no match for the clever Roth. Not only was Roth difficult to hit but he seemed able to send in straight lefts and uppercuts almost as and when he pleased. At the same time it did not help Merlo's cause that he lacked the power required to turn the fight around with one punch. Roth's balance and movement were a joy to watch in terms of ring science, but with Merlo's corner at a loss to advise their man tactically the decision was a formality.

1 May 1937. Gustave Roth w pts 15 John Andersson.
Venue: Sports Palace, Antwerp, Belgium. **Recognition:** IBU. **Referee:** Mr Desmerts.
Fight Summary: Articled for the IBU version of the world championship as well as being a European title defence for Roth, although no weights were reported on the day of the fight two days earlier Roth scaled 169¾lbs to Andersson's 172. In what was a clash of styles, Andersson attacked from the first bell, shaking up the clever Roth in the third round before the latter was cut over both eyes in the fourth due to an accidental clash of heads. In the fourth and the fifth the Swede was warned for head butts. While Andersson was always aggressive, Roth, displaying excellent defensive skills, was scoring at will in the tenth. He then dominated the 13th and 14th prior to going toe-to-toe in the 15th. Following the contest Andersson's manager filed a complaint with the IBU, arguing that the fourth round had lasted five minutes, 45 seconds due to the referee allowing Roth time out after being cut. Needless to say, the protest was quickly dismissed.

3 June 1937. John Henry Lewis w rsc 8 (15) Bob Olin.
Venue: The Arena, St Louis, Missouri, USA. **Recognition:** GB/NBA/NY. **Referee:** Walter Heisner.
Fight Summary: Having kept Olin (174¾) at arm's length during the opening two sessions, Lewis (174) opened up in the third with a vicious body attack. After putting Olin down in the fourth with a cracking right under the heart that fractured a rib, Lewis continued to attack the body from there onwards. Those tactics certainly paid dividends, and at 1.20 of the eighth with the challenger down for the second time in the round the referee stopped the fight.

On 15 July, the fourth-rated Tiger Jack Fox met Deacon Leo Kelly, who was one place above him, in what was reported to be an elimination contest to find Lewis's next challenger. Kelly, who had spent almost two years campaigning in Australia, had temporarily been *The Ring* magazine's top-rated fighter in May 1936 after beating Ambrose Palmer, and had an interesting sideline as a Deacon in a Los Angeles Baptist Church. Contested over 15 rounds Fox beat Kelly (w rsc 6 at Madison Square Garden, Manhattan, NYC, New York), but found himself no nearer to a title crack as it was clear at this time that Lewis was eyeing up the heavyweight division.

Along with Fox, Al Gainer, Jock McAvoy, George Black, Jack Gibbons, Eddie Wenstob, Fred Lenhart, Gus Lesnevich, Oscar Rankins and Ray Actis constituted *The Ring* magazine's top ten at the end of September, all of them looking to make progress in a division that was rapidly stagnating.

Although it was reported in December that Lewis would be making a defence against Lenhart in January 1938 it did not happen. Then, after being pressed by both the NYSAC and NBA to make a defence, it was announced on 29 January 1938 that Lewis would relinquish the title if he could get a crack at Joe Louis for the heavyweight crown. At the same time the NYSAC stated that they would look favourably at the winner of a contest at 175lbs between Fox and Lou Brouillard at The Garden, Boston, Massachusetts on 18 February 1938 being given an opportunity to meet Lewis for the title. Fox won by a count-out in the seventh round.

It was reported on 24 February 1938 that contracts were in place for Lewis to defend against Gainer, but when that match was agreed for June (eventually moved on to October) Lewis continued fighting over-the-weight contests before signing up on 8 April 1938 for a title match against Emilio Martinez.

Light Heavyweight Division

1 December 1937. Gustave Roth drew 15 Karel Sys.
Venue: Sports Palace, Brussels, Belgium. **Recognition:** IBU. **Referee:** Marcel Falony.
Fight Summary: This was a contest in which a clash of styles meant that more often than not Roth (169¾) and his challenger cancelled each other out as both were too cautious when it came to making the first move. It was soon clear that Sys' strategy was to draw Roth in, but with the latter apparently not happy to make the running there was little action. If he wanted to win the title it was really up to Sys (172½) to set the pace, and although occasionally letting the punches go Roth's defence was too sound to break down. There were far too many clinches and too many warnings, with both men seemingly happy for things to continue the way they were. Finally, in the 12th, the fight livened up when Roth decided to throw more punches, but with Sys negating his aggression the bout fizzled out completely.

21 January 1938. Gustave Roth w pts 15 Jupp Besselmann.
Venue: Sports Palace, Berlin, Germany. **Recognition:** IBU. **Referee:** M. Murello.
Fight Summary: Defending the IBU version of the title for the sixth time Roth (168½) took on Besselmann (155½), Germany's leading middleweight, and after a hard contest came away with the unanimous decision. Although the heavy-handed Besselmann gave of his best he could not move the crafty, skilful Roth, who was cautioned for holding in the 11th. However, to his great credit he never gave up trying. Decked in the ninth, but up immediately, Besselmann continued to come forward right up to the final bell despite being outboxed by a very good champion.

Meanwhile, in order to find Roth's next opponent, Adolf Heuser outpointed Karel Sys over 12 rounds at the Olympic Stadium, Berlin on 10 February.

25 March 1938. Adolf Heuser w rsc 7 (15) Gustave Roth.
Venue: Olympic Stadium, Berlin, Germany. **Recognition:** IBU.
Fight Summary: Setting about Roth (175) from the opening bell, on recognising that he had to stop his rival from dictating the contest Heuser (175) got inside with vicious non-stop swings and hooks to batter the champion from his title. By the sixth round it had become clear that Heuser would not be checked, and in the seventh Roth was floored three times before his manager realised the hopelessness of his charge's task when throwing in the towel. At that point, the referee stopped the contest. Roth, who had tried all he knew to stem the tide, was cheered from the ring for his game display.

During an international boxing convention held in Rome in April, which was attended by many leading authorities within the sport (not including the New York State Athletic Commission, who could not agree to designate any part of its function to a foreign body as it was ruled by State legislative law), the IBU agreed to refuse to recognise all individually-made world champions, including their own, in an effort to stand by one universally acknowledged champion, who, in turn, would have to concede to regular defences decided by the new Federation.

25 April 1938. John Henry Lewis w co 4 (15) Emilio Martinez.
Venue: The Auditorium, Minneapolis, Minnesota, USA. **Recognition:** GB/NBA/NY. **Referee:** Britt Gorman.
Fight Summary: Jabbing and moving with great skill, Lewis (174¾) hurt Martinez (174) badly in the opening session before scoring at will with telling lefts and rights in the second and third rounds. In the fourth, Lewis, having set Martinez up with the left, caught him flush with a right to the jaw, a punch that saw the challenger counted out on the 0.54 mark.

On 27 July, Lewis was warned that he would forfeit NYSAC recognition under the six-monthly defence ruling after refusing to fight in the 'Empire City'. He was then given until the end of October to defend in New York. At the same time the NYSAC named Tiger Jack Fox, Gus Lesnevich, Melio Bettina and Al Gainer, who was already contracted to challenge Lewis for the title, as the men they would be selecting to contest the vacant title if need be. This action, which was followed by Lewis taking the NYSAC to the Supreme Court, resulted in him being granted the right to appeal against the NYSAC's decision.

28 October 1938. John Henry Lewis w pts 15 Al Gainer.
Venue: The Arena, New Haven, Connecticut, USA. **Recognition:** GB/NBA. **Referee:** Dave Fitzgerald.

Fight Summary: Carrying the fight to Gainer (170) from the off Lewis (174) jabbed, hooked and sunk his right repeatedly under the heart to win at least ten of the 15 rounds, according to Nat Fleischer of *The Ring* magazine. Although the challenger looked to counter most of the time Lewis's blocking of blows was superb, and when Gainer got through he was unable push on. Gainer's best rounds were the eighth through to the 11th when he fought viciously to turn the tide, but Lewis came back strongly right through to the end even though he had to take several stiff punches to the jaw before retaining his title by a unanimous decision. Prior to the fight there was much controversy after Lewis and Gainer weighed in at 10am instead of 1pm without the press being present.

With many wondering whether Lewis could continue to make the weight it was reported that he would be challenging Joe Louis for the heavyweight crown at Madison Square Garden, Manhattan, NYC, New York on 25 January 1939.

Further to this, the NYSAC announced that because Gus Lesnevich had taken himself off to Australia, the remaining three men that they saw contesting their vacant title, Melio Bettina, Gainer and Tiger Jack Fox, would go into the hat with first two out meeting in a semi-final leg. Thus, on 29 November, despite Lewis still claiming to be the champion, after Fox defeated Gainer (w pts 15 at The Coliseum, Bronx, NYC, New York) he went forward to fight Bettina to decide the championship. Meanwhile, Lewis lost his heavyweight title challenge against Louis when he was put down three times in the opening round and stopped.

3 February 1939. Melio Bettina w rsc 9 (15) Tiger Jack Fox.
Venue: Madison Square Garden, Manhattan, NYC, New York, USA. **Recognition:** NY. **Referee:** Eddie Joseph.
Fight Summary: Contesting the vacant NYSAC version of the title Bettina (172½) began well when taking the play away from the hard-hitting Fox (174¾) almost from the start, and despite it being a dull affair he kept plugging away while waiting for the opportunity to open up. Unorthodox, game and aggressive, the hard-hitting southpaw eventually caught up with Fox in the eighth, dropping him with a left hook, and when the latter made it to his feet at 'nine' he was battered into the ropes for another count. Picking it up where he left off, when Bettina came out for the ninth with only one thing on his mind the referee rescued Fox, who was being pounded against the ropes without reply. The finish was times at 1.22. Really, there was no way that Fox should have been in the ring that night as he had been stabbed near the heart a couple of months earlier and had been on the critical list for several days, which would explain why he threw so few solid blows during the fight. The contest was also given plenty of advance publicity due to Bettina's manager, Jimmy Grippo, a magician of some repute, claiming that his charge would be in a hypnotic state come the night.

Following Bettina v Fox, John Henry Lewis, who was still claiming the title, went forward to defend against Dave Clark in the latter's home city on 31 March. However, the fight was prevented from taking place when two doctors failed Lewis on his eyesight. At this point, John Roxborough, Clark's manager, claimed the title on behalf of his charge, while Grippo wrote to the NBA asking them to consider Bettina as their champion. Both claims were immediately rebuffed. Nat Fleischer, of *The Ring* magazine, then attacked the NYSAC for allowing Lewis to fight Joe Louis when it must have been obvious that his eyesight had already failed.

It did not stop there, however. With Lewis still claiming the championship, having travelled to England to defend against Len Harvey in London on 22 June, after the BBBoC doctors inspected his eyesight on arriving they immediately stopped him from fighting in Britain. Prior to that, the NBA had actually implied that Lewis's eye damage was not as bad as first thought and were still considering him to be their champion.

Back in America, Lewis was banned from fighting on 19 June due to failing eyesight, even though he was continuing to claim the championship and refusing to retire. At that juncture the NBA said that they would support a fight between Bettina and Billy Conn, who had won 45 of 56 since turning pro at 17 four years earlier, and had twice beaten the reigning NBA middleweight champion, Solly Krieger, along with the NYSAC equivalent, Fred Apostoli. After ignoring the claims of Australia's Ron Richards, who had beaten Gus Lesnevich (w pts 15 at the Sports Ground, Sydney, Australia on 27 October 1938), and Harvey, the British and British Empire champion, it should have been no surprise when the BBBoC decided to recognise a match between the latter and Jock McAvoy as being for their version of the title.

Light Heavyweight Division

10 July 1939. Len Harvey w pts 15 Jock McAvoy.
Venue: White City Stadium, Shepherds Bush, London, England. **Recognition:** GB. **Referee:** Charlie Thomas.
Fight Summary: Coming together for the fourth time, and also involving the British and British Empire titles, McAvoy (171) made the early pace while Harvey (174) stood back with the left jab, relying on a superb defence to break down the latter's aggression. McAvoy appeared to be leading at the half-way stage, but Harvey, damaged around both eyes, came back strongly to land telling blows to head and body from then on before surviving a battering in the 13th round to earn the referee's decision. There were 80,000 fans in attendance, which was a British record.

With the war looming Harvey joined the RAF, and had, to all intents and purposes, retired when he was called upon to defend the British version of the title in June 1942 against the younger Freddie Mills, who was also serving in the RAF. Mills had taken part in 74 contests (58 wins, ten losses and six draws) and had recently stopped McAvoy (w rsc 1 at the Royal Albert Hall, Kensington, London on 23 February 1942) in an official eliminator for the British, British Empire and world titles, all currently held by Harvey.

13 July 1939. Billy Conn w pts 15 Melio Bettina.
Venue: Madison Square Garden, Manhattan, NYC, New York, USA. **Recognition:** NBA/NY. **Referee:** Frank Fullam.
Scorecards: 9-6, 8-7, 10-5.
Fight Summary: For five rounds Bettina (173¾) more than held his own against the fast moving Conn (170¼), fighting out of a crouch that made for a difficult target while baffling the latter with his southpaw stance. However, by the sixth Conn had worked Bettina out when beginning to get home solidly with the left jab despite being caught at times. Although Conn had to hold on occasionally when Bettina opened up, he was the one who was dictating the contest over the last five sessions, and in the 13th he cut the latter badly on the cheekbone following a cracking left hand. Because the fight was close enough to warrant a return the two men were signed up almost immediately.

25 September 1939. Billy Conn w pts 15 Melio Bettina.
Venue: Forbes Field, Pittsburgh, Pennsylvania, USA. **Recognition:** NBA/NY. **Referee:** Red Robinson.
Fight Summary: As in their previous fight, Conn (172¼) was kept at bay for the opening six rounds as the clever Bettina (174½) continually confused him with his southpaw stance. Cut under the left eye the champion began to pick things up in the seventh, and ducking and countering well he began to outbox Bettina for the rest of the contest bar the 13th. In that session it was all Bettina, who took Conn to the ropes to batter away with blows to head and body while generally roughing him up. Although taken out of his stride Conn came back well to shower Bettina with lefts and rights to maintain his lead on all three cards, but despite having the latter badly hurt a couple of times he was unable to floor him.

17 November 1939. Billy Conn w pts 15 Gus Lesnevich.
Venue: Madison Square Garden, Manhattan, NYC, New York, USA. **Recognition:** NBA/NY. **Referee:** Johnny McAvoy.
Scorecards: 8-5-2, 10-5, 9-6.
Fight Summary: Setting out aggressively, banging in blows to the body, Lesnevich (174¾) took the fight to Conn (171½) in the early stages before the latter came back strongly from the fourth round onwards. This was never an easy fight for the champion, with Lesnevich always looking to attack the body, and he was made to fight every inch of the way. However, from the 12th, with both men cut under their left eyes, it was all Conn as he ripped into Lesnevich with hooks, jabs and uppercuts to make sure of the verdict. Despite seemingly lacking a heavy punch, Conn proved once again that he was an excellent boxer who was more than capable of dealing with hard-hitting rivals.

5 June 1940. Billy Conn w pts 15 Gus Lesnevich.
Venue: Olympia Stadium, Detroit, Michigan, USA. **Recognition:** NBA/NY. **Referee:** Sam Hennessey.
Scorecards: 8-5-2, 6-3-6, 7-6-2.
Fight Summary: Taking on Lesnevich (173½) in a return match, Conn (173½) was again made to fight all the way in order to retain his title in what would be his last contest at the weight. Showing an excellent range of punches, apart from taking the odd breather Conn outboxed the always dangerous Lesnevich most of the way. Throwing

every punch in the book Conn cut Lesnevich over the left eye in the 11th before momentarily dropping him in the final session to run out a clear winner, even though one judge showed just one round between them.

At the end of December, with Conn concentrating on the heavyweight division, the NBA withdrew recognition from him in favour of a match between Anton Christoforidis, who had recently beaten Jimmy Bivins (w pts 10 at The Arena, Cleveland, Ohio on 2 December), and Melio Bettina for their version of the vacant title.

Then, with the likelihood that Conn would remain among the heavyweights, the NYSAC set up an elimination series in which Jimmy Webb, *The Ring* magazine's number one rated light heavy, stopped Tommy Tucker in the ninth round of a scheduled 15 at Madison Square Garden, Manhattan, NYC, New York on 21 February 1941. Ultimately, it would be a long and fruitless wait for Webb as Conn only vacated the NYSAC version of the title on 3 June 1941.

13 January 1941. Anton Christoforidis w pts 15 Melio Bettina.
Venue: The Arena, Cleveland, Ohio, USA. **Recognition:** NBA. **Referee:** Joe Sedley.
Fight Summary: In a savage and bloody contest for the vacant title Christoforidis (168½) made a slow start while trying to work his southpaw opponent out, but by the fifth he was beginning to find the range. Getting off solid right hooks he started to hurt Bettina (174), and in the seventh the latter was cut over the left eye. The battle was fairly even with first one man then the other picking it up, before Christoforidis came on fast in the latter rounds with two-fisted body attacks that forced Bettina to the ropes. In the 13th session Bettina had been at his best. However, after Bettina had the round deducted for butting, the Greek had the advantage, eventually being awarded the unanimous decision.

Following the result, Abe Greene, the Vice President of the NBA, stated that he would be asking the NBA executive to work with the NYSAC in deciding the next American champion when Billy Conn officially abdicated.

22 May 1941. Gus Lesnevich w pts 15 Anton Christoforidis.
Venue: Madison Square Garden, Manhattan, NYC, New York, USA. **Recognition:** NBA. **Referee:** Frank Fullam.
Fight Summary: Contested in New York despite it being billed for the NBA title, it was also seen as the semi-final leg of an elimination series that would ultimately decide the American title. Making his first defence of the NBA crown, Christoforidis (166) was soon under pressure as Lesnevich (175) attacked him with solid lefts to the body and jarring rights to the head. It was only in the fifth round that the champion had any joy when staggering Lesnevich with heavy blows to the head, but in the seventh through to the ninth he was badly hurt and cut under the left eye. Christoforidis bravely kept going right through to the final bell, even after being blasted into the ropes in the final session and seemingly at the mercy of Lesnevich. But the New Jersey man, who had punched himself out, had to be satisfied with the unanimous decision.

Tami Mauriello would be Lesnevich's next challenger after Jimmy Webb, who had earlier qualified for the final leg of the NYSAC version of the title, got himself badly beaten when the unranked Mose Brown knocked him out inside two rounds at Hickey Park, Pittsburgh, Pennsylvania on 28 July. Having defeated Tommy Tucker in the eliminators back in February, with Webb basically marking time the Brown defeat was a massive setback. Twice more he was given the chance to overturn the defeat, but twice more he was defeated in Pittsburgh by Brown (l rsc 5 at Hickey Park on 20 August and l co 6 at Forbes Field on 15 September) before dropping out of the title race altogether. Despite his three victories over Webb, which gained him a top-three ranking, after Brown was beaten in quick succession by former world middleweight champion Ken Overlin, Melio Bettina and Kid Tunero, he too quickly dropped out of the reckoning.

26 August 1941. Gus Lesnevich w pts 15 Tami Mauriello.
Venue: Madison Square Garden, Manhattan, NYC, New York, USA. **Recognition:** NBA/NY. **Referee:** Eddie Joseph.
Scorecards: 8-7, 8-6-1, 5-10.
Fight Summary: Almost beaten before he started, having been dropped by a tremendous left hook in the second round for a count of 'nine', Mauriello (170¾) came right back to give the NBA champion all manner of problems. One judge had him winning by five rounds, which was supported by Nat Fleischer of *The Ring* magazine, and there was so much all-round confusion when the decision was announced that both men signed up for an immediate

return. From the third session Mauriello was very much back in the fight, and apart from the eighth when Lesnevich (175) scored heavily he was the one forcing the action. Leading with conviction Mauriello had the flat-footed Lesnevich, who'd had trouble making the weight, under real pressure in the final four rounds without being able to make it pay.

Having outscored Red Burman, a day later Booker Beckwith took over *The Ring* magazine's number one spot, and despite being beaten by two heavyweights in Bob Pastor and Melio Bettina he maintained it until knocked out inside nine rounds by Ezzard Charles. During that period Beckwith had beaten Joey Maxim, but would never attain such lofty heights again.

14 November 1941. Gus Lesnevich w pts 15 Tami Mauriello.
Venue: Madison Square Garden, Manhattan, NYC, New York, USA. **Recognition:** NBA/NY. **Referee:** Arthur Donovan.
Scorecards: 9-4-2, 9-6, 10-2-3.
Fight Summary: A return fight, this one was nothing like their first encounter with the champion producing his best form to outwit the inexperienced Mauriello (173½) who was well beaten but not disgraced. With straight lefts finding their mark and solid body shots slowing his rival down Lesnevich (173¾) always seemed to be in control, and although Mauriello fought back strongly on occasions he was well beaten. Three times the challenger was almost dropped by powerful blows to head and body, his great conditioning saving him, but while still in the contest he was unable to halt Lesnevich's forward march.

In an effort to keep boxing alive, with Lesnevich inactive between March 1942 and January 1946 due to military service, Ohio initiated a light heavyweight 'duration' title. It was won by Jimmy Bivins, who outscored Anton Christoforidis over 15 rounds at The Arena, Cleveland on 26 February 1943, but not before Ezzard Charles and Joey Maxim had been eliminated in the earlier stages. Bivins' one and only defence came when he knocked out Lloyd Marshall inside 13 rounds at the Lakefront Stadium, Cleveland on 8 June 1943, and by September he had moved up a division, having been the number one light heavy according to *The Ring* magazine since July 1942. At the same time Bivins had topped the heavyweight rankings since January 1943.

After Bivins, *The Ring* magazine's next top-rated man was Marshall (October 1943), followed by Nate Bolden (November 1943), Marshall again (December 1943 to May 1945), Archie Moore (June 1945 to August 1945), Fitzie Fitzpatrick (September 1945) and once again Moore right through and beyond Lesnevich's return to the ring.

Back in action on 11 January 1946, Lesnevich forced Joe Kahut to take the full count in the opening round, before having to retire at the end of the fourth of a heavyweight contest against Lee Oma. Having shaken off some of the ring rust, Lesnevich then signed up for a match against Freddie Mills.

20 June 1942. Freddie Mills w co 2 (15) Len Harvey.
Venue: White Hart Lane, Tottenham, London, England. **Recognition:** GB. **Referee:** Eugene Henderson.
Fight Summary: Inactive since winning the British version of the world title almost three years earlier, and rapidly approaching 35 years of age, Harvey (171¼) was no match for the 22-year-old Mills (173½). Having ended the first round with a crunching left hook to Harvey's jaw, after Mills tore out for the second he soon had the champion on the floor, a similar punch doing the damage. Although Harvey got to his feet he was again under siege, and after taking several solid blows he was sent crashing through the ropes before being counted out on the 53-second mark, still outside the ring.

With the war raging in Europe Mills had just six more contests, including an unsuccessful crack at the vacant British and British Empire heavyweight titles against West Hartlepool's Jack London, before arriving home from service in India and being matched in March 1946 against Gus Lesnevich in order to decide the championship. According to *The Ring* magazine ratings of the time only Archie Moore was considered to be in front of Mills, but with the latter claiming a share of the world title his match-up with Lesnevich was the most logical one to get out of the way first. Although Moore, who was considered to be the division's danger man, would eventually get a crack at the world title it would not be for another six years and 66 fights.

14 May 1946. Gus Lesnevich w rsc 10 (15) Freddie Mills.
Venue: The Arena, Harringay, London, England. **Recognition:** World. **Referee:** Eugene Henderson.
Fight Summary: In a fight that would be remembered for a long time by all those who saw it, Lesnevich (175) came back from the brink to beat the British champion and unify the title. Dropped four times in the second round, Mills (174) finished the session in a parlous state when having great difficulty in finding his corner. Despite that, Mills came right back in the third with solid blows of his own to have Lesnevich carrying a cut and badly swollen left eye. He then went on to outbox the American champion for the next few rounds and break his nose in the sixth. Lesnevich, though, remained strong, and by the end of the ninth he was having some success before opening up in the tenth to have Mills in real trouble. After Mills went to the canvas three times from rights to the jaw, with just four seconds of the round remaining the referee rescued him halfway through the final count.

Managed by Frank 'Blinky' Palermo, an underworld figure, Billy Fox, who had a fantastic record with 43 inside the distance wins from 43 starts, was chosen to be Lesnevich's next challenger.

28 February 1947. Gus Lesnevich w rsc 10 (15) Billy Fox.
Venue: Madison Square Garden, Manhattan, NYC, New York, USA. **Recognition:** World. **Referee:** Johnny Burns.
Fight Summary: This was a contest in which an inexperienced challenger, despite being unbeaten and carrying a kayo punch, was unable to finish Lesnevich (174½) off following two powerful rights in the third that had the latter all at sea. Although boxing well to take the fourth, from there onwards Fox (172) was continuously being punished as Lesnevich sent in heavy blows from both hands and denied him any space. At 2.19 of the tenth the contest was over after Fox had got to his feet at 'eight', having been floored by a long right to the jaw that followed punch after punch. Failing to realise that the fight was over Lesnevich raced in, and despite not hitting Fox both men went to the floor for the last action of the fight.

With Lesnevich lining himself up to meet Joe Louis for the heavyweight crown, there were moves to get him to make a defence against his number one challenger, Ezzard Charles, but he too seemed more intent on meeting Louis and nothing was signed. Since removing Fox from his path Lesnevich had beaten Melio Bettina and Tami Mauriello (twice), but after Louis made a successful defence of the heavyweight crown against Jersey Joe Walcott on 5 December and was signed up for a return the following summer Lesnevich again came under pressure from the NBA to defend his title.

Although Charles had earlier stalled when a match between him and Lesnevich was first mooted, when the latter signed in December to defend against Fox again he was stunned. Since being beaten by Lesnevich, Fox had run up seven more inside the distance wins. However, he had looked suspect on a number of occasions and had been floored several times. His last contest, which had been a four-round kayo defeat of Jake LaMotta at Madison Square Garden on 14 November, had also ended in suspicious circumstances. Years later, LaMotta admitted that he had taken a dive in order to obtain himself a crack at the middleweight title.

At the end of 1947 Charles was the outstanding challenger, having twice beaten Archie Moore, the number two rated contender, Lloyd Marshall, Oakland Billy Smith, Jimmy Bivins and Fitzie Fitzpatrick since returning to action after the war. After failing to obtain better support from the national bodies, a leading Cleveland promoter, Larry Atkins, branded Charles' treatment as 'skulduggery', stating that Lesnevich had already turned down $50,000 to meet him and was running scared. Bearing that in mind, and presumed to have been supported by the Cleveland Boxing Commission, Atkins billed a contest between Charles and Moore at The Arena, Cleveland, Ohio on 13 January 1948 as being for the 'world title'. In a contest set for 15 rounds Charles knocked out Moore inside eight rounds, but on getting nowhere with Lesnevich he would concentrate on the heavyweight division from thereon in.

5 March 1948. Gus Lesnevich w co 1 (15) Billy Fox.
Venue: Madison Square Garden, Manhattan, NYC, New York, USA. **Recognition:** World. **Referee:** Frank Fullam.
Fight Summary: Regardless of the fact that Lesnevich (175) was having difficulty making the weight he was still far too good for the hapless Fox (172¼), who had been given a title shot despite having already been beaten by him just over a year earlier. This time round Lesnevich took just 118 seconds to finish Fox off. Dropped three times by

clubbing right hands to the jaw, the final knockdown saw Fox counted out after making a big effort to get to his feet in time before toppling over again.

26 July 1948. Freddie Mills w pts 15 Gus Lesnevich.
Venue: White City Stadium, Shepherds Bush, London, England. **Recognition:** World. **Referee:** Teddy Waltham.
Fight Summary: A return contest that lacked the thrills and sparkle of the first fight saw Mills (171½) take the referee's decision by a very close margin. Nat Fleischer, of *The Ring* magazine, felt that Mills had won by a point under the British system of scoring, while stating that had the fight taken place under NYSAC Rules in America the champion would have retained his crown. There was far less action than before, but the two knockdowns that Lesnevich (174¾) suffered in the tenth round and Mills' fast finish were the deciding factors. Lesnevich was severely handicapped from the opening session onwards after being cut over both eyes, and the extra problems of making the weight ultimately took the sheen off his performance.

With Mills contracted to fight South Africa's Johnny Ralph in November for the right to meet the British and British Empire heavyweight champion, Bruce Woodcock, during the following summer, the NBA set up an eliminating contest between Joey Maxim and Lesnevich to decide his next opponent. Billed for the American title, Maxim outpointed Lesnevich over 15 rounds at The Garden, Cincinnati, Ohio on 23 May 1949, which was followed by the London promoter, Jack Solomons, provisionally booking the winner to meet Mills early in 1950.

Having been a pro since 1941, Maxim had run up 87 fights, losing 16 mainly against heavyweights, and had recently lost a 15-round split decision to Ezzard Charles in a heavyweight elimination tournament. With wins over Lee Oma, Nate Bolden (twice), Red Burman, Lou Brooks (twice), Curtis Sheppard (twice), Buddy Scott, Buddy Walker (twice), Ralph DeJohn, Phil Muscato (twice), Jersey Joe Walcott, Jimmy Webb, Bob Foxworth, Olle Tandberg, Tony Bosnich, Joe Kahut (twice), Bob Satterfield, Jimmy Bivins and Pat McCafferty, he was certainly ready. Although Maxim had beaten Foxworth, the latter was lying second in *The Ring* magazine ratings until being forced to retire with a detached retina, his last contest being a stoppage win over Leonard Morrow inside four rounds on 1 September. In a brief career of 23 bouts, losing three, Foxworth had knocked out or stopped Satterfield, Johnny Colan (twice), Fitzie Fitzpatrick, Enrico Bertola and Morrow.

Another meteoric rise saw Sylvester Perkins jump into the number two spot in the November ratings after beating Tommy Yarosz and McCafferty, but following a points defeat at the hands of Bert Lytell he dropped out of the rankings as quickly as he had entered them.

24 January 1950. Joey Maxim w co 10 (15) Freddie Mills.
Venue: Exhibition Centre, Earls Court, London, England. **Recognition:** World. **Referee:** Andrew Smyth.
Fight Summary: Starting fast, Mills (171½) nearly had his challenger over when landing a heavy overarm right to the jaw in the opening round but was unable to press home the advantage. Although Mills was still dangerous in the second, come the third Maxim (174¼) was beginning to take control, his straight left and knowledge on the inside taking him to the front. With the fight going against him Mills made a final attempt to knock his man out in the eighth, but the American's speed and extra class saw him through the session. After getting back to business in the ninth, when Maxim began to unload in the tenth a left-right to the chin eventually sent Mills crashing down to be counted out on the 1.54 mark. So hard was the finishing blow that four of Mills' teeth were embedded in his gum shield.

After winning the title, Maxim spent the next 12 months up among the heavyweights before being brought to task in January 1951 by the NBA, who ordered him to defend by 31 March against Bob Murphy, Bob Satterfield or Archie Moore. By the end of March, Maxim, who was by now contracted to challenge Ezzard Charles for the American version of the heavyweight title on 30 May, was also booked to meet Satterfield in the same town on 27 June. However, because of the beating he received at the hands of Charles (l pts 15 at the Stadium, Chicago, Illinois), Maxim agreed a postponement of the Satterfield fight with the International Boxing Club, who would later substitute Murphy for Satterfield and Chicago for New York, leaving Satterfield on the back burner and the victim of a fight that never happened.

An out-and-out two-fisted slugger, Murphy was at number three in *The Ring* magazine ratings having beaten 60 of 66 opponents (54 inside the distance). Although he had been outpointed by Harry Matthews who was one place above him in the rankings, he had beaten Milo Savage, Eddie Cotton, Lloyd Marshall, Dave Whitlock (twice), Dick Wagner, Jimmy Beau, Henry Brimm, Dan Bucceroni, Cecil Hudson, Danny Nardico and Jake LaMotta, and would be 5-12 favourite going into the bout.

22 August 1951. Joey Maxim w pts 15 Bob Murphy.
Venue: Madison Square Garden, Manhattan, NYC, New York, USA. **Recognition:** World. **Referee:** Ruby Goldstein.
Scorecards: 10-3-2, 10-5, 10-5.
Fight Summary: Favoured by many to become the new champion, the hard-punching Murphy (174½) was outboxed in every round bar the opener when he staggered the champion with a long left hook. Stabbing out the left jab almost endlessly into Murphy's face Maxim (173½) was the master of the situation, and by the eighth the challenger's right eye was closed shut. Tied up at close range where he was expected to be at his best, although Murphy was on the end of a boxing lesson throughout he never gave up and was never floored.

The collapse of a proposed Maxim v Don Cockell fight, due to the latter's defeat at the hands of the unheralded Jimmy Slade, saw the champion under a lot of pressure to finally defend against Archie Moore. Harry Matthews was another option, but he refused to meet Maxim in New York. Unsurprisingly, Moore, who was considered a non-drawing card according to Maxim's management, was shunted sideways yet again to allow for a big-money fight against Sugar Ray Robinson, the world middleweight champion.

While Matthews remained among the top-rung of challengers until May 1953, following a win over Rex Layne and a forthcoming heavyweight title eliminator against Rocky Marciano to all intents and purposes he was fighting in the latter weight class from June 1952 onwards.

25 June 1952. Joey Maxim w rtd 13 (15) Sugar Ray Robinson.
Venue: Yankee Stadium, Bronx, NYC, New York, USA. **Recognition:** World. **Referee:** Ruby Goldstein.
Fight Summary: Setting a tremendous pace the world middleweight champion was the master of Maxim (173) from the opening bell right up until the 11th round when tiredness took over. Even the referee had to be replaced (by Ray Miller) and then treated after the ninth round, having been exhausted by the heat. It was noticeable in the 11th that Robinson (157½) was suffering when he began to stumble. The next two sessions saw much of the same as Robinson struggled with the heat, and at one stage in the 13th he fell flat on his face after missing with a punch. Miles in front on the cards by dint of accurate left jabs, hooks and right crosses, Robinson was retired on his stool at the end of the 13th, having failed in his attempt to become a three-time world champion at different weights.

With the British promoter, Jack Solomons, looking to match Maxim against Randy Turpin, who had stopped Don Cockell inside 11 rounds at the White City Stadium, Shepherds Bush, London on 10 June to win the British and British Empire titles, the NYSAC stated that Maxim should meet Archie Moore, a pro for 16 years, before all else. That was rich coming from a body, which along with the NBA, had ignored the persistent claims of Moore, who had, within reason, been rated by *The Ring* magazine as the division's leading contender for seven years. However, at that point the NYSAC did not have access to the contractual arrangements between Solomons and Jack Kearns, Maxim's manager.

Having decided he could make more money by fighting Robinson again or Jake LaMotta, Maxim decided to give Turpin a miss. This decision was then followed by Maxim being suspended by the NYSAC in September for his failure to honour a contract made with Solomons, which called for him to meet the winner of Turpin v Cockell. At the beginning of September the NBA ordered Maxim to fight Moore within 60 days with the winner to meet Turpin within 90 days. Just days prior to Maxim v Moore, the New York Commission lifted the champion's suspension when Turpin announced that he had relinquished his British light heavyweight crown in order to concentrate on regaining the world middleweight title.

17 December 1952. Archie Moore w pts 15 Joey Maxim.
Venue: The Arena, St Louis, Missouri, USA. **Recognition:** World. **Referee:** Harry Kessler.

Scorecards: 76-74, 82-58, 87-63.
Fight Summary: The number one challenger for several years Moore (172½) finally got his opportunity, taking it with both hands when outscoring the champion by a wide margin. Although the referee's scorecard was much closer than those of the two judges, apart from the opening six rounds when he was well in the fight Maxim (174½) ran second best from thereon in. It was the body punishment dished out by Moore, especially in the second and tenth rounds that won the fight for him. While there were no knockdowns Maxim was forced to take plenty of punishment, and several times he was on the verge of going down. At the age of 39, and after 166 fights and almost 17 years in the ring, Moore had finally become the champion of all he surveyed.

24 June 1953. Archie Moore w pts 15 Joey Maxim.
Venue: Municipal Stadium, Ogden, Utah, USA. **Recognition:** World. **Referee:** Ray Miller.
Scorecards: 7-6-2, 8-7, 8-5-2.
Fight Summary: Starting positively in what was a return match Maxim (175) was in front by the eighth round, jabbing and moving well, but from then on to the 13th the champion came back strongly. As Maxim tired from the body assaults he was forced to hang on as Moore (173¾) got himself back in the fight. Realising he needed to win the final two sessions Maxim hurt Moore with a couple of solid blows to the jaw, but it was the latter who stayed on to retain his title by a unanimous, if relatively narrow margin.

In the aftermath of Moore's second victory over Maxim, the champion said he would be off to the Argentine to honour a couple of non-title commitments before thinking of his next defence. However, that did not stop Maxim's manager, Jack Kearns, sitting down with Moore's people to discuss a return.

At an NBA convention in September the Association turned down Kearns' request that Maxim be named as the leading challenger on the grounds that they recognised Harold Johnson as the next man in line, providing that he met an obligation to box in Wisconsin, which he did on 7 November. Regardless of the edict, Moore would make another defence against Maxim.

27 January 1954. Archie Moore w pts 15 Joey Maxim.
Venue: Orange Bowl, Miami, Florida, USA. **Recognition:** World. **Referee:** Cy Gottfried.
Scorecards: 145-137, 148-135, 148-134.
Fight Summary: The third fight between the pair saw the champion exert his authority over Maxim (174¼) when twice dropping him for counts of 'eight' in the eighth and 'seven' in the 11th. This time round, despite having difficulty in making the weight Moore (175) controlled the fight, wearing Maxim down with solid body blows and bringing up hooks and uppercuts for good measure. Even though Maxim was under the cosh on several occasions, Moore had to be satisfied with a clear points victory. Maxim had given of his best, but it had not been enough.

With pressure being exerted on Moore to defend against the number one challenger, Harold Johnson, by the NYSAC, NBA and World Boxing Commission (WBC), the bout was scheduled for some time in June prior to it being switched to 11 August. A pro since 1946 Johnson had clocked up 51 fights, winning 46 of them, and in four meetings with Moore he had won once. Men he had beaten included Arturo Godoy, Henry Hall (three times), Jimmy Bivins, Bert Lytell, Chuck Hunter, Chubby Wright (twice), Clarence Henry, Leonard Morrow, Bob Satterfield, Niño Valdés, Jimmy Slade (twice), Ezzard Charles, Charley Doc Williams and Paul Andrews, all good fighters. When Johnson was knocked out inside three rounds by Jersey Joe Walcott in 1950 the latter created a bit of a record, having stopped Harold's father, Phil, also in three rounds, in 1936.

11 August 1954. Archie Moore w rsc 14 (15) Harold Johnson.
Venue: Madison Square Garden, Manhattan, NYC, New York, USA. **Recognition:** World. **Referee:** Ruby Goldstein.
Fight Summary: Right up to the finish the contest had been closely fought with both men boxing well and cleverly negating each other's work at times. In the tenth round Johnson (172½) had Moore (173) down from a right to the jaw for 'four', the champion being angry when the referee counted on to 'eight' which was contrary to the rules at the time. Realising he could be behind in the scoring and despite tiring Moore began to go up a gear in the 13th before finally catching up with Johnson in the following session. After feinting Johnson into position, Moore smashed home a left-right-left combination to the jaw to put his challenger on the floor. Although he was up at

'six' again the referee counted to 'eight' before allowing the contest to continue. But within moments of the resumption when it was clear that Johnson, who was being hammered from head to body without return, was in serious trouble the fight was halted on the 56 second mark.

Fast running out of opposition in his own division, Moore looked towards the heavyweights and a big-money fight against world heavyweight champion, Rocky Marciano. After eliminating Nino Valdes he moved in that direction, while his next title defence would be against the middleweight champion, Carl Bobo Olson, who had outpointed Joey Maxim over ten rounds at the Cow Palace, San Francisco, California on 13 April 1955 to gain his opportunity in a higher weight class. Alarmingly, prior to the Valdes fight Moore was temporarily suspended by the Californian Boxing Commission due to an alleged organic heart condition which ultimately proved negative.

Despite losing to Moore, Johnson was still seen by *The Ring* magazine as the top-rated challenger for the title. It was therefore a bit of a shock when he was knocked out inside two rounds at The Arena, Philadelphia, Pennsylvania by Oakland Billy Smith on 8 October in a stunning upset. A hard-hitting veteran who had been a pro since 1941, when Smith failed to build on his new status, having lost two out of three, he retired.

22 June 1955. Archie Moore w co 3 (15) Carl Bobo Olson.
Venue: Polo Grounds, Manhattan, NYC, New York, USA. **Recognition:** World. **Referee:** Ruby Goldstein.
Fight Summary: Defending his title against the world middleweight champion, Moore (175) ultimately proved to be too powerful and too good for the naturally lighter man. The opening two rounds saw Olson (170¼) moving around Moore and stabbing out the left jab before banging away inside. But towards the end of the second Moore had started to work the body, and in the third he made his move. Although the session started quietly, with both men probing, on the 1.19 mark Olson had been counted out after taking a solid straight right to the face that was followed by two crunching left hooks to the jaw.

Following the fight, Moore took time out from the light heavies to make an unsuccessful challenge for Rocky Marciano's heavyweight title on 21 September, losing by a ninth-round knock-out at the Yankee Stadium, Bronx, NYC, New York, before announcing that he would be defending his championship in Britain against Yolande Pompey on 13 March 1956. However, whether that was a ruse to keep the commissions off his back is unclear, but a number of excuses and a reluctance to make that date saw the fight eventually put back to June.

Since arriving in England from his native Trinidad in 1951, Pompey had proved a difficult man to beat, being tough and aggressive with no mean skill. In 36 contests prior to meeting Moore he had run up 31 wins, beating men of the calibre of Dave Sands, which was an incredible win for him, Mel Brown, Ray Barnes, Jimmy King, Arthur Howard, Polly Smith and Yvon Durelle. He had also reversed the two defeats on his record against Bobby Dawson and Moses Ward, as well as going one better against Gentle Daniel and Jimmy Slade, two of the three men he had drawn with.

5 June 1956. Archie Moore w rsc 10 (15) Yolande Pompey.
Venue: The Arena, Harringay, London, England. **Recognition:** World. **Referee:** Jack Hart.
Fight Summary: Having taken 32lbs off in just over three weeks it was clear that the champion would have to conserve as much energy as he could, something that would have explained his slow start against Pompey (171¼). By the end of the seventh Pompey was well in front and boxing well, but by the end of the eighth Moore (174½) was beginning to get going. The round ended with him cornering and hurting the challenger. Pompey was now cut on the left eye, and having taken a battering in the ninth he walked back to his corner with his right eye swollen. Moore was soon at work in the tenth. After dropping Pompey for counts of 'eight', 'nine' and 'eight' from heavy rights and lefts to the head, the latter was not fighting back when the referee rescued him with 2.50 on the clock.

After eliminating Nino Valdes and James J. Parker to become the number one contender for the heavyweight title, following Rocky Marciano's retirement Moore was matched against Floyd Patterson to decide the new champion. When Moore was knocked out in the fifth round at The Stadium, Chicago, Illinois on 30 November it was back to the light heavies for him.

At the beginning of 1957, the top-rated man in *The Ring* magazine ratings at that time was Gerhard Hecht, Germany's European champion. That situation changed on 25 January 1957 when Pompey knocked him out inside two rounds at the Sports Palace, Berlin, Germany in what was seen as another eliminator. The World Championship Committee were then asked to adjudicate on behalf of Pompey, but before they reached a conclusion he lost on points over ten rounds to Willi Hoepner at the Ernst Merck Hall, Hamburg, Germany on 10 May 1957.

Despite Moore again looking to fight on his own terms it was announced in February 1957 that Chuck Spieser would be meeting Tony Anthony to decide whom he would be fighting in his next title defence. Said to satisfy both the NBA and NYSAC, after Anthony scored a third-round kayo at the Olympia Stadium, Detroit, Michigan on 5 April 1957 he went forward to face Moore.

With an over-the-weight Moore in Germany, booked to fight a heavyweight in June 1957 with no intention of meeting Anthony, in his absence Anthony drew over ten rounds at the Olympia Stadium, Detroit on 14 June 1957 with the soon to be crowned British Empire champion, Yvon Durelle. Surprisingly, the Canadian was completely ignored by the World Championship Committee when they met two days later and decided that Moore must sign to meet Anthony by 7 July 1957 or be stripped. The Committee went on to say that in the event of Moore failing to agree to a fight against Anthony, a match between the latter and either Pompey or Harold Johnson would be considered for the vacant title. Even though Moore had still to sign up for Anthony, having broken the deadline, while the NBA stated that they were prepared to give him another week the World Boxing Committee declared the title vacant. The Committee then had a change of heart after Moore signed for 20 September 1957, but right up to the day of the fight it was rumoured that he would never make the required weight.

20 September 1957. Archie Moore w co 7 (15) Tony Anthony.
Venue: Olympic Auditorium, Los Angeles, California, USA. **Recognition:** World. **Referee:** Mushy Callahan.
Fight Summary: Clearly having difficulty making 175lbs, taking three attempts to do so, when the champion started slowly, with the cross-armed defence that he had become associated with, the opening three rounds saw Anthony (172) jabbing out the left but doing little else. By the fifth Moore (175) had begun to go to work, mixing up the jab with bobbing and weaving on the inside, and in the sixth Anthony shipped plenty of punishment before being on the floor when the bell rang. Although tearing out of his corner showing plenty of fight at the start of the seventh, with Anthony soon on the defensive he was eventually counted out at 2.29 of the session after being dropped by a terrific right to the head.

When Moore asked for a $33,000 guarantee from any man wishing to challenge for his title, bearing in mind the fact that he had already beaten his two leading contenders, Harold Johnson and Anthony, who had stopped the third-rated Yvon Durelle inside seven rounds at Madison Square Garden, Manhattan, NYC, New York on 14 March 1958, it was anyone's guess as to who would be selected as his next opponent. What also did not help was the weakness of the commissions, especially the NBA, who were trying to force Moore into accepting Johnson as his next defence despite being powerless to do so legally unless it suited the champion's time frame.

Following an eight-round retirement victory over South Africa's Mike Holt at the Forum, Montreal, Canada on 16 July 1958 it appeared that Durelle, who successfully defended his British Empire title on the result, was the favourite to get the next crack at the title. Confirmation that the fight had been made came at the end of September 1958.

10 December 1958. Archie Moore w co 11 (15) Yvon Durelle.
Venue: The Forum, Montreal, Canada. **Recognition:** World. **Referee:** Jack Sharkey.
Fight Summary: Having to get off the floor three times in the opening session just a few days short of his 45th birthday, the champion proved once and for all that he should be recognised as one of the sport's top fighters. With Moore (173¾) making a great recovery several rounds went by until Durelle (172) picked it up again. When Moore was floored again from a right to the head, in the fifth, after getting to his feet at 'five' he finally began to assume control from there on. In the seventh it was Durelle's turn to be dropped, a left-right to the jaw doing the damage, and on getting up he was subjected to all manner of punches. From the eighth through to the tenth

Durelle had almost become a punch-bag as Moore hit him with everything he had. Saved by the bell at the end of the tenth, having taken an 'eight' count, after Durelle came out for the 11th he was soon on the floor again, this time for 'nine'. Back on his feet, with blood pouring from his nose, Durelle was smashed to the floor by solid lefts and rights to the head and counted out after 49 seconds.

Despite all the talk about Moore meeting Sugar Ray Robinson he could see the sense in taking on Durelle again, especially on a financial front, and at the back end of March 1959 a deal was finally struck with a return clause in place if the champion lost. Scheduled to take place on 15 July 1959, it was postponed on the eve of the fight after Moore bruised a heel in training before being re-scheduled.

12 August 1959. Archie Moore w co 3 (15) Yvon Durelle.
Venue: The Forum, Montreal, Canada. **Recognition:** World. **Referee:** Jack Sharkey.
Fight Summary: A return match, this time around the champion gave Durelle (173) no real opportunities when boxing in a crab-like fashion and giving the Canadian no room to target. Even then Moore (174¼) was forced to take some heavy blows to get his own shots off, and in the third he went after Durelle with a vengeance. After a tremendous right to the chin had Durelle down for 'seven', on getting up he went straight on the attack only to be dropped three more times from heavy rights and lefts, the final knockdown seeing him counted out with eight seconds of the session remaining.

When Moore forfeited NBA recognition on 25 October 1960, having not made a defence for more than a year, the Association had initially planned an elimination series involving Erich Schoppner v Chic Calderwood and Harold Johnson v Willie Pastrano. However, with Schoppner more intent on a match with Moore, Calderwood pulling out through injury and then Pastrano being outpointed over ten rounds by Jesse Bowdry at The Auditorium, Miami Beach, Florida on 27 December 1960, a straight NBA title bout between Johnson and Bowdry was the next best option.

Moore's reaction was that as he had agreed to meet Schoppner in a title defence in July 1960 it was not his fault the promoters had failed to make it happen. Moore's comments came after he had withdrawn due to his wife's illness and the promoters had lost interest. Having lost an overweight match to Giulio Rinaldi (l pts 10 at the Sports Palace, Rome, Italy on 29 October 1960), Moore stated that as far as he was concerned he could defend his version of the title against Schoppner, Rinaldi or Calderwood. Given until 11 January 1961 by the NYSAC to make a defence a tentative agreement for Moore to meet Schoppner was put in place for 21 March 1961, but Moore ruined those plans by requesting a postponement until 27 May 1961 to allow him time to make the weight. Surprisingly, with Schoppner unable to come to an agreement with the promoters due to Moore wanting too much, instead of stripping Moore the NYSAC gave him until the end of February 1961 to make a match with Rinaldi.

Rated the number two contender by *The Ring* magazine, Rinaldi was seen as a strong, durable and solid puncher even if he was lacking in the fine arts. Having beaten Artenio Calzavara (the former European champion), Rocco Mazzola, Santo Amonti, Germinal Ballarin, Donnie Fleeman, Johnny Halafihi, Sonny Ray, Freddie Mack and Sixto Rodriguez, as well as Moore, Rinaldi was expected to go close.

7 February 1961. Harold Johnson w rsc 9 (15) Jesse Bowdry.
Venue: Convention Hall, Miami, Florida, USA. **Recognition:** NBA. **Referee:** Cy Gottfried.
Fight Summary: Fighting for the vacant NBA title, Johnson (172) finally became a champion when stopping Bowdry (173) after 45 seconds of round nine when the latter's corner threw the towel in and the referee concurred. Johnson, boxing in classical mode, had too much for the bobbing and weaving Bowdry, knocking him down for the first time in round six following a short right to the jaw. Having taken an 'eight' count, Bowdry weathered the seventh before being dropped again by a similar punch in the eighth. This time he was saved by the bell. Somehow making it for the start of the ninth, Bowdry took two more counts before being rescued.

24 April 1961. Harold Johnson w rsc 2 (15) Von Clay.
Venue: The Arena, Philadelphia, Pennsylvania, USA. **Recognition:** NBA. **Referee:** David Beloff.

Fight Summary: Making his first defence Johnson (174) did not waste much time in going after Clay (175), soon having the latter in trouble when a right to the head had him face down with his chin on the bottom strand at the bell. Picking up where he left off Johnson stormed into Clay in the second, and after being dropped three times the challenger was stopped on the 2.23 mark under the 'three knockdowns in a round' ruling in Pennsylvania. It took Clay almost five minutes before he was able to get up unattended.

10 June 1961. Archie Moore w pts 15 Giulio Rinaldi.
Venue: Madison Square Garden, Manhattan, NYC, New York, USA. **Recognition:** EBU/NY. **Referee:** Ruby Goldstein.
Scorecards: 11-3-1, 11-4, 9-5-1.
Fight Summary: Although Rinaldi (173¾) was in the fight for three or four rounds, thereafter floundering and incapable of working the champion out, he ended the fight bleeding from both eyes along with nose and mouth injuries. Moore (174½) was a clear winner, but having failed to hurt Rinaldi had the Italian been more adventurous the result might have been different. Once again weight-making problems were blamed on the champion's sluggish performance and lack of zip in his punches.

Moore forfeited NY/EBU recognition in February 1962 for failing to defend against either Harold Johnson or Doug Jones.

29 August 1961. Harold Johnson w pts 15 Eddie Cotton.
Venue: Sick's Stadium, Seattle, Washington, USA. **Recognition:** NBA. **Referee:** Jimmy Rondeau.
Scorecards: 147-145, 147-145, 144-148.
Fight Summary: While Cotton (170) gave the champion plenty of problems, once his left eye was badly damaged in the seventh and he was cut on the right eye a round later his options became limited. With both men good defensively the battle was fought at a fast pace, Johnson (173) carrying the harder punch of the two. While there were no knockdowns, and little sign of one occurring, the fight was decided by Johnson's strong finish over the final five rounds.

Although Johnson remained idle while waiting to accommodate Archie Moore, following the NYSAC taking the latter's title away in February 1962 it was announced that the winner of Johnson v Doug Jones would be recognised by them as the champion. Almost immediately a match was made for May 1962.

12 May 1962. Harold Johnson w pts 15 Doug Jones.
Venue: The Arena, Philadelphia, Pennsylvania, USA. **Recognition:** World. **Referee:** David Beloff.
Scorecards: 74-61, 73-64, 71-63.
Fight Summary: In a battle to unify the title, Johnson (171½), the NBA champion, proved a bit too experienced for Jones (171½), his left hand keeping the latter at bay for much of the time. In control from the fifth onwards Johnson made a big effort to stop Jones in the 11th, throwing right after right, but with the latter not budging when the bell rang the pair continued to fight on. Thereafter, Johnson went back to his tried and trusted left jab, outboxing the younger man through to the final bell when bringing him on to punches.

23 June 1962. Harold Johnson w pts 15 Gustav Scholz.
Venue: Olympic Stadium, Berlin, Germany. **Recognition:** World. **Referee:** Ike Powell.
Scorecards: 73-70, 72-64, 72-70.
Fight Summary: Fighting outside America for the first time the champion was up against a very experienced southpaw in Scholz (171), who gave him plenty of trouble in what turned into a gruelling fight. Although Johnson (172½) took an early lead Scholz was never far behind. Having been hurt by a right to the jaw in the sixth, Scholz came back strongly in the tenth with a left-right to the head to stagger his rival. Scholz looked like being stopped in the final session when suffering a badly gashed left eyebrow, but he was allowed to continue to the relief of his camp.

Following his win over Scholz the authorities were looking for Johnson's next defence to be against the number one contender, Mauro Mina. After Mina beat Eddie Cotton (w pts 10 at the National Stadium, Lima, Peru on 18 January 1963), the way was clear for the match to be made. Unfortunately, within a matter of weeks of the announcement that Johnson would be meeting Mina in Nevada on 4 May 1963 it was reported that Mina had an arthritic right hand, as well as a serious eye problem, and was out of the fight. It was then announced that Henry Hank would replace Mina, the date being shifted to 1 June 1963, but before anyone could hold their breath Hank suffered a fractured cheekbone in training. Following that, Willie Pastrano, having beaten Wayne Thornton (w pts 10 at the Convention Centre, Las Vegas, Nevada on 4 May 1963), was quickly drafted in.

Known as 'Willie the Wisp' for his movement around the ring, his hand-speed and ability to avoid punches coming his way, Pastrano had turned pro at 16 as a welterweight and had boxed for long periods as a heavyweight. Not even rated when he got the call, Pastrano had won 57 of 76 contests, beating the likes of Jimmy Martinez (twice), Jacques Royer-Crecy, Bobby Dykes, Al Andrews, Joey Maxim, Chuck Spieser (twice), Paddy Young, Rex Layne, Pat McMurtry, Charley Norkus, John Holman, Dick Richardson, Willi Besmanoff, Brian London, Joe Bygraves, Franco Cavicchi, Jerry Luedee, Alonzo Johnson, Sonny Ray, Tom McNeeley and Thornton.

1 June 1963. Willie Pastrano w pts 15 Harold Johnson.
Venue: Convention Centre, Las Vegas, Nevada, USA. **Recognition:** World. **Referee:** Jim Olivas.
Scorecards: 69-68, 69-67, 68-69.
Fight Summary: Having spent most of his career fighting heavyweights, with Pastrano (174) making the most of his opportunity the split decision in his favour saw him finally become a champion. For the entire contest Pastrano jabbed and moved while the counter-punching Johnson (173½) failed to take the fight to his challenger. On two occasions, in the fifth and 13th, the harder-punching Johnson had Pastrano at his mercy after landing heavy rights to the jaw, but when he failed to follow up the latter was able to recover. It was the higher work-rate that won the fight for Pastrano, and at the finish he was unmarked while Johnson had a badly swollen nose and damage to his left eye.

At the beginning of August when Pastrano refused to meet Henry Hank (now fully fit), the Michigan Boxing Federation decided to hold their own version of the championship, bringing in a leading contender, Eddie Cotton, to face the local man. Hank, who had been a pro since 1953, had won 56 of 76 bouts and had never ducked anyone, beating Charley Cotton (twice), Rudy Ellis (twice), Jimmy Beecham, Charley Joseph, Willie Vaughn, Neal Rivers (twice), Holly Mims, George Benton, Jesse Bowdry (twice), Sixto Rodriguez (twice), Rory Calhoun, Victor Zalazar, Hank Casey, Randy Sandy, Joey Giardello, Chic Calderwood, Allan Harmon and Jimmy Ellis, prior to winning the Michigan State title in his last contest.

Meanwhile, Pastrano took in three non-title bouts, losing to Gregorio Peralta on points over ten rounds at The Auditorium, Miami, Florida on 20 September in one of them.

In January 1964, Angelo Dundee, Pastrano's manager, was reported to be negotiating a title fight against Peru's Mauro Mina, who had come through a successful detached retina operation and had been given the all-clear by the doctors. With the prospect of that fight coming off quickly not seeming too good a few weeks later, following pressure from the authorities to defend or be stripped, Pastrano signed for a defence against Peralta. For Mina it was almost the end of the line, and having lost to Peralta he had just five more contests before bowing out of boxing after beating the future European champion, Piero Del Papa, on 5 November 1965.

29 October 1963. Eddie Cotton w pts 15 Henry Hank.
Venue: IMA Auditorium, Flint, Michigan, USA. **Recognition:** Michigan. **Referee:** Jack Stein.
Scorecards: 146-140, 148-147, 146-140.
Fight Summary: Fighting for the vacant Michigan version of the title, Cotton (172½) used his longer reach to keep Hank (175) continually at bay when stabbing out the left jab. Hank, a heavy hitter, seemed to have no answer to the punch as every time he got set he found himself unbalanced by the jab. There were no knockdowns, although Cotton, who finished with a cut left eye, was shaken up a couple of times. While Cotton concentrated on the jab his rights to the body were also effective, and despite a late charge by Hank the veteran just about deserved the win. Under Michigan rules this contest had a break of 90 seconds instead of the normal 60 between rounds.

Cotton forfeited Michigan recognition after a ten-rounds split decision defeat at the hands of Johnny Persol at Madison Square Garden, Manhattan, NYC, New York on 21 February 1964.

10 April 1964. Willie Pastrano w rsc 6 (15) Gregorio Peralta.
Venue: Municipal Auditorium, New Orleans, Louisiana, USA. **Recognition:** World. **Referee:** Pete Giarusso.
Fight Summary: In what was a thrilling bout from start to finish the challenger was stopped at the start of the sixth round after sustaining a long gash on the left eyelid that had come about following a long right to the head in the fourth. Peralta (174¾) was aggressive right from the first bell, especially with body punches, but Pastrano (174¾) was always alert and showing much cleverness, scoring well with crisp blows from either hand. With the fifth session being Peralta's best as he began to slow Pastrano down with solid blows to the body, the Argentine was shocked when the referee waited for the sixth to start before stopping the contest. Nat Fleischer, the editor of *The Ring* magazine, had Pastrano 3-2 ahead at the finish.

Having safely come through his first defence, Pastrano announced that he would fight anyone of the top-rated men as long as the money was right. With that in mind, at the end of June Gustav Scholz flew to America to negotiate a title bout in Germany for September or October, but on failing to get a contract went back to Germany to defend his European title against Giulio Rinaldi. Another man waiting in the wings was the former world middleweight champion, Terry Downes, and towards the end of August it was reported that Harry Levene, the English promoter, had clinched a fight between him and Pastrano for 28 September. The date was later moved on to 30 November to allow the champion more time to recover from a haemorrhoid operation.

30 November 1964. Willie Pastrano w rsc 11 (15) Terry Downes.
Venue: Belle Vue, Manchester, England. **Recognition:** World. **Referee:** Andrew Smyth.
Fight Summary: Given an opportunity to contest the title from out of the blue the former middleweight champion, Downes (171), giving it everything was thought to be ahead at the start of the 11th. Always on the front foot and always working despite being puzzled by the movement of Pastrano (174¾), the Englishman kept up the attack. It all went horribly wrong for Downes, however, in the 11th when Pastrano came off his stool quickly to drop him for an 'eight' count following a right to the head. Back in action Downes was under immediate pressure, and after being hit with lefts and rights and unable to fight back he was dropped again, at which point the referee stopped the contest. The time of the stoppage was announced as being 1.17.

Pastrano's next challenger would be Jose Torres, who beat the former middleweight champion, Carl Bobo Olson (w co 1 at Madison Square Garden, Manhattan, NYC, New York on 27 November), in what was an eliminating contest. Prior to the fight, Teddy Brenner, the Madison Square Garden matchmaker, had announced that the winner would probably meet Pastrano on 1 March 1965.

30 March 1965. Jose Torres w rsc 9 (15) Willie Pastrano.
Venue: Madison Square Garden, Manhattan, NYC, New York, USA. **Recognition:** World. **Referee:** John LoBianco.
Fight Summary: Taking command right from the start Torres (171¼) hurt Pastrano (174½) with heavy left hooks to the head in the opening two rounds, while continually bemusing him with his bobbing-and-weaving tactics. Pastrano seemed to have no answer to the challenger's attacks, a left hook to the body putting him down in the sixth for the first time in his career. From there onwards it was just a matter of time, and after damage to his left eye worsened in the eighth Pastrano was stopped at the end of the ninth, seemingly having co-ordination problems.

Hospitalised in San Juan, Puerto Rico after suffering a pancreas ailment in August, Torres was suspended by the NYSAC. He was then told that he would not be required to make a defence for six months, dependant on medical reports. Signed off at the end of February 1966, he began training to meet either Wayne Thornton or Roger Rouse.

21 May 1966. Jose Torres w pts 15 Wayne Thornton.
Venue: Shea Stadium, Queens, NYC, New York, USA. **Recognition:** World. **Referee:** John LoBianco.
Scorecards: 12-2-1, 10-4-1, 10-4-1.

Fight Summary: Dropped twice in the first round with solid left hooks, the challenger somehow kept going despite being cut over both eyes and subjected to a bombardment of punches from Torres (175) throughout. Badly hurt on several occasions, and looking unlikely to last out the contest, Thornton (174) was warned repeatedly by the referee to stop wrestling and to start fighting. The fight was as one-sided as you could get, and while Thornton managed to last the distance he spent the night in hospital recovering from the battering to the body he had been forced to endure. In the aftermath, Torres claimed that he would have stopped Thornton had he not had blurred vision up until the tenth session.

15 August 1966. Jose Torres w pts 15 Eddie Cotton.
Venue: Convention Centre, Las Vegas, Nevada, USA. **Recognition:** World. **Referee:** Nate Morgan.
Scorecards: 70-67, 68-67, 69-67.
Fight Summary: After taking the opening two rounds when hurting Cotton (173½) with heavy body shots, Torres (173) was outboxed from the fourth to the eighth as the veteran challenger got his left jab going. Cotton also did well with solid rights to the body before tiring and letting Torres back in the fight. Having been deducted a point for going low in the tenth, Cotton came right back to put Torres on the defensive for the next couple of sessions. With two rounds to go Torres at last opened up to make sure of the verdict, but it had been a close call.

15 October 1966. Jose Torres w co 2 (15) Chic Calderwood.
Venue: Hiram Bithorn Stadium, San Juan, Puerto Rico. **Recognition:** World. **Referee:** Teddy Martin.
Fight Summary: Getting a crack at the title after several years of waiting Calderwood (175) made a reasonable start, as did the champion, and there were no early signs of what was to come. The second round began in much the same fashion, but once Torres (175) had thrown a tremendous right over the top of Calderwood's guard the fight was over when the latter crashed to the floor to be counted out on the 2.06 mark.

16 December 1966. Dick Tiger w pts 15 Jose Torres.
Venue: Madison Square Garden, Manhattan, NYC, New York, USA. **Recognition:** World. **Referee:** John LoBianco.
Scorecards: 10-5, 8-6, 10-4.
Fight Summary: Having recently lost his world middleweight title, when Tiger (167) was given an immediate crack at Torres (175) he took the opportunity with both hands. Right from the opening bell Tiger charged into Torres with both hands banging away, slamming in heavy punches when close up and managing to make Torres miss on any number of occasions. Listless in the middle rounds, Torres started to get going thereafter, but left his finish too late as Tiger pressed on relentlessly to deservedly take the title. After the fight Tiger's manager was quoted as saying "Tiger is a fighter who will follow instructions. All he had to do was bob and weave under Torres' best punches and come up with combinations to the body."

16 May 1967. Dick Tiger w pts 15 Jose Torres.
Venue: Madison Square Garden, Manhattan, NYC, New York, USA. **Recognition:** World. **Referee:** Harold Valan.
Scorecards: 8-7, 8-7, 7-8.
Fight Summary: This, a return contest, saw the challenger starting well when scoring with solid blows to the head while Tiger (167) concentrated on the body, and in the third round both men let their punches go and both were staggered. The fight followed a similar pattern as their previous go, but this time around with Torres (167) being more effective it was much closer. Following the decision there was a riot as Torres' partisan fans began throwing chairs and bottles towards the ring after their man failed to regain the title. Even Torres thought he had won, stating that he would seriously think about retiring.

17 November 1967. Dick Tiger w rsc 12 (15) Roger Rouse.
Venue: Convention Centre, Las Vegas, Nevada, USA. **Recognition:** World. **Referee:** Jim Olivas.
Fight Summary: For four rounds the challenger held his own but thereafter, when punching with power and authority, Tiger (168¼) took over. By the fifth, with Rouse (174½) failing to use his reach advantage to good effect he was slowing as Tiger's work on the body was beginning to pay dividends. Having been hurt in the third by a heavy left hook, as the fight went on Rouse took more and more of them. In the ninth he was dropped by a left hook prior to taking another count in the tenth when floored by a right to the jaw following a body attack.

Extremely tired in the 11th Rouse made it through the bell, only to be floored in the 12th by a big right and stopped 36 seconds into the session.

Tiger's next defence would be against Bob Foster, who had taken part in 33 contests since turning pro in March 1961. A dangerous puncher, Foster had wins over Henry Hank (twice), Andres Antonio Selpa and Eddie Cotton (w rsc 3 at The Coliseum, Washington DC on 8 May), in what was effectively an eliminator with both men weighing in at 174lbs.

24 May 1968. Bob Foster w co 4 (15) Dick Tiger.
Venue: Madison Square Garden, Manhattan, NYC, New York, USA. **Recognition:** World. **Referee:** Mark Conn.
Fight Summary: Making his third defence Tiger (168) made a great start when moving inside the challenger's long arms to power in the solid shots to the body, but thereafter he found few opportunities to get close. From that point onwards Foster (173½) dictated matters with his huge reach advantage enabling him to keep Tiger at bay with left jabs, hooks and uppercuts that found their target with alacrity. Tiger was still trying to reach the body in the fourth, but without success, and when Foster evaded one of the champion's rushes a right uppercut followed by a terrific left sent him down to be counted out on the 2.05 mark.

In mid-August Foster was made an offer to defend against Roger Rouse, reportedly the biggest he'd had to date. Although refusing to put his title on the line against Rouse, Foster was quite happy to take him on in a non-title affair, winning by a five-round stoppage at The Coliseum, Washington DC on 9 September.

Meanwhile, Tiger, looking to get back in the frame, faced a young Frankie DePaula (at Madison Square Garden) on 25 October, winning on points over ten rounds in a dramatic and exciting contest in which he came close to losing. Following a record crowd for a non-title fight of more than 14,000 fans, it was the loser's management who sat down in November to negotiate a first defence for Foster. The sixth-ranked DePaula, who was obviously not the rightful challenger, was chosen because he could fill the Garden.

23 January 1969. Bob Foster w rsc 1 (15) Frankie DePaula.
Venue: Madison Square Garden, Manhattan, NYC, New York, USA. **Recognition:** World. **Referee:** John LoBianco.
Fight Summary: This one was all over at 2.17 of the first round after Foster (171½) had enforced the 'three knockdowns in a round' ruling. Having been dropped by a left to the head and a right to the body in the opening minute, Foster got up without a count and decked DePaula (173) with a right to the temple. Although DePaula was on his feet almost immediately a battery of blows to head and body had him over again, and he was put down for the final time after being measured by a series of solid left hooks and a right to the head. The unfortunate challenger had just two more fights before being gunned down in a gang fight and dying on 14 September 1970.

24 May 1969. Bob Foster w rsc 4 (15) Andy Kendall.
Venue: Eastern States Coliseum, West Springfield, Massachusetts, USA. **Recognition:** World. **Referee:** Bill Connelly.
Fight Summary: Looking to move inside the champion's long reach from the opening bell Kendall (175) was an easy mark for the long left jab, and in the second round he was cut over the left eye by a cracking uppercut. In the third Kendall charged into Foster (174), having some joy, but after trying the same tactics in the fourth he came unstuck. Angry about being butted several times Foster smashed away at Kendall, who was trapped in a corner, and eventually dropped his man heavily. With Kendall in the process of getting to his feet the referee stopped the fight, the finish being announced as 2.17.

By this time Foster was eyeing up the heavyweight division, taking in four non-title fights before being pressured into another defence by the authorities. Earlier, in July, Mike Barrett, the English promoter, announced that he had signed up Foster to meet the British Empire champion, Bob Dunlop, in Sydney before the year was out. When the fight never materialised, Dunlop, who had beaten Bobby Stininato (twice), Tony Montano, Young John McCormack, Jose Menno and Giulio Rinaldi, retired early in 1970 after being beaten by Henry Clark. Following that, Roger Rouse signed up in February 1970 to meet Foster, having already been beaten by the champion in a non-title contest. Foster was quoted as saying "Rouse should have waited until I had won the heavyweight title, as he would have been favoured to win the elimination series."

4 April 1970. Bob Foster w rsc 4 (15) Roger Rouse.
Venue: Adams Fieldhouse, Missoula, Montana, USA. **Recognition:** World. **Referee:** Lee Sala.
Fight Summary: In control from the start with the left jab paving the way, Foster (174) had too much of everything for his challenger who was under pressure and floored twice in the opening round. When Rouse (173½) received a bad cut over the left eye in the second session before being dropped again, courtesy of a solid right to the head, it was almost the end of the line for him. The third session saw much of the same, and after Rouse was put down for a fourth time, a right to the jaw doing the damage, when the bell rang to start the fourth the referee, under the doctor's orders, stopped the contest.

27 June 1970. Bob Foster w co 10 (15) Mark Tessman.
Venue: Civic Centre, Baltimore, Maryland, USA. **Recognition:** World. **Referee:** Terry Moore.
Fight Summary: An unknown quantity Tessman (170) began moving away from the champion as early as the first round, and although he occasionally scored with the left jab he was being stalked. Despite Foster (173¾) being in control for much of the time Tessman occasionally surprised him with bouts of activity, especially in the seventh when he moved in and out with stinging punches. Cut over the right eye in the eighth, instead of backing off Tessman began to pick up the fight in the ninth before Foster dropped him heavily with a left hook to the jaw in the tenth. Counted out on the two-minute mark, Tessman had nothing to be ashamed of according to *The Ring* magazine.

Having been knocked out in the second round when challenging Joe Frazier for the world heavyweight title on 18 November, at the Cobo Hall, Detroit, Michigan, Foster required more time to prepare for a 175lbs title defence. The WBC was prepared to wait but the WBA were not. After getting back into training following the Frazier fight, a few weeks later Foster signed to meet Hal Carroll.

Foster eventually forfeited WBA recognition in December for consistently failing to defend his title against top-rated contenders during the last two years. Those were the words of the WBA, who shortly afterwards announced that a match had been arranged between the two leading challengers, Jimmy Dupree and Vicente Rondon, for the Association's version of the title.

27 February 1971. Vicente Rondon w rsc 6 (15) Jimmy Dupree.
Venue: New Circus Bullring, Caracas, Venezuela. **Recognition:** WBA. **Referee:** Zach Clayton.
Fight Summary: Contesting the vacant WBA title, Dupree (173½) almost had an early win to his name when he came out for the second round swinging in punches from all angles before dropping Rondon (175) with a cracking left hook to the head. Getting to his feet Rondon somehow lasted out the final minute of the session, surprisingly coming back to trade punches in the third as if nothing had happened. The round ended with Dupree cut on the right temple. From then on Rondon took over, and in the sixth a left hook had Dupree staggering around the ring taking punches without reply before the referee stepped in on the 2.58 mark to rescue him.

2 March 1971. Bob Foster w co 4 (15) Hal Carroll.
Venue: Catholic Youth Centre, Scranton, Pennsylvania, USA. **Recognition:** WBC. **Referee:** Manny Gelb.
Fight Summary: Coming back after being knocked out by Joe Frazier in an unsuccessful challenge for the heavyweight title Foster (174) quickly imposed himself on Carroll (171½), flooring him three times in the second round before opening up a deep gash on his left eye in the third. Having great difficulty in dealing with Foster's huge reach advantage Carroll was there to be taken, and following a smashing right cross to the head he was counted out at 2.32 of the fourth.

24 April 1971. Bob Foster w pts 15 Ray Anderson.
Venue: Curtis Hixon Hall, Tampa, Florida, USA. **Recognition:** WBC. **Referee:** Lee Sala.
Scorecards: 145-140, 148-139, 149-138.
Fight Summary: Taken the 15-round distance for the first time, although angered by Anderson (172½), the champion appeared content to pace himself despite having several opportunities to drop his man. The pattern of the fight was clear from the start as Anderson moved backwards and Foster (170¼) made no effort to chase him, happy to counter whenever he could. As the fight moved towards the final third Anderson's speed had diminished

following Foster's ability to rifle in solid left jabs to his body. He had also been cut under the left eye in the ninth. Forced to attack more as he was well behind on points, Anderson came in for a fair amount of punishment before making it to the final bell.

5 June 1971. Vicente Rondon w co 1 (15) Piero Del Papa.
Venue: New Circus Bullring, Caracas, Venezuela. **Recognition:** WBA. **Referee:** Zach Clayton.
Fight Summary: After tearing out of his corner at the opening bell, Del Papa (172) landed two heavy lefts before the champion replied with several short hooks to the head prior to moving in with a steady flow of combination punches. With Rondon (174¾) showing no sign of slowing down Del Papa was finally dropped by a right uppercut to the jaw and counted out in a kneeling position at 2.35 of the session.

21 August 1971. Vicente Rondon w pts 15 Eddie Jones.
Venue: New Circus Bullring, Caracas, Venezuela. **Recognition:** WBA. **Referee:** Jesus Celis.
Scorecards: 148-144, 148-145, 146-145.
Fight Summary: In what was a hard-hitting affair from start to finish, Jones (173¾) was able to withstand the heavier punches of the champion to come firing back with solid blows of his own. The title might well have changed hands had Jones not been cut badly over the left eye in the fourth as it hindered him from thereon in and was continually being inspected by the doctor. It was a disappointing performance by Rondon (175), who had looked ordinary in a non-title bout just a few weeks earlier and had failed to shake off the lethargy.

26 October 1971. Vicente Rondon w rsc 12 (15) Gomeo Brennan.
Venue: Convention Hall, Miami, Florida, USA. **Recognition:** WBA. **Referee:** Eddie Eckert.
Fight Summary: Taking the fight to Rondon (175) from the opening bell the challenger was well in the fight during the first five rounds, scoring with sharp left jabs to the head and banging in right hands. In the fifth Brennan (167½) had to cope with his left eye beginning to swell, and by the 11th it was closed shut. From the fifth onwards Rondon began to take control of the fight, his solid right uppercuts from close range always bothering Brennan who never really found a way of avoiding them. With the eye causing real problems for Brennan he was given one more round, the 12th, before the doctor advised the referee to pull him out at the end of the session.

29 October 1971. Bob Foster w rsc 8 (15) Tommy Hicks.
Venue: Catholic Youth Centre, Scranton, Pennsylvania, USA. **Recognition:** WBC. **Referee:** Manny Gelb.
Fight Summary: Even though he was pulled out of the contest at 1.04 of the eighth round with a bad cut over the right eye impairing his vision, Hicks (171) maintained his record of never being off his feet in 25 contests. The challenger certainly came to fight, when pressing Foster (174) all the way despite being cut in the second, and at the finish the official scorecards showed him winning two rounds. Unable to knock Hicks out, it was Foster's trusty left jab that did the damage.

15 December 1971. Vicente Rondon w co 8 (15) Doyle Baird.
Venue: The Arena, Cleveland, Ohio, USA. **Recognition:** WBA. **Referee:** John Christopher.
Fight Summary: Having started at a fair pace, Baird (170) was beginning to feel it by the fourth as Rondon (175) got down to work with short lefts and rights to the head that stopped him in his tracks. Regardless, the challenger continued to come forward, but by the seventh, badly cut over both eyes and bleeding profusely from the nose, he could hardly see. In the eighth it was all over for the game Baird after he was dropped three times and counted out on the last occasion, the finish timed at 2.10.

16 December 1971. Bob Foster w rsc 3 (15) Brian Kelly.
Venue: Fairgrounds Arena, Oklahoma City, Oklahoma, USA. **Recognition:** WBC. **Referee:** Earle Keel.
Fight Summary: Following a quiet opening round the champion got busy in the second after being caught by a right to the head, the only punch of note that Kelly (175) threw throughout the fight. With a seven-inch-reach advantage and power in both hands, when Foster (174) opened up Kelly had no defence against what was coming his way. Dropped twice in the second and again in the third when a left hook flattened him, Kelly was rescued by the referee at 1.56 of the session, his unbroken run of 22 contests shattered along with any hopes he may have had regarding the championship.

7 April 1972. Bob Foster w co 2 (15) Vicente Rondon.
Venue: Convention Hall, Miami, Florida, USA. **Recognition:** World. **Referee:** Cy Gottfried.
Fight Summary: In a match made to unify the title it was soon clear that Foster (175), the WBC champion, was too good for his WBA counterpart when getting down to business at the opening bell, landing solid left jabs and taking his man to the ropes. From the start Rondon (175) had looked apprehensive. Dropped early in the second by a solid left hook, his nose damaged and bleeding badly, Rondon was given the standing 'eight' count before being allowed back into action. From there onwards it would be just a matter of time, and when Foster let the combinations roll followed by two cracking left hooks Rondon crashed down to be counted out with just five seconds of the session remaining.

27 June 1972. Bob Foster w co 4 (15) Mike Quarry.
Venue: Convention Centre, Las Vegas, Nevada, USA. **Recognition:** World. **Referee:** Harry Krause.
Fight Summary: Giving it his best shot Quarry (175) gave the champion a few early problems, but by the third round he was being jabbed around the ring on the end of a stiff left jab. Swollen under the right eye Quarry came out for the fourth, gamely taking the fight to Foster (173½), but after being hurt by a heavy right a tremendous left hook to the jaw had him down just as the bell rang to end the session. Flat on his back, Quarry was counted out ten seconds after the round had finished.

On his way to a crack at the title, having beaten Tony Montano and Brian Kelly, Pat O'Connor was derailed when he was stopped inside seven rounds by Andy Kendall at the Metro Sports Centre, Bloomington, Minnesota on 14 September. Ranked at number three by *The Ring* magazine with 31 straight wins to his credit, when O'Connor's form fell away, 15 fights later he retired.

Chris Finnegan, an Olympic gold medallist from 1968 would be Foster's next challenger. Ranked at number four by *The Ring* magazine, he had won 23 out of 26 contests since turning pro and was the reigning British, Commonwealth and European champion. A durable and clever southpaw, he had beaten Harry Scott, Eddie Avoth, Roger Rouse, Hal Carroll and Conny Velensek.

26 September 1972. Bob Foster w co 14 (15) Chris Finnegan.
Venue: The Arena, Wembley, London, England. **Recognition:** World. **Referee:** Roland Dakin.
Fight Summary: After being subjected to heavy punches at the start of the contest Finnegan (173¾) came back hard and effectively to give the champion plenty of trouble. The former Olympic champion was right back in the fight, matching Foster (174½) up until the tenth when he was floored by a heavy right to the head and forced to take a count of 'eight'. Finnegan's southpaw blows to head and body still bothered Foster, but the latter was getting on top. By the 13th, although Finnegan, now cut around both eyes, was still exchanging blows with Foster he was beginning to wilt under the pressure. And after 55 seconds of the 14th the Englishman was dropped by a vicious right to the jaw and counted out. It had been a valiant attempt, with Finnegan matching the champion blow for blow at times.

Following this defence Foster was allowed time out to take on Muhammad Ali for the North American Boxing Federation (NABF) heavyweight title, but was knocked out inside eight rounds on 21 November. Suitably rested, Foster was talking up a defence against Jimmy Dupree for March 1973 but, after that appeared to die a death, by early April 1973 he was being asked to defend against the number one contender, Pierre Fourie.

Negotiations for this fight to take place in South Africa had been ongoing for six months. However, for it to happen the Government would have to change the clause in the Boxing Act which prohibited whites from fighting non-whites. When it was recognised that the Government were not going to act the promoters looked at Swaziland as a replacement venue, but by that time Foster's management team was looking towards a defence on home territory. At this stage the WBA demanded that the pair meet, regardless, and a match was finally agreed for New Mexico on 21 August 1973.

21 August 1973. Bob Foster w pts 15 Pierre Fourie.
Venue: University Arena, Albuquerque, New Mexico, USA. **Recognition:** World. **Referee:** Jim Cleary.

Light Heavyweight Division

Scorecards: 148-120, 149-130, 149-138.
Fight Summary: Despite being cut over the right eye as early as the first round, Fourie (168) stuck to his battle plan of trying to negate the champion's huge reach advantage by staying as close to him as possible. Although Foster (173) used the jab well Fourie occasionally found a way inside where he could work the body, but for much of the time he was kept at bay. Cut over the left eye in tenth and starting to tire, when Foster began to coast knowing that his challenger lacked the power to damage him his trusty left did the rest.

1 December 1973. Bob Foster w pts 15 Pierre Fourie.
Venue: Rand Stadium, Johannesburg, South Africa. **Recognition:** World. **Referee:** Roland Dakin.
Scorecards: 103-99, 103-95, 101-98.
Fight Summary: Giving Foster (174) another tough fight the South African appeared to be ahead at the halfway stage as he covered up well against the left and countered effectively with left hooks to the jaw. However, from the eighth onwards Foster began to score more with heavy right uppercuts, and although Fourie (167) made a great effort in the 11th and 12th the last three sessions saw him struggling to survive. Badly hurt several times towards the end, the challenger was physically sick at the final bell as his exertions caught up with him.

17 June 1974. Bob Foster drew 15 Jorge Ahumada.
Venue: University Arena, Albuquerque, New Mexico, USA. **Recognition:** World. **Referee:** Jim Cleary.
Scorecards: 148-143, 142-145, 144-144.
Fight Summary: With his punch power seemingly leaving him, Foster (174) came close to losing his title as Ahumada (173½) pressed him throughout. Regardless of the blows coming his way, and there were plenty of them, the outreached Ahumada made the body his target which led to far too much clinching. It was in the 12th that Foster seemed to have his best chance of stopping Ahumada, who had damage to his nose and a left eye that was fast closing, but the Argentine weathered the storm and continued where he left off.

Foster relinquished the title on announcing his retirement in September, and while the WBC supported the claims of John Conteh (who beat Chris Finnegan by a sixth-round stoppage at the Wembley Pool, London, England on 21 May) and Ahumada (who beat Angel Oquendo over 12 rounds at Madison Square Garden, Manhattan, NYC, New York on 29 July) who had both come through eliminating bouts, the WBA backed Victor Galindez and Len Hutchins in a straight fight for their version of the title.

1 October 1974. John Conteh w pts 15 Jorge Ahumada.
Venue: The Arena, Wembley, London, England. **Recognition:** WBC. **Referee:** Harry Gibbs.
Scorecard: 147-142.
Fight Summary: Contesting the vacant WBC title Conteh (174¼) fought an excellent tactical battle to beat Ahumada (174), and although he failed to knock the latter over he was always in the driving seat. It was Conteh's left that won the fight for him, both in defence and attack, and he had far more variety than did the Argentine who lacked his accuracy. By the two thirds stage Conteh was well in control, showing his total domination from the 12th onwards when driving his rival around the ring. With Conteh punch-picking at this stage he never let up right through to the final bell, the verdict in his favour being a formality.

7 December 1974. Victor Galindez w rtd 12 (15) Len Hutchins.
Venue: Luna Park Stadium, Buenos Aires, Argentina. **Recognition:** WBA. **Referee:** Jesus Celis.
Fight Summary: In a battle for the vacant WBA title Galindez (174) proved to be the master of Hutchins (172¼), flooring him for mandatory 'eight' counts at the end of the first round and then in the fourth, eighth and 12th. Galindez had his best rounds between the fifth and ninth when it looked as though Hutchins would crumble but, with the American made of stern stuff, in the tenth and 11th both men slugged it out. The 12th was a tough round for Hutchins, and he was battered endlessly before being retired during the interval.

11 March 1975. John Conteh w rsc 5 (15) Lonnie Bennett.
Venue: The Arena, Wembley, London, England. **Recognition:** WBC. **Referee:** Roland Dakin.
Fight Summary: Boxing quite brilliantly, Conteh (174) began to get on top of the always dangerous Bennett (172½) in the second round after the American had taken the opener. The third and fourth sessions saw both men

matching their skills, but it was Conteh who looked the most likely to finish it when buckling Bennett's legs on a couple of occasions. Storming out for the fifth, Conteh was pounding Bennett with rights and lefts when the latter suddenly pulled away with a badly cut left eye. When it was seen that there was no way Bennett could box on with that injury the referee stopped the fight on the 1.10 mark.

Taking a trip to America, Conteh outpointed Willie Taylor over ten rounds of a non-title fight at the Catholic Youth Centre, Scranton, Pennsylvania on 16 August. Although he looked good he had unfortunately broken his right hand in the fifth round and was forced to take a long lay-off to allow the bone to knit properly.

At the end of December the WBC ordered Conteh to defend against a nominated contender, and at the same time honour his commitment to Mickey Duff. Having settled his argument with Duff, Conteh was then booked to defend against Yaqui Lopez in Kampala, Uganda on 28 March 1976, prior to it being postponed. Bad luck then struck again, Conteh breaking his right hand in the same place as before and being sidelined for at least three or four months. Given until October to defend against Lopez or face being stripped, a date of 9 October 1976 and a new venue were eventually confirmed.

7 April 1975. Victor Galindez w pts 15 Pierre Fourie.
Venue: Ellis Park Stadium, Johannesburg, South Africa. **Recognition:** WBA. **Referee:** Waldemar Schmidt.
Fight Summary: Having his third crack at a world title Fourie (168¾), keeping Galindez (172) at bay for the first six rounds, looked to be on his way to the title at that stage. In the eighth he seemed to be even closer to that objective when opening up a bad cut over the champion's right eye. It was then that Galindez got himself going, and from the 12th session onwards he battered away at a very tired Fourie, his sheer strength taking him to a very narrow victory. Although the scorecards were not given out, as was the general practice in South Africa at the time, it was generally felt that Galindez won by just one point in what was a unanimous verdict.

30 June 1975. Victor Galindez w pts 15 Jorge Ahumada.
Venue: Madison Square Garden, Manhattan, NYC, New York, USA. **Recognition:** WBA. **Referee:** Jimmy Devlin.
Scorecards: 9-5-1, 10-3-2, 6-2-7.
Fight Summary: After winning twice in three meetings between the pair Galindez (174) was expected to retain his title against Ahumada (175), and when a left hook to the jaw sent the latter hurtling to the floor at the end of the third that looked to be on the cards. Showing great character, Ahumada battled his way back and was going well when a clash of heads opened up a bad cut on Galindez's left eye. Stirred up, Galindez began his charge for home, being well in control by the 11th as his strength pushed Ahumada back. With it remaining that way, even when Galindez was cut on the right eye from another head clash in the 13th, the last three sessions were among the most brutal seen in recent times.

13 September 1975. Victor Galindez w pts 15 Pierre Fourie.
Venue: Rand Stadium, Johannesburg, South Africa. **Recognition:** WBA. **Referee:** Waldemar Schmidt.
Fight Summary: This was the fourth occasion that Fourie (174½) had challenged for a world title, but for this one he decided to change his style in an effort to get more power in his punches. Level at the end of the fifth Galindez (175) began to warm to the task, swinging in punches from both hands, and although Fourie stayed with him the champion won the tenth, 11th and 12th by sheer belligerence. After the 13th saw Fourie come back into it the next two sessions had him matching Galindez punch for punch right through to the final bell. Although the scores were not given out, the result was announced as being a split decision win for the champion.

28 March 1976. Victor Galindez w rsc 3 (15) Harald Skog.
Venue: Ekeberg Hall, Oslo, Norway. **Recognition:** WBA. **Referee:** Tony Perez.
Fight Summary: Clearly a mismatch, with Skog (173½) flicking out left jabs and not landing anything of note, once the champion opened up in the second round the writing was on the wall for the Norwegian. Much taller than Galindez (173½), after being hurt at the end of the first, Skog was dropped by a right uppercut at the end of the second. Storming out for the third Galindez forced a mandatory 'eight' count on Skog when the latter was hanging halfway out of the ring, and after smashing in lefts and rights to drop challenger the referee stopped what had become an uneven contest on the 1.45 mark.

22 May 1976. Victor Galindez w co 15 (15) Richie Kates.
Venue: Rand Stadium, Johannesburg, South Africa. **Recognition:** WBA. **Referee:** Stan Christodoulou.
Fight Summary: Once again Galindez (174½) was involved in a vicious affair that had the large crowd enthralled for most of the time. When an accidental clash of heads in the third round saw the champion suffer a serious cut over the right eye pandemonium reigned until it was announced that there would be a break of five minutes to allow for the damage to be patched up. From that point on Galindez fought like a wounded tiger in every round, while Kates (173¾) showed how durable he was when remaining upright and even trying to fight back under the onslaught. At the start of the 14th Galindez was dropped by a low blow, and when getting to his feet he took another one in the groin which saw Kates warned and told he was losing the round. Although Kates steamed into Galindez in the final session, after getting the worst of it, eventually two cracking left hooks to the jaw sent him crashing down to be counted out with just one second of the fight remaining.

5 October 1976. Victor Galindez w pts 15 Kosie Smith.
Venue: Rand Stadium, Johannesburg, South Africa. **Recognition:** WBA. **Referee:** Waldemar Schmidt.
Scorecards: 104-91, 105-95, 105-92.
Fight Summary: On the floor in the opening round, when Smith (174) was given the mandatory 'eight' count after slipping rather than being knocked down it was all downhill thereafter as he allowed the champion to control the fight. Smith had a go at Galindez (175) in the fourth, but in the main he was on the end of solid lefts and rights throughout. Cut over the left eye in the middle of the contest, Smith received another mandatory count after falling through the ropes in the tenth following a savage attack by Galindez. The result was a formality.

9 October 1976. John Conteh w pts 15 Yaqui Lopez.
Venue: The Forum, Copenhagen, Denmark. **Recognition:** WBC. **Referee:** Rudolf Durst.
Scorecards: 149-145, 149-145, 148-146.
Fight Summary: Boxing well with solid left jabs and hooks constantly slamming into the challenger's face, Conteh (174¼) showed much of his old form apart from limited use of his twice broken right hand. Although the taller Lopez (173) was always second best and the decision in Conteh's favour was unanimous the scores were surprisingly close, especially when most experts at ringside gave the Mexican no more than a round or so at best. When caught by long lefts and rights Conteh immediately hit back to take the play away from Lopez, who after being cut over the left eye in the 11th was content to take it easy for the last three sessions.

5 March 1977. John Conteh w rsc 3 (15) Len Hutchins.
Venue: The Stadium, Liverpool, England. **Recognition:** WBC. **Referee:** Sid Nathan.
Fight Summary: Both men started confidently, but before the opening session ended heads accidentally came together leaving the challenger with a badly gashed left eye. The second round saw Conteh (175) at his best, stabbing in solid left jabs followed by heavy rights, and Hutchins (173¾), who was beginning to be taken apart, was unable to match the power. Going after Hutchins with a vengeance in the third, Conteh battered his man with solid blows from both hands before a terrific left hook to the jaw had the American down. Up at around 'seven', when it was clear that Hutchins was not fit to fight on the referee wisely terminated the contest after 1.05 of the round had elapsed.

Conteh forfeited the WBC version of the title in May when he withdrew from a scheduled defence against Miguel Angel Cuello less than a week before the contest was due to take place. Luckily, Jesse Burnett, a man who had lost narrowly to Victor Galindez and beaten Australia's Tony Mundine, was able to take Conteh's place at short notice. It was thought that the prime reason for Conteh pulling out was due to him requiring better safeguards over his purse money, the matter going to London's High Court as a matter of some urgency. The result was that the BBBoC were instructed to do everything in their power to stop the WBC from dethroning Conteh, although the Court had no powers to place an injunction on the WBC. While Cuello and Burnett were told that the winner would have to defend against the European champion, Mate Parlov, within 90 days, Conteh's once glittering future lay in shreds.

21 May 1977. Miguel Angel Cuello w co 9 (15) Jesse Burnett.
Venue: Louis II Stadium, Monte Carlo, Monaco. **Recognition:** WBC. **Referee:** Ray Solis.

Fight Summary: Fighting for the vacant title Cuello (173) eventually put paid to Burnett (169), who was counted out at 2.49 of the ninth round after a punishing fight that saw both men in trouble at varying stages. Pressing right from the start despite carrying an already damaged left eye, Cuello generally forced Burnett around the ring before being decked by a cracking right hand in the fourth. It was clear that Burnett was the classier man, and throughout the contest he would pick his punches with accuracy although Cuello would always come back slugging. In the seventh and eighth Burnett had Cuello rocking on several occasions but, unable to find a finishing blow and tiring rapidly, the ninth round would be his last.

Told that he must defend the title against Mate Parlov within 90 days of beating Burnett, a succession of injuries suffered by Cuello forced repeated postponements that pushed the date on from 1 October to 7 January 1978.

18 June 1977. Victor Galindez w pts 15 Richie Kates.
Venue: Sports Palace, Rome, Italy. **Recognition:** WBA. **Referee:** Waldemar Schmidt.
Scorecards: 146-139, 151-144, 148-140.
Fight Summary: Coming out fast the champion won the opening three rounds, hurting Kates (173¾) with right-left combinations in the second and third before the latter began to hit back in the fifth with some solid rights. From the sixth through to the ninth it was Kates who was dictating things with solid blows from both hands bringing Galindez (174) up straight on occasion. But when Kates began to tire in the tenth after shipping heavy punches to the body it was Galindez all the way from thereon in, the American holding on desperately for much of the time in order to make it to the final bell.

17 September 1977. Victor Galindez w pts 15 Yaqui Lopez.
Venue: Sports Palace, Rome, Italy. **Recognition:** WBA. **Referee:** Stan Christodoulou.
Scorecards: 147-146, 148-146, 146-145.
Fight Summary: Having great difficulty in dealing with the challenger's long reach Galindez (174½) went behind during the opening seven rounds, being badly hurt in the sixth. Beginning his fight-back from the eighth onwards Galindez continued to have problems, but it was not until the last four rounds that he really got on top as he threw punch after punch at a tiring Lopez (174½). Many of Galindez's blows were wild, Lopez claiming afterwards that he had been fouled on any number of occasions by rabbit punches.

20 November 1977. Victor Galindez w pts 15 Eddie Gregory (Eddie Mustafa Muhammad).
Venue: Sports Palace, Turin, Italy. **Recognition:** WBA. **Referee:** Luis Sulbaran.
Scorecards: 147-145, 147-146, 148-147.
Fight Summary: Winning most of the early rounds on sheer aggression, and dropping Gregory (174) in the fifth with a cracking left hook to the jaw, the champion looked to be on his way to a comfortable win. It was in the eighth that Gregory eventually got to grips with Galindez (173½), cutting him under the right eye and making full use of his left jab and solid right-hand hitting. Gregory was still not throwing enough punches, but after being warned for a low blow in the 13th he came on like a train when hammering Galindez with solid rights to the head and fighting hard to the final bell. Although it had been a close call for Galindez he just about held on.

7 January 1978. Mate Parlov w co 9 (15) Miguel Angel Cuello.
Venue: Sports Palace, Milan, Italy. **Recognition:** WBC. **Referee:** Sid Nathan.
Fight Summary: Parlov (173½), a former Olympic and World amateur champion, had control right from the opening bell. Although Cuello (174) was on the attack throughout he was unable to inflict too much damage on his adversary, other than in the eighth after landing with a heavy right. From the fourth onwards the southpaw challenger was producing the much cleaner shots, boxing effectively on the back foot as Cuello concentrated on the body. With Cuello tiring fast, when Parlov stepped up the pace in the ninth a solid straight left to the chin sent the Argentine down to be counted out on the 2.43 mark.

6 May 1978. Victor Galindez w pts 15 Yaqui Lopez.
Venue: Circus Tent, Viareggio, Italy. **Recognition:** WBA. **Referee:** Mario Riva.
Scorecards: 148-146, 148-145, 146-144.

Fight Summary: Fighting a cautious battle the challenger failed to do enough work to warrant the decision, going down narrowly on all three cards as in their previous contest. Although he came forward for much of the time, because Lopez (172) allowed Galindez (172) too much space he was open to countering right uppercuts and left hooks. Galindez, who finished with a swollen right eye, even showed a smart left jab at times that flummoxed Lopez and made him even more wary. At the final bell it was agreed that Lopez had fought well, but had failed to do enough work to warrant the decision.

17 June 1978. Mate Parlov w pts 15 John Conteh.
Venue: Red Star Stadium, Belgrade, Yugoslavia. **Recognition:** WBC. **Referee:** Rudy Ortega.
Scorecards: 145-141, 143-140, 141-147.
Fight Summary: Despite coming to the ring with both eyes heavily protected with grease, Parlov (175) was allowed to start the fight after a delay of 20 minutes due to pressure being exerted by the TV executives. At that point the champion still had two layers of covering on his eyes, giving him an unfair advantage from the start. Although Parlov was still amateur regarding technique, often flicking out his southpaw jab rather than landing solidly, it took Conteh (173) a fair time to work him out. With Conteh being cautioned throughout when getting to close quarters, in frustration he butted Parlov in the eighth after opening up a cut on the latter's right eye. From the tenth onwards, however, Conteh hurt Parlov with all manner of body shots as well as scoring solidly to the head. At the start of the 15th it appeared that Conteh was in total command and although deducted a point for use of the elbow he continued to batter away at Parlov. With the referee scoring it for Conteh by a six-point margin, it seemed incredible that the other two judges leant towards the champion.

15 September 1978. Mike Rossman w rsc 13 (15) Victor Galindez.
Venue: The Superdome, New Orleans, Louisiana. **Recognition:** WBA. **Referee:** Stan Christodoulou.
Fight Summary: Right from the opening bell Rossman (173) took the fight to Galindez (174), boxing in a cool fashion, picking his punches well and protecting himself from the expected counters with a high guard. Cut on the right eye in the second, and having had difficulty in making the weight, the champion found Rossman a tough nut to crack, being badly hurt by solid rights to the jaw in the eighth and ninth rounds. Galindez tried to fight back in the 11th and 12th, but by now it was all Rossman. Under real pressure in the 13th, when the champion was hit with heavy blows without return, the referee stopped the contest 55 seconds into the session.

2 December 1978. Marvin Johnson w rsc 10 (15) Mate Parlov.
Venue: Sports Palace, Marsala, Italy. **Recognition:** WBC. **Referee:** Roland Dakin.
Fight Summary: In a battle of southpaws Johnson (175) proved too much for Parlov (174¾), opening up cuts over the champion's eyes as early as the second round and generally dominating him. Scoring with solid body punches, Johnson had Parlov tired and clinching at every opportunity from the third onwards. It all caught up with Parlov in the ninth when he could barely keep going, and in the tenth he was rescued by the referee on the 2.33 mark having taken two standing counts and unable to defend himself. Parlov's corner had already indicated that they wanted the fight stopped.

Johnson's next challenger would be Matthew Franklin (Saad Muhammad), a man who had knocked him out inside 12 rounds of a battle for the vacant NABF title at the Spectrum, Philadelphia, Pennsylvania on 26 July 1977. Since then Franklin had successfully defended three times at the same venue, against Billy Douglas, Richie Kates and Yaqui Lopez, and fully warranted a crack at the championship. Franklin would later change his name to that of Matthew Saad Muhammad on becoming a Muslim.

5 December 1978. Mike Rossman w rsc 6 (15) Aldo Traversaro.
Venue: The Spectrum, Philadelphia, Pennsylvania, USA. **Recognition:** WBA. **Referee:** Jesus Celis.
Fight Summary: Traversaro (173½), the European champion, certainly came to fight and by the third he had warmed to the task despite being cut over the left eye in the first round. Having been shaken up by two right uppercuts in the fourth, the champion picked up the pace in the fifth and stung Traversaro with a right to the head in the closing seconds. Unfortunately, in the sixth Traversaro was seriously cut on the right side of his head and with blood pouring down his face and Rossman (171) hacking away at him the referee was forced to call the contest off at 1.15 of the round.

14 April 1979. Victor Galindez w rtd 9 (15) Mike Rossman.
Venue: The Superdome, New Orleans, Louisiana, USA. **Recognition:** WBA. **Referee:** Stan Christodoulou.
Fight Summary: Galindez (174¼) became the first light heavyweight to regain his title when Rossman (174¼) was retired at the end of the ninth round due to a broken right hand. It was a different fight to their last one, and after Rossman had been hurt by a left hook-right uppercut at the end of the fourth it was downhill from there onwards. Although he was cut above the right eye in the fourth Galindez was able to shrug it off, dominating every round until the finish when scoring with solid lefts and rights to head and body as Rossman began to lose heart.

22 April 1979. Matthew Franklin (Saad Muhammad) w rsc 8 (15) Marvin Johnson.
Venue: Market Square Arena, Indianapolis, Indiana, USA. **Recognition:** WBC. **Referee:** George DeFabis.
Fight Summary: With both men looking for an early finish it was the champion who struck first with southpaw rights and lefts hitting the target in the second round, before Franklin (175) hit back with a burst of punches prior to being wobbled himself. From that moment on both men went head-to-toe, ripping in punches from both hands in an effort to finish early. The fight changed in Franklin's favour when he almost had Johnson (175) over in the seventh and saved by the bell. Racing out of his corner at the start of the eighth Franklin poured in punch after punch on the stricken Johnson and, even though he was badly cut on the left eye by a stray blow, the referee stopped the fight in his favour on the 2.44 mark after the latter had got to his feet at 'nine' following a tremendous right to the jaw. From here on Franklin would be known by his Islamic name of Matthew Saad Muhammad.

18 August 1979. Matthew Saad Muhammad w pts 15 John Conteh.
Venue: Resorts International Hotel, Atlantic City, New Jersey, USA. **Recognition:** WBC. **Referee:** Carlos Padilla.
Scorecards: 146-142, 144-143, 146-141.
Fight Summary: After boxing well behind the left jab, dictating the fight and making Muhammad (172½) miss, when Conteh (175) was caught by two solid rights in the fifth he looked shaken prior to a head clash that left the champion with a terrible gash on the left eye. Once again Conteh got on top in the sixth, but by the 11th both men were landing with heavy shots, and towards the end of the 12th the Englishman had Muhammad all but beaten when he was lying on the ropes taking heavy punishment from both hands. Inexplicably, Conteh backed off, a decision that ultimately cost him the fight. Well ahead by the 13th, the fight turned again as Conteh was battered throughout the session and dropped twice in the 14th before somehow coming back to hurt Muhammad in the 15th. The scorecards failed to tell the true picture after a tough fight, but the referee's score on 144-143 was about right.

30 November 1979. Marvin Johnson w co 11 (15) Victor Galindez.
Venue: The Superdome, New Orleans, Louisiana, USA. **Recognition:** WBA. **Referee:** Jesus Celis.
Fight Summary: Boxing coolly, the southpaw challenger had the fight well under control by the sixth, having cut Galindez (174¾) on the left eye while generally dominating him, and although the latter came back well with rights and lefts to the body in the eighth and ninth rounds it was not enough. Blow for blow in the tenth, within moments of the 11th getting underway Johnson (173½) sent Galindez crashing to the floor to be counted out after just 20 seconds of the session after catching the Argentine with a tremendous left to the jaw. Just short of a year and one fight later, Galindez was killed on 26 October 1980 in Argentina during an automobile race when struck by another car.

29 March 1980. Matthew Saad Muhammad w rsc 4 (15) John Conteh.
Venue: Resorts International Hotel, Atlantic City, New Jersey, USA. **Recognition:** WBC. **Referee:** Octavio Meyran.
Fight Summary: Although not looking his normal self the challenger stayed with Muhammad (175) in the opening three sessions, but in the fourth it all changed when he was dropped heavily by a right-left hook to the head. Put down again a further three times and given the mandatory 'eight' counts, when Conteh (175) went to the floor for the fifth time the referee stopped the contest after he had got up at 'five', 2.27 into the session. Conteh would have just one more fight, a winning one, before retiring.

31 March 1980. Eddie Gregory (Eddie Mustafa Muhammad) w rsc 11 (15) Marvin Johnson.
Venue: Stokely AC, Knoxville, Tennessee, USA. **Recognition:** WBA. **Referee:** Carlos Berrocal.

Fight Summary: Having enforced the mandatory count of 'eight' in the third round following blows to head and body, the challenger, carrying a cut left eye, was well ahead by the eighth as Johnson (174½) laboured. Although Johnson occasionally found the target he was unable to shake Gregory (174), who always came right back at him. Wobbled in the ninth and hurt again in the tenth Johnson was caught heavily in the 11th by a right to the jaw, and after Gregory kept firing in blows without return at 2.43 of the session the fight was halted. From then on Gregory would be known by his Islamic name of Eddie Mustafa Muhammad.

11 May 1980. Matthew Saad Muhammad w rsc 5 (15) Louis Pergaud.
Venue: Metro Centre, Halifax, Nova Scotia, Canada. **Recognition:** WBC. **Referee:** Rudy Ortega.
Fight Summary: Taking control from the opening bell Muhammad (174½) was soon targeting the body with solid blows, and although the challenger landed two solid southpaw lefts to his jaw in the second and third they were shrugged off. Pergaud (174½) began the fourth throwing wild punches from either hand, but having been hurt downstairs at the end of the session he was more than wary at the start of the fifth. Opening up, Muhammad was soon on top of Pergaud, who tried to hold him up with long lefts and rights before being rescued by the referee at 1.19 despite getting to his feet after being dropped by a left hook to the body.

13 July 1980. Matthew Saad Muhammad w rsc 14 (15) Yaqui Lopez.
Venue: Great Gorge Playboy Hotel, McAfee, New Jersey, USA. **Recognition:** WBC. **Referee:** Waldemar Schmidt.
Fight Summary: In what was his fourth attempt to win a title Lopez (173¾) seemed to be in front coming into the ninth, having landed well with both hands and forced the champion back on several occasions. However, this stage of the fight saw Muhammad (174¼) finally get going when sending in unanswered blows to head and body, the pressure paying off for him as the rapidly tiring Lopez began to give ground in the 13th. Coming out fast for the 14th Muhammad waded in to Lopez, and after dropping the latter four times for mandatory 'eight' counts the referee came to his rescue with 57 seconds of the round remaining.

20 July 1980. Eddie Mustafa Muhammad w rsc 10 (15) Jerry Martin.
Venue: Great Gorge Playboy Hotel, McAfee, New Jersey, USA. **Recognition:** WBA. **Referee:** Tony Perez.
Fight Summary: Showing some of his best form the champion outboxed Martin (173½) from the start, and at the end of the fourth round had his man down from a straight right. Subsequently, Martin, unable to get back in the fight, was forced to take many hooks and uppercuts as Muhammad (175) gradually upped the pace. The contest was terminated after 28 seconds of the tenth when Martin, who had risen from a knockdown that followed a series of heavy blows to the head, was deemed unable to defend himself on being backed up against the ropes.

28 November 1980. Matthew Saad Muhammad w co 4 (15) Lottie Mwale.
Venue: Sports Arena, San Diego, California, USA. **Recognition:** WBC. **Referee:** Tony Perez.
Fight Summary: Mwale (172½) made a good start when boxing the champion on even terms, but towards the end of the third round after being stunned by a big left hook he somehow survived the two-handed punches coming his way to last out the session. Chasing Mwale down with right and left swings to the body in the fourth, Muhammad (175) eventually found a tremendous left uppercut to the jaw that sent the Commonwealth champion down to be counted out on the 2.25 mark. Afterwards, Muhammad said that the finishing blow was probably the hardest that he had ever thrown.

29 November 1980. Eddie Mustafa Muhammad w rsc 3 (15) Rudy Koopmans.
Venue: Olympic Auditorium, Los Angeles, California, USA. **Recognition:** WBA. **Referee:** Larry Rozadilla.
Fight Summary: Moving back at speed from the opening bell, with Koopmans (175) making it difficult for the champion to catch up with him the contest turned into a non-event. There had hardly been any punches landed when the two men came together towards the end of the third, but when pulling away from Muhammad (175) it could be seen that the European champion was carrying a cut left eye. At the end of the round, and following an inspection, the doctor told the referee to stop the fight.

Muhammad's next defence would be against Michael Spinks, the 1976 Olympic gold medal winner at middleweight, who gained his opportunity after 16 unbeaten pro contests and defeating men such as Murray

Sutherland, Yaqui Lopez, Willie Taylor and Marvin Johnson (w co 4 at the International Resorts Centre, Atlantic City, New Jersey on 28 March 1981) in what was effectively an eliminator.

28 February 1981. Matthew Saad Muhammad w rsc 11 (15) Vonzell Johnson.
Venue: Bally's Park Place Hotel, Atlantic City, New Jersey, USA. **Recognition:** WBC. **Referee:** Tony Perez.
Fight Summary: Making his sixth defence Muhammad (174¼) was up against it for the opening five rounds, the 6'4" Johnson (174) confusing him when picking up points and moving out of range. The fight changed at the end of the sixth, Johnson going to the floor after what seemed to be a slip and incurring a mandatory 'eight' count much to his chagrin. From there onwards Muhammad picked up the pace, and by the ninth Johnson was getting hit more often and was fast tiring. Cut over the left eye in the tenth Johnson gamely fought on, but after being dropped by a right to the jaw following a steady battery of blows and then being badly hurt by another big right the referee stopped the fight, the finish being timed at 1.13 of the 11th.

25 April 1981. Matthew Saad Muhammad w co 9 (15) Murray Sutherland.
Venue: Resorts International Hotel, Atlantic City, New Jersey, USA. **Recognition:** WBC. **Referee:** Paul Venti.
Fight Summary: Winning the first four rounds, scoring well with left jabs and follow-up rights, Sutherland (173) took advantage of the champion's lethargy. That all changed in the sixth when Muhammad (175) finally began to unload, and in the seventh he had Sutherland down for 'nine' from a volley of punches and cut over the left eye. Although Sutherland fought back well in the eighth, Muhammad, now on top, dropped the challenger in the ninth with a big right to the jaw. Counted out at 1.16 of the session Sutherland was angry at not being allowed to continue as he had been on his feet at 'nine', and despite the New Jersey commissioner and former heavyweight champion, Jersey Joe Walcott, initially thinking that the referee had stopped the fight the result stood.

18 July 1981. Michael Spinks w pts 15 Eddie Mustafa Muhammad.
Venue: Imperial Palace Hotel, Las Vegas, Nevada, USA. **Recognition:** WBA. **Referee:** Richard Greene.
Scorecards: 146-138, 144-140, 145-139.
Fight Summary: Unbeaten in 16 pro fights, Spinks (173¼), the former Olympic champion, took seven rounds to find his feet as Muhammad (175), despite having weight-making problems, looked to be on his way to successfully defending his title. That all changed in the eighth when Muhammad's right eye suddenly closed, and although he was still in the fight a knockdown in the 12th following a cracking right to the jaw put Spinks firmly in the driving seat. Despite Muhammad continuing to fight hard, with Spinks letting the punches go, his title drifted away from him.

26 September 1981. Matthew Saad Muhammad w rsc 11 (12) Jerry Martin.
Venue: Golden Nugget Casino, Atlantic City, New Jersey, USA. **Recognition:** WBC. **Referee:** Larry Hazzard.
Fight Summary: Despite forcing the fight for the opening two rounds Martin (172½) was badly hurt in the third when the champion opened up with heavy lefts and rights the head, which led to the action going back and forth for several sessions. After taking some heavy shots in the sixth Martin came right back in the seventh to blitz Muhammad (172) almost without response and an early night seemed on the cards. From then on both men exploded punches on each other, Muhammad's appearing to carry more power, and in the 11th two massive rights to the jaw had Martin wobbling. Although Martin was still on his feet the referee called it off after 28 seconds of the session due to the challenger suffering what he called "a concussive period".

Having beaten Mike Rossman and James Scott in his last two fights, and rated at number three by *The Ring* magazine, Dwight Braxton (Muhammad Qawi) would be Muhammad's next challenger. The heavy-handed, two-fisted Braxton had lost just once in 17 contests against Johnny Davis, before gaining revenge at a later date. The fight against Scott, held in Rahway Prison, New Jersey, where the latter was serving time, was made even more interesting by the fact that Braxton had also served a term there.

7 November 1981. Michael Spinks w rsc 7 (15) Vonzell Johnson.
Venue: Playboy Hotel, Atlantic City, New Jersey, USA. **Recognition:** WBA. **Referee:** Larry Hazzard.
Fight Summary: In what was his first defence Spinks (173) was in control most of the way, and although Johnson (174¼) fought well at times his best punches had no real effect on the champion. The fifth was Johnson's best

round when taking the fight to Spinks, but after being cut by the left eye in the sixth and blowing heavily he was under attack in the seventh before being dropped by a right to the jaw following a left hook to the body. Boxing on after the 'eight' count Johnson was immediately in trouble when staggered by a left to the head, the referee stopping the contest with 1.13 on the clock.

19 December 1981. Dwight Braxton (Dwight Muhammad Qawi) w rsc 10 (15) Matthew Saad Muhammad.
Venue: Playboy Hotel, Atlantic City, New Jersey, USA. **Recognition:** WBC. **Referee:** Arthur Mercante.
Fight Summary: After having trouble making the weight the champion was unable to get going, being forced around the ring for round after round as Braxton (174½) battered him with punches from both hands. Never at any stage was Braxton concerned, and although Muhammad (174½) occasionally put some solid punches together it had no real effect on the man in front of him. After suffering bad rounds in the eighth and ninth when he was forced on the ropes and belted without firing much back, Muhammad was finally dropped in the tenth. Despite looking distinctly unsteady Muhammad was allowed to box on, but after Braxton had smashed him into the ropes and blasted away at him the referee finally called it off with six seconds of the session remaining.

13 February 1982. Michael Spinks w rsc 6 (15) Mustafa Wasajja.
Venue: Playboy Hotel, Atlantic City, New Jersey, USA. **Recognition:** WBA. **Referee:** Tony Perez.
Fight Summary: Although the champion was unable to drop Wasajja (174½) he was always in control, and never at any stage was it likely that the squat Ugandan southpaw could find a punch that could turn the fight his way. Wasajja was badly shaken in the in the fourth by lefts and rights to the jaw, as he was in the fifth, but when he was hit flush with a left hook in the sixth his legs turned to jelly. The referee gave Wasajja every chance. However, with Spinks (173¾) driving him around the ring and throwing solid blows from both hands, with nothing coming back the fight was stopped at 1.36 of the session.

21 March 1982. Dwight Braxton (Dwight Muhammad Qawi) w rsc 6 (15) Jerry Martin.
Venue: Showboat Hotel, Las Vegas, Nevada, USA. **Recognition:** WBC. **Referee:** Davy Pearl.
Fight Summary: Making his first defence, despite having to shift some excess before making the required weight Braxton (175) was soon into his stride, a right to the head in the first round warning Martin (173½) of what was likely to come. Twice Martin was put down in the second from a succession of heavy blows before returning to his corner with a cut over his right eye. Having somehow managed to get through the third and fourth Martin was under heavy pressure in the next two rounds, and when his gumshield was knocked out in the sixth the referee rescued him with 30 seconds of the session remaining.

11 April 1982. Michael Spinks w rsc 8 (15) Murray Sutherland.
Venue: Playboy Hotel, Atlantic City, New Jersey, USA. **Recognition:** WBA. **Referee:** Zack Clayton.
Fight Summary: For several rounds Sutherland (173¾) made a good showing, but after hurting the champion with a right to the jaw in the sixth the pattern of the fight changed. It seemed to be the wake-up call that Spinks needed, and when the round ended Sutherland was under a big attack from both hands. From then on, with Spinks (172) knowing that he had Sutherland where he wanted him, he forced a standing count in the eighth when the Scottish-born challenger was sent spinning by a heavy right to the head. Now in a bad way, Sutherland was dropped twice more before the referee rescued him on the 1.24 mark.

12 June 1982. Michael Spinks w rsc 8 (15) Jerry Celestine.
Venue: Playboy Hotel, Atlantic City, New Jersey, USA. **Recognition:** WBA. **Referee:** Jimmy Rondeau.
Fight Summary: Having sparred Spinks (173¾) on many occasions, Celestine (174¼) certainly made life difficult for the champion in the opening seven rounds as he showed good defensive moves. At the start of the eighth, when Spinks began to unload, a terrific right uppercut to the jaw dropped Celestine heavily. It certainly looked to be all over, and despite Celestine getting up before the count could be completed the referee stopped the contest, the finish being timed at 1.58.

7 August 1982. Dwight Braxton (Dwight Muhammad Qawi) w rsc 6 (15) Matthew Saad Muhammad.
Venue: The Spectrum, Philadelphia, Pennsylvania, USA. **Recognition:** WBC. **Referee:** Carlos Padilla.

Fight Summary: In a return contest, Braxton (174½) having won the title from Muhammad (175), the champion took over from the opening bell whether it was inside or at long range. Badly hurt in the second, Muhammad had his gumshield knocked out in the third as well as being dropped for the mandatory 'eight' count following an assortment of heavy blows. Having fought back as best as he could in the next two rounds Muhammad was soon up against it in the sixth as Braxton ploughed forward and when unable to fight back the contest was stopped at 1.23 of the session. From then on Braxton would be known by his Islamic name of Dwight Muhammad Qawi.

18 September 1982. Michael Spinks w rsc 9 (15) Johnny Davis.
Venue: Sands Hotel, Atlantic City, New Jersey, USA. **Recognition:** WBA. **Referee:** Larry Hazzard.
Fight Summary: For three rounds Davis (172¾) had Spinks (173¼) backing off before covering up well to thwart the champion's attempts to nail him, but by the fifth it was all about survival. Gradually softening Davis up with body punches and solid shots to the head Spinks eventually had his man over in the eighth. Back in action, carrying a cut on the left eye, Davis made it to the bell. However, with Spinks unloading big punches in the ninth, the referee stopped the contest to rescue the challenger at 2.27 of the round following a right to the jaw that left him an open target.

20 November 1982. Dwight Muhammad Qawi w rsc 11 (15) Eddie Davis.
Venue: Convention Hall, Atlantic City, New Jersey, USA. **Recognition:** WBC. **Referee:** Tony Perez.
Fight Summary: Put down in the first round by a right uppercut to the jaw, a dazed Davis (175) beat the count and survived the next two sessions before coming right back at the champion in the fourth. By now cut over the left eye, Davis slugged it out with the squat Qawi (174½) right up to the end of the ninth before the pace told on him. Hammered by punches from both hands in the tenth Davis somehow held up, but in the 11th with Qawi on the attack a big right to the head dropped him. Although he got to his feet in time the referee stopped the fight 28 seconds into the round.

Towards the end of the year the WBC announced that all world title bouts held under their banner would be contested over 12 rounds as from 1 January 1983.

18 March 1983. Michael Spinks w pts 15 Dwight Muhammad Qawi.
Venue: Convention Hall, Atlantic City, New Jersey, USA. **Recognition:** World. **Referee:** Larry Hazzard.
Scorecards: 144-141, 144-141, 144-140.
Fight Summary: Fighting to unify the title, Spinks (173) came out on top as he kept his left jab going against the much smaller Qawi (174) despite being dropped in the eighth by a right to the body. Most of those watching thought it was a slip as Qawi was standing on Spinks' foot before the latter fell down. Qawi was always in the fight as he rumbled forward but never able to get close enough to do any real damage and even in the last two sessions, when he tried to turn the fight his way, Spinks was unruffled. Although the match was made at the WBA's scheduled distance of 15 rounds, as opposed to the WBC's 12, it was fully supported by the latter.

Booked to make his first defence of the title against Eddie Mustafa Muhammad at The Armoury, Washington DC on 15 July, Spinks was furious when his opponent came in two and a half pounds overweight and flatly refused to shed the excess, claiming the scales had been tampered with. With the show being called off, Muhammad was suspended indefinitely by the District of Columbia Boxing Commission as well as being dropped from the WBA and WBC ratings.

Spinks had been seen as the champion by the United States Boxing Association/International (USBA/I) when they were formed in April, but in late October at their first ever convention, and now renamed the International Boxing Federation (IBF), they stated that they were recognising Eddie Davis as their title-holder.

25 November 1983. Michael Spinks w rsc 10 (15) Oscar Rivadeneyra.
Venue: Pacific Coliseum, Vancouver, Canada. **Recognition:** WBA/WBC. **Referee:** Joe Cortez.
Fight Summary: Despite being contested under WBA rules with the referee scoring, the WBC still recognised Spinks (173¾) as the world champion. Although badly cut over the left eye in the second round the elusive Rivadeneyra (173¼) managed to stay in the fight, slipping the jab and countering whenever the opportunity

presented itself, and gave the ring-rusty Spinks a difficult time up until the finish. Spinks, who was cut over the left eye in the second, eventually caught up with Rivadeneyra in the tenth when dropping him with a right uppercut-left hook to the head. Although Rivadeneyra got back into the fray he was stopped at 1.42 of the session after he had been put down again by another right uppercut. Earlier, in the seventh, Rivadeneyra had suffered a cut over his right eye.

25 February 1984. Michael Spinks w pts 12 Eddie Davis.
Venue: Resorts International Hotel, Atlantic City, New Jersey, USA. **Recognition:** World. **Referee:** Frank Cappuccino.
Scorecards: 119-109, 115-114, 118-111.
Fight Summary: Although the cagey Davis (173½) presented the champion with plenty of problems he lacked the firepower to take the title by storm, ultimately going down on points. In the early rounds Spinks (172) had difficulty with Davis's movement and was unable to get his punches off properly, but by the sixth he was beginning to find the target. Davis continued to make life tough for Spinks, who had been cut over the left eye in the fourth, and even forced the fight in the last two sessions. However, Spinks, who always landed the better quality punches, well deserved the decision even if it had not been one of his better performances. Prior to the contest the WBC had threatened to strip Spinks if he met the IBF's Davis over the WBA's distance of 15 rounds, stating they had an agreement with the WBA that this defence should be over 12 rounds. Common sense eventually prevailed when the fight went ahead supported by all three bodies.

In mid-July it was announced that Spinks would be defending his title in Reno, Nevada on 7 September over 12 rounds against Dwight Muhammad Qawi. It was later confirmed as a 15-round fight when the WBA and WBC agreed that Spinks should alternate between 12 and 15-round defences to satisfy both authorities. Unfortunately, after all that had gone on, Qawi pulled out within days of the fight taking place when complaining he had damaged his left shoulder in training.

Following that, Spinks said he was keen to move up to challenge Carlos de Leon for the WBC cruiser title if he could not make serious matches at light heavyweight, especially as two defences had now fallen through costing him a total of $2,000,000 in lost purses and there seemed to be no viable challengers in sight. Then, at the beginning of 1985, it was reported that he would be defending the title against the undefeated David Sears in February 1985. Scheduled for 15 rounds, the WBA's scheduled distance, it was supported by the WBC on the grounds that Spinks' next defence would be over 12 rounds. While not being involved in either promotion, Spinks was recognised by the IBF as champion.

23 February 1985. Michael Spinks w rsc 3 (15) David Sears.
Venue: Sands Hotel, Atlantic City, New Jersey, USA. **Recognition:** World. **Referee:** Larry Hazzard.
Fight Summary: Sears (173¾) made a bright start, shaking Spinks (170½) up with a left hook in the second round, before being advised by his corner to throw more of the same in the third. That proved to be Sears' downfall. Up until then Spinks had been pacing himself, and when he countered with a right over the top Sears was down and virtually beaten. Having taken the 'eight' count Sears tried to hang on but, with Spinks in full flow, when a right to the head had the challenger almost out on his feet the referee made a timely intervention with 1.02 on the clock.

6 June 1985. Michael Spinks w rsc 8 (12) Jim MacDonald.
Venue: Riviera Hotel, Las Vegas, Nevada, USA. **Recognition:** World. **Referee:** Davy Pearl.
Fight Summary: Outscored in every round the outclassed challenger did well to get beyond the seventh, having been knocked down in the fifth and seventh and carrying a swollen left eye. Although MacDonald (172¼) was taking a beating there was always the chance that he might nail Spinks (175) with one of his big punches as he had already hurt the latter a couple of times. Giving it one last effort MacDonald charged out for the eighth, but Spinks opened up to drop him with a cracking left hook to the jaw. Although MacDonald was up at 'eight' the referee called the fight off on the 1.30 mark.

Both the WBA and WBC vacated Spinks' light heavy title early in November after he had won the IBF version of the heavyweight crown from Larry Holmes (w pts 15 at the Riviera Hotel, Las Vegas on 21 September) and showed no interest in defending his 175lbs crown.

With no eliminators required just straight contests to decide the vacant titles, the WBA matched Leslie Stewart and Marvin Johnson, while the WBC settled on Prince Mama Mohammed and J. B. Williamson. A week later, at a press conference, Spinks officially relinquished the WBA, WBC and IBF titles, which was followed by the announcement that Eddie Mustafa Muhammad would be meeting the former Olympic gold medallist, Slobodan Kacar, for the last named title belt.

10 December 1985. J. B. Williamson w pts 12 Prince Mama Mohammed.
Venue: Inglewood Forum, Los Angeles, California, USA. **Recognition:** WBC. **Referee:** Marty Denkin.
Scorecards: 116-112, 117-111, 117-111.
Fight Summary: In a fight to decide a new champion Williamson (173) was a clear winner on all three cards, but lacked the power to finish his southpaw opponent off. There were no knockdowns, and Mohammed (171½), who finished the fight cut over the left eye and badly swollen on the right, was indecisive and lacked the know-how required at that level. It was an easy night for Williamson, who both started and finished scoring with rights through the middle that Mohammed had no answer to.

21 December 1985. Slobodan Kacar w pts 15 Eddie Mustafa Muhammad.
Venue: Sports Palace, Pesaro, Italy. **Recognition:** IBF. **Referee:** Joe Cortez.
Scorecards: 144-141, 145-143, 143-145.
Fight Summary: Now that Michael Spinks was up among the heavyweights, with Kacar (173½) and Muhammad (173½) looking to put their seal on the IBF version of the title at times it seemed that neither of them were that bothered. There were far too many clinches, and while the former Olympic champion looked amateurish at times Muhammad was not the fighter he had once been. Kacar, cut on the forehead in the fourth, appeared to be ahead at the halfway stage with his jab picking up the points, but although Muhammad occasionally hurt his rival with right crosses he was unable to follow up. Tiring fast, and with Muhammad being warned for butting, Kacar just about kept going to take the split points decision.

9 February 1986. Marvin Johnson w rsc 7 (15) Leslie Stewart.
Venue: Market Square Arena, Indianapolis, Indiana, USA. **Recognition:** WBA. **Referee:** Franco Priami.
Fight Summary: Johnson (174½) became the first man to win a light heavyweight title three times after stopping Stewart (175) 56 seconds into the seventh round. Cut on his right eye in the first, Stewart stuck to his boxing but found it difficult to keep his southpaw opponent at bay as he continuously rumbled forward throwing punches. Johnson was warned several times for butting, although it seemed to make no difference. Both men had battled hard during the opening five rounds, but in the sixth Stewart was badly cut over the left eye. Then, with Johnson pouring in solid shots in the seventh and the blood flowing the referee called it off after 56 seconds.

30 April 1986. Dennis Andries w pts 12 J. B. Williamson.
Venue: Picketts Lock Leisure Centre, Edmonton, London, England. **Recognition:** WBC. **Referee:** Angelo Poletti.
Scorecards: 116-114, 118-116, 113-115.
Fight Summary: Fighting as if his life depended on it the British champion never left Williamson (172) alone as he punched his way to the title in what became an extremely close and gruelling contest. The fight seemed to be going in the cleverer Williamson's favour at the end of the ninth, but after Andries (173) made a big push in two of the last three rounds his work-rate and effort was recognised favourably by two of the judges. It had been an untidy fight, and while Williamson was carrying a cut under the left eye from the fifth round onwards it hardly affected the result.

6 September 1986. Bobby Czyz w rsc 5 (15) Slobodan Kacar.
Venue: Hilton Hotel, Las Vegas, Nevada, USA. **Recognition:** IBF. **Referee:** Joey Curtis.
Fight Summary: Despite having a good reach advantage the champion failed to make it pay off, being outworked during the first three rounds before coming back hard in the fourth to temporarily take the play away from Czyz

(172¾). Coming back strongly in the fifth, after Czyz hurt Kacar (175) with lefts and rights to the jaw the latter lost his balance and went to the floor. Ruled a slip, Kacar was quickly under pressure as Czyz smashed in right after right, and after reeling against the ropes and not hitting back the fight was stopped in the latter's favour at 1.10 of the session.

10 September 1986. Dennis Andries w rsc 9 (12) Tony Sibson.
Venue: Alexandra Pavilion, Muswell Hill, London, England. **Recognition:** WBC. **Referee:** Sid Nathan.
Fight Summary: It was an uphill fight all the way for Sibson (172) as he found Andries (174½) just too big and strong for him. Even when he landed his best punches they seemed to bounce off the champion. Cut over the right eye and hurt by solid blows in the fourth, Sibson was in even worse shape at the end of the fifth when saved by the bell after taking a battering. Surprisingly, Sibson took the next two sessions as Andries had a breather, but when the latter opened up in the eighth and carried the pounding over into the ninth the writing was on the wall. With it being clear at that stage that Sibson had little left to offer, following four counts he was rescued on the 2.04 mark.

20 September 1986. Marvin Johnson w rsc 13 (15) Jean-Marie Emebe.
Venue: Market Square Arena, Indianapolis, Indiana, USA. **Recognition:** WBA. **Referee:** Luis Rivera.
Fight Summary: Defending his new title for the first time Johnson (175) was in a real war with the hard-hitting Emebe (174), having to take some heavy punches before finally coming through at 1.41 of the 13th. There were no knockdowns, but both men handed out plenty of punishment. In the 11th the doctor was called upon by the referee to inspect Emebe's facial damage, his left eye that was cut in the eighth and his right eye that was swollen shut giving concern. Although all three judges had the southpaw champion ahead by a couple of rounds coming into the 13th Emebe was still in with a chance, but after taking a heavy left hand and with the blood flowing the referee called the fight off.

26 December 1986. Bobby Czyz w rsc 1 (15) David Sears.
Venue: South Mountain Arena, West Orange, New Jersey, USA. **Recognition:** IBF. **Referee:** Joe Cortez.
Fight Summary: Making a fast start in what was his first defence, Czyz (175) stepped right into Sears (175), firing in heavy punches to the body before moving upstairs to land several big right hands to the head, the last of which sent the latter crashing to the floor. Although Sears got to his feet, the referee had already stopped the contest 61 seconds into the round after realising that it was pointless carrying on.

21 February 1987. Bobby Czyz w co 2 (15) Willie Edwards.
Venue: Trump Plaza Hotel, Atlantic City, New Jersey, USA. **Recognition:** IBF. **Referee:** Rudy Battle.
Fight Summary: Having retained his title in double-quick time some seven weeks earlier Czyz (174¼) went all out to finish off Edwards (175) in the same manner, but he was the one who was floored at the end of the round and saved by the bell. A moment earlier, following a head clash, Czyz had been cut on the left eye. With both men coming out quickly for the second, before too long Edwards was cut above the right eye. Charging into Edwards, who was now in disarray, after Czyz had the challenger backing into his own corner a tremendous right to the head sent him crashing to the floor to be counted out at 2.16 of the session.

7 March 1987. Thomas Hearns w rsc 10 (12) Dennis Andries.
Venue: Cobo Hall, Detroit, Michigan, USA. **Recognition:** WBC. **Referee:** Isaac Herrera.
Fight Summary: With the left jab consistently picking up points the challenger took no risks against the hefty swings of Andries (173½), especially after being cut over the left eye in the second round. The fight only came to life in the sixth when Andries was sent crashing from a right over the top, and even though he was dropped twice more and slipped over a couple of times he still managed to make it to the end of the session. The seventh saw Andries have his best round, but by the eighth Hearns (173¾) was back in control before having the champion over again in the ninth. Clearly this could not continue for much longer, and after Andries had been dropped again and then got up somewhat disorientated the referee stepped in to rescue him at 1.26 of the tenth. Even though Andries had shown tremendous courage to keep going as long as he did, in the end it was more fatigue than Hearns' punches that finished him.

Hearns relinquished the WBC version of the title in August to challenge for the vacant WBC middleweight crown, which was followed by Donny Lalonde, the WBC Continental Americas champion, being matched against Eddie Davis to decide the vacancy.

3 May 1987. Bobby Czyz w rsc 6 (15) Jim MacDonald.
Venue: Convention Centre, Atlantic City, New Jersey, USA. **Recognition:** IBF. **Referee:** Tony Orlando.
Fight Summary: After two quick defences of his title Czyz (174¼) picked his punches this time round, and although he staggered MacDonald (175) in the second and third rounds he stuck to the game plan. In the fourth Czyz began to go to the body more in an effort to slow MacDonald down, carrying on that line of attack into the sixth before nailing the latter with solid blows to the head from both hands. Despite MacDonald being stunned he did not go down, but following a solid left uppercut to the chin that wobbled him the referee decided to stop the contest 37 seconds into the session.

23 May 1987. Leslie Stewart w rtd 8 (15) Marvin Johnson.
Venue: National Stadium, Port of Spain, Trinidad, USA. **Recognition:** WBA. **Referee:** Bernie Soto.
Fight Summary: Cheered on by his local fans, Stewart (175) turned the tables on the southpaw champion despite having had difficulty making the weight immediately prior to the weigh-in. With his hard career fast catching up with him, Johnson (175) was dropped twice in the opening round before being outpunched from there onwards as Stewart took revenge. Although Stewart was cut on the left eye in the second round there was no let-up in his work, and while unable to drop Johnson the latter was so exhausted that he was retired by his corner after the eighth.

5 September 1987. Virgil Hill w rsc 4 (15) Leslie Stewart.
Venue: Trump Plaza Hotel & Casino, Atlantic City, New Jersey, USA. **Recognition:** WBA. **Referee:** Vincent Rainone.
Fight Summary: Boxing on the back foot and countering well, the challenger made a solid start before opening up in the fourth round after cutting Stewart (174¾) over the left eye. With Stewart in disarray Hill (173¾) came on strong, a left hook-right cross having the Trinidadian over. Up at 'eight', Stewart looked like a beaten man as Hill tore in throwing punches from all angles, and he was soon on the floor again. Although Stewart tried to make it to his feet in time it was a wasted effort, the referee stopping the fight without completing the count as the bell rang to end the round.

During their convention held in October, the WBA announced that in future all world title bouts contested under their auspices would be over 12 rounds.

29 October 1987. Charles Williams w rtd 9 (15) Bobby Czyz.
Venue: Hilton Hotel, Las Vegas, Nevada, USA. **Recognition:** IBF. **Referee:** Carlos Padilla.
Fight Summary: It looked likely to be an early night when Czyz (173¾) floored Williams (172¼) with a right to the head in the second round, and in the next session he sent the latter heavily into the ropes which brought about a standing 'eight' count. At the same time Czyz's right eye was starting to close, which probably explained the reason for Williams' spirited fight-back from the fourth round onwards. Having made up any lost ground and ahead on the cards Williams came out for the ninth, boxing coolly and sending in hurtful blows. Although Williams picked up a cut over right eye in that session it made no difference to the result, the champion being retired on his stool at the end of the session.

21 November 1987. Virgil Hill w pts 12 Rufino Angulo.
Venue: Pierre de Coubertin Stadium, Paris, France. **Recognition:** WBA. **Referee:** John Coyle.
Scorecards: 118-111, 120-107, 120-107.
Fight Summary: Having dropped Angulo (173¼) with a left hook counter in the opening round the champion settled down to control the contest with an accurate lead, picking his man off throughout. Angulo was always a danger, being strong and aggressive, but lacking the tools to worry Hill (174½) unduly many of his wild swings were avoided with ease. Occasionally Hill was forced to give ground, but with it never more than momentarily Angulo was usually made to pay.

27 November 1987. Donny Lalonde w rsc 2 (12) Eddie Davis.
Venue: National Stadium, Port of Spain, Trinidad. **Recognition:** WBC. **Referee:** Ismael Quinones Falu.
Fight Summary: Contesting the title vacated by Thomas Hearns, Davis (173) made a bright start before being hammered to the floor by a right after Lalonde (173¼) had set him up with the jab. Back in action the moment the mandatory 'eight' count had been completed, Davis was dropped again right at the end of the first round. Coming out shakily for the second Davis was soon at the mercy of Lalonde, who had actually been cut on the left eye in the opening session, and when another big right had sent him crashing to the floor the referee called the fight off after just 22 seconds had elapsed.

3 April 1988. Virgil Hill w rsc 11 (12) Jean-Marie Emebe.
Venue: Civic Centre, Bismarck, North Dakota, USA. **Recognition:** WBA. **Referee:** Roberto Ramirez.
Fight Summary: In his first defence Hill (174) was far too good for his game challenger, who was effectively boxed to a standstill before he was dropped in the 11th. Emebe (173) was rescued by the referee at 1.29 of the session after getting up and being hammered without respite. Although Emebe had his moments, especially in the eighth when Hill was cut over the left eye after a two-fisted attack, they were few and far between. By the end of the tenth Emebe looked a beaten fighter, his right eye badly swollen and his body weary from the pounding he had received, and it was no surprise that he succumbed in the 11th.

29 May 1988. Donny Lalonde w rsc 5 (12) Leslie Stewart.
Venue: National Stadium, Port of Spain, Trinidad. **Recognition:** WBC. **Referee:** Marty Denkin.
Fight Summary: Despite Stewart (173¼) being knocked down by a right to the jaw in the second he came back strongly. Fighting on equal terms through the next two rounds, Stewart was throwing right hands of his own before Lalonde (172½) caught up with him in the fifth when dropping him with a solid right to the head. Making it to his feet at the count of 'nine' Stewart was allowed back into the fray, but with punches incessantly raining in on him and not fighting back the referee rescued him at 2.27 of the session.

6 June 1988. Virgil Hill w pts 12 Ramzi Hassan.
Venue: Hilton Hotel, Las Vegas, Nevada, USA. **Recognition:** WBA. **Referee:** Mills Lane.
Scorecards: 118-109, 116-112, 118-109.
Fight Summary: Making hard work of what should have been a relatively easy defence, Hill (174½) was forced to travel the full distance as Hassan (175) ultimately proved to be a tough nut to crack. Although outboxing Hassan for most of the way, landing with left jabs, left hooks and right crosses, with the durable man from Jordan taking everything in his stride Hill never looked likely to win inside the distance. Docked a point for going low in the 11th hardly changed anything for Hill, but what was a surprise was the fact that one of the judges actually gave Hassan three rounds.

Following much dissent at the WBA convention in October, in which 27 of the 71 delegates walked out, the World Boxing Organisation (WBO) was formed. A few weeks later, after Michael Moorer (175) stopped Ramzi Hassan (173¼) inside five rounds to win the vacant Continental Americas title at the International Exposition Centre, Cleveland, Ohio on 3 December, the WBO recognised him as their first world champion at the weight.

10 June 1988. Charles Williams w rsc 11 (15) Richard Caramanolis.
Venue: Sports Park, Annecy, France. **Recognition:** IBF. **Referee:** Randy Neumann.
Fight Summary: Defending the title for the first time Williams (172½) was quick off the mark when flooring Caramanolis (174½) towards the end of the opening round, only for the latter to come back hard with straight rights in the next four sessions. By the fifth, however, Caramanolis was beginning to be worn down as Williams countered with solid rights of his own. He was then badly cut down the left side of his nose. In the ninth Williams' left eye began to swell, and stepping up the pace he worked from head to body as Caramanolis sagged. After being floored twice in the 11th, Caramanolis was rescued by the referee following the second knockdown when the towel was thrown in by the latter's corner.

Subsequently, all world title bouts would be contested over 12 rounds when the IBF announced that they were falling into line with the WBA and WBC from 1 September.

21 October 1988. Charles Williams w rsc 3 Rufino Angulo.
Venue: Space Arena, Villenave d'Ornon, France. **Recognition:** IBF. **Referee:** Joe O'Neil.
Fight Summary: After a fairly even first round Williams (174¾) got down to work, dropping his challenger twice in the second and twice in the third before the referee halted the contest at 2.21 of the third. Right from the start Williams proved to be far too strong for Angulo (174), belabouring him with left jabs and rights to the head while working him over with left hooks to the body. Angulo finished the contest with his right eye cut and a gashed forehead.

7 November 1988. Sugar Ray Leonard w rsc 9 Donny Lalonde.
Venue: Caesar's Palace, Las Vegas, Nevada, USA. **Recognition:** WBC. **Referee:** Richard Steele.
Fight Summary: In a contest for the inaugural WBC super middleweight title, and with Lalonde's light heavyweight title also on the line, most of the money was on Leonard (165). But after four rounds he was behind on all the scorecards, having been knocked down by a right in that session. From there on, however, Leonard made it his fight when gradually cutting Lalonde (167) down to size, his combination punching being the main difference between them. Eventually, in the ninth, Leonard backed Lalonde up on the ropes and hammered him with lefts and rights before a left hook sent the latter down, blood coming from his mouth, bringing about an immediate stoppage with 30 seconds of the session remaining.

Lalonde, who entered the ring one pound inside the super middleweight limit, should not have been forced to put his 175lbs crown on the line at the same time, although the situation went some way to righting itself when Leonard relinquished the WBC light heavyweight title following the fight in order to concentrate on defending his lighter belt. Further to that, a match was made between Dennis Andries and Tony Willis, the North American Boxing Federation (NABF) champion, to find a successor.

11 November 1988. Virgil Hill w rsc 10 Willie Featherstone.
Venue: Civic Centre, Bismarck, North Dakota, USA. **Recognition:** WBA. **Referee:** Steve Smoger.
Fight Summary: Dominating the contest with the left jab the champion proved to be too good for the tough Featherstone (174), who despite getting through with an occasional big right was unable to follow up any advantage he may have had. Dropped by a countering left hook in the third and cut under the right eye in the sixth, Featherstone was up against it when he slipped over in the seventh. Starting to throw more rights in the ninth Hill (174) went after Featherstone in the tenth and following a big right uppercut that sent the latter across the ring and into the ropes the referee stopped the fight on the 2.05 mark.

14 January 1989. Michael Moorer w rsc 2 Victor Claudio.
Venue: Auburn Hills Palace, Detroit, Michigan, USA. **Recognition:** WBO. **Referee:** Sam Williams.
Fight Summary: Coming in as a late substitute after Art Jimmerson was forced to pull out with a bad ear infection, Claudio (173¼) was no match for the new champion, being quickly under attack. This, despite the Puerto Rican throwing punches from both hands in a hectic start. Saved by the bell at the end of the first, having been dropped by a southpaw left, although Claudio made it out for the second round Moorer (175) was on to him in a flash. With the challenger on the ropes taking an unmerciful battering the moment he dropped to his knees the referee stopped the fight, 25 seconds into the session.

19 February 1989. Michael Moorer w rsc 6 Frankie Swindell.
Venue: The High School Gym, Monessen, Pennsylvania, USA. **Recognition:** WBO. **Referee:** Andy DePaul.
Fight Summary: Building up a good lead in the opening three rounds with solid southpaw jabs, crosses and body shots, Moorer (174) seemed to be well on his way to victory before Swindell (175) shook him up badly at the end of the fourth. Although Moorer came back to some degree in the fifth his left eye was beginning to close. Getting his jab to work in the sixth was the key for Moorer, and after catching Swindell with heavy combinations the referee stopped the contest on the 2.50 mark when the latter was on the ropes being battered without return.

21 February 1989. Dennis Andries w rsc 5 Tony Willis.
Venue: Convention Centre, Tucson, Arizona, USA. **Recognition:** WBC. **Referee:** Carlos Padilla.

Fight Summary: In a fight for the vacant title, and looking to get back his old belt, Andries (173) immediately chased down Willis (173½), throwing in punches from both hands and generally looking much stronger than his opponent. All the unbeaten Willis seemed able to do was to hold and it came as no surprise when he was deducted a point at the end of the third. The fourth saw much of the same from Willis, and after being dropped by a left-right-left in the fifth he was deemed unable to carry on with ten seconds of the session remaining.

4 March 1989. Virgil Hill w pts 12 Bobby Czyz.
Venue: Civic Centre, Bismarck, North Dakota, USA. **Recognition:** WBA. **Referee:** Tony Perez.
Scorecards: 117-112, 117-111, 119-110.
Fight Summary: Despite being comprehensively outboxed the challenger was at his most dangerous early on, dropping Hill (174½) with a cracking right to the jaw in the third round. Strangely ruled a slip, Czyz (174½) was unable to repeat the feat. Even though he caught Hill with the occasional right he was unable to follow up. Cut over the left eye in the seventh Hill never let it worry him, and although being made to work hard he continued to jab Czyz's head back throughout the remainder of the contest.

22 April 1989. Michael Moorer w rsc 1 Freddie Delgado.
Venue: Auburn Hills Palace, Detroit, Michigan, USA. **Recognition:** WBO. **Referee:** Bobby Watson.
Fight Summary: Trying to unsettle Moorer (171), Delgado (171) came out throwing wild blows, some of them low. However, he was made to pay when the southpaw champion almost smashed him out of the ring, an action that enforced a standing count. Badly shaken, Delgado tried to fight back before being dumped by a right-left that saw him taking the mandatory 'eight' count. There was no way that Moorer was going to let this one slip, and he was battering Delgado without reply when the referee stopped the contest after just 66 seconds.

27 May 1989. Virgil Hill w rsc 7 Joe Lasisi.
Venue: Civic Centre, Bismarck, North Dakota, USA. **Recognition:** WBA. **Referee:** Hubert Earle.
Fight Summary: A difficult task for Lasisi (173) became even harder when he was dropped by a left-hand counter before being comprehensively outboxed by the champion for round after round. Never really in the fight, although Lasisi caught Hill (173) with an overarm right in the fifth and occasionally landed solidly to the body the latter remained unperturbed. It was Hill's speed and accuracy with left jabs and hooks that did the damage and by the sixth Lasisi was banged up around both eyes and looking like a beaten man. The seventh finally saw Hill unload. With Hill going through the gears, after battering the tough Lasisi with lefts and rights the referee stopped the fight 116 seconds into the session when there was no response.

24 June 1989. Jeff Harding w rsc 12 Dennis Andries.
Venue: Convention Centre, Atlantic City, New Jersey, USA. **Recognition:** WBC. **Referee:** Joe Cortez.
Fight Summary: Although taking a beating for much of the time, been dropped in the fifth, cut over both eyes, as well as carrying a badly damaged nose, it was almost miraculous that Harding (174½) reached the 12th round. Harding had been a replacement for Donny Lalonde, who decided to retire a month earlier, and at times he must have wondered whether it had been a good idea to take the Canadian's place. However, by the eighth Andries (175) was beginning to show signs of weariness, but although managing to keep things together he suddenly ran out of gas in the 11th. Even though Harding picked up a badly cut right eye Andries was a spent force in the 12th, being floored twice before the referee rescued him just 97 seconds from the final bell.

25 June 1989. Charles Williams w rtd 10 Bobby Czyz.
Venue: Convention Centre, Atlantic City, New Jersey, USA. **Recognition:** IBF. **Referee:** Rudy Battle.
Fight Summary: Trying to reclaim his old title, even though Czyz (175) gave it his best shot it was not enough as Williams (174½) took his hardest blows and continually hit back. Having taken the opening round and cut the champion over the right eye in the third Czyz had his successes, but thereafter he was gradually ground down. In the eighth round, Czyz, his left eye badly damaged, was knocked down twice by powerful rights to the head before being saved by the bell when in a precarious position. Although Czyz was allowed to come out for the next two sessions, with Williams in full flight it was a hopeless task. Under constant pressure and his left eye closed shut, Czyz was finally retired by his corner at the end of the tenth.

25 June 1989. Michael Moorer w rsc 8 Leslie Stewart.
Venue: Convention Centre, Atlantic City, New Jersey, USA. **Recognition:** WBO. **Referee:** Ted Pick.
Fight Summary: Starting badly, the undefeated champion was picked off by left jabs and rights over the top for several rounds, and at the end of the seventh all three judges had Stewart (174¼) ahead. It was at that point things dramatically changed. Taking on a new lease of life Moorer (173¾) finally caught up with Stewart, southpaw lefts and rights having the latter down for the mandatory 'eight' count. Dropped again, Stewart was stopped with 36 seconds of the eighth left after getting up and being battered without return.

24 October 1989. Jeff Harding w rtd 2 Tom Collins.
Venue: Boondall Entertainment Centre, Brisbane, Australia. **Recognition:** WBC. **Referee:** Lou Filippo.
Fight Summary: Dropped in the opening round by a right to the head Collins (171¾) came back hard in the second when landing rights of his own to shake the champion up. However, upon going back to his corner he retired himself, claiming that Harding (172) had hit him in the throat and that he was unable to continue.

24 October 1989. Virgil Hill w rsc 1 James Kinchen.
Venue: Civic Centre, Bismarck, North Dakota, USA. **Recognition:** WBA. **Referee:** Billy Yohan.
Fight Summary: After making the challenger miss right at the start of the contest, Hill (175) got down to work quickly and precisely with big left hooks to shake his rival up. Caught cold, Kinchen (174) was hit from both hands as Hill opened up with powerful blows, and on being dropped he rolled on to the ring apron. Although getting to his feet, when it could be seen that Kinchen was still badly dazed, the referee had no hesitation in stopping the fight with just eight seconds of the opening session remaining.

16 November 1989. Michael Moorer w rsc 1 Jeff Thompson.
Venue: Resorts International Hotel, Atlantic City, New Jersey, USA. **Recognition:** WBO. **Referee:** Earl Morton.
Fight Summary: Having looked pedestrian in his last title defence, Moorer (175) soon had his fellow southpaw in some difficulty. Knocked over by a solid jab and cut over the left eye, with it being clear that Thompson (175) was in real trouble, Moorer was not going to let him off the hook. Unleashing a tremendous right hook Moorer sent Thompson crashing down again, but this time the referee called the fight off on the 1.46 mark without bothering to take up the count.

22 December 1989. Michael Moorer w rsc 6 Mike Sedillo.
Venue: Auburn Hills Palace, Detroit, Michigan, USA. **Recognition:** WBO. **Referee:** Sam Williams.
Fight Summary: Under pressure right from the opening bell the lanky challenger did well to remain upright for so long as Moorer (175) pounded him from both hands. Cut and swollen on the right eye in the third round, Sedillo (175) remained upright well into the sixth before finally succumbing after a big southpaw left had sent him staggering into the ropes. With Moorer letting the punches go from both hands to floor Sedillo, when the latter got up at 'seven', his right cheek gashed, the referee stopped the contest. The finish was timed at 2.07.

7 January 1990. Charles Williams w rsc 8 Frankie Swindell.
Venue: Tropicana Hotel & Casino, Atlantic City, New Jersey, USA. **Recognition:** IBF. **Referee:** Tony Orlando.
Fight Summary: Making his fourth defence Williams (172½) took a few rounds to get the measure of Swindell (175), who had initially struggled to make the weight. Working at distance before moving inside Williams had taken over by the fifth, accurate left jabs and uppercuts being his best weapons, and in the eighth he dropped Swindell following a barrage of rights to the head. Although still dazed, Swindell got up to make it to his stool at the bell before the referee, on the advice of the doctor, stopped the contest during the interval.

3 February 1990. Michael Moorer w rtd 9 Marcellus Allen.
Venue: Convention Hall, Atlantic City, New Jersey, USA. **Recognition:** WBO. **Referee:** Frank Cappuccino.
Fight Summary: Refusing to stand in front of Moorer the light-hitting Allen (175) was soon on his bike, a tactic that initially made life difficult for the southpaw champion. Instead of cutting the ring down Moorer (175) chased Allen for round after round without being able to get heavy shots off. Moorer was obviously well ahead on aggression alone, but it was only in the ninth that the fast tiring Allen began to get caught with heavy punches which led to his corner sensibly retiring him during the interval.

25 February 1990. Virgil Hill w pts 12 David Vedder.
Venue: Civic Centre, Bismarck, North Dakota, USA. **Recognition:** WBA. **Referee:** Eddie Eckert.
Scorecards: 119-111, 119-110, 119-107.
Fight Summary: Forced to go the distance by an extremely tough and willing challenger, Hill (174¾) ended the contest with a damaged right hand after hurting it early on. Relying on the left hand was not a problem for Hill, as that was his best mode of attack anyway, but it possibly allowed Vedder (175) to stay in the fight. Despite the injury Hill stepped up the pace in the last two sessions, the ropes keeping Vedder upright in the 11th following a big attack, and he came close to a stoppage in the last as the latter held on to survive.

18 March 1990. Jeff Harding w rsc 11 Nestor Giovannini.
Venue: Resorts International Hotel, Atlantic City, New Jersey, USA. **Recognition:** WBC. **Referee:** Joe Cortez.
Fight Summary: In what was another tough battle for Harding (174), who chose to walk through the punches from first to last, it was probably just as well for him that the challenger injured his right hand in the second round. Dropped by a left hook to the head in the third, Giovannini (175) was immediately galvanised into action before taking a low one and given time out to recover. Cut over the left eye in the seventh due to a coming together of heads, Harding continued to take the fight to Giovannini, and in the tenth he floored him with a solid left hook. Despite that, Giovannini came out for the 11th as if nothing had happened, but after being sent crashing by heavy lefts to the head he was rescued on the 56-second mark without the referee bothering to take up the count.

28 April 1990. Michael Moorer w co 1 Mario Melo.
Venue: Taj Mahal Hotel & Casino, Atlantic City, New Jersey, USA. **Recognition:** WBO. **Referee:** Joe O'Neil.
Fight Summary: Yet another contest where the opposition could have been better saw Moorer (174) go for his fellow southpaw right from the opening bell, staggering him with straight lefts and putting him on alert. Having hurt Melo (174) with a left to the body, the champion quickly brought the bout to a finish with a cracking left to the head that sent the Argentine crashing to the floor to be counted out at 1.52 of the session.

7 July 1990. Virgil Hill w pts 12 Tyrone Frazier.
Venue: Civic Centre, Bismarck, North Dakota, USA. **Recognition:** WBA. **Referee:** Billy Yohan.
Scorecards: 120-109, 120-108, 120-108.
Fight Summary: Despite a wide points win, Hill (175) failed to impress against a challenger who was only just recovering from an operation for a detached retina. There was very little fighting of note from Hill throughout, apart from a big left that sent Frazier (173) through the ropes in the second and a few solid right hands, one of which stunned him in the 11th. Afterwards, Hill could not really explain what was wrong, although those around him felt that the left thumb he had broken a few months earlier, which had to be pinned, had something to do with it.

28 July 1990. Dennis Andries w co 7 Jeff Harding.
Venue: Rod Laver Arena, Melbourne, Australia. **Recognition:** WBC. **Referee:** Arthur Mercante.
Fight Summary: Regaining his old title from the man he lost it to, Andries (174) showed once again his remarkable powers of recovery as he battled to overcome the champion's lead. After a couple of sticky rounds Harding (175) had won four straight, and although swollen above the left eye he came out for the seventh confident of victory. At this stage of the fight the tiring Andries knew what he had to do as he continually pushed Harding back while taking shots himself, before landing with a tremendous overarm right that sent the latter down. Although Harding, his left eye pouring blood, made a mighty effort to get to his feet he just failed to do so, being counted out with 45 seconds of the session remaining.

10 October 1990. Dennis Andries w rsc 4 Sergio Merani.
Venue: Royal Albert Hall, Kensington, London, England. **Recognition:** WBC. **Referee:** Franz Marti.
Fight Summary: Making the first defence of the title he had regained for the second time, Andries (173¾) temporarily looked as though he might lose it quickly after Merani (173½) made a confident start when winning the opening two rounds. What was not known at the time was that heavy rights and lefts from Andries at the end of the second had broken Merani's jaw. The third session saw Andries get right back into the fight and in the fourth, although the challenger kept going, it was apparent that there was something wrong with his jaw, which

led to an inspection by the referee. At the end of the fourth when it was discovered that Merani could not open his mouth the doctor advised the referee that the Argentine could not continue.

15 December 1990. Michael Moorer w co 8 Danny Stonewalker.
Venue: Civic Arena, Pittsburgh, Pennsylvania, USA. **Recognition:** WBO. **Referee:** Frank Cappuccino.
Fight Summary: Retaining his title for the ninth time, Moorer (175) had little trouble with his challenger after putting him down in the opening round with a southpaw jab. Unsteady on his feet in the second and cut on the nose in the fifth Stonewalker (174¾) was still there even if he was not a threat, and in the seventh he was dropped again, this time after taking an overarm left to the head. Rescued by the bell after being floored again, Stonewalker was counted out just 11 seconds into the eighth, having been decked by the first punch of the session, a straight left to the body.

When Moorer relinquished the WBO version of the title in April 1991 to campaign as a heavyweight, Tom Collins was matched against Leeonzer Barber to find a new champion.

6 January 1991. Virgil Hill w pts 12 Mike Peak.
Venue: Civic Centre, Bismarck, North Dakota, USA. **Recognition:** WBA. **Referee:** Eddie Eckert.
Scorecards: 120-108, 120-108, 119-109.
Fight Summary: Once again flattering to deceive, after Hill (174) was cut under the left eye in the first round following a head clash he generally failed to look like a champion. It was not until the fourth that he began to find the range with his left jab, but it was clear at that stage that Peak (173) had come to survive, boxing off the back foot and infrequently hitting the target. Almost a shut-out win for Hill, in real terms it was no more than a workout against a man who was not of championship class.

12 January 1991. Charles Williams w pts 12 Mwehu Beya.
Venue: Sports Palace, St Vincent, Aosta, Italy. **Recognition:** IBF. **Referee:** Frank Cappuccino.
Scorecards: 116-112, 115-113, 116-113.
Fight Summary: Not at his best, the champion was forced to hang on for the last two rounds as Beya (172) made a big effort to make up lost ground. Although Williams (172½) started well enough, making the fight as Beya backed off, he failed to capitalise mainly due to injuring his right hand in the fourth. The further the fight went the more confident Beya became, and had he got his left jab working earlier it could have been different. Beya was cut over the left eye in the fifth.

19 January 1991. Dennis Andries w pts 12 Guy Waters.
Venue: Memorial Drive Tennis Centre, Adelaide, Australia. **Recognition:** WBC. **Referee:** Richard Steele.
Scorecards: 115-114, 116-112, 117-113.
Fight Summary: By fighting in safety-first mode, especially in the first half of the fight, the challenger failed to press home any openings he had as Andries (174¾) bulled his way to the unanimous decision. Although Waters (173½) proved that he had plenty of boxing ability and a strong chin it was clear that he had difficulty in working Andries out, but while there was never a great deal between them in points he was unable to move up a gear when required.

20 April 1991. Charles Williams w rsc 2 James Kinchen.
Venue: Caesar's Hotel & Casino, Atlantic City, New Jersey, USA. **Recognition:** IBF. **Referee:** Frank Cappuccino.
Fight Summary: Walking straight into Kinchen (175) from the bell, the champion immediately made his extra power pay as he whacked in punches from both hands. Towards the end of the opening session Kinchen was caught by a cluster of blows before being dropped by a right to the head. Despite getting up he was being battered by Williams (174) when the gong came to his aid. In the second round, with Kinchen rapidly being taken apart, the referee rescued him after 23 seconds had elapsed.

9 May 1991. Leeonzer Barber w rtd 5 Tom Collins.
Venue: Town Hall, Leeds, England. **Recognition:** WBO. **Referee:** Roberto Ramirez.

Fight Summary: Fighting for the title relinquished by his stable-mate, Michael Moorer, Barber (173½) was soon taking the fight to Collins (174½), who landed just one worthwhile punch in the whole of the contest before being retired at the end of the fifth. Barber, a 12-fight novice, was on top all the way as Collins stayed mainly on the ropes. Having been dropped by a right to the head in the second round, which left a bad swelling on his forehead, and with Collins doing little more than take punishment, his subsequent decision not to continue came as a welcome relief. It was only after the bell rang to start the sixth that the referee realised that Collins would not be fighting on.

3 June 1991. Thomas Hearns w pts 12 Virgil Hill.
Venue: Caesar's Palace, Las Vegas, Nevada, USA. **Recognition:** WBA. **Referee:** Mills Lane.
Scorecards: 116-112, 115-113, 115-113.
Fight Summary: In a battle of left jabs the champion was outscored by Hearns (174), who took the honours and showed that he still had plenty left in the tank. Hill (173) was always in the fight, occasionally slamming in big punches of his own, but despite coming on strong in the latter rounds he lacked the power required to stop Hearns in his tracks. Marked around both eyes at the finish, although Hill gave it his best shot, he was unable to stop Hearns from becoming a five-weight champion.

20 July 1991. Charles Williams w co 3 Vincent Boulware.
Venue: Ariston Theatre, San Remo, Italy. **Recognition:** IBF. **Referee:** Joe O'Neil.
Fight Summary: Moving at speed the champion soon had Boulware (173¼) where he wanted him; the opening two sessions seeing the latter backed against the ropes where he was forced to take a mixture of heavy blows to head and body. At the start of the third round, when Williams (174¼), carrying a cut over his right eye, began to open up with body shots Boulware, despite hitting back, was eventually dropped by two short rights. On getting back into the fray Boulware was given no respite, and following some heavy punches to the head he dropped down to be counted out with 11 seconds of the round remaining.

11 September 1991. Jeff Harding w pts 12 Dennis Andries.
Venue: Odeon Cinema, Hammersmith, London, England. **Recognition:** WBC. **Referee:** Joe Cortez.
Scorecards: 115-114, 115-113, 114-114.
Fight Summary: Despite losing his title Andries (175) yet again proved his mettle in what was the third championship fight between him and Harding (175). The first five rounds saw Andries at his best as he dished out punishment to leave swellings over both of Harding's eyes and put himself in front. Although each man continued to throw heavy shots, as the fight progressed it appeared that Harding was lasting better and was more accurate. Harding, showing a sound chin, was still under pressure though as Andries continued to give everything he had, and the decision could have gone either way. In such a close contest, neither man deserved to lose.

19 October 1991. Charles Williams w rsc 2 Freddie Delgado.
Venue: Williamsburg Memorial Fieldhouse, Brooklyn, NYC, New York, USA. **Recognition:** IBF. **Referee:** Al Rothenberg.
Fight Summary: Defending the title for the eighth time, Williams (172) started fast to have Delgado (173) in some difficulty before a series of blows from both hands to the head had the latter down for a mandatory count in the opening session. On coming out for the second there was a bad clash of heads that left Williams cut over the left eye, but instead of nursing it through the session the champion ripped into Delgado with all he had. Battered endlessly thereafter, Delgado was rescued by the referee on the 2.24 mark when not fighting back.

7 January 1992. Leeonzer Barber w pts 12 Anthony Hembrick.
Venue: Auburn Hills Palace, Detroit, Michigan, USA. **Recognition:** WBO. **Referee:** Frank Cappuccino.
Scorecards: 114-113, 115-113, 113-115.
Fight Summary: Closely fought, when a countering right to the jaw put Hembrick (174) down in the 11th round it was almost certainly the difference between the champion winning or losing his title. Although Hembrick's jab was a point scorer it was the power of Barber (172) that was most noticeable, and at the start of the ninth he sent his rival stumbling to the floor. At the start of the tenth Barber's left eye was swelling up fast, but after having Hembrick over again in the 11th the latter began to tire rapidly and was happy to hear the final bell.

20 March 1992. Iran Barkley w pts 12 Thomas Hearns.
Venue: Caesar's Palace, Las Vegas, Nevada, USA. **Recognition:** WBA. **Referee:** Mills Lane.
Scorecards: 114-113, 115-113, 113-114.
Fight Summary: Having struggled to make the weight probably explained the champion's disappointing display, but that should not detract from a best-ever performance by Barkley (174). Outboxed for the opening three rounds Barkley suddenly found a thudding left hook to the jaw in the fourth that sent Hearns (174½) down for the mandatory count, and from thereon in he had his nose just about in front. Although Hearns continued to fire in heavy blows, it was Barkley's work-rate that won the day. Both men finished with swellings over their eyes, and Barkley, carrying a broken left hand, stated afterwards that by staying in close had won him the fight as it took away much of Hearns' power.

Following Barkley's decision to relinquish the WBA version of the title in April to concentrate on defending his IBF super middleweight crown, Virgil Hill and Frank Tate were matched to find a successor.

5 June 1992. Jeff Harding w rsc 8 Christophe Tiozzo.
Venue: Sports Palace, Marseille, France. **Recognition:** WBC. **Referee:** Richard Steele.
Fight Summary: Tiozzo (174¾) made the better start, moving well and sending in left jabs to the champion's face, and it was not until the sixth round that the tide began to turn. At that point Harding (174¾) stepped it up to get his left jab working, while Tiozzo, cut under the left eye, began to show signs of tiring despite continuing to throw good punches. Coming out for the eighth, Tiozzo decided to punch it out on the inside with Harding, a tactic that proved to be his downfall. Eventually beaten to the punch Tiozzo was dropped by a cracking left hook to the jaw, and although he got up he was rescued by the referee as Harding, cut and swollen over both eyes, was battering him from both hands with nothing coming back. The time of the finish was not reported.

29 September 1992. Virgil Hill w pts 12 Frank Tate.
Venue: Civic Centre, Bismarck, North Dakota, USA. **Recognition:** WBA. **Referee:** Bernie Soto.
Scorecards: 116-112, 118-116, 120-109.
Fight Summary: Fighting for the title that Iran Barkley had relinquished, and for the belt he once held, Hill (175) boxed an excellent tactical campaign to beat Tate (175), forcing the fight with left jabs and hooks. Tate, who was cut over the right eye in the third, failed to throw enough leather and was caught up in clinches far too often. In the 11th Tate shook up Hill with a right to the jaw before the latter came back with rights of his own in the final session.

3 December 1992. Jeff Harding w pts 12 David Vedder.
Venue: Franklyn Rooms, Paris, France. **Recognition:** WBC. **Referee:** Arthur Mercante.
Scorecards: 117-113, 116-114, 118-114.
Fight Summary: Once again coming from behind to retain his title, Harding (170¾) had to call on all his resources to get past Vedder (169¾), who made an impressive start. His good work had him in front after six rounds before Harding moved up a notch in the seventh to get himself in with a shout. Despite being cut on the left eye Harding poured it on from the eighth, banging in solid jabs and hooks as a tiring Vedder tried to counter before being pushed back.

Ruled out by a cut eye a week before defending his WBC crown against Mike McCallum, Harding had to sit it out while the former stopped Randall Yonker in the fifth round at the MGM Grand, Las Vegas, Nevada, USA on 4 March 1994 to win the WBC 'interim' title. The pair would eventually get it on in July 1994 after months of promotional difficulties had finally been overcome.

20 February 1993. Virgil Hill w tdec 11 Adolpho Washington.
Venue: The Dome, Fargo, North Dakota, USA. **Recognition:** WBA. **Referee:** Steve Smoger.
Scorecards: 109-99, 110-98, 109-99.
Fight Summary: Pressing from the bell the challenger made a good start, banging in solid left jabs, and by the end of the opening round Hill (175) had been cut over the right eye. Things changed dramatically in the second when Washington (175) was dropped heavily by a countering left hook and then had his nose broken. Although the

brave Washington, swollen over the left eye, kept going he was now severely handicapped, Hill making him pay with stabbing left hands to the face and rights over the top. Having got back to his corner at the end of the 11th, with the referee still deciding whether to let Washington out for the final session, when a cameraman got too close for a shot he inadvertently slipped and cut the challenger's eye right open. Following that, the referee was forced to go to the cards.

27 February 1993. Leeonzer Barber w pts 12 Mike Sedillo.
Venue: Capital City Gym, Beijing, China. **Recognition:** WBO. **Referee:** James Jen-Kin.
Scorecards: 116-111, 117-112, 116-111.
Fight Summary: In what was China's first professional boxing promotion for over 40 years, Sedillo (174) started well, banging in punches from both hands and pressing forward at every opportunity. However, once Barber (175) found his rhythm and got his left jab to work the challenger, while still dangerous, had great difficulty in closing his man down. Towards the end it had become one-sided as Barber picked his shots, but in not following up his advantage he allowed the game Sedillo to survive to the final bell.

20 March 1993. Henry Maske w pts 12 Charles Williams.
Venue: Philips Hall, Dusseldorf, Germany. **Recognition:** IBF. **Referee:** Al Rothenberg.
Scorecards: 116-111, 118-110, 116-111.
Fight Summary: A gold medallist from the 1988 Olympics, Maske (174) quickly made his imprint on the fight with southpaw jabs and crosses making it difficult for the champion to get set. Returning to the ring after suffering two broken left hands and having encountered problems in making the weight Williams (174½) was up against it from the off. Although Williams damaged both of Maske's eyes early on the latter was content to box on the back foot. Eventually, when realising he was behind on the cards, Williams put in big effort in the final couple of sessions, but it was too little and too late.

3 April 1993. Virgil Hill w pts 12 Fabrice Tiozzo.
Venue: Marcel Cerdan Sports Palace, Levallois-Perret, France. **Recognition:** WBA. **Referee:** Carlos Berrocal.
Scorecards: 115-112, 115-110, 113-115.
Fight Summary: Getting a shot at another version of the title, Tiozzo (174) gave Hill (174) plenty to think about despite being put down in rounds one and two after the latter had made an excellent start. A change of tactics in the fifth saw Tiozzo finally picking up speed, and having cut Hill over the left eye and marked him up somewhat he was then the benefactor of two points when hit low in the sixth and ninth. Towards the end, when it was clear that Tiozzo's big effort had drained him, Hill took the contest by the scruff of the neck to make sure of the win.

28 August 1993. Virgil Hill w pts 12 Sergio Merani.
Venue: Civic Centre, Bismarck, North Dakota, USA. **Recognition:** WBA. **Referee:** Bernie Soto.
Scorecards: 119-109, 119-112, 119-112.
Fight Summary: Coming back to the ring following an operation on his left shoulder in April Hill (174¾) took a while to find his feet, but after landing a terrific left hook to the challenger's body in the second round he was on his way. Even though it took Hill several sessions to develop his sharpness, Merani (174½) was unable to take advantage due to his lack of mobility. From the sixth onwards Hill was back to his best, firing in blows from both hands and generally keeping the tough Argentine on the defensive. However, although controlling the fight Hill never appeared likely to force a stoppage.

18 September 1993. Henry Maske w pts 12 Anthony Hembrick.
Venue: Philips Hall, Dusseldorf, Germany. **Recognition:** IBF. **Referee:** Bobby Ferrara.
Scorecards: 119-109, 119-108, 119-108.
Fight Summary: Outboxing the cagey Hembrick (171½) from first to last, the southpaw champion's main problem came in the sixth round when the doctor was called to inspect a cut over his left eye. Allowed to box on, despite picking up more cuts around the same eye Maske (172½) seemed unperturbed even though Hembrick was dangerous with his head throughout. Taking Maske's best shots without ever looking likely to go down, Hembrick had a point deducted in the ninth for foul tactics.

29 September 1993. Leeonzer Barber w pts 12 Andrea Magi.
Venue: Ice Palace, Pesaro, Italy. **Recognition:** WBO. **Referee:** Ismael Fernandez.
Scorecards: 116-113, 115-114, 115-113.
Fight Summary: Aggressive from the opening bell, and fighting in front of his home fans, the tough challenger gave Barber (174½) plenty of problems before going down on points. Prior to this contest Magi (174¼) was unbeaten in 16 bouts, but this was a real step up in class for him. At his best in the middle sessions it was Barber's left jab backed up by accurate combinations that gained him the win.

9 November 1993. Virgil Hill w rsc 10 Saul Montana.
Venue: The Dome, Fargo, North Dakota, USA. **Recognition:** WBA. **Referee:** Hubert Earle.
Fight Summary: Having a massive reach advantage, the champion outboxed the limited Montana (175) for round after round with the latter unable to get close enough to do any damage. Stringing left jabs, hooks and crosses together, despite shaking Montana up on several occasions Hill (175) was unable to drop him. And it was only when the referee was prompted that the well-beaten Mexican was rescued at 2.26 of the tenth.

11 December 1993. Henry Maske w pts 12 David Vedder.
Venue: Philips Hall, Dusseldorf, Germany. **Recognition:** IBF. **Referee:** Norbert Krosch.
Scorecards: 118-110, 120-107, 120-108.
Fight Summary: Piling up the points with a southpaw jab that was backed up with solid lefts to head and body, the champion dominated Vedder (172½) throughout the contest without ever looking likely to knock him over. Deducted a point for careless use of the head in the seventh Vedder's challenge was all about closing in and holding, and on one occasion, in the tenth, he virtually threw Maske (174¾) over his shoulder. Surprisingly, Maske finished the contest without the normal problems of cuts while Vedder was marked over both eyes.

17 December 1993. Virgil Hill w pts 12 Guy Waters.
Venue: Municipal Auditorium, Minot, North Dakota, USA. **Recognition:** WBA. **Referee:** Waldemar Schmidt.
Scorecards: 120-108, 119-110, 120-108.
Fight Summary: Being out of the ring for some 14 months was not the best preparation for the challenger, who was outspeeded and outboxed throughout as Hill (175) showed his class. With both men at their best as counter punchers there were few thrills, but Waters (173½) manfully stuck to his task despite having difficulty with his nose from the third round onwards. There were no knockdowns.

29 January 1994. Leeonzer Barber w rsc 9 Nicky Piper.
Venue: National Ice Rink, Cardiff, Wales. **Recognition:** WBO. **Referee:** Ismael Quinones Falu.
Fight Summary: Carrying the fight to the champion and excelling with the left hook, Piper (174¾) got away to a great start. Barber (175) was always dangerous, but by the third there was an ominous swelling under his right eye. Although Barber occasionally showed his class, when his right eye was closed in the eighth he looked to be heading for certain defeat. Then, with most of the fans sensing that Barber would soon have to be retired, the latter pulled out a tremendous left hook to the jaw in the ninth to send Piper crashing. Even though Piper managed to get to his feet he was immediately dropped again and rescued by the referee at 1.40 of the round.

26 March 1994. Henry Maske w rsc 9 Ernesto Magdaleno.
Venue: Westphalia Hall, Dortmund, Germany. **Recognition:** IBF. **Referee:** Sam Williams.
Fight Summary: Although Magdaleno (174¾) tried to turn the contest into a slugging session from the opening bell, the southpaw champion was having none of it when rocking his man with straight lefts. Always in control despite it being a tough fight that saw him sustaining a swelling to his left eye, Maske (174¾) continued to bang away with jabs and hooks. Maske's persistence paid off in the ninth, the referee stopping the fight in his favour on the 2.14 mark after Magdaleno was badly cut over the left eye and his right eye was almost closed.

4 June 1994. Henry Maske w pts 12 Andrea Magi.
Venue: Westphalia Hall, Dortmund, Germany. **Recognition:** IBF. **Referee:** Robert Gonzalez.
Scorecards: 117-114, 117-112, 119-110.

Fight Summary: With both men boxing cautiously it was not an exciting fight, but Maske (173¾) did more than enough to retain his title against the tough challenger despite being cut on the left eye in the sixth and dropped by a right hand in the tenth. Eventually warned for careless use of the head in the eighth, and then cut over the left eye in the ninth, Magi (174½) lacked the quality of his southpaw opponent whose returns were mainly crisp and accurate. While not an exciting contest it was always an interesting one.

23 July 1994. Mike McCallum w pts 12 Jeff Harding.
Venue: Civic Centre, Bismarck, North Dakota, USA. **Recognition:** WBC. **Referee:** Marty Denkin.
Scorecards: 116-112, 115-114, 115-113.
Fight Summary: Out of action for over 18 months, mainly due to promotional problems that stopped his fight with McCallum (174½) from happening earlier, the champion was being worked over from head to body before too long. Deducted a point in the fourth round for continuously going low, McCallum merely got back to work as Harding (174) tried desperately tried to find some form. Although McCallum was going well, especially when sending in cracking uppercuts, he could not put Harding down as hard as he tried, and while observers generally thought that the latter had won two rounds at most the official scoring showed there was not much between them. Afterwards, it was said that the judges had penalised McCallum for continuing to blitz Harding with low punches.

23 July 1994. Virgil Hill w pts 12 Frank Tate.
Venue: Civic Centre, Bismarck, North Dakota, USA. **Recognition:** WBA. **Referee:** Bernie Soto.
Scorecards: 119-108, 119-107, 118-110.
Fight Summary: In a battle of jabs the champion generally outscored Tate (174¼), who probably made the mistake of sticking to his boxing, and in the sixth a solid right had the latter staggering around the ring. The fight should have been over there and then, but Hill failed to take advantage even after Tate had fallen into a corner. Hill's explanation afterwards was that he needed to conserve his energy against a tough opponent. From the ninth onwards it was all Hill (174½) as Tate, marked over both eyes, fell further behind. But even though the champion was totally dominant at this stage of the fight, Tate always fought back when hurt.

10 September 1994. Dariusz Michalczewski w pts 12 Leeonzer Barber.
Venue: Alsterdorfer Sports Hall, Hamburg, Germany. **Recognition:** WBO. **Referee:** Raul Caiz.
Scorecards: 117-109, 116-111, 116-111.
Fight Summary: It was the challenger who made the better start of the pair, and while Barber (174½) was always dangerous with the right hand he was being outworked. Despite being cut on the left eye in the eighth Michalczewski (174½) continued to outjab Barber, who appeared to be relying on the big right to get himself out of trouble. In the final session Michalczewski was given time out after being struck low but was soon back in charge once recovered.

8 October 1994. Henry Maske w rtd 9 Iran Barkley.
Venue: Gerry Weber Stadium, Halle, Germany. **Recognition:** IBF. **Referee:** Bobby Ferrara.
Fight Summary: Leading with fast southpaw jabs that were backed up by solid lefts and rights the champion simply had too much skill for Barkley (171½), who continued to barge his way forward even after both of his eyes began to swell in the fifth. With Maske (174¼) always moving well, although Barkley was taking a beating, a badly damaged bottom lip adding to his woes, he kept up the attack. By the ninth Barkley's time was limited, and at the end of the session he was retired by his corner when it was becoming clear that the doctor was not going to allow him to continue.

11 February 1995. Henry Maske w pts 12 Egerton Marcus.
Venue: Festival Hall, Frankfurt, Germany. **Recognition:** IBF. **Referee:** Chris Wollenson.
Scorecards: 118-110, 118-109, 118-110.
Fight Summary: Despite having lost to Maske (174) in the 1988 Olympic final the challenger fancied his chances in this one before going the way of all of the German's previous opponents. Marcus (173½) made a good start, winning the opening two rounds, but having run out of ideas by the fourth he failed to win a single session thereafter. Following being put down in the eighth by a southpaw left, that his corner felt was more of a push than

a punch, Marcus continued his aggressive pitch. Regardless of that, even when Maske was cut on the left eye in the tenth he remained unconcerned.

25 February 1995. Mike McCallum w rsc 7 Carl Jones.
Venue: London Arena, Millwall, London, England. **Recognition:** WBC. **Referee:** Larry O'Connell.
Fight Summary: At the age of 38 there were those who thought that the champion might have been stripped of his title by the tough Jones (171), but it was quickly clear that the latter did not belong in the same league. Outboxed from the start, Jones was under pressure the moment McCallum (174) started to double up the jab and smash in rights to head and body, and at the end of the fourth he was dropped heavily by a right to the body. Even though the bell saved Jones at that point it did not stop the punches from raining in on him from there onwards. Although not floored again, at 1.17 of the seventh with the left side of his face damaged and taking a beating, Jones was rescued by the referee after a barrage of lefts and rights had forced him back to the ropes.

11 March 1995. Dariusz Michalczewski w co 2 Roberto Dominguez Perez.
Venue: Sports Hall, Cologne, Germany. **Recognition:** WBO. **Referee:** Genaro Rodriguez.
Fight Summary: Making a terrific start when using his feet and hand-speed effectively, Dominguez Perez (173¼) had the champion down with a heavy punch to the jaw in the opening round. At that point, Michalczewski (173¾), looking extremely groggy, was saved by the bell. Despite Michalczewski landing several solid lefts to the body at the start of the second that did not deter Dominguez Perez, who fired back with rights to the head. Then, after Dominguez Perez hurt Michalczewski and moved in for the kill he was smashed to the floor and counted out at 1.05 of the session, having taken a booming left hook to the jaw.

1 April 1995. Virgil Hill w pts 12 Crawford Ashley.
Venue: Buffalo Bill's Casino & Hotel, Stateline, Nevada, USA. **Recognition:** WBA. **Referee:** Richard Steele.
Scorecards: 117-113, 118-110, 118-110.
Fight Summary: Getting away fast the champion quickly moved into gear, jabbing Ashley (174) up and down, as the latter found it hard to find a way through. It looked as though Ashley was in for a tough night, but Hill (175) was much more cautious after the fourth, later claiming to have broken his left hand. Ashley had his best rounds in the seventh and eighth, sending in some good shots but, unable to follow up, any advantage he may have had disappeared. The final session was the best of the fight, Ashley doing well to make it to the bell as Hill opened up for the first time. Both men finished with swellings around their eyes.

20 May 1995. Dariusz Michalczewski w co 4 Paul Carlo.
Venue: Alsterdorfer Sports Hall, Hamburg, Germany. **Recognition:** WBO. **Referee:** Genaro Rodriguez.
Fight Summary: Erring on the side of caution in the opening moments against his little-known challenger, Michalczewski (172¾) took a few solid southpaw lefts before stepping up the pace in the second round. Having shaken Carlo (174¼) up in the third with some heavy left hooks, when Michalczewski went to town in the fourth with the same punch the American was counted out on his knees at 2.46 of the session after being blasted to the floor.

27 May 1995. Henry Maske w pts 12 Graciano Rocchigiani.
Venue: Westphalia Hall, Dortmund, Germany. **Recognition:** IBF. **Referee:** Bobby Ferrara.
Scorecards: 116-114, 116-112, 117-111.
Fight Summary: In a battle of southpaws the challenger was on the attack from the opening bell, hurting Maske (174) with a left hook to the head and keeping up the pressure right to the end despite being cut over both eyes. In most rounds Maske just about kept his nose in front, but in the ninth he was almost dropped after taking several hard lefts and rights to the head as Rocchigiani (173½) desperately tried to gain the upper hand. Again, in the 12th, Maske should have received a count when he fell to the canvas after holding on for dear life, only for the referee to help him to his feet.

16 June 1995. Fabrice Tiozzo w pts 12 Mike McCallum.
Venue: Gerland Sports Palace, Lyon, France. **Recognition:** WBC. **Referee:** Joe Cortez.
Scorecards: 115-112, 116-112, 116-112.

Fight Summary: Following a slow start there was nothing to suggest that the fight would change so suddenly, but after being cut by the side of the left eye when heads clashed Tiozzo (174¼) roared into McCallum (174¼) to administer a standing count. Back in action, McCallum was lucky to last out the session before doing well in the fourth and fifth when fighting on even terms. With McCallum tiring badly in the seventh there was a ruction when the referee noticed that one of the challenger's gloves was cut and had to be replaced. Although McCallum made a bit of a comeback in the tenth, having been steamrollered in the remaining two sessions he was almost out on his feet at the finish.

19 August 1995. Dariusz Michalczewski w co 5 Everardo Armenta.
Venue: Ice Palace, Dusseldorf, Germany. **Recognition:** WBO. **Referee:** Ismael Fernandez.
Fight Summary: Defending his title against yet another southpaw Michalczewski (175) was in control all the way, and Armenta (174½), who took several heavy shots, did well to last into the fifth round. Eventually, when Michalczewski picked it up, a couple of rights to the head and a cracking left hook to the jaw saw Armenta counted out with just one second of the fifth remaining.

2 September 1995. Virgil Hill w pts 12 Drake Thadzi.
Venue: The Stadium, Wembley, London, England. **Recognition:** WBA. **Referee:** Stan Christodoulou.
Scorecards: 117-111, 119-110, 118-112.
Fight Summary: Boxing cleverly, showing an excellent left jab, Hill (174¾) disappointed when only doing enough to make sure of victory over a limited challenger on foreign soil. Thadzi (172¾) tried hard enough, always looking to land the right hand when he could, but in the main Hill was one step ahead of him, picking his target off with stinging left jabs before holding at close quarters. Although the last round saw Thadzi lashing in right-handers at the tiring Hill he was unable to find one that would count.

7 October 1995. Dariusz Michalczewski w pts 12 Philippe Michel.
Venue: Festival Hall, Frankfurt, Germany. **Recognition:** WBO. **Referee:** Jose Rivera.
Scorecards: 117-109, 120-107, 120-107.
Fight Summary: Even though the limited challenger tried his best he was ultimately no match for Michalczewski (174), who picked his shots throughout and won every round according to two of the judges' cards. Badly hurt in the ninth when taking several heavy blows to the head, Michel (173) did well to survive, especially when standing up to Michalczewski's powerful left hook. Deducted two points for head butts, Michel finished strongly but to no avail.

14 October 1995. Henry Maske w pts 12 Graciano Rocchigiani.
Venue: Olympic Hall, Munich, Germany. **Recognition:** IBF. **Referee:** Robert Byrd.
Scorecards: 117-111, 116-112, 115-113.
Fight Summary: A return meeting of southpaws saw the champion showing up well, jabbing and moving fluently as Rocchigiani (173¼) piled in while looking to get heavy punches off. Rocchigiani was clearly on top in the fourth and fifth, forcing Maske (173¾) to the ropes and scoring well on the inside before tiring at the halfway stage and dropping behind. Despite Rocchigiani winning two of the last three rounds on pressure alone, never in any real difficulty, Maske cruised through to the final bell.

13 January 1996. Fabrice Tiozzo w pts 12 Eric Lucas.
Venue: Sports Palace, St Etienne, France. **Recognition:** WBC. **Referee:** Arthur Mercante.
Scorecards: 119-108, 117-110, 118-109.
Fight Summary: Working off the jab well, although the champion had Lucas (174) over in the third following a left-right he was unable to find a finishing blow. Always looking to trade with Tiozzo (174¾), Lucas proved to be a tough nut to crack as he always came back after being hurt. Despite losing by a wide margin, Lucas was cheered to the rafters for showing such spirit and resolve in lasting the distance.

With Tiozzo inactive, Roy Jones outpointed Mike McCallum over 12 rounds for the WBC 'interim' title at the Ice Palace, Tampa, Florida, USA on 22 November. When the Frenchman forfeited his crown in February 1997 due to continued inactivity Jones was named champion.

17 February 1996. Henry Maske w pts 12 Duran Williams.
Venue: Westphalia Hall, Dortmund, Germany. **Recognition:** IBF. **Referee:** Pete Podgorski.
Scorecards: 117-110, 118-110, 117-111.
Fight Summary: Showing plenty of aggression Williams (174) made Maske (174½) work hard for his points win, especially in the second round when he shook the southpaw champion up with big rights to the head and body. After he got going in the third, Maske assumed complete control up to the eighth, his jabs and hooks being very effective, and it was only in the ninth that Williams got through with some good shots. The computer statistics showed Maske, who finished with a cut under the right eye, landing 359 punches to his rival's 261.

6 April 1996. Dariusz Michalczewski w co 5 Asluddin Umarov.
Venue: Sports Centre, Hannover, Germany. **Recognition:** WBO. **Referee:** Ismael Fernandez.
Fight Summary: Although making a brave stand the challenger was no match for Michalczewski (174¾) who quickly targeted him with solid left jabs. Cut over the right eye in the fourth Umarov (174¼) was allowed to fight on, but continued to walk into big punches as Michalczewski began to unload blows from head to body. It could not last. Eventually, at 2.30 of the fifth, Umarov was counted out after being smashed to the floor by a terrific left hook to the jaw. The referee completed the count despite it being obvious that the challenger would not get up in time.

20 April 1996. Virgil Hill w pts 12 Lou Del Valle.
Venue: Engelstad Arena, Grand Forks, North Dakota, USA. **Recognition:** WBA. **Referee:** Hubert Earle.
Scorecards: 114-113, 116-112, 116-114.
Fight Summary: Taking on a challenger who was virtually unknown seemed like easy pickings for Hill (174½) but, following a second round in which he was virtually saved by the bell after being dumped by a southpaw left, all in attendance knew better. Although Hill made it out for the third and ran up the next four sessions he failed to find any rhythm against the awkward, ungainly Del Valle (175). The seventh saw Del Valle landing more solid punches, and in the last three sessions he ripped into Hill, who was damaged around both of his eyes, stunning him several times and forcing him around the ring. Had Del Valle not looked for a one-punch finish, who knows what might have happened.

25 May 1996. Henry Maske w pts 12 John Scully.
Venue: New Fair Hall, Leipzig, Germany. **Recognition:** IBF. **Referee:** Stan Christodoulou.
Scorecards: 119-109, 120-108, 120-108.
Fight Summary: After being posed a few problems by Scully (174¼) in the opening two rounds the southpaw champion got his act together by the third to outbox his man from there onwards. Scully was soon cut and swollen over the right eye as Maske (174¾) used his height and reach to good advantage, and although the American connected with the occasional right no damage was done. Showing much spirit, despite being picked off throughout Scully was warmly applauded at the final bell.

8 June 1996. Dariusz Michalczewski w pts 12 Christophe Girard.
Venue: Sporting Hall, Cologne, Germany. **Recognition:** WBO. **Referee:** Andre Van Grootenbruel.
Scorecards: 117-112, 117-112, 117-111.
Fight Summary: Making a sixth defence, Michalczewski (175) failed to get going when plodding to a points win that was made easier after Girard (175) damaged his right elbow in the ninth round. Prior to that Girard had posed all kinds of problems, often beating the champion to the punch and generally messing him about. In the 11th Girard was deducted a point for an accidental head butt, but by then his chance had gone.

10 August 1996. Dariusz Michalczewski w disq 7 Graciano Rocchigiani.
Venue: St Pauli Stadium, Hamburg, Germany. **Recognition:** WBO. **Referee:** Joe O'Neill.
Fight Summary: Starting well, the southpaw challenger stunned Michalczewski (174) badly in the opening round with cracking left to the jaw, and although the latter came back to shade the third and fourth sessions he was always under pressure. Despite Rocchigiani (173½) being cut over the left eye in the third and on the right in the fifth he continued to push on, looking to be ahead before dropping Michalczewski with a solid left to the head in the seventh. After counting to 'eight' the referee stopped the count to allow the doctor to attend the champion,

the finish coming on the 2.35 mark. Initially, the officials deemed it to be a technical draw, but as this was not in the rules a few days later it was reclassified as a disqualification win for Michalczewski when it was clear that Rocchigiani had landed the final blow on the break.

23 November 1996. Virgil Hill w pts 12 Henry Maske.
Venue: Olympic Hall, Munich, Germany. **Recognition:** IBF/WBA. **Referee:** Carlos Berrocal.
Scorecards: 116-113, 115-113, 112-116.
Fight Summary: In a battle to unify two titles it was the WBA champion, Hill (174¾), who was adjudged to have won the split decision after what was generally described as a disappointing contest. Hill made the better start whereas the southpaw IBF champion, Maske (174¼), took time to settle and, although the latter controlled the middle of the ring, too often he allowed himself to be picked off and tied up. Boxing on the back foot and carrying damage to his left eye at the finish, Hill did just enough to be sure of the win despite one of the judges marking him down as having lost by four rounds.

13 December 1996. Dariusz Michalczewski w rsc 8 Christophe Girard.
Venue: Stadium Sports Hall, Hannover, Germany. **Recognition:** WBO. **Referee:** Joe Cortez.
Fight Summary: A return match between the pair saw the champion produce his best form this time round, and it was only in the third that Girard (174½) shaded a round before being systematically taken apart. Girard (174½) had come into the fight as a late replacement for Eddy Smulders. Dropped in the fifth by a right to the body and saved by the bell Girard was seriously up against it. Continually under pressure from there onwards, after Girard had been floored by a right to the head in the eighth the referee stopped the contest on seeing the latter's corner throw the towel in when the count had reached 'six'. The finish was timed at 1.35 of the session.

21 March 1997. Montell Griffin w disq 9 Roy Jones.
Venue: Taj Mahal Resort & Casino, Atlantic City, New Jersey, USA. **Recognition:** WBC. **Referee:** Tony Perez.
Fight Summary: Defending for the first time, and a huge favourite, Jones (175) lost his unbeaten record when being disqualified at 2.27 of the ninth round after twice hitting Griffin (175) when he was down. Prior to that, the fight was virtually even after Griffin had come back well after being dropped in the seventh by a short left to the chin. Coming into the ninth with his left eye swollen, when Jones picked up the pace again a right to the head had Griffin all over the place and in a bad way. Eventually dropping to the floor on one knee, Griffin was shocked to be hit by a right-left hook before toppling over face first on the canvas. Initially, the referee began to count over Griffin before disqualifying Jones, an action that was later explained away as being one where the stricken fighter was given every chance of continuing if he had been able.

13 June 1997. Dariusz Michalczewski w pts 12 Virgil Hill.
Venue: The Arena, Oberhausen, Germany. **Recognition:** IBF/WBA/WBO. **Referee:** John Coyle.
Scorecards: 117-112, 116-113, 118-110.
Fight Summary: Fighting for three championship belts, despite the WBO saying that their title was not involved, Michalczewski (174½) took over from the third round onwards as Hill (173¾) began to fade. The American had won the first two rounds, scoring with good left jabs, but once Michalczewski had got into a rhythm there was no stopping him. Cutting off the ring and pushing Hill back he began to control the fight with excellent left jabs and crosses right through to the final bell. Hill, who was cut above the left eye in the fourth, blamed a foot injury on his lack of mobility, while there were those who felt his future lay in a higher weight class.

Michalczewski relinquished the IBF version of the title a week later rather than defend against William Guthrie, who was matched against Darrin Allen to decide the vacancy. After Michalczewski handed back the WBA Championship Belt, the former European champion, Eddy Smulders, was selected to meet Lou Del Valle to contest the vacant title.

19 July 1997. William Guthrie w rsc 3 Darrin Allen.
Venue: Fantasy Springs Casino Resort, Indio, California, USA. **Recognition:** IBF. **Referee:** Robert Byrd.
Fight Summary: Looking to win the title relinquished by Dariusz Michalczewski, Guthrie (173) made the better start. Into his stride from the opening bell he soon had Allen (174) backing off as he pitched in with southpaw

rights and lefts. By now well on top Guthrie floored Allen with a solid left hook at the beginning of the third, and following two more visits to the canvas in quick succession the latter was stopped at 2.38 of the session under the 'three knockdowns in a round' ruling.

7 August 1997. Roy Jones w co 1 Montell Griffin.
Venue: Foxwoods Resort & Casino, Ledyard, Connecticut, USA. **Recognition:** WBC. **Referee:** Arthur Mercante.
Fight Summary: Billed as 'Unfinished Business', Jones (175) made no mistake this time around, sending the champion down with a left hook early on. Although looking to have overcome the early storm the 5'7" Griffin (174) was in trouble again towards the end of the session, and after being caught heavily by a terrific left uppercut he made several desperate attempts to get up before being counted out with 29 seconds of the opening round still remaining.

Jones was reported to have relinquished the WBC version of the title in early November after refusing to meet Michael Nunn, stating that HBO, the cable network who had him under contract, would not be televising the fight. Following the announcement, Nunn v Graciano Rocchigiani, the WBC's number two ranked fighter, went out for purse bids to decide the vacant title.

Meanwhile, within a day or so of the match being made towards the end of November, Jones was saying he would like time to negotiate a fight with Nunn despite contracts being in place for the latter to contest the title with Rocchigiani. With it being difficult enough for Rocchigiani and Nunn to prepare with all this going on, come the week of the fight the former picked up a bad dose of flu which saw the date moved on to 21 March 1998. Although Rocchigiani beat Nunn (w pts 12 at the Max Schmeling Hall, Berlin, Germany), if the WBC, who were now calling it an 'interim' title bout while continuing to rate Jones as champion, believed the problem was going to go away they should have thought again. Over four years later, in the District Court of Manhattan, New York, Rocchigiani, who had been released on bail while serving a 12-month prison sentence, won a landmark case against one of the alphabet boys when the WBC were ordered to pay him $31 million in compensation. Also, for what it was worth, the Court retroactively handed Rocchigiani back the title in April 2003, but only for the period 28 March 1998 to 15 April 2000 when he lost in a WBO title bout against Dariusz Michalczewski.

20 September 1997. Lou Del Valle w rsc 8 Eddy Smulders.
Venue: Tivoli Ice Rink, Aachen, Germany. **Recognition:** WBA. **Referee:** John Coyle.
Fight Summary: Contesting the title vacated by Dariusz Michalczewski, with Del Valle (174¾) starting the better of the pair, a left hook towards the end of the opening round cut Smulders (175) under the left eye. The second was even worse for Smulders, who took two counts after being caught by heavy southpaw lefts and struggled to make it to the end of the session. Smulders surprised all and sundry when he charged out of his corner to take the next two rounds, hurting Del Valle with right hands while looking to make a real fight of it. Del Valle was even sent out minus his gumshield in the fourth. From the fifth Del Valle began to get back on top again, and in the seventh two left hooks sent Smulders to the floor. Although the Dutchman got up and made it to the bell he was immediately in trouble at the start of the eighth, whereupon the referee rescued him with just 22 seconds on the clock.

4 October 1997. Dariusz Michalczewski w rtd 7 Nicky Piper.
Venue: Stadium Sports Hall, Hannover, Germany. **Recognition:** WBO. **Referee:** Raul Caiz.
Fight Summary: Dropped twice in the opening session was the worst possible start for Piper (174½), but it did not stop him from displaying indomitable courage to hit back whenever he could. The problem that the challenger had was in keeping Michalczewski (175) at bay long enough to take stock, the latter merely walking through the punches thrown at him. Fighting on bravely, Piper continued to work well at times before being overpowered in the seventh. Having been knocked down by a right to the head Piper got up and defied Michalczewski to drop him again, taking everything coming his way before being retired by his corner during the interval.

13 December 1997. Dariusz Michalczewski w rtd 6 Darren Zenner.
Venue: Alsterdorfer Sports Hall, Hamburg, Germany. **Recognition:** WBO. **Referee:** Raul Caiz.
Fight Summary: Even though the champion won every round Zenner (175) was not disgraced, occasionally landing solid rights to the jaw and always trying to stay on the front foot. The problem for Zenner was that Michalczewski

(175) was just too good for him, being continuously battered by powerful left jabs that left him off balance. With a cut over the right eye, which was closing rapidly, it was no surprise when Zenner was retired by his corner at the end of the sixth.

6 February 1998. Reggie Johnson w co 5 William Guthrie.
Venue: Mohegan Sun Casino, Uncasville, Connecticut, USA. **Recognition:** IBF. **Referee:** Steve Smoger.
Fight Summary: In a battle of southpaws it was the challenger who made the better start despite having just five fights in the previous four years, and by the third round Guthrie (174) was being outboxed. On several occasions Johnson (172½) should have had point deductions when going low with right hooks, but all he received were warnings before finally getting one towards the end of the fourth. Having been caught by solid counters throughout by the fifth, even though Guthrie was decidedly more careful, he was counted out at 1.58 of the session after being poleaxed by a tremendous countering right hook.

20 March 1998. Dariusz Michalczewski w rsc 4 Andrea Magi.
Venue: Ball Sports Hall, Frankfurt, Germany. **Recognition:** WBO. **Referee:** Raul Caiz.
Fight Summary: Despite the challenger putting up stiff resistance, even breaking Michalczewski's nose, after being outgunned all the way an early finish was continually on the cards. It was in the fourth that Michalczewski (174¼) finally found a terrific left hook to send Magi (174¾) crashing, and on realising the latter was not going to get up the referee stopped the fight on the 2.35 mark.

29 May 1998. Reggie Johnson w pts 12 Ole Klemetsen.
Venue: BPA Sports Palace, Pesaro, Italy. **Recognition:** IBF. **Referee:** Sam Williams.
Scorecards: 117-107, 115-109, 114-112.
Fight Summary: Notwithstanding that Klemetsen (174¾) had Johnson (173) down for a mandatory count in the opening round he was unable to capitalise on it, the southpaw champion coming back strongly to take the play away from him. Docked a point in the third for use of the elbow, Klemetsen was then cut over the right eye in the fifth before sending in some solid rights to the head as Johnson relaxed. In the 11th Johnson was deducted a point for going low before dropping Klemetsen, who was forced to take another count after being hit below the belt yet again. Despite Klemetsen fighting on strongly in the final session, it was too late to make a difference.

18 July 1998. Roy Jones w pts 12 Lou Del Valle.
Venue: MSG Theatre, Manhattan, NYC, New York, USA. **Recognition:** WBA/WBC. **Referee:** Jim Santa.
Scorecards: 118-109, 118-109, 119-108.
Fight Summary: Fighting to decide two titles Jones (175) stormed to the front, winning the opening seven rounds before running into a tremendous southpaw left to the head in the eighth that dropped him for the first time in his pro career. The battle-hardened Del Valle (175), who had been cut over the left eye by an accidental head butt in the seventh, was unable to get to Jones again prior to going down by a wide points margin. While Jones proved he could take a punch, having got up at the count of 'four' in the eighth, Del Valle showed his gameness when continuing to come forward regardless.

19 September 1998. Dariusz Michalczewski w rsc 8 Mark Prince.
Venue: Centrum Arena, Oberhausen, Germany. **Recognition:** WBO. **Referee:** Rudy Battle.
Fight Summary: Even though he worked hard from the opening bell Prince (173¾) was always up against it as Michalczewski (174¾) picked his punches with care and cut the ring down to size before opening up. Prince had his best rounds in the third and fourth when letting the punches go, but when he was cut over the right eye in the fifth the writing was on the wall. Yet again Michalczewski impressed with his quality, his left jabs and hooks being sharp, accurate and powerful, and he never wasted a punch. Even though the challenger may have held his own in the sixth he was tiring fast, having expended so much energy. When Prince was sent crashing through the ropes on to the ring apron by a terrific left hook in the eighth the referee immediately closed the show with three seconds of the session remaining.

14 November 1998. Roy Jones w rsc 10 Otis Grant.
Venue: Foxwoods Resort Casino, Ledyard, Connecticut, USA. **Recognition:** WBA/WBC. **Referee:** Arthur Mercante.

Fight Summary: After being caught heavily in the opening session the southpaw challenger went on the defensive, and it was only due to Jones (171) playing to the gallery that he lasted so long. Initially standing back to admire his work Jones almost overwhelmed Grant (172) in the fourth before having him over with a right uppercut in the sixth. With Grant never in the contest, Jones being too fast for him, after the former was sent crashing by a right hand the referee called the fight off at 1.18 of the tenth when one of the stricken fighter's seconds jumped into the ring.

With Jones unavailable, Richard Hall stopped Anthony Bigeni in the third round of their WBA 'interim' title fight held at the Convention Centre, Atlantic City, New Jersey on 5 December. Hall would eventually meet Jones in May 2000.

12 December 1998. Dariusz Michalczewski w rsc 9 Drake Thadzi.
Venue: Ball Sports Hall, Frankfurt, Germany. **Recognition:** WBO. **Referee:** Lou Moret.
Fight Summary: Having taken several rounds to warm up after being hurt in the second by the tough Thadzi (174) the champion eventually got himself going in the fourth. Picking up the pace and timing his punches better Michalczewski (175) began driving Thadzi back with uppercuts and solid jabs, and at 1.45 of the ninth the referee rescued the latter after a cracking right to the head had sent him staggering towards his corner.

9 January 1999. Roy Jones w rsc 2 Richard Frazier.
Venue: Civic Centre, Pensacola, Florida, USA. **Recognition:** WBA/WBC. **Referee:** Armando Garcia.
Fight Summary: Seen as a terrible mismatch, the 39-year-old Frazier (174), who worked by day as a New York City policeman, immediately went on the defensive before a left-right dropped him at the end of the first round. Saved by the bell the southpaw Frazier was soon racing around the ring to avoid punishment as Jones (175) chased him down, and after being floored by a left hook-right uppercut the referee terminated the contest with one second of the second remaining. Frazier had failed to land any anything of note.

27 February 1999. Reggie Johnson w pts 12 Will Taylor.
Venue: Miccosukee Indian Gaming, Miami, Florida, USA. **Recognition:** IBF. **Referee:** Max Parker Jnr.
Scorecards: 115-112, 115-112, 114-113.
Fight Summary: The 6'3" Taylor (173) certainly gave the southpaw champion a run for his money despite being unable to dominate at any stage, his long left jab being his best weapon. Although Johnson (172) always had his nose in front, with him not being at his best it took several rounds before he found any sustainable rhythm. Eventually, Johnson found some heavy punches with which to hurt Taylor in the last four rounds before having to suffer the ignominy of being caught square by a right to the jaw that dropped him in the final session. Even though Johnson was badly cut over the right eye with almost the last punch of the fight it came too late for the upright Taylor.

3 April 1999. Dariusz Michalczewski w rsc 7 Muslim Biarslanov.
Venue: Stadium Hall, Bremen, Germany. **Recognition:** WBO. **Referee:** Michael Ortega.
Fight Summary: Caught early on by the aggressive challenger, Michalczewski (174¼) came back strongly towards the end of the opening session when landing heavily with left hooks and rights over the top. To his credit Biarslanov (174¾) was always in Michalczewski's face regardless of having to take plenty of stick, and he was cut over the right eye in the fourth before coming right back again. With Biarslanov not giving way, taking heavy blows from both hands as Michalczewski pushed on, it took the referee to bring the contest to a close at 1.41 of the seventh after the challenger had been constantly battered without response.

5 June 1999. Roy Jones w pts 12 Reggie Johnson.
Venue: Mississippi Coast Coliseum, Biloxi, Mississippi, USA. **Recognition:** IBF/WBA/WBC. **Referee:** Elmo Adolph.
Scorecards: 120-106, 120-106, 120-106.
Fight Summary: In a battle for three titles Jones (174) showed far too much speed for the IBF champion, who must have felt that he was being ambushed at times when hit at the rate of five punches to one. Smashed to the floor in the third round by a left hook-right counter the southpaw Johnson (171) was cut over the right eye and bewildered

at the bell. Having survived that round Johnson was not dropped again and, although he was in big trouble in the last two sessions as Jones went for a kayo, he bravely made it to the finishing line.

28 August 1999. Dariusz Michalczewski w rsc 4 Montell Griffin.
Venue: Stadium Hall, Bremen, Germany. **Recognition:** WBO. **Referee:** Joe Cortez.
Fight Summary: It was virtually all Griffin (175) in the opening three rounds as he moved in on the champion from the start, whacking in lefts and rights to head and body, while generally controlling the pace of the fight. It was only in the fourth that Michalczewski (175) found his feet, and with Griffin tiring from his exertions he was forced to take several heavy punches without return. With just one second of the session remaining the fight was over after Griffin, cut over the right eye and in a sorry state, was rescued by the referee.

15 January 2000. Roy Jones w pts 12 David Telesco.
Venue: Radio City Music Hall, Manhattan, NYC, New York, USA. **Recognition:** IBF/WBA/WBC. **Referee:** Arthur Mercante.
Scorecards: 120-108, 120-108, 120-106.
Fight Summary: While not winning a round on the cards, being on the receiving end throughout, the challenger made it to the final bell mainly due to the fact that Jones (175), who had hurt his left hand prior to the fight, was forced to use it sparingly. That did not stop Jones from using his right, however, and Telesco (175) was forced to show how tough he was when taking many heavy shots to the head without ever looking likely to go down. Telesco finished the fight with damage to both eyes, but for Jones it was little more than a sparring session.

15 April 2000. Dariusz Michalczewski w rtd 9 Graciano Rocchigiani.
Venue: Preussag Arena, Hannover, Germany. **Recognition:** WBO. **Referee:** Rudy Battle.
Fight Summary: Although the southpaw challenger took the second round on all three judges' cards that was the last one he would win; Michalczewski (175) setting the pace and staying on top despite having to absorb several heavy punches. Rocchigiani (175) never stopped trying, forcing Michalczewski to work, but he fell further and further behind before being dropped for the first time in his career following a left hook to the body in the ninth. With Rocchigiani in real trouble, continually protecting his rib cage, he was retired on his stool during the interval.

13 May 2000. Roy Jones w rsc 11 Richard Hall.
Venue: Conseco Fieldhouse, Indianapolis, Indiana, USA. **Recognition:** IBF/WBA/WBC. **Referee:** Wayne Kelly.
Fight Summary: Never winning a round and shipping far more punches than a fighter should take the southpaw challenger fought an uphill battle from the opening bell as Jones (173½) went into overdrive at times. Down twice in the first from heavy combinations, Hall (174½) bravely stayed with it despite being hurt in virtually every round and unable to live with Jones' speed. Still there in the 11th, Hall, his face a bloody mess, was finally rescued by the referee at 1.41 of the session after being bombarded and left helpless on the ropes.

9 September 2000. Roy Jones w rtd 10 Eric Harding.
Venue: The Arena, New Orleans, Louisiana, USA. **Recognition:** IBF/WBA/WBC. **Referee:** Johnny Femia.
Fight Summary: Clearly frustrated by his southpaw challenger, who came to the ring in safety-first mode, Jones (173½) failed to deliver in the early rounds, especially in the second and third as he looked to be countered. However, Jones' tremendous speed took him to the front from thereon in and apart from the eighth when Harding (173¾) caught him with some solid shots to the head he remained on top. Although Jones won the tenth he was still not at his best against the awkward Harding, but it was still a surprise when the latter decided to retire during the interval, naming a torn muscle in his left arm as the reason for not continuing.

16 December 2000. Dariusz Michalczewski w rsc 7 Ka-Dy King.
Venue: Gruga Hall, Essen, Germany. **Recognition:** WBO. **Referee:** Genaro Rodriguez.
Fight Summary: Having overcome an injured back and nose suffered in training, along with personal problems, with the champion not being at his best in this one King (175) made good in the opening three sessions. Showing a distinct lack of defence, Michalczewski (175), who took far too many punches needlessly, suffered a cut right eye in the second round following a head clash. In the fourth Michalczewski finally got going, with heavy rights and lefts

finding the target, and in the seventh the tiring King was rescued by the referee on the 28-second mark. With King in real trouble after shipping heavy rights and lefts to the temple it was a timely stoppage.

24 February 2001. Roy Jones w rtd 10 Derrick Harmon.
Venue: Ice Palace, Tampa, Florida, USA. **Recognition:** IBF/WBA/WBC. **Referee:** Frank Santore Jnr.
Fight Summary: With the durable southpaw challenger failing to win a round, by the sixth the contest had become extremely one-sided after he had run out of ideas. Although Harmon (175) continued to go forward whenever he could it was little more than a sparring session for Jones (174), who was picking his punches effortlessly, and at the end of the tenth it was all over. Going back to his corner, when it was clear that Harmon had problems communicating, having sustained damage to his right eardrum, he was retired.

5 May 2001. Dariusz Michalczewski w co 9 Alejandro Lakatos.
Venue: Volkswagen Hall, Braunschweig, Germany. **Recognition:** WBO. **Referee:** Michael Ortega.
Fight Summary: Once again Michalczewski (175) failed to start well enough when conceding the opening three rounds to a challenger who was not considered to be in his class. The situation changed in the fourth when Michalczewski pulled himself together, and by the bell Lakatos (174½) had been slowed up by body shots and was carrying a swollen right eye. With Michalczewski's left jab working well by the sixth he eventually dropped Lakatos with a combination of blows for the mandatory 'eight' in the ninth before a left hook to the jaw saw the latter counted out at 1.35 of the round.

28 July 2001. Roy Jones w pts 12 Julio Cesar Gonzalez.
Venue: Staples Centre, Los Angeles, California, USA. **Recognition:** IBF/WBA/WBC. **Referee:** Raul Caiz.
Scorecards: 119-106, 118-107, 119-106.
Fight Summary: Dropped in the opening round by a left hook counter Gonzalez (174¼) did his utmost to get into the fight when on his feet again, but with someone as fast as Jones (173) in front of him he had great difficulty in landing solidly. Although Gonzalez won the second round on the judges' cards it was more to do with the champion's lack of effort, and in the fifth another cracking left hook had him down again. For the remainder of the contest Gonzalez proved his toughness when shipping all manner of blows to head and body, but to his credit he took all that Jones could throw at him to stay on to the final bell.

As the WBA was now recognising Jones as their 'super' champion, Bruno Girard and Lou Del Valle met to decide who should be their 'second tier' kingpin. However, with the fight ending in a split 12-round draw at the Prado Seaside Park, Marseilles, France on 4 August the so-called title remained vacant. Later, on 22 December, at The Zenith, Orleans, France, Girard finally landed the WBA 'second tier' title when stopping Robert Koon in the 11th round.

15 December 2001. Dariusz Michalczewski w rsc 11 Richard Hall.
Venue: Estrel Convention Centre, Berlin, Germany. **Recognition:** WBO. **Referee:** Mark Nelson.
Fight Summary: After starting slowly as usual, Michalczewski (174½) eventually shook Hall (173½) up in the fourth with a series of solid combinations. He also got his left jab to work effectively. At that stage of the fight the southpaw challenger was throwing more punches than Michalczewski, but once his right eye had begun to swell up in the seventh his days were numbered despite him not being subdued. Even though the referee was continually looking at Hall's damage, putting him under extra pressure, he appeared to be getting stronger. However, the fight came to an end at 1.50 of the 11th after the referee decided that it was too dangerous to let Hall carry on, despite the doctor not having advised him to take that action, as well as the boxer begging for more time. That was the final straw for Hall who earlier had witnessed the referee allowing his opponent to walk away for a break following a long right hook to the kidney area, even though the official had not called a foul punch. It was all largely academic though, as at the time of the stoppage all three judges had Michalczewski ahead by scores of 98-93, 97-93, 97-93.

2 February 2002. Roy Jones w co 7 Glen Kelly.
Venue: American Airlines Arena, Miami, Florida, USA. **Recognition:** IBF/WBA/WBC/The Ring. **Referee:** Max Parker Jnr.

Fight Summary: Kelly (174½), who was never in with a chance at any stage of the contest, was eventually counted out at 1.55 of the seventh round after being dropped by a right to the head. Prior to that Jones (172) had hurt his challenger badly in the second, knocked him down with a cracking left hook to the head in the third, and almost had him over again in both the fourth and fifth sessions before dropping him with a left to the body in the sixth. Apart from his other three titles, Jones was also defending *The Ring* Championship Belt he had been awarded in November 2001

At the Marcel Cerdan Sports Palace, Levallois-Perret, France, on 23 May, Bruno Girard defended the WBA 'second tier' title when outpointing Thomas Hansvoll over 12 rounds. He then defended it when outscoring Lou Del Valle over 12 rounds at the Cordoba Arena, Palavas les Flots, France on 13 July.

20 April 2002. Dariusz Michalczewski w co 2 Joey DeGrandis.
Venue: Stoczniowiec Arena, Gdansk, Poland. **Recognition:** WBO. **Referee:** Joachim Jacobsen.
Fight Summary: Although the challenger gave it a real go in the opening session, sending in overarm rights in a bid to catch Michalczewski (175) cold, once the latter got his left jab to work the end was never far away. Despite winning six fights in a row, DeGrandis (175) was soon on the back foot in the second after feeling the power of Michalczewski's jab. It came as no surprise when he was set up by a right hook before being counted out at 1.58 of the session following a terrific left uppercut that smashed him to the floor.

7 September 2002. Roy Jones w rsc 6 Clinton Woods.
Venue: Rose Garden Arena, Portland, Oregon, USA. **Recognition:** IBF/WBA/WBC/The Ring. **Referee:** Jay Nady.
Fight Summary: Outboxed and outpunched in the opening two rounds Woods (174) went after Jones (174¾), who was defending four championship belts, only to receive more problems to deal with when badly hurt by a body shot on the bell. The fourth and fifth sessions saw Jones show-boating his skills before going to work with a vengeance in the sixth. Woods, now carrying a cut over his left eye, had very little left at that stage, and after being badly hurt by a big right to the head he was rescued by the referee on the 1.29 mark.

Jones forfeited the IBF title in November, having decided to take on John Ruiz for the WBA heavyweight title on 1 March 2003.

Meanwhile, the WBA 'second tier' champion, Bruno Girard, was stopped by his fellow countryman, Mehdi Sahnoune, in the seventh at the Sports Palace, Marseilles, France on 8 March 2003, and following the announcement that Jones would be relinquishing the WBC and WBA 'super' titles in early April 2003, having won the WBA heavyweight crown, Sahnoune automatically took over full recognition as the WBA light heavyweight champion. Further to that, it was announced that Antonio Tarver and Montell Griffin would contest the vacant WBC and IBF titles.

14 September 2002. Dariusz Michalczewski w rsc 10 Richard Hall.
Venue: Volkswagen Hall, Braunschweig, Germany. **Recognition:** WBO. **Referee:** Rudy Battle.
Fight Summary: Hall (175), who had previously lost to the champion in dubious circumstances, made a very fast start. Cut over the left eye after a clash of heads in the opening round, and cut on the bridge of the nose in the second, Michalczewski (175) looked a sorry sight before getting his left jab to open up his southpaw opponent in the fourth. Despite his left eye swelling up, with Michalczewski gradually getting on top it was Hall who was now under pressure. However, when Michalczewski, who later admitted that he could not see out of his left eye at that point, went after Hall at the start of the tenth, following several hard unanswered punches the referee stepped in to rescue the latter at 1.12 of the session. As before, Hall had a lot to be unhappy about.

29 March 2003. Dariusz Michalczewski w co 9 Derrick Harmon.
Venue: Color Line Arena, Hamburg, Germany. **Recognition:** WBO. **Referee:** Eddie Cotton.
Fight Summary: Starting slowly as usual Michalczewski (174½) conceded the opening three sessions as his awkward challenger used his southpaw jab and low stance to confuse him. Persevering, Michalczewski gradually got his left jab working, and by the sixth round he was in control as Harmon (175) began to feel the pace. Holding

more and more Harmon was still making life difficult for Michalczewski, but in the ninth a solid left to the body that was followed by several heavy shots saw him drop on one knee to be counted out on the 1.08 mark.

26 April 2003. Antonio Tarver w pts 12 Montell Griffin.
Venue: Foxwoods Resort Casino, Mashantucket, Connecticut, USA. **Recognition:** IBF/WBC. **Referee:** Michael Ortega.
Scorecards: 120-106, 120-106, 120-106.
Fight Summary: On top from the start Tarver (175) won the vacant WBC and IBF titles by a wide margin in what was a messy affair against a man who was outreached by seven inches. Having slipped over earlier, the 5'7" Griffin (175) was dropped by a cracking southpaw left cross in the first round, and finding it too difficult to reach Tarver he was forced to take a battering. Way behind with cuts on both eyes Griffin was smashed to the floor in the 12th by a big left to the head before getting up and making it to the final bell.

When Tarver relinquished the IBF title at the end of October in order to defend his WBC Championship Belt against Roy Jones, Clinton Woods was matched against Glen Johnson to find a new champion.

10 October 2003. Silvio Branco w rsc 11 Mehdi Sahnoune.
Venue: Sports Palace, Marseilles, France. **Recognition:** WBA. **Referee:** Guillermo Perez.
Fight Summary: Making his first defence Sahnoune (175) made a reasonable start before the 37-year-old Branco (175) got his left jab going well to take control of the contest. Badly hurt in the fourth Sahnoune battled on before a badly swollen right eye made it even more difficult for him. Coming out for the 11th, way down on the scorecards, Sahnoune was dropped by a big right to the head as Branco went for the finish, and at 2.15 of the session the referee stopped what had become an unequal contest.

18 October 2003. Julio Cesar Gonzalez w pts 12 Dariusz Michalczewski.
Venue: Color Line Arena, Hamburg, Germany. **Recognition:** WBO. **Referee:** Joe Cortez.
Scorecards: 116-112, 116-112, 113-115.
Fight Summary: Unbeaten in 48 fights the champion came into the contest with Gonzalez (174¼) as a hot favourite to retain his title and move level with the legendary Rocky Marciano on 49 straight. Unfortunately for Michalczewski (174¼) the Mexican had not read the script, and after being cut over the left eye by a head butt in the second round and attacked with body shots and long jabs at every opportunity the fight gradually slipped away from him. Although Michalczewski came on strongly in the latter stages, having Gonzalez desperately hanging on in the final session, he was unable to find the punches needed to turn things around.

7 November 2003. Glen Johnson drew 12 Clinton Woods.
Venue: Hillsborough Leisure Centre, Sheffield, England. **Recognition:** IBF. **Referee:** Ian John-Lewis.
Scorecards: 116-112, 113-115, 114-114.
Fight Summary: In a match that was originally intended to be an eliminator it assumed full title status at the end of October 2003 when Antonio Tarver opted to return his belt ahead of a WBC title showdown with Roy Jones on 8 November. Although Johnson (173¾) appeared to win handily it was more to do with him clearly winning rounds on the judges' cards with plenty to spare, whereas Woods (174) marginally edged or nicked his winning rounds. Contested under the 'ten-point must' system, because there were no knockdowns all winning rounds were scored 10-9. Johnson looked to be the better craftsman of the two, but Woods, who damaged his left hand, certainly warranted a rematch for his dogged persistence.

8 November 2003. Roy Jones w pts 12 Antonio Tarver.
Venue: Mandalay Bay Resort & Casino, Las Vegas, Nevada, USA. **Recognition:** WBC/The Ring. **Referee:** Kenny Bayless.
Scorecards: 116-112, 117-111, 114-114.
Fight Summary: Having won the WBA heavyweight title Jones (175) dropped down a couple of divisions to take on Tarver (175), and after a tough fight against the dangerous southpaw he successfully retained *The Ring* Championship Belt and won back his WBC title at the same time. The contest was a difficult one to score as Jones would send in single shots while Tarver threw punches in clusters. And when one looked at the way the judges saw

the action it was clear that they were seeing it differently in most rounds. Jones, who finished the fight with damage to his left eye and tiring badly, probably won the last two sessions, but as far at Tarver was concerned he should have been the winner.

17 January 2004. Zsolt Erdei w pts 12 Julio Cesar Gonzalez.
Venue: DM Arena, Karlsruhe, Germany. **Recognition:** WBO. **Referee:** John Coyle.
Scorecards: 118-110, 118-110, 117-111.
Fight Summary: Putting his title up for the first time Gonzalez (172½) was comprehensively outboxed by the former world amateur champion, who settled quickly and was soon blocking and countering accurately. Despite being outreached, with Erdei (172) getting his left jab working well he was already pulling away by the third round as Gonzalez rumbled forward. It was the same pattern from thereon in, and even though Erdei hurt Gonzalez badly in the final session he failed to follow up, being content to box his way to the bell.

6 February 2004. Glen Johnson w pts 12 Clinton Woods.
Venue: Ponds Forge Leisure Centre, Sheffield, England. **Recognition:** IBF. **Referee:** Dave Parris.
Scorecards: 116-112, 115-113, 115-113.
Fight Summary: Following on from their previous fight it was again closely contested, but this time around Johnson (174½) ensured that he won enough rounds on the judges' scorecards to land the vacant title in his 35th year. Although Woods (174) had the longer reach and worked the jab well at times Johnson always replied quickly, and it was he who landed the heavier shots. Both men were all-in at the final bell, in what again had been a hard battle despite a lack of knockdowns and injuries.

20 March 2004. Fabrice Tiozzo w pts 12 Silvio Branco.
Venue: Sports Palace, Lyon, France. **Recognition:** WBA. **Referee:** Rudy Battle.
Scorecards: 114-112, 114-112, 113-113.
Fight Summary: Despite making a slow start the champion picked it up in the second round to win the next three sessions and, although being outboxed in the fifth and sixth as Tiozzo (175) hit back, he saved his best work for the eighth. Dropped by left-right combinations to the head, Tiozzo was then hit twice while in a kneeling position without the referee taking any action. He then had to endure a tough ninth round before taking the fight to Branco (173¾). It was in the 11th that Tiozzo, who had dropped down a division, made sure of victory when twice sending Branco slipping to the floor prior to flooring him with a right to the head.

After Roy Jones signed up to meet Antonio Tarver for the WBC title on 15 May the WBA announced that they had appointed Jones as their 'super' champion, which would have left Tiozzo as the 'second tier' champion. However, when that decision was later rescinded, possibly in the wake of the Graciano Rocchigiani legal stand against the WBC, Tiozzo remained the champion.

8 May 2004. Zsolt Erdei w pts 12 Hugo Hernan Garay.
Venue: Westphalia Hall, Dortmund, Germany. **Recognition:** WBO. **Referee:** Jose Rivera.
Scorecards: 115-113, 116-112, 114-114.
Fight Summary: In what was a difficult defence Erdei (173¾) just about deserved the win over the tough Garay (174¾), who started fast when attacking the body. Several times Garay was warned by the referee to keep his punches up, but it failed to deter him as he looked to slow Erdei down. Although Erdei always came back with good jabs and accurate counters he was happy to see the fight out after Garay came on strongly to take the last two rounds in an aggressive fashion.

15 May 2004. Antonio Tarver w rsc 2 Roy Jones.
Venue: Mandalay Bay Resort & Casino, Las Vegas, Nevada, USA. **Recognition:** WBC/The Ring. **Referee:** Jay Nady.
Fight Summary: With both men up for their return, Jones (174) boxed well to take the opening session, but coming in to the second it was clear that the southpaw challenger was relishing the battle ahead. Staying in the middle of the ring Tarver (175) was happy for Jones to come to him, and despite the two-belt champion being caught by the left a couple of times he failed to spot the warning signs. Having landed a solid right to the head before following up with a left hook, Jones was dropped heavily by an overarm left counter to the jaw. After just about making it to

his feet before the count reached 'ten' Jones stumbled over yet again. Although getting to his feet for the second time he was stopped on the 1.41 mark when the referee rightly stated that he was unable to defend himself.

Having collected *The Ring* Championship Belt on winning, Tarver relinquished the WBC title in November in favour of taking on the dangerous Glen Johnson in a fight that would be recognised by *The Ring* as being for the world title.

To find a new champion the WBC decided that Tomasz Adamek, unbeaten in 28 contests, should meet Paul Briggs, who had won two eliminators, against Jesus Ruiz (w pts 12 at the Panthers World of Entertainment, Penrith, NSW, Australia on 7 March) and Stipe Drews (w pts 12 at the State Sports Centre, Homebush Bay, Sydney, Australia on 15 August).

11 September 2004. Zsolt Erdei w pts 12 Alejandro Lakatos.
Venue: Ice Hockey Stadium, Budapest, Hungary. **Recognition:** WBO. **Referee:** Joachim Jacobsen.
Scorecards: 116-112, 118-109, 116-111.
Fight Summary: Although the champion had Lakatos (174¼) in some difficulty early on when scoring with solid counters and won the opening five rounds, he began to tire in the middle stages. Fighting sparingly Erdei (174) did enough to influence the judges with last-minute bursts in every session, but after Lakatos was finally docked a point for going low in the seventh it was an uphill battle for him.

25 September 2004. Glen Johnson w co 9 Roy Jones.
Venue: FedEx Forum, Memphis, Tennessee, USA. **Recognition:** IBF. **Referee:** Bill Clancy.
Fight Summary: Coming back from his bad defeat at the hands of Antonio Tarver, Jones (175) was a long way short of being the fastest man around. Badly hurt in the fifth, although Jones sucked it up it was clear at that stage that he could not hurt Johnson (174), who walked through the punches to get his own off. Coming into the ninth Johnson was ahead on all three judges' cards, but there were no signs of what was to come. The contest came to a sudden conclusion after 48 seconds of the session when Jones was caught by a smashing right over the top, followed by a left hook, and was counted out. Badly shaken, Jones was treated at ringside before being taken to hospital suffering concussion.

Further to Johnson vacating the IBF title in November in favour of a prestigious fight against Tarver, Clinton Woods and Rico Hoye were matched to find a new champion. Both men had won eliminating bouts - Woods beating Jason DeLisle (w rsc 12 at the Octagon Centre, Sheffield, England on 24 October) and Hoye winning over Richard Hall (w co 4 Mandalay Bay Resort & Casino, Las Vegas, Nevada on 15 May) and Montell Griffin (w pts 12 at the Kewadin Casino, Sault Sainte Marie, Michigan on 16 September).

18 December 2004. Glen Johnson w pts 12 Antonio Tarver.
Venue: Staples Centre, Los Angeles, California, USA. **Recognition:** The Ring. **Referee:** Pat Russell.
Scorecards: 115-113, 115-113, 112-116.
Fight Summary: Billed for *The Ring* Championship Belt, even though they said it could not get any better for the 35-year-old Johnson it did. Although the southpaw champion was always looking to unload, with there never being much between them it was Johnson (174¼) who took the verdict, his work-rate being a key factor. Afterwards, Tarver (175) blamed his lack of finishing power on an injury to his left hand early on, while Johnson said that it was his sound defence which enabled his inspired victory.

26 February 2005. Fabrice Tiozzo w rsc 6 Dariusz Michalczewski.
Venue: Color Line Arena, Hamburg, Germany. **Recognition:** WBA. **Referee:** Stan Christodoulou.
Fight Summary: Looking ring rusty, the former WBO champion lost the opening three rounds as Tiozzo (174¼) quickly got down to work with solid blows from both hands going in. His attacks on the body were also softening up Michalczewski (175). Although Michalczewski came back to take the fourth round he was soon running out of ideas before being dropped in round six and then stopped at 2.05 of the session when under terrific pressure from lefts and rights to the head.

On 27 July 2006, Silvio Branco won the vacant WBA 'interim' title when outpointing Manny Siaca over 12 rounds at the Vigorelli Velodrome, Milan, Italy. Branco was installed as the champion on 21 October 2006 after Tiozzo, who had been due to defend against Hugo Hernan Garay, announced his retirement from the ring on 19 October 2006.

26 February 2005. Zsolt Erdei w pts 12 Hugo Hernan Garay.
Venue: Color Line Arena, Hamburg, Germany. **Recognition:** WBO. **Referee:** Luis Pabon.
Scorecards: 110-118, 116-112, 115-113.
Fight Summary: Following on from their earlier hard-fought contest this one was even closer at the finish, with the American judge giving it to the tough Argentine challenger by ten rounds to two. Very aggressive, Garay (175) again started fast as he went for the body, and continuing to press throughout with his greater strength being dominant, it was not until the third that Erdei (173) began to get his boxing together. Although Erdei landed the better quality it was Garay, often slinging punches in, who came on strongly in the last three rounds when making what turned out to be a vain effort to swing the fight his way.

4 March 2005. Clinton Woods w rsc 5 Rico Hoye.
Venue: Magna Centre, Rotherham, England. **Recognition:** IBF. **Referee:** Ian John-Lewis.
Fight Summary: In taking on the dangerous, heavy-handed American in a battle for the vacant title Woods (174) showed he was really up for it by first outboxing his rival and then outpunching him. While Hoye (174¼), who had spent ten years in prison for a gangland killing, tried to blast his way to victory the Sheffield man kept his defences together despite taking a number of low blows which saw his rival deducted two points. In the fifth Woods eventually upped the pace when correctly believing his time had come, and was driving Hoye before him without reply when the referee called it off with just one second of the round remaining.

21 May 2005. Tomasz Adamek w pts 12 Paul Briggs.
Venue: United Centre, Chicago, Illinois, USA. **Recognition:** WBC. **Referee:** Tim Adams.
Scorecards: 117-113, 115-113, 114-114.
Fight Summary: Fighting for the title vacated by Antonio Tarver, Adamek (175) started the better of the pair when taking the opening four rounds, banging in right hands. Briggs (175) had been severely handicapped when gashed over the left eye after heads came together in the second. It remained close though as Briggs hit back with solid right hands of his own, and damage to Adamek's right eye as well as a broken nose was not helping his cause by the middle rounds. In the eighth Briggs almost had Adamek over from several vicious rights to the head before being pegged back by jabs, and in the final two rounds the latter mixed it up with the Australian to make sure of the verdict.

18 June 2005. Antonio Tarver w pts 12 Glen Johnson.
Venue: FedEx Forum, Memphis, Tennessee, USA. **Recognition:** The Ring. **Referee:** Bill Clancy.
Scorecards: 116-112, 116-112, 115-113.
Fight Summary: Gaining his revenge, Tarver (173) used his three-inch-reach advantage to better effect this time round as he repeatedly backed the champion up. It was hardly surprising that both men were tiring in the middle rounds, but by then Johnson (173½) was feeling it more than Tarver. With Johnson's left eye swelling fast, despite giving it one final effort, it was Tarver who produced the better work in the closing stages to warrant the unanimous verdict.

9 September 2005. Clinton Woods w pts 12 Julio Cesar Gonzalez.
Venue: Hallam FM Arena, Sheffield, England. **Recognition:** IBF. **Referee:** Mickey Vann.
Scorecards: 117-111, 118-112, 116-112.
Fight Summary: Working off the left jab the champion took the first four rounds due to his better boxing before Gonzalez (175) came back with a few blows of his own to take the play away from him in the fifth. Although Woods (174¾) came back strongly it had become a tough battle as Gonzalez sensed that he could win, but by the ninth he was being outworked and was tiring fast. The last three sessions all belonged to Woods as he picked his punches, raised a swelling on Gonzalez's left eye and remained in the driving seat until the final bell.

1 October 2005. Antonio Tarver w pts 12 Roy Jones.
Venue: St Petersburg Times Forum, Tampa, Florida, USA. **Recognition:** The Ring. **Referee:** Tommy Kimmons.
Scorecards: 116-112, 116-112, 117-111.
Fight Summary: Despite not being the fighter of old, plus the fact that his legs occasionally let him down, Jones (173) made the southpaw champion pull out all the stops in order to retain his title. There was never much between them other than Tarver (175) doing that little bit more, and in the 11th a right hook to the jaw had Jones in big trouble before he fought back to make it to the bell. Following the contest, while there were many calls for the 36-year-old Jones to quit they fell on deaf ears.

15 October 2005. Tomasz Adamek w co 6 Thomas Ulrich.
Venue: Multipurpose Hall, Dusseldorf, Germany. **Recognition:** WBC. **Referee:** Ian John-Lewis.
Fight Summary: Setting off at a fast pace the challenger was always in the fight right up until the sixth round. Ulrich (174¾) certainly made Adamek (174¾) work hard even though he was cut over the left eye as early as the second round. With both men throwing quality punches from both hands the fight was exciting as Ulrich continually came forward before tiring towards the end of the fifth. Picking it up in the sixth Adamek began to work on Ulrich's damaged eye, and after slipping inside an overarm right he smashed in a right-hand counter of his own that landed flush on the jaw. Crashing to the floor, Ulrich was counted out at 1.57 of the session.

22 October 2005. Zsolt Erdei w rsc 12 Mehdi Sahnoune.
Venue: Fire Mountains Arena, Halle, Germany. **Recognition:** WBO. **Referee:** Joe Cortez.
Fight Summary: Making the contest from the opening bell, the challenger, a former WBA champion, forced Erdei (174¼) to pull out all the stops in order to hang on to his title. With every round closely contested and solid blows delivered by both men, coming into the final session there was little to choose between them, even though Erdei had been up against it in the fifth, sixth and ninth. In the 12th Erdei finally began to hurt Sahnoune (175), and after driving the latter into a corner and battering him with both hands the referee stopped the fight with just 43 seconds remaining on the clock. Afterwards, Erdei claimed that a rib injury had held him back.

6 May 2006. Zsolt Erdei w rsc 10 Paul Murdoch.
Venue: Castle Guard Arena, Dusseldorf, Germany. **Recognition:** WBO. **Referee:** Mark Nelson.
Fight Summary: Defending his title successfully for the fifth time, the clever Erdei (172¾) took over from the opening bell with solid combinations, battering Murdoch (172½) throughout. The Australian was always game, but was unable to test Erdei. In the eighth round Murdoch was sent crashing following three left hooks to the head, and although he got to his feet and made it through the ninth he was shipping punishment when the referee rescued him after 19 seconds of the tenth.

13 May 2006. Clinton Woods w rsc 6 Jason DeLisle.
Venue: Ponds Forge International Sports Centre, Sheffield, England. **Recognition:** IBF. **Referee:** Dave Parris.
Fight Summary: During their previous contest, a non-title affair, Woods (174½) had to climb off the floor to secure a win, but this time there were no such problems as he outboxed the challenger from start to finish. Using lefts and rights to keep DeLisle (172½) at bay, Woods nearly got the job done in the second when the Australian reeled away from some solid blows. Sticking to his boxing Woods bided his time before he finally pounced in the sixth. Following a terrific right uppercut, Woods took his man to the ropes and after unleashing a whole range of punches another big uppercut dropped DeLisle so heavily that the referee immediately called it off at 1.55 of the session.

10 June 2006. Bernard Hopkins w pts 12 Antonio Tarver.
Venue: Boardwalk Hall, Atlantic City, New Jersey, USA. **Recognition:** The Ring. **Referee:** Benjy Esteves Jnr.
Scorecards: 118-109, 118-109, 118-109.
Fight Summary: With Tarver's *Ring* Championship Belt at stake, the 41-year-old Hopkins (174) stepped up from middleweight after two losing fights against Jermain Taylor to administer a lesson in boxing skills as his southpaw opponent continually floundered. Dropped in the fifth by a right, Tarver (174) tried to turn things his way in the eighth before tiring as Hopkins dug to the body. Although Tarver, his right eye swelling fast, made a big effort in the 11th he was a spent force in the final session as Hopkins breezed to the unanimous points verdict.

29 July 2006. Zsolt Erdei w pts 12 Thomas Ulrich.
Venue: Konig Pilsener Arena, Oberhausen, Germany. **Recognition:** WBO. **Referee:** Eddie Cotton.
Scorecards: 118-110, 116-112, 120-108.
Fight Summary: In a battle of stablemates, with the champion controlling the action throughout, Ulrich (174¼) finished the contest with cuts and bruises to the left-hand side of his face after taking stiff jabs for round after round. The superior technician, Erdei (172¼) did enough to win most of the sessions without getting out of first gear, while Ulrich threw many punches that missed the target. There were no knockdowns.

2 September 2006. Clinton Woods w pts 12 Glen Johnson.
Venue: Reebok Stadium, Bolton, England. **Recognition:** IBF. **Referee:** Howard Foster.
Scorecards: 116-112, 115-113, 113-115.
Fight Summary: There was never much in this one, the champion ultimately taking a split decision. Despite being the taller man, Woods (175) was often forced to take solid jabs from Johnson (172) as well as hard body blows when the latter forced his way inside. Johnson's plan to slow Woods down was clear enough, but the challenger's camp had ignored the undoubted spirit and toughness of the Englishman, who finished like a train to impress the judges.

7 October 2006. Tomasz Adamek w pts 12 Paul Briggs.
Venue: Allstate Arena, Rosemont, Illinois, USA. **Recognition:** WBC. **Referee:** Tim Adams.
Scorecards: 114-112, 115-111, 113-113.
Fight Summary: Looking to gain revenge for the narrow verdict that went against him in their previous contest, a Briggs (175) left hook had the champion down in the opening session for the first time in his career. However, Adamek (174) came back strongly to whistle off the next two rounds before being put under pressure again as Briggs let both hands go in the fourth and fifth. Having dropped Briggs in the ninth with a low blow Adamek was deducted a point while Briggs took a short rest. Although Briggs took the tenth with heavy punches finding the mark, it was Adamek who took the 11th and 12th with solid left jabs and rights through the middle.

27 January 2007. Zsolt Erdei w rsc 8 Danny Santiago.
Venue: Castle Guard Arena, Dusseldorf, Germany. **Recognition:** WBO. **Referee:** Genaro Rodriguez.
Fight Summary: Having dropped Santiago (174½) in the second round with a cracking left hook, the champion further tightened his grip on the fight with the use of solid jabs and combinations. His excellent defence also meant that the hard-working Santiago rarely found a way through. In the seventh Erdei (173) began to open up, and the following session saw him drop Santiago for 'seven' with a three-punch combination before badly staggering the latter enough for the referee to make a timely intervention on the 1.56 mark.

3 February 2007. Chad Dawson w pts 12 Tomasz Adamek.
Venue: Silver Spurs Arena, Kissimmee, Florida, USA. **Recognition:** WBC. **Referee:** Jorge Alonso.
Scorecards: 117-109, 118-108, 116-110.
Fight Summary: Making his play right from the opening bell, Dawson (175) took to the periphery of the ring with southpaw rights and left crosses keeping the cumbersome champion at bay for much of the time. Hurt in the fifth and sixth from heavy right hands, Adamek (174), also cut under the left eye, suffered more misery when he was dropped by a left to the body in the eighth. Although the unbeaten Adamek came back strongly in the tenth, flooring Dawson with a short right to the jaw, he took a lot out of himself in that session when trying to bring the contest to a conclusion and was badly hurt by a solid left in the 11th. Dawson then made sure of the win by staying out of trouble in the 12th.

28 April 2007. Stipe Drews w pts 12 Silvio Branco.
Venue: Konig Pilsener Arena, Oberhausen, Germany. **Recognition:** WBA. **Referee:** Steve Smoger.
Scorecards: 116-113, 116-112, 115-113.
Fight Summary: Defending the title that was handed to him after it was relinquished by Fabrice Tiozzo, for several rounds the 40-year-old Branco (174¼) was picked off by southpaw jabs as Drews (174¼) made his way into the fight. In the fifth, however, Branco began to find his distance with right hooks to the head getting through, and in the seventh a body blow doubled Drews up. Having turned away from Branco, who was cut over the left eye, the

Croat was given a slightly fortunate break by the referee when allowed to box on. Putting that behind him, Drews got back to his boxing in the eighth and closed out strongly to take the unanimous decision.

9 June 2007. Chad Dawson w rsc 6 Jesus Ruiz.
Venue: Connecticut Convention Centre, Hartford, Connecticut, USA. **Recognition:** WBC. **Referee:** Johnny Callas.
Fight Summary: The southpaw champion, making his first defence, was far too good for Ruiz (174¾), who had his nose broken in the fourth after being clubbed by left hands before being forced to take solid shots to both head and body in the fifth. Clearly one-sided, by the sixth, Dawson (174) waded into Ruiz with some big punches to force an intervention by the referee at 2.00 of the session when the latter was unable to fight back and was on his way down.

16 June 2007. Zsolt Erdei w rsc 11 George Blades.
Venue: SYMA Sports & Leisure Centre, Budapest, Hungary. **Recognition:** WBO. **Referee:** Joe Cortez.
Fight Summary: Although Blades (174¼) went on the offensive from the opening bell he was soon pulled up short after the champion started to bring solid straight lefts into play. From the third onwards it was one-way traffic as Erdei (172) picked up the pace to go further and further ahead. In the 11th when it was clear that Blades, who was under the cosh, was so far behind on the cards and had little chance winning the referee halted the contest at 2.27 of the session.

21 July 2007. Bernard Hopkins w pts 12 Ronald Wright.
Venue: Mandalay Bay Resort & Casino, Las Vegas, Nevada, USA. **Recognition:** The Ring. **Referee:** Robert Byrd.
Scorecards: 116-112, 117-111, 117-111.
Fight Summary: Happy to defend his prestigious *Ring* Championship Belt, Hopkins (167) proved to be too clever for the southpaw Wright (167), who ultimately found himself bullied by the battle-hardened champion. Despite being cut over the left eye in the third, Wright had his best rounds in the fourth and fifth with left crosses finding their mark. By the sixth, however, Wright was beginning to tire as Hopkins leaned on him and started to work the body. The final session saw Hopkins unload, a heavy right almost smashing Wright down, but the latter kept going to hear the bell.

29 September 2007. Chad Dawson w rsc 4 Epifanio Mendoza.
Venue: Arco Arena, Sacramento, California, USA. **Recognition:** WBC. **Referee:** Jon Schorle.
Fight Summary: Coming in at 12 days' notice after Adrian Diaconu pulled out with an injured wrist, Mendoza (175) found himself outclassed by the hard-hitting southpaw champion. It was never going to be easy for him, and so it proved. By the second round Mendoza was already reduced to throwing single head punches, and towards the end of the session he was battered to the ropes by a steady stream of solid lefts and rights. Having finished the third taking a beating, Mendoza was finally rescued in the fourth by the referee on the 2.30 mark as Dawson (172¾) belted him with heavy rights to the body without return.

29 September 2007. Clinton Woods w pts 12 Julio Cesar Gonzalez.
Venue: Hallam FM Arena, Sheffield, England. **Recognition:** IBF. **Referee:** Dave Parris.
Scorecards: 115-113, 117-111, 116-112.
Fight Summary: Giving a great display of boxing against the tough Gonzalez (173½) in a return match, the champion once again had a hard night's work. With both men relatively even after four rounds, it was Gonzalez who took the next two sessions as he tore into Woods (174½) with both hands to head and body before the latter got his jab going, backed up by solid hooks. In the 11th Woods almost took Gonzalez out with some fierce blows from both hands that left the Argentine badly cut on the right eye, but was then forced to protect his lead in the 12th as the latter went for broke. Woods also finished with a cut right eye.

24 November 2007. Zsolt Erdei w pts 12 Tito Mendoza.
Venue: Freiberger Arena, Dresden, Germany. **Recognition:** WBO. **Referee:** Samuel Viruet.
Scorecards: 116-112, 117-111, 111-117.
Fight Summary: In what was a difficult defence, Erdei (173½), who was badly hurt in the fourth when a Mendoza (174) left hook nearly took him out, struggled to contain his rival. Erdei had made a reasonable start, but after the

fourth he was up against it as Mendoza walked through his jab, throwing hurtful right hands and uppercuts. According to one report, Erdei had problems with his stamina and was lucky to get the split decision as he had clearly lost the last four rounds when wilting under pressure. With two judges scoring 117-111, one for and one against Erdei, it did not give a fair reflection of the contest.

16 December 2007. Danny Green w pts 12 Stipe Drews.
Venue: Challenge Stadium, Mount Claremont, Perth, Australia. **Recognition:** WBA. **Referee:** Takeshi Shimakawa.
Scorecards: 118-111, 118-110, 120-108.
Fight Summary: Always looking to go forward against the negative southpaw champion, Green (174½) fully deserved the win with solid right hooks and left hands guiding the way. For a champion, Drews (174½) displayed little ambition, preferring to stay on the outside after feeling the weight in Green's punches. Drews even resorted to throwing Green to the floor as early as the third, and continually clutched his rival when under attack in a one-sided contest that was devoid of two-way action.

Having fulfilled his lifetime ambition of winning a title, Green announced at the end of March 2008 that he was hanging up his gloves with immediate effect to concentrate on his family and to preserve his health. Following that, the WBA matched Hugo Hernan Garay, the WBA FEDELATIN (Latin American Boxing Federation) champion, and Yuriy Barashian, the former European champion, to contest the vacant title.

12 April 2008. Antonio Tarver w pts 12 Clinton Woods.
Venue: St Petersburg Times Forum, Tampa, Florida, USA. **Recognition:** IBF. **Referee:** Frank Santore Jnr.
Scorecards: 119-109, 117-111, 116-112.
Fight Summary: Getting off to a slow start when dropping the opening three rounds, having taken several big left uppercuts in the process from the 39-year-old Tarver (173¾), the champion came back to win the fourth before the fight ran away from him. From there on it was clear that the southpaw Tarver just had too much for the hardy Woods (175), who just could not get going, and was happy to counter with heavy blows whenever the latter came forward. There were no knockdowns, but Woods finished the fight with plenty of facial damage.

12 April 2008. Chad Dawson w pts 12 Glen Johnson.
Venue: St Petersburg Times Forum, Tampa, Florida, USA. **Recognition:** WBC. **Referee:** Tommy Kimmons.
Scorecards: 116-112, 116-112, 116-112.
Fight Summary: With the challenger starting as he meant to carry on when failing to give ground and advancing throughout with the left jab, it was Dawson (173¾) who was deemed to have delivered the better scoring shots by the judges. While several of the rounds were close and difficult to score, Dawson threw solid southpaw blows that landed cleanly, whereas Johnson (172½) was happy to mix it up, the two best punches of the fight coming from him in the third and tenth when he almost had the champion over. Once again it was a contest where Johnson, with some validity, would state that he was unlucky.

On 19 April, at the Tineretului Park Arena, Bucharest, Romania, Adrian Diaconu outpointed Chris Henry over 12 rounds to win the vacant WBC 'interim' title.

Rather than be forced into a defence against Diaconu in July, Dawson handed in his belt to challenge Antonio Tarver for the IBF title. The Romanian was then upgraded to full championship status.

19 April 2008. Joe Calzaghe w pts 12 Bernard Hopkins.
Venue: Thomas & Mack Centre, Las Vegas, Nevada, USA. **Recognition:** The Ring. **Referee:** Joe Cortez.
Scorecards: 115-112, 116-111, 113-114.
Fight Summary: Moving up from super middle to take on the holder of *The Ring* Championship Belt, the unbeaten Calzaghe (173) yet again proved to be a master of his craft when winning the split decision after being knocked down by a left-right for 'three' in the opening session. Although Hopkins (173) landed the heavier shots, Calzaghe did the better work, his southpaw right bemusing the champion at times. In the tenth Hopkins complained of being hit low when going down, and made sure that he got a good rest before resuming. Following the win, Calzaghe was looking forward to making a match with Roy Jones.

26 April 2008. Zsolt Erdei w pts 12 DeAndrey Abron.
Venue: Freiberger Arena, Dresden, Germany. **Recognition:** WBO. **Referee:** Roberto Ramirez.
Scorecards: 119-109, 119-109, 119-109.
Fight Summary: Making his tenth defence Erdei (173¼) was far too good for Abron (173), who won just one round, the third, at most. Whether it was on the inside or at distance, Erdei was the boss. It was clear early on that the taller Abron, whose right eye was badly swollen at the finish, did not have the skill or the tools to beat Erdei, but despite that the latter was content to waltz his way to the unanimous points win.

Due to defend his WBO title against Yuriy Barashian at the Borderland Hall, Magdeburg, Germany, on 10 January 2009, Erdei went ahead with the contest despite the Armenian coming in over the weight, winning on points over 12 rounds.

At the SYMA Sport & Leisure Centre, Budapest, Hungary, on 22 August 2009, Juergen Braehmer stopped Aleksy Kuziemski in the 11th round to win the vacant WBO 'interim' title. Braehmer was handed full title status on 13 November 2009, eight days before Erdei challenged Giacobbe Fragomeni for the WBC cruiser title.

3 July 2008. Hugo Hernan Garay w pts 12 Yuriy Barashian.
Venue: Luna Park Stadium, Buenos Aires, Argentina. **Recognition:** WBA. **Referee:** Roberto Ramirez.
Scorecards: 118-111, 120-108, 118-110.
Fight Summary: In a contest for the vacant title after Danny Green had announced his retirement, Garay (174¾), who was making his third attempt at a version of the world championship, overcame Barashian (175) by a wide margin on the cards. Throwing punches from head to body, Garay outworked his hard-hitting southpaw opponent in all rounds except the ninth and tenth. It was in the latter session that Barashian staggered Garay with a big left hook, but unable to follow it up his chance had gone.

11 October 2008. Chad Dawson w pts 12 Antonio Tarver.
Venue: Palms Casino, Las Vegas, Nevada, USA. **Recognition:** IBF. **Referee:** Jay Nady.
Scorecards: 118-109, 117-110, 117-110.
Fight Summary: Having given up his WBC Championship Belt in order to challenge Tarver (174), Dawson (174) completely dominated the champion in what was a battle of southpaws. Winning just three rounds, the third, sixth and 11th, Tarver lost all chances of victory when a right to the head in the 12th saw him given an 'eight' count after his hand touched the floor. Expected to have trouble with Tarver's punch power, Dawson surprised many when standing up to anything thrown at him. After the fight Tarver admitted that it was not so much Dawson's speed that won it but his high work-rate.

18 November 2008. Joe Calzaghe w pts 12 Roy Jones.
Venue: Madison Square Garden, NYC, New York, USA. **Recognition:** The Ring. **Referee:** Hubert Earle.
Scorecards: 118-109, 118-109, 118-109.
Fight Summary: Despite being floored for 'six' by a wide right hand in the opening session the southpaw holder of *The Ring* Championship Belt got up to beat the once great Jones (174½) in some style, his all-round work-rate taking him to the front and keeping him there. It took Calzaghe (174½) a while to read Jones' right hand and left hook combinations, but once he had he was on his way. Being cut on the left eye in the sixth further hindered Jones' chances. However, by this time Calzaghe's speed of foot and hands were making life extremely difficult for Jones, who despite landing some pretty meaty punches found that they had no effect on the champion.

When Calzaghe announced his retirement early in February 2009, *The Ring* Championship Belt was made available for the next outstanding candidate.

22 November 2008. Hugo Hernan Garay w pts 12 Juergen Braehmer.
Venue: Stadium Hall, Rostock, Germany. **Recognition:** WBA. **Referee:** Stan Christodoulou.
Scorecards: 118-110, 117-112, 116-115.
Fight Summary: Taking the opening two sessions with a fast start, even though the champion lost the next two as Braehmer (174¼) opened up with solid southpaw punches the latter failed to make it stick. By the sixth it was clear

that Garay (175) was the stronger of the two, when firing back with volleys of blows every time he was put under pressure. Coming into the final round, having lost the last four, Braehmer landed with two heavy lefts as he looked to make a late comeback, but when Garay took them without flinching the game was up.

9 May 2009. Chad Dawson w pts 12 Antonio Tarver.
Venue: Hard Rock Hotel & Casino, Las Vegas, Nevada, USA. **Recognition:** IBF. **Referee:** Robert Byrd.
Scorecards: 116-112, 117-111, 117-111.
Fight Summary: Contested in front of a small audience, Dawson (175) won the battle of the two southpaws just as he had done in their previous meeting. As before, Dawson got away well, firing in combinations and concentrating on the body, before Tarver (172) found any kind of rhythm in the third. Having taken a few solid shots in the eighth, Dawson came right back in the ninth when he stunned Tarver with a batch of solid combinations, and although the latter never stopped trying the champion cruised through the remaining sessions to retain his title.

On 27 May, Dawson relinquished the IBF title to negotiate a rematch against Glen Johnson for the WBC 'interim' title and Tavoris Cloud was matched against Clinton Woods to find a successor. Both men had won eliminating contests, Cloud beating Julio Cesar Gonzalez (w rsc 10 at the Aragon Ballroom, Chicago, Illinois on 8 August 2008) and Woods defeating Elvir Muriqi (w pts 12 at the France Hotel, St Helier, Jersey, England on 14 February).

19 June 2009. Jean Pascal w pts 12 Adrian Diaconu.
Venue: Bell Centre, Montreal, Quebec, Canada. **Recognition:** WBC. **Referee:** Frank Garza.
Scorecards: 116-112, 116-111, 115-112.
Fight Summary: Defending the title that was handed to him after it was relinquished by Chad Dawson, the champion's reign turned out to be a short one after Pascal (174¼) took the unanimous points verdict. Making a strong start when showing excellent speed, his left jab and right cross working well, Pascal floored Diaconu (173¼) with a cracking left hook in the fifth. Although being hurt and forced to take more heavy blows prior to the end of the session, Diaconu came back well in the sixth and seventh before Pascal took over again. However, in the 11th an overarm right had the challenger all at sea, but despite battering him until the bell Diaconu was unable to find a finish, Pascal closing out the final session with a boxing lesson.

20 June 2009. Gabriel Campillo w pts 12 Hugo Hernan Garay.
Venue: Freedom Club Stadium, Sunchales, Santa Fe, Argentina. **Recognition:** WBA. **Referee:** Steve Smoger.
Scorecards: 115-114, 114-113, 114-114.
Fight Summary: Not expected to cause the champion a problem, Campillo 174¼) threw a spanner in the works when edging the majority decision. Despite Garay (175) going well for several rounds the weight-making problems he had been suffering in the lead-up to the fight eventually caught up with him in round five, when Campillo came on strong behind the southpaw jab. By the end of the 11th Garay was exhausted however, by rallying strongly in the 12th, he made one last despairing effort to retain his title, but the judges decided otherwise.

15 August 2009. Gabriel Campillo w pts 12 Beibut Shumenov.
Venue: Daulet Sports Complex, Astana, Kazakhstan. **Recognition:** WBA. **Referee:** Steve Smoger.
Scorecards: 114-113, 115-111, 113-113.
Fight Summary: The southpaw champion wasted little time in making the first defence of his new title, the unbeaten Shumenov (174) being a dangerous opponent for him on enemy turf. Regardless of having had just eight contests, Shumenov had beaten two former world champions and was the WBA's number one contender. After five rounds Shumenov was ahead, his power punching proving troublesome for Campillo (174¾), but the latter came back well in the next three rounds before running into a left hook that decked him in the ninth. Despite that seeming to be it for Campillo, the latter surprised the crowd by taking the last three sessions and putting Shumenov down in the last with a left to the body to make sure of the win.

28 August 2009. Tavoris Cloud w pts 12 Clinton Woods.
Venue: Seminole Hard Rock Hotel, Hollywood, Florida, USA. **Recognition:** IBF. **Referee:** Telis Assimenios.
Scorecards: 116-112, 116-112, 116-112.

Fight Summary: In a contest to decide the vacant title after Chad Dawson handed in his belt, it was the unbeaten Cloud (174), a man with 19 wins, 18 of them inside the distance, who triumphed over the former champion, Woods (173½). The Englishman had stood up well to heavy-handed blows for the opening five rounds, being still in the fight, but from the sixth through to the tenth he was given a hard time as Cloud upped the pace and landed some hurtful blows. Although Woods, both eyes swollen, came back gamely in the last two it had been Cloud's fight.

25 September 2009. Jean Pascal w rsc 10 Silvio Branco.
Venue: Bell Centre, Montreal, Canada. **Recognition:** WBC. **Referee:** Gerry Bolen.
Fight Summary: After making a quiet start in the opener Pascal (175) was up to speed by the fourth, his hand-speed being too much for Branco (174¼) to deal with, the latter eventually going down from what seemed to be a less than hard blow to the back of the head. Given a standing 'eight' count despite the referee not signifying a knockdown, Branco continued throwing long punches prior to being dropped in the seventh after being caught by a heavy overarm right. By this time Branco was complaining about being hit by rabbit punches, and in the ninth he suffered what seemed to be another knockdown that was not registered. However, in the tenth it was all over for Branco as he was floored twice before the corner threw the towel in and the referee enforced the stoppage.

At the XL Centre, Hartford, Connecticut, USA on 7 November, Chad Dawson outpointed Glen Johnson to win the WBC 'interim' title.

11 December 2009. Jean Pascal w pts 12 Adrian Diaconu.
Venue: Bell Centre, Montreal, Canada. **Recognition:** WBC. **Referee:** Michael Griffin.
Scorecards: 117-111, 117-111, 118-110.
Fight Summary: Meeting the man he took the title from in a rematch, Pascal (174) was forced to deal with a right shoulder that became dislocated on two separate occasions during the contest. Both men started well, Pascal boxing at distance with Diaconu (174¾) looking to get close. After hurting the challenger in the third with a corking left hook, Pascal dislocated his right shoulder for the first time when going for a finish and was then on the end of some hurtful blows as he retreated. Losing the next couple of sessions when only using his left, Pascal somehow kept in the fight before coming back hard in the eighth and ninth. Having Diaconu under severe pressure in the tenth, and looking to finish it, Pascal was then forced to back off when the shoulder popped out again. The last two rounds saw Pascal keep up the attack despite the pain as Diaconu, his right eye badly swollen, failed to take advantage of the champion's injury woes.

19 December 2009. Juergen Braehmer w pts 12 Dmitry Sukhotsky.
Venue: Sport & Congress Centre, Schwerin, Germany. **Recognition:** WBO. **Referee:** Michael Ortega.
Scorecards: 118-110, 116-112, 116-112.
Fight Summary: Making his first defence of the title that was handed to him after it was relinquished by Zsolt Erdei, Braehmer (175) had a difficult night against the largely unknown Sukhotsky (172¾). Controlling the action for the opening seven rounds, the southpaw champion found Sukhotsky a different proposition for the next three sessions as he began to tire. After scoring well in the eighth, Sukhotsky battered away at Braehmer in the ninth before really working the latter over in the tenth. Suffering a bad cut over the right eye and being subjected to a rare old pounding without firing back, it was only when Sukhotsky ran out of fuel that Braehmer came back to take the 11th and 12th, and the verdict.

29 January 2010. Beibut Shumenov w pts 12 Gabriel Campillo.
Venue: Hard Rock Hotel & Casino, Las Vegas, Nevada, USA. **Recognition:** WBA. **Referee:** Jay Nady.
Scorecards: 117-111, 115-113, 111-117.
Fight Summary: As far as many were concerned, including *Boxing News* and *The Ring* magazine, Campillo (175) was robbed of his title, especially when he landed 320 punches to Shumenov's 219 and appeared to be a good winner in all eyes bar two of the judges. Starting slowly, the 6'2" southpaw champion did not get going until the third round of this return bout, showing good defensive skills, an accurate jab and solid countering. Cut over the left eye in the fifth, Campillo upped the rate in the seventh as Shumenov (174½) tired, and in the ninth he let loose with punch after punch getting home. Happy to see out the tenth, Campillo came back strongly in the last two

sessions, only to be denied the verdict. Although a protest was filed on behalf of Campillo immediately after the fight, in March the WBA rejected any claims for a third meeting between the pair.

24 April 2010. Juergen Braehmer w rsc 5 Mariano Nicolas Plotinsky.
Venue: Alsterdorfer Sports Hall, Hamburg, Germany. **Recognition:** WBO. **Referee:** Paul Thomas.
Fight Summary: Not taking a backward step the challenger tore into Braehmer (174½) from the opening bell, but was soon up against it as solid southpaw left counters found their mark. Although Plotinsky (174¼) was on the floor from a left hook in the second it did not count on the cards as the referee had already called 'break'. Repeatedly countered or tied up in close, Plotinsky was out of ideas in the fifth, and having taken some heavy blows and sent staggering by a left hook the referee rescued him at 2.36 of the session.

On 11 December, at the Echo Arena, Liverpool, England, Nathan Cleverly outpointed Nadjib Mohammedi over 12 rounds to win the vacant WBO 'interim' title.

Just days before making a defence against Cleverly, Braehmer pulled out stating an injury as the reason for his withdrawal, and the Welshman was installed as the champion on 19 May 2011. The contest had already been postponed earlier in the year to allow Braehmer time to deal with a number of legal issues.

23 July 2010. Beibut Shumenov w pts 12 Vyacheslav Uzelkov.
Venue: Tachi Palace Hotel & Casino, Lemoore, California, USA. **Recognition:** WBA. **Referee:** Jon Schorle.
Scorecards: 117-109, 116-108, 118-108.
Fight Summary: Making a bright start Uzelkov (172) dropped Shumenov (175) with a cracking left hook in the opener, but was himself smashed down at the end of the third after the champion connected with a heavy right to the head. With both men affected by the heat it was Shumenov, cut over the right eye in the fourth, who produced the better boxing and lasted the pace well to win virtually every round thereafter.

7 August 2010. Tavoris Cloud w pts 12 Glen Johnson.
Venue: Scot Trade Centre, St Louis, Missouri, USA. **Recognition:** IBF. **Referee:** Steve Smoger.
Scorecards: 116-112, 116-112, 116-112.
Fight Summary: If Cloud (174½) ever thought that Johnson (173) might have seen better days, in what his first defence, he was mistaken after a big overarm right in the second round settled him down. Although Johnson won the second and third sessions, Cloud came back strongly, especially when hurting the challenger in the fifth with a left hook on the head that had him on wobbly legs. All three judges had Johnson winning the ninth before Cloud came back strongly in the 11th and 12th. In the main, Johnson boxed behind the jab while looking for openings to get the right-hand across, as Cloud produced the heavier blows that would ultimately gain him the unanimous decision.

14 August 2010. Jean Pascal w tdec 11 Chad Dawson.
Venue: Bell Centre, Montreal, Canada. **Recognition:** WBC/The Ring. **Referee:** Michael Griffin.
Scorecards: 106-103, 108-101, 106-103.
Fight Summary: In a contest that also attracted the vacant *Ring* Championship Belt, Pascal (174¼) successfully defended his WBC title against his southpaw challenger by means of a technical decision. Showing great speed, Pascal won the opening three rounds before Dawson (174¼) got going in the fourth with good combinations and a solid jab. At the end of the eighth Pascal was in front, having hurt Dawson on a couple of occasions with heavy hooks, but the latter came back strongly in the ninth as he looked for a stoppage. The next two sessions saw Dawson landing the heavier blows, but when Pascal came in low in the 11th and heads came together the former came off worse, his right eye spouting blood. Although deducted a point for an accidental head butt, it was Pascal who was ahead on the cards after the doctor declared that Dawson was unfit to carry on at 2.07 of the session.

17 December 2010. Tavoris Cloud w pts 12 Fulgencio Zuniga.
Venue: American Airlines Arena, Miami, Florida, USA. **Recognition:** IBF. **Referee:** Telis Assimenios.
Scorecards: 118-108, 117-109, 117-109.

Fight Summary: Despite his punches not disturbing the champion too much, Zuniga (174) gave a courageous display when staying on the front foot while taking plenty in return. Being cut above the left eye early in the fight did not unduly concern Cloud (175) as he set about the Colombian with vigour, dropping his man in the fifth with a hard right to the head and again in the final session following a left-right to the jaw. The sixth and seventh were Zuniga's best rounds when outworking Cloud.

18 December 2010. Jean Pascal drew 12 Bernard Hopkins.
Venue: Pepsi Coliseum, Quebec City, Quebec, Canada. **Recognition:** WBC/The Ring. **Referee:** Michael Griffin.
Scorecards: 113-113, 114-114, 112-114.
Fight Summary: After taking a pounding early on, being knocked down in the first by a right to the head and again in the third by a couple of cracking left hooks, Hopkins (174¾) boxed his way back into the fight when giving the WBC champion and holder of *The Ring* Championship Belt all kinds of problems. At the age of 45 Hopkins showed all his mettle and class, even having Pascal (174¾) on the back foot on occasion as he clawed his way back when winning the last three rounds. With two judges making it a draw and another giving it to Hopkins by two rounds there were calls for a return.

8 January 2011. Beibut Shumenov w co 6 William Joppy.
Venue: Ice Sports Palace, Shymkent, Kazakhstan. **Recognition:** WBA. **Referee:** Nabijon Ismanov.
Fight Summary: Fighting on home turf the champion took on the 38-year-old Joppy (174½), who had come in at five days' notice after Juergen Braehmer pulled out. Having prepared for three months to fight a southpaw, Shumenov (175) adjusted fairly quickly when winning the opening four rounds before taking Joppy out in the sixth. It was clear that Joppy was not going to last much longer after being dropped by a heavy right to the head in the fifth, and just 15 seconds into the sixth a left hook to the body saw him floored and counted out.

21 May 2011. Bernard Hopkins w pts 12 Jean Pascal.
Venue: Bell Centre, Montreal, Canada. **Recognition:** WBC/The Ring. **Referee:** Ian John-Lewis.
Scorecards: 116-112, 115-114, 115-113.
Fight Summary: Having drawn with the WBC champion and holder of *The Ring* Championship Belt at the start of the year the 46-year-old Hopkins (175) got the rematch he badly wanted, and this time around stayed on his feet to edge it on all three cards in another close fight. At the same time he broke George Foreman's record as the oldest man to win a world title by 192 days. There was never much between them other than Hopkins' class and excellent defensive ability, Pascal (175) always giving it his best despite being outmanoeuvred by the wily old fox. Hurt in the third by a big right to the head, Pascal regrouped and came right back at Hopkins for round after round without a great deal of success. Realising he was down on the cards Pascal came on like a train in the last two sessions, winning them despite being badly hurt in the 11th. However, it was not enough.

21 May 2011. Nathan Cleverly w rsc 4 Aleksy Kuziemski.
Venue: O2 Arena, Millwall, London, England. **Recognition:** WBO. **Referee:** Mark Nelson.
Fight Summary: With Cleverly (174¾) defending the title that was handed to him after Juergen Braehmer was stripped, the Welshman was far too good for his last-minute opponent. Coming out fast, he was soon hitting Kuziemski (174¾) with every punch in the book as he looked for an early finish. Despite being caught wide open in the third by a left hook the unperturbed Cleverly kept up the assault, and with Kuziemski carrying a cut on the right eye, his face badly swollen, the referee called the fight off at 1.27 of the fourth.

25 June 2011. Tavoris Cloud w rsc 8 Yusaf Mack.
Venue: Family Arena, St Charles, Missouri, USA. **Recognition:** IBF. **Referee:** Sam Williams.
Fight Summary: Ultimately, Cloud (175) proved too strong for his challenger, who despite giving him problems in the opening three rounds with his movement and speed was eventually ground down. Battered by left hooks to head and body in the fourth, Mack (174¼) was forced to fight Cloud's fight from thereon and even won the seventh before coming under the cosh in the eighth. Hurt by a left hook Mack was then dropped by heavy body shots, and although getting to his feet the referee rescued him at 2.57 of the session.

29 July 2011. Beibut Shumenov w rsc 9 Danny Santiago.
Venue: South Point Hotel Casino, Las Vegas, Nevada, USA. **Recognition:** WBA. **Referee:** Tony Weeks.
Fight Summary: Although competitive early on, the challenger began losing every round on the cards as Shumenov (175) picked up the pace after a slow start. Shaken up by a hard right to the head towards the end of the fifth, when Santiago (173) was saved by the bell it was a sign of things to come. With Santiago's face badly swollen the sixth, seventh and eighth saw him shipping plenty of punches as Shumenov warmed to the task, and in the ninth he was pulled out by the referee after 46 seconds following a tremendous barrage of blows with nothing coming back.

15 October 2011. Bernard Hopkins tdraw 2 Chad Dawson.
Venue: Staples Centre, Los Angeles, California, USA. **Recognition:** WBC/The Ring. **Referee:** Pat Russell.
Fight Summary: Dawson (174¼) made a fair start against the WBC champion and holder of *The Ring* Championship Belt, working behind a southpaw right jab, as Hopkins (173½) seemed happy to move around the ring while eyeing his man up. Having upped the pace in the second, Dawson was pushed to the floor unintentionally before Hopkins charged in and ended up on the floor with an injury to his left elbow after what appeared to be a shove from the former. With Hopkins still grounded, at 2.48 of the session the referee stopped the fight and Dawson was announced as the winner and new champion by a stoppage. That was after the referee stated that no foul had been committed. A few days later the WBC overturned the decision, claiming that it was a push by Dawson that caused a separation of the collar bone and shoulder blade and that the result should be seen as a technical draw.

15 October 2011. Nathan Cleverly w pts 12 Tony Bellew.
Venue: Echo Arena, Liverpool, England. **Recognition:** WBO. **Referee:** Richie Davies.
Scorecards: 117-112, 116-113, 114-114.
Fight Summary: Making his first defence, Cleverly (174¼) was forced to fight all the way as Bellew (175) gave it everything and more. It started with Bellew being warned for headwork, but once the contest got going it was a corker with the latter's aggression pitted against Cleverly's better boxing. A Cleverly left hook that went low in the fourth produced another warning while Bellew was given a rest. With the pace catching up with him, Cleverly boxed more at range from the eighth onwards as Bellew continued to storm forward while looking for a punch that would finish it. There was never a great deal in it, but it was Cleverly's more correct punching that gave him the win.

18 February 2012. Tavoris Cloud w pts 12 Gabriel Campillo.
Venue: American Bank Centre, Corpus Christi, Texas, USA. **Recognition:** IBF. **Referee:** Mark Nelson.
Scorecards: 116-110, 114-112, 111-115.
Fight Summary: Yet again Campillo (173½) felt hard done by when losing a decision in a world title fight, even though he suffered two knockdowns in the opening session when floored firstly by a hard right and then by a left uppercut. Surprisingly, the southpaw challenger came back strongly in the second when sending in good blows from the outside, and although Cloud (175) tried to close him down he had little success. A cut over the left eye in the fourth did not aid Cloud much, especially when Campillo drove forward with both hands. Coming into the last three sessions realising his title was at risk Cloud picked up the action, and after hurting Campillo with a solid right to the head in the 11th the latter was forced to give ground in the final session.

25 February 2012. Nathan Cleverly w pts 12 Tommy Karpency.
Venue: Motorpoint Arena, Cardiff, Wales. **Recognition:** WBO. **Referee:** Terry O'Connor.
Scorecards: 120-108, 120-108, 120-108.
Fight Summary: Defending the title in front of his home fans Cleverly (174) marched to a shut-out points win over Karpency (172½), who appeared happy to remain behind a tight guard as the champion loaded up on him. It was almost the same every round, as Cleverly looked to land punches wherever there was an opening, Karpency proving his toughness and durability as the blows rained in. It was only in the 11th that the southpaw challenger took up the gauntlet but, following some heavy shots from the Welshman finding their mark, he went back into his shell.

28 April 2012. Chad Dawson w pts 12 Bernard Hopkins.
Venue: Boardwalk Hall, Atlantic City, New Jersey, USA. **Recognition:** WBC/The Ring. **Referee:** Eddie Cotton.
Scorecards: 117-111, 117-111, 114-114.
Fight Summary: In a return match between Hopkins (173½), the WBC champion and holder of *The Ring* Championship Belt, and Dawson (174½) that was ordered following the disappointing end to their previous affair the latter made sure he stuck to task in hand this time round, and in doing so won the fight. However, it was still very tactical. In the main it was Dawson picking up points from the outside with the southpaw jab and generally trying to do enough to win the rounds. Cut in the fourth on the left eye from what was ruled to be an accidental head butt, Dawson moved up a gear in the fifth while keeping himself out of trouble as best he could. As the rounds progressed, with Hopkins conserving energy it was a poor fight for the fans, but for Dawson it was a badly needed win even if one of the judges had them level at the finish.

2 June 2012. Beibut Shumenov w pts 12 Enrique Ornelas.
Venue: Hard Rock Hotel, Las Vegas, Nevada, USA. **Recognition:** WBA. **Referee:** Joe Cortez.
Scorecards: 120-108, 120-108, 120-108.
Fight Summary: Despite having been out of the ring for nearly a year, the champion started fast when throwing solid rights over the jab. Although Ornelas (174½) gamely stuck to his task every time he had a success of sorts Shumenov (174½) would come roaring back to take the play away from him. For round after round Shumenov dominated the action as he walked to a shut-out points win. Following the fight Shumenov's camp stated that their man had damaged his right forearm in sparring ten days earlier, an injury that forced him to hold back at times.

11 November 2012. Nathan Cleverly w rsc 8 Shawn Hawk.
Venue: Staples Centre, Los Angeles, California, USA. **Recognition:** WBO. **Referee:** Tony Crebs.
Fight Summary: Originally due to defend his title against Ryan Coyne, when the latter pulled out a week before due to a legal dispute with Don King, South Dakota's Hawk (173¾) was substituted. Winning the first six rounds emphatically, his speed of foot and hand making it a tough night's work for Hawk, Cleverly (174½) had his man down twice in the seventh before finishing the contest in the eighth. Setting about Hawk from the bell to start the session and swiftly moving up through the gears the referee finally rescued the outgunned American on the 1.53 mark after he had taken a battery of heavy lefts and rights and was not fighting back.

9 March 2013. Bernard Hopkins w pts 12 Tavoris Cloud.
Venue: Barclays Centre, Brooklyn, NYC, New York, USA. **Recognition:** IBF. **Referee:** Earl Brown.
Scorecards: 116-112, 116-112, 117-111.
Fight Summary: Coming back at 48 years of age to win another version of the world title was truly remarkable, but that is what Hopkins (174½) did when outsmarting the champion. It was Cloud (173¾) who made the better start, hurting his man with left hooks in the second, but over the next few rounds it was fairly even as Hopkins countered the champion's aggression. Cut over the left eye in the sixth from an accidental butt Cloud went after Hopkins, but the latter moved adroitly to avert any danger. From the ninth Hopkins took over, tying Cloud up and more often than not beating him to the punch with solid jabs and right hands.

20 April 2013. Nathan Cleverly w pts 12 Robin Krasniqi.
Venue: The Arena, Wembley, London, England. **Recognition:** WBO. **Referee:** Mark Nelson.
Scorecards: 115-112, 118-109, 118-111.
Fight Summary: Once again the champion put on an excellent display of boxing, his left jab and combinations to head and body being too much for Krasniqi (173) to handle. Pushing on to a shut-out points win, Cleverly (174) occasionally got caught by heavy rights as Krasniqi tried to get into the fight, but they made no real impression on the Welshman who continued at his own pace.

8 June 2013. Adonis Stevenson w rsc 1 Chad Dawson.
Venue: Bell Centre, Montreal, Canada. **Recognition:** WBC/The Ring. **Referee:** Michael Griffin.
Fight Summary: Seen as a huge shock by many, the WBC champion and holder of *The Ring* Championship Belt was halted inside 1.16 of the opening round by a rampant, hard-hitting Stevenson (174¼). Meeting a fellow southpaw, Dawson (173½) was expected to be too experienced for the Haiti-born puncher, but he was given little time to find

his feet before hitting the floor. Both men started cautiously, feeling each other out, before Stevenson smashed home a tremendous overarm left that dropped Dawson heavily. Although getting up at the count of 'seven' it was clear to the referee that Dawson could not continue and the fight was stopped.

17 August 2013. Sergey Kovalev w rsc 4 Nathan Cleverly.
Venue: Motorpoint Arena, Cardiff, Wales. **Recognition:** WBO. **Referee:** Terry O'Connor.
Fight Summary: Kovalev (173½), who had only gone the distance twice in 22 contests and had recently finished off Gabriel Campillo inside three rounds, was quite rightly seen as a dangerous opponent for the champion, and so it proved. Under pressure throughout, the Welshman stated afterwards that every punch that landed had felt like a hammer blow. Although Cleverly (174) got through the opening two rounds, when Kovalev, cut by the right eye, opened up with lefts and rights in the third he was dropped twice and very nearly did not see out the session, slumping onto his stool at the bell. Having been allowed out for the fourth the referee made a timely intervention just 20 seconds later when Cleverly was taking heavy punishment and unable to defend himself.

28 September 2013. Adonis Stevenson w rtd 7 Tavoris Cloud.
Venue: Bell Centre, Montreal, Canada. **Recognition:** WBC/The Ring. **Referee:** Michael Griffin.
Fight Summary: Making the first defence of his WBC title and *The Ring* Championship Belt, Stevenson (173¾) proved that he could also box as well as punch when defeating Cloud (174½). Cut over the left eye in the first Cloud was up against it from the start as Stevenson moved in with heavy southpaw blows, and after feeling the effects of a heavy straight left in the opener he looked to fight on the outside rather than taking too many risks. Stevenson's clever movement made life even more difficult for Cloud, who took a beating in virtually every round before being retired by his corner at the end of the seventh after he had been further gashed.

26 October 2013. Bernard Hopkins w pts 12 Karo Murat.
Venue: Boardwalk Hall, Atlantic City, New Jersey, USA. **Recognition:** IBF. **Referee:** Steve Smoger.
Scorecards: 119-108, 119-108, 117-110.
Fight Summary: Happy to take on his mandatory challenger, Hopkins (172½) once again showed that he still had what it takes when outmanoeuvring the tough Murat (174). There was no doubt that Murat, who was docked a point for hitting on the break in the seventh, came to fight, but he was up against a master craftsman in Hopkins. Cut around the left eye in the eighth, Murat continued his march without great success as Hopkins cruised through the last session to win by a good margin on all three cards.

30 November 2013. Adonis Stevenson w rsc 6 Tony Bellew.
Venue: The Coliseum, Quebec City, Quebec, Canada. **Recognition:** WBC/The Ring. **Referee:** Michael Griffin.
Fight Summary: Putting up a good fight Bellew (175) held the WBC champion and holder of *The Ring* Championship Belt at bay for the opening five rounds when making him miss before moving but was unable to mount any real offensive. Pursuing Bellew hard in the sixth Stevenson (174½) finally caught up with his man, a terrific southpaw straight left to the head dropping the game Englishman. Although up quickly Bellew was unable to get going, and after taking several solid lefts without return the referee pulled him out on the 1.50 mark.

30 November 2013. Sergey Kovalev w rsc 2 Ismayl Sillakh.
Venue: The Coliseum, Quebec City, Quebec, Canada. **Recognition:** WBO. **Referee:** Marlon Wright.
Fight Summary: Having boxed reasonably well in the opening session, the challenger was blasted out of the fight just 56 seconds into the second after Kovalev (174¾) had unleashed his heavy armoury. Initially dropped by a right to the head Sillakh (174½) took the 'eight' count before being allowed back into the action, and following a tremendous left-right combination he crashed down under the ropes to be rescued by the referee.

14 December 2013. Beibut Shumenov w rsc 3 Tomas Kovacs.
Venue: The Alamodome, San Antonio, Texas, USA. **Recognition:** WBA. **Referee:** Rafael Ramos.
Fight Summary: Coming back to the ring after 18 months away from boxing due to injury and a self-promotion scheme that failed to produce a fight, Shumenov (175) patiently moved in after his challenger before dropping him with a left hook towards the end of the first. Having floored Kovacs (174½) again in the second, Shumenov chased

after his man in the third, finally blasting him to the floor with a crashing right hand to the jaw. At this point the referee, who had seen enough, immediately stopped the contest with five seconds of the session remaining.

The same day, at the Jahn Sports Forum, Neubrandenburg, Germany, Juergen Braehmer won the vacant WBA 'second tier' title when outpointing Marcus Oliveira over 12 rounds. On 5 April 2014, Braehmer followed this up with a successful defence when he stopped Enzo Maccarinelli inside six rounds at the Stadium Hall, Rostock, Germany.

29 March 2014. Sergey Kovalev w co 7 Cedric Agnew.
Venue: The Ballroom, Boardwalk Hall, Atlantic City, New Jersey, USA. **Recognition:** WBO. **Referee:** Samuel Viruet.
Fight Summary: On 26 straight, and having beaten Yusaf Mack to get the opportunity, Agnew (174½) tried to confuse the champion when coming out for the opening session as a southpaw. It may have confused Kovalev (174½) momentarily, but before too long he was hunting Agnew down, dropping him with a left hook near the end of the second. Although suffering a cut right eye in the fourth and another one under the left eye in the sixth Kovalev was still in total control, and towards the end of the sixth he floored Agnew with a hard right to the body. Not wasting much time in the seventh Kovalev launched himself at Agnew, a left to the ribs seeing the latter counted out on one knee after 58 seconds of the session.

19 April 2014. Bernard Hopkins w pts 12 Beibut Shumenov.
Venue: The Armoury, Washington DC, USA. **Recognition:** IBF/WBA. **Referee:** Earl Brown.
Scorecards: 116-111, 116-111, 113-114.
Fight Summary: This was a unification fight between the IBF's 49-year-old Hopkins (172½) and Shumenov (174½), the WBA champion, and it was the former who came out on top by a split decision, two of the judges scoring it as a five round margin of victory with the other judge favouring the Kazakh. Although Shumenov was always dangerous, Hopkins used the jab superbly well and closed his man down when he had to, giving him no room to get his punches off. All three judges gave Shumenov the ninth and tenth rounds as he finally got his right hand going as Hopkins tired, but in the 11th he was dumped by a heavy right. It was all Hopkins in the final session, Shumenov stating after the fight that while his opponent was a great champion he had got his tactics wrong.

Juergen Braehmer retained his WBA 'second tier' title when outpointing Roberto Feliciano Bolonti over 12 rounds at the Sport & Congress Centre, Schwerin, Germany on 7 June.

24 May 2014. Adonis Stevenson w pts 12 Andrzej Fonfara.
Venue: Bell Centre, Montreal, Canada. **Recognition:** WBC/The Ring. **Referee:** Frank Garza.
Scorecards: 116-109, 115-110, 115-110.
Fight Summary: Dropped in the first round by a solid southpaw left to the head, Fonfara (174½) got up and fought his way back strongly in the face of the champion's attacks. Winning the fourth by dint of his jab and left hook, Fonfara showed that he had not come to be swept away by Stevenson (173½) despite being subjected to solid blows to the body, one of which dropped him in the fifth. Continuing to show his mettle, Fonfara hurt the tiring Stevenson with a body shot before driving on into the ninth where he floored the champion with a left-right. However, it was Stevenson who quickly regrouped to win the last three sessions as Fonfara faded, having given it his best. As well as his WBC title, Stevenson's *Ring* Championship Belt was also at stake in this one.

2 August 2014. Sergey Kovalev w rsc 2 Blake Caparello.
Venue: Revel Resort, Atlantic City, New Jersey, USA. **Recognition:** WBO. **Referee:** Sparkle Lee.
Fight Summary: With a big unification match in the offing against Bernard Hopkins, despite taking a count in the opening session when Caparello (174) caught him off balance with a southpaw left hander, the champion was never going lose this one. Having threatened with the right throughout the first round Kovalev (174) finally used it to drop Caparello with a body shot in the second, and following two more knockdowns the latter was rescued by the referee on the 1.47 mark.

8 November 2014. Sergey Kovalev w pts 12 Bernard Hopkins.
Venue: Boardwalk Hall, Atlantic City, New Jersey, USA. **Recognition:** IBF/WBA/WBO. **Referee:** David Fields.

Scorecards: 120-107, 120-107, 120-106.
Fight Summary: Another unification battle saw Kovalev (174½), the WBO champion, take on the 49-year-old Hopkins (173½), the holder of the WBA and IBF titles. Into his stride quickly, Kovalev dropped Hopkins with an overarm right before going on to wrap up the rounds with his speed and power taking the play away from the latter. Although Hopkins had been hurt by cracking rights in several rounds he was still there at the start of the 12th, even wobbling Kovalev with a left hook prior to holding on to the final bell as punch after punch rained in on him.

Yet again, Juergen Braehmer successfully defended the WBA 'second tier' title when knocking out Pawel Glazewski inside a round at the EWE Arena, Oldenburg, Germany on 6 December.

19 December 2014. Adonis Stevenson w co 5 Dmitry Sukhotsky.
Venue: Pepsi Coliseum, Quebec City, Canada. **Recognition:** WBC/The Ring. **Referee:** Michael Griffin.
Fight Summary: Taking over from the start the WBC champion was soon forcing Sukhotsky (173½) back with the southpaw jab, and in the second round the latter was pushed down after a left to the head had hurt him. By the fifth there was little coming back from Sukhotsky as Stevenson (174½) loaded up, a straight left dropping him before he was floored twice more by vicious lefts. After the third knockdown, Sukhotsky was rescued by the referee with 18 seconds of the session remaining. Stevenson's *Ring* Championship Belt was also at risk in this one.

14 March 2015. Sergey Kovalev w rsc 8 Jean Pascal.
Venue: Bell Centre, Montreal, Canada. **Recognition:** IBF/WBA/WBO. **Referee:** Luis Pabon.
Fight Summary: Putting his three titles up for grabs Kovalev (174¼) was forced to fight hard against a determined Pascal (175), whose best form of attack was when countering the champion with crunching right hands over the top. Having been forced to take a count in the third after a battery of heavy blows had left him stuck between the ropes, Pascal came back with solid shots of his own in the fifth and sixth that forced Kovalev on the defensive. However, the seventh saw Kovalev back in control with the jab as Pascal tired from his exertions and in the eighth, with the latter all at sea, after a terrific right to the head had wobbled him the referee stopped the fight at 1.03 of the session.

Defending his WBA 'second tier' title, Juergen Braehmer forced Robin Krasniqi to retire at the end of the ninth round of their contest at the Stadium Hall, Rostock, Germany on 21 March.

4 April 2015. Adonis Stevenson w pts 12 Sakio Bika.
Venue: Pepsi Coliseum, Quebec City, Quebec, Canada. **Recognition:** WBC/The Ring. **Referee:** Michael Griffin.
Scorecards: 115-111, 116-110, 115-110.
Fight Summary: Moving up a division and looking to upset Stevenson (174½), the tough challenger made life difficult for his southpaw opponent with his brawling tactics and ability to absorb heavy shots. Having pulled Stevenson to the floor in the fifth as he stumbled, despite being ruled a slip, Bika (174½) was officially dropped in the sixth by a cracker of a left to the head. Following that Bika visibly slowed as the accumulation of blows took their toll, and in the tenth he was dumped by a solid left to the jaw. The final two sessions saw Stevenson box his way through to the final bell without too much coming his way. Stevenson's *Ring* Championship Belt was also on the line.

25 July 2015. Sergey Kovalev w co 3 Nadjib Mohammedi.
Venue: Mandalay Bay Hotel & Casino, Las Vegas, Nevada, USA. **Recognition:** IBF/WBA/WBO. **Referee:** Kenny Bayless.
Fight Summary: Following a feeling-out opening round the champion stepped it up in the second, having Mohammedi (173) on the floor three times, once from a two fisted assault, then a shove before a trip made it a hat-trick. Although Mohammedi came out firing in the third he was soon being pushed back as Kovalev (174½) chased him down, and following a cracking right hand and a straight left he was sent to the floor where he was counted out at 2.38 of the session.

On 23 August, Felix Valera won the vacant WBA 'interim' title when outpointing Stanislav Kashtanov over 12 rounds at the Rixos Mriya Resort Hotel, Yalta, Russia.

The 'second tier' champion, Juergen Braehmer, successfully defended his title at the EnergieVerbund Arena, Dresden, Germany, by way of a seventh-round retirement win over Konni Konrad on 5 September.

11 September 2015. Adonis Stevenson w rsc 3 Tommy Karpency.
Venue: Ricoh Coliseum, Toronto, Canada. **Recognition:** WBC/The Ring. **Referee:** Hector Afu.
Fight Summary: After giving it his best shot in the opening session, in a battle of southpaws Karpency (174½) began to buckle under the weight of the champion's punches in the second, a left-right putting him down heavily for a 'nine' count. At the start of the third Stevenson (175) wasted no further time when he marched out with both hands before dropping Karpency with a cracking left, and after 21 seconds had elapsed the fight was over when the referee rescued the latter who was up at 'nine' but in no position to defend himself. Once again, Stevenson's *Ring* Championship Belt was at stake.

Stevenson forfeited *The Ring* Championship Belt at the end of November after failing to meet a top-five-rated opponent for over two years.

30 January 2016. Sergey Kovalev w rtd 7 Jean Pascal.
Venue: Bell Centre, Montreal, Canada. **Recognition:** IBF/WBA/WBO. **Referee:** Michael Griffin.
Fight Summary: Impressing as the man to beat in the division, the champion successfully defended his three titles against Pascal (174¼), who was retired at the end of the seventh round following a severe beating. Using a solid left jab to the body to bring Pascal's defences down, as in their previous contest, Kovalev (174½) was merciless when banging in heavy right hands to the head and left hooks to the body. Put down in the first by a stiff left which was called a slip, Pascal was always prepared to throw heavy rights at Kovalev, but at the end of the third a big right sent him through the ropes for a count. Saved by the bell, Pascal continued to plug away, but after being given one more round by his corner at the start of the seventh and with his right eye swelling they had seen enough.

Juergen Braehmer successfully defended his WBA 'second tier' title when outpointing Eduard Gutknecht over 12 rounds at the Jahn Sports Forum, on 12 March.

Dmitry Bivol won the WBA 'interim' title when outscoring the holder, Felix Valera, over 12 rounds at the Khodynka Ice Palace, Moscow, Russia on 21 May.

11 July 2016. Sergey Kovalev w pts 12 Isaac Chilemba.
Venue: DIVS Sports Palace, Ekaterinburg, Russia. **Recognition:** IBF/WBA/WBO. **Referee:** Michael Griffin.
Scorecards: 117-110, 118-109, 116-111.
Fight Summary: Taken the distance for only the fourth time in 31 fights, the champion was not at his best in this one as Chilemba (174¾) moved away from the firing line and became a difficult target. It was only Chilemba's lack of power that allowed Kovalev (174½) to get away scot-free, but in the seventh he finally caught up with his Malawi-born opponent. Dropped by a heavy right to the head, although Chilemba made it to the end of the session he was now in survival mode. Having taken a bit of a beating in the eighth, Chilemba somehow managed to make it to the final bell despite looking likely to go at any time.

Nathan Cleverly won the WBA 'second tier' title when forcing the champion, Juergen Braehmer, to retire at the end of the sixth round at the Jahn Sports Forum, Neubrandenburg, Germany on 1 October.

29 July 2016. Adonis Stevenson w co 4 Thomas Williams.
Venue: Videotron Centre, Quebec City, Quebec, Canada. **Recognition:** WBC. **Referee:** Michael Griffin.
Fight Summary: In a match-up between southpaws it was the 38-year-old champion who came out on top of Williams (174½), putting his younger rival down with a cracking left to the head in the opening session and serving notice on those who felt that his best days were behind him. Coming back strongly in the second, Williams showed

he had plenty left in the tank when stunning Stevenson (173½) with some big lefts and rights to head and body even though he was forced to take another heavy left hand. Having regained control in the third, Stevenson had Williams down with a low blow in the fourth, something he was admonished for. Given time out, Williams threw himself at Stevenson, but when a clash of heads left him with a bad cut over the left eye his days were numbered. Chased to the ropes, when Williams was chinned by a crashing left he went to the floor face first to be counted out with just six seconds of the session remaining.

Light Heavyweight Boxers' Index:
(Country of birth where known/Domicile - birthplace and domicile are the same unless stated)

A
DeAndrey Abron (USA)
Ray Actis (USA)
Tomasz Adamek (Poland/USA)
Cedric Agnew (USA)
Jorge Ahumada (Argentina)
Muhammad Ali (USA)
Darrin Allen (USA)
Marcellus Allen (USA)
Santo Amonti (Italy)
Lee Anderson (USA)
Ray Anderson (USA)
John Andersson (Sweden)
Al Andrews (USA)
Paul Andrews (USA)
Dennis Andries (Guyana/England)
Rufino Angulo (France)
Tony Anthony (USA)
Fred Apostoli (USA)
Everardo Armenta (Mexico)
Crawford Ashley (England)
Eddie Avoth (Egypt/Wales)

B
Abie Bain (Russia/USA)
Doyle Baird (USA)
Germinal Ballarin (Luxembourg/France)
Joe Banovic (USA)
Yuriy Barashian (Russia/Ukraine)
Leeonzer Barber (USA)
Iran Barkley (USA)
Ray Barnes (USA)
Jimmy Beau (USA)
Jack Beauscholte (USA)
Booker Beckwith (USA)
Jimmy Beecham (USA)
Charley Belanger (USA)
Tony Bellew (England)
Lonnie Bennett (USA)
George Benton (USA)
Paul Berlenbach (USA)
Enrico Bertola (Italy)
Willi Besmanoff (Germany/USA)
Jupp Besselmann (Germany)
Melio Bettina (USA)
Mwehu Beya (DR Congo/USA)
Muslim Biarslanov (Russia)
Anthony Bigeni (New Zealand)
Sakio Bika (Cameroon/Australia)

Jimmy Bivins (USA)
Dmitry Bivol (Kyrgyzstan/Russia)
George Black (USA)
George Blades (USA)
Tom Bogs (Denmark)
Nate Bolden (USA)
Roberto Feliciano Bolonti (Argentina)
Jack Bonner (USA)
Tony Bosnich (USA)
Vincent Boulware (USA)
Jesse Bowdry (USA)
Battling Bozo (USA)
Jim Braddock (USA)
Juergen Braehmer (Germany)
Silvio Branco (Italy)
Dwight Braxton-Muhammad Qawi (USA)
Gomeo Brennan (Bahamas/USA)
Paul Briggs (New Zealand/Australia)
Henry Brimm (Puerto Rico/USA)
Lou Brooks (USA)
Lou Brouillard (Canada/USA)
George KO Brown (Greece/USA)
Mel Brown (USA)
Mose Brown (USA)
Dan Bucceroni (USA)
Red Burman (USA)
Jesse Burnett (USA)
Tommy Burns (Canada)
Willie Bush (USA)
George Byers (Canada/USA)
Joe Bygraves (Jamaica/England)

C
Chic Calderwood (Scotland)
Rory Calhoun (USA)
Baxter Calmes (USA)
Joe Calzaghe (England/Wales)
Artenio Calzavara (Italy)
Mario Campi (Italy/USA)
Gabriel Campillo (Spain)
Blake Caparello (Australia)
Tony Caponi (USA)
Richard Caramanolis (France)
Paul Carlo (USA)
Frank Carpenter (USA)
Georges Carpentier (France)
Hal Carroll (USA)
Kid Carter (USA)
Hank Casey (USA)

Franco Cavicchi (Italy)
Jerry Celestine (USA)
Ezzard Charles (USA)
Clyde Chastain (USA)
Isaac Chilemba (Malawi/South Africa)
George Chip (USA)
Joe Choynski (USA)
Gus Christie (USA)
Anton Christoforidis (Turkey/USA)
Dave Clark (USA)
Henry Clark (USA)
Victor Claudio (Puerto Rico)
Von Clay (USA)
Louis Clement (Switzerland)
Nathan Cleverly (Wales)
Tavoris Cloud (USA)
Don Cockell (England)
Johnny Colan (USA)
Tom Collins (Curacao/England)
Billy Conn (USA)
John Conteh (England)
Fred Cooley (USA)
Charley Cotton (USA)
Eddie Cotton (USA)
George Courtney (USA)
Ryan Coyne (USA)
Dan Creedon (New Zealand/Australia)
Miguel Angel Cuello (Argentina)
Humberto Curi (Argentina/USA)
Bobby Czyz (USA)

D
Gentle Daniel (Trinidad)
Terry Daniels (USA)
Eddie Davis (USA)
Johnny Davis (USA)
Bobby Dawson (USA)
Chad Dawson (USA)
Carlos De Leon (Puerto Rico)
Joey DeGrandis (USA)
Ralph DeJohn (USA)
Piero Del Papa (Italy)
Lou Del Valle (USA)
Jack Delaney (Canada/USA)
Freddie Delgado (Puerto Rico)
Jason DeLisle (Australia)
Jack Dempsey (USA)
Frank DePaula (USA)
Adrian Diaconu (Romania/Canada)
Jack Dillon (USA)
Roberto Dominguez Perez (Spain)
Billy Douglas (USA)
Terry Downes (England)

Stipe Drews (Croatia)
Mickey Dugan (USA)
Bob Dunlop (Australia)
Wilson Dunn (USA)
Jimmy Dupree (USA)
Yvon Durelle (Canada)
Bobby Dykes (USA)

E
Harry Ebbets (USA)
Willie Edwards (USA)
Sailor Einert (Germany/USA)
Jimmy Ellis (USA)
Rudy Ellis (USA)
Armand Emanuel (Canada/USA)
Jean-Marie Emebe (Cameroon/France)
Harry English (USA)
Larry English (USA)
Zsolt Erdei (Hungary)

F
Frank Farmer (USA)
Willie Featherstone (Canada)
Pret Ferrar (Cuba/USA)
Chris Finnegan (England)
Young Fisher (USA)
Jack Fitzgerald (USA)
Fitzie Fitzpatrick (USA)
Bob Fitzsimmons (England/USA)
Donnie Fleeman (USA)
Tiger Flowers (USA)
Fireman Jim Flynn (USA)
Harry Foley (USA)
Andrzej Fonfara (Poland/USA)
Bob Foster (USA)
Pierre Fourie (South Africa)
Billy Fox (USA)
Tiger Jack Fox (USA)
Bob Foxworth (USA)
Giacobbe Fragomeni (Italy)
Matthew Franklin-Matthew Saad Muhammad (USA)
Joe Frazier (USA)
Richard Frazier (USA)
Tyrone Frazier (USA)
Harry Fuller (USA)

G
Al Gainer (USA)
Victor Galindez (Argentina)
Hugo Hernan Garay (Argentina)
George Gardner (Ireland/USA)
Joey Giardello (USA)
Jack Gibbons (USA)

Mike Gibbons (USA)
Tommy Gibbons (USA)
Nestor Giovannini (Argentina)
Bruno Girard (France)
Christophe Girard (France)
Pawel Glazewski (Poland)
Bob Godwin (USA)
Julio Cesar Gonzalez (Mexico/USA)
Sailor Grande (Italy/USA)
Otis Grant (Jamaica/Canada)
Harry Greb (USA)
Danny Green (Australia)
Eddie Gregory-Eddie Mustafa Muhammad (USA)
Montell Griffin (USA)
William Guthrie (USA)
Eduard Gutknecht (Kazakhstan/Germany)

H
Johnny Halafihi (Tonga/England)
Jim Hall (Australia)
Richard Hall (Jamaica/USA)
Henry Hank (USA)
Wild Bill Hanrahan (USA)
Vic Hansen (USA)
Thomas Hansvoll (Norway)
Eric Harding (USA)
Jeff Harding (Australia)
Allan Harmon (Jamaica/USA)
Derrick Harmon (USA)
Marvin Hart (USA)
Len Harvey (England)
Ramzi Hassan (Jordan/USA)
Shawn Hawk (USA)
Thomas Hearns (USA)
Gerhard Hecht (Germany)
Anthony Hembrick (USA)
Chris Henry (USA)
Clarence Henry (USA)
Adolf Heuser (Germany)
Freddie Hicks (USA)
Tommy Hicks (USA)
Virgil Hill (USA)
Willi Hoepner (Germany)
John Holman (USA)
Mike Holt (South Africa)
Bernard Hopkins (USA)
Arthur Howard (England)
Johnny Howard (USA)
Rico Hoye (USA)
Cecil Hudson (USA)
Chuck Hunter (USA)
Len Hutchins (USA)

J
Alonzo Johnson (USA)
Glen Johnson (Jamaica/USA)
Harold Johnson (USA)
Larry Johnson (USA)
Marvin Johnson (USA)
Reggie Johnson (USA)
Vonzell Johnson (USA)
Young Jack Johnson (USA)
Billy Jones (USA)
Carl Jones (USA)
Doug Jones (USA)
Eddie Jones (USA)
Gorilla Jones (USA)
Roy Jones (USA)
William Joppy (USA)
Charley Joseph (USA)

K
Slobodan Kacar (Bosnia/Serbia)
Joe Kahut (USA)
Tommy Karpency (USA)
Stanislav Kashtanov (Ukraine/Russia)
Richie Kates (USA)
Fay Keiser (USA)
Brian Kelly (USA)
Glen Kelly (Australia)
Hugo Kelly (Italy/USA)
Leo Kelly (USA)
Andy Kendall (USA)
Bert Kenny (Canada)
Stanley Ketchel (USA)
Jamaica Kid (Belize/USA)
Zulu Kid (USA)
James Kinchen (USA)
Jimmy King (USA 1915-35)
Jimmy King (USA 1946-61)
Ka-Dy King (USA)
Ed Kinley (USA)
Ole Klemetsen (Norway)
Joe Knight (USA)
Konni Konrad (Montenegro/Germany)
Robert Koon (USA)
Rudy Koopmans (Netherlands)
Tomas Kovacs (Slovakia)
Sergey Kovalev (Russia/USA)
Robin Krasniqi (Kosovo/Germany)
Solly Krieger (USA)
Aleksy Kuziemski (Poland)

L
Alejandro Lakatos (Romania/Spain)
Donny Lalonde (Canada)

Jake LaMotta (USA)
Sam Langford (Canada/USA)
Joe Lasisi (Nigeria/USA)
Pete Latzo (USA)
Alejandro Lavorante (Argentina)
Bob Lawson (USA)
Rex Layne (USA)
Heinz Lazek (Austria)
Fred Lenhart (Czech Republic/USA)
Sugar Ray Leonard (USA)
Gus Lesnevich (USA)
Battling Levinsky (USA)
John Henry Lewis (USA)
Ted Kid Lewis (USA)
Tait Littman (USA)
Leo Lomski (USA)
Brian London (England)
Jack London (England 1931-49)
Jack London (USA 1917-20)
Yaqui Lopez (Mexico/USA)
Tommy Loughran (USA)
Joe Louis (USA)
Eric Lucas (Canada)
Jerry Luedee (USA)
Bert Lytell (USA)

M
Enzo Maccarinelli (Wales)
Jim MacDonald (USA)
Freddie Mack (USA)
Yusaf Mack (USA)
Ernesto Magdaleno (USA)
Andrea Magi (Italy)
Dave Maier (USA)
George Manley (USA)
Roscoe Manning (USA)
Frank Mantell (Germany/USA)
Rocky Marciano (USA)
Egerton Marcus (Guyana/Canada)
Lloyd Marshall (USA)
Jerry Martin (Antigua/USA)
Emilio Martinez (USA)
Jimmy Martinez (USA)
Tony Marullo (USA)
Henry Maske (Germany)
Harry Matthews (USA)
Tami Mauriello (USA)
Joey Maxim (USA)
Rocco Mazzola (Italy)
Bob McAllister (USA)
Buddy McArthur (USA)
Jock McAvoy (England)
Pat McCafferty (USA)

Mike McCallum (Jamaica/USA)
Young John McCormack (Ireland/England)
Al McCoy (USA)
Charles Kid McCoy (USA)
Eddie McGoorty (USA)
Tom McMahon (USA)
Pat McMurtry (USA)
Tom McNeeley (USA)
Mike McTigue (Ireland/USA)
Mario Melo (Argentina)
Epifanio Mendoza (Colombia)
Tito Mendoza (Panama)
Jose Menno (Argentina)
Sergio Merani (Argentina)
Preciso Merlo (Germany/Italy)
Dariusz Michalczewski (Poland/Germany)
Philippe Michel (France)
Freddie Mills (England)
Holly Mims (USA)
Mauro Mina (Peru)
Billy Miske (USA)
Bob Moha (USA)
Prince Mama Mohammed (Ghana/USA)
Nadjib Mohammedi (France)
Saul Montana (Mexico)
Tony Montano (USA)
Archie Moore (USA)
Dick Moore (Ireland/USA)
Michael Moorer (USA)
Jack Moran (USA)
Howard Morrow (USA)
Leonard Morrow (USA)
Eddie Mustafa Muhammad (USA)
Tony Mundine (Australia)
Karo Murat (Armenia/Germany)
Paul Murdoch (Australia)
Elvir Muriqi (Kosovo/USA)
Bob Murphy (USA)
Billy Murray (USA)
Phil Muscato (USA)
Lottie Mwale (Zambia)

N
Danny Nardico (USA)
George Nichols (USA)
Kid Norfolk (USA)
Charley Norkus (USA)
Al Norton (USA)
Michael Nunn (USA)

O
Philadelphia Jack O'Brien (USA)
Pat O'Connor (USA)
Dan O'Dowd (Poland/USA)
Tim O'Neil (USA)
Yale Okun (USA)
Bob Olin (USA)
Marcus Oliveira (USA)
Carl Bobo Olson (Hawaii)
Lee Oma (USA)
Angel Oquendo (USA)
Enrique Ornelas (Mexico/USA)
Willie Oster (USA)
Ken Overlin (USA)

P
Ambrose Palmer (Australia)
Jack Palmer (England)
James J. Parker (Canada)
Mate Parlov (Croatia)
Jean Pascal (Haiti/Canada)
Bob Pastor (USA)
Willie Pastrano (USA)
Floyd Patterson (USA)
Mike Peak (USA)
Gregorio Peralta (Argentina)
Louis Pergaud (Cameroon/Germany)
Sylvester Perkins (USA)
Johnny Persol (USA)
Jack Petersen (Wales)
Don Petrin (USA)
Sailor Ed Petroskey (USA)
Owen Phelps (USA)
Eddie Phillips (England)
Nicky Piper (Wales)
Mariano Nicolas Plotinsky (Argentina)
Yolande Pompey (Trinidad/England)
Mark Prince (England)

Q
Dwight Muhammad Qawi (USA)
Mike Quarry (USA)

R
Johnny Ralph (South Africa)
Oscar Rankins (USA)
Sonny Ray (USA)
Pal Reed (USA)
Bandsman Dick Rice (England)
Ron Richards (Australia)
Dick Richardson (Wales)
Giulio Rinaldi (Italy)
Babe Risko (USA)

Oscar Rivadeneyra (Peru)
Neal Rivers (USA)
Sugar Ray Robinson (USA)
Graciano Rocchigiani (Germany)
Al Rodrigues (USA)
Antonio Rodrigues (Portugal/Brazil)
Sixto Rodriguez (Puerto Rico/USA)
Vicente Rondon (Venezuela)
Jack Root (Czech Republic/USA)
Rosy Rosales (USA)
Maxie Rosenbloom (USA)
Mike Rossman (USA)
Gustave Roth Belgium)
Roger Rouse (USA)
Russ Rowsey (USA)
Jacques Royer-Crecy (France)
John Ruiz (USA)
Australian Jim Ryan (Australia/USA)

S
Matthew Saad Muhammad (USA)
Mehdi Sahnoune (France)
Randy Sandy (USA)
Danny Santiago (USA)
Bob Satterfield (USA)
Milo Savage (USA)
Gustav Scholz (Germany)
Erich Schoppner (Germany)
Buddy Scott (USA)
Harry Scott (England)
James Scott (USA)
Lou Scozza (USA)
John Scully (USA)
David Sears (USA)
Mike Sedillo (USA)
Andres Antonio Selpa (Argentina)
Billy Shade (USA)
Dave Shade (USA)
Curtis Sheppard (USA)
Tony Shucco (USA)
Beibut Shumenov (Kazakhstan/USA)
Manny Siaca (Puerto Rico)
Tony Sibson (England)
Battling Siki (Senegal/France)
Ismayl Sillakh (Ukraine)
Harald Skog (Norway)
Jimmy Slade (USA)
Jimmy Slattery (USA)
Dick Smith (England)
Jim Smith (USA)
Kosie Smith (South Africa)
Oakland Billy Smith (USA)
Polly Smith (Bermuda/England)

Eddy Smulders (Netherlands)
Chuck Spieser (USA)
Michael Spinks (USA)
Adonis Stevenson (Haiti/Canada)
Leslie Stewart (Trinidad/USA)
Al Stillman (USA)
Bobby Stininato (USA)
Danny Stonewalker (Canada)
Young Stribling (USA)
Dmitry Sukhotsky (Russia)
Murray Sutherland (Scotland/USA)
Frankie Swindell (USA)
Karel Sys (Belgium)

T
Olle Tandberg (Sweden)
Antonio Tarver (USA)
Frank Tate (USA)
Will Taylor (USA)
Willie Taylor (USA)
David Telesco (USA)
Mark Tessman (USA)
Drake Thadzi (Malawi/Canada)
Cyclone Johnny Thompson (USA)
Jeff Thompson (USA)
Wayne Thornton (USA)
Dick Tiger (Nigeria/USA)
Christophe Tiozzo (France)
Fabrice Tiozzo (France)
Jose Torres (Puerto Rico)
Aldo Traversaro (Italy)
Jim Tremble (USA)
Tommy Tucker (USA)
Kid Tunero (Cuba)
Gene Tunney (USA)
Clay Turner (USA)
Randy Turpin (England)

U
Thomas Ulrich (Germany)
Asluddin Umarov (Kazakhstan/USA)
Paulino Uzcudun (Spain)
Vyacheslav Uzelkov (Ukraine)

V
Nino Valdes (Cuba)

Felix Valera (Dominican Republic)
Willie Vaughn (USA)
David Vedder (USA)
Conny Velensek (Slovenia/Germany)

W
Dick Wagner (USA)
Jersey Joe Walcott (USA)
Buddy Walker (USA)
Mickey Walker (USA)
Moses Ward (USA)
Rough House Ware (USA)
Mustafa Wasajja (Uganda/Denmark)
Adolpho Washington (USA)
Guy Waters (Australia)
Jimmy Webb (USA)
Charley Weinert (Hungary/USA)
Eddie Wenstob (Canada)
Whitey Wenzel (USA)
Dave Whitlock (USA)
Chuck Wiggins (USA)
Jess Willard (USA)
Charley Doc Williams (USA)
Charles Williams (USA)
Duran Williams (Jamaica/USA)
Thomas Williams (USA)
Tiger Roy Williams (USA)
J. B. Williamson (USA)
Tony Willis (USA)
Harry Wills (USA)
Adolf Witt (Germany)
Bruce Woodcock (England)
Clinton Woods (England)
Chubby Wright (USA)
Ronald Wright (USA)

Y
Tommy Yarosz (USA)
Randall Yonker (USA)
Paddy Young (USA)

Z
Victor Zalazar (Argentina)
Darren Zenner (Canada/USA)
Fulgencio Zuniga (Colombia)

Cruiserweight Division

A name that was once used to describe light heavyweights, and emanating from the description of battleships of a lighter build rather than of maximum size, the cruiserweight class came into being in 1979 when the World Boxing Council (WBC) introduced it at 190lbs to give more opportunities to men too light to take on full-blown heavies. It is also known as the junior heavyweight division.

In order to find a champion the WBC set up eliminators involving Marvin Camel (who had recently won the vacant North American Boxing Federation (NABF) cruiserweight title when outpointing Bill Sharkey over 12 rounds at the Adams Fieldhouse, Missoula, Montana, USA on 5 June 1979) against David Cabrera, and Mate Parlov versus Tony Mundine. Having knocked Cabrera out in the third round at the Villa Real Convention Centre, McAllen, Texas, USA on 30 August 1979, Camel went on to fight Parlov, who had outscored Mundine over 12 rounds at the Sports Palace, Gorizia, Italy on 26 September 1979.

Weight Band/Amendments

175lbs to 190lbs (8 December 1979 to 25 November 1981)
175lbs to 195lbs (At their end of November Convention in 1981 the WBC increased the poundage to 195lbs, while the WBA remained at 190lbs)
175lbs to 190lbs (In November 1988 the WBC dropped their weight-class limit from 195lbs to 190lbs, thus falling into line with the IBF and WBA)
175lbs to 200lbs (Both the WBA and WBC increased the weight limit from 190lbs in early October 2003 to allow small heavyweights an even chance when competing for a title, and were soon followed by the IBF and WBO)

Cruiserweight World Championship Fights:

8 December 1979. Marvin Camel drew 15 Mate Parlov.
Venue: Gripe Sports Centre, Split, Yugoslavia. **Recognition**: WBC. **Referee:** Raymond Baldeyrou.
Scorecards: 147-142, 143-143, 144-144.
Fight Summary: In what was the inaugural 190lbs title fight, and a battle between southpaws, Parlov (189¾) started well with jabs and crosses finding Camel (184¼) early on before the latter came on strong in the middle rounds. From the ninth through to the 12th Camel was on top as Parlov suffered a cut and swollen left eye, but from the 13th session onwards the Yugoslav just about shaded it despite being forced to take some heavy head shots. With the result announced as being a draw the pair would have to go head-to-head yet again.

31 March 1980. Marvin Camel w pts 15 Mate Parlov.
Venue: Caesar's Palace, Las Vegas, Nevada, USA. **Recognition:** WBC. **Referee:** Ferd Hernandez.
Scorecards: 144-141, 148-141, 149-141.
Fight Summary: Yet again the two southpaws fought for the right to become the division's first champion, but this time around it was Camel (185¾), a member of the Flathead Indian tribe, who took the fight by the scruff of the neck to win the unanimous decision. Parlov (189) made the better start, hammering in rights and lefts, and from the fourth round onwards both men were carrying bad cuts – Camel over the right eye and Parlov under his right eye. Starting to find the range in the fifth, by the ninth Camel was in full flow, being credited with taking five of the last six sessions when outpunching Parlov and almost having him over in the 14th.

25 November 1980. Carlos De Leon w pts 15 Marvin Camel.
Venue: The Superdome, New Orleans, Louisiana, USA. **Recognition:** WBC. **Referee:** Carlos Padilla.
Scorecards: 145-142, 145-141, 145-145.
Fight Summary: Although the challenger made the better start, by the fourth round Camel (182) was scoring well with the southpaw jab and solid left crosses. Carrying cuts around the eyes from early on and being chased down by the stocky De Leon (182½) made life difficult for Camel. To De Leon's credit he never stopped throwing punches even if many of them were wayward. By the ninth it had become a war of attrition, but after De Leon had battered

Camel all over in the 11th he made sure of victory in the eyes of two of the judges when putting in a grandstand finish.

Inactive for over a year, when a defence for De Leon against Tony Mundine in August 1981 failed to materialise the WBC set up an eliminator between Camel and Bash Ali, which was won on points over 12 rounds by the former champion at the Cow Palace, San Francisco, California on 2 October 1981. Meanwhile, De Leon began preparations for the fight by winning a non-title warm-up contest in mid-December 1981.

With the WBA also finally recognising the need for a weight class between the light heavyweight and heavyweight divisions they announced that Ossie Ocasio and Robbie Williams would meet to decide their first ever championship fight at the weight.

13 February 1982. Ossie Ocasio w pts 15 Robbie Williams.
Venue: Rand Stadium, Johannesburg, South Africa. **Recognition:** WBA. **Referee:** Yusaku Yoshida.
Scorecards: 146-144, 147-143, 144-148.
Fight Summary: Ocasio (188¾) made the better start, scoring well from both hands, especially with body blows, but following a couple that strayed below the belt he had a point deducted in the fourth round. Around that time Williams (186¾) came into the fight more, favouring jabs and crosses. At that point things were nicely balanced before Ocasio came on strongly from the eighth through to the 12th. It was in the 12th that Williams had Ocasio going after a big left hook landed, and for the next three sessions the South African fighter went after the latter, banging in blows from all angles, and finishing the stronger of the two. Although the referee thought that Williams had done enough the two judges felt otherwise.

24 February 1982. Carlos De Leon w rsc 7 (15) Marvin Camel.
Venue: Playboy Hotel & Casino, Atlantic City, New Jersey, USA. **Recognition:** WBC. **Referee:** Juan Jose Guerra.
Fight Summary: Getting solid blows off from the start De Leon (182¾) was soon in charge, and in the third round Camel (183½) was hurt by a cracking left hook, finishing the session with a bad cut over the right eye. Although Camel kept going with the southpaw jab he was unable to stop the champion's right hand regularly smashing into his features, causing even more blood to flow. At the end of the seventh, with Camel's face badly bloodied and swollen, it was no surprise when the doctor advised the referee to stop the fight.

27 June 1982. S.T. Gordon w rsc 2 (15) Carlos De Leon.
Venue: Front Row Theatre, Cleveland, Ohio, USA. **Recognition:** WBC. **Referee:** Carlos Padilla.
Fight Summary: Following a fairly even opening round, when the champion was caught by a big right to the jaw after taking the fight to Gordon (189), a barrage of blows put him on the floor. Forced to take the mandatory 'eight' count it was soon clear that De Leon (187) was still dazed, and after being backed into a corner and taking a steady shellacking from both hands the referee stopped the contest with nine seconds of the session remaining. In the aftermath, the winner claimed he was unaware until shortly before the fight that the WBC had increased the weight-class limit from 190 to 195lbs. He went on to say that had he known he would have obviously come in heavier.

Later in the year, the WBA announced that all world title bouts held under their auspices would be contested over 12 rounds from 1 January 1983.

15 December 1982. Ossie Ocasio w pts 15 Young Joe Louis (Eddie Taylor).
Venue: Aragon Ballroom, Chicago, Illinois, USA. **Recognition:** WBA. **Referee:** Isidro Rodriguez.
Scorecards: 147-143, 146-142, 147-144.
Fight Summary: Booked to take place in Gary, Indiana, the fight was moved to Chicago on the day of the promotion taking place due to a dispute over local judges covering the fight other than the WBA's own officials. The better boxer of the pair, Ocasio (188½) got away well with sharp scoring punches from both hands while outworking the challenger for considerable periods. Ocasio was just too quick for Taylor (187½), who despite landing well with body shots and rights to the head was unable to build on his advantage for any length of time.

Taylor did have some success in the tenth and 11th, but by then he had picked up a swelling over the left eye which allowed Ocasio to get back in control.

16 February 1983. S.T. Gordon w rsc 8 (12) Jesse Burnett.
Venue: Byrne Meadowlands Arena, East Rutherford, New Jersey, USA. **Recognition:** WBC. **Referee:** Vincent Rainone.
Fight Summary: Defending his title for the first time Gordon (194) started aggressively when taking the opening three rounds, stunning Burnett (183) in the third with a left hook before the latter came back strongly in the fourth. Burnett began well in the fifth, but was being broken down by the end of the session as the champion hit back hard. Stepping the pace up in the seventh Gordon began to up the ante before unleashing his full armoury in the eighth, and after battering Burnett with heavy blows from both hands a right to the head dropped the latter at the end of the session. After getting up and staggering to his corner, the befuddled Burnett was stopped from continuing by the referee seven seconds into the interval.

20 May 1983. Ossie Ocasio w pts 15 Randy Stephens.
Venue: Dunes Hotel, Las Vegas, Nevada, USA. **Recognition:** WBA. **Referee:** Isidro Rodriguez.
Scorecards: 148-144, 147-143, 146-142.
Fight Summary: Making good use of the ring the champion was fast out of the blocks to run up a big points margin before relaxing and allowing Stephens (188¾) some respite. It was an uphill battle for Stephens, who had picked up a cut and swollen eye in an early round, and although manfully sticking to the task he lacked the know-how to trouble Ocasio (188¾) unduly. Despite Stephens coming back in the final third, especially when landing solid left hooks, any chance he had of winning had drifted away from him by then. Possibly due to injury, Ocasio remained out of action for just under a year before being called upon to make a defence.

17 July 1983. Carlos De Leon w pts 12 S.T. Gordon.
Venue: Dunes Hotel, Las Vegas, Nevada, USA. **Recognition:** WBC. **Referee:** Carlos Padilla.
Scorecards: 119-109, 119-109, 118-112.
Fight Summary: In regaining his title from the man who took it from him, De Leon (191¼) came back much stronger this time round to comprehensively outbox the champion after dropping him with a right over the top in the opening session. Picking up points with a stinging left jab and making sure that the slower moving Gordon (194¾) was unable to corner him, De Leon was way out in front entering the final third. Cruising through to the last round De Leon capped a top-class display when forcing Gordon to take another mandatory 'eight' count after landing some heavy head shots. The fight ended with De Leon all over Gordon, by now carrying a badly swollen left eye, but he was unable to find the finisher.

21 September 1983. Carlos De Leon w rsc 4 (12) Yaqui Lopez.
Venue: Municipal Stadium, San Jose, California, USA. **Recognition:** WBC. **Referee:** Henry Elesperu.
Fight Summary: Getting away fast, De Leon (188¾) had his 42-year-old challenger on the deck inside the opening 40 seconds, but then allowed him to recover. After outboxing Lopez (188¾) in the second De Leon was forced to defend in the third as the Mexican moved his attack to the body, a pattern that continued into the fourth. With Lopez back in the fight it all changed when a long left from De Leon opened up a bad cut over his right eye and led to the referee calling it off at 2.51 of the fourth.

Back in April, the recently formed United States Boxing Association/International (USBA/I) had stated that they would recognise S.T. Gordon as champion, but following his defeat at the hands of De Leon the organisation agreed to recognise De Leon. However, in late October, the USBA/I, reconstituted as the International Boxing Federation (IBF), announced that they would now be recognising Marvin Camel (who held the United States Boxing Association title) as their champion as it had not been possible to induce De Leon to fight under their banner. They then nominated Roddy MacDonald as Camel's first challenger.

13 December 1983. Marvin Camel w rsc 5 (15) Roddy MacDonald.
Venue: Metro Centre, Halifax, Nova Scotia, Canada. **Recognition:** IBF. **Referee:** Bob Beaton.

Fight Summary: Contesting the inaugural IBF title, the former WBC champion, Camel (186), mainly controlled the fight with southpaw jabs and counters as the slower MacDonald (177) came looking for him. Dropped in the second and third rounds by vicious body shots, MacDonald appeared to be on the way out before dropping Camel in the fifth with a right to the jaw. On getting up Camel immediately unleashed another cracking body shot that had MacDonald down again, claiming it to be a low blow. Although the referee was unsighted, after consulting with the judges he stopped the fight in Camel's favour on the 2.49 mark due to MacDonald being down for at least 15 seconds.

9 March 1984. Carlos De Leon w pts 12 Anthony Davis.
Venue: Convention Centre, Las Vegas, Nevada, USA. **Recognition:** WBC. **Referee:** Carlos Padilla.
Scorecards: 118-113, 118-112, 115-112.
Fight Summary: Proving far too fast for his slow-moving challenger, De Leon (190) started well when hurting his man with a big right to the jaw in the opening session. Well ahead after six rounds De Leon was pegged back in the seventh and eighth before dropping Davis (194¼) with a right to the jaw in the ninth. Although De Leon tried hard to finish the fight there and then, and banged away at Davis's now swollen left eye in the tenth, he virtually stopped working in the final two rounds due to a damaged right hand.

5 May 1984. Ossie Ocasio w rsc 15 (15) John Odhiambo.
Venue: Mets Pavilion, Guaynabo, Puerto Rico. **Recognition:** WBA. **Referee:** Isidro Rodriguez.
Fight Summary: It was clear from the start that the challenger was no pushover for Ocasio (189) and, using his longer reach well, by the end of the seventh round he was in front. Unfortunately, in that session Odhiambo (187½) was cut over the left eye following a clash of heads, which encouraged Ocasio to pick up the pace. Still very much in the contest at that point, it was only when Odhiambo was badly hurt by a right to the jaw in the 13th that Ocasio took over. Fighting in extreme heat Odhiambo finally wilted, and although making it into the final session he was rescued by the referee with just 36 seconds of the fight remaining when unable to defend himself properly following a two-fisted attack from Ocasio.

2 June 1984. Carlos De Leon w pts 12 Bash Ali.
Venue: Coliseum Arena, Oakland, California, USA. **Recognition:** WBC. **Referee:** Henry Elesperu.
Scorecards: 118-112, 118-112, 117-111.
Fight Summary: Taking control from the first bell the champion had far too much ability for the outclassed Ali (190), romping to an easy win without being pressed. De Leon (192½) had been expected to win early, but for whatever reason he rarely threw more than one punch at a time. Ali, who had been out of the ring for over a year after suffering a broken jaw, hardly ever threatened De Leon, being more often than not on the receiving end of the latter's left jab.

6 October 1984. Lee Roy Murphy w rsc 14 (15) Marvin Camel.
Venue: Yellowstone MetraPark, Billings, Montana, USA. **Recognition:** IBF. **Referee:** Dan Janjic.
Fight Summary: Defending the IBF Championship Belt for the first time, Camel (190) got his nose in front of Murphy (190) early on when opening the latter up with solid southpaw jabs. Even when he was cut over the right eye in the fifth and dropped by a right to the head in the eighth he remained in control. Murphy was always dangerous, but with Camel ether riding or avoiding his big shots he went further behind before getting lucky in the 14th. After being caught in that session by a heavy right Camel received another cut, this time over his left eye, and although leading the fight handily the doctor advised the referee to stop the fight during the interval.

1 December 1984. Piet Crous w pts 15 Ossie Ocasio.
Venue: Super Bowl, Sun City, South Africa. **Recognition:** WBA. **Referee:** Carlos Berrocal.
Scorecards: 147-143, 147-140, 144-143.
Fight Summary: Forced to box on the back foot from the off the champion resorted to weak left jabs and an occasional right counter in an effort to hold the powerful Crous (180) at bay. Despite being badly cut over the left eye in the eighth Crous continued to be one step ahead of Ocasio (187¾), who held on more and more as the fight progressed. The last three rounds saw Crous make sure of the win, Ocasio being pushed around the ring without sending much back in reply.

20 December 1984. Lee Roy Murphy w rsc 12 (15) Young Joe Louis (Eddie Taylor).
Venue: Bismarck Hotel, Chicago, Illinois, USA. **Recognition:** IBF. **Referee:** Stan Berg.
Fight Summary: In what was a tough first defence for Murphy (190) he was forced to chase Taylor (190) around the ring for almost half the contest before being able to catch up with him, having been held up by solid counters. Come the tenth round Taylor was tiring as Murphy chased him down, and he was forced to go toe-to-toe before being cut over the left eye and hurt on several occasions. By that stage of the contest Taylor's excellent left jab had deserted him. Although landing with a few heavy rights Taylor was overwhelmed in the 12th when a two-handed attack from Murphy had him all over the place prior to the referee stopping the fight on the 1.37 mark.

30 March 1985. Piet Crous w rsc 3 (15) Randy Stephens.
Venue: Super Bowl, Sun City, South Africa. **Recognition:** WBA. **Referee:** Ismael Fernandez.
Fight Summary: Following a settling-down period the champion picked up the pace in the second round before finally catching up with Stephens (188¼) in the third when landing heavy blows to the head. Ducking under the punches and under real pressure Stephens suddenly found a big right to the head that dropped Crous (185¾), stunning the crowd into silence. Even though the referee failed to take up the count, which allowed Crous valuable breathing space, from there onwards it became a slogging match. Both men were hurt, but after Stephens was caught heavily and appeared dazed the referee quickly terminated the contest with 38 seconds of the session remaining.

6 June 1985. Alfonzo Ratliff w pts 12 Carlos De Leon.
Venue: Riviera Hotel, Las Vegas, Nevada, USA. **Recognition:** WBC. **Referee:** Carlos Padilla.
Scorecards: 116-113, 117-114, 114-117.
Fight Summary: After making a solid start the champion found himself in a battle of attrition as Ratliff (192½) came on strongly in the third round, throwing punches from both hands, and by the eighth both men were showing distinct signs of wear. With Ratliff cut over both eyes and De Leon (187¾) over the left it seemed set for an early night, but there was no let-up in the action. Thereafter, both men punched away. In the 11th De Leon caught Ratliff heavily, only for the latter to stun the champion with a big right to the head immediately prior to the announcement that he had won the title by a split decision.

27 July 1985. Dwight Muhammad Qawi w co 11 (15) Piet Crous.
Venue: Super Bowl, Sun City, South Africa. **Recognition:** WBA. **Referee:** Enzo Montero.
Fight Summary: With not too much in it after eight rounds the fight came to life when Qawi (189¼) hammered the champion all over the ring in the ninth. Subsequently, it was all downhill for Crous (182), who was battered from pillar to post before being dropped by a barrage of blows in the 11th and barely beat the count. There was to be no let-up, and as soon as Crous was allowed back into action he was sent crashing by a left-right combination and counted out at 1.47 of the session.

21 September 1985. Bernard Benton w pts 12 Alfonzo Ratliff.
Venue: Riviera Hotel, Las Vegas, Nevada, USA. **Recognition:** WBC. **Referee:** Joey Curtis.
Scorecards: 117-112, 115-113, 115-113.
Fight Summary: Never giving the champion a moment's respite, Benton (190) kept up the pressure for round after round to walk off with the title. Although both men were cut over their left eyes early on it failed to stop Benton's forward march, and even when Ratliff (194) caught him with solid counters it made no difference. Despite Ratliff having a good reach advantage he was unable to keep Benton off with the jab, spending much of the fight trying to get himself going. At the final bell it was Benton who found favour with the judges, regardless of the fact that many of his blows failed to hit the target.

19 October 1985. Lee Roy Murphy w co 12 (15) Chisanda Mutti.
Venue: Louis II Stadium, Monte Carlo, Monaco. **Recognition:** IBF. **Referee:** Larry Hazzard.
Fight Summary: Mixing his punches up well the stylish Mutti (188) looked to be well ahead by the tenth, having dropped the champion heavily in the ninth and generally being on top. Although hurt on several occasions Murphy (190) had somehow managed to keep going, and in the tenth he found a second wind when it looked as though Mutti was tiring rapidly. The 11th saw a complete reversal of form as Mutti, under the cosh for the first time, was

lucky to last out the round after being dropped by a cracking left hook. Still behind on points Murphy came out slugging in the 12th as he looked to find a winning blow, but Mutti had the same idea and both men went toe-to-toe. Dramatically, the fight ended when both men landed heavy rights to the head and both went to the floor at the same time, with Murphy just making it to his feet as Mutti was counted out on the 1.53 mark.

22 March 1986. Carlos De Leon w pts 12 Bernard Benton.
Venue: Lawlor Events Centre, Reno, Nevada, USA. **Recognition:** WBC. **Referee:** Mills Lane.
Scorecards: 117-114, 115-113, 114-114.
Fight Summary: After what was a difficult fight to judge, with the champion pressing throughout as De Leon (185) scored with jabs and right-hand counters, it was the latter's cleaner work that ultimately won the day. There was never much between them, but it was De Leon's double left jab that continually bemused Benton (185) and kept the former titleholder marginally ahead. Eventually, De Leon began to open up in the tenth, and in the 11th he twice stunned Benton with combinations before going back to his boxing in the 12th.

22 March 1986. Dwight Muhammad Qawi w rsc 6 (15) Leon Spinks.
Venue: Riviera Hotel, Las Vegas, Nevada, USA. **Recognition:** WBA. **Referee:** Joey Curtis.
Fight Summary: Having dropped down a division the former world heavyweight champion, Spinks (190), was given a real battering at the hands of Qawi (189) before being rescued by the referee at 2.56 of the sixth round. Right from the opening bell the champion went for Spinks' body, knowing that the latter had found it difficult to make the weight, and before too long the pattern of the fight was set. While going from body to head was reaping dividends for Qawi, although Spinks tried to fight back he was constantly being driven into corners and pounded prior to being pulled out.

19 April 1986. Lee Roy Murphy w co 9 (15) Dorcy Gaymon.
Venue: The Casino, San Remo, Italy. **Recognition:** IBF. **Referee:** Joe Santarpia.
Fight Summary: Defending his title on foreign ground, Murphy (189), whose left eye was swollen early on, bided his time when allowing Gaymon (188½) to make the running right through to the eighth. The third had been a big round for Gaymon, but he had been unable to build on it. With Murphy beginning to pick it up, coming into the ninth both men were level on the scorecards. It was then that Murphy got down to business, and at 2.31 of the session Gaymon was counted out after being flattened by a left-right to the head.

12 July 1986. Evander Holyfield w pts 15 Dwight Muhammad Qawi.
Venue: Omni Coliseum, Atlanta, Georgia, USA. **Recognition:** WBA. **Referee:** Vincent Rainone.
Scorecards: 144-140, 147-138, 141-143.
Fight Summary: In only his 12th pro fight Holyfield (186) won the title on a split decision after coming on strong from the tenth round onwards. How one of the cards should be so wide was ridiculous, with the contest being in question most of the way, as first one man scored with heavy shots and then the other. With both men taking heavy blows without blinking it was Holyfield's quality and speed that surprised Qawi (189¾). Knowing that he had to put on a show in the final session Qawi came out firing, but after being deducted a point for going low and with Holyfield happy to keep out of trouble his reign was over.

10 August 1986. Carlos De Leon w rsc 8 (12) Michael Greer.
Venue: Parking Lot, Sant Alfphio, Giardini Naxos, Sicily, Italy. **Recognition:** WBC. **Referee:** Rudy Ortega.
Fight Summary: Fighting well for the opening seven rounds the challenger more than held his own with De Leon (188¼), hurting him with left hooks and scoring with the jab. He was also ahead on all three scorecards. It was only in the eighth that De Leon came to life, Greer (186¼) being pushed back to the ropes after he had been hurt by solid uppercuts to the jaw. At that stage of the contest, when it was clear that Greer was unable to fight back, the referee came to his aid at 1.45 of the session.

25 October 1986. Ricky Parkey w rsc 10 (15) Lee Roy Murphy.
Venue: Sports Palace, Marsala, Italy. **Recognition:** IBF. **Referee:** Frank Cappuccino.
Fight Summary: Coming to the ring as a big outsider the challenger soon showed his mettle when taking the fight to Murphy (190) from the start, beating him to the punch time and again. The signs that Murphy was going to have

a tough night were there for all to see, especially when Parkey (190) continually caught him with rights over the top and left hooks to the body, and in the seventh a long right to the head had the champion over. Although it looked as though Murphy was getting back into the fight following that shock, doing well in the eighth and ninth rounds, he was put down again in the tenth. Despite Murphy fighting on, with five seconds of the session remaining he was rescued by the referee after being blasted on to the ring apron.

14 February 1987. Evander Holyfield w rsc 7 (15) Henry Tillman.
Venue: Bally's Hotel & Casino, Reno, Nevada, USA. **Recognition:** WBA. **Referee:** Carlos Padilla.
Fight Summary: Making his first defence, against his former Olympic Games team-mate, Holyfield (188½) was quickly down to business, having his rival over with a right to the face in the second round. Although Tillman (189) got to his feet and tried to fight back it was noticeable that Holyfield had the power. Attacking Tillman to the body was paying dividends, the latter running out of ideas by the sixth as Holyfield kept coming on. In the seventh Tillman finally crumbled, and after being dropped three times by heavy lefts and rights the fight was terminated at 1.43 of the session under the 'three knockdowns in a round' ruling.

21 February 1987. Carlos De Leon w rsc 4 (12) Angelo Rottoli.
Venue: Sports Palace, Bergamo, Italy. **Recognition:** WBC. **Referee:** Franz Marti.
Fight Summary: Being cut over the right eye so early ruined any hopes of victory the challenger may have had, and with De Leon (188¼) concentrating on the injury there was little chance of a distance fight. At the end of the third the doctor allowed Rottoli (189½) one more round, but with De Leon totally in control and the wound pouring blood the referee stopped the contest after the fourth session ended.

28 March 1987. Ricky Parkey w rsc 12 (15) Chisanda Mutti.
Venue: Sports Palace, Camaiore, Italy. **Recognition:** IBF. **Referee:** Vincent Rainone.
Fight Summary: Proving to be a tough opponent the challenger made Parkey (189½) fight every inch of the way, scoring with left hooks to the body and also showing up well with two-fisted attacks. Although Parkey took many of the blows on his arms and gloves he was occasionally forced back as Mutti (187¼) took the fight to him. Parkey, who had looked dangerous throughout with wide left hooks and overarm rights regularly hitting the target, finally had Mutti over in the 12th with a big left. Back in action after the 'eight' count, with Mutti quickly in trouble as Parkey opened up he was rescued by the referee on the 54-second mark when not fighting back.

15 May 1987. Evander Holyfield w rsc 3 (15) Ricky Parkey.
Venue: Caesar's Palace, Las Vegas, Nevada, USA. **Recognition:** IBF/WBA. **Referee:** Davey Pearl.
Fight Summary: Battling for two titles, despite the WBA refusing to sanction the bout due to their dispute with the State of Nevada, Holyfield (188) quickly proved to be a cut above the IBF's Parkey (187½). By the second round it was noticeable that Holyfield had the hand-speed to bother Parkey, and although the latter hit back the body shots were already wearing him down. After being dropped twice in the third from brutal lefts and rights Parkey tried to come back, but when a two-handed attack sent him into the ropes the referee halted the contest with 16 seconds of the session remaining.

15 August 1987. Evander Holyfield w rsc 11 (15) Ossie Ocasio.
Venue: Outdoor Arena, St Tropez, France. **Recognition:** IBF/WBA. **Referee:** John Coyle.
Fight Summary: Fighting on the back foot Ocasio (190) made life difficult for the double champion, especially as his main tactic was clinching immediately after throwing a burst of punches. Holyfield (189), who always looked like winning and was in charge throughout, remained patient for round after round while waiting for Ocasio to wear himself out before stepping up the pace in the tenth. It could be seen that Ocasio had little left, and in the 11th he was stunned and then floored after being hammered by lefts and rights to the head. Although the former champion got up and tried to use the ring in order to survive, Holyfield, quickly in pursuit, had him on the ropes when the referee stopped the fight at 1.24 of the session.

During their convention, held in October, the WBA announced that all world title bouts held under their banner in the future would be contested over 12 rounds.

5 December 1987. Evander Holyfield w co 4 (15) Dwight Muhammad Qawi.
Venue: Convention Centre, Atlantic City, New Jersey, USA. **Recognition:** IBF/WBA. **Referee:** Randy Neumann.
Fight Summary: A return match, this one was a bridge too far for Qawi (190), as the champion both outjabbed and outpunched him right from the start. Surprisingly, Qawi showed some of his old form in the third, landing solidly from both hands, but in the fourth Holyfield (187) made his move, and following a two-handed assault he had Qawi over with a left hook. Although Qawi made it to his feet he was soon under attack again before being counted out in a sitting position at 2.30 of the session after being hit by a heavy right to the head. Prior to the fight the WBA stated that their version of the title was technically not at stake as they recognised 12 rounds as the championship distance, not 15. They went on to say that if Qawi won they would vacate their portion of the title, but would support Holyfield if he was successful.

22 January 1988. Carlos De Leon w pts 12 Jose Maria Flores Burlon.
Venue: Convention Centre, Atlantic City, New Jersey, USA. **Recognition:** WBC. **Referee:** Frank Cappuccino.
Scorecards: 119-110, 118-111, 118-110.
Fight Summary: Having been booked to meet Pinklon Thomas in an overweight match, when the latter pulled out, De Leon (188) found himself taking on Burlon in a title defence instead. Clearly unprepared, De Leon let Burlon (189), a most inept challenger, stay the full course when it was clear to most of those in attendance that he could have ended the contest as and when he liked. Apart from a brief spell in the sixth when hitting back with both hands after being stunned, and in the 11th when winging in wide hooks, Burlon did very little to suggest that he wanted to be a champion.

9 April 1988. Evander Holyfield w rsc 8 (12) Carlos De Leon.
Venue: Caesar's Palace, Las Vegas, Nevada, USA. **Recognition:** World. **Referee:** Mills Lane.
Fight Summary: Prior to the fight the WBC stipulated 195lbs as being the division's limit, while the IBF and WBA agreed on 190lbs. However, with both men inside 190lbs, and all three titles at stake, from then on the poundage would be standardised. The fight itself saw the WBC's De Leon (188) spend much of the fight with his back to the ropes trying to counter the hard-hitting Holyfield (190), who complained afterwards that he was being butted when at close quarters. Several times De Leon was badly hurt, but he remained on his feet and occasionally troubled Holyfield with sneak punches until coming undone. Having been cut over the left eye in the sixth De Leon was still there in the eighth, but after Holyfield cut loose with both hands and he was left unable to defend himself the referee stopped the fight on the 1.08 mark.

Although the IBF recognised 15 rounds to be the world championship distance they still supported Holyfield as the champion. It came as no surprise when they announced at their annual summer convention that all world title bouts held under their auspices from 1 September would be contested over 12 rounds, thus bringing them into line with the other bodies. There was such a paucity of talent around that when Holyfield relinquished his titles in November in order to campaign as a heavyweight the three major organisations were hard pressed to find a championship bout of any consequence, let alone be in a position to organise elimination tournaments. Eventually, matches were made between Taoufik Belbouli and Michael Greer (WBA), Carlos De Leon and Sammy Reeson (WBC), Glenn McCrory and Patrick Lumumba (IBF) to decide the respective vacancies.

The situation was further complicated when the World Boxing Organisation (WBO) was formed in November after 27 of the 71 delegates had walked out of the WBA convention a month earlier in disgust at the way things were being run in that organisation. However, after their number one contender, Anaclet Wamba, pulled out the WBO matched Boone Pultz against Magne Havnaa to contest their version of the vacant title.

25 March 1989. Taoufik Belbouli w rsc 8 Michael Greer.
Venue: Sheraton Hotel, Casablanca, Morocco. **Recognition:** WBA. **Referee:** Nicasio Drake.
Fight Summary: Fighting for one of the titles relinquished by Evander Holyfield, Belbouli (189½) was just too strong for Greer (189½), who was dropped heavily by a big right to the head in the fourth and just about survived the round. From then on Belbouli was very much in control, and even though Greer gave it an almighty effort in the seventh the latter was being overwhelmed in the eighth when the referee came to his rescue.

After Belbouli relinquished the WBA version of the title in August following a long-term knee injury, Robert Daniels and Dwight Muhammad Qawi were matched to find a successor.

17 May 1989. Carlos De Leon w rsc 9 Sammy Reeson.
Venue: London Arena, Millwall, London, England. **Recognition:** WBC. **Referee:** Arthur Mercante.
Fight Summary: In winning the title for a record fourth time De Leon (189¾) proved to be too good for the former British and European champion, Reeson (189½), who had been waiting for this opportunity for some while and had been out of the ring for over a year. The fight came about after Evander Holyfield stepped up to the heavyweight ranks and vacated the title. Cut around the right eye in the first round Reeson already had his back to the wall, and when a long vertical gash appeared over his right eye in the third his days were numbered. Although the wounds were being controlled by good corner work, Reeson was unable to bother De Leon too much apart from in the eighth when he got his southpaw jab working. Then, in the ninth, after Reeson had been dropped twice the fight was halted at 2.04 of the session.

3 June 1989. Glenn McCrory w pts 12 Patrick Lumumba.
Venue: Louisa Centre, Stanley, England. **Recognition:** IBF. **Referee:** Randy Neumann.
Scorecards: 118-110, 116-111, 118-111.
Fight Summary: Billed for the title vacated by Evander Holyfield, it was McCrory (190) all the way as Lumumba (187¾), who got his chance when beating Jeff Lampkin some 13 months earlier, offered little. Boxing more like a sparring partner Lumumba occasionally stung McCrory with sharp blows, but it was not enough to influence the scoring. Even in the last third Lumumba failed to step up the pace which could have made it closer. As it was, McCrory boxed well within himself, the left jab and solid rights winning the fight for him, and at the final bell Lumumba was completely sold-out despite his lack of effort.

21 October 1989. Glenn McCrory w co 11 Siza Makathini.
Venue: Eston Leisure Centre, Middlesbrough, England. **Recognition:** IBF. **Referee:** Rudy Battle.
Fight Summary: Making his first defence McCrory (190) found himself under the cosh during the opening five rounds as the much smaller Makathini (187) got inside, banging in hooks to head and body and being generally on top. McCrory, who'd had difficulty making the weight, had been sluggish, but in the sixth all that changed as he went for Makathini as if his life depended on it when battering the South African from pillar to post. Although the action slowed somewhat after that, McCrory got more and more on top as Makathini tired and drew public warnings for holding, and in the 11th the latter was sent crashing in his own corner after taking lefts and rights without response. Making no attempt to get up, the challenger was counted out at 1.07 of the session.

28 November 1989. Robert Daniels w pts 12 Dwight Muhammad Qawi.
Venue: Baltard Pavilion, Nogent sur Marne, France. **Recognition:** WBA. **Referee:** Bernie Soto.
Scorecards: 115-113, 116-113, 114-115.
Fight Summary: Contesting the title left vacant by Taoufik Belbouli, both Daniels (188½) and Qawi (188½) came to fight, and at times it turned into a good old-fashioned slugging session. While Daniels was the better boxer, scoring well with the jab, all too often he was prepared to get drawn in by the slower man, who relished the close-quarter work, and he often took punches he should have avoided. Coming out for the final session it was clear that Daniels thought he was ahead, doing little work and dancing out of danger, but it was much closer than he imagined when one of the judges voted for Qawi in what was a difficult fight to score.

3 December 1989. Boone Pultz w pts 12 Magne Havnaa.
Venue: Scandinavia Hotel, Copenhagen, Denmark. **Recognition:** WBO. **Referee:** Stan Christodoulou.
Scorecards: 116-113, 115-114, 115-118.
Fight Summary: Fighting to decide the WBO's first champion at the weight it was the switch-hitting Pultz (182) who impressed two of the judges, despite his work-rate slumping in the final third. Even a cut over his right eye suffered in the seventh failed to slow Havnaa (189) down, and having forced the fight for much of the time he appeared to have done enough to win, his left jab and body attacks being prominent. At the bell Havnaa was odds on favourite, but following the incredulity and commotion afterwards he was given an early opportunity of a return.

Cruiserweight Division

27 January 1990. Carlos De Leon drew 12 Johnny Nelson.
Venue: City Hall, Sheffield, England. **Recognition:** WBC. **Referee:** Bob Logist.
Scorecards: 116-115, 111-117, 115-115.
Fight Summary: Unable to lift his game against a very ordinary champion Nelson (190) stayed out of range for much of the time, trying to nick points with a flicking jab. With it never being much of a fight, in the 11th the referee called for more action but to no avail. Throughout, De Leon (188¾) barely exerted himself, realising that Nelson had to work harder if he wanted to take his title, and there was so little action that there was booing from the fourth round onwards. A difficult fight to score, it would have been a travesty had Nelson won.

22 March 1990. Jeff Lampkin w co 3 Glenn McCrory.
Venue: Leisure Centre, Gateshead, England. **Recognition:** IBF. **Referee:** Randy Neumann.
Fight Summary: Continuing to have difficulty making the weight McCrory (189½) soon found that his challenger meant business, even though the opening two rounds were relatively close. Coming into the third, when it was clear that Lampkin (188¼) had the power he began closing down the space to get in jabs and hooks to head and body as McCrory's jabs lost their way. It was the body that Lampkin was concentrating on, and getting closer and closer to McCrory he suddenly found a tremendous left hook to the ribs that sent the latter down on one knee to be counted out with 40 seconds of the session remaining. Unable to get to his feet, McCrory was taken to hospital where it was discovered that he had a badly swollen liver but no broken bones.

17 May 1990. Magne Havnaa w rsc 5 Boone Pultz.
Venue: Nordjysk Exhibition Centre, Jutland, Denmark. **Recognition:** WBO. **Referee:** Denny Nelson.
Fight Summary: In a return fight that came about after Havnaa (190) appeared to have been robbed in their previous bout, the champion made an aggressive start before coming under fire in the third. By now, having taken over, Havnaa totally dominated in the fourth as Pultz (190) was forced to take punches to head and body without being able to get going. One-way traffic in the fifth, eventually Pultz was dropped by rights and lefts to the head, and although getting up he was momentarily dropped again before being rescued by the referee at 2.54 of the session.

19 July 1990. Robert Daniels w pts 12 Craig Bodzianowski.
Venue: The Kingdome, Seattle, Washington, USA. **Recognition:** WBA. **Referee:** Lou Moret.
Scorecards: 119-110, 118-109, 118-109.
Fight Summary: Bodzianowski (190), who had his right foot amputated after a motorcycle accident six years earlier, became the first man ever to contest a world title with such a disability, and although being soundly outpointed gave hope to many would-be sportsmen. Right from the start it was noticeable that Bodzianowski lacked the mobility to trouble the champion, his job being made even more difficult when sustaining damage to his ribs in the second round. Even when Daniels (188) got home with solid shots to the head, unable to dent Bodzianowski he was forced to travel the full distance to retain his title.

27 July 1990. Massimiliano Duran w disq 11 Carlos De Leon.
Venue: Outdoor Arena, Capo D'Orlando, Italy. **Recognition:** WBC. **Referee:** Bob Logist.
Fight Summary: With just 15 bouts to his credit, two of them being losses, the Italian champion started confidently when scoring well with the left jab and crossing the right before De Leon (189) began to come more and more into it. At the start of the 11th, with Duran (183) marginally ahead on two of the scorecards and dead level on the other, the desperate De Leon finally picked up the pace to have Duran over with a push rather than a punch. Although De Leon was cautioned by the referee for clipping Duran when he was down before taking up the count, when the latter got to his feet he drove the champion into a corner where he punched away non-stop until the bell rang to end the round. It was then that the trouble started. After the referee had parted the two men De Leon went after Duran, knocking him to the floor with a right hander, and following several minutes of uproar it was announced that the referee had disqualified the champion.

29 July 1990. Jeff Lampkin w co 8 Siza Makathini.
Venue: Hilton Hotel, St Petersburg, Florida, USA. **Recognition:** IBF. **Referee:** Bill Connors.

Fight Summary: Defending his title for the first time Lampkin (190) found Makathini (187) a tough customer to handle, and one who always tried to hit back, especially in the sixth and seventh when backing him up with solid combinations. There was not a great deal in it coming into the eighth, but after 2.04 of the session Makathini had been counted out after being set up by a right to the jaw followed by a crunching left hook to the body.

When Lampkin relinquished the IBF version of the title in July 1991 on signing with promoter Don King, James Warring, the NABF champion, was matched against James Pritchard, the IBF Inter-Continental champion, to decide the vacancy.

22 November 1990. Robert Daniels drew 12 Taoufik Belbouli.
Venue: Sports Palace, Madrid, Spain. **Recognition:** WBA. **Referee:** Ernesto Magana.
Scorecards: 115-114, 115-115, 114-114.
Fight Summary: Giving the former undefeated champion a crack at his title, Daniels (186½) was in the lead after eight rounds, scoring well to head and body, and generally controlling the fight. The ninth session saw Belbouli (188½) make his push for home before he really went to work in the tenth, hammering Daniels all over the ring and having him all but out. Daniels, to his credit, somehow remained upright and even finished the last two rounds fresher than Belbouli, who was still looking for a knockout blow. It had been a tough battle with neither deserving to lose.

8 December 1990. Magne Havnaa w pts 12 Daniel Neto.
Venue: Congress & Culture Centre, Aalborg, Denmark. **Recognition:** WBO. **Referee:** Bill Connors.
Scorecards: 119-109, 120-108, 119-109
Fight Summary: Dominating the contest with solid jabs and hooks the champion won every round going away despite being cut on his left eye at the start, and was far too good for the limited Neto (190). In fact, Havnaa (190) was a class above his man, who showed little aggression and seemed happy to cover up apart from in the latter rounds when he realised that he needed a kayo to win. An excellent boxer, the only disappointment for Havnaa's fans was his lack of a knockout punch.

8 December 1990. Massimiliano Duran w disq 12 Anaclet Wamba.
Venue: Sports Palace, Ferrara, Italy. **Recognition:** WBC. **Referee:** Larry O'Connell.
Fight Summary: Making his first defence, Duran (187) was hardly convincing when relying on left hands alone to keep Wamba (189¾) at bay, and the contest degenerated into a brawl with the latter being deducted five points for head butts. The first came in round three when Duran's left eye was cut, although the latter was partly at fault for continually holding and stopping Wamba from getting his punches off. Even with the points deductions Duran was only just ahead coming into the final session, but that counted for nothing when Wamba was disqualified with just nine seconds remaining when putting his head in yet again.

15 February 1991. Magne Havnaa w pts 12 Tyrone Booze.
Venue: Sports Hall, Randers, Denmark. **Recognition:** WBO. **Referee:** Ismael Quinones Falu.
Scorecards: 116-115, 117-113, 114-115.
Fight Summary: This was a difficult fight for Havnaa (190), and he even had to get off the floor in the 11th round after Booze (186¼) had caught him with a terrific right uppercut to the jaw. The left jab was the champion's best weapon, but whenever Booze was able to get inside it he would pound the body and get the uppercut off whenever he could. With Booze's defence also good it was probably Havnaa's big effort in the final session, despite being tired, that gave him the win.

Further to Havnaa's decision to relinquish the WBO version of the title in February 1992 due to increasing weight problems, it was thought that Derek Angol would be meeting Yuri Vaulin to contest the vacant title. However, after a change of management held things up Angol was eventually matched against Tyrone Booze.

9 March 1991. Bobby Czyz w pts 12 Robert Daniels.
Venue: Trump Taj Mahal, Atlantic City, New Jersey, USA. **Recognition:** WBA. **Referee:** Rudy Battle.
Scorecards: 119-112, 116-114, 114-116.

Fight Summary: Starting at a brisk pace Czyz's left jab was soon finding its way through the champion's high guard, something that set the pattern for the rest of the fight. Well in front after six rounds Czyz (186½) was also firing in right crosses and hooks to the body to wear Daniels (188¼) down. The remainder of the contest saw Daniels pressing Czyz before coming on strong from the ninth onwards with solid, if not heavy combinations to close the gap. Realising that his lead was being pegged back the former IBF light heavyweight champion made a big effort in the final session and, despite being totally exhausted as Daniels attacked the body, he held on for the win.

20 July 1991. Anaclet Wamba w rsc 11 Massimiliano Duran.
Venue: Athletic Track, Palermo, Sicily. **Recognition:** WBC. **Referee:** Arthur Mercante.
Fight Summary: Following their controversial earlier meeting, Wamba (189½) was given another crack at the champion. Boxing behind the left jab Duran (183¾) made a fair start, but after being cut over the right eye in the second round he was happy to jab and hold in order to protect the damage. Deducted a point in the fourth for excessive holding on Duran tired as the fight moved on, and in the eighth he continually pushed Wamba into the ropes without being cautioned. Never really able to use his jab to advantage, at the end of the tenth Wamba was marginally ahead on the cards despite being deducted a point in that session for dangerous headwork. In the 11th, having slipped over due to exhaustion, after Wamba sent Duran to the floor following a two-fisted attack the referee called the fight off with 42 seconds on the clock.

9 August 1991. Bobby Czyz w pts 12 Bash Ali.
Venue: Convention Hall, Atlantic City, New Jersey, USA. **Recognition:** WBA. **Referee:** Steve Smoger.
Scorecards: 120-108, 120-108, 120-108.
Fight Summary: Although his challenger was willing, Czyz (188) chose to box with caution throughout. Every round was virtually the same as Czyz jabbed away before driving in hooks to the body and right crosses to the head, and while Ali (188) proved his durability he was unable to pose any danger. After winning by a shut-out scoreline, Czyz stated that he had decided against going for a stoppage in order to avoid being cut.

6 September 1991. James Warring w co 1 James Pritchard.
Venue: Municipal Stadium, San Giacomo Salemi, Italy. **Recognition:** IBF. **Referee:** Joey Curtis.
Fight Summary: In a contest to decide a new champion after Jeff Lampkin had sent his belt back, Warring (186¼) knocked out Pritchard (189¾) after just 36 seconds following a cracking right to the jaw. With only 12 fights behind him the part-time actor and former kick-boxer caught his man cold without having taken a punch. Fought in the open air, Warring looked a good bet to stir up a weight class that was considerably weakened by the loss of Evander Holyfield. Some reports gave the time of the finish as being 24 seconds.

15 November 1991. James Warring w co 5 Donnell Wingfield.
Venue: Valley Sports Arena, Roanoke, Virginia, USA. **Recognition:** IBF. **Referee:** Al Rothenberg.
Fight Summary: Not letting the dust settle Warring (188½) was quickly back in action to defend his new title against Wingfield (185¾), who started well when taking two of the opening three rounds. It was only in the fourth that Warring found the distance, catching Wingfield with heavy rights as he attacked, and at 1.05 of the fifth the fight was ended when the latter was smashed to the floor by a cracking right uppercut and counted out.

13 December 1991. Anaclet Wamba w rsc 11 Massimiliano Duran.
Venue: Bercy Sports Palace, Paris, France. **Recognition:** WBC. **Referee:** Richard Steele.
Fight Summary: The third contest between the pair saw the champion get his left jab working early on, and apart from the fifth when Duran (184½) scored well with jabs and hooks he was pretty well dominant thereafter. By the ninth the pace had dropped considerably as the men tired, but in the tenth things became even more difficult for Duran when he was cut between both eyes. It got even worse for Duran in the 11th when he was cut over the left eye, Wamba (189½) seizing on the opportunity to batter him with both hands. When it was clear that Duran, who was extremely tired, was unable to defend himself properly the referee came to his rescue at 1.16 of the session.

8 May 1992. Bobby Czyz w pts 12 Donny Lalonde.
Venue: Riviera Hotel & Casino, Las Vegas, Nevada, USA. **Recognition:** WBA. **Referee:** Richard Steele.
Scorecards: 117-111, 116-110, 116-113.

Fight Summary: Smashed to the floor in the opening seconds of the fight by a cracker of a left hook and badly cut over the left eye, the challenger, a shadow of his former self, was there to be finished off. However, for whatever reason, Czyz (187) was unable to complete the job. With Czyz continually going below the belt for which he was warned on several occasions, things got worse for Lalonde (184½) in the fifth when he was cut above the right eye. When both men began to tire in the middle rounds it was Czyz who was landing the heavier punches. The tenth round saw Czyz finally being deducted a point for punching low, but with it making little difference Lalonde was forced to take a few more for good measure as the contest wound down.

After Czyz forfeited the WBA version of the title in September 1993 due to inactivity, Orlin Norris and Marcelo Figueroa were signed up to contest the vacancy.

16 May 1992. James Warring w pts 12 Johnny Nelson.
Venue: Hugo's Nightclub, Fredericksburg, Virginia, USA. **Recognition:** IBF. **Referee:** Chris Wollesen.
Scorecards: 118-111, 120-108, 117-111.
Fight Summary: Up against the hard-punching champion, Nelson (189¼) went down by a big margin on the scorecards as he generally stayed out of range and failed to threaten. It was only the inexperience of Warring (188) that allowed Nelson to go the distance, and even when he caught up with his man he failed to get his punches off apart from landing a big right in the eighth. According to the press Nelson froze, while it was left to Brendan Ingle, his manager, to state that his man had every chance of winning but was just too tense.

13 June 1992. Anaclet Wamba w rsc 5 Andriy Rudenko.
Venue: Marcel Cerdan Sports Palace, Levallois-Perret, France. **Recognition:** WBC. **Referee:** Joe Cortez.
Fight Summary: Trying to pressure the champion early on Rudenko (186½) showed plenty of gumption, but by the fourth he was being opened up and caught by solid right counters and body punches. Rudenko continued his forward march in the fifth despite being caught by lefts and rights to the head, and when Wamba (189¾) realised that his rival was hurt he opened up with two heavy rights to drop him. Although Rudenko made it to his feet before being counted out, when his corner threw the towel in the referee stopped the contest after two minutes of the session had elapsed.

25 July 1992. Tyrone Booze w co 7 Derek Angol.
Venue: G-Mex Centre, Manchester, England. **Recognition:** WBO. **Referee:** Roy Francis.
Fight Summary: Contesting the vacant title Angol (190) got away to a flier, firing in blows from both hands and looking to take Booze (189½) out early. Unfortunately for him, though, the American had not read the script and was content to let his rival punch himself out. By the fourth round it could be seen that Angol, now under a sustained body attack from Booze, was landing with 'arm' punches and tiring rapidly. Almost put down in the fifth, Angol was now under pressure with long rights to the head and hooks from both hands to the ribs finding their way through his defences, and in the sixth he barely made it back to his corner. For a man who had not boxed for close on 18 months Booze was doing a good job. Eventually, after taking a sustained battering in the seventh Angol was put down and counted out with 28 seconds of the session remaining.

30 July 1992. Alfred Cole w pts 12 James Warring.
Venue: Waterloo Village Open Air Arena, Stanhope, New Jersey, USA. **Recognition:** IBF. **Referee:** Rafael Ramos.
Scorecards: 116-111, 117-110, 114-113.
Fight Summary: In what was a difficult fight to score, with the champion mainly on the back foot and Cole (190) trying to catch him, it was made even more difficult for the latter when he was cut over the left eye in the second round after being held in a bear-hug. Warring (188) continued to hold on despite being deducted a point in the third, and it was not until the middle rounds that he got down to work when catching Cole with big right hands in the seventh and eighth. Two of the final three rounds went to Cole after he had rocked Warring in the tenth before following up with good blows to head and body.

2 October 1992. Tyrone Booze w pts 12 Ralf Rocchigiani.
Venue: National Hall, Berlin, Germany. **Recognition:** WBO. **Referee:** Genaro Rodriguez.
Scorecards: 114-113, 116-113, 116-112.

Fight Summary: Defending the title for the first time Booze (187) did just enough to win against the less than mobile Rocchigiani (184¼), who was always in the fight regardless of the fact that many of his punches missed the target or were taken on the champion's gloves. It was soon clear that neither man had the power necessary for a kayo win, but Booze's hooks and uppercuts were accurate enough to gain the points even though he was warned on several occasions for punches that landed at the back of the head. While Rocchigiani did well in the sixth and ninth sessions when pushing Booze on to the back foot, unable to set up sustained attacks his time would come at a later date.

16 October 1992. Anaclet Wamba w pts 12 Andrew Maynard.
Venue: Pierre de Coubertin Stadium, Paris, France. **Recognition:** WBC. **Referee:** Mickey Vann.
Scorecards: 118-110, 118-112, 116-113.
Fight Summary: After making a disastrous start, being knocked down heavily by a right to the jaw in the opening round, Maynard (179¾) somehow made it to the bell. Even though Maynard was cut over the left eye in the second and hurt by more right hands he recovered to pose problems for the champion in the third. In several rounds Maynard outworked Wamba (184¾), the latter being given a rest in the seventh when another one went low. By then Maynard's left eye was closing, but he was still there giving Wamba problems right up until the end despite the champion's better work gaining him a clear win on the cards.

13 February 1993. Markus Bott w pts 12 Tyrone Booze.
Venue: Alsterdorfer Sports Hall, Hamburg, Germany. **Recognition:** WBO. **Referee:** Ismael Quinones Falu.
Scorecards: 117-113, 117-112, 117-112.
Fight Summary: Staying with the champion throughout Bott (188) was good value for his win, landing the better punches, but he was made to fight every inch of the way. Booze (188) had not arrived in Germany to lose, and even when he was being outworked he would quickly bounce back. As the contest moved into the final stages, although Bott picked up the pace, Booze was still fighting hard at the final bell.

28 February 1993. Alfred Cole w pts 12 Uriah Grant.
Venue: Trump Castle, Atlantic City, New Jersey, USA. **Recognition:** IBF. **Referee:** Tony Orlando.
Scorecards: 116-112, 115-113, 117-111.
Fight Summary: Despite what the scorecards said this was a very close fight. It was also one that the champion could quite easily have lost as Grant (189) consistently used his left jab to get inside where he could attack the body. Even with his long reach Cole (190) found it difficult to keep Grant at bay, being forced to trade more often than he would have wished before getting back to the jab. Although Grant did well in the eighth and ninth rounds, Cole came on strongly in the last three sessions to secure the victory, a left hook-right uppercut hurting the Jamaican in the tenth before he repeated the dose in the 11th.

6 March 1993. Anaclet Wamba w pts 12 David Vedder.
Venue: Marcel Cerdan Sports Palace, Levallois-Perret, France. **Recognition:** WBC. **Referee:** Larry O'Connell.
Scorecards: 117-113, 118-111, 116-113.
Fight Summary: Once the champion had taken a good look at Vedder (187½), who started well with fast left hands, there was only going to be one winner. Really a jumped-up light heavy Vedder was too small for the lumbering Wamba (190), but apart from being hurt by a countering right in the tenth the American comfortably made it to the final bell. It was Wamba's sheer strength at the weight that was making him a difficult customer to beat, and Vedder ultimately went the same way as all bar two of his previous 41 opponents.

26 June 1993. Nestor Giovannini w pts 12 Markus Bott.
Venue: Alsterdorfer Sports Hall, Hamburg, Germany. **Recognition:** WBO. **Referee:** Paul Thomas.
Scorecards: 114-113, 114-113, 113-114.
Fight Summary: A disappointing fight saw Bott (189) losing his title to Giovannini (185½) 133 days after winning it, but there was so little between the two men that it could have gone either way. It was a poor performance by the champion, his punches lacking snap throughout, and there was a case for the referee to answer when Giovannini fell out of the ring in the tenth only to be helped back in again by his brother. There was so much dissent about the

way the referee allowed Giovannini to duck below the waist line for much of the fight, as well as putting up with both men continually holding on in every round, that a rematch was ordered in the aftermath.

16 July 1993. Alfred Cole w pts 12 Glenn McCrory.
Venue: Prospect Mira Sports Palace, Moscow, Russia. **Recognition:** IBF. **Referee:** Rudy Battle.
Scorecards: 118-109, 118-109, 117-110.
Fight Summary: Given the opportunity to regain his old title, McCrory (190) gave it his best shot but was ultimately found wanting against a champion who pressured him throughout and carried more firepower. Fought at a fast pace, McCrory did well to stand up against Cole (190) despite having to get off the floor twice in the sixth round in order to do so. Although Cole was a clear winner, McCrory, who had to get weight off at the weigh-in, showed his mettle in the tenth when gamely hanging on to make it to the final bell after being hurt by a body shot.

16 October 1993. Anaclet Wamba w rtd 7 Akim Tafer.
Venue: Marcel Cerdan Sports Palace, Levallois-Perret, France. **Recognition:** WBC. **Referee:** Rolando Barrovecchio.
Fight Summary: In an all-French title fight the champion retained his title when Tafer (189¾) failed to come out for the eighth, having sustained a swelling on his left eye in the sixth and being all but out on his feet. At that point Tafer was ahead on two of the judges' cards, but had little left in the tank while Wamba (190) was just as strong as when he started. Although Tafer boxed well, left jabs, hooks and combinations surprising Wamba at times, it was the latter's greater power that was the deciding factor.

6 November 1993. Orlin Norris w co 6 Marcelo Figueroa.
Venue: Winter Velodrome, Paris, France. **Recognition:** WBA. **Referee:** Franco Priami.
Fight Summary: With Bobby Czyz forfeiting the title due to inactivity, Norris (188¼) and Figueroa (188¼) were matched to decide a new champion. The fight was almost over before it started when Figueroa was dropped by the first two blows, a left hook-right cross, and although stunned he managed to get back into contention when working hard. For three rounds it became a contest of the Argentine's left jab and the punching power of Norris before the latter got totally on top, hurting his man every time he connected. Cut under the left eye after a clash of heads in the third, Figueroa then endured very tough fourth and fifth sessions prior to being counted out after 45 seconds of the sixth following a chopping right to the head that sent him to the floor face down.

17 November 1993. Alfred Cole w rsc 5 Vincent Boulware.
Venue: Caesar's Hotel & Casino, Atlantic City, New Jersey, USA. **Recognition:** IBF. **Referee:** Robert Palmer.
Fight Summary: Making his third defence Cole (190) was soon banging in long lefts and rights to Boulware's head and body, and even though the latter fought back it was already clear that it was going to be a tough night for him. By the third both men were going toe-to-toe, with Boulware (190) prepared to go down fighting. However, beginning to get ground down, after Boulware's gumshield came out for the third time in the fourth he looked ready to go. Then, having been dropped by a big right uppercut in the fifth Boulware somehow managed to get back into the fray, but after being endlessly battered around the ring and almost out on his feet he was rescued by the referee on the 1.08 mark.

20 November 1993. Nestor Giovannini w pts 12 Markus Bott.
Venue: Alsterdorfer Sports Hall, Hamburg, Germany. **Recognition:** WBO. **Referee:** Joe O'Neil.
Scorecards: 118-109, 117-110, 117-110.
Fight Summary: Following their earlier controversial fight Bott (189) was given an early chance to regain his title but, although going the distance, there were no complaints when he was well beaten. Getting off to a bad start when given a standing 'eight' count after being caught by a big right to the head in the opening session and bereft of his old form, Bott was outboxed throughout by Giovannini (189). It was also extremely tough with plenty of holding and work on the inside, Bott being thrown to the floor at least six times. Giovannini had a bit of a scare in the ninth when the doctor inspected a cut over his right eye but, allowed to box on, the result was a formality.

On 1 October 1994, Giovannini (184) forced Larry Carlisle (179) to retire inside six rounds in Buenos Aires, Argentina, in a fight that was billed for the title but not sanctioned by the WBO.

4 March 1994. Orlin Norris w pts 12 Arthur Williams.
Venue: MGM Grand, Las Vegas, Nevada, USA. **Recognition:** WBA. **Referee:** Toby Gibson.
Scorecards: 114-112, 118-110, 112-114.
Fight Summary: Thought to be the leading light of the cruiserweight division the champion almost came unstuck in his first defence against the unheralded Williams (189), who took him to a split decision. Dropped by a big right in the opening session Williams looked a beaten man for several rounds, despite cutting Norris (187) over the right eye in the second, before having a barnstorming sixth in which he had the latter all over the place. Thereafter, every round was tightly contested, both men being shaken badly in the 11th, and even though Williams' cleaner work in the 12th gave him the round on two of the cards it was too little and too late.

2 July 1994. Orlin Norris w rsc 3 Arthur Williams.
Venue: Mirage Hotel & Casino, Las Vegas, Nevada, USA. **Recognition:** WBA. **Referee:** Richard Steele.
Fight Summary: Ordered to defend his title against Williams for the second time following their earlier contest, Norris (188) made no mistake this time round. For whatever reason it was clear that Williams (190) was but a pale shadow of the man who had come close to beating the champion, and by the end of the second he had already been set up for the finish. Even though lacking composure, with Norris continually throwing punches in the third eventually Williams, floored by several terrific overarm rights to the head, was rescued at 1.08 of the session.

14 July 1994. Anaclet Wamba drew 12 Adolpho Washington.
Venue: Sporting Club, Monte Carlo, Monaco. **Recognition:** WBC. **Referee:** Mickey Vann.
Scorecards: 116-114, 115-115, 116-116.
Fight Summary: Despite being cut on the forehead in the opening round Washington (189¾) proved to be a tough opponent for the champion. Fighting in a lethargic manner Wamba (189½) did just enough to retain his title, barely raising his game while allowing Washington to dictate on occasion. Even when Washington, his left swelling up, was tiring in the eighth Wamba failed to take advantage, and it was not until the 11th that he realised he needed to work harder. At the final bell, with opinion divided, all talk of Wamba unifying the title appeared to be way off the mark.

23 July 1994. Alfred Cole w pts 12 Nate Miller.
Venue: Civic Centre, Bismarck, North Dakota, USA. **Recognition:** IBF. **Referee:** Denny Nelson.
Scorecards: 115-113, 117-111, 117-111.
Fight Summary: Closely contested over the opening eight rounds it was only in the latter stages that Cole (188) made sure of retaining his title. Even then he had to come through difficult times when hurt by heavy rights to the head, especially in the ninth and 11th when Miller (190) opened up. The loudest cheer of the night came when Cole, who blamed his poor performance on damaging his right hand early on, backed into the referee in the tenth, knocking him to the floor. Although Miller showed his mettle when pressing throughout he was ultimately unable to make his hard work pay off.

12 November 1994. Orlin Norris w rsc 2 James Heath.
Venue: The Bullring, Mexico City, Mexico. **Recognition:** WBA. **Referee:** Julio Alvarado.
Fight Summary: In what was an easy defence for Norris (187¾), his challenger barely bothered him before being stopped at 2.46 of the second round. Having dropped Heath (187¾) with a cracking left uppercut in the opening session Norris remained on the attack in the second, concentrating on the body before backing his man to the ropes and dropping him with an overarm right to the jaw. Although Heath managed to beat the count the fight was immediately halted when he was deemed unable to defend himself.

3 December 1994. Anaclet Wamba w pts 12 Marcelo Dominguez.
Venue: Delmi Stadium, Salta, Argentina. **Recognition:** WBC. **Referee:** Mickey Vann.
Scorecards: 116-115, 115-113, 114-114.
Fight Summary: Finding it hard to make the weight the champion looked distinctly lucky to have retained his title after a poor performance against the tough Dominguez (188¾) that saw him unable to keep the latter away from him while being drawn into slugging sessions. Although the fight perked up in the ninth, Wamba (190) still was not doing enough against an opponent who merely swiped and lacked accuracy. However, in the tenth Wamba picked

up the pace to just about get his nose in front, aided and abetted by Dominguez being docked a point in the tenth for carrying on fighting when the referee was picking up his misplaced gumshield. Wamba, damaged over both eyes at the finish, should also have been deducted a point at the same time as Dominguez for the very same offence, but the referee failed to spot it.

Following an injury that forced Wamba to withdraw from a prospective defence against Akim Tafer, the latter met Dominguez at the Jai-Alai Stadium, Saint Jean de Luz, France on 25 July 1995 to contest the 'interim' title; Dominguez winning on a ninth-round stoppage. Having successfully defended the 'interim' crown against Reinaldo Gimenez (w rsc 12 at the United Youth Club Stadium, Gualeguaychu, Argentina on 2 September 1995) and Sergey Kobozev (w pts 12 at the Marcel Cerdan Sports Palace, Levallois-Perret, France on 24 October 1995), Dominguez was proclaimed champion in April 1996 after Wamba had failed to make the weight for their title fight.

17 December 1994. Dariusz Michalczewski w co 10 Nestor Giovannini.
Venue: Alsterdorfer Sports Hall, Hamburg, Germany. **Recognition:** WBO. **Referee:** Genaro Rodriguez.
Fight Summary: Stepping up a weight division, Michalczewski (181) showed his class when unseating the champion after knocking him out at 1.25 of the tenth round. The fight did not warm up until the fifth when Michalczewski forced a count on Giovannini (182), who slipped over rather than being punched, while in the sixth the German fell foul of the referee when he was deducted a point for pushing. Although Giovannini, cut over the left eye in the fourth, scored well with overarm rights and left hooks it was Michalczewski's solid left-rights that began to dominate proceedings. Dropped heavily by a left at the end of the ninth, when Giovannini failed to recover properly he was eventually undone by another cracking left after being set up by solid blows from both hands.

Michalczewski vacated the WBO version of the title in January 1995 after failing to secure a defence against Thomas Hearns and deciding to continue as the WBO light heavyweight champion. Following that, Carl Thompson, the former British and European champion, was matched against Ralf Rocchigiani for the vacant title.

18 March 1995. Orlin Norris w pts 12 Adolpho Washington.
Venue: Memorial Auditorium, Worcester, Massachusetts, USA. **Recognition:** WBA. **Referee:** Hubert Earle.
Scorecards: 115-114, 115-114, 115-114.
Fight Summary: Yet again Washington (190) lost a title challenge that could have gone either way, this time when up against Norris (190). In fact it was Washington who landed some of the heavier shots of the fight, looking as though he was taking over in the sixth as Norris's work-rate dropped. Boxing cleverly, Washington was making life tough for Norris, and even with his left eye swelling up in the ninth and fast tiring he was still right in the fight. Although Norris made up some ground in the tenth and 11th, with it still being desperately close at the final bell it was too tight to guess.

10 June 1995. Ralf Rocchigiani w rsc 11 Carl Thompson.
Venue: G-Mex Centre, Manchester, England. **Recognition:** WBO. **Referee:** Genaro Rodriguez.
Fight Summary: Contested for the title vacated by Dariusz Michalczewski, Thompson (188) won the first seven rounds on all three cards, cutting Rocchigiani (187½) over the left eye in the fourth prior to flooring him in the fifth. Earlier in the session, Thompson had also been on the floor. Staggered several times in the eighth things began to look ominous for Thompson, and in the tenth he went down complaining that his right arm was damaged. Although coming out for the 11th, with Thompson's arm a real problem he dropped down before walking to his corner before the referee stopped the contest after 38 seconds.

24 June 1995. Alfred Cole w pts 12 Uriah Grant.
Venue: Convention Centre, Atlantic City, New Jersey, USA. **Recognition:** IBF. **Referee:** Steve Smoger.
Scorecards: 118-110, 117-111, 117-111.
Fight Summary: With this being Grant's second crack at Cole (190) for the latter's title, once again the result went against him. Both men landed well at times, but Cole was the most hurtful, a powerful left hook almost felling Grant (188) in the eighth. Although Grant boxed in clever fashion, rarely wasting his shots and slipping punches well, Cole's left jab was the match winner, and even though the champion was cut over the right eye by a clash of heads in the tenth he remained calm to win going away.

Unable to make the weight any longer, when Cole relinquished the IBF version of the title in July 1996, Adolpho Washington was matched against Torsten May to decide the vacancy.

22 July 1995. Nate Miller w co 8 Orlin Norris.
Venue: London Arena, Millwall, London, England. **Recognition:** WBA. **Referee:** John Coyle.
Fight Summary: Having had trouble making the weight Norris (188¾) boxed very much in a subdued fashion, and by the seventh he looked completely exhausted after running out of ideas against a challenger who, although behind on the cards, had barely exerted himself. All at sea in the eighth, having been hurt by a left hook and an overarm right to the head earlier on as Miller (186¾) picked up the pace, Norris was counted out at 2.04 of the session. Driven to the floor by solid blows from both hands, Norris tried to get up before falling back to the canvas where he was administered oxygen prior to leaving the ring.

30 September 1995. Ralf Rocchigiani w pts 12 Marc Randazzo.
Venue: Sports Centre, Hannover, Germany. **Recognition:** WBO. **Referee:** Raul Caiz.
Scorecards: 117-111, 118-110, 116-113.
Fight Summary: Making his first defence Rocchigiani (186½) had trouble with Randazzo (186) in the early rounds, especially in the opening two, before getting behind the left jab to rack up the points. As with most unbeaten fighters the American was always dangerous, but once Rocchigiani had his measure he was comprehensively outboxed and outpunched. According to Jack Tree, writing in *Boxing News*, this was a career best performance for Rocchigiani.

25 November 1995. Ralf Rocchigiani w rsc 8 Dan Ward.
Venue: Stadium Hall, Brunswick, Germany. **Recognition:** WBO. **Referee:** Luis Pabon.
Fight Summary: The challenger started the better of the pair, proving to be a far cleverer and technically accomplished fighter than what had been expected, his fast hands giving Rocchigiani (186¼) plenty to think about. Ward (187) was also dangerous at close quarters though. With his left eye cut Rocchigiani possibly got too involved, but after the fifth round Ward became less of a threat before being rescued by the bell at the end of the seventh having been caught by a left-right combination. Totally one-sided in the eighth, when Ward was sent reeling from a cluster of heavy blows and was not fighting back the referee came to his rescue with just five seconds of the session remaining.

13 January 1996. Nate Miller w rtd 4 Reinaldo Gimenez.
Venue: Jai-Alai Fronton, Miami, Florida, USA. **Recognition:** WBA. **Referee:** Bernie Soto.
Fight Summary: Walking into his challenger from the opening bell Miller (188½) was happy to keep the fight at close quarters where he could drive in solid shots to the body and determine the way the contest went. Gimenez (189), who had recently been beaten by Marcelo Dominguez, was never really up to the challenge, doing very little other than throw one punch at a time before retreating and covering up. Ironically, the Argentine's best round came in the fourth when he connected with several heavy punches before retiring himself at the end of the session, claiming that he had nothing left in the tank.

16 March 1996. Ralf Rocchigiani w rsc 4 Jay Snyder.
Venue: National Hall, Berlin, Germany. **Recognition:** WBO. **Referee:** Genaro Rodriguez.
Fight Summary: Starting as he meant to carry on Rocchigiani (184½) was in control of his challenger from the opening bell, landing good shots to head and body before stepping on the gas in the fourth round. Having been forced to take the mandatory 'eight' count following a left-right to the jaw, Snyder (189¾) was still on shaky legs when he was dropped heavily by Rocchigiani for the second time. At that point, with 2.05 on the clock, the referee stopped the fight immediately.

23 March 1996. Nate Miller w rsc 9 Brian LaSpada.
Venue: The Arena, Miami, Florida, USA. **Recognition:** WBA. **Referee:** Bill Connors.
Fight Summary: Little more than a club fighter the challenger hardly deserved a crack at Miller (188¼), and the fight had barely started when he was floored by a right over the top. Although LaSpada (187) was ready to be taken Miller failed to finish him off, being happy to give him time and space. Only in the fifth did LaSpada, who

offered up a weak left jab in resistance, remotely come close to winning a round. Even then Miller continually failed to finish his man off despite hurting him in every session. Eventually the fight came to an end, much to the relief of the crowd, with LaSpada receiving a badly gashed left eye in the ninth following a head clash prior to the referee calling it a day 36seconds into the session.

5 July 1996. Marcelo Dominguez w rtd 9 Patrice Aouissi.
Venue: Space Arena, Hyeres, France. **Recognition:** WBC. **Referee:** Bob Logist.
Fight Summary: Defending the title that was awarded to him after Anaclet Wamba forfeited his right to the championship Dominguez (190) battered his way to victory over Aouissi (188) when the latter was retired at the end of the ninth round. Strong, but lacking in skill, Dominguez hurt Aouissi several times, especially in the fourth, fifth and sixth. However, he was unable to drop his challenger who continued to rally and was ahead on points at the end of the ninth prior to being retired by his corner. It had been a game showing by Aouissi, but with the ninth round being a bad one for him he had nothing left.

13 July 1996. Ralf Rocchigiani w pts 12 Bash Ali.
Venue: Gruga Hall, Essen, Germany. **Recognition:** WBO. **Referee:** Rudy Battle.
Scorecards: 115-113, 116-112, 116-112.
Fight Summary: Making a strong start the champion took the opening four rounds before Ali (189¾) had some success in the fifth and gradually upped his game from the seventh onwards. Despite the fight becoming more even from that point Rocchigiani (187½) was still in the driving seat, almost having Ali over with a heavy left to the jaw in the eighth. With nothing to lose Ali made one final effort to dislodge Rocchigiani in the 12th, but was unable to turn things around in what would be his third and final attempt to become a champion.

31 August 1996. Adolpho Washington w pts 12 Torsten May.
Venue: Balear Bullring, Palma de Mallorca, Spain. **Recognition:** IBF. **Referee:** Randy Neumann.
Scorecards: 115-114, 117-111, 116-112.
Fight Summary: Fighting for the right to succeed Alfred Cole, who had relinquished the title in order to move up to heavyweight, Washington (189¾) became champion in his fourth attempt when outscoring May (188½). Having made a bad start, being cut over the right eye in the opening round, May found it difficult to find a foothold in the fight, especially with Washington concentrating his attacks on the damage. However, he had a good second round and went on to win three of the next four sessions when using his southpaw jab to advantage before Washington took over. Washington's left eye had begun to swell in the fifth, but it did not stop him from negating May's reach advantage and taking the fight to close quarters where he rolled off the last five rounds for the win. Unfortunate to receive a further cut, this time over the left eye in the sixth, May never looked likely to be floored at any stage.

31 August 1996. Nate Miller w rsc 7 James Heath.
Venue: Point Theatre, Dublin, Ireland. **Recognition:** WBA. **Referee:** Carlos Berrocal.
Fight Summary: In control throughout, the champion took his time regardless of the fact that he had Heath (187½) on the floor from a left hook in the opening session. Never at risk, Miller (189½) had Heath at his mercy right up until the finish. Picking off Heath at close quarters or at distance, Miller wore his man down with solid blows to head and body before stepping it up in the seventh. Clearly without a chance, Heath was rescued by the referee with six seconds of the session remaining after being decked by a right-left hook to the head.

6 December 1996. Marcelo Dominguez w rtd 7 Jose Arimatea Da Silva.
Venue: Palomar Athletic Club, Buenos Aires, Argentina. **Recognition:** WBC. **Referee:** Luis Carlos Guzman.
Fight Summary: For the opening two rounds Da Silva (188½) used his greater reach to keep Dominguez (189¼) at bay, but in the third the tide turned as the latter found his range. From there onwards the champion dominated with left hooks and straight rights before flooring Da Silva with a solid right to the jaw in the fifth. While the Brazilian made it to his feet he was badly used up, and after being under terrific pressure for the next couple of sessions he was retired by his corner at the end of the seventh.

13 December 1996. Ralf Rocchigiani w pts 12 Stefan Angehrn.
Venue: Stadium Sports Hall, Hannover, Germany. **Recognition:** WBO. **Referee:** Joe Cortez.

Scorecards: 119-109, 117-112, 118-110.

Fight Summary: Dropping two rounds at most the champion boxed well within himself to dominate Angehrn (186½), who despite being a skilled practitioner lacked the power to be a real threat. Although Angehrn had his best round in the seventh, winning the session on all three cards, he was unable to build on it after Rocchigiani (187½) came back strongly in the eighth to have him hanging on at the bell. Angehrn gave it a real go in the 12th, but with Rocchigiani in cruise control he had left it too late.

22 February 1997. Nate Miller w rsc 2 Alexander Gurov.
Venue: The Theatre, Fort Lauderdale, Florida, USA. **Recognition:** WBA. **Referee:** Jorge Alonso.

Fight Summary: Boxing for the first time in America Gurov (190) was unable to bother the champion with his southpaw stance even though he was a good three inches taller. With Miller (188) looking to jab and work the body in the opening session it was already obvious that Gurov was in for a tough night, and in the second he was quickly in trouble. Just about making it up at the count of 'nine', having been dropped by a right to the jaw, the former European champion was floored twice more before being stopped at 1.54 on the 'three knockdowns in a round' ruling.

26 April 1997. Ralf Rocchigiani w pts 12 Stefan Angehrn.
Venue: Stadium Hall, Zurich, Switzerland. **Recognition:** WBO. **Referee:** Joe Cortez.
Scorecards: 119-109, 115-114, 114-114.

Fight Summary: Handed another opportunity to take the title from Rocchigiani (187¼), Angehrn (187¼) went much closer this time around when losing on a majority decision. He also gave the champion all manner of problems. There were no knockdowns, but with both men showing wear and tear at the finish after giving everything Rocchigiani only retained his crown when winning three of the last four sessions. How one of the judges gave Rocchigiani 11 of the 12 rounds was a mystery as there were many who thought that Angehrn deserved a draw at the very least.

21 June 1997. Uriah Grant w pts 12 Adolpho Washington.
Venue: South Florida University Sun Dome, Tampa, Florida, USA. **Recognition:** IBF. **Referee:** Brian Garry.
Scorecards: 116-112, 116-112, 114-114.

Fight Summary: Seen as a major surprise the supposed trial-horse, Grant (187¼), won the IBF title at his third attempt when outscoring the champion by eight rounds to four on two of the judges' scorecards. Working hard, Grant had more than held his own with Washington (190) during the first six rounds, and in the seventh he almost had the latter over when connecting with two big rights to the head. From thereon in he held the upper hand as Washington seemed unable to find an answer.

16 August 1997. Marcelo Dominguez w pts 12 Akim Tafer.
Venue: Sports Palace, Le Cannet, France. **Recognition:** WBC. **Referee:** Richard Steele.
Scorecards: 115-114, 116-114, 117-112.

Fight Summary: After stopping Tafer (189¼) to win the 'interim' title, Dominguez (190) was favoured to beat the Frenchman again but had to go the whole route to do so in what was a much harder contest. Twice hit below the belt in the third, Tafer, who had come to the ring with tendon damage to his right elbow, was given a fair rest. Then, when Dominguez repeated the foul in the 11th he had a point deducted from his score. Between rounds seven and nine, in his own words Tafer admitted that he'd had a bad day at the office, lacking sharpness and failing to take advantage of his extra reach as Dominguez pressed him. Those three sessions were the difference between winning and losing. Afterwards, Tafer had two teeth removed due to the battering he had received in the eighth.

4 October 1997. Carl Thompson w pts 12 Ralf Rocchigiani.
Venue: Stadium Sports Hall, Hannover, Germany. **Recognition:** WBO. **Referee:** Max Parker Jnr.
Scorecards: 117-111, 119-109, 113-115.

Fight Summary: Despite failing against Rocchigiani (185¾) in an earlier title challenge after dislocating his right shoulder when leading on points, Thompson (188½) made no mistake this time round despite one of the judges unbelievably marking him down as a loser. Working well with left jabs and solid rights Thompson pressured Rocchigiani throughout, and although the champion came on strong in the seventh when the pace dropped he was unable maintain that effort. Even though Rocchigiani, his left eye swollen and bleeding made another big effort in the final session it was just too little and too late.

8 November 1997. Fabrice Tiozzo w pts 12 Nate Miller.
Venue: Thomas & Mack Centre, Las Vegas, Nevada, USA. **Recognition:** WBA. **Referee:** Richard Steele.
Scorecards: 115-113, 115-113, 117-114.
Fight Summary: Having earlier been a WBC light heavyweight champion, Tiozzo (190) became a 'double' titleholder when outscoring Miller (190). Taking all the champion could throw at him, which included several heavy rights to the head, Tiozzo began to push Miller back in the last few rounds, his cause being helped when a clash of heads saw the American cut over the left eye in the ninth. Realizing he had to do something in order to retain his title Miller gave it everything in the final session, but was unable to dislodge Tiozzo despite catching him with some solid blows.

8 November 1997. Imamu Mayfield w pts 12 Uriah Grant.
Venue: Thomas & Mack Centre, Las Vegas, Nevada, USA. **Recognition:** IBF. **Referee:** Jay Nady.
Scorecards: 115-112, 117-110, 116-111.
Fight Summary: Making his first defence the 35-year-old Grant (190) lost his title to the virtually unknown Mayfield (188), who proved to have a punch in either hand when shaking the champion up in the third before dropping him in the fifth with a left hook. At that point of the fight it looked as though Mayfield would force a stoppage, but Grant came back strongly in the sixth to cut him over the left eye prior to taking the seventh when exerting plenty of pressure. From there onwards though, with Grant unable to sustain his work-rate, it was the 18-fight Mayfield who came through to land the title.

21 February 1998. Juan Carlos Gomez w pts 12 Marcelo Dominguez.
Venue: Pan America Stadium, Mar del Plata, Argentina. **Recognition:** WBC. **Referee:** Richard Steele.
Scorecards: 116-112, 116-112, 115-113.
Fight Summary: Defending his title for the sixth time, Dominguez (190), up against the Cuban-born Gomez (189½), was outpointed in what was a tough fight for both men. Cut over the left eye early on was not helpful to Dominguez's cause, and he also had difficulty finding a way through the challenger's long-armed southpaw guard. Regardless of the problems he faced Dominguez made Gomez fight every inch of the way, the last two rounds seeing both men going blow for blow despite being extremely tired.

28 March 1998. Imamu Mayfield w co 11 Terry Dunstan.
Venue: Ice Arena, Hull, England. **Recognition:** IBF. **Referee:** John Coyle.
Fight Summary: Both men started slowly before the champion almost had Dunstan (189¾) over after connecting with a big right to the head in the fourth, only for the latter to come back with a good right uppercut as the round closed. In the fifth Dunstan cut Mayfield (188) over the right eye, but was then was deducted a point for backhanding in what had been a good round for him. Fairly even for the next few sessions, Dunston, cut over the right eye in the ninth, was ahead on one of the cards at the end of the tenth before the roof fell in a round later. Beaten to the punch by a big right to the head in the 11th Dunstan crashed to the boards, and although getting up he was caught by another right and counted out on the 1.35 mark on being floored again.

18 April 1998. Carl Thompson w pts 12 Chris Eubank.
Venue: Nynex Arena, Manchester, England. **Recognition:** WBO. **Referee:** Roy Francis.
Scorecards: 114-113, 114-113, 116-113.
Fight Summary: In what was his first defence, Thompson (189), who had to dig deep after being badly hurt in the second round, was dropped in the fourth by a right uppercut and almost floored on several further occasions as the former WBO middleweight and super middleweight champion looked for a finish. In the fifth Eubank (186½) picked up a swollen left eye as Thompson regrouped, and it was this injury more than anything that changed the way the fight went. From the seventh onwards Thompson won five of the six remaining rounds despite having to take some heavy shots, while Eubank was exhausted and beginning to come apart at the seams by the end of the tenth. He bravely continued, but at the final bell he was desperately holding on as Thompson, throwing punches from both hands, was making sure that his title would remain in his hands.

2 May 1998. Fabrice Tiozzo w rsc 1 Terry Ray.
Venue: Astro Bullet Arena, Villeurbanne, France. **Recognition:** WBA. **Referee:** John Coyle.
Fight Summary: After exchanging left jabs from the opening bell the champion quickly took advantage of an opening when dropping the 35-year-old Ray (187¾) with a left hook-right cross. Although getting up Ray was almost immediately downed again by heavy shots from both hands as Tiozzo (189½) opened up. Clambering to his feet, Ray was rescued by the referee on the 60-second mark after being put down for the third time and in no condition to defend himself even though he was upright.

5 June 1998. Juan Carlos Gomez w rsc 6 Guy Waters.
Venue: Wandsbek Sports Hall, Hamburg, Germany. **Recognition:** WBC. **Referee:** Jay Nady.
Fight Summary: On top from the opening bell the southpaw champion was the harder puncher of the two, and although Waters (185¼) got his shots off they were virtually brushed aside. In the fifth round Gomez (189½) was deducted a point for holding and hitting, but it barely mattered as by that stage Waters was taking a shellacking. At 1.30 of the sixth it was all over after the referee had stopped the contest to save the outclassed Waters from taking further punishment when he was not firing back.

18 July 1998. Carl Thompson w rsc 9 Chris Eubank.
Venue: The Arena, Sheffield, England. **Recognition:** WBO. **Referee:** Paul Thomas.
Fight Summary: Starting well the aggressive Eubank (189) took the opening six rounds on the cards when boxing cleverly to make the champion miss with heavy shots while banging home solid punches of his own. Boxing well within himself in what was a return match, although occasionally hurt, Thompson (189½) managed to avoid more than he was hit with. When Eubank's left eye began to close up in the fifth it was ominous, and after going punch for punch with Thompson in the seventh it was closed shut at the bell. Thereafter, with Eubank having little chance of winning, being caught by right hands he would normally have avoided, the doctor advised the referee to call the fight off at the end of the ninth. At that point the scorecards showed Eubank leading 87-84, 87-84, 86-86.

3 October 1998. Juan Carlos Gomez w rsc 2 Alexey Ilyin.
Venue: Prinz Garden Hall, Augsburg, Germany. **Recognition:** WBC. **Referee:** Tony Perez.
Fight Summary: Making a solid start Gomez (189) had a good look at Ilyin (189¼) before opening up in the second round and driving his challenger into the ropes from where there would be no way out for him. It was all one way, and with 25 seconds of the session remaining the referee stopped the fight after Ilyin had been dropped by a steady battery of southpaw blows to head and body and was unlikely to get up.

30 October 1998. Arthur Williams w rsc 9 Imamu Mayfield.
Venue: Grand Casino, Biloxi, Mississippi, USA. **Recognition:** IBF. **Referee:** Elmo Adolph.
Fight Summary: Although the challenger was dropped in the second round he came right back at Mayfield (186½), who seemed content to let his man off the hook, a tactic that would ultimately prove costly. Towards the end of the fourth Williams (187) finally got himself going, dropping Mayfield heavily with a heavy right to the head, and despite the latter being all over the shop he was unable to find a finishing blow. Hurt again in the fifth it looked as though Mayfield would not last too long, but he surprised Williams when putting him down with a left hook in the sixth. By now Mayfield was cut over the left eye. After doing reasonably well in the next two sessions Mayfield came under a sustained attack in the ninth before being rescued by the referee on the 1.10 mark following two knockdowns.

14 November 1998. Fabrice Tiozzo w co 2 Ezequiel Paixao.
Venue: Francois Mitterrand Space Arena, Mont de Marsan, France. **Recognition:** WBA. **Referee:** John Coyle.
Fight Summary: Tiozzo (189) was never under any kind of threat whatsoever from a challenger who appeared to be short of ideas and power and after finding his range with the left jab he dropped the Brazilian with a right cross at the end of the opening session. Starting the second as he left off, with Tiozzo hurting Paixao (183½) almost every time he connected, the latter was counted out at 1.04 of the round having taken another heavy right to the jaw.

12 December 1998. Juan Carlos Gomez w rsc 2 Rodney Gordon.
Venue: Ball Sports Hall, Frankfurt, Germany. **Recognition:** WBC. **Referee:** Luis Carlos Guzman.
Fight Summary: The champion had been matched to meet a fellow southpaw in England's Rob Norton, but when the latter pulled out with flu Gordon (190) was quickly substituted. Clearly out of his depth Gordon was soon under attack, and towards the end of the opening session a solid left from Gomez (190) dropped him, reportedly fracturing his skull. Coming out for the second Gomez bided his time as the unfortunate Gordon was forced to endure further pain before a cracking left to the head sent him down to be rescued by the referee with 41 seconds of the session remaining.

13 March 1999. Juan Carlos Gomez w pts 12 Marcelo Dominguez.
Venue: Hanseatic Hall, Lubeck, Germany. **Recognition:** WBC. **Referee:** Marty Denkin.
Scorecards: 119-111, 119-111, 119-110.
Fight Summary: Defending his title against the man he won it from Gomez (189½) was in charge all the way, apart from when he got back to his corner at the end of the sixth and asked to be retired after feeling too tired to carry on. Luckily his corner talked him out of it, saying that Dominguez (188½) was just as exhausted as he was. There were no knockdowns due to Dominguez's toughness, but the Argentine was forced to take southpaw jabs and crosses all night as Gomez plied his trade. The contest had originally been set for 20 February before being cancelled due to Gomez contracting flu.

27 March 1999. Johnny Nelson w rsc 5 Carl Thompson.
Venue: Storm Arena, Derby, England. **Recognition:** WBO. **Referee:** Paul Thomas.
Fight Summary: Finally putting the bad memory of his two previous attempts at winning a world title behind him the switch-hitting Nelson (190) started well pumping out lefts and rights, continually having the champion bemused with his hand-speed. At the end of the third round Nelson was already forging ahead, and in the fourth a solid right hook dropped Thompson (189½) who, although forced to take the mandatory 'eight' count when up at 'three', ultimately made it to the bell. Thompson had survived what had been a difficult couple of minutes, but in the fifth after taking several heavy shots without reply the referee stopped the fight on the 1.42 mark having decided that he was absorbing too much punishment.

15 May 1999. Johnny Nelson w pts 12 Bruce Scott.
Venue: Ponds Forge Leisure Centre, Sheffield, England. **Recognition:** WBO. **Referee:** John Coyle.
Fight Summary: Far too fast for his challenger, Nelson (190) used his reach advantage to good effect to win all but two or three rounds on his way to an easy defence. Scott (187) came to fight, but was outmanoeuvred throughout and knocked down in the third when caught by a short right counter. Although he was up quickly, Scott, his left eye swollen, never remotely came close to unseating Nelson who controlled him whether it was on the inside or at distance.

5 June 1999. Vassiliy Jirov w rsc 7 Arthur Williams.
Venue: The Coliseum, Biloxi, Mississippi, USA. **Recognition:** IBF. **Referee:** Paul Sita.
Fight Summary: Despite making a reasonable start the champion was soon under duress as Jirov (188) cut him over the right eye in the second round before smashing him to the floor with a long southpaw left to the body in the third. Back in the fight by the fifth it looked as though Williams (188) might have weathered the storm, but in the next session he was once again looking to survive after being hurt again. The seventh then saw Williams floored by a cracking left followed by a right to the body, and upon getting to his feet and being battered without reply he was rescued by the referee at 1.59 of the session.

17 July 1999. Juan Carlos Gomez w rsc 6 Bruce Scott.
Venue: Philips Hall, Dusseldorf, Germany. **Recognition:** WBC. **Referee:** Daniel Van de Wiele.
Fight Summary: Coming in at short notice after just two weeks of training Scott (188½) was no match for the hard-hitting southpaw champion, who not only had the advantages in height and reach but with fast hands as well. After comprehensively outboxing Scott for five rounds Gomez 188½) went for the finish in the sixth, punching away without return for a good 30 seconds before the referee decided to call a halt with 14 seconds of the session

remaining. Scott was a strange opponent for Gomez, having been well beaten by Johnny Nelson when challenging for the WBO title just two months earlier.

7 August 1999. Johnny Nelson w rtd 4 Willard Lewis.
Venue: Goresbrook Leisure Centre, Dagenham, England. **Recognition:** WBO. **Referee:** Dave Parris.
Fight Summary: With huge advantages in height and reach the champion found Lewis (189¾) an easy target, landing so many punches in the fourth that two of the judges marked it a 10-8 round. Two solid right crosses opened a cut over Lewis's left eye as Nelson (189½) went to work in that session, being followed by a left hook ripping open a cut over the Canadian's right eye. Having taken a pounding and with serious eye damage making a difficult task even harder, it came as no surprise when Lewis was retired by his corner during the interval.

18 September 1999. Johnny Nelson w pts 12 Sione Asipeli.
Venue: Mandalay Bay Resort & Casino, Las Vegas, Nevada, USA. **Recognition:** WBO. **Referee:** Joe Cortez.
Fight Summary: Defending his title in America, Nelson (190) began jabbing the tough Asipeli (190) at random, and the fight quickly became one-sided when the latter was unable to get his punches off. For round after round Nelson treated Asipeli as if he was a sparring partner, banging in lefts and rights before moving on, and even going southpaw at times. In the tenth Nelson finally made his domination pay off when flooring Asipeli with a heavy right through the middle, prior to being docked a point later in the round when throwing back-hands. The last two sessions saw Nelson firing away with both hands as he waltzed to a virtual shut-out win over the always willing but outclassed Asipeli.

18 September 1999. Vassiliy Jirov w co 10 Dale Brown.
Venue: Mandalay Bay Resort & Casino, Las Vegas, Nevada, USA. **Recognition:** IBF. **Referee:** Richard Steele.
Fight Summary: Making his first defence, Jirov (188) quickly moved to the centre of the ring, soon having the challenger moving away from vicious southpaw rights to head and body. Although Brown (188) did reasonably well in the third, in the fifth he was cut over the left eye and dropped by two heavy lefts just before the bell. However, he came back well to unbalance Jirov on several occasions, cutting him by the side of the right eye before being counted out with just eight seconds of the tenth remaining after being flattened by a terrific left to the body.

6 November 1999. Johnny Nelson w co 4 Christophe Girard.
Venue: Kingsway Leisure Centre, Widnes, England. **Recognition:** WBO. **Referee:** Mickey Vann.
Fight Summary: Starting in confident mode the champion was soon sending out lefts and rights while Girard (182½) was happy to move away. Due to the negative tactics employed the contest failed to get going until the fourth round, one of the judges even giving Girard the third as Nelson (189¼) threw so few punches. That all changed in the fourth when Nelson began to open up, sending Girard to the floor when landing with a right-hand counter, and after the latter got up he was eventually counted out on the 2.34 mark having been dropped by a long right uppercut to the face.

13 November 1999. Fabrice Tiozzo w rtd 7 Ken Murphy.
Venue: Thomas & Mack Centre, Las Vegas, Nevada, USA. **Recognition:** WBA. **Referee:** Joe Cortez.
Fight Summary: Having been sidelined by injuries - to the jaw and back - since his last defence, Tiozzo (189½) was happy to be back in action. It did not take him too long to get going, Murphy (188) being in trouble from a left hook to the body towards the end of the second round. Although Murphy was prepared to fight it had become one-sided by the fourth, and in the sixth it was noticeable that Tiozzo had picked up the pace as he looked for an early night. Still walking forward in the seventh, after Murphy found himself on the end of a short right to the head that downed him on getting back to his corner he was retired at the end of the session.

11 December 1999. Juan Carlos Gomez w co 9 Napoleon Tagoe.
Venue: Alsterdorfer Sports Hall, Hamburg, Germany. **Recognition:** WBC. **Referee:** Laurence Cole.
Fight Summary: The champion started as he meant to finish, banging in southpaw punches from both hands and looking to hurt Tagoe (189½) at every opportunity. Towering six inches over his rival the 6'4" Gomez (189¼) wobbled Tagoe in the third before driving his man around the ring in the fourth and dropping him with a solid left to the jaw in the fifth. Although managing to keep out of trouble in the sixth Tagoe was floored again in the

seventh, being finally put out of his misery at 1.25 of the ninth when counted out after a left uppercut delivered on the inside had sent him crashing.

12 February 2000. Vassiliy Jirov w rsc 9 Saul Montana.
Venue: Bank of America Centre, Boise, Idaho, USA. **Recognition:** IBF. **Referee:** Jerry Armstrong.
Fight Summary: In what was a very competitive fight up until the eighth when the champion finally gained control, the hard-hitting Montana (189½) was always in with a chance. Starting behind the southpaw right jab Jirov (189½) scored well in the opening two sessions, but took some heavy two-handed shots in the third as Montana eventually got going. The fourth and fifth rounds saw both men trading from head to body before Montana came on with hard rights to the body in the sixth and seventh, which were his best rounds. At that stage of the contest Jirov took over, scoring well with heavy blows to the head. With five seconds of the ninth remaining the fight was stopped by the referee after Montana had been shaken up badly following a left to the temple and several additional punches. Montana then slumped to the floor where he lay for several minutes prior to recovering.

11 March 2000. Juan Carlos Gomez w rsc 2 Mohamed Siluvangi.
Venue: Hanse Hall, Lubeck, Germany. **Recognition:** WBC. **Referee:** Larry O'Connell.
Fight Summary: Right from the opening bell it was clear that Siluvangi (187½) had no realistic chance of beating the heavy-handed champion, who boxed as he pleased in the first round before finishing him off in the second. Caught again and again with the southpaw jab Siluvangi had nowhere to go as Gomez (189½) hunted him down, the fight being stopped at 2.35 of the second after the African-born Frenchman was deemed unable to defend himself on getting up from a countering left to the jaw.

8 April 2000. Fabrice Tiozzo w rsc 6 Valeriy Vykhor.
Venue: Bercy Sports Palace, Paris, France. **Recognition:** WBA. **Referee:** John Coyle.
Fight Summary: When a cracking countering right to the jaw had dropped Vykhor (188½) half a minute into the first it appeared that the referee might call a halt, but he let it continue when the champion failed to follow up. Boxing patiently Tiozzo (189½) kept the jab going before working from head to body, which led to Vykhor being cut on the right eye as heads came together in the third. Although Vykhor was strong he was unable to bother Tiozzo, and at 1.45 of the sixth the fight was called off by the referee after the Ukranian had been floored by a mixture of right uppercuts to the head and body shots.

8 April 2000. Johnny Nelson w rsc 7 Pietro Aurino.
Venue: York Hall, Bethnal Green, London, England. **Recognition:** WBO. **Referee:** Paul Thomas.
Fight Summary: Despite flooring Aurino (189½) in the opening session with a solid left hook that was followed by a right uppercut to the head, the champion sat back on his laurels for several rounds and bided his time. The Italian southpaw even won the second and fourth rounds on one of the judges' cards, which was more by default than by excellent work as Nelson (189¼) failed to show any initiative. With both men looking to counter it was not a great fight to watch, but Nelson picked it up in the sixth when a long right had Aurino down momentarily, and after heads came together in the seventh the referee stopped the contest on the 2.23 mark when it was clear that the latter did not want to continue.

6 May 2000. Juan Carlos Gomez w rsc 3 Imamu Mayfield.
Venue: Swiss Hotel & Resort, Dusseldorf, Germany. **Recognition:** WBC. **Referee:** Lupe Garcia.
Fight Summary: Having had a good look at Mayfield (189¾) the southpaw champion opened up in the third when the latter began to succumb to his sheer power. The finish was not long in coming. After almost doubling Mayfield up with a heavy right to the body Gomez (189¾) immediately followed through with a left to the jaw, and although the latter just about made it to his feet the referee called the fight off just 50 seconds into the session.

7 October 2000. Johnny Nelson w rsc 5 Adam Watt.
Venue: The Dome, Doncaster, England. **Recognition:** WBO. **Referee:** Dave Parris.
Fight Summary: For three rounds the champion did very little, being quite happy to make Watt (189¾) come to him as he pulled away, and it was not until the fourth that he began to use his jab as an attacking weapon rather than as a defensive one. Nelson (189¼) was still cautious in the fifth, but after Watt appeared to be slowing the

latter was given a mandatory 'eight' count when floored by a countering short right. Although Watt did not appear to be hurt, on racing in to Nelson he was floored by a crunching left-right to the jaw. Not even bothering to count Watt out, fearing a badly broken nose and concussion, the referee stopped the contest on the 2.12 mark to allow him immediate medical attention.

9 December 2000. Virgil Hill w rsc 1 Fabrice Tiozzo.
Venue: Astro Bullet Arena, Villeurbanne, France. **Recognition:** WBA. **Referee:** Luis Pabon.
Fight Summary: On becoming the oldest man to win the cruiserweight title the 36-year-old former light heavyweight champion, who had not boxed for over 18 months, created a major shock when stopping Tiozzo (190) with just one second of the opening round remaining. Immediately on the attack behind a solid left jab the much faster Hill (190) soon had Tiozzo over from a right to the face, and although the champion was quickly back into the fray a left to the jaw had him down again. With Hill not letting up, following a battery of blows from both hands Tiozzo was on his way down for the third time when mercifully rescued by the referee.

16 December 2000. Juan Carlos Gomez w rsc 10 Jorge Castro.
Venue: Gruga Hall, Essen, Germany. **Recognition:** WBC. **Referee:** Larry O'Connell.
Fight Summary: Starting as he meant to carry on Gomez (189) had his southpaw right jab in Castro's face right from the off, and for round after round the latter was pounded by a steady array of blows to head and body without looking to go down. With Castro (183) not winning anything, at the end of the eighth the referee allowed him to carry on after the doctor had given the all-clear. The same thing happened at the end of the ninth, but in the tenth Gomez decided enough was enough. After dropping Castro with a big left to the jaw the referee stopped the contest at 1.56 of the session in Gomez's favour even though the former WBA middleweight champion was back on his feet. For record purposes alone, Gomez was deducted a point in the eighth for going low.

27 January 2001. Johnny Nelson w pts 12 George Arias.
Venue: York Hall, Bethnal Green, London, England. **Recognition:** WBO. **Referee:** Bill Connors.
Scorecards: 119-110, 120-108, 120-110.
Fight Summary: In his seventh defence Nelson (189¾) once again settled for a clear points win, even after having Arias (189¼) badly hurt in the opening session from an explosive countering right uppercut. There was no doubting that Arias was tough, going forward throughout the contest. However, although Nelson hit him with some good punches including some solid body shots in the seventh and eighth he could not stop the Brazilian's march. Despite both men turning southpaw at times it did little to change the nature of the contest and, apart from the tenth when Arias earned a share of the round, Nelson was always in control.

6 February 2001. Vassiliy Jirov w co 1 Alex Gonzales.
Venue: Ice Palace, Almaty, Kazakhstan. **Recognition:** IBF. **Referee:** Eddie Cotton.
Fight Summary: There was plenty of action while it lasted. Gonzales (189¾) certainly came to fight, hurting Jirov (188) with a couple of solid shots before the latter responded with some of his own. However, once the southpaw champion had the bit between his teeth there was no stopping him, and at 1.35 of the opening round Gonzales was counted out after being floored by cracking uppercuts to the head and body. Badly stunned, Gonzales had to be carried to the dressing room.

24 March 2001. Vassiliy Jirov w co 1 Terry McGroom.
Venue: MGM Grand, Las Vegas, Nevada, USA. **Recognition:** IBF. **Referee:** Tony Weeks.
Fight Summary: Less than two months after his last defence Jirov (190) was at it again when destroying another challenger inside the opening round, this time it was McGroom (190) who was knocked out on the 1.22 mark. Prior to the finish there was little action as Jirov looked to set up McGroom for his explosive punches, but once he had cornered the latter a terrific left to the body had him over and unable to get up in time to beat the 'ten' count.

21 July 2001. Johnny Nelson w pts 12 Marcelo Dominguez.
Venue: Ponds Forge Leisure Centre, Sheffield, England. **Recognition:** WBO. **Referee:** Bill Connors.
Scorecards: 117-110, 117-110, 119-108.

Fight Summary: Although the tough challenger caused Nelson (189¾) a few problems early on with his aggression and efforts to get inside he was ultimately unable to find the punches that would count in his favour. In the sixth, a round he was actually winning, Dominguez (187½) was docked a point for repeated low blows, and thereafter Nelson stepped up the pace to go well clear when banging in lefts and rights to leave the Argentine gasping. Despite being apprehensive at times, with Nelson happy to outbox Dominguez after several heavy shots from both hands had failed to move him it was another clear, if unexciting, win for him.

8 September 2001. Vassiliy Jirov w rsc 8 Julian Letterlough.
Venue: Lawlor Events Centre, Reno, Nevada, USA. **Recognition:** IBF. **Referee:** Jay Nady.
Fight Summary: Winning every round on the cards the champion had a field day against the tough, six-inch shorter Letterlough (186½), who came out fast before being almost finished off by powerful southpaw blows in the opening session. Taking a steady beating at the hands of Jirov (190) for round after round the only surprise was that Letterlough stayed upright for so long, looking to be one punch away from defeat on several occasions. In the seventh, Letterlough, battered to head and body, was virtually done for. Finally, in the eighth, the referee pulled him out at 1.24 of the session when he was almost knocked senseless by a left uppercut to the jaw after being hit by all manner of heavy shots.

3 November 2001. Juan Carlos Gomez w rsc 6 Pietro Aurino.
Venue: Hanse Hall, Lubeck, Germany. **Recognition:** WBC. **Referee:** Mark Green.
Fight Summary: Outclassing his fellow-southpaw challenger in every round Gomez (190) continued to part-dominate a weight division with a distinct paucity of talent. Dramatically outreached Aurino (190) never had a chance, being dropped by a left cross to the head in the third and on the floor three more times, twice in the fifth and once in the sixth. At 1.42 of the sixth the referee jumped in to rescue the embattled Aurino, who appeared powerless to fight back.

Gomez relinquished his title in early March 2002 in order to campaign in the heavyweight division. To decide the vacancy, Wayne Braithwaite, who had beaten Louis Azille in an eliminator on 17 November, was matched against Vincenzo Cantatore, the WBC International champion.

1 February 2002. Vassiliy Jirov w pts 12 Jorge Castro.
Venue: Celebrity Theatre, Phoenix, Arizona, USA. **Recognition:** IBF. **Referee:** Bobby Ferrara.
Scorecards: 119-109, 119-109, 120-108.
Fight Summary: Challenging for Jirov's title the tubby Castro (187), way above his best fighting weight, went down on points despite rocking the champion every now and again to remind the onlookers of better days. Boxing at distance Jirov (189) was the master, his southpaw jab finding Castro without fail, and it was only when he was at close quarters that he was exposed. A 30-1 underdog, with Castro never in with a chance, it was only his solid chin that enabled him to make it to the final bell.

23 February 2002. Jean-Marc Mormeck w rtd 8 Virgil Hill.
Venue: Sports Palace, Marseilles, France. **Recognition:** WBA. **Referee:** Stan Christodoulou.
Fight Summary: Having reeled off the opening two rounds with some ease the champion could be forgiven for thinking that it was going to be an easy night's work against the cumbersome Mormeck (185). Clearly, Mormeck had not read the script, literally steamrolling Hill (189¾) who began to go downhill as age finally caught up with him. Advancing from the third onwards, pounding the body with solid blows from both hands, Mormeck got right on top of Hill, and at the end of the eighth the latter was retired on his stool after being badly cut over the left eye and driven around the ring in that session.

6 April 2002. Johnny Nelson w co 8 Ezra Sellers.
Venue: Circus Building, Copenhagen, Denmark. **Recognition:** WBO. **Referee:** Andre Van Grootenbruel.
Fight Summary: With Nelson (189½) unable to get going over the first six or seven rounds, having been floored when losing his balance in the fourth round and being hurt in the seventh, he finally put it together in the eighth with a right hander that landed on the dangerous challenger's head and sent him down. While there were those

who thought that Sellers (189) could beat the count, with his eye swelling ominously and obviously still dazed he was counted out in the act of rising.

10 August 2002. Jean-Marc Mormeck w rsc 8 Dale Brown.
Venue: Gaston Deferre Beach Arena, Marseilles, France. **Recognition:** WBA. **Referee:** Luis Pabon.
Fight Summary: Very competitive for five rounds, with the challenger winning at least two of the rounds, by the sixth Mormeck (188) was building up his work-rate. In the seventh, Brown (189½), who was forced to take heavy blows to head and body, was cut on both cheeks and ended the session with his right eye closed. With Mormeck totally on top in the eighth, driving Brown before him and taking nothing in return, the referee rescued the latter on the two-minute mark when it was clear that he had nothing left.

11 October 2002. Wayne Braithwaite w rsc 10 Vincenzo Cantatore.
Venue: The Casino, Campione d'Italia, Italy. **Recognition:** WBC. **Referee:** Lupe Garcia.
Fight Summary: Following Juan Carlos Gomez's abdication, Braithwaite (186) and Cantatore (190) were brought together to contest the vacant crown. In a gruelling contest, it was Braithwaite who ultimately prevailed when the referee rescued the tough Cantatore at 2.03 of the tenth round after he had been badly hurt by big southpaw rights and lefts and was stumbling around the ring. Although both men scored with hard punches Braithwaite was soon at the forefront, flooring Cantatore with a smashing right to the head in the fifth before being cautioned for going low. The eighth round saw Cantatore come on strongly, and after hurting Braithwaite in the ninth the latter was docked a point for holding before raising his game for the finish.

23 November 2002. Johnny Nelson drew 12 Guillermo Jones.
Venue: Storm Arena, Derby, England. **Recognition:** WBO. **Referee:** Paul Thomas.
Scorecards: 116-113, 113-115, 114-114.
Fight Summary: Lucky to escape with his title intact, with *Boxing News* reporting that he won only two rounds at best, Nelson (189) somehow got a draw due to some surprising scoring by two judges to say the least. Whatever fighting there was came from Jones (189), but as an untidy affair with much cuffing and slapping it fell far below championship standard.

21 February 2003. Wayne Braithwaite w rsc 4 Ravea Springs.
Venue: Miccosukee Indian Gaming Centre, Miami, Florida, USA. **Recognition:** WBC. **Referee:** Tommy Kimmons.
Fight Summary: Making his first defence Braithwaite (186) quickly got down to business against his fellow southpaw opponent, but with Springs (184½) up for the battle by the end of the first round it had already become a slugging session. By the third there was only going to be one winner, Braithwaite finally catching up with Springs when dropping him with a couple of rights to the head in the fourth. On being allowed to fight on Springs was then put down by two heavy lefts to the head, and at 2.41 of the session the referee stopped the fight when ruling that the challenger was unable to continue.

1 March 2003. Jean-Marc Mormeck w rsc 8 Alexander Gurov.
Venue: Thomas & Mack Centre, Las Vegas, Nevada, USA. **Recognition:** WBA. **Referee:** Kenny Bayless.
Fight Summary: Appearing in America for the first time Mormeck (187½) made a slow start as his southpaw challenger got his jab going, and it was not until he began working the body that he found success. In what was an exciting fight, when Mormeck picked up the pace in the sixth, landing several solid punches to the head, by the seventh Gurov (188½) was visibly weakening as he was hit with increasing regularity. Given a standing count at the end of the seventh, having been hurt by lefts and rights to the head and sagging on the ropes, Gurov was stopped after just 32 seconds of the eighth following a steady battering from both hands. At the finish two of the judges had Gurov two points ahead.

26 April 2003. James Toney w pts 12 Vassiliy Jirov.
Venue: Foxwoods Resort Casino, Mashantucket, Connecticut, USA. **Recognition:** IBF. **Referee:** Steve Smoger.
Scorecards: 116-110, 117-109, 117-109.
Fight Summary: Despite not being in the greatest shape Toney (190) still had too much for the champion, and after losing the opening two rounds he won the next five when picking up speed. Jirov (188) was never out of the

contest, still managing to hurt Toney now and again with jolting southpaw punches, but in the eighth round he was deducted a point for going low and failed to win a round thereafter. Looking for a finish in the 12th, Toney eventually had Jirov over with a right-left-right combination that followed several unanswered shots to the head, but the bell rang before any further damage could be done.

After Toney handed in his belt in January 2004 to concentrate on the heavyweight division, Kelvin Davis, who had outpointed Louis Azille in an eliminator on 24 October, was matched against Ezra Sellers to decide the vacancy.

15 November 2003. Johnny Nelson w pts 12 Alexander Petkovic.
Venue: Upper Franconia Arena, Bayreuth, Germany. **Recognition:** WBO. **Referee:** Genaro Rodriguez.
Scorecards: 115-113, 115-113, 114-114.
Fight Summary: Geared up for his number one contender Nelson (189½) gave very few chances to Petkovic (188¾), while controlling the fight with the jab and looking sharp. There were no knockdowns, and while it was clear that the challenger would be a tough nut to crack it was also clear that he had no idea as to how to break the champion's defences down, merely following him around and swinging punches in the vain hope that they might connect. What did surprise was the scoring of the three judges, who must have awarded rounds to Petkovic merely on the grounds of coming forward rather than landing scoring punches.

13 December 2003. Wayne Braithwaite w co 1 Luis Andres Pineda.
Venue: Boardwalk Hall, Atlantic City, New Jersey, USA. **Recognition:** WBC. **Referee:** Eddie Cotton.
Fight Summary: Starting out as he meant to win the title in a hurry Pineda (199) began unloading heavy blows from either hand before being badly hurt by a big left as Braithwaite (189) momentarily switched to southpaw. Following that success Braithwaite sent Pineda crashing from a right to the head, and although the latter was almost up at 'six' he fell back down and was counted out.

17 April 2004. Wayne Braithwaite w pts 12 Louis Azille.
Venue: Madison Square Garden, Manhattan, NYC, New York, USA. **Recognition:** WBC. **Referee:** Eddie Claudio.
Scorecards: 119-108, 120-107, 118-107.
Fight Summary: Having earlier knocked out Azille (193¾) in an eliminator, with the champion expected to repeat the feat he came close to doing just that when dropping his man with a terrific left hook to the head in the third round. Unfortunately for Braithwaite (188) both of his hands were damaged early on, an injury that allowed Azille to stay in the fight. Despite the much shorter Azille landing the occasional heavy shot, Braithwaite took virtually every round as he biffed and banged away at his tough rival without ever being able to finish him off.

1 May 2004. Kelvin Davis w rsc 8 Ezra Sellers.
Venue: Jai-Alai Fronton, Miami, Florida, USA. **Recognition:** IBF. **Referee:** Frank Santore Jnr.
Fight Summary: Fighting for the title vacated by James Toney, who failed to make a defence, the chunky Davis (190) won every round when wearing Sellers (190) down for a stoppage win at 2.33 of the eighth. Early on it was clear that Sellers, a southpaw, was looking for an early victory, but after hitting Davis with his best punches he was dropped heavily in the fourth by a big right to the head. Thereafter, it would be only a matter of time for Sellers, who was badly cut on the left eye in the seventh, and in the eighth after taking a one-sided beating the referee finally called it off.

When Davis was stripped on 9 February 2005 for failing to agree a defence against O'Neil Bell, the latter was matched against Dale Brown to decide the vacant title.

22 May 2004. Jean-Marc Mormeck w pts 12 Virgil Hill.
Venue: Carnival City Big Top Arena, Brakpan, South Africa. **Recognition:** WBA. **Referee:** Wally Snowball.
Scorecards: 115-114, 115-113, 115-113.
Fight Summary: Just a mere shadow of his former self Hill (194¾) lost his return match against the champion by a unanimous decision, taking a battering in the process as his long career caught up with him. Although Hill was in survival mode for much of the time, being forced to take heavy blows to head and body, he continued to show his defensive skills as Mormeck (196¼) forced the fight. Sustaining a swollen left eye in the third made Hill's task even

more difficult, and after he was dropped by a right to the jaw in the eighth his case looked hopeless. That Hill came back to take three of the remaining four rounds as Mormeck relaxed the pressure did not distort the fact he was past his best, something he recognised when announcing his retirement from the ring.

4 September 2004. Johnny Nelson w rsc 7 Ruediger May.
Venue: Gruga Hall, Essen, Germany. **Recognition:** WBO. **Referee:** Axel Zielke.
Fight Summary: Despite being firm friends it counted for nothing once the action got underway as May (198¾) took the early initiative while the champion settled in. However, by the third round, Nelson (199½) was beginning to go on the offensive, getting in solid combinations, and following a situation where he was deducted two points for pushing in the sixth he cut loose. Thereafter, it was all Nelson as the challenger tired. Having dropped May with a heavy right to the head in the seventh, on getting to his feet it was apparent that the latter was through as Nelson stormed in with damaging blows hitting the target. With May all over the place and not fighting back the referee called it off on the 2.29 mark.

2 April 2005. Jean-Marc Mormeck w pts 12 Wayne Braithwaite.
Venue: DCU Centre, Worcester, Massachusetts, USA. **Recognition:** WBA/WBC/The Ring. **Referee:** Richard Flaherty.
Scorecards: 116-110, 114-112, 115-111.
Fight Summary: In a battle to unify two titles and involving the vacant *Ring* Championship Belt, Mormeck (198), the WBA champion, proved too good for the switch-hitting Braithwaite (188), his WBC counterpart. For five rounds it was very competitive, both men getting home with heavy shots, but in the sixth Mormeck got on top when driving in solid blows to Braithwaite's head and body. That was followed by Mormeck having Braithwaite down from a cracking right to the head in the seventh. Docked a point for holding in the eighth and badly cut over the left eye in the same session, Braithwaite dug deep to somehow stay in the contest when taking two of the last three rounds as Mormeck tired.

20 May 2005. O'Neil Bell w pts 12 Dale Brown.
Venue: Seminole Hard Rock Casino, Hollywood, Florida, USA. **Recognition:** IBF. **Referee:** Armando Garcia.
Scorecards: 115-113, 116-112, 117-111.
Fight Summary: After Kelvin Davis was stripped for failing to defend against Bell, the man from Georgia made good his opportunity when outscoring Brown (198¾) in a tough fight that many thought could have gone either way. It was the skill and punch-picking of Brown against the constant aggression of Bell (199), but by the fourth he was cut over the right eye and had a swelling on the other optic, testament to Bell's headwork and punching power. Despite boxing on the back foot Brown continued to pick Bell off with the jab and right-hand counters, and although ahead on the punch stats at the final bell it was Bell who got the decision.

26 August 2005. O'Neil Bell w co 11 Sebastiaan Rothmann.
Venue: Seminole Hard Rock Casino, Hollywood, Florida, USA. **Recognition:** IBF. **Referee:** Tommy Kimmons.
Fight Summary: Realising that he to stick and move if he wanted to stay in the fight, after taking heavy punishment in the opening session the challenger took over the next four rounds, almost knocking Bell (200) over in the fifth after catching him with several good punches followed by a right to the jaw. Badly damaged around both eyes Rothmann (194) fought on bravely, giving and taking in equal numbers, and going into the 11th was level on two cards and ahead on the other. Desperately trying to hang on to his title, Bell was still taking the jab. All of that counted for nothing when Bell finally sent Rothmann down to be counted out at 2.09 of the session after catching him with two long rights to the temple. It had been a hard night's work for Bell, made even more difficult when he was deducted points in the seventh and ninth for low blows.

26 November 2005. Johnny Nelson w pts 12 Vincenzo Cantatore.
Venue: Sports Palace, Rome, Italy. **Recognition:** WBO. **Referee:** Roberto Ramirez.
Scorecards: 116-111, 115-112, 112-115.
Fight Summary: Continuing to surprise all boxing people alike the champion stayed one step ahead of Cantatore (199¼), jabbing, moving and making the latter miss more often than not before he was dropped by a big left hook in the ninth and had to fight hard to stay in the contest. With Nelson (198½) in trouble the round was timed at 4.20, something that was par for the course when an Italian fighter had an opponent on the go, and he did well to

hang on in until the bell. After a quiet tenth Nelson was badly hurt in the 11th by another heavy blow to the temple, but to his great credit he got through the session and held on well to the final bell to be the recipient of a split decision.

At the Millennium Stadium, Cardiff, Wales, on 8 July 2006, Enzo Maccarinelli stopped Marcelo Dominguez in the ninth round to win the vacant WBO 'interim' title.

Following Nelson's decision to retire after breaking down in training in September 2006, Maccarinelli was immediately upgraded to full champion status.

7 January 2006. O'Neil Bell w rsc 10 Jean-Marc Mormeck.
Venue: MSG Theatre, Manhattan, NYC, New York, USA. **Recognition:** IBF/WBA/WBC/The Ring. **Referee:** Wayne Kelly.
Fight Summary: Challenging for three more championship belts to add to his IBF title, Bell (199½) was forced to take plenty of hits in the opening six sessions as Mormeck (197¾) threw everything but the kitchen sink at him. However, by the seventh Mormeck was visibly tiring from his efforts and it was Bell's turn to go on the offensive, one judge making it a 10-7 round. Although Mormeck just about held Bell at bay in the eighth and ninth, the tenth saw his demise as the latter poured in punch after punch, the referee eventually halting the contest on the 2.50 mark with the Frenchman on the floor.

On 27 January, at the Tropicana Hotel & Casino, Atlantic City, New Jersey, Virgil Hill won the vacant WBA 'second tier' title when outpointing Valery Brudov over 12 rounds.

Meanwhile, in April, Bell forfeited the IBF title for not fulfilling his mandatory requirements, and to fill his shoes a match was made between Steve Cunningham, who had outpointed Kelvin Davis over 12 rounds at the Gund Arena, Cleveland, Ohio on 3 September 2005 in an eliminator, and Guillermo Jones. When the contest was called off at the last moment due to a contractual dispute, Cunningham was later matched against Krzysztof Wlodarczyk, a fighter who had lost just once in 36 contests.

Valery Brudov won the vacant WBA 'interim' title on 2 December, at the Bercy Sports Palace, Paris, France, when stopping Luis Andres Pineda in the 11th round.

14 October 2006. Enzo Maccarinelli w rsc 1 Mark Hobson.
Venue: MEN Arena, Manchester, England. **Recognition:** WBO. **Referee:** Terry O'Connor.
Fight Summary: Having been handed the title on Johnny Nelson's retirement Maccarinelli (199) did not hang around against an old opponent and, following a short period of feeling his way in, a heavy right to the side of the head sent Hobson (200) crashing to the floor. Although he was just about upright at 'nine' the referee continued the count, but because Hobson was standing the result was classified as a stoppage.

25 November 2006. Krzysztof Wlodarczyk w pts 12 Steve Cunningham.
Venue: Torwar Sports Hall, Warsaw, Poland. **Recognition:** IBF. **Referee:** Tony Weeks.
Scorecards: 116-112, 115-113, 109-119.
Fight Summary: Contested for the vacant title after O'Neil Bell had been stripped, it was Wlodarczyk (192¼) who took the split decision when finishing stronger than Cunningham (193½) in a well contested match-up. Both men had struggled to gain control throughout, Wlodarczyk landing heavy punches in the seventh before Cunningham came back with a cracking uppercut in the eighth. Despite the closeness of the fight, one judge gave Cunningham 11 rounds.

17 March 2007. Jean-Marc Mormeck w pts 12 O'Neil Bell.
Venue: Marcel Cerdan Sports Palace, Levallois-Perret, France. **Recognition:** WBA/WBC/The Ring. **Referee:** Massimo Barrovecchio.
Scorecards: 115-113, 115-113, 116-112.

Fight Summary: Bell (198½) lost his remaining three championship belts after being generally outboxed by Mormeck (198¼) in what was a return bout. Once again Mormeck started strongly when pushing Bell back with solid combinations, but the latter always looked dangerous with heavy counters, especially in the sixth when catching the Frenchman with solid blows from both hands. Under pressure several times in the second half of the contest, Mormeck began to use his better skills, boxing and moving, as Bell continually got frustrated with his inability to land a finisher.

At the SYMA Sport & Leisure Centre, Budapest, Hungary, on 16 June, Firat Arslan outpointed, the holder, Valery Brudov, over 12 rounds to win the WBA 'interim' title.

7 April 2007. Enzo Maccarinelli w rsc 1 Bobby Gunn.
Venue: Millennium Stadium, Cardiff, Wales. **Recognition:** WBO. **Referee:** Mark Nelson.
Fight Summary: A bad mismatch saw the champion batter the much shorter Gunn (195) almost from the opening bell, landing solid blows from either hand. At one point Gunn was given an 'eight' count after the ropes saved him from going down and with his nose badly damaged, as Maccarinelli (200) worked him over, he was rescued by the referee after 2.35 of the first had elapsed.

26 May 2007. Steve Cunningham w pts 12 Krzysztof Wlodarczyk.
Venue: Spodek Arena, Katowice, Poland. **Recognition:** IBF. **Referee:** Dave Parris.
Scorecards: 116-112, 115-112, 114-114.
Fight Summary: In a reversal of fortunes, Cunningham (194) outpointed the champion by a majority decision after a rematch had been ordered when it was discovered that neither fighter had undergone a post-fight urine test in their previous bout. This time around with Cunningham throwing far more punches than Wlodarczyk (196), despite many being blocked, enough got through to convince the judges. The only knockdown came in the fourth when Wlodarczyk went on one knee following a jab to the eye, and although he came on strongly towards the finish it was not enough.

21 July 2007. Enzo Maccarinelli w pts 12 Wayne Braithwaite.
Venue: International Arena, Cardiff, Wales. **Recognition:** WBO. **Referee:** Mickey Vann.
Scorecards: 118-109, 120-107, 119-108.
Fight Summary: Up against a tough southpaw challenger, Maccarinelli (194) proved good value for his points win, knocking Braithwaite (195¼) down in the fifth with solid combinations and boxing well within himself. For his part, Braithwaite, who finished with a badly swollen right eye, spent too much time on the ropes looking to counter, and while he posed a threat with his power punching he failed to take the fight to Maccarinelli. Apart from the third round when a cracking right to the jaw put Maccarinelli at risk that was it from Braithwaite.

3 November 2007. Enzo Maccarinelli w rsc 4 Mohamed Azzaoui.
Venue: Millennium Stadium, Cardiff, Wales. **Recognition:** WBO. **Referee:** Dave Parris.
Fight Summary: Although Azzaoui (197¾), who replaced Ezra Sellers at short notice, had the heavy-hitting champion down in the first from what was ruled as a slip, the Welshman eventually caught up with him in the fourth when a crunching left to the body saw the Algerian rolling around the floor before the referee halted the fight on the 58-second mark. Despite losing the opening three rounds the unbeaten Azzaoui had given Maccarinelli (197¾) something to think about, his high guard and fast jab causing early problems. However, once Maccarinelli had found the range there was only going to be one winner.

10 November 2007. David Haye w rsc 7 Jean-Marc Mormeck.
Venue: Marcel Cerdan Sports Palace, Levallois-Perret, France. **Recognition:** WBA/WBC/The Ring. **Referee:** Franco Ciminale.
Fight Summary: Finally getting his chance of a crack at Mormeck (199), the holder of three championship belts, Haye (199½) started strongly before coming under pressure from rights to the head, one of which floored him in the fourth following a terrific left hook. Keeping his cool Haye gradually recovered his strength, coming back well with solid blows to the head in the fifth. In the sixth, despite being cut over the right eye Haye began to dominate, his speed and movement being too much for Mormeck, and in the seventh he dropped the latter following a burst

of heavy punches from both hands. Although Mormeck was on his feet at the count of 'eight' the referee quickly decided that he was in no fit state to continue. The finish was timed at 1.05 of the session.

On 24 November, at the Freiberger Arena, Dresden, Germany, Firat Arslan won the WBA 'second tier' title when outpointing the champion, Virgil Hill, over 12 rounds. Earlier, it had been incorrectly reported that Hill had been stripped after losing a non-title fight at the weight.

29 December 2007. Steve Cunningham w rsc 12 Marco Huck.
Venue: Seidensticker Hall, Bielefeld, Germany. **Recognition:** IBF. **Referee:** Marlon Wright.
Fight Summary: While Huck (198½) started well there were early signs that this would not be his night when the tough champion took a crashing right to the head in the opener without blinking. Even though the brawling Huck kept on coming, Cunningham (192¾) generally tied his man up while working the body. Several times Cunningham was pushed or thrown to the floor, but it did not change his focus even though Huck grew more and more wild. By the 12th, sensing that Huck was behind on points and extremely tired Cunningham opened up, dropping his man for what the referee deemed to be a slip before really going to town. With Huck being battered non-stop the referee finally called the fight off at 1.56 of the session after the challenger's corner threw the towel in.

8 March 2008. David Haye w rsc 2 Enzo Maccarinelli.
Venue: O2 Arena, Greenwich, London, England. **Recognition:** WBA/WBC/WBO/The Ring. **Referee:** John Keane.
Fight Summary: Putting up his three championship belts against Maccarinelli (197), the holder of the WBO title, Haye (198) started in confident fashion, finding his distance and showing excellent speed as he looked to measure his rival. Even though he was cut by the left eye in the second nothing was going to stop Haye, who moved in menacingly with both hands before cornering Maccarinelli and smashing in heavy blows. When the Welshman eventually slid to the floor, prior to getting up in a dazed state, the referee stopped the fight at 2.04 of the session.

Firat Arslan outpointed Darnell Wilson over 12 rounds at the Hanns Martin-Schleyer Hall, Stuttgart, Germany on 3 May to retain the WBA 'second tier' title.

Having decided to move up to the heavyweight division, Haye relinquished the WBC title on 12 May and a few days later he notified the WBA that he would be sending back his belt. He also stated on 23 May that he would not be defending *The Ring* Championship Belt again. Following that, Arslan was handed full WBA title honours on 16 June, while the WBC set up a match between Giacobbe Fragomeni and Rudolf Kraj to decide their vacancy. Fragomeni's only defeat in 26 contests had been at the hands of Haye, while Kraj was getting his chance due to his win over Matt Godfrey (w pts 12 König Arena, Krefeld, Germany on 8 March) in an eliminator.

Although Haye relinquished the WBO title on 22 July, it took the body some while to fill his boots. Eventually, Victor Emilio Ramirez contested and won the vacant WBO 'interim' title when forcing Alexander Alekseev to retire after nine rounds at the Castle Guard Arena, Dusseldorf, Germany on 17 January 2009, before being promoted to full championship status a few days after. Following that decision, Ola Afolabi knocked out Maccarinelli in the ninth round to win the vacant WBO 'interim' title at the MEN Arena, Manchester, England on 14 March 2009. Maccarinelli had initially been matched against Johnathon Banks, but when he pulled out Afolabi stepped in at relatively short notice.

27 September 2008. Guillermo Jones w rsc 10 Firat Arslan.
Venue: Color Line Arena, Hamburg, Germany. **Recognition:** WBA. **Referee:** Luis Pabon.
Fight Summary: Arslan (198¼), who was making his first defence after being appointed champion when David Haye decided to move up among the heavyweights, came unstuck when winning just two rounds at best before being halted at 2.33 of the tenth. The southpaw champion appeared early on to have no defence against a steady stream of uppercuts from both hands as Jones (199½) imposed himself, and suffered a damaged nose, a cut over the right eye and a badly cut lower lip. Although there were no knockdowns the game Arslan was taking a battering and at 2.33 of the tenth, when he was under steady fire and not fighting back, the referee called the fight off.

Steve Herelius won the vacant WBA 'interim' title when forcing Firat Arslan to retire at the end of the 11th round at the Porsche Arena, Stuttgart, Germany on 3 July 2010.

24 October 2008. Giacobbe Fragomeni w tdec 8 Rudolf Kraj.
Venue: Sports Palace, Milan, Italy. **Recognition:** WBC. **Referee:** Yuji Fukuchi.
Scorecards: 77-74, 76-75, 77-74.
Fight Summary: Contested for the vacant title after David Haye decided to move up to heavyweight, it was Fragomeni (194½) who became the new champion after being awarded the technical decision at the end of the eighth round. Although winning the opening two rounds, Kraj (198½) was soon under pressure from an aggressive Fragomeni who continuously went forward. In the seventh an accidental butt that saw Kraj being deducted a point left Fragomeni with a bad cut over the right eye. Allowed to fight on it was clear that Fragomeni would be unable to continue for long, and after an inspection by the ringside doctor it was all over.

11 December 2008. Tomasz Adamek w pts 12 Steve Cunningham.
Venue: Prudential Centre, Newark, New Jersey, USA. **Recognition:** IBF/The Ring. **Referee:** Earl Morton.
Scorecards: 115-112, 116-110, 112-114.
Fight Summary: As well as Cunningham's IBF title being on the line, the vacant *Ring* Championship Belt was also up for grabs in this one. In an exciting fight of give and take the tough Adamek (198) picked up the two belts that were on offer after dropping Cunningham (197) three times; in the second, fourth and eighth. The knockdown in the fourth came when Cunningham, who had been giving Adamek a real going over, was dropped by a big right that strangely saw only one of the judges making it a 10-8 round. Following the fight Cunningham stated that he had planned to box but getting carried away when looking for a kayo win had cost him.

27 February 2009. Tomasz Adamek w rsc 8 Johnathon Banks.
Venue: Prudential Centre, Newark, New Jersey, USA. **Recognition:** IBF/The Ring. **Referee:** Eddie Cotton.
Fight Summary: With Adamek (199) defending two championship belts, Banks (200) made an excellent start when winning three of the opening four rounds, solid lefts and rights keeping the champion at distance. However, by the fifth Adamek was taking the fight to Banks when targeting the body, and in the sixth the latter was given time out after one went low. Although caught heavily by a right himself in the eighth, Adamek shook it off before twice blasting Banks to the canvas and forcing the referee to intervene at 1.30 of the session.

16 May 2009. Giacobbe Fragomeni drew 12 Krzysztof Wlodarczyk.
Venue: Grand Theatre, Rome, Italy. **Recognition:** WBC. **Referee:** Ian-John Lewis.
Scorecards: 114-113, 112-116, 114-114.
Fight Summary: This was a tough give and take affair in which the 39-year-old champion retained his title by means of a split draw despite being knocked down twice in the ninth by Wlodarczyk (198½). With only one of the knockdowns counting due to hitting Fragomeni (197¼) while he was down, Wlodarczyk lost his chance of becoming champion when the round was scored as 10-8 instead of 10-7. Apart from that there was never much between them, especially after Fragomeni came back strongly to win two of the last three sessions on work-rate alone.

16 May 2009. Victor Emilio Ramirez w pts 12 Ali Ismailov.
Venue: Luna Park Stadium, Buenos Aires, Argentina. **Recognition:** WBO. **Referee:** Michael Ortega.
Scorecards: 116-112, 115-113, 113-115.
Fight Summary: Having been handed the title after David Haye returned his belt Ramirez (198½) made his first defence a successful one when taking a hard-earned split decision over Ismailov (197½). Contested at a fast pace both men had their successes when landing heavy shots, but with neither able to make much headway it was always going to be close. Although Ismailov was the first to show any form of tiredness, when beginning to clinch more in the last two or three sessions, Ramirez was unable to take advantage.

11 July 2009. Tomasz Adamek w rtd 4 Bobby Gunn.
Venue: Prudential Centre, Newark, New Jersey, USA. **Recognition:** IBF/The Ring. **Referee:** Earl Brown.

Fight Summary: Regardless of the fact that Gunn (194) had been beaten easily by Enzo Maccarinelli, he was matched against a two-belt champion who had lost just one fight in 38 and had mixed at a much higher level. There was no doubting Gunn's spirit as Adamek (199) walked through him, but the latter was unable to score a knockdown despite the result being inevitable. However, at the end of round four, having taken many unanswered blows and being saved by the bell, Gunn was retired by his corner.

After Adamek relinquished the IBF title on 18 October, having decided to fight in the heavyweight division, Steve Cunningham and Troy Ross were signed up to find a new champion. Since losing the IBF title to Adamek, Cunningham had beaten Wayne Braithwaite (w pts 12 at the Bank Atlantic Centre, Sunrise, Florida on 11 July) to win an eliminator and become the top-ranking fighter in *The Ring*, while Ross was rated at number five in the same magazine.

When it was clear that Adamek was staying in the heavyweight division, *The Ring* Championship Belt became available on 20 February 2010 for the next pair of outstanding candidates to contest as and when.

29 August 2009. Marco Huck w pts 12 Victor Emilio Ramirez.
Venue: Gerry Weber Stadium, Halle, Germany. **Recognition:** WBO. **Referee:** Mark Nelson.
Scorecards: 116-111, 115-112, 116-111.
Fight Summary: In a battle of sluggers, it was Huck (198½) who prevailed over the champion when taking the unanimous decision. Most of the fans thought that Huck would be drawn into a war of attrition, but he surprised all bar his corner by sticking to a game plan that kept Ramirez (199) busy for much of the time. When Huck did take Ramirez on at his own game in the main he was successful, although he was eventually deducted a point in the 11th for going low, having transgressed earlier. While Ramirez was the stronger, Huck was more controlled.

21 November 2009. Zsolt Erdei w pts 12 Giacobbe Fragomeni.
Venue: Sparkassen Arena, Kiel, Germany. **Recognition:** WBC. **Referee:** Vic Drakulich.
Scorecards: 115-113, 115-113, 114-114.
Fight Summary: It was the lighter challenger who came through in an extremely close contest to nick the title from the hard-working Fragomeni (196) who never let up. Having outboxed Fragomeni for the opening four rounds Erdei (179) began to be pegged back as the Italian's strength took its toll but, despite tiring, the latter fought on well, his better quality punches just about getting him home.

Further to Erdei vacating the WBC title on 22 January 2010 in favour of fighting in the light heavyweight division, Fragomeni and Krzysztof Wlodarczyk were matched to find a new champion.

5 December 2009. Marco Huck w pts 12 Ola Afolabi.
Venue: The Arena, Ludwigsburg, Germany. **Recognition:** WBO. **Referee:** Joe Cortez.
Scorecards: 115-113, 115-112, 116-112.
Fight Summary: Making his first defence against the English-born Afolabi (196½), the 'interim' champion, Huck (196) prevailed in a difficult fight to score. Ultimately, it was Huck's work-rate against the better skills of Afolabi. Known for his aggressive, charging tactics Huck was always likely to be involved close up, and in the fifth he was badly hurt by a clash of heads followed by a heavy right uppercut that had him hanging on. However, Afolabi was unable to sustain the pressure that was building, while Huck continued to take the eye with short bursts of action.

13 March 2010. Marco Huck w rsc 3 Adam Richards.
Venue: Max Schmeling Hall, Berlin, Germany. **Recognition:** WBO. **Referee:** Mark Nelson.
Fight Summary: Initially happy to weigh his challenger up, midway through the second round Huck (198½) picked up the pace when sending in solid shots to the head, although many were blocked. The third saw more of the same as Huck moved forward with intent before a clash of heads left Richards (199¼) with a badly cut scalp. Having taken a count to gain some respite Richards was then subjected to some heavy hits and, as the referee stepped in to halt proceedings after two crashing rights had landed, he toppled over. The finish was timed at 2.30 of the session.

Cruiserweight Division

1 May 2010. Marco Huck w rtd 9 Brian Minto.
Venue: Weser-Ems Hall, Oldenburg, Germany. **Recognition:** WBO. **Referee:** Robert Byrd.
Fight Summary: Fighting out of a crouch, the tough challenger tore into Huck (199) from the start, only to be countered heavily for his pains virtually throughout the contest. Down in the third from a straight right to the head at one stage Minto (198½) threw himself to the floor when missing wildly, and he was downed again in the fifth by a solid right hook. Although Minto continued his forward march, by the end of the ninth his corner wisely pulled him out following another tough round.

15 May 2010. Krzysztof Wlodarczyk w rsc 8 Giacobbe Fragomeni.
Venue: Atlas Arena, Lodz, Poland. **Recognition:** WBC. **Referee:** Frank Garza.
Fight Summary: With the vacant title up for grabs after Zsolt Erdei decided to move up to heavyweight, by the fifth round Wlodarczyk (197) had begun to impose himself on Fragomeni (197¾), eventually dropping the latter in the sixth. From this point on Wlodarczyk's extra power and height and reach advantages showed and in the eighth a solid jab followed by a crunching right uppercut set Fragomeni up for the finish. Unable to fight back and under constant pressure from a barrage of punches, Fragomeni was floored by a left hook before being rescued by the referee after 44 seconds of the session.

5 June 2010. Steve Cunningham w rsc 4 Troy Ross.
Venue: Jahn Sports Forum, Neubrandenburg, Germany. **Recognition:** IBF. **Referee:** Bill Clancy.
Fight Summary: Contested for the vacant title after Tomasz Adamek decided to move up among the heavyweights, Cunningham (193) regained his old title when Ross (193¾), a southpaw, was pulled out of the contest by the referee at the end of the fourth round on the advice of the ringside doctor. It had been fairly even up to that point, with Cunningham marginally ahead despite being dropped by a straight left to the chest in the fourth. Towards the end of the session Ross's swollen left eye began pouring blood after taking a hard hit, and it was that injury that ultimately ended the fight.

21 August 2010. Marco Huck w rsc 5 Matt Godfrey.
Venue: Fair Hall, Erfurt, Germany. **Recognition:** WBO. **Referee:** Genaro Rodriguez.
Fight Summary: Keeping up the pressure from the opening bell, despite being outboxed at times, the champion caught up with Godfrey (198¾) in the second round when a hard left-right dropped the American southpaw. In the third the wild-punching Huck (198½) went low with a blow that floored Godfrey, and although the latter was given the benefit of time out there was no points deduction. Having battered Godfrey in the fourth Huck stepped it up in the fifth, dropping the challenger twice before the referee finally stepped in at 2.18 of the session.

25 September 2010. Krzysztof Wlodarczyk w pts 12 Jason Robinson.
Venue: Torwar Sports Hall, Warsaw, Poland. **Recognition:** WBC. **Referee:** Daniel Van de Wiele.
Scorecards: 117-111, 116-112, 115-113.
Fight Summary: Making his first defence, Wlodarczyk (197¼) generally initiated the majority of attacks, solid right hands to the head that followed the left lead notching up the points over his awkward southpaw opponent. Although Robinson (199½) came into the fight more, after the halfway stage he did not do enough to impress the judges, going down by a unanimous decision. Showing good defensive skill, had Robinson upped his work-rate and gone on the offensive the result could well have been different.

2 October 2010. Guillermo Jones w rsc 11 Valery Brudov.
Venue: Roberto Duran Arena, Panama City, Panama. **Recognition:** WBA. **Referee:** Luis Pabon.
Fight Summary: Out of the ring for over two years and making his first defence, Jones (200) came back slowly before finding his feet in the second half of the contest. It had been a battle of jabs up until then, but once Jones had worked off his ring rust and let the punches flow the tide turned as solid combinations forced Brudov (193) on to the back foot. By round nine a cut over Brudov's left eye was giving cause for concern, and with the latter shipping punishment the referee called the bout off at 2.16 of the 11th.

On 12 February 2011, Steve Herelius was stopped in the seventh round by Yoan Pablo Hernandez at the RWE Rhein-Ruhr Sports Hall, Mulheim, Germany, thus losing his WBA 'interim' title. Hernandez vacated the title on challenging Steve Cunningham for the IBF crown.

18 December 2010. Marco Huck w pts 12 Denis Lebedev.
Venue: Max Schmeling Hall, Berlin, Germany. **Recognition:** WBO. **Referee:** Eddie Cotton.
Scorecards: 115-113, 115-113, 112-116.
Fight Summary: Up against yet another southpaw challenger, Huck (199¼) changed his normal style for this one, boxing well on the back foot while sending in solid counters from both hands. The champion complained afterwards that he had suffered damage to his ribs in the fourth, which probably explained the fact that Lebedev (198¼) had his best rounds in the fifth, sixth and seventh when forcing Huck to the ropes and sending in powerful blows to the body. When Huck won two of the last three sessions on two of the judges' cards the split decision was his, but had Lebedev pushed on there would almost certainly have been a new champion.

12 February 2011. Steve Cunningham w pts 12 Enad Licina.
Venue: RWE Rhein-Ruhr Sports Hall, Mulheim, Germany. **Recognition:** IBF. **Referee:** Charlie Fitch.
Scorecards: 118-110, 117-111, 115-113.
Fight Summary: The challenger was never out of the contest, continually trying to get to close quarters where he could work Cunningham (198½) over with the right hand. Cunningham, however, was the better boxer of the pair, and although Licina (198¼) gave him a run for his money he was nearly always second best. Generally boxing on the back foot the taller Cunningham controlled the fight with his left jab, but when he had to he was able to call on solid right hands as Licina tried to turn the contest into a brawl.

2 April 2011. Krzysztof Wlodarczyk w pts 12 Francisco Palacios.
Venue: Sports Hall, Bydgoszcz, Poland. **Recognition:** WBC. **Referee:** Luigi Muratore.
Scorecards: 116-113, 118-112, 113-115.
Fight Summary: In what was a much closer fight than two of the scorecards suggested, according to reports, the challenger made life difficult for Wlodarczyk (198½), his tactics negating much of the latter's work. Despite the fight being a bore, Palacios (197¾), switching from orthodox to southpaw and back again, confused Wlodarczyk who mainly followed his man around the ring with the left jab, whilst the Puerto Rican favoured left-hand counters. There were few solid punches thrown and rarely any moments of excitement.

2 April 2011. Marco Huck w pts 12 Ran Nakash.
Venue: Gerry Weber Stadium, Halle, Germany. **Recognition:** WBO. **Referee:** Joe Cortez.
Scorecards: 118-110, 116-112, 118-110.
Fight Summary: Defending his title for the sixth time, Huck (198½) met Israel's Nakash (199¾), a late substitute for Giacobbe Fragomeni and a man with 25 wins in a row on his record. Making Huck fight all the way, his charging in head-first tactics followed up with swinging blows to head and body, Nakash made it an exciting fight. Regardless of that Huck stuck to his boxing, using the jab well to set up heavy uppercuts from either hand as Nakash came forward, and although the latter received a badly swollen left eye in the seventh he managed to make it to the final bell.

16 July 2011. Marco Huck w rsc 10 Hugo Hernan Garay.
Venue: Olympia Ice Sports Centre, Munich, Germany. **Recognition:** WBO. **Referee:** Luis Pabon.
Fight Summary: Down in the opening round the challenger came back strongly to provide Huck (197½) with a real test, closing the ring down and banging away with both hands. In the third Huck was deducted a point for hitting Garay (197½) behind the head, but by now he was beginning to assert his authority on the tough Argentine. Despite Garay's hardy work ethic Huck's two-handed assaults were giving him plenty of problems and after being dropped heavily in the tenth, following a right cross that was backed up by a left hook, the referee came to his rescue at 1.10 of the session.

1 October 2011. Yoan Pablo Hernandez w tdec 6 Steve Cunningham.
Venue: Jahn Sports Forum, Neubrandenburg, Germany. **Recognition:** IBF. **Referee:** Mickey Vann.

Scorecards: 59-54, 58-55, 56-57.
Fight Summary: Knocked down by a southpaw left hook from Hernandez (200) in the opener, from which he required two attempts to make it to his feet, the champion was saved by the bell and then spent most of the second trying to regain his equilibrium before coming back strongly in the third. In that session, however, a clash of heads saw Hernandez cut on the left temple and in the sixth another accidental coming together left him badly cut over the right eye too. With Hernandez having great difficulty in seeing clearly, the referee, on advice from the ringside doctor, stopped the contest at the end of the session and called for the cards. Although one of the judges had Cunningham (199¼) in front at that stage, he lost his title on a split decision.

22 October 2011. Marco Huck w co 6 Rogelio Omar Rossi.
Venue: The Arena, Ludwigsburg, Germany. **Recognition:** WBO. **Referee:** Paul Thomas.
Fight Summary: The tall southpaw challenger certainly came to fight, several of his punches going low, and in the third he was docked a point as Huck (198½) took yet another downstairs. It did not deter Huck, however, and shortly after he dropped Rossi (197½) with a blow to the back of the head. It was now clear that Rossi, badly swollen under the right eye, did not have the power to bother Huck but then the latter dropped his rival with a blow delivered after the bell, to end the fourth round, and received a two-point deduction. Having already been knocked down twice in the fifth, the fight ended for Rossi when a batch of combinations followed by a cracking right to the jaw saw him counted out at 1.09 of the sixth.

On 3 March 2012, at the Esprit Arena, Dusseldorf, Germany, Ola Afolabi won the vacant WBO 'interim' title when Valery Brudov retired at the end of the fifth round.

5 November 2011. Guillermo Jones w rsc 6 Michael Marrone.
Venue: Seminole Hard Rock Live Arena, Hollywood, Florida, USA. **Recognition:** WBA. **Referee:** Telis Assimenios.
Fight Summary: Coming down from heavyweight the challenger was way out of his depth in this one, being forced to take heavy punishment as Jones (197) picked him apart from head to body. In the second, one of the judges gave it as a 10-7 round, so dominant was Jones. It did not get much better for Marrone (198¾), who was dropped by a right to the head in the fifth and saved by the bell. Although Marrone came out for the sixth, after he was floored by a volley of combinations to the head, when he made it to his feet the referee called the fight off on advice from his corner, the finish being timed at 1.55 of the session.

Denis Lebedev won the vacant WBA 'interim' title when outpointing an ageing James Toney over 12 rounds at the Khodynka Ice Palace, Moscow, Russia on 4 November. The Russian Lebedev next defended the WBA 'interim' title against Shawn Cox, winning by a second-round kayo at the Crocus City Hall, Myakinino, Russia, on 4 April 2012.

After backing out of a scheduled title defence against Andres Taylor and then refusing to fight the 'interim' champion, Lebedev, the WBA gave Jones the title of 'champion in recess' before upgrading the Russian on 30 October 2012.

30 November 2011. Krzysztof Wlodarczyk w rsc 11 Danny Green.
Venue: Challenge Stadium, Mount Claremont, Australia. **Recognition:** WBC. **Referee:** Michael Griffin.
Fight Summary: A former WBA light heavyweight titleholder, the 37-year-old Green (197½) failed to put a dent in the champion's armour and was eventually rescued by the referee at 2.15 of the 11th. Although he had battled away bravely, hurting Wlodarczyk (199¼) in the fifth with some solid shots, when Green eventually ran out of steam his challenge was almost over. Having fought at a slow pace for several rounds Wlodarczyk picked it up in the 11th and, following a cracking right-left that deposited Green on the canvas, the referee halted the bout with the latter on his feet but deemed unable to defend himself.

4 February 2012. Yoan Pablo Hernandez w pts 12 Steve Cunningham.
Venue: Fraport Arena, Frankfurt, Germany. **Recognition:** IBF/The Ring. **Referee:** Eddie Cotton.
Scorecards: 115-111, 116-110, 116-110.
Fight Summary: In a return fight that was called for following the unsatisfactory ending in their previous go, Hernandez (198½) put his IBF title on the line against Cunningham (197½), while *The Ring* Championship Belt, that

was vacant, was also up for grabs. Making a fast start, Hernandez caught up with Cunningham with a southpaw left hook that left the latter on his back. Getting to his feet and then being put down again, Cunningham somehow survived before coming back hard in the sixth. From thereon in both men took and gave hard shots, and although Cunningham made a great effort in the final session Hernandez would not be denied.

5 May 2012. Marco Huck drew 12 Ola Afolabi.
Venue: Fair Hall, Erfurt, Germany. **Recognition:** WBO. **Referee:** Robert Byrd.
Scorecards: 115-113, 114-114, 114-114.
Fight Summary: Having challenged Alexander Povetkin for the WBA heavyweight championship last time out, Huck (198½) returned to the cruiserweight division to defend his title against Afolabi (199). The contest began well for the challenger, who had lost a close one to Huck in 2009, when boxing well with the left jab from the centre of the ring. It was only in the sixth that Huck got himself going as Afolabi tired, but after the ninth it became a slugging match with both men dishing it out in equal measure. Although the majority draw saved the title for Huck, a rubber match was clearly on the cards.

15 September 2012. Yoan Pablo Hernandez w pts 12 Troy Ross.
Venue: Stechert Arena, Bamberg, Bayern, Germany. **Recognition:** IBF/The Ring. **Referee:** David Fields.
Scorecards: 114-113, 115-112, 116-112.
Fight Summary: Defending two championship belts in a battle of southpaws, Hernandez (200) was given plenty of trouble by the hard-hitting Ross (193½). Shaken up in the third by a solid left hook, Hernandez was floored in the fifth from the same punch and was lucky to get through the round, almost falling down several times from the after effects. Although still dazed in the sixth Hernandez gradually got his boxing together, coming back well in the ninth to hurt Ross. At that point it was all to play for, but with Hernandez winning three of the last four rounds on the cards he picked up the unanimous points verdict.

22 September 2012. Krzysztof Wlodarczyk w pts 12 Francisco Palacios.
Venue: Centennial Hall, Wroclaw, Poland. **Recognition:** WBC. **Referee:** Massimo Barrovecchio.
Scorecards: 116-112, 117-112, 116-113.
Fight Summary: Following their controversial contest in April, Wlodarczyk (199) again put his title on the line against Palacios (195). In what was a pretty even affair, Wlodarczyk edged many of the rounds in the first half of the contest until Palacios stepped it up with solid shots to the body, having successes in rounds seven and nine. However, Wlodarczyk came back strongly in the tenth with a cracking left hook to the jaw that almost finished the fight there and then, before Palacios recovered somewhat to see out the remaining sessions.

3 November 2012. Marco Huck w pts 12 Firat Arslan.
Venue: Gerry Weber Stadium, Halle, Germany. **Recognition:** WBO. **Referee:** Celestino Ruiz.
Scorecards: 115-113, 115-113, 117-111.
Fight Summary: Although Huck (199) retained his title against the 42-year-old Arslan (198½), the unanimous decision in his favour was roundly booed by a crowd who felt that the southpaw challenger deserved more. For six rounds it seemed that Arslan's work-rate and ability to cut the ring down, allied to heavy shots from either hand, would give him victory. It was only in the latter rounds when Arslan began to tire that Huck found the room to get solid blows off, but the challenger was still in there firing off left hooks right up to the final bell.

17 December 2012. Denis Lebedev w co 4 Santander Silgado.
Venue: Crocus City Hall, Myakinino, Russia. **Recognition:** WBA. **Referee:** Mikael Hook.
Fight Summary: This was the first defence of the title that Lebedev (197½) had been handed after Guillermo Jones was stripped, and he wasted little time in putting Silgado (193¾) under pressure when winning the opening session. However, not deterred, the unbeaten Silgado quickly found an answer when taking the fight to Lebedev with some confidence before slipping up in the fourth. Whether it was overconfidence or not, Silgado failed to defend himself properly and was counted out at 2.14 of the session after being dropped heavily following a tremendous southpaw left to the jaw.

17 May 2013. Guillermo Jones w co 11 Denis Lebedev.
Venue: Crocus City Hall, Moscow, Russia. **Recognition:** WBA. **Referee:** Stan Christodoulou.
Fight Summary: Ahead on points, 96-94, 97-93, 96-94 at the time of the finish, Lebedev (199½) had fought on despite being unable to see out of his right eye for at least two-thirds of the fight. As early as the first round the champion had been cut over the right eye by the 41-year-old Jones (198¾), the so-called 'champion in recess', but despite this the Russian southpaw attacked his man relentlessly, especially in the fourth and sixth through to the eighth. It was only in the ninth, when Jones began concentrating on Lebedev's right eye that the fight turned, the latter being eventually counted out at 1.54 of the 11th after taking several hefty blows to head and body.

Lebedev was handed back the title on 17 October when Jones, who had failed a drugs test following the fight, was eventually stripped. Following that decision the WBA stated that a rematch should be negotiated as soon as possible, while eventually recognising Jones as a 'champion in recess' yet again. With the return made for 25 April 2014 in Moscow, the fight was cancelled just hours before after Jones failed a drugs test for the second successive time.

On 21 June 2014, Youri Kayembre Kalenga won the vacant WBA 'interim' title when outpointing Mateusz Masternak at the Medecin Casino, Monte Carlo, Monaco.

8 June 2013. Marco Huck w pts 12 Ola Afolabi.
Venue: Max Schmeling Hall, Berlin, Germany. **Recognition:** WBO. **Referee:** Eddie Cotton.
Scorecards: 117-111, 115-113, 114-114.
Fight Summary: Meeting for the third time, Huck (198¾) held on to his title when outpointing Afolabi (198) by a majority decision. In what was a difficult fight to score, *Boxing News* having it for Afolabi 115-113, the latter concentrated on the champion's body in an effort to slow him down while the German-based Serb worked away in bursts, his best rounds being the third and fourth. Coming on strong, Afolabi loaded up in the tenth and 11th when shaking Huck with solid punches, but unable to floor his man he ultimately lost out. Afolabi forfeited his WBO 'interim' title on the result.

21 June 2013. Krzysztof Wlodarczyk w rsc 8 Rakhim Chakhkiev.
Venue: Dynamo Sports Palace, Moscow, Russia. **Recognition:** WBC. **Referee:** Daniel Van de Wiele.
Fight Summary: The Russian southpaw challenger certainly came to fight, cutting Wlodarczyk (198¾) over the right eye in the first before dropping him with a solid right in the third. The next two sessions were much of the same before Wlodarczyk floored Chakhkiev (196¼) with a cracking left hook to the jaw towards the end of the sixth. From thereon in the fight turned in the champion's favour, Chakhkiev being dropped again by another left in the seventh prior to being on the canvas twice more in the eighth before being rescued by the referee at 2.03 of the session. At the finish Chakhkiev was ahead on all three cards.

23 November 2013. Yoan Pablo Hernandez w co 10 Alexander Alekseev.
Venue: Stechert Arena, Bamberg, Bayern, Germany. **Recognition:** IBF/The Ring. **Referee:** Lindsey Page.
Fight Summary: In a battle between southpaws, Hernandez (198½) put both of his championship belts on the line against his mandatory challenger, Alekseev (198½). Hernandez started the better of the pair when dropping Alekseev in the second following a left hook to the jaw, and continued as the aggressor until being boxed-off in the fourth. Still going well, his jab and right hooks being effective, Alekseev was suddenly dumped by a cracking overarm right in the fifth. Despite that, Alekseev came back strongly to win three of the next four rounds, hurting Hernandez enough to force him to hold, before a crashing right to the head in the tenth sent him down to be counted out on the 1.35 mark.

6 December 2013. Krzysztof Wlodarczyk w rsc 6 Giacobbe Fragomeni.
Venue: UIC Pavilion, Chicago, Illinois, USA. **Recognition:** WBC. **Referee:** Rocky Burke.
Fight Summary: Meeting for the third time, the champion again imposed himself on the 44-year-old Fragomeni (198) when using a solid left jab to keep the smaller Italian on the outside looking in. Smashed to the deck in the fourth, following a hefty left hook to the chin and bleeding from a cut under the left eye, Fragomeni came back

well in the fifth before his eye began to swell rapidly in the sixth. At the end of the session, following advice from the ringside doctor the referee declared the fight to be over.

25 January 2014. Marco Huck w rsc 6 Firat Arslan.
Venue: Hanns-Martin Schleyer Hall, Stuttgart, Germany. **Recognition:** WBO. **Referee:** Mark Nelson.
Fight Summary: Although the southpaw challenger made all of the running in this rematch it was Huck (199½), boxing off the back foot, who landed the heavier shots. In the fourth round Arslan (198¾) was hurt by a body shot and in the sixth he was down twice before the referee came to his rescue at 1.56 of the session. In their first contest Arslan had been extremely dangerous with the left uppercut but on this occasion such a punch was hardly in use.

16 August 2014. Yoan Pablo Hernandez w pts 12 Firat Arslan.
Venue: Exhibition Centre, Erfurt, Germany. **Recognition:** IBF/The Ring. **Referee:** Randy Neumann.
Scorecards: 115-113, 116-113, 113-115.
Fight Summary: Having failed to lift the WBO title from Marco Huck two fights earlier, the 43-year-old Arslan (199¾) came within a whisker of taking Hernandez's two championship belts in an all-southpaw battle. Although Hernandez (199¾) made a good start, by the fourth he was being pegged back as Arslan's good inside work nullified many of his offensive efforts. One of the judges had Arslan winning seven of the last nine rounds while the other two saw him taking five but ultimately it was Hernandez's better work in the closing stages, as Arslan tired, that gained him the split decision.

Victor Emilio Ramirez outpointed Ola Afolabi over 12 rounds to win the vacant IBF 'interim' title on 10 April 2015, at the Villa La Nata Sporting Club, Benavidez, Buenos Aires, Argentina.

Due to defend his IBF title against Ramirez, Hernandez forfeited his belt on 21 September 2015 after injuring his knee and being unable to go through with the fight. Following that, Ramirez was handed full title status.

Hernandez was eventually stripped of *The Ring* Championship Belt at the end of November 2015 after not meeting a top-five-rated opponent for over two years.

30 August 2014. Marco Huck w pts 12 Mirko Larghetti.
Venue: Gerry Weber Stadium, Halle, Germany. **Recognition:** WBO. **Referee:** Jack Reiss.
Scorecards: 118-110, 116-112, 116-112.
Fight Summary: Boxing well beyond expectation, Larghetti (195¼) gave the champion plenty of tough moments before going down on all three cards. While Huck (200) carried the heavier punch the Italian matched him for aggression, and even when stunned he more often than not fired back. In the seventh through to the ninth Larghetti came on strong when backing Huck on to the ropes, but in the 11th he was badly shaken up by a solid right to the head before coming apart in the final session. In the 12th, having sustained a terrific onslaught, Larghetti was eventually sent crashing following a burst of heavy blows. Although out to the world the referee stated that as Larghetti had hit the deck after the final bell had gone it would be the judges who would decide the winner.

27 September 2014. Denis Lebedev w rsc 2 Pawel Kolodziej.
Venue: Krylatskoye Dynamo Sports Palace, Moscow, Russia. **Recognition:** WBA. **Referee:** Guillermo Perez Pineda.
Fight Summary: Defending his title after 16 months out of the ring, Lebedev (200) did not hang around for long before despatching the unbeaten Kolodziej (198¾) with a southpaw straight left to the chin in the second round. Although Kolodziej regained his feet at the count of 'eight', on being asked if he was able to continue and not responding the referee stopped the contest on the 2.08 mark.

Youri Kayembre Kalenga successfully defended the WBA 'interim' title when stopping Denton Daley in the final round at the Hershey Centre, Mississauga, Ontario, Canada on 15 November.

27 September 2014. Grigory Drozd w pts 12 Krzysztof Wlodarczyk.
Venue: Krylatskoye Dynamo Sports Palace, Moscow, Russia. **Recognition:** WBC. **Referee:** Ian John-Lewis.
Scorecards: 118-109, 119-108, 119-108.
Fight Summary: With just one defeat in his 39-fight record, against Firat Arslan back in 2006, Drozd (198¼) was not going to let the opportunity pass him by after spending 13 years in the pro ranks. Fighting behind the left jab, the challenger countered hard when Wlodarczyk (199) moved in before smothering any attack coming his way. Although Wlodarczyk hurt Drozd in the third and fourth with heavy rights to the head, it did not deter the latter from coming back well in the fifth through to the seventh before dropping the champion with a hard right in the eighth. From thereon in it was all Drozd who, despite being weary, was able to hold Wlodarczyk off with left-rights to the head right up to the final bell.

10 April 2015. Denis Lebedev w pts 12 Youri Kayembre Kalenga.
Venue: Luzhniki Stadium, Moscow, Russia. **Recognition:** WBA. **Referee:** Guillermo Perez Pineda.
Scorecards: 116-111, 115-112, 116-110.
Fight Summary: Controlling the fight for the opening three rounds, the southpaw champion was surprised more than hurt when Kalenga (198¾) had him over from what was termed a slip by the referee after taking a hard left to the head. That spurred Kalenga on to more success, but having been floored heavily in the seventh he was put under real pressure as Lebedev (198½) pushed forward. Despite tiring and taking some heavy left hooks in the process, Kalenga came back well to win three of the last four sessions.

Beibut Shumenov won the vacant WBA 'interim' title when outscoring BJ Flores over 12 rounds at the Palms Casino Resort, Las Vegas, Nevada, USA on 25 July.

22 May 2015. Grigory Drozd w rsc 9 Lukasz Janik.
Venue: Luzhniki Sports Palace, Moscow, Russia. **Recognition:** WBC. **Referee:** Ian John-Lewis.
Fight Summary: Putting his title on the table for the first time, Drozd (199¾) immediately settled down to work when winning every round against Janik (200), stabbing in left hands and solid body shots that would eventually weaken the challenger. Dropped by a body blow in the seventh and pushed down in the eighth Janik looked sold-out, and in the ninth he was rescued by the referee after just 50 seconds when he was taking a two-fisted pounding and seemed unable to defend himself.

Originally due to meet Ilunga Makabu in November, the fight was rescheduled after Drozd suffered an injury in training, and on being injured again Drozd was given 'champion in recess' status on 14 March 2016. Meantime, it was announced that Makabu and Tony Bellew would contest the vacant title.

14 August 2015. Krzysztof Glowacki w rsc 11 Marco Huck.
Venue: Prudential Centre, Newark, New Jersey, USA. **Recognition:** WBO. **Referee:** David Fields.
Fight Summary: Having successfully defended his title 13 times and looking to break the divisional record jointly held with Johnny Nelson, Huck (199) made a slow start when dropping the opening three rounds. At this stage of the fight Huck was still shaking off the ring rust after being idle for almost a year. However, he picked up the pace in the fourth before sending Glowacki (198) crashing in the sixth following a left hook to the jaw. Although Glowacki came back hard Huck soon regained some momentum, all three cards having the latter ahead at the end of the tenth. The contest changed dramatically in the 11th as Glowacki took up the offensive when blasting Huck to the ropes and after dropping the latter for the 'eight' count, with a southpaw left hook and straight right, he was battering away at his defenceless opponent who was then quickly rescued by the referee at 2.39 of the session.

2 October 2015. Victor Emilio Ramirez drew 12 Ovill McKenzie.
Venue: Villa La Nata Sporting Club, Benavidez, Buenos Aires, Argentina. **Recognition:** IBF. **Referee:** Benjy Esteves Jnr.
Scorecards: 115-113, 113-115, 114-114.
Fight Summary: Making the first defence of the title that was handed to him after Yoan Pablo Hernandez had been stripped, Ramirez (200) took on McKenzie (191¼) who had accepted the contest at 11 days' notice. Boxing on the back foot showing a good jab, McKenzie took the opening three rounds before being forced to take some heavy

shots as Ramirez came more into the fight as it progressed. Fighting with great desire the tenth belonged to McKenzie, and although Ramirez came back strongly in the 11th it was the challenger who finished the better. *Boxing News*, who gave McKenzie the fight by 115-114, felt that the Jamaican-born Englishman certainly deserved another crack at Ramirez in view of the split draw on away territory.

4 November 2015. Denis Lebedev w rsc 8 Lateef Kayode.
Venue: Basket-Hall Arena, Kazan, Russia. **Recognition:** WBA. **Referee:** Steve Smoger.
Fight Summary: After coming down from heavyweight to challenge the southpaw champion, Kayode (199½) started reasonably well before falling behind on points and coming under fire in the seventh when a hard left hook sent him down. From thereon in it became a hard night's work for Kayode as Lebedev (198¾) upped the pace while sending in heavy left hands and with the challenger forced against the ropes, taking solid blows without return, the referee stepped in at 1.22 of the eighth to save him.

Yunier Dorticos stopped Youri Kayembre Kalenga inside ten rounds to win the WBA 'interim' title that had been vacated by Beibut Shumenov at the Versailles Sports Palace, Paris, France on 20 May 2016.

16 April 2016. Krzysztof Glowacki w pts 12 Steve Cunningham.
Venue: Barclays Centre, Brooklyn, NYC, New York, USA. **Recognition:** WBO. **Referee:** Arthur Mercante Jnr.
Scorecards: 115-109, 115-109, 116-108.
Fight Summary: Despite being dropped on four separate occasions the 40-year-old challenger not only made it to the final bell against the hard-punching Glowacki (199) but actually won five rounds on the cards. Floored in the second by a southpaw left hook and moments later by a stiff right it looked as though it would be an early night for Cunningham (194¼), but back he came until a short right downed him in the tenth. With his right eye swollen he gave it one last try in the 12th until another big right put him down again and finally took the sting out of his tail.

21 May 2016. Denis Lebedev w rsc 2 Victor Emilio Ramirez.
Venue: Khodynka Ice Palace, Moscow, Russia. **Recognition:** IBF/WBA. **Referee:** Steve Smoger.
Fight Summary: In a battle between two champions, Ramirez (198½) representing the IBF and Lebedev (198¾) the WBA, it was the latter who came away with two belts after stopping his rival at 1.57 of the second. Following a relatively even opening round, after Lebedev got home with a southpaw left uppercut and followed it up with a short left Ramirez was decked. Although the Argentine regained his feet and appeared not too interested in carrying on, the contest was only halted when he was once again under the cosh and not fighting back.

On the same day at the Cosmopolitan, Las Vegas, Nevada, USA, Beibut Shumenov won the vacant WBA 'second tier' title when stopping Junior Anthony Wright inside ten rounds.

29 May 2016. Tony Bellew w rsc 3 Ilunga Makabu.
Venue: Goodison Park Stadium, Liverpool, England. **Recognition:** WBC. **Referee:** Victor Loughlin.
Fight Summary: Contesting the vacant title after Grigory Drozd was handed 'champion in recess' status on being injured, Bellew (199¼) took full advantage of the opportunity to pound Makabu (196½) into submission. That was after Makabu had dropped the Englishman with a solid southpaw left in the opener. Not deterred, Bellew gritted his teeth and hit back hard in the third when crashing right hands to the head sent Makabu into the ropes. Having followed up with a heavy right uppercut and left hook, Makabu was sent down and when it was clear that he was never going to make it to his feet in time the referee ignored the count and stopped the fight on the 1.20 mark.

17 September 2016. Oleksandr Usyk w pts 12 Krzysztof Glowacki.
Venue: Ergo Arena, Gdansk, Poland. **Recognition:** WBO. **Referee:** Robert Byrd.
Scorecards: 117-111, 117-111, 119-109.
Fight Summary: The inexperienced Usyk (198¾), with just nine contests on his tab coming into the fight, showed what a good prospect he was when going 12 rounds for the first time and picking up a unanimous decision over the hard-hitting champion in a match-up of southpaws. A former European and World amateur gold medallist, Usyk used his longer reach and fast hands to shoot in solid jabs that were followed up by heavy rights and lefts

which Glowacki (199¼) seemed unable to avoid. Having been cut on the right eye following a clash of heads in the third Glowacki had some good rounds but in the latter stages, as he tired and his eye began to swell, he became wilder as Usyk took the fight by the scruff of the neck. Despite slipping over in the final session, Usyk, who was awarded the last three rounds on the cards, was a clear winner regardless of the downcast Glowacki receiving hand and elbow injuries during the fight.

15 October 2016. Tony Bellew w rsc 3 BJ Flores.
Venue: Echo Arena, Liverpool, England. **Recognition:** WBC. **Referee:** Ian John-Lewis.
Fight Summary: Although the challenger made a decent enough start, taking the opening session, he was soon under pressure in the second after Bellew (199¼) opened up with some heavy shots. Having complained about a low blow, Flores (199¼) was still complaining when he was dropped by a left hook to the head. Getting up at 'eight', the American was soon on the floor from another left hook, and despite making it to his feet he was put down again from a two-handed attack. Saved by the bell Flores came right back at Bellew in the third, but following yet another left hook that sent him crashing the referee halted the contest on the 2.11 mark.

Cruiserweight Boxers' Index:
(Country of birth where known/Domicile - birthplace and domicile are the same unless stated)

A
Tomasz Adamek (Poland/USA)
Ola Afolabi (England/USA)
Alexander Alekseev (Uzbekistan/Germany)
Bash Ali (Nigeria)
Stefan Angehrn (Switzerland)
Derek Angol (England)
Patrice Aouissi (France)
George Arias (Brazil)
Jose Arimatea Da Silva (Brazil)
Firat Arslan (Germany)
Sione Asipeli (Tonga/USA)
Pietro Aurino (Italy)
Louis Azille (Dominica/USA)
Mohamed Azzaoui (Algeria/France)

B
Johnathon Banks (USA)
Taoufik Belbouli (Tunisia/France)
O'Neil Bell (Jamaica/USA)
Tony Bellew (England)
Bernard Benton (USA)
Craig Bodzianowski (USA)
Tyrone Booze (USA)
Markus Bott (Germany)
Vincent Boulware (USA)
Wayne Braithwaite (Guyana/USA)
Dale Brown (Canada)
Valery Brudov (Russia)
Jesse Burnett (USA)

C
David Cabrera (Mexico)
Marvin Camel (USA)
Vincenzo Cantatore (Italy)
Larry Carlisle (USA)
Jorge Castro (Argentina)
Rakhim Chakhkiev (Russia)
Alfred Cole (USA)
Shawn Cox (Barbados)
Piet Crous (South Africa)
Steve Cunningham (USA)
Bobby Czyz (USA)

D
Denton Daley (Canada)
Robert Daniels (USA)
Anthony Davis (USA)
Kelvin Davis (USA)

Carlos De Leon (Puerto Rico)
Marcelo Dominguez (Argentina)
Yunier Dorticos (Cuba/USA)
Grigory Drozd (Russia)
Terry Dunstan (England)
Massimiliano Duran (Italy)

E
Zsolt Erdei (Hungary)
Chris Eubank (England)

F
Marcelo Figueroa (Argentina)
Jose Maria Flores Burlon (Uruguay/Argentina)
BJ Flores (USA)
Giacobbe Fragomeni (Italy)

G
Hugo Hernan Garay (Argentina)
Dorcy Gaymon (USA)
Reinaldo Gimenez (Argentina/USA)
Nestor Giovannini (Argentina)
Christophe Girard (France)
Krzysztof Glowacki (Poland)
Matt Godfrey (USA)
Juan Carlos Gomez (Cuba/Germany)
Alex Gonzalez (Puerto Rico)
S. T. Gordon (USA)
Rodney Gordon (USA)
Uriah Grant (Jamaica/USA)
Danny Green (Australia)
Michael Greer (USA)
Bobby Gunn (Canada/USA)
Alexander Gurov (Ukraine)

H
Magne Havnaa (Norway)
David Haye (England)
James Heath (USA)
Steve Herelius (France)
Yoan Pablo Hernandez (Cuba/Germany)
Virgil Hill (USA)
Mark Hobson (England)
Evander Holyfield (USA)
Marco Huck (Serbia/Germany)

I
Alexey Ilyin (Russia)
Ali Ismailov (Ukraine/Russia)

J
Lukasz Janik (Poland)
Vassiliy Jirov (Kazakhstan/USA)
Guillermo Jones (Panama)

K
Youri Kayembre Kalenga (DR Congo/France)
Lateef Kayode (Nigeria/USA)
Sergey Kobozev (Russia/USA)
Pawel Kolodziej (Poland)
Rudolf Kraj (Czech Republic/Germany)

L
Donny Lalonde (Canada)
Jeff Lampkin (USA)
Mirko Larghetti (Italy)
Brian LaSpada (USA)
Denis Lebedev (Russia)
Julian Letterlough (USA)
Willard Lewis (Canada)
Enad Licina (Serbia/Germany)
Yaqui Lopez (Mexico/USA)
Young Joe Louis-Eddie Taylor (USA)
Patrick Lumumba (Kenya/Sweden)

M
Enzo Maccarinelli (Wales)
Roddy MacDonald (Canada)
Ilunga Makabu (DR Congo/South Africa)
Siza Makathini (South Africa)
Michael Marrone (USA)
Mateusz Masternak (Poland)
Ruediger May (Germany)
Torsten May (Germany)
Imamu Mayfield (USA)
Andrew Maynard (USA)
Glenn McCrory (England)
Terry McGroom (USA)
Ovill McKenzie (Jamaica/England)
Dariusz Michalczewski (Poland)
Nate Miller (USA)
Brian Minto (USA)
Saul Montana (Mexico)
Jean-Marc Mormeck (Guadeloupe/France)
Tony Mundine (Australia)
Ken Murphy (USA)
Lee Roy Murphy (USA)
Chisanda Mutti (Zambia/Germany)

N
Ran Nakash (Israel)
Johnny Nelson (England)
Daniel Neto (Argentina)

Orlin Norris (USA)
Rob Norton (England)

O
Ossie Ocasio (Puerto Rico)
John Odhiambo (Kenya/Denmark)

P
Ezequiel Paixao (Brazil)
Francisco Palacios (USA/Puerto Rico)
Ricky Parkey (USA)
Mate Parlov (Croatia)
Alexander Petkovic (Germany)
Luis Andres Pineda (Panama)
James Pritchard (USA)
Boone Pultz (USA)

Q
Dwight Muhammad Qawi (USA)

R
Victor Emilio Ramirez (Argentina)
Marc Randazzo (USA)
Alfonzo Ratliff (USA)
Terry Ray (USA)
Sammy Reeson (England)
Adam Richards (USA)
Jason Robinson (USA)
Ralf Rocchigiani (Germany)
Troy Ross (Guyana/Canada)
Rogelio Omar Rossi (Argentina)
Sebastiaan Rothmann (Israel/South Africa)
Angelo Rottoli (Italy)
Andrey Rudenko (Russia)

S
Bruce Scott (Jamaica/England)
Ezra Sellers (USA)
Bill Sharkey (USA)
Beibut Shumenov (Kazakhstan/USA)
Santander Silgado (Colombia/USA)
Mohamed Siluvangi (DR Congo/France)
Jay Snyder (USA)
Leon Spinks (USA)
Ravea Springs (USA)
Randy Stephens (USA)

T
Akim Tafer (France)
Napoleon Tagoe (Ghana/USA)
Andres Taylor (USA)
Carl Thompson (England)
Henry Tillman (USA)

Fabrice Tiozzo (France)
James Toney (USA)

U
Oleksandr Usyk (Ukraine)

V
Yuri Vaulin (Latvia)
David Vedder (USA)
Valeriy Vykhor (Ukraine)

W
Anaclet Wamba (Congo/France)
Dan Ward (USA)
James Warring (USA)
Adolpho Washington (USA)
Guy Waters (Australia)
Adam Watt (Australia)
Arthur Williams (USA)
Robbie Williams (South Africa)
Darnell Wilson (USA)
Donnell Wingfield (USA)
Krzysztof Wlodarczyk (Poland)
Junior Anthony Wright (USA)

Heavyweight Division

Known as the richest prize in sport the heavyweight division as we know it today has its roots in England, the history of modern pugilism taking us right back to the 1720s when James Figg, an expert with the sword and quarterstaff, opened his theatre on Oxford Road, London. Over the years Figg has become recognised as being the man who brought bare-fist fighting into the public domain. A little-known fact unearthed by Tony Gee in his excellent book, *Up to Scratch*, records that Figg had been a scholar of the noted Timothy Buck in Clare Market, London and had risen to the position of 'Master of the Noble Science of Defence' by 1714 under his tutor.

It is Jack Broughton, however, who is generally credited with bringing the sport into prominence, and as its true founder he was the man who should be seen retrospectively as being the first real champion of the bare-knuckle era prior to laying down the prize ring's first set of rules in 1743. Some of the big names who followed him included Jack Slack, Tom Johnson, Ben Bryan (sometimes known as Brian, Brain or Bryant), Daniel Mendoza, Gentleman John Jackson, Jem Belcher, Hen Pearce, John Gully, Tom Cribb, Tom Spring, Jem Ward, James Deaf Burke, William Bendigo Thompson, Ben Caunt, William Perry, Tom Sayers and Jem Mace. Incidentally, it was only after Mace that I can find the term 'heavy weight' regularly in use, but by the 1870s it was prevalent on both sides of the Atlantic.

The first glove fight of 25 rounds or more took place at the Cambridge Hall, Newman Street, Westminster, London, England on 4 September 1877 between Jack Knifton and Tom Scrutton. Although *The Sportsman* and *Sporting Life* reported it to be for the English title it should not be seen as such, with Scrutton being an amateur and Knifton, a newcomer with just three three-round fights behind him. With both men totally out of condition it was a farce right from the beginning, the referee calling it off in semi-darkness during the ninth round and refusing to give a decision. Almost two months later, Tom Allen, who had been claiming the English title without donning the gloves, took on Tompkin Gilbert in a defence of his claim. A year earlier, in 1876, Allen had lost his bare-knuckle title in America to fellow-Englishman, Joe Goss, after being disqualified in the 21st round.

With bare knuckles becoming popularised in America by the mid-1800s and maintained mainly by British-born fighters, it was left to John L. Sullivan, 'The Boston Strong Boy' from America, to bring the curtain down on championships under London Prize Ring Rules when defeating Jake Kilrain in 75 rounds on 8 July 1889.

At the start of gloved boxing it was pretty much accepted in Britain that men under 158/160lbs were middleweights while those above were heavyweights. However, because there were many men who boxed in catchweight contests above that weight and who were too light for the heavyweight ranks prior to the light heavyweight division being introduced in 1899, I have set the heavyweight band at all weights above 166lbs.

Prior to Jess Willard beating Jack Johnson on 5 April 1915, I have listed all English, black and white title bouts regardless of the fact that there was a generally recognised line of succession following James J. Corbett's victory over Sullivan on 7 September 1892. This has been done in order to show a clear picture of how the weight class evolved at championship level.

Weight Band/Amendments
166lbs + (1877 to 18 August 1899)
170lbs + (On 29 August 1899, Joe Choynski beat Australian Jim Ryan on points to win the inaugural light heavyweight title, thus setting up a weight class for men between 160 and 170lbs)
175lbs + (Although the light heavyweight division had not really taken off, on 22 April 1903 a contest between Jack Root and Charles Kid McCoy further established the weight class, with the limit rising to 175lbs. Following the National Sporting Club (NSC) formally introducing eight named weight divisions on 11 February 1909, with the light heavyweight division recognised in Britain for the first time, and shortly after in Europe, the minimum poundage became well and truly established)

190lbs + (On 8 December 1979, the new cruiserweight division got underway for men weighing between 175 and 190lbs, a contest between Marvin Camel and Mate Parlov deciding the championship. With heavyweights getting bigger all the time, this was implemented to allow the lighter men among the weight class more of a chance against men of similar weight)
195lbs + (At the end of their November Convention in 1981 the WBC increased the cruiserweight poundage to 195lbs)
190lbs + (In November 1988 the WBC dropped their cruiserweight limit from 195lbs to 190lbs, thus falling into line with the IBF and WBA)
200lbs + (Both the WBA and WBC increased the cruiserweight limit from 190lbs to 200lbs in early October 2003, followed by the WBO and IBF a short while later)

Heavyweight World Championship Fights and Title Claims:

29 October 1877. Tom Allen w rtd 7 (finish) Tompkin Gilbert.
Venue: Sadler's Wells Theatre, Clerkenwell, London, England. **Referee:** Robert Watson.
Fight Summary: Articled for the gloved championship under Marquess of Queensberry (MoQ) Rules, it somehow got confused with London Prize Ring Rules with several rounds ending short and the whole contest lasting just over 16 minutes. Although the articles called for the meeting to be contested in gloves it was apparent that the gloves used had no padding and were more in keeping with knuckle dusters. The fight itself saw Gilbert (175), a novice, badly beaten by the far more experienced Allen (168) who claimed the English title on winning. That was what it said in *Bells Life*, which reported on boxing generally, but in the *Lincolnshire Chronicle* a far different account of what took place was reported. The paper went on to state that after Gilbert unsuccessfully tried to 'throw' Allen, the latter picked him up, raised him on a level with his head and dashed him with great force on the wooden stage, the thud resounding throughout the building. At this point Gilbert's seconds claimed a foul, and after much consultation with the referee on the articles the claim was upheld, although it was not publicly made known in order to prevent a disturbance. The truth of the matter was that Gilbert had been outclassed throughout, being knocked down at least four times and badly cut, and had been the one who instigated the 'throwing' session. On the basis of that the initial result stood amongst those involved in the sport.

4 April 1878. Tom Allen w disq 5 (finish) Charley Davis.
Venue: The Skating Rink, Cambridge Heath, London, England. **Referee:** Charles Conquest.
Fight Summary: Billed for the English title, and contested in gloves under MoQ Rules, Davis, outweighed by almost three stone, was a badly beaten man when his trainer deliberately entered the ring to automatically get his fighter disqualified. Having been severely hurt several times, he had been dropped in the second and fourth before pluckily coming out for the fifth. With little left, Davis was treated to some heavy uppercuts that put him down for three further counts prior to the fight being concluded. Ultimately, Allen (189) had proved far too big for his outgunned rival, the finish being timed at 2.25 of the session.

22 April 1879. Tom Allen drew 24 (finish) Jem Stewart.
Venue: St James' Hall, Piccadilly, London, England. **Referee:** Charles Conquest.
Fight Summary: Press reports showed it to be a billed world title contest under MoQ Rules and using gloves, with virtually all the bout being contested in Stewart's corner as the Scot merely waited for Allen (184) to come to him. It seemed that Allen, who was the odds-on favourite at the end of the tenth, could win as he pleased, having Stewart (170) just where he wanted him when the bell to end the 14th rang. However, when he failed to take advantage of the situation the fight became a huge disappointment with just four punches being struck in rounds 21 to 24. At that stage, because the owners had stated that the hall had to be vacated by 11pm the referee brought matters to a halt. With no decision given, it was only after the participants had met the following day at the offices of the *Sporting Life* that a draw was announced. Englishman Allen returned to the USA in May 1880.

6 September 1879. Jem Stewart w disq 13 (one hour limit) Tompkin Gilbert.
Venue: Springfield Grounds, Glasgow, Scotland. **Referee:** John Riddell.

Fight Summary: The first five rounds were relatively even before Stewart (168) began to gain control, landing at the rate of two to one. Although Gilbert (164) came back well in the 12th, the 13th saw him pick Stewart up and throw him to the floor before continuing to hit the Scot while he was down. This action brought Gilbert an immediate disqualification. According to the *Sportsman*, Stewart was seen as the English champion by the following January.

26 February 1880. Alf Greenfield w disq 20 (finish) Jem Stewart.
Venue: King's Road Baths, Chelsea, London, England. **Referee:** Charles Bedford.
Fight Summary: Despite not being billed as a championship contest, following his victory Greenfield (157) was claiming the English heavyweight title. Although he slipped down in the opening session it quickly became noticeable that Greenfield was far too good for Stewart (166), and even when his right hand was disabled in the third he continued to outclass his rival. Apart from the tenth when Stewart made a bit of a showing Greenfield went further ahead using just one hand, the fight ending when he was deliberately thrown in the 20th session.

On 19 May 1881, Jack Burke outpointed William Coddy Middings over three rounds at the Griffin Public House, Shoreditch, London to win a championship competition, while Tug Wilson challenged all England and claimed the title on hearing that Greenfield had retired in April 1882.

After deciding to go to America, Wilson was signed up by Richard K. Fox to meet the bare-knuckle champion, John L. Sullivan, in a four-round exhibition with gloves at Madison Square Garden, Manhattan, NYC, New York on 17 July 1882. Having contractually agreed to halt Wilson inside four rounds, Sullivan failed to get his hands on the $9,000 purse money after Wilson, who was dropped to the floor 27 times in all, made it to the final bell. When Wilson, who was contracted to return to the States to fight Jimmy Elliott, Joe Goss and Sullivan, failed to honour the agreement with Fox it became extremely difficult for other British fighters to acquire American backers in the future.

Charlie Mitchell won a championship competition when outpointing Dick Roberts over three rounds at St George's Hall, Mayfair, London on 23 December 1882. Not long after he was reported to be the English champion by the *Sporting Life* before signing to fight Sullivan at Madison Square Garden on 14 May 1883. Scheduled for four rounds with gloves, the bout was stopped in the third when Mitchell was knocked off the stage, which coincided with the arrival of the police.

Greenfield then won Jem Mace's championship competition when outpointing Burke over three rounds at the Free Trade Hall, Manchester on 29 June 1883, prior to meeting Sullivan in two-losing four-rounders with gloves in America.

23 February 1883. George Godfrey w rsc 6 (6) Charles Hadley.
Venue: Cribb Club, Boston, Massachusetts, USA. **Referee:** John L. Sullivan.
Fight Summary: Billed as a battle for the 'black heavyweight title' in two-ounce gloves and held under MoQ Rules, both men were badly punished in what became a slugging match. The fight came to an end after Godfrey (170) had fought Hadley (174) to a standstill and the latter was unable to continue.

The first 'black champion' with gloves appears to have been C. C. Smith, who claimed the title after challenging all America in 1876. He was followed by Morris Grant, who was said to have won a three-round 'black tournament' in 1878, and then by Hadley, who twice outpointed Grant over three rounds in 1881.

Even at this stage it was becoming clear that black fighters were generally finding it difficult to obtain matches to their advantage, and early in 1882 Richard K. Fox set up a *Police Gazette* championship medal competition specifically for that purpose. Contested over three or four rounds at Harry Hill's Theatre, Manhattan, NYC, New York, the idea was that any man who won the tournament three times would keep the medal.

Having won six of ten contests against Grant in 1882, including a walkover, Hadley duly collected the medal and went forward to meet Godfrey after knocking out Harry Woodson in two rounds on 10 January 1883. Following his win over Hadley, Godfrey, who had also been claiming the 'black title' since September 1881 when John L. Sullivan walked away immediately prior to a contest between the pair taking place, next took on McHenry Johnson on 10 May 1883. Billed as a four-round spar at the Revere Hall, Boston, the contest was stopped by the police in the fourth session after Johnson was floored. Godfrey had been well on top. Further short-distance fights for Godfrey in Boston where his 'black title' claim was at stake came against Johnson again (drew 4 at the Concert Hall on 10 May 1884), George Taylor (drew 4 at the Earley Athletic Club on 6 December 1884) and C. C. Smith (drew 6 on 15 January 1885). I have been unable to locate a venue for the last named contest, but in all probability it was held at Tom Earley's club.

Regardless of further competition, with Godfrey generally recognised at this time as being the best black fighter in America all others would remain in his slipstream.

14 October 1884. Jack Knifton w rtd 10 (finish) Woolf Bendoff.
Venue: London, England.
Fight Summary: In a private show in London that was advertised for the English title and Championship Belt, Knifton (197), known as the '81-Tonner', came close to being beaten in the opening round when he was nearly knocked out by a heavy blow to the jaw. However, recovering well he gradually got on top of the smaller Bendoff (165) before dropping him in a heap at the end of the fifth. Bendoff eventually retired at the end of the tenth, having nothing left.

Knifton claimed the English championship on the result, but although efforts were made to put together a fight against Jem Smith it never happened. The closest he got to a fight with Smith, having signed articles on 31 July 1886, was with bare-knuckles. And even that was called off, with stakes being drawn on 12 December.

Apart from four three-round exhibition contests in 1887, against Alf Greenfield (Grand Circus, Campbell Street, Leicester on 11 February), Toff Wall (Royal Agricultural Hall, Islington, London on 15 February), Charlie Mitchell (Royal Agricultural Hall on 16 February) and Greenfield again (Royal Agricultural Hall on 17 February) that appears to be the end of Knifton's short ring career. Having been totally outclassed in all four exhibition bouts it came as no surprise when he walked away from the ring, his backer later saying that he was a better orator than fighter.

17 December 1884. Jem Smith w rtd 12 (finish) Woolf Bendoff.
Venue: London, England.
Fight Summary: Held in the West End of London in private, Smith won a £50 trophy and claimed the English title after Bendoff, down in the 12th and saved by the bell, was retired during the interval. Using a long lead, although Bendoff made the fight he could not really hurt Smith, who continually backed off and waited for the former to become exhausted. At the finish Bendoff was still in front, but Smith, who had played a waiting game, remained unhurt throughout.

Smith followed this up when outpointing Tom Longer over three rounds to win a championship competition at the Blue Anchor Public House, Shoreditch, London on 26 February 1885. Later in the year Smith put down a deposit and accepted a challenge from Jack Davis, but the latter never covered it. Following that, Smith then disputed Alf Greenfield's right to also be called the English champion. Smith and Davis would eventually come together on 16 December in a bare-knuckle fight, the latter being knocked out inside six rounds.

29 August 1885. John L. Sullivan w disq 7 (finish) Dominick McCaffrey.
Venue: Chester Driving Park, Cincinnati, Ohio, USA. **Referee:** Billy Tait.
Fight Summary: According to the *Chicago Tribune* Sullivan (208) v McCaffrey (167½) was contracted for six rounds in three-ounce gloves, with a draw to be given in the event that both men were still standing at the final bell, and was billed as a contest with gloves that would decide the MoQ championship of the world. However, the *Boston Globe* account of the affair gives a rather different impression when reporting, the day before, that it was to be a finish fight as per an advertisement that ran in the *Enquirer*. This is more likely to be closer to the truth, as anything other than gloved exhibitions were banned in much of America at the time and promoters would not have wanted to tip off the authorities. Throughout the contest Sullivan was the aggressor, having McCaffrey over in the third,

fourth and fifth rounds, but the latter was making life difficult for the favourite who was beginning to flag during the seventh. Following the fight, the *Sunday Boston Globe* stated that it had been stopped at 1.45 of the seventh round and given to Sullivan on a foul, the referee stating that he had disqualified McCaffrey for using his legs illegally. The paper went on to say that there had been 26 minutes and 20 seconds on the clock at the finish, broken down by four rounds of three minutes each, one of 3.20, one of 3.15 and one of 1.45, with six minutes lost between rounds. Regarding the breakdown of rounds contested, it would appear that MoQ Rules got mixed up with London Prize Ring Rules. There was no doubt that McCaffrey believed it to be a finish fight, and not expecting it to end at that point a riot ensued after his brother pulled a gun and clubbed the former London Rules lightweight champion, Arthur Chambers (one of Sullivan's seconds), on the head. Although Sullivan continued his career with fists, he would be claiming the gloved title from there on despite it being hardly a fight to remember.

For Sullivan, another gloved fight for him that had a dubious ending came against Patsy Cardiff at the Washington Rink, Minneapolis, Minnesota on 18 January 1887. Supposedly made for six rounds or a finish, Sullivan was said to have broken his left forearm, and with Cardiff having the best of it he called it quits at the end of the sixth. At that point, a draw was announced by the referee, Pat Sullivan. As far as the champion's wife was concerned her husband had tricked all concerned yet again and was perfectly okay.

Jake Kilrain challenged Sullivan on 17 May 1987 to decide the championship of America with fists or two-ounce gloves for $2,500 up to $5,000, the winner to receive the *Police Gazette* Championship Belt. When Sullivan refused Kilrain's challenge, failing to cover his deposit, the belt was awarded to the latter on 4 June 1887 in Baltimore on condition that he defended it against all comers from either side of the Atlantic. Kilrain was then challenged with knuckles by Jem Smith, who received a draw after 150 minutes (106 rounds) of fighting on 19 December 1887 in France.

Meanwhile, Sullivan, on the verge of defeat, held on to his version of the bare-knuckle championship against Charlie Mitchell in Chantilly, France on 10 March 1888, when a draw was given after 190 minutes of fighting. He then beat Kilrain in his final bare-knuckle defence, in a fight that lasted 136 minutes in Richburg, Mississippi on 8 July 1889.

25 January 1888. McHenry Johnson w disq 4 (finish) George Godfrey.
Venue: Boulder County, Colorado, USA. **Referee:** Dick Williams.
Fight Summary: Contested in four-ounce gloves, about 15 miles from Denver on a branch of the Burlington Road, after two tame rounds Godfrey (168) almost knocked Johnson (171) senseless in the third, continuing to pound the latter around the ring at will. In the fourth Godfrey was again completely on top, Johnson being unable to do much about it, other than hold on for dear life. Told to break by the referee, Godfrey continued to pound away, eventually knocking Johnson to the floor with a right to the jaw. Although Johnson, who had been down three times, was comprehensively beaten, when his seconds claimed a foul the referee went along with it. Following the fight, although allowing the result to stand the organisers decided that as far as the stake money was concerned Godfrey should receive the lion's share. This appears to be the last fight for Johnson, while Godfrey continued to claim the 'black title'.

On 14 May, Godfrey challenged John L. Sullivan, who refused point blank. That was followed by the *Boston Police News* stating that Godfrey had every right to the 'black title'. In fact, Sullivan infamously refused to fight any black boxer and drew what came to be known as boxing's 'colour line' (or 'Colour Bar'), stating "I will not fight a Negro. I never have, and I never shall."

24 August 1888. Peter Jackson w rtd 19 (finish) George Godfrey.
Venue: California AC, San Francisco, California, USA. **Referee:** Hiram Cook.
Fight Summary: Billed for the 'black heavyweight title', Jackson (195), who was at least three inches taller and 30lbs heavier than Godfrey (165), made a good start when dropping the latter in the second with a solid uppercut. Having gained a decided advantage in the opening ten rounds, Jackson pushed on despite Godfrey making him work for every point. By the 19th session Godfrey was weakening, and after Jackson rained in punches

continuously the American, realising his hopeless position, retired himself. The fight was contested in two-ounce gloves.

In what was a risk fight of sorts Jackson put his 'black title' claim on the line against George Peters in a four-round contest at Whitney's Opera House, Detroit, Michigan on 25 July 1889. The result was never in doubt, the referee stopping the contest in Jackson's favour in the third. Like Godfrey before him, Jackson was constantly ignored by many of the white fighters of the day who were happy to use the 'Colour Bar' as a reason when choosing not to fight him.

30 September 1889. Jem Smith w pts 10 Jack Wannop.
Venue: Novelty Theatre, The Strand, London, England. **Referee:** W. J. King.
Fight Summary: Although not billed for the English championship, with Smith (192) being the recognised champion it was seen as a defence despite it not meeting championship conditions. A poor contest, it did not really warm up until the ninth round when Smith dropped his rival with a terrific right to the ribs. On getting up, Wannop (178) somehow survived the rest of the session before spending the tenth trying to nail Smith, who was happy to cruise to the bell.

The 36-year-old Wannop, who was a famous wrestler, next won a catchweight contest when forcing Josh Coshett to retire inside 12 rounds at the Ormonde Club, Walworth, London on 21 April 1890, but never made his mark in boxing.

11 November 1889. Peter Jackson w disq 2 (10) Jem Smith.
Venue: New Pelican Club, Soho, London, England. **Referee:** George Vize.
Fight Summary: After several pre-fight disputes the boxing finally got underway, being fast and furious with Jackson holding the upper hand. At the end of the first round Smith looked as though he had already taken a beating. Not letting up, after starting the second session Jackson produced even more powerful hitting. Barely able to land a punch Smith was being overwhelmed, and having back-heeled and thrown Jackson he was quite rightly disqualified. Although there was no championship billing attached, Jackson had much credibility as the 'black champion' at the time. He also claimed the Imperial British Empire title on the result.

A few weeks later, on 23 December, Smith took part in the last of the big bare-knuckle contests when meeting Frank Slavin in Bruges, Belgium. With Smith on the verge of defeat, when his supporters broke the fight up, a draw was announced after 14 rounds.

At the Gaiety Theatre, Glasgow, Scotland, on 7 February 1890, Charlie Mitchell outpointed the 58-year-old Jem Mace over four rounds in what was advertised as being for the English championship. In reality it was nothing of the kind, being merely a publicity stunt, and following the event the pair went on a sparring exhibition of the country. Mace would have lasting fame as the undefeated holder of the London Prize Ring title.

Meanwhile, after defeating the English champion Jackson had a run of victories over men such as Woolf Bendoff, Peter Maher and Denver Ed Smith before setting sail for America where he would meet America's James J. Corbett in a finish fight at the California AC, San Francisco, California on 21 May 1891. The contest was stopped during the 61st round by Hiram Cook, the referee, and declared to be a no contest after there had been no knockdowns and both men were extremely tired and stalling. Prior to the fight the newspapers were reporting that the result would open the way to settling the question of the championship of the world, as it was generally understood that the winner would eventually meet Slavin or any other man who might come forward now that John L. Sullivan was thought to have retired.

27 September 1890. Frank Slavin w rtd 2 (15) Joe McAuliffe.
Venue: Ormonde Club, Walworth, London, England. **Referee:** Bernard J. Angle.
Fight Summary: With George Vize and B. J. Angle acting as umpires (referees/judges) from outside the ring, the fight had initially been set for 30 rounds or more, but on the insistence of the police it was rescheduled for 15 with both men to use four-ounce gloves. Billed for the world championship, both fighters started as if they meant

business, and prior to the end of the opening round, following a clinch, Slavin (183) dropped McAuliffe (210) heavily. Although McAuliffe made it back to his corner, before too long in the second he began to cut a sorry figure as Slavin chased him down. With the blows raining in on him McAuliffe was dropped twice more before his seconds tossed in the towel following the second knockdown. Slavin won the *Police Gazette* Championship Belt on his victory.

Earlier in the year McAuliffe was reported to have agreed a match with John L. Sullivan for purse offers as high as $15,000, but this was denied by the 'Boston Strong Boy'. That was followed by McAuliffe claiming the American glove title by forfeit.

16 June 1891. Frank Slavin w rsc 9 (10) Jake Kilrain.
Venue: Granite Club, Hoboken, New Jersey, USA. **Referee:** Jerry Dunn.
Fight Summary: Slavin, who defended the *Police Gazette* Championship Belt in this one, had initially gone to America for the purpose of challenging John L. Sullivan, only to be told by the 'great' man himself that he had retired. Then, on learning that two of the other leading contenders, James J. Corbett and Peter Jackson, were already articled to fight, a match was made with Kilrain. Starting like a hurricane, Slavin (186) roared into Kilrain (190), having the latter over four times in the third round. Although he survived the fourth, Kilrain was knocked down repeatedly in the fifth before somehow managing to make it into the ninth where he continued to be pounded at will. It could not continue the way it was, and after Kilrain had just about made it to his feet following another knockdown the referee told him it was all over. The fight was contested in four-ounce gloves.

27 July 1891. Ted Pritchard w rtd 3 (finish) Jem Smith.
Venue: Wrestlers Public House, New Cross, London, England.
Fight Summary: Articled to decide the English title, Smith (181½) took a decided lead in the opening round when driving Pritchard (152) around the ring and flooring him twice before time was called. Although both of them went down twice in the second, it was Smith who looked all-in at the end of the session before retiring from the fray in the third after being dropped heavily. Following the fight, Pritchard's backer stated that his charge would not be defending the title as he was not big enough to take on all comers. He went on to say that Pritchard would concentrate on defending his middleweight championship.

30 May 1892. Peter Jackson w rsc 10 (20) Frank Slavin.
Venue: NSC, Covent Garden, London, England. **Referee:** Bernard J. Angle.
Fight Summary: It was evident after a few rounds that Slavin (185), his left eye already closed, had no chance against the bigger man. However, despite shipping punishment he was always trying to fight back. In the tenth Jackson (196) went all out for the win, and within two minutes of the session had forced a stoppage with a badly beaten Slavin lying helpless against the ropes. Although only billed for the championships of England and Australia, by his victory Jackson took over Slavin's *Police Gazette* Championship Belt. Jackson's Imperial British Empire title claim would have also been involved.

Unfortunately for Jackson, who was recognised as the 'black champion' after beating George Godfrey in 1888, John L. Sullivan continually ignored his challenges, preferring to put up a 'Colour Bar' instead. Sullivan was adamant that it had nothing to do with Jackson, but more to do with him being twice matched against Godfrey only for the fights to be called off by the promoter at the last minute following police interference. Eventually, it was James J. Corbett who grasped the opportunity while Jackson remained inactive for six years. Sadly, after returning to the ring for four more contests Jackson became a victim to the ravages of consumption, passing away on 13 July 1901.

7 September 1892. James J. Corbett w co 21 (finish) John L. Sullivan.
Venue: Olympic Club, New Orleans, Louisiana, USA. **Recognition:** World. **Referee:** John Duffy.
Fight Summary: As the world bare-knuckle champion since 1882 Sullivan had also been claiming to be the Queensberry Rules champion and, although the majority of boxing people accepted this fight as settling the world-gloved title, outside of America Peter Jackson should have had a fair bit of recognition also. Forcing the fight from the opening bell Sullivan (212) found Corbett (178) a difficult target, and by the 15th round he seemed to be all-in, having been unable to dislodge the much younger man. At the age of 44 it was all getting too much for Sullivan.

And although Corbett had boxed a defensive if not negative fight, when he began to open up Sullivan was dropped four times in the 21st session, the last time seeing him counted out. The fight was contested in regulation five-ounce gloves.

Having signed for a return bout with Jackson to take place early in 1893, after the contest fell through due to the latter's poor health, Corbett went on tour with the stage play, 'Gentleman Jack', and was out of the ring for over a year.

Meantime the middleweight champion, Bob Fitzsimmons, was also making waves, having already beaten Peter Maher (w co 12 at the Olympic Club on 2 March), and was considered in some parts of America as a future champion.

25 January 1894. James J. Corbett w co 3 (finish) Charlie Mitchell.
Venue: Duval AC, Jacksonville, Florida, USA. **Recognition:** World. **Referee:** John Kelly.
Fight Summary: Scheduled for 20 rounds or more in five-ounce gloves, Mitchell (158) made a reasonable start, despite being inactive for such a long time, before being knocked down in the second round. Fighting like a madman, when Corbett (184) proceeded to hit at the downed Mitchell he had to be pulled off, many believing he deserved to be disqualified at that point. The third session saw Mitchell battered to the floor three times, being counted out on the last occasion, but even then the referee had to hold Corbett back. Following the fight Mitchell announced his retirement.

Peter Jackson, the holder of the *Police Gazette* Championship Belt, was reported as the obvious man to meet Corbett having already defeated the best of four continents. However, the fight most people were hoping for was Corbett v Bob Fitzsimmons, the middleweight champion, who was now looking to add the heavyweight title to his collection.

On 18 June, Fitzsimmons met Joe Choynski in an eight-rounder at The Theatre, Boston, Massachusetts, the contest being stopped by police in the fifth with the middleweight champion well on top. Announced as a draw in line with the Articles, Fitzsimmons then successfully defended his middleweight title against Dan Creedon on 26 September while continually pushing for a fight with Corbett. Eventually, contracts were signed on 11 October for a finish fight to take place in Jacksonville, Florida no earlier than 1 July 1895, but with deposits in place a local Government Bill prohibiting boxing there was passed in early 1895. Under the terms of the contract if the fight in Jacksonville fell through there was a clause that allowed it to go out to best purse offers. Following all of the problems encountered, Dallas, Texas was chosen as the next venue, but when the Governor there refused support it was quickly transferred to Hot Springs, Arkansas. Unfortunately, for all concerned, the Governor of Arkansas issued a statement to the effect that he would not allow the staging of an event that was brutal and morally wrong, which was followed by the Sheriff of Hot Springs actually giving his blessing to the bout. However, when the Governor called all parties concerned to a meeting on 7 November 1895 to tell them that if they defied him they would be in serious trouble the fight was finally called off.

By now, with there being so much animosity between the two fighters, it was almost impossible for them to agree on anything and the fight was cancelled indefinitely. A few days later, immediately following a first-round kayo victory for Peter Maher over Corbett's sparring partner, Steve O'Donnell, at the Empire AC, Maspeth, Queens, NYC, New York on 11 November, Corbett jumped into the ring and announced his retirement. At the same time he awarded his title to the winner. Scheduled for 25 rounds, Maher had been quick out of the blocks, having O'Donnell down three times in the opening session from rights and lefts to the jaw before the latter was counted out by Tim Hurst on the 1.30 mark. A short while later Corbett admitted that he had been wrong in reacting in this peculiar fashion but was angry with Fitzsimmons for allowing himself to be talked out of their prospective fight in Hot Springs and, continually making derogatory remarks, he decided on teaching his rival a lesson. Out of action, apart from a couple of exhibitions since breaking his left hand during a sparring session in December, Fitzsimmons was matched against Maher, who was now calling himself the champion of the heavyweights.

10 May 1895. Jem Smith w co 2 (20) Ted Pritchard.
Venue: Central Hall, Holborn, London, England. **Referee:** Joe Steers.
Fight Summary: In a battle that was billed for the English heavyweight title it was reckoned to be one of the fiercest fights ever seen while it lasted, with Smith being allowed to get away with some of the most blatant fouls witnessed in a boxing ring. After both men had been floored in the opening session, Smith (175) four times and Pritchard (160) once, it quickly developed into a win at all costs affair, and coming up for the second round all involved were sensing that it was going to be more of the same. With the fighting intense, both men standing toe-to-toe and hammering in punch after punch to head and body, it was plainly obvious that it could not last. The first to show the effects was Pritchard, who eventually dropped down exhausted. The *Sporting Life* reported that the ring was then invaded by enthusiasts whose common sense had completely left them. Amidst the pandemonium, after the referee had spoken with the timekeeper and discovered that Pritchard had been on the floor for 15 seconds prior to getting up he declared Smith the winner. Although Smith could claim to be the national champion he was never really considered to be world class.

26 November 1895. Jem Smith w disq 9 (20) Dick Burge.
Venue: Bolingbroke Club, Clapham, London, England. **Referee:** Bernard J. Angle.
Fight Summary: Smith (178) successfully defended the English title against Burge (143½) in a contest that should never have been made, with the champion carrying more than 30 pounds advantage in weight. Right from the start Smith went after his rival, knocking him down once in the third round and five times in the seventh prior to coming up for the ninth session. It had been all one way with Burge just not heavy enough to hurt Smith, the challenger going down on one knee in virtually every round to avoid taking more punishment. Smith made it clear in the ninth that he was aiming to bring matters to a close, and to that end he had Burge over twice and all at sea. When Burge went down again without being hit the referee finally disqualified him for repeatedly using that tactic to save himself.

27 January 1896. Dan Creedon w co 2 (20) Jem Smith.
Venue: NSC, Covent Garden, London, England. **Referee:** Bernard J. Angle.
Fight Summary: Billed for the Imperial British Empire title that was considered vacant with Peter Jackson seemingly retired, it decided nothing with the winner being little more than a middleweight. The contest itself saw Smith (180) taking up the attack with Creedon (162) content to counter, and in the second round it continued in much the same vein. By now it was noticeable that Smith was falling well short, especially when going to the body, and after Creedon had finessed his rival forward one more time he drove in the right with such force on the Englishman's jaw that he was floored and counted out on the 1.25 mark.

21 February 1896. Bob Fitzsimmons w co 1 (finish) Peter Maher.
Venue: Near Langtry, Texas, USA. **Referee:** George Siler.
Fight Summary: This fight took place on a sandbar in the Rio Grande, therefore beyond the reach of the law, a short train journey from El Paso on the US/Mexico border. It was due to be the first major fight captured on film with the promoter and certainly not the fighters, which deeply angered Fitzsimmons, due to benefit from the film rights. After only 95 seconds Maher (180) was knocked out following a short right to the jaw from Fitzsimmons (165). Having stepped inside Maher's swinging right to deliver the kayo Fitzsimmons was somewhat pleased when he found that the Kinetoscope operators had been unable to set the machine up in time to film any of the action whatsoever.

A great deal of people still thought a champion should lose his title in the ring, and with the public refusing to fully recognise Fitzsimmons after his defeat of Maher, Corbett eventually regained his taste for boxing, being matched to meet Tom Sharkey over four rounds at the Mechanics' Pavilion, San Francisco, California on 24 June. Not at his best, Corbett had a tough time controlling the rushing tactics of Sharkey and was in a bad way after being twice bundled to the floor before being rescued by police intervention. The decision to stop matters in the final session was taken by the authorities when it was felt that the contest had turned into a brawl and was inciting the crowd. Although he had come close to being beaten, Corbett agreed to give Sharkey a return with the title at stake but, after protracted negotiations with nothing signed, it was announced on 13 September that the champion had signed up to meet Fitzsimmons prior to 1 March 1897. Meantime, Fitzsimmons was matched to fight Sharkey in a warm-up.

At The Amphitheatre, Johannesburg, South Africa on 7 November, Australia's Joe Goddard knocked out Denver Ed Smith inside four rounds of a scheduled 20. Billed for the South African open title, with some reports mistakenly giving it world championship status, Goddard, despite regularly challenging the world, was unable to build on that performance.

2 December 1896. Tom Sharkey w disq 8 (10) Bob Fitzsimmons.
Venue: Mechanics' Pavilion, San Francisco, California, USA. **Referee:** Wyatt Earp.
Fight Summary: Announced as being the world champion, Fitzsimmons (173½) moved into Sharkey (182) from the off before having the sailor down in the first, fifth and sixth rounds. The last occasion saw Sharkey hauled back into the ring in a dazed state. After hammering away non-stop in the seventh, Fitzsimmons tore into Sharkey in the eighth, and following right and left swings to the head the latter was sent crashing from a left uppercut to the jaw. To the surprise of all those present, the famous Marshall, Wyatt Earp, who was acting as referee, disqualified Fitzsimmons, claiming that the champion had struck Sharkey in the groin as he was on the way down. Sharkey was unconscious for nearly 15 minutes.

The victim of what most people described as a diabolical decision, despite Fitzsimmons going to court to get the result overturned the judge decided that the referee's verdict should stand. Earp was rumoured to have been a member of a betting ring who had money on Sharkey. However, with everybody present knowing who the better man was, Fitzsimmons' forthcoming championship fight with James J. Corbett continued to attract a great deal of interest.

Regardless of that, Sharkey, who next drew with Jim Williams in an eight-round no-decision contest at the Athletic Club, Salt Lake City, Utah on 5 April 1897, still laid claim to the title even though there was little recognition forthcoming.

21 December 1896. Bob Armstrong w co 19 (20) Charley Strong.
Venue: Broadway AC, Manhattan, NYC, New York, USA. **Referee:** Dick Roche.
Fight Summary: With these two reckoned to be among the top flight they were matched to contest the vacant 'black title' in a fight that came about due to the leading black fighters of the day being sidelined for championship matches. The match itself saw Strong fighting gamely despite being outclassed by Armstrong, who used his greater reach to good effect, and in the 19th he was sent to the boards by a left swing to the head and counted out.

It has been reported down the years that Armstrong was knocked out by Joe Butler in the second round of a Philadelphia, Pennsylvania six-round no-decision contest at the beginning of 1897. As yet, I have not found evidence of that fight taking place.

19 February 1897. George Chrisp w disq 5 (8) Jem Smith.
Venue: Ginnett's Circus, Newcastle, England. **Referee:** Ed Plummer.
Fight Summary: On undertaking to stop Chrisp (164) inside the distance Smith (188) had great difficulty in catching the fleet-footed northerner, who showed that he was able to keep on the move and keep his distance in the early stages. Having had little success, Smith completely lost his head in the fifth round. After cornering and cutting up Chrisp with rough tactics while continually taking no notice of the referee's call to break, Smith paid the consequences when being disqualified. Although there was no title billing, it not being contested over a championship distance, this did not stop Chrisp from claiming the English title despite scant support.

6 March 1897. Bob Armstrong w rsc 6 (15) Joe Butler.
Venue: Broadway AC, Manhattan, NYC, New York, USA. **Referee:** Dick Roche.
Fight Summary: This was recognised as a contest for the 'black title'. Outweighed by at least 20 pounds Butler was unable to get close enough to Armstrong, who jabbed at will, and was floored in the second round by a straight

left. Bleeding badly, by the sixth Butler was being battered relentlessly and ready to drop when the referee called it off with 45 seconds on the clock.

The following day, according to some records Armstrong was supposed to have lost a six-round points decision in Philadelphia, Pennsylvania to Frank Childs, another black fighter, but I have yet to find notification of that fight taking place.

17 March 1897. Bob Fitzsimmons w co 14 (finish) James J. Corbett.
Venue: Racetrack Arena, Carson City, Nevada, USA. **Recognition:** World. **Referee:** George Siler.
Fight Summary: From the start Corbett's skilful boxing had Fitzsimmons (167) bleeding, especially from stiff left jabs, and when he was put down from a right to the jaw in the sixth it looked as though the end was not too far away. After getting up at the count of 'nine' (Corbett and his manager claimed it was at least 13 seconds), when Fitzsimmons started to go for the body, by the end of the tenth Corbett looked tired out, so much so that the odds had shrunk to evens. Corbett (183) still had something left, but it was not enough. In the 14th session, with the champion sufficiently weakened, Fitzsimmons, feigning a southpaw stance, drove in a tremendous left hook under the heart. Lifted off his feet by the sheer force of the punch, Corbett went crashing down to be counted out. It was a blow that Fitzsimmons had perfected over a long period of time and it gained fame as the 'solar plexus punch', a left hook to the body. It was Robert H. Davis, the author and reporter, who coined the phrase, but according to Joe Choynski it was a punch to the liver that paralysed Corbett.

Immediately following the fight, Fitzsimmons announced that he was retiring to go on the music halls and was resigning the title. Several times during the next few months he reiterated this, but no one seemed to take it seriously. It later transpired that when Corbett had asked for a return he was told by Mrs Fitzsimmons, the new champion's manager, her husband would be going on a theatrical tour and would not fight again for at least two years.

Two days after Fitzsimmons' victory over Corbett, on 19 March, Sharkey again laid claim to the title, stating that the championship was his until his colours were lowered. Following that, on 27 April, it was reported that Peter Jackson had challenged Corbett for the vacant title, but with the Australian not in the greatest of condition it came to nothing.

Meanwhile, with Fitzsimmons continuing to state that he had retired, he sent letters out to all the leading newspapers on 4 October formally relinquishing the title. Regardless, there were many who felt that Fitzsimmons was bluffing, for whatever reason. On 26 January 1898, Charles Kid McCoy challenged either Corbett or Fitzsimmons to a bout to decide the world championship, stating that if the challenges were not accepted he would be claiming the title. While Corbett ignored the challenge, Fitzsimmons at first accepted before stating that he would only box McCoy if the latter beat Peter Maher first. With Fitzsimmons continuing to posture about retirement, McCoy claimed the title on 9 March 1898 and after the champion had failed to cover a forfeit the *New York Herald* reported that McCoy would be fighting Gus Ruhlin for the championship.

23 April 1897. Bob Armstrong w rtd 1 (10) Sam Pruitt.
Venue: National AC, Woodward's Pavilion, San Francisco, California, USA. **Referee:** Hiram Cook.
Fight Summary: Right from the opening bell Pruitt looked a beaten man, his whole demeanour giving the general impression that he would rather be somewhere else than be facing up to the 'black title' claimant. Taking the initiative Armstrong was soon banging in lefts to head and body, and having received a hefty blow to the stomach Pruitt walked to his corner after telling the referee that he was through for the night. The fight had lasted a matter of seconds.

In defence of his 'black title' claim, Armstrong forced Jack Douglass to retire in the second of an eight-round contest at the Second Regiment Armoury, Chicago on 13 September.

9 June 1897. Tom Sharkey drew 7 (20) Peter Maher.
Venue: Palace AC, Manhattan, NYC, New York, USA. **Referee:** Jimmy Colville.

Fight Summary: After five tame rounds that had angered the fans, Sharkey (173) got first blood when he dropped Maher (173) in the sixth with a straight left to the face. Maher came back somewhat in the seventh when flooring Sharkey for a short count, but when the two men carried on after the bell had rung to end the session the fight was stopped by the police. Despite it being a thoroughly unsatisfactory ending the referee had no option other than giving a draw.

Following the contest, Sharkey departed for Britain, knocking out four limited 'home-based' fighters in Joe Craig (1st round), Pat McCourt (2nd), Tom Parks (1st) and Punch Vaughn (3rd) before returning home in September.

On 3 November, Maher challenged the world to decide the vacant title, Sharkey and Peter Jackson preferred, and two weeks later the *Sporting Life* reported that Maher, having been turned down by James J. Corbett, was being favoured by many as the next world heavyweight champion. Although Maher tried for matches against all the leading men he failed to get any of them into the ring, and while waiting he took on four six-round contests at The Arena in Philadelphia, Pennsylvania in 1898, knocking out Yank Kenney in the first on 21 January, C. C. Smith in the third on 15 February and stopping Steve O'Donnell in the second on 16 March before being knocked out by Joe Goddard after just 1.50 of the opening session on 12 May, thereby dramatically reducing his stock. Given the chance to fight Goddard again, this time over 25 rounds, Maher gained revenge on 8 July 1898 when forcing his opponent to retire himself in the eighth at the Lenox AC, Manhattan, but the damage had already been done.

18 November 1897. Tom Sharkey w rsc 6 (20) Joe Goddard.
Venue: Mechanics' Pavilion, San Francisco, California, USA. **Referee:** Bob McArthur.
Fight Summary: Having dropped Goddard (193) twice in the opening two rounds Sharkey (178) resorted to rushing his man in the next three sessions with very little happening. In the sixth Sharkey continued to bore in, and after sending Goddard down with a right to the head he proceeded to fall on top of him with great force. Although Goddard beat the count he was in no condition to continue, the referee stopping the fight. Sharkey stated afterwards that he would be challenging Bob Fitzsimmons again and, if after a reasonable time the champion had failed to accept his offer, he would continue to claim the title.

29 January 1898. Frank Childs w co 2 (6) Bob Armstrong.
Venue: Athletic Association Gym, Chicago, Illinois, USA. **Referee:** George Siler.
Fight Summary: Only a six-rounder, but the 'black title' changed hands on the result after Armstrong gave up in the second round. Having dropped Armstrong in the first, Childs tore into his rival in the second to put him down again with a right to the jaw. Getting up at 'nine' Armstrong was soon under attack, and after being dropped twice more he was counted out.

Childs next risked his 'black title' claim in Chicago six-rounders at the Athletic Association Gym against George Grant (w pts 6 on 7 February) and Klondike (on 26 February). Depending on what papers you read the fight against Klondike ended in Childs' favour by a disqualification, either in the third or fourth round. On 3 June, at Tattersall's, Chicago, Childs put his 'black title' claim on the line against Charley Strong over six rounds, the result being a draw.

11 March 1898. Tom Sharkey drew 8 (20) Joe Choynski.
Venue: Woodward's Pavilion, San Francisco, California, USA. **Referee:** George Green.
Fight Summary: Yet another rough and tumble of a contest instigated by Sharkey (178) saw him rush Choynski (168) time and again, repeatedly fouling him. Choynski was easily the better boxer of the two, sending in stiff left jabs but, after being dropped more by a push than a punch in the fifth, on getting up he was forced over the ropes before help arrived in the shape of the attending police. Hurt in the sixth, when Sharkey continued his rushing tactics in the eighth, dropping Choynski with a dubious punch, he then pushed him through the ropes. At that point, the referee, calling the fight off on the instructions of the police, announced a drawn decision.

6 May 1898. James J. Jeffries w pts 20 Tom Sharkey.
Venue: Mechanics' Pavilion, San Francisco, California, USA. **Referee:** Alex Greggains.
Fight Summary: With just ten contests under his belt Jeffries (205) showed great maturity when handling the rough, tough Sharkey with some ease in the opening four rounds. Regardless that some sessions were slow Jeffries

landed well to force Sharkey to the ropes, while the latter often fell short with his best efforts. Dropped by a right to the ear in the 11th Sharkey was then hit repeatedly, being in some distress on occasions. Both men were tired from the 17th onwards, but both fought viciously to the final bell, with Jeffries cheered to the rafters on the decision. Although taking over Sharkey's title claim Jeffries stated that he would be looking to make a match with Peter Maher before trying to get it on with Bob Fitzsimmons.

On 25 July, in most of the newspapers of the day, it was reported that Jeffries was one of several men now claiming the heavyweight title.

Agreeing to fight two ten-round contests at the Lenox AC, Manhattan, NYC, New York on 5 August, Jeffries easily outpointed Bob Armstrong, but was unable to meet Steve O'Donnell after breaking his left arm on the former 'black champion's' head. Subsequently, following several months out of the ring, Jeffries, who was now being acclaimed by many as the unbeaten heavyweight champion, signed to meet the returning Fitzsimmons on 30 March 1899.

20 May 1898. Charles Kid McCoy w pts 20 Gus Ruhlin.
Venue: Empire Club, The Alhambra, Syracuse, New York, USA. **Referee:** George Siler.
Fight Summary: Reported as the first defence of his heavyweight title claim, having been turned down by both Bob Fitzsimmons and James J. Corbett, McCoy (157) soon proved to be far more mobile than Ruhlin (180), utilising the jab well and cutting the bigger man up. The last four rounds saw Ruhlin looking by far the stronger as both men tired, but McCoy remained alert to the big punches coming his way before taking the decision.

Despite his victory McCoy received little or no recognition whatsoever. However, when terms were agreed on 11 July for McCoy to meet Corbett at the Hawthorne AC, Buffalo, New York on 27 August it seemed as though the public would see a real title battle. Unfortunately, after hearing that his father and mother had died following a shooting on 16 August, Corbett, who had reclaimed his old title, called the fight off. It transpired that Pat Corbett, the fighter's father, had shot his mother, Kate, before turning the gun on himself.

In a six-round contest on 16 December, McCoy beat Joe Goddard, the 'Barrier champion' (a region near his home town in New South Wales, Australia), by a fifth-round disqualification at The Arena, Philadelphia, Pennsylvania, before going on to defend his claim against Tom Sharkey.

14 September 1898. George Byers w pts 20 Frank Childs.
Venue: Lenox AC, Manhattan, NYC, New York, USA. **Referee:** Johnny White.
Fight Summary: Billed for the 'black title', with Childs' claim on the line, Byers (165) made a good start when having his rival bleeding badly from damage to the left eye in the fourth round following a succession of left jabs. Continuing to play on the injury Byers moved ahead as Childs, whose eye was closed shut as the fight moved along, held on to reach the final bell after failing to find a finishing blow.

As in other instances, with Childs not letting a defeat get in the way of his 'black title' aspirations he carried on defending his claim in six-round contests against Charley Strong (w pts 6 at the American AA, Chicago, Illinois on 8 November) and Joe Butler (w disq 2 at Tattersall's Club, Chicago on 21 January 1899).

22 November 1898. Tom Sharkey w disq 9 (20) James J. Corbett.
Venue: Lenox AC, Manhattan, NYC, New York, USA. **Referee:** John Kelly.
Fight Summary: Effectively the first defence of Corbett's title claim, it all went wrong for the ex-champion when he was dropped heavily by Sharkey (176) in the second round before twisting an ankle in the third. Although Corbett (182) came back well Sharkey's strength was gaining him the upper hand. However, by the seventh the contest had turned into a brawl, and with punches from both men going below the belt in the ninth Corbett's seconds rushed into the ring and their man was disqualified. The sailor would next take on Charles Kid McCoy, with both men's poorly regarded versions of the title being at stake.

10 January 1899. Tom Sharkey w co 10 (20) Charles Kid McCoy.
Venue: Lenox AC, Manhattan, NYC, New York, USA. **Referee:** Tim Hurst.
Fight Summary: Although being a fight that was not recognised by many as involving the heavyweight championship, McCoy (156), who made Sharkey (173) look like a selling-plater for much of the time, sent the latter to the floor twice in the third and battered him at will on occasion. It was only Sharkey's superb conditioning that kept him in the fight up until the middle rounds, but in the eighth he came on strongly to drop McCoy heavily with a body punch. Although the referee counted to 'eight' McCoy seemed to have been down for well over ten seconds. Having taken a battering in the ninth, McCoy was sent crashing from a left hook to the neck in the tenth and counted out. However, in the din Sharkey had not heard the count, and after McCoy got to his feet the sailor smashed in three vicious blows to drop him yet again. At this point the referee stopped the contest, stating that he had already counted McCoy out on his previous visit to the canvas.

With McCoy losing his claim in this one, it was Sharkey who went on to meet James J. Jeffries in a title decider after he had beaten Jack McCormick by a second-round knockout at The Arena, Philadelphia, Pennsylvania on 30 January.

4 March 1899. Frank Childs w rtd 6 (10) Bob Armstrong.
Venue: Stag AC, Cincinnati, Ohio, USA. **Referee:** Johnny Murphy.
Fight Summary: Reduced from 15 rounds due to State law, Armstrong, who was far the taller of the pair, started well with the left jab before being staggered in the second round by a solid right to the jaw. Picking it up in the third Childs soon had Armstrong in trouble, dropping him with a right swing to the head. Both men gave it everything they had in the fourth and fifth sessions before Childs got right on top. In the sixth Armstrong was sent crashing into the ropes from a heavy right to the jaw, and when he rebounded off them another big right sent him staggering around the ring in a befuddled state, whereupon his corner threw up the sponge.

6 May 1899. Klondike w co 5 (6) Jack Johnson.
Venue: Howard Theatre, Chicago, Illinois, USA. **Referee:** Malachy Hogan.
Fight Summary: Even though he had little more than a handful of fights under his belt, as a recent winner of a 'battle royal' in Springfield, Illinois Johnson was reckoned to be a good match for Klondike by none other than George Siler, the famed referee and boxing writer. Once Siler began eulogising about Johnson's potential it was not long before they were matched for the 'black title', regardless of the fact that George Byers already had a claim and it was just a six-round affair. After the bout quickly exploded into life it was only the bell bringing the first round to an end that saved Klondike, who had been dropped heavily by a left big uppercut. Years later the referee admitted that he had given Klondike a long count that enabled him to eventually get up at 'nine'. Although Klondike was still groggy at the start of the second, quickly getting his legs back he was soon matching Johnson blow for blow. Towards the end of the fifth Klondike dropped Johnson with a solid left to the midsection, and after the latter had rolled over into a more comfortable sitting position he was counted out. If those at ringside were surprised at Johnson's actions they were even more taken aback when he got up the moment the count had been completed and headed for the dressing room, looking to be still full of fight. Conflicting reports stated that the fight took place on 8 May and that it was the end of the fourth round the fight ended, not the fifth.

Three risk fights for Klondike came in six-rounders in Chicago against George Grant (w pts 6 at Fort Dearborn AC on 12 May), Scaldy Bill Quinn (w rsc 2 at the Illinois AC on 27 May) and Frank Childs (l pts 6 at Fort Dearborn AC on 11 August), but despite losing on points to the latter he continued with his claim.

9 June 1899. James J. Jeffries w co 11 (25) Bob Fitzsimmons.
Venue: Greater New York AC, Brooklyn, NYC, New York, USA. **Recognition:** World. **Referee:** George Siler.
Fight Summary: Fitzsimmons (167) made the early running but found it difficult to reach the crouching Jeffries' body before he was dropped in the second round from a straight left. Swinging rights to the ribs were also beginning to hurt Fitzsimmons. By now fighting an uphill battle, having hit the challenger with his best punches to no avail Fitzsimmons was floored twice in the tenth prior to being taken out by a left-right to the jaw in the 11th. Thus Jeffries (206) won the championship after just 12 contests, a record he shared with James J. Corbett.

However, history shows him to have then drawn the 'Colour Bar', an action that precluded great fighters such as Jack Johnson from getting the chance to fight for the title during his tenure.

Following exhibition bouts against George Chrisp and Jack Scales in London on successive nights in August, Jeffries claimed that the latter was, in his opinion, the best heavyweight in England. Following that Scales challenged all England, with Chrisp being the preferred opponent. When Chrisp failed to sign for an English championship contest against him on 5 December of that year Scales claimed the title by forfeit.

24 July 1899. George Byers w rsc 9 (10) Charley Strong.
Venue: Coney Island AC, Brooklyn, NYC, New York, USA.
Fight Summary: Defending the 'black title', Byers was floored by Strong in the second round by a heavy left. He was then cut on the left eye in the third. Although fighting viciously, Strong, who came in as a replacement for Frank Childs, was knocked down twice in the eighth before the referee rescued him when he was almost out on his feet in the ninth.

28 October 1899. Frank Childs w co 3 (6) Klondike.
Venue: Athletic Association Gym, Chicago, Illinois, USA. **Referee:** Joe Choynski.
Fight Summary: Childs, who was superior in every way to his rival, took over Klondike's 'black title' claim when a left uppercut dropped the latter like a log to be counted out at 60 seconds of the third round. Prior to that Childs had controlled the fight, avoided Klondike's rushes and scored with heavy blows to the body.

With both fighters' title claims at stake, Childs drew over six rounds with George Byers at the Star AC, Chicago on 16 March 1900. In what was a strange one, Childs next defended his claim with a fourth-round kayo win over Joe Butler at the Athletic Association Gym, Chicago on 15 December 1900. Having gone down in the second round and been counted out sitting on the floor looking for a foul, Butler, despite being talked into carrying on, was knocked out again a couple of rounds later.

3 November 1899. James J. Jeffries w pts 25 Tom Sharkey.
Venue: Greater New York AC, Brooklyn, NYC, New York, USA. **Recognition:** World. **Referee:** George Siler.
Fight Summary: Fighting under the glare of 400 arc lights to enable filming, the arena was like a hot house but it did not appear to affect Jeffries (215) or Sharkey (183) who battled away throughout. After putting Sharkey down in the second round, despite the majority of the crowd thinking that the champion would finish his rival off, the tough sailor got up and went toe-to-toe. Neither took a backward step, and when Jeffries was given the verdict in what was a close fight Sharkey lost any claim he may have had to the title.

9 February 1900. Dick Burge w co 1 (20) Jack Scales.
Venue: New Palace Club, Westminster, London, England. **Referee:** Ed Plummer.
Fight Summary: Despite Burge (146) being far too light to be considered a heavyweight title claimant, within five seconds of the opening round he had dropped Scales (174) and had the latter at his mercy. On Scales rising, Burge smashed in lefts and rights on his stricken foe to floor him yet again. Down fell Scales time after time only to rise and receive more hard blows before eventually being deposited over the lower rope and counted out. With Burge moving on, Scales continued to claim the championship after what appeared to be a decided 'fix' in the eyes of many of those present.

Among the men to challenge all England were John Jackson (28 February) and Pat Daly, who won a championship competition at Wonderland, Mile End, London on 5 March when knocking out Jim Styles in the first round of the final.

Earlier, Daly, making his debut as a heavyweight, eliminated Scales from the competition following a three-round points win. However, when Daly, who always claimed his victory over Scales was by a third-round kayo, was challenged by the latter to decide the championship over 20 rounds he declined the offer, thus forfeiting any right he had to be called champion.

Meanwhile, Scales knocked out Cloggy Saunders in the second of their scheduled ten two-minute rounds contest at the same venue on 7 January 1901 before being knocked out in the fourth by Harry Neumier (again in the same ring) on 22 April 1901. Also reported as a first-round kayo defeat by the *Mirror of Life*, Scales' stock slumped even though it was a mere six two-minute rounder and contested over a non-championship distance.

6 April 1900. James J. Jeffries w co 1 (10) Jack Finnegan.
Venue: Light Guard Armoury, Detroit, Michigan, USA. **Recognition:** World. **Referee:** George Siler.
Fight Summary: Only scheduled for ten rounds, Jeffries (240) did not even know who his opponent was until three days before the fight. Even though there was little or no media coverage whatsoever, it has to be seen as a defence of Jeffries' title. As a warm-up for his forthcoming contest against James J. Corbett the champion wasted little time in scoring a 55-second kayo win, flooring Finnegan (180) twice before knocking him out with a left to the body.

11 May 1900. James J. Jeffries w co 23 (25) James J. Corbett.
Venue: Greater New York AC, Brooklyn, NYC, New York, USA. **Recognition:** World. **Referee:** Charlie White.
Fight Summary: Having almost walked the first 22 rounds Corbett (188) was entitled to think that he was well on the way to getting his title back, especially as Jeffries' left eye was closed and his face was a mess. Told that he was miles behind on points Jeffries (218) prepared himself for one almighty effort in the 23rd, and when the dancing Corbett slowed to deliver a right cross he was beaten to the punch by a mighty left hook thrown by a desperate champion. With Corbett badly shaken, when the second punch went in a moment later he crashed to the floor to be counted out.

17 December 1900. George Chrisp w co 14 (20) Harry Smith.
Venue: Ginnett's Circus, Newcastle, England. **Referee:** Thomas Gale.
Fight Summary: Made at catchweights but given English heavyweight title billing locally, Chrisp (170) had not fought seriously since losing to the American, Frank Craig, in November 1898. Although Chrisp's blows had more venom than those of his opponent it was soon noticeable that Smith (167) was scoring more effectively as he began to build up a lead. By the third, with the pace being terrific it was hardly surprising that the men were already tiring. In the fifth, Chrisp, scoring heavily with uppercuts and swings to both head and body, was looking the stronger. Keeping up the momentum he had Smith groggy in the seventh, and although the latter was landing more he was struggling to keep clear of the punishment, especially to the body. Coming into the 13th, with Smith slowing considerably Chrisp picked up the pace before sending the Birmingham man to the floor following four heavy rights to the jaw. Gamely getting to his feet Smith was at the mercy of Chrisp before the bell came to his rescue, but he would not be so lucky in the 14th when a terrific left hook to the jaw saw him smashed to the floor and counted out. With Jack Scales not that highly thought of as an English title claimant, Chrisp immediately put in a claim of his own.

16 March 1901. Frank Childs w co 17 (20) George Byers.
Venue: The Arena, Whittington Park, Hot Springs, Arkansas, USA. **Referee:** Bat Masterson.
Fight Summary: Looking to relieve Byers of his 'black title' honours while defending his own claim in this one, Childs had it all his own way, scoring three knockdowns before applying the finishing blow in the 17th. Although much the cleverer, Byers, who was giving away both height and weight, was unable to hurt Childs.

Fighting in Chicago, Illinois six-rounders in 1902, Childs risked all against Walter Johnson (w pts 6 at the Athletic Association Gym on 18 January), Denver Ed Martin (l pts 6 at the American AC on 24 February) and Joe Walcott (nc 3 at the Apollo Hall on 9 October). Following the Martin bout the latter was also claiming the 'black title' on being given the verdict, but as it was contested over a short distance it carried little weight.

1 April 1901. George Chrisp w co 8 (20) Ben Taylor.
Venue: Standard Theatre, Gateshead, England. **Referee:** Eugene Corri.
Fight Summary: Effectively putting up his British title claim against the 20-year-old Taylor in a catchweight contest, Chrisp showed up well when following up left jabs to the face with heavy rights under the heart to ultimately subdue the erratic youngster. Although showing up as a heavy puncher Taylor was easy to hit, and in the fourth he

was down twice from right-hand counters. As strong as ever in the fifth, despite being cautioned for using the illegal pivot punch, Taylor held his own against Chrisp for the next couple of rounds before being dropped by a right to the jaw at the end of the seventh and saved by the bell. Taylor seemed fine when coming out for the eighth, but was soon sent down for the full count after right-lefts to the point had opened him up.

In his very next contest Chrisp (170lbs) was knocked out in 11 rounds by the 154lbs Philadelphia Jack O'Brien at Ginnett's Circus, Newcastle on 20 May. He later forfeited any right he had to the English title when kayoed by Jack Mullen in a non-descript 15 rounder, not contested under championship conditions, at the same venue on 23 February 1903. While Mullen declined to claim the English title on the result, Chrisp announced his retirement.

23 September 1901. Jack Scales w co 11 (20) Jack Palmer.
Venue: Ginnett's Circus, Newcastle, England. **Referee:** George Dunning.
Fight Summary: Stated at the time to be a defence of his English title claim, Scales (175) took on a much lighter man in Palmer (154), who showed up well early on before being brought to the boards in the fourth with a right swing to the jaw, following a sustained burst of body blows. After being punched all around the ring in the fifth Palmer came back well in the sixth to have Scales over towards the end of the session. Palmer continued to take the fight to his man, and although Scales had him over three times in the eighth he was also forced to take a count. Down once in the ninth and twice in the tenth, when Palmer was battered down by lefts and rights in the 11th and counted-out a terrible uproar ensued due to an objection that the count was just five seconds. Immediately following the decision the referee stated that he had no other course open to him as he had nothing to do with the timekeeper, upon whom both men had agreed.

15 November 1901. James J. Jeffries w rtd 5 (20) Gus Ruhlin.
Venue: Mechanics' Pavilion, San Francisco, California, USA. **Recognition:** World. **Referee:** Harry Corbett.
Fight Summary: Ruhlin (194) was hammered throughout by Jeffries (211), it being only his cleverness that enabled him to last as long as he did. Knocked down in the third round and saved by the bell he was immediately under pressure in the fourth as Jeffries hooked in short rights to the body. However, by the end of the fifth, with Ruhlin appearing to have recuperated, it was a surprise when he failed to answer the bell to open the sixth.

Shortly after the contest Jeffries stated that he would not be meeting Denver Ed Martin under any circumstances as, in the event of losing, he had no wish to see a black world heavyweight champion.

25 June 1902. Denver Ed Martin w rsc 5 (10) Sandy Ferguson.
Venue: NSC, Covent Garden, London, England.
Fight Summary: Due to meet Bob Armstrong in a 'black title' fight, with the latter indisposed Martin was matched against Ferguson who had outpointed Woolwich's Ben Taylor over ten rounds at Wonderland, London on 3 March. Strangely, Taylor had been spoken of as the English champion in the *Sporting Life* on 14 May. Reported as an English title fight, which it was not, according to Martin it was a defence of the world heavyweight title he was claiming due to James J. Jeffries' refusal to meet him. With Martin soon on top, his physical strength and aggression wearing Ferguson down, after the latter became reckless it would be just a matter of time before the contest came to an end. Early in the fifth Martin floored Ferguson with a right hook to the jaw, and on getting up in a dazed condition the Canadian was dropped three more times before the referee finally rescued him.

25 June 1902. Jack Scales w pts 10 Ben Taylor.
Venue: New Adelphi Theatre, The Strand, London, England. **Referee:** Eugene Corri.
Fight Summary: Billed for the English Coronation Championship Belt, both men were down early on before Scales started to impose himself on Taylor by the fifth round. There was never a lot between them, other than Scales providing the more skilful boxing and Taylor always being dangerous with his heavy hitting right through to the final bell.

On 13 September, Jack Palmer knocked out Harry Slounch Dixon inside five rounds of a scheduled ten at Ginnett's Circus, Newcastle. Despite being given no title billing as such, Palmer put in an English title claim on the result.

A month later, on 13 October, Scales also beat Dixon (w co 7 at the NSC, Covent Garden, London) in a contest scheduled for ten three-minute rounds. It was hardly contested under championship conditions, but Scales' right to the English title was automatically at stake. When he was knocked out inside three rounds by Charlie Wilson at Wonderland, Mile End, London on 8 November, Scales' title claim all but disintegrated, whereas the winner would go on to challenge all England on the result, that, despite it being contested over six two-minute rounds. In December it was announced that a contest for the English title between Scales and Dixon had been cancelled due to the former having an abscess on his shoulder.

Another contest that had some bearing on the English title came on 16 March 1903, when Dixon drew with Taylor at Wonderland. Billed for the English title despite it being contested over 12 (one extra added on to try and find a winner) two-minute rounds, neither man was accorded much recognition. Things became even more confused a few days later when Pat Daly, the winner of an English championship competition in March 1900, challenged all England on 21 March.

25 July 1902. Denver Ed Martin w pts 15 Bob Armstrong.
Venue: Crystal Palace Grounds, Sydenham, London, England. **Referee:** Tom Scott.
Fight Summary: Reported to be for the 'black world championship' it was quickly apparent that Martin (186) was the better stylist of the two men, especially when using smart footwork to avoid Armstrong's rushes while sending in pile-driving left jabs. In the fifth round Martin's better work paid off when he dropped Armstrong (196) with a heavy right uppercut, but he was lucky to get away without a warning when he hit the latter who was still on the floor. Although Armstrong's powers of recovery were good he could not hold off Martin indefinitely, and in the 11th a right to the jaw had him down again. Despite Armstrong being second best over the remaining four sessions Martin was unable to take further advantage, having to settle for the points decision.

25 July 1902. James J. Jeffries w co 8 (20) Bob Fitzsimmons.
Venue: Athletic Club Arena, San Francisco, California, USA. **Recognition:** World. **Referee:** Ed Graney.
Fight Summary: Given the opportunity to regain his old title Fitzsimmons (172) started well, his left hand picking off the slower champion whose face was covered in blood after three rounds. At the end of the fifth Fitzsimmons was still going strong, making Jeffries (219) miss while jabbing and dropping in right hands. In the sixth Jeffries at last began to weaken Fitzsimmons with tremendous rights to the body. Although Fitzsimmons came back well to take the seventh, after being caught by a cracking right to the body in the eighth he dropped down in agony to be counted out.

At Sutton's Broadway Theatre, Butte, Montana, on 19 December, Jeffries took on Jack Munroe in a four-round exhibition in which he was contracted to stop his rival inside the distance or lose both the decision and the $500 stake money. With Munroe still on his feet at the final bell he would eventually meet Jeffries for the championship in August 1904.

16 August 1902. Denver Ed Martin w rtd 3 (10) Frank Craig.
Venue: Ginnett's Circus, Newcastle, England. **Referee:** Sam Francis.
Fight Summary: Recognised as being a contest for the 'black title', having undertaken to stop Craig inside the distance, Martin was soon in control. To ease the pressure Craig kept dropping down early on before surprising all when flooring Martin in the second. However, Martin came back strongly to deck Craig towards the end of the third, and after the latter failed to claim a foul he was retired at the end of the session.

30 August 1902. Denver Ed Martin w co 4 (10) Frank Craig.
Venue: Ginnett's Circus, Newcastle, England. **Referee:** Sam Francis.
Fight Summary: In defence of his 'black title' claim, Martin, who had met Craig just two weeks earlier, was again contracted to stop his rival inside ten rounds. Having been dropped twice in the second round Craig came back strongly towards the end of the session to stagger his fellow-American, and although he got through the third without too many problems he was soon under pressure in the fourth. After going down without taking a punch early on, following another visit to the canvas from a right to the jaw, a similar blow sent Craig crashing to be counted out moments later.

That was Martin's last contest in England before returning to America, where he next risked his claim against Bob Armstrong (nd-w pts 6 at the Penn Art Club, Philadelphia, Pennsylvania on 11 December). Some reports give this as a six-round no contest.

21 October 1902. Jack Johnson w rtd 12 (20) Frank Childs.
Venue: Hazzard's Pavilion, Los Angeles, California, USA. **Referee:** John Brink.
Fight Summary: Johnson took over Childs' 'black title' claim after the latter's corner threw in the towel, arguing that their man was suffering badly from a dislocated right elbow. Up to that point Childs had backed off from the advancing Johnson round after round, the general feeling being that he was looking for the room to let go with a big swing that would put the latter down and out. When it came to the 11th Childs was spitting blood and looking out of one eye, testament to Johnson's punches, and in the 12th his corner had seen enough and pulled their man out. Later on, after two physicians examined Childs' right arm and decided that there was nothing wrong with it, the Century Athletic Club stated that unless the loser could bring proof of an injury then some of the gate receipts due to him would go to charity.

5 February 1903. Jack Johnson w pts 20 Denver Ed Martin.
Venue: Hazzard's Pavilion, Los Angeles, California, USA. **Referee:** Harry Stuart.
Fight Summary: Reported as involving the 'black title', Johnson (180) unified it following an excellent victory over Martin (203) in one of the best fights seen at the venue. After ten rounds of clever boxing Johnson finally caught up with Martin in the 11th, knocking him down twice with right-hand smashes to the head and almost forcing the win, only for the latter to be saved by the bell. Making a great recovery in the 12th Martin gradually picked himself up, having a shade the best of the leading-off for the remainder of the contest, while Johnson relied on countering his man. There was never much between them other than the knockdowns suffered by Martin in the 11th, and it was Johnson's good work in that session which ultimately afforded him the decision.

26 February 1903. Jack Johnson w pts 20 Sam McVea.
Venue: Hazzard's Pavilion, Los Angeles, California, USA. **Referee:** Harry Stuart.
Fight Summary: Defending his 'black title' claim, Johnson was given a hard time of it by McVea, having to be at his cleverest to avoid the heavy rights thrown at him by his aggressive opponent. Although McVea received severe punishment, mainly from Johnson's solid left jab, he made it to the final bell where it could be seen that neither man was in great condition.

Again risking his 'black title' claim, Johnson successfully came through a six rounder against Joe Butler (nd-w co 3 at the Washington AC, Philadelphia, Pennsylvania on 11 May).

2 May 1903. Jack Palmer w co 12 (20) Ben Taylor.
Venue: Ginnett's Circus, Newcastle, England. **Referee:** Sam Francis.
Fight Summary: Billed for the English title, with Palmer going for the body Taylor was down twice in the opening two sessions. Twice decked from body blows in the fourth, floored four times in the sixth and three times in the seventh, it was amazing that Taylor was able to fight back strongly in the eighth. His resurgence did not last long however and, after being down again in the tenth and 11th, Taylor was eventually put down for the full count in the 12th following lefts and rights to the jaw. By his victory, Palmer had every right to see himself as the prime claimant to be called English champion.

Although Taylor came back to kayo Jack Mullen inside 16 rounds at Ginnett's Circus on 30 May, whilst the result let him back into the title picture he was unable to take advantage of it.

On 25 March 1904, the *Sporting Life* reported that Gunner Hewitt of the Royal Marines was undoubtedly the best man in Britain, but he was another who was ultimately unable to make the transition.

Continuing to claim the English title, Jack Scales drew over ten rounds with Canada's Mike Shallow at the Artillery Barracks, Newport, Wales on 15 December 1904. Articled for two-minute rounds and advertised as involving the

English title, although reported in some papers as an eight rounder, not only was Shallow not eligible but without championship conditions being in place it was farcical.

Meanwhile, on 9 December 1905, Scales challenged all of the English title claimants, specifically naming Taylor, Charlie Wilson, Geoff Thorne, Harry Slounch Dixon, Palmer and Sergeant Sunshine (who had kayoed Dixon inside two rounds at the NSC, Covent Garden, London on 20 November) to decide the English championship once and for all. Strangely, at the time of his challenge to all England Scales had been out of the ring for eight months. It would be a further year before Scales got back into training, his English title aspirations all but dead and buried.

14 August 1903. James J. Jeffries w rtd 10 (20) James J. Corbett.
Venue: Mechanics' Pavilion, San Francisco, California, USA. **Recognition:** World. **Referee:** Ed Graney.
Fight Summary: Given another chance to regain his old title, Corbett (190) boxed well enough in the opening round before being put down for 'nine' by a left to the body in the second. Corbett, who felt that his ribs had gone on the right side, later estimated that he had been down for at least 17 seconds but had been given a break by the referee. Although in terrible pain Corbett fought on bravely, but with Jeffries (220) showing great improvement in speed and skill, five times over the next few rounds the challenger went to the floor. Then, after being dropped twice from heavy blows to the body in the tenth Corbett was rescued at the count of 'seven' on the second occasion when his corner threw the towel in.

27 October 1903. Jack Johnson w pts 20 Sam McVea.
Venue: Hazzard's Pavilion, Los Angeles, California, USA. **Referee:** Charles Eyton.
Fight Summary: Recognised as a 'black title' fight, Johnson had the best of it this time around as he pounded McVea at will and knocked him down three times on his way to an easy defence.

Johnson next risked his claim against Black Bill (nd-w pts 6 at the Lenox AC, Philadelphia, Pennsylvania on 15 February 1904).

22 April 1904. Jack Johnson w co 20 (20) Sam McVea.
Venue: Mechanics' Pavilion, San Francisco, California, USA. **Referee:** Ed Graney.
Fight Summary: A defence of Johnson's 'black title' claim saw a relatively tame affair take place until a terrific right swing took McVea (207) out of the fight in the last session. Johnson scaled 190lbs.

Another fight where Johnson risked the 'black title' came against Frank Childs (w pts 6 at the Empire AC, Chicago, Illinois on 2 June).

26 August 1904. James J. Jeffries w rsc 2 (20) Jack Munroe.
Venue: Mechanics' Pavilion, San Francisco, California, USA. **Recognition:** World. **Referee:** Ed Graney.
Fight Summary: Three times Munroe (186) was sent to the floor from rights and lefts to the jaw in the first round, and it would have been curtains had the bell not rung to end the session. With Jeffries (219) unrelenting in the second the referee stopped the contest on the 1.45 mark after Munroe had been dropped twice, firstly from body blows and then by a terrific right to the head. Munroe, who had failed to land a punch worthy of a title battle, had been a huge disappointment.

Jeffries relinquished the title on announcing his retirement as undefeated champion in May 1905, having run out of worthy 'white' opposition. He then nominated the winner of a match between Marvin Hart and Jack Root as his successor. At the same time, Philadelphia Jack O'Brien, Bob Fitzsimmons, Al Kaufman and Tommy Burns all laid claim to the title.

18 October 1904. Jack Johnson w co 2 (20) Denver Ed Martin.
Venue: Hazzard's Pavilion, Los Angeles, California, USA.
Fight Summary: Billed for the 'black title', although Martin started well enough with solid left jabs he was soon in trouble from heavy blows to the body, being dropped twice in the opening round. At this stage Johnson looked awesome, and after Martin had been down twice more in the second from cracking body shots he was knocked

out by a right-hand smash to the jaw that lifted him fully two feet in the air. Many people left the building fearing for Martin's life, such was the crash made when he hit the floor, and it took some ten minutes before he came round.

Afterwards, Johnson stated that he would not rest until he got the opportunity to fight for the world title, claiming that James J. Jeffries was happy to fight black men before becoming champion and it was pure hypocrisy for him to have put up a 'Colour Bar'. Although Johnson lost some credence when he was outpointed over 20 rounds at Woodward's Pavilion, San Francisco, California on 28 March 1905 by Marvin Hart, the winner going on to contest what some perceived to be the world title, he was convinced that he had been duped out of the verdict.

Johnson next risked his 'black title' claim in a series of six-round fights at the Knickerbocker AC, Philadelphia, Pennsylvania, against Black Bill (nd-w co 4 on 2 May 1905), Walter Johnson (nd-w co 3) and Joe Jeannette (nd-drew 3). The last two contests took place on 9 May 1905, with Johnson contracted to knock both men out. I have been unable to locate a six-round no-decision contest between Johnson and Jeannette that, according to some record books, took place in Philadelphia on 19 May 1905.

At the Broadway AC, Philadelphia, on 13 July 1905, with the 'black title' up for grabs Johnson met two men on the same day over three rounds apiece, beating Black Bill (nd-w pts 3) and Morris Harris (nd-w co 1). He again risked his 'black title' claim against Jeannette (nd-l disq 2 at the National AC, Philadelphia on 25 November 1905). Although the latter tried to claim the title he was given very little credit with the fight being over six rounds and the decision being a strange one.

3 July 1905. Marvin Hart w co 12 (20) Jack Root.
Venue: The Arena, Reno, Nevada, USA. **Referee:** James J. Jeffries.
Fight Summary: Although the retired champion, Jeffries, gave his belt to the winner, Hart was never really seen as a real champion despite beating the 'black titleholder', Jack Johnson, a few months earlier. With both men making the body their main target, the battle being mainly consigned to close quarters, it was not until the seventh round that there was a knockdown when Hart (190) was dropped by a terrific right to the head and saved by the bell. Surprisingly, after Hart came out fresh for the eighth it was punch for punch most of the way. Coming into the 12th Root (171) appeared to be marginally ahead, but after being hit by a heavy right to the ribs he went down to be counted out.

27 October 1905. Philadelphia Jack O'Brien w co 17 (20) Al Kaufman.
Venue: Woodward's Pavilion, San Francisco, California, USA. **Referee:** Jack Welch.
Fight Summary: Not recognised as a title bout within the record books, and not indicated as being one in the *Philadelphia Item* fight report, it did not stop O'Brien from claiming the title following his victory. The inexperienced Kaufman, who had been beaten to a bloody pulp, his eyes and nose severely damaged, was finally put out of his misery 14 seconds from the end of the 17th round after a short right to the jaw knocked him out.

1 December 1905. Jack Johnson drew 12 Young Peter Jackson.
Venue: Eureka AC, Germania Maennerchor Hall, Baltimore, Maryland, USA.
Fight Summary: Despite his defeat at the hands of Marvin Hart earlier in the year, Johnson, who was still recognised as a man to avoid, undertook to knock Jackson out inside 12 rounds in defence of his 'black title' or be forced to accept just 25% of the purse. Outweighed by at least 40 pounds Jackson proved rather elusive, showing good defence and keeping out of range for much of the time. Only when Johnson caught up with him was he punished unmercifully, but he stood his ground to hear the final bell. At the conclusion of the contest, despite no verdict being given due to the agreements in place it was reported as a draw regardless of Johnson having had the better of it.

A day later, Johnson put his claim at further risk against Joe Jeannette (nd-w pts 6 at the National AC, Philadelphia, Pennsylvania) before meeting the same opponent again, at the Sharkey AC, Manhattan, NYC, New York on 16 January 1906, and taking the three-round press verdict.

18 December 1905. Jack Palmer w co 4 (20) Geoff Thorne.
Venue: NSC, Covent Garden, London, England.
Fight Summary: Prior to the contest, which was billed for the vacant English title, and following much criticism, it was reported that Thorne (who won four Amateur Boxing Association (ABA) titles as an amateur under his real name of Geoffrey Townsend) had every right to meet Palmer as British heavyweights were of such poor standard. Palmer made a good start when breaking through Thorne's guard several times with rights and lefts to the head, momentarily dropping his man just before the first round ended. Down again in the second, when Palmer went to help him up Thorne was heard to exclaim "It's all right, thank you". In the fourth Palmer started to play for the body, and on knocking Thorne flat on his face following a heavy blow to that region cries of "Foul" went up as the latter was counted out. However, the ruling official judged that as Thorne had partially pushed the blow downwards the decision was the right one.

Palmer, who had cemented his right to be called the English champion on winning, immediately challenged the world. Palmer's first defence of the English title would come against Gunner Moir, who had knocked out Jim Casey inside eight rounds of a final eliminator at the NSC on 26 February 1906.

20 December 1905. Philadelphia Jack O'Brien w rtd 13 (20) Bob Fitzsimmons.
Venue: Mechanics' Pavilion, San Francisco, California, USA. **Referee:** Ed Graney.
Fight Summary: Although seen by some as one of a series of eliminators to decide the heavyweight title, the *Boston Daily Globe* and others reported it to involve both the world light heavyweight and heavyweight championships. O'Brien was already claiming the heavyweight title, while Fitzsimmons' light heavyweight crown was on the line at the same time. Once the fight got underway it was clear that O'Brien (164) was the faster, using good footwork to get away from trouble, while Fitzsimmons (165) looked for the punch to finish it. Throughout, O'Brien showed his ability to hit and shift, hurting Fitzsimmons badly in the fourth and flooring his rival in the eighth with a stiff right to the jaw. Although Fitzsimmons continued to come forward he was taking more and more punishment, and at the end of the 13th he collapsed in his corner, blood pouring from his nose and mouth. Obviously unable to continue, when his corner tossed the towel into the ring the referee awarded the fight to O'Brien. Fortunately, Fitzsimmons quickly recovered and left the ring unassisted.

Following O'Brien's victory, he was regarded by 'certain sporting men' as winning the heavyweight title based upon the theory that the championship had reverted to Fitzsimmons on James J. Jeffries' retirement.

23 February 1906. Tommy Burns w pts 20 Marvin Hart.
Venue: Naud Junction Pavilion, Los Angeles, California, USA. **Referee:** Charles Eyton.
Fight Summary: Billed as a championship fight, at 5'7" Burns (180) became the shortest man to win a version of the heavyweight title when taking over Hart's claim. From start to finish, with the possible exception of the tenth and 12th, Burns had the upper hand over the bigger man, outfighting and outmanoeuvring him at every turn. With never a knockdown in sight the contest became monotonous as Burns handled Hart (188) like he would a novice, going from head to body. In the fifth Hart's right eye opened up, allowing Burns to systematically work it over until the final bell.

On 28 March, at the National AC, San Diego, California, in what were billed as ten-round championship exhibition bouts, Burns took on two opponents in the same evening – Jim O'Brien and James J. Walker - and knocked both of them out in the first round. At this moment in time Burns would not be fully recognised until he had cleared Philadelphia Jack O'Brien from his path.

14 March 1906. Jack Johnson w pts 15 Joe Jeannette.
Venue: Eureka AC, Germania Maennerchor Hall, Baltimore, Maryland, USA. **Referee:** Fred Sweigert.
Fight Summary: Still anxious for a crack at what he considered to be the 'white title', Johnson (205) continued to defend the black version, eliminating Jeannette (185) in this one. The *Baltimore Sun* reported that with Johnson the cleverer and Jeannette eager to mix it after a fast clip neither man was hurt. Johnson, who was easily the heavier, looked well able to put his rival out. According to the paper, Johnson had to make a living, and exhibitions

Heavyweight Division

like this enabled him to do so. Johnson was given the decision because he landed the greater number of punches, but even when he opened up he never did more than what was necessary to stay ahead of his rival.

Risking his 'black title' claim, Johnson knocked out Black Bill in the seventh of a ten-round no-decision fight held at the Peerless AC, Pittston, Pennsylvania on 16 April.

26 April 1906. Jack Johnson w pts 15 Sam Langford.
Venue: Lincoln AC, Chelsea, Massachusetts, USA. **Referee:** Martin Flaherty.
Fight Summary: In what was seen as a 'black title' fight, Langford (156), outweighed by at least 40 pounds, gave Johnson (185) a run for his money. Even after being dropped in the sixth round he came back strongly, finishing in good shape. Although Johnson won handily it was more to do with his cleverness than his power.

Johnson next risked his claim against Joe Jeannette (nd-w pts 6 at the Broadway AC, Philadelphia, Pennsylvania on 20 September).

2 October 1906. Tommy Burns w co 15 (20) Fireman Jim Flynn.
Venue: Naud Junction Pavilion, Los Angeles, California, USA. **Referee:** Eddie Robinson.
Fight Summary: Defending his title claim, having felt the weight of Flynn's punches early on Burns (170) decided that the best way of winning was to fight at close quarters where he could nullify the challenger's best efforts. Proving to be a master of the craft Burns gradually slowed Flynn (169) down, and in the 15th set about him with a vengeance. Dropped for two counts of 'nine', Flynn finally took the full count after being battered with thudding lefts and rights to the body that were followed by a terrific uppercut to the jaw.

29 October 1906. Gunner Moir w disq 9 (20) Jack Palmer.
Venue: NSC, Covent Garden, London, England. **Referee:** J. H. Douglas.
Fight Summary: The way Moir (180) started when working the body looked like giving him an early win, but after Palmer (173) got through the opening session, despite being extremely groggy at times, by the third he was making it interesting. Having gone well in the fourth Palmer was badly shaken up by head shots, and although he got through the round he never posed a threat thereafter. On being brought to his knees by a smashing right to the jaw in the ninth Palmer got up and charged into Moir, both holding and punching, before going low and suffering an immediate disqualification.

Looking to build on his victory, Moir challenged America's Philadelphia Jack O'Brien to decide the world title.

26 November 1906. Jack Johnson drew 10 Joe Jeannette.
Venue: The Auditorium, Portland, Maine, USA. **Referee:** Martin J. Sullivan.
Fight Summary: Only too happy to risk his 'black title' claim, Johnson met the much lighter Jeannette, who put up an excellent argument against his burly opponent. The *Portland Evening Express* stated that had Jeannette stood up and mixed it with Johnson he would have been beaten quickly. There was little doubt that Johnson was inclined to be merciful as twice he had Jeannette in real trouble but failed to follow up his advantage. The paper reported that it was a splendid, fast exhibition of boxing, and had Jeannette been up against anyone other than Johnson he probably would have been the favourite. The draw was obviously agreed prior to the contest.

28 November 1906. Tommy Burns drew 20 Philadelphia Jack O'Brien.
Venue: Naud Junction Pavilion, Los Angeles, California, USA. **Referee:** James J. Jeffries.
Fight Summary: Fighting like a bulldog from beginning to end Burns (172) just about deserved to win the decision from O'Brien (163½), who was never far behind in the scoring. With both fighters' title claims at stake, despite there being no knockdowns the fight was unrelenting and there was plenty of hard hitting. Both men were damaged; O'Brien's right eye being cut early on and Burns' left optic closed shut at the final bell. According to O'Brien the fight was pre-arranged with Burns to be drawn. He explained "The promoter, McCarey, had figured it out that if we fought a spirited draw he could bill the return match during fiesta week and make a small fortune by charging top prices." Although billed for the heavyweight title there were those who saw it also involving O'Brien's light heavyweight claim.

Following the fight, C. B. Cochrane, the British promoter, deposited £100 with the *Sporting Life* to bind a match between O'Brien and Gunner Moir that would decide the vacant world heavyweight title. On 26 December, the *Sporting Life* stated that there were just four men in the running to contest the vacant world title, naming them as O'Brien, Burns, Moir and James Tiger Smith.

Before taking some time out, Burns met Joe Grim in a three-round exhibition bout at the Lyceum Theatre, Philadelphia, Pennsylvania on 10 January 1907.

19 February 1907. Jack Johnson w co 1 (20) Peter Felix.
Venue: Gaiety Athletic Hall, Sydney, Australia. **Referee:** Mr Beckett.
Fight Summary: Johnson successfully defended his 'black title' when despatching Felix at 2.20 of round one, dropping the man from Saint Croix, US Virgin Islands, twice before finishing him off with a right uppercut to the jaw.

Further to this, having beaten Bill Lang and Bob Fitzsimmons, Johnson took in another couple of six-round fights before meeting Fireman Jim Flynn in what was seen as an eliminating contest to decide Tommy Burns' next opponent. Taking place in California at the Mission Street Arena, Colma, San Francisco, and scheduled for 45 rounds, Johnson won easily, knocking Flynn out in 11 rounds on 2 November. The promoter, Jim Coffroth, then made plans to bring Burns home to defend his title against Johnson, but had no joy as the champion decided to stay in Europe.

After taking in a three-round exhibition contest against Joe Jeannette at the beginning of January 1908 Johnson stopped off for another exhibition in Montreal, Canada before sailing for England to force a fight with Burns. When arriving in England Johnson found to his dismay that Burns had moved on to Australia. Deciding to make the best of his trip, and having stopped Britain's Ben Taylor inside eight rounds at the Cosmopolitan Club, Plymouth on 31 July 1908 two days later Johnson was matched to meet Mike Schreck over 20 rounds at the NSC, Covent Garden, London in what would be a billed world title bout. At this point Johnson was claiming the title as Burns had refused to meet him under reasonable conditions. Unfortunately, when Schreck was unable to get himself in condition in the allotted time the fight was called off. It was then announced on 12 September 1908 that Johnson had signed to meet Burns in Australia over 20 rounds sometime in December. With that agreed, Johnson set sail from London six days later.

25 February 1907. Gunner Moir w co 1 (20) James Tiger Smith.
Venue: NSC, Covent Garden, London, England. **Referee:** Tom Scott.
Fight Summary: Smith (161) made the first move, hanging in southpaw lefts to Moir's face, but once the latter had overcome that problem it was all downhill for the Welshman. Dropped by a right swing, after Smith got to his feet he even troubled Moir (180) for a moment or two before being floored five more times by hammer-fisted blows, the last occasion seeing him counted out on the 2.49 mark.

On 26 April, the *Sporting Life* reported that both Jem Roche and Charlie Wilson were claiming the English title, to which Moir responded that if either put down a £500 deposit the match could be made for October. Wilson had stopped Moir inside two rounds at Wonderland, Mile End, London on 26 September 1903, and was sure he could repeat the exercise. According to Moir it was only his fourth contest and he had got out of a sick bed to take it before a twisted ankle brought matters to a conclusion. He went on to state that if Wilson cared to put the money up he could have the fight. A few months later, on 6 July, it was reported in the *Sporting Life* that Moir had challenged Tommy Burns to decide the world title for the best purse in the USA.

15 April 1907. Mike Schreck w co 19 (20) John Wille.
Venue: The Casino, Tonopah, Nevada, USA. **Referee:** Otto Floto.
Fight Summary: This one was given American title status and carried a $10,000 purse. Up until the tenth round Wille had given a reasonable account of himself, keeping Schreck at distance with a long left lead, but from there onwards the latter picked up the pace and began to do some damage. Hammering in blows to head and body Schreck had Wille staggering badly in the 18th and 19th sessions, and in the 19th a heavy blow to the jaw saw the

latter counted out. Even though both men had been forced to wear seven-ounce gloves there had been plenty of slugging and wrestling before the finish.

3 May 1907. Mike Schreck w co 13 (finish) Tony Ross.
Venue: Gymnastic Club, Dayton, Ohio, USA.
Fight Summary: With both men scaling around 180lbs Schreck drew first blood, jabbing well to the head, and although many early rounds were slow it came to life in the 11th with Ross, tiring fast, being chased around the ring. In the 13th, after Schreck dropped Ross for 'seven' with a punch to the neck, when the latter got to his feet he was quickly sent to the floor again by a swinging right hook to be counted out. This was seen to be a defence of Schreck's American title claim.

8 May 1907. Tommy Burns w pts 20 Philadelphia Jack O'Brien.
Venue: Naud Junction Pavilion, Los Angeles, California, USA. **Referee:** Charles Eyton.
Fight Summary: In a return bout between the two claimants which was nothing like their previous set-to, each and every round became repetitive as Burns (180) chased after O'Brien (167). Although Burns came the closest to ending the fight with the occasional wild swing, O'Brien was too clever to be caught napping, being more interested in getting to the final bell in one piece. Clearly, O'Brien was not up to the task, especially following revelations afterwards that he had offered Burns the winner's end of the purse to take a dive in the 11th round. Fearing that O'Brien would not accept the fight under any other circumstances, although Burns agreed to his terms, he had no intention whatsoever of complying with them. According to Burns, having made up his mind to double-cross his opponent at the onset he immediately reported the matter to the promoter. The decision was then made to get both men into the ring before all bets were called off.

30 May 1907. Mike Schreck w rtd 21 (finish) Marvin Hart.
Venue: The Casino, Tonopah, Nevada, USA. **Referee:** George Siler.
Fight Summary: Now that Schreck was claiming the championship due to Tommy Burns' inability to make a match with him, this was seen as involving the world title in some quarters. Hart was the aggressor most of the way, nearly finishing Schreck off in the 18th round, but by then he was carrying severe damage to his right wrist. After fierce fighting in the 19th and 20th, with Schreck smashing in punches to head and body, Hart was pulled out by his corner midway through the 21st session, having been down several times.

When Schreck was defeated by Al Kaufman (l co 7 at the Auditorium Rink, San Francisco, California on 29 August) it undoubtedly cost him a crack at Burns. Regardless of whether he bothered to pick up Schreck's title claim or not, Kaufman's continued good form, with successive victories over Dave Barry, Jack Twin Sullivan, Joe Grim, Battling Johnson, Fireman Jim Flynn, Fred Bradley, Terry Mustain, Jim Barry and Tony Ross, would eventually pave the way for a shot at the title.

4 July 1907. Tommy Burns w co 1 (20) Bill Squires.
Venue: Mission Street Arena, Colma, San Francisco, California, USA. **Referee:** James J. Jeffries.
Fight Summary: Starting out as if he meant business, Squires (181) charged into Burns (180), who initially stood off before tossing in a long right hand to the jaw that dropped the Australian champion. Although Squires made it to his feet, still groggy, he was soon decked again by a similar blow. Getting up for the second time Squires was a sitting target. When a short right to the chin put him down again this time he was counted out on the 2.08 mark.

Firmly in the mix, on 10 July England's Gunner Moir challenged Burns to defend his title claim against him either in the USA or Britain. With Moir having much support in Britain it was clear that if Burns wanted worldwide recognition he would have to eliminate the British champion.

2 December 1907. Tommy Burns w co 10 (20) Gunner Moir.
Venue: NSC, Covent Garden, London, England. **Recognition:** World. **Referee:** Eugene Corri.
Fight Summary: Billed for the undisputed world heavyweight championship (Jack Johnson would have had something to say about that), Burns (177) was far too good for the Englishman, whether it be boxing or landing solidly, and apart from the fourth round he was on top all the way. Badly cut over the right eye in the fifth and

nearly put out in the ninth Moir (204) was in a bad state, and when Burns dropped him three times in the tenth he was unable to make it to his feet after the third knockdown.

Away from the ring for over 16 months, Moir lost his English title (which had been renamed as British on 11 February 1909 when the NSC introduced the eight named weight divisions) to Iron Hague by a first-round kayo at the Club on 19 April of that year.

10 February 1908. Tommy Burns w co 4 (20) Jack Palmer.
Venue: Wonderland, Mile End, London, England. **Recognition:** World. **Referee:** Robert Watson.
Fight Summary: On the attack right from the start as Palmer (168) froze, Burns (175), who had the Englishman down twice in the first round, continued to batter away at him during the next two sessions. Finally, in the fourth, after Burns put Palmer down several more times the latter was counted out on his knees.

Two weeks later, Burns reportedly offered to fight James Tiger Smith, Gunner Moir and Bill Squires on the same night.

17 March 1908. Tommy Burns w co 1 (20) Jem Roche.
Venue: Theatre Royal, Dublin, Ireland. **Recognition:** World. **Referee:** Robert Watson.
Fight Summary: As soon as the fight began it could be seen that the challenger would be out of his depth, and after Burns (176) feinted his left and shot over a right to the jaw Roche (180) went crashing on to his face to be counted out at 1.28 of the opening session.

18 April 1908. Tommy Burns w co 5 (10) Jewey Smith.
Venue: Neuilly Bowling Palace, Paris, France. **Recognition:** World. **Referee:** Dr Phelin Roux.
Fight Summary: Although billed as a world title defence for Burns (176¼), this was really scraping the barrel as Smith (187½) was little more than a novice fighting only his third traced pro fight. What is more, the Englishman received just £25 plus expenses for two. Although Smith started reasonably well, sending in some lusty hits to the body, he was soon being taken apart by Burns who had him down with a left to the head in the third. Knocked down twice in the fourth Smith rallied gamely in the fifth, but had no answer to the agile champion before being put down and out following a terrific right to the jaw.

13 June 1908. Tommy Burns w co 8 (10) Bill Squires.
Venue: Neuilly Bowling Palace, Paris, France. **Recognition:** World. **Referee:** Dr Phelin Roux.
Fight Summary: Squires (183) gave Burns (184) a fair bit of bother until tiring in the seventh round, having gone punch for punch at times. Coming out for the eighth, mustering all of his remaining energy, Squires tore into Burns, only to be stopped in his tracks by a blow to the body that dropped him for the full count.

24 August 1908. Tommy Burns w co 13 (20) Bill Squires.
Venue: The Stadium, Sydney, Australia. **Recognition:** World. **Referee:** Harry Nathan.
Fight Summary: A return match between the pair, only this time in Australia, Squires (184), who gave the champion all the trouble he could handle in many of the rounds, had his man groggy on at least two occasions. As the fight progressed it became difficult to call but, having hurt Squires in the 12th, when Burns (181) opened up in the 13th he soon put the Australian down for 'nine'. Although Squires was soon back on his feet, after taking another count a right hand to the jaw put him down and out.

2 September 1908. Tommy Burns w co 6 (20) Bill Lang.
Venue: West Melbourne Stadium, Melbourne, Australia. **Recognition:** World. **Referee:** Harry Nathan.
Fight Summary: Putting up a better fight than expected Lang (187) dropped Burns (183) in the second with a heavy right swing to the jaw, but was soon made to pay for the indiscretion. After settling down it was all Burns as he pummelled Lang with left and right swings to head and body, sending the latter to the floor repeatedly in every round before closing the fight with a right to the jaw in the sixth.

Having put pen to paper on 1 October 1908 to meet Burns, Jack Johnson would become the first black man allowed to contest the world heavyweight title, thus ushering in what I would recognise as the start of the modern era. Prior to this contest taking place, most champions had the 'Colour Bar' in place, as well as certain parts of the boxing world not wishing to have a fight between black and white men staged on their territory.

26 December 1908. Jack Johnson w rsc 14 (20) Tommy Burns.
Venue: The Stadium, Sydney, Australia. **Recognition:** World. **Referee:** Hugh McIntosh.
Fight Summary: The 'black champion' for close on six years, but unable to force a match with Burns, Johnson followed him first to England and then to Australia. The fight was eventually made after Burns accepted a $30,000 guarantee from promoter, Snowy Baker; a huge sum for those days. Inside the first 20 seconds Burns (168) was down, having taken a heavy right uppercut to the jaw, and he was soon dropped again from a similar blow. Fighting courageously, Burns threw everything he had at a goading Johnson (192) to little effect. Down again from a left to the body in the seventh Burns did his utmost, but Johnson appeared to be toying with him, calling him names and ridiculing him. Round after round Johnson failed to put Burns out of his misery until the 14th when he battered the champion to the floor with a constant barrage of blows. Having got up at 'eight' Burns was there to be taken, but with the crowd at fever pitch the police asked the referee to stop the contest to save the Canadian from being badly hurt.

With Johnson now generally recognised as the world champion, Sam McVea outpointed Joe Jeannette over 20 rounds at The Circus, Paris, France on 20 February 1909 to win what was considered by the black population as being a fight for the vacant 'black title'.

This was followed by Johnson boxing an exhibition bout against Victor McLaglen over six rounds at the Athletic Club, Vancouver, Canada on 10 March 1909. In later years, although McLaglen, who went on to become a famous film star, was said to have fought for the world title in this one it was nothing more than studio publicity.

Contesting the 'black title', McVea knocked out Cyclone Billy Warren inside two rounds at The Circus, Paris on 9 April 1909 before being forced to retire in the 49th round of a return finish fight at the same venue against Jeannette on 17 April 1909. There were 38 knockdowns recorded in the latter contest, Jeannette going down on 27 occasions to McVea's 11.

24 May 1909. Sam Langford w co 4 (20) Iron Hague.
Venue: NSC, Covent Garden, London, England. **Recognition:** NSC. **Referee:** Eugene Corri.
Fight Summary: Although Langford should have been meeting Jack Johnson at the NSC on this date, when the latter failed to honour the agreement Hague was drafted in. The contract with Johnson had stated that he would meet Langford at the NSC on 22 February 1909, but when he took the fight with Burns both parties agreed that he should come back to the Club to meet Langford on 24 May regardless of the outcome of his fight with Burns. Thus, Hague, who had recently knocked out Gunner Moir in the first round to win the British title at the NSC on 19 April, would participate in the NSC's version of the vacant world title in his very next fight. Even though Langford was at a disadvantage in weight and reach, his cleverness and hard hitting would ultimately prove too much for Hague despite being dropped by a wild right swing that partially closed his eye near the end of the third round. Shaken up, Langford was a different man in the fourth and, having decided to end it, a terrific right to Hague's jaw saw the latter counted out.

Not recognised as a world champion outside of the NSC Langford was by now also claiming the 'black title', which he risked in a subsequent contest against Klondike (nd-w pts 6 at the Bijou Theatre, Pittsburgh, Pennsylvania on 13 July). Having presented Langford with a belt emblematic of the world championship it is difficult to know if and when the NSC discontinued recognising him as being the world champion, but under their own ruling that a champion should defend the belt every six months it was possibly before the end of the year. Anyway, it is quite clear that just about everyone throughout the world of boxing at this time, even those who ran the NSC, grudgingly recognised Johnson regardless of the fact that they wanted him beaten.

9 September 1909. Jack Johnson nd-w pts 10 Al Kaufman.
Venue: Mission Street Arena, Colma, San Francisco, California, USA. **Recognition:** World. **Referee:** Edward J. Smith.
Fight Summary: Despite being a no-decision bout although Johnson's title was at stake, Kaufman (191), unable to take advantage of his opportunity, landed very few punches throughout the contest. At times Johnson (209) appeared to be taking it easy, but when he did open up Kaufman was often in distress. With the fight at an end the referee stated to the newspaper men present that while he could not give a verdict Johnson was the better man, having outboxed and outpunched Kaufman in virtually every round.

Just a matter of days before taking on Stanley Ketchel, Johnson met Gunboat Smith in a four-round exhibition bout at the Seal Rock House, San Francisco on 11 October. According to the *New York Herald* the champion was floored and badly dazed in the fourth, whereupon his manager cut the round short.

Earlier, on 28 September, at the Armoury AA, Boston, Massachusetts, Sam Langford forced the Dixie Kid to retire inside five rounds of a defence of his 'black title' claim.

16 October 1909. Jack Johnson w co 12 (20) Stanley Ketchel.
Venue: Mission Street Arena, Colma, San Francisco, California, USA. **Recognition:** World. **Referee:** Jack Welch.
Fight Summary: An historic battle that had both men agreeing to a no-knockdown clause (a contract stating that neither man would look for a kayo), saw Johnson (205½) break the agreement when smashing Ketchel (170¼) to the floor in the second round, having whipped in a right uppercut. Realising what he had done from there onwards Johnson kept Ketchel at bay with the left hand, but the middleweight champion was biding his time before getting lucky in the 12th round. Having just grazed Johnson's chin with a sweeping right, when Ketchel slammed in another right that landed just behind the ear the champion was down. With Johnson back on his feet, as Ketchel roared in for the kill he was lifted off the ground by a tremendous right uppercut. There was no way Ketchel was going to get up, and after being counted out it took several minutes to bring him round.

Meanwhile, defending his version of the 'black title' Sam Langford took on Klondike (w co 2 at The Armoury AA, Boston, Massachusetts on 2 November), the Dixie Kid (w co 3 at the Phoenix AC, Memphis, Tennessee on 10 January 1910) and Battling Jim Johnson (nd-w pts 6 at the National AC, Philadelphia, Pennsylvania on 14 May 1910), while the other claimant, Joe Jeannette, drew over 30 rounds with Sam McVea at The Circus, Paris, France on 11 December 1909 prior to taking on Morris Harris (nd-drew 10 at the National AC, NYC, New York on 1 July 1910).

4 July 1910. Jack Johnson w rsc 15 (45) James J. Jeffries.
Venue: The Amphitheatre, Reno, Nevada, USA. **Recognition:** World. **Referee:** Tex Rickard.
Fight Summary: The former champion was coaxed out of retirement on the grounds that he was expected to win for the 'white race' and put Johnson (208) firmly in his place. Unfortunately for his supporters, after six years out of the ring and at the age of 35 the weary Jeffries (227) was just not up to the task. Systematically beaten, at the end of the 11th round Jeffries' corner wanted to retire him but he would not hear of it. With Johnson taunting Jeffries while hitting him at will it could not last, and in the 15th the latter was dropped three times before the referee brought proceedings to an end on the 2.20 mark. Some reports state that the timekeeper had already knocked off ten seconds and the result should have been a knockout, others say that when the referee's count had reached 'seven' he saw Jeffries' seconds entering the ring and brought the fight to an end. I have gone with the latter as it was clear that Rickard was out of step with the count and that neither he nor the majority of the crowd wished to see a once great champion knocked out.

Following what had been an unedifying slaughter, from that moment on many people involved in boxing, whether it be administering, organising or reporting, felt that it was imperative that America found a 'white champion' to supplant the arrogant Johnson. With men such as the famous author and boxing fan, Jack London, beating the drum, thus began in earnest the period which came to be known as 'The Era of the Great White Hope', with tournaments springing up around the country to find a successor to Johnson. Men who were either already claiming the 'white title' or were likely candidates included Luther McCarty, Al Palzer, Fireman Jim Flynn, Jim Barry, Frank Moran, Carl Morris, Arthur Pelkey, Gunboat Smith, Tom Kennedy, Jess Willard, Al Kaufman, and Bombardier

Billy Wells. The *Fort Wayne Indiana Sentinel* even reported that a ten-round no-decision contest between Palzer and Kennedy at the Royal AC, Clermont Rink, Brooklyn, NYC, New York on 29 November 1911, was billed for the 'white title'. The fight went the distance, with Kennedy credited by the press as being the winner.

At the Armoury AA, Boston, Massachusetts, on 6 September 1910, Sam Langford outpointed Joe Jeannette over 15 rounds, and in doing so was generally recognised as the 'black champion'. Langford then went on to successfully defend against Jeff Clark (w rsc 2 at the Business Men's AC Auditorium, Joplin, Missouri on 10 November 1910), Morris Harris (w co 2 at the Armoury AA, Boston on 6 December 1910), Jeannette (w pts 12 at the Armoury AA, Boston on 10 January 1911), Fred Atwater (nd-w rsc 3 at the State Armoury, Utica, New York on 16 January 1911), Sam McVea (drew 20 at The Circus, Paris, France on 1 April 1911), Ralph Calloway (nd-w rsc 4 at The Alhambra, Syracuse, New York on 30 May 1911) and Jeannette (nd-w pts 10 at Madison Square Garden, Manhattan, NYC, New York on 5 September 1911) before losing to McVea (l pts 20 at The Stadium, Sydney, Australia on 26 December 1911). However, Langford soon regained the 'black title', outpointing McVea over 20 rounds at The Stadium, Sydney on 8 April 1912.

Earlier, a title fight proposed for 5 August 1911 between Johnson and PO Curran in Belfast, Ireland was called off after the former refused to box in Ireland. That was followed by another championship fight, set for 2 October 1911 at the Empress Hall, Earls Court, London, England, between Johnson and Wells being called off just days before. This came about after the Home Secretary and a London County Council representative intervened, having taken into account protests by an anti-boxing lobby. The official objection, despite lawyers pointing out the legality of boxing, was against a white man meeting a black man for money.

4 July 1912. Jack Johnson w rsc 9 (45) Fireman Jim Flynn.
Venue: The Arena, Las Vegas, New Mexico, USA. **Recognition:** World. **Referee:** Edward W. Smith.
Fight Summary: Having been inactive for two years Johnson took on Flynn, virtually toying with him throughout as the latter continually rushed in. There was no other way for Flynn (175) to get near Johnson (195½), and he was soon bleeding badly before resorting to foul tactics. Warned for use of the head five times in the sixth round, in the eighth, even though Flynn was given a final warning, it seemed to make no difference. With Flynn carrying on where he had left off, butting Johnson several times in the ninth as the champion held on to him, the policeman in charge ordered the referee to stop the fight on the grounds that there had been too much fouling. When the referee brought the fight to a close he gave the decision as a stoppage win for Johnson rather than deciding it on a disqualification. Although the better man, Johnson had held Flynn rather than box him off, tactics that fuelled the latter's anger.

With the authorities desperately looking for ways and means to take Johnson out of circulation, having earlier tried to get him indicted on charges of smuggling, he was arrested under the Mann Act (legislation intended to stop the interstate trafficking of women) on 12 October and charged with 'Transporting a White Woman for Immoral Purposes'. This one stuck, despite Johnson marrying the woman involved, and he was convicted and sentenced to one year's imprisonment on 4 June 1913. However, released on bail and given two weeks to appeal, Johnson skipped the country, fleeing to Europe via Canada. The American public were outraged, and with the Government intent on bringing Johnson back he was recognised as champion only in Europe.

Meanwhile, in Australia, Sam Langford, who was seen as the 'black champion', successfully defended his claim in three further matches against Sam McVea, winning on points over 20 rounds at The Stadium, Sydney on 3 August, by an 11th-round stoppage at the Exhibition Stadium, Perth on 9 October and a 13th-round kayo at The Stadium, Sydney on 26 December. By the end of 1912, with the first 'white champion' due to be crowned, there was no way a black man was going to be allowed to contest the championship in America at that moment in time, but, nevertheless, Langford should be considered as having a claim equal to all his rivals if not better.

From here until 5 April 1915, the date that Jess Willard unified the title, I have listed black and white championship contests, along with Johnson's, separately.

1 January 1913. Luther McCarty w rsc 18 (20) Al Palzer.
Venue: Vernon Arena, Los Angeles, California, USA. **Referee:** Charles Eyton.
Fight Summary: This was considered to be the final of the 'white tournament' following wins by McCarty over Al Kaufman and Fireman Jim Flynn, and Palzer's third-round kayo of the British champion, Bombardier Billy Wells. Prior to those contests McCarty had eliminated Carl Morris, while Palzer had quick wins over Tom Kennedy and Kaufman. In spite of his superior height, weight and reach advantages Palzer (227) was no match for McCarty (205), who was just too clever for him. For much of the time McCarty used him as a punch-bag, especially from the 13th onwards. Both men were cut. However, by the 18th Palzer was reeling around the ring unable to see through the blood pouring into his eyes, which left the referee with no other option than stopping the fight. There had been no knockdowns, but there was only going to be one winner. Palzer had just three more fights before being tragically shot dead by his father on 26 July 1914.

On 16 April, McCarty risked his newly won title against Flynn (nd-w pts 6 at the Olympia AC, Philadelphia, Pennsylvania), cutting the latter up and winning easily.

24 March 1913. Sam Langford drew 20 Sam McVea.
Venue: Olympic Stadium, Brisbane, Australia. **Referee:** Major Fred Craig.
Fight Summary: Recognised as a 'black title' defence for Langford, for the opening few rounds he was forced to play second fiddle to McVea who used the left jab to keep his man at bay. Eventually, the aggressive tactics of Langford began to pay off as the taller man tired and began to be caught on the ropes. By the 11th Langford looked to be getting on top as McVea, carrying damage to his left eye, appeared to be wilting. However, it was McVea who scored the first knockdown a round later. Regardless of that, from there on through to the final bell it was Langford, with lefts and rights to the head and solid rights to the body, who carried the fight to McVea. The referee's decision of a draw was received in uproar.

30 April 1913. Luther McCarty nd-w pts 10 Frank Moran.
Venue: St Nicholas Arena, Manhattan, NYC, New York, USA.
Fight Summary: Fought at a fast pace for heavyweights, there was very little good work as both men threw punches that more often than not missed the target. McCarty (204¾) did his best work with the left jab, but was continually countered by the left hook. Having been butted to the floor in the ninth, the 'white champion' came right back in the tenth and last session to send Moran (194¾) staggering around the ring. Although Moran was up against it he somehow remained on his feet to the bell, McCarty missing with crude swings as he tried to find a finishing blow.

24 May 1913. Arthur Pelkey w co 1 (10) Luther McCarty.
Venue: Manchester Arena, Calgary, Alberta, Canada. **Referee:** Edward W. Smith.
Fight Summary: McCarty's first proper title defence as the 'white champion' ended in tragedy when, having been knocked down and failing to regain consciousness, he was pronounced dead. The contest had only just begun when McCarty (200) dropped to the floor after taking a left to the jaw and a right under the heart from Pelkey (210), being counted out amidst a brilliant ray of sunshine that suddenly blazed through the roof on to the ring platform at that very moment. The autopsy showed that McCarty's neck had been dislocated which led to a rupture of the spinal cord and haemorrhaging of the spine and brain. With all the main participants arraigned, it was left to a jury to clear them on discovering that McCarty had fallen from his horse a few days earlier, something they believed to have contributed greatly to his death. Two days after the fight arsonists burnt the new arena to the ground, and within the week the Alberta Boxing Commission had banned professional boxing.

9 September 1913. Sam Langford nd-w co 1 (10) John Lester Johnson.
Venue: Atlantic Gardens AC, Manhattan, NYC, New York, USA. **Referee:** Billy Moore.
Fight Summary: Defending his 'black title' claim Langford (185) soon had Johnson (170) in trouble, and after sending in some heavy body shots the latter was put down for 'eight'. Back up on his feet, when Johnson was quickly dropped from another vicious punch to the midsection it was all over after just 32 seconds.

3 October 1913. Sam Langford nd-drew 10 Joe Jeannette.
Venue: Madison Square Garden, Manhattan, NYC, New York, USA. **Referee:** Billy Joh.
Fight Summary: Another 'black title' fight for Langford (200) saw him put under a lot of pressure early on by the well-conditioned Jeannette (196), especially with left jabs, before heavy rights and lefts to the head rocked him in the fourth. There were no knockdowns, but Langford, who was forced to hang on from the sixth onwards, finished extremely weak from his exertions while Jeannette looked as though he could have carried on all night.

19 December 1913. Jack Johnson drew 10 Battling Jim Johnson.
Venue: Elysee Montmartre Centre, Paris, France. **Referee:** Emile Maitrot.
Fight Summary: Although the New York State Athletic Commission (NYSAC) strangely cabled the promoter their backing of Jack Johnson (213¾) as champion, it is doubtful whether the International Boxing Union (IBU) saw it as a championship contest as they had already vacated the title in early December. The first few rounds had Jack playing with his namesake, Jim (222¾), but after supposedly breaking his left arm in the third the contest degenerated into continuous holding and clutching. Both men slipped to the floor in the tenth, with Jack looking decidedly groggy, and at the end of the session the referee hurriedly offered up a drawn decision. The result was strange to say the least, especially as Jack had undertaken to stop Jim inside ten rounds.

20 December 1913. Sam Langford w pts 20 Joe Jeannette.
Venue: Luna Park, Paris, France. **Referee:** Franz Reichel.
Fight Summary: Putting his 'black title' claim on the line yet again, Langford (199½) forced the contest throughout, dropping Jeannette (188¼) for counts of 'nine' three times in the 13th. Although Jeannette landed heavily in the 15th and 19th sessions, after it failed to halt Langford's forward march he was hardly able to stand up in the 20th before being cheered for his bravery at the final bell.

1 January 1914. Gunboat Smith w co 15 (20) Arthur Pelkey.
Venue: Daly City Arena, San Francisco, California, USA. **Referee:** Jim Griffin.
Fight Summary: Billed for the 'white title', the smaller man took over Pelkey's title claim when knocking him out in the 15th round. Although the fight was fairly even up to the sixth, after that Smith (180) was never in danger as he danced around Pelkey (205) while sending in lefts and rights to the Canadian's head and body. Pelkey, who was slow and cumbersome, was a big disappointment to many, seldom taking the fight to Smith and lacking the experience to corner his man. In the 15th Smith feinted with the left before sending in a terrific right to the jaw that dropped Pelkey in a heap. Up at 'nine' Pelkey was a sitting target, and a right-hand smash to the back of his head sent him down on his face to be counted out. Pelkey went downhill from then on, winning just eight fights from 32, before retiring to become a police officer and suddenly dying from a sleeping sickness at the age of 36 in 1921.

23 March 1914. Sam Langford nd-w rsc 1 Bill Watkins.
Venue: National SC, Manhattan, NYC, New York, USA. **Referee:** Patsy Haley.
Fight Summary: In a defence of his 'black title' Langford (200) made short work of Watkins (186), who appeared out of his depth. It did not take long for Langford to find his rival and after landing heavily to the ear in the opening session Watkins fell to the floor claiming he could not see. With Watkins sitting on the floor complaining, the referee stopped the fight.

27 March 1914. Sam Langford nd-w pts 10 Battling Jim Johnson.
Venue: Empire AC, Maspeth, Queens, NYC, New York, USA.
Fight Summary: Making another successful defence of the 'black title', Langford (200), who was outweighed by Johnson (226), took eight of the ten rounds in a contest with little action and no knockdowns. Many of the sessions resembled a peace conflict until they got going near the end to uncork some vicious blows. At times Johnson got angry with the amount of straight lefts coming his way, but although he occasionally assumed a warlike attitude it quickly subsided.

Langford next risked the 'black title' in two eight-rounders, against George Kid Cotton (w pts 8 at the City Auditorium, Chattanooga, Tennessee on 15 April) and Rough House Ware (w rsc 5 at the Phoenix AC, Memphis, Tennessee on 20 April).

1 May 1914. Sam Langford nd-drew 10 Harry Wills.
Venue: National Baseball Park, New Orleans, Louisiana, USA. **Referee:** Buddy Griffin.
Fight Summary: Even though only a short distance fight, and a no-decision one at that, Wills (210) claimed the 'black title' after being awarded the press decision over Langford (187) by the *New Orleans Daily Picayune*, who gave him seven rounds. The *New Orleans Item* gave it to Langford by a narrow margin. Wills had the better of the opening four rounds, closing Langford's left eye, but the latter was fighting strongly at the final bell. While Wills used his long reach to good advantage, Langford was far happier at close quarters where he could stay out of trouble and work the body. There were no knockdowns.

25 May 1914. Sam Langford nd-w co 4 (10) Bill Watkins.
Venue: Olympic AC, Rochester, New York, USA. **Referee:** Harry Pollock.
Fight Summary: Meeting for the second time in two months, it took the 'black champion' a little longer this time round as Watkins (180) skated around the ring for all he was worth. However, once Langford (186) finally caught up with his man in the fourth the result was inevitable.

9 June 1914. Harry Wills nd-drew 10 Joe Jeannette.
Venue: National Baseball Park, New Orleans, Louisiana, USA. **Referee:** Buddy Griffin.
Fight Summary: Announced as a 'black title' fight, with Wills seen as the champion, the *Daily Picayune* reported it to be a contest that lacked interest as both men held on throughout and neither would lead. In the fourth round Wills picked up Jeannette and threw him to the floor in sheer frustration, but although the latter was definitely weakened by the action he was able to continue as before. While Wills was more effective with body blows in the clinches, with Jeannette smashing in a few telling left hooks, the press were equally divided on who should be named as the winner.

Wills risked his 'black title' claim when taking on Jim Cameron (w pts 4 at the Dreamland Rink, San Francisco, California on 30 October) in a short-distance affair.

27 June 1914. Jack Johnson w pts 20 Frank Moran.
Venue: Bicycle Velodrome, Paris, France. **Referee:** Georges Carpentier.
Fight Summary: Prior to the contest taking place, on 15 March the IBU had stated that Johnson v Moran could go ahead under French Federation Rules on the grounds that it was not billed as a world title bout, as only Sam Langford and Joe Jeannette were eligible to compete for that crown. However, on 18 April, the same body said that Johnson must box Langford on or before 5 August if he wanted to retain the title, a title that they were showing to be vacant in their latest listings. At this stage of his career, Johnson (221), who was only recognised in certain parts of Europe, was virtually into semi-retirement, living the 'gay life' and squandering his fortune. However, he got himself into shape for Moran (203), and although being unable to knock his rival out he was well worth the decision. Hardly exciting, although never boring, Moran tried throughout to land his big right, which he had christened 'Mary Ann', as he chased after Johnson, but the latter proved to be just too quick for him. Round after round seemed the same as Johnson moved out of danger, held on tight, or used Moran for target practice. There were no knockdowns. The referee and sole judge was 20-year-old Georges Carpentier, who would be the next challenger for Gunboat Smith's 'white title' and an admitted admirer of Johnson.

16 July 1914. Georges Carpentier w disq 6 (20) Gunboat Smith.
Venue: Olympia, Kensington, London, England. **Referee:** Eugene Corri.
Fight Summary: Recognised as a contest involving the 'white title', both Smith (182) and Carpentier (170) got down to business quickly, landing solid blows and looking to find openings they could take advantage of. Although being cautioned for foul tactics in the third round Smith continued to rough the Frenchman up, but in the fourth he was dropped by a right to the kidney region and took a count of 'six'. Carpentier continued to look for a finishing blow from there on before running into a right to the jaw in the sixth that floored him. Hurt, but in control

of his senses, Carpentier got to his knees quickly and was looking to rise when Smith jumped in with a heavy blow to his neck. With the crowd in an uproar the referee immediately disqualified Smith, who in a moment of madness had all but dashed his chances of meeting Jack Johnson.

Following the outbreak of war in Europe, when Carpentier relinquished the 'white title' in favour of military service it was Jess Willard who would eventually challenge Johnson. Willard had not taken up boxing until nearing the age of 30, but at 6'6" and weighing in the region of 250 pounds he was an imposing figure. Having beaten George Rodel (w rsc 6 at the Orpheum Theatre, Atlanta, Georgia, USA on 28 April) in what was seen to be a final eliminator for the 'white title' held by Smith, the latter had then gone to Europe to fight Carpentier instead of meeting Willard, who had been promised first crack at the Gunboat. Smith had already outpointed Willard over 20 rounds, albeit narrowly, at the Mission Street Arena, Colma, San Francisco, California on 20 May 1913, but the latter had vastly improved since that meeting and was being seen as a future champion.

Meanwhile, Smith, who was now back in America and had reclaimed the 'white title', met Cyclone Johnny Thompson (nd-w pts 6 at the Duquesne Gardens, Pittsburgh, Pennsylvania on 28 September) and Battling Levinsky (nd-l pts 10 at the Empire AC, Maspeth, Queens, NYC, New York on 9 October) before taking on the former 'black champion', Sam Langford. Knocked out in the third round at the Atlas AA, Boston, Massachusetts on 20 October, having been floored several times, Smith's title claim never took off, being seen as just another heavyweight thereafter.

Earlier, at the end of July, it had been reported widely that in principle Johnson was prepared to fight Willard if a deal could be struck. Jack Curley, an American fight promoter, was the man behind Johnson meeting Willard, but there would be plenty of negotiating to do before terms could be agreed. However, on 17 November it was announced that Johnson had signed Articles of Agreement to meet Willard in March 1915 at a place yet to be decided. To that end, a short while later, the Juarez Race Track in Mexico was set aside as the venue. In order to prepare himself the 36-year-old Johnson took part in three one-round exhibitions against three little known fighters on 10 January 1915 in Argentina. Meanwhile, with there being problems in getting Johnson to fight in Mexico, it was finally agreed that the fight would take place in Cuba on 5 April. Two days before meeting Willard, Johnson boxed a six-round exhibition with Sam McVea at The Stadium, Havana, Cuba, but gave little away other than he was no longer the man who strode imperiously over all he surveyed.

12 August 1914. Sam Langford nd-w pts 10 Battling Jim Johnson.
Venue: Stadium AC, Manhattan, NYC, New York, USA. **Referee:** Billy Joh.
Fight Summary: Outfighting Johnson in at least seven rounds, making the body his target, the 'black title' claimant was far too good for the heavier man despite being much smaller. Although taking terrific punishment to the body while continuing to come forward, Johnson hammered in several heavy rights to the jaw in the eighth. It might have slowed Langford somewhat, but the latter was soon back in charge during the final two sessions as Johnson slowed. Johnson, who made the mistake of not using his long left jab enough, generally failed to take advantage of openings when they appeared.

25 August 1914. Sam Langford w co 4 (12) George Kid Cotton.
Venue: Atlas AA, Boston, Massachusetts, USA. **Referee:** Jack Sheehan.
Fight Summary: Having started the fight with a cracking left hook to the jaw, Langford was quickly on top of his opponent who scuttled away at every opportunity. Coming into the fourth, when Langford opened up from head to body with both hands the signs were ominous. It was obvious that Cotton could not take too much more, and after about half a minute he went down on his hands and knees, only getting up when the count had been completed. There had never been any doubt that Langford's 'black title' claim would remain intact.

15 September 1914. Sam Langford drew 12 Battling Jim Johnson.
Venue: Atlas AA, Boston, Massachusetts, USA. **Referee:** George Tuohy.
Fight Summary: With Langford's 'black title' claim up for grabs, Johnson, showing much improvement from their fight a month earlier, made it difficult for his rival to take control, regardless of the fact that much of the action was at close quarters. While Johnson made the kidneys his target, Langford often used his head, an act that

angered the recipient considerably. It was a close-run thing with neither man gaining a clear lead, and at the final bell the decision appeared to suit all in attendance.

1 October 1914. Sam Langford nd-drew 10 Joe Jeannette.
Venue: Stadium AC, Manhattan, NYC, New York, USA. **Referee:** Billy Joh.
Fight Summary: In a contest between two fighters who knew each other too well, and with Langford's 'black title' claim at stake, for eight rounds it was a hugging match. It was clear that neither man wished to exert himself or take unnecessary risks, and even though Jeannette (196) scored well with the jab in the last two sessions it was not enough to persuade the majority of the press to give him the advantage over Langford (199½).

26 October 1914. Sam Langford nd-l pts 10 Jeff Clark.
Venue: Business Men's AC, Joplin, Missouri, USA.
Fight Summary: Contested over ten fast rounds, despite the 'black title' claimant scoring a second-round knockdown it was Clark's fight from thereon in. Staying out of range to avoid Langford's heavy body attacks while using a solid jab, at the final bell the press were clearly in favour of the local man, justifiably nicknamed 'The Joplin Ghost'.

On 16 November, Jim Cameron retired during the sixth round of a scheduled eight against Langford at the Arctic Arena, San Diego, California, claiming a broken hand.

26 November 1914. Sam Langford w co 14 (20) Harry Wills.
Venue: Vernon Arena, Los Angeles, California, USA. **Referee:** George Blake.
Fight Summary: Billed for the 'black title', despite twisting an ankle in the opening round Langford (190) stayed with his bigger rival to eventually outlast him. Both men were knocked down repeatedly, Langford taking advantage of four counts early on and doing well to stave off Wills' straight-arm smashes throughout. From the 12th onwards Langford showed up well and in the 14th, following a torrent of blows that made Wills (210) groggy, he finished the latter off with a left swing to the jaw halfway through the session. Langford, who would never be able to challenge for the world title due to the damage wreaked by Jack Johnson, joined a long list of great black fighters who were beaten by the 'Colour Bar'.

5 April 1915. Jess Willard w co 26 (45) Jack Johnson.
Venue: Oriental Racetrack, Havana, Cuba. **Recognition:** World. **Referee:** Jack Welch.
Fight Summary: To his dying day Johnson insisted that he had been forced to throw the fight, often pointing to a picture of himself on the canvas shading his eyes from the sun as his proof. Because there has always been doubt the fight remains one of the sport's great mysteries. Promoted by Jack Curley, the story goes that Johnson would get $30,000, win, lose or draw, as well as a share of the moving picture rights. He would also be helped to gain re-entry to the United States. Although winning easily, Johnson (205½) was tiring rapidly. It was rumoured that once he had received the signal from his wife, who was in the audience, that the remainder of the guarantee had been paid he took the full count at 1.26 of the 26th session after walking into a solid right uppercut. Curley's account was different. With Willard (230) being so big and strong, Curley stated that he made the fight for 45 rounds, knowing full well that the challenger would outlast the out-of-condition Johnson.

Following his defeat Johnson moved on to Spain, fighting four times while there before moving on to Mexico and having seven more fights. On deciding to go back to America, having surrendered himself to Federal agents, Johnson was sent to Leavenworth Penitentiary for a year, being released on 9 July 1921. Whilst in prison Johnson took part in six exhibition bouts before having nine further contests prior to retiring and eventually being killed in a car crash at the age of 68.

Although the 'white title' stopped with Willard's victory, the 'black title' would survive, mainly due to the fact that it was believed with some conviction that black fighters would continue to be avoided when it came to world title bouts. At this point in time the recognised 'black champion' was Sam Langford, who defended against Battling Jim Johnson (nd-w pts 10 at the 135th Street AC, Manhattan, NYC, New York on 6 April) before being outpointed over 12 rounds at the Atlas AA, Boston, Massachusetts seven days later by Joe Jeannette.

Having claimed the 'black title', Jeannette met Battling Brooks (nd-w co 4 at the Vanderbilt AC, Brooklyn, NYC, New York on 19 April), but could only draw over 12 rounds with Sam McVea at the Atlas AA on 27 April prior to meeting Battling Jim Johnson (nd-l pts 10 at Sohmer Park, Montreal, Canada on 10 May). Shown in some record books, Jeannette supposedly met Brooks again (nd-w co 5 in NYC on 14 May), but as yet I have been unable to trace it happening.

Dissatisfied with the decision after the Jeannette fight McVea claimed the 'black title', putting it up for grabs against Harry Wills (nd-w pts 10 at the St Nicholas Arena, Manhattan on 19 May) and Battling Jim Johnson (nd-w pts 10 at the Gaiety Theatre, Montreal on 9 June). Then, on 29 June, at the Atlas AA, following a 12-round points win over Langford, the *Boston Post* reported that the winner, McVea, should be seen as the 'black champion'. This comment was made regardless of the fact that Jeannette, who defended his claim against Bill Watkins (nd-w pts 10 at the Nicholas Rink on 2 July), had recently beaten Langford and drawn with McVea in the same city.

Further to McVea losing his claim when outpointed over 12 rounds by Wills at the Atlas AA on 7 September, the winner defended against Langford (nd-w pts 10 at the Harlem AC, Manhattan on 3 December). Wills again made a successful defence against Langford (w pts 20 at the Tulane AC, New Orleans, Louisiana on 3 January 1916) prior to the latter turning the tables with a 19th-round kayo win at the Tommy Burns Arena, New Orleans on 11 February 1916.

Langford then gained a ten-round press decision over McVea at Madison Square Garden, Manhattan just six days later, on 17 February 1916, while Jeannette risked his 'black title' claim when beating Silas Green (nd-w co 6 at the Canadian AC, Montreal on 25 February 1916) and George Kid Cotton (nd-w co 2 at the East New York AC, Brooklyn, NYC on 24 March 1916). In three no-decision bouts, Langford extended his claim when meeting Cleve Hawkins (nd-w pts 10 at the Long Acre AC, Manhattan on 28 February 1916), Wills (nd-l pts 10 at the Broadway SC, Brooklyn on 7 March 1916) and Dave Mills (nd-w rsc 2 at The Arena, Syracuse, New York on 23 March 1916).

25 March 1916. Jess Willard nd-w pts 10 Frank Moran.
Venue: Madison Square Garden, Manhattan, NYC, New York, USA. **Recognition:** World. **Referee:** Charlie White.
Fight Summary: Making his first defence, Willard (225) was just too big, too strong and too good for the Pittsburgh man, and had he not broken his right hand in the second round the result may have been quite different. Towering above his opponent the champion used his tremendous reach advantage to dictate the fight, winning at least seven rounds, but Moran (203) was always dangerous with the right hand. There were no knockdowns.

After this, which had been followed by a two-round exhibition for Willard against Soldier Kearns, Sam Langford continued to press for a title shot by taking on all comers in defence of the 'black title', including Jeff Clark (nd-w rsc 5 at the Future AC, St Louis, Missouri on 31 March), Sam McVea (nd-l pts 10 at The Arena, Syracuse, New York on 7 April), Harry Wills (nd-l pts 8 at the Future AC, St Louis on 25 April), McVea again (nd-drew 12 at the Market Street Rink, Akron, Ohio on 2 May) and Joe Jeannette (nd-w co 7 at The Arena, Syracuse on 12 May). This win, in what was a risk for both fighters in a scheduled ten-round no-decision contest, brought Langford overall control of the 'black heavyweight title'. Next up for Langford was McVea (drew 20 at the Avellaneda Roma Theatre, Buenos Aires, Argentina on 12 August) yet again, followed by Bill Tate (nd-drew 10 at The Arena, Syracuse on 30 November) and Battling Jim Johnson (nd-w co 12 at the Future AC, St Louis on 12 December).

1917 started well enough for Langford when outpointing Battling Jim Johnson over 12 rounds at the Academy AC, Kansas City, Missouri on 1 January, before Tate took a 12-round points decision and the 'black title' from him at the Grand Opera House, Kansas City, Missouri on 25 January. While the 37-year-old Willard remained inactive, Langford, no spring chicken himself, regained the 'black title' from Tate (nd-w co 5 at the Future AC, St Louis on 1 May) and then notched up defences over Wills (nd-l pts 6 at the Cambria AC, Philadelphia, Pennsylvania on 11 May), Jeannette (nd-w pts 12 at The Coliseum, Toledo, Ohio on 14 September), Andy Johnson (nd-w co 2 at the Maryland AC, Ardmore, Maryland on 17 September), Wills (nd-l pts 10 at the Clermont Rink, Brooklyn, NYC on 20 September), Wills again (nd-drew 12 at The Coliseum, Toledo on 12 November) and Kid Norfolk (nd-w co 2 at Stockyards Stadium, Denver, Colorado on 17 December). Langford's 'black title' reign came to an end on 14 April 1918 in Panama City, Panama, when he was knocked out by Wills inside six rounds.

Wills then stopped Langford in seven rounds at the same venue on 19 May 1918 before defeating McVea (w pts 20 at the Vista Alegre Bullring, Panama City, Panama on 16 June 1918) and risking the title in short distance no-decision fights against Clark (nd-w rsc 5 at the Sporting Club Arena, Atlantic City, New Jersey on 19 August 1918), Jack Thompson (nd-w pts 6 at the National AC, Philadelphia on 14 September 1918), Thompson again (nd-nc 8 at the Sporting Club Arena, Atlantic City on 15 November 1918), John Lester Johnson (nd-w pts 8 at the Armoury AA, Jersey City, New Jersey on 10 June 1919) and Langford (nd-w pts 8 at the Sportsman's Park, St Louis on 4 July 1919).

Meantime, Willard had remained inactive for over three years, apart from a couple of ten-round exhibition bouts against two nonentities in July 1918, and had spent much of his time travelling with a circus, taking part in sparring sessions. It was not the ideal preparation for a title defence. By now, Tex Rickard, the promoter, was scouring the country looking for a man who could defeat the 37-year-old Willard, eventually hitting upon Jack Dempsey, who would come to be known as 'The Manassa Mauler'. Dempsey had come up the hard way, beating men such as Fireman Jim Flynn, thus reversing an earlier loss, Carl Morris, Gunboat Smith (twice), Arthur Pelkey, Battling Levinsky and Fred Fulton. Rickard had been thinking of matching Fulton against Willard, but after Dempsey knocked him out in 23 seconds at the Baseball Park, Harrison, New Jersey on 27 July 1918 he became the obvious choice to meet the champion.

4 July 1919. Jack Dempsey w rtd 3 (12) Jess Willard.
Venue: Bay View Park Arena, Toledo, Ohio, USA. **Recognition:** World. **Referee:** Ollie Pecord.
Fight Summary: With nearly 20,000 fans packed into the arena that Tex Rickard had built for the fight they would not be disappointed. Having knocked Willard (245) down a record seven times in the opening round Dempsey (187) actually left the ring feeling he had already won, only to be called back to finish the job. After punishing Willard throughout the second session Dempsey came out with a rush in the third, hitting the champion almost at will. Staggering back to his corner in a pitiful state, his right eye closed and face battered, Willard slumped down on his stool a badly beaten fighter after which his corner advised the referee that their man was through for the night. Incidentally, although taking place in Ohio, a State more accustomed to contests of a no-decision variety, Dempsey v Willard was billed for 12 rounds of boxing with a points verdict to be given if necessary. Tex Rickard had taken the fight to Toledo when he discovered that under Ohio law at the time it was up to the local authority not the Governor, as to whether boxing took place within the town. The day after his victory, Dempsey was quoted as saying that he would be drawing the 'Colour Line' and would be paying no attention to black challengers forthwith.

Meanwhile, Harry Wills, the 'black champion', was gunning for Dempsey, and in keeping busy he defended against Jeff Clark (nd-w rsc 4 at The Arena, Syracuse, New York on 18 August), Sam Langford (nd-w pts 10 at The Arena, Syracuse, New York on 30 September) and Joe Jeannette (nd-w pts 8 at the 4th Regiment Armoury, Jersey City, New Jersey on 20 October).

On 21 October, Langford drew with Jack Thompson over 15 rounds of an advertised 'black title' fight at the Convention Hall, Tulsa, Oklahoma. Even though there was a belt at stake it did not do either man much good as Wills quickly eliminated both of them: Langford (w pts 15 at the Convention Hall, Tulsa on 5 November) came first followed by Thompson (nc 3 at The Coliseum, San Francisco, California on 1 January 1920 and w pts 15 at the Convention Hall, Tulsa on 12 January 1920). On a run, Wills' next three defences were against Andy Johnson (nd-w co 1 at the Auditorium, St Paul, Minnesota on 17 March 1920), Langford (w pts 15 at the Stockyards Stadium, Denver, Colorado on 23 April 1920) and Ray Bennett (w rsc 1 at the Armoury AA, Bridgeport, Connecticut on 1 June 1920).

6 September 1920. Jack Dempsey nd-w co 3 (10) Billy Miske.
Venue: The Arena, Benton Harbor, Michigan, USA. **Recognition:** World. **Referee:** Jack Dougherty.
Fight Summary: Although Miske (187) was badly hurt by a ramrod left to the body in the first round he held on until the bell and seemed to have recovered before being floored by a crashing right to the body in the second. It was the first time in his career the 'The St Paul's Thunderbolt' had been dropped. The third had barely started when Dempsey (185) was sent staggering with a left hook, but when the champion came back with one of his own

Miske was dropped for 'nine'. How he managed to get up was a mystery, but with the still groggy Miske all at sea a tremendous right hand to the jaw sent him down to be counted out on the 1.13 mark.

This affair left a nasty taste in the mouth when it was later learned that Miske was already suffering from 'Bright's Disease' (a chronic inflammation of the kidneys). Although he knew his rival had been ill there was never any proof that Dempsey ever realised it was terminal, and he was exonerated from all blame after the unfortunate Miske died on 1 January 1924, having taken part in 23 more fights and beaten Bill Brennan just six weeks earlier.

Two days after Dempsey v Miske, Harry Wills defended his 'black title' against Sam McVea (nd-nc 6 at the Ice Palace, Philadelphia, Pennsylvania on 8 September) before taking on Jeff Clark (nd-w rsc 4 at the Auditorium, Atlanta, Georgia on 15 September).

14 December 1920. Jack Dempsey w co 12 (15) Bill Brennan.
Venue: Madison Square Garden, Manhattan, NYC, New York, USA. **Recognition:** World. **Referee:** Johnny Haukaup.
Fight Summary: In an extremely hard defence Dempsey (188¼) eventually came through to knock the tough challenger out, but he had taken far more punches than he cared for. Both men were hard at it in the early rounds with Dempsey just about getting the better of things. Having hurt Brennan (197) to the body in the fifth, Dempsey, working downstairs well, hammered his challenger from pillar to post in the eighth. Brennan hit back with a big left in the ninth, but Dempsey, not to be denied, went all out for victory in the tenth. With both men taking a fair amount of punishment, Dempsey, bleeding badly from both eyes and mouth, scored with a terrific left the body that doubled Brennan up in the 12th. Following that, after Dempsey smashed in a big right to the head to floor Brennan, the latter was counted out in the act of rising at 1.57 of the session. This was the first heavyweight title fight held under Walker Law (which, once again, legalised professional boxing in New York State).

A series of 'black title' defences for Harry Wills in the first half of 1921 saw him successfully deal with Bill Tate (w co 2 at the Broadway Auditorium, Buffalo, New York on 17 January), Jeff Clark (w rsc 2 at The Coliseum, Baltimore, Maryland on 11 February), Jack Thompson (nd-w pts 8 at The Odeon, St Louis, Missouri on 8 April), Andy Johnson (w co 1 at the Broadway Arena, Brooklyn, NYC on 27 May), Battling Jim McCreary (w co 7 at The Arena, Syracuse, New York on 3 June), Ray Bennett (w co 1 at Queensboro Stadium, Long Island City, Queens, NYC, New York on 4 June) and Tate again (w rsc 6 at Queensboro Stadium on 2 July).

2 July 1921. Jack Dempsey nd-w co 4 (12) Georges Carpentier.
Venue: Rickard's Oval, Jersey City, New Jersey, USA. **Recognition:** World. **Referee:** Harry Ertle.
Fight Summary: Even though a decision could not be rendered in New Jersey at that time, as a billed title fight it has achieved lasting fame as being the first million-dollar gate after 80,183 fans passed through the turnstiles. However, by defending his title under no-decision conditions Dempsey (188) forced the Frenchman to look for a kayo victory, and thus negated his shrewd boxing skills. Carpentier (172) was hugely popular for both his looks and the fact that he was a war hero, while many saw Dempsey, who avoided the war, as a slacker. The contest started with Carpentier diving in to swap blows before feeling the weight of Dempsey's punches and dropping to his knees. In the second round the fight almost certainly slipped away from Carpentier when he broke his right thumb on Dempsey's head, and although he walked into the champion during the third he was being noticeably outpunched. When Dempsey went all out in the fourth, smashing in lefts and rights to Carpentier's body, after a right to the jaw dropped the Frenchman it appeared to be over. Despite Carpentier springing to his feet at 'nine' he was immediately targeted by Dempsey, it coming as no surprise when a right-hand smash saw the challenger counted out with just 1.16 of the session on the clock.

Further to this, Dempsey appeared in a number of exhibition bouts. Interestingly, what has been uncovered recently is the fact that Dempsey risked his title in what was to have been an exhibition bout against Jimmy Darcy, a light heavyweight stable-mate, at the Broadway Auditorium, Buffalo, New York, on 24 July 1922. This came about after Dempsey, who won the four-round points decision, was told by the local boxing commissioner that under the NYSAC regulations the State made no distinction between exhibition and regulation contests.

With much support, Harry Wills, who was clamouring for a title shot in 1921, defended his 'black title' against Denver Ed Martin (w co 1 at the Milwaukie Arena, Portland, Oregon on 18 November), Jack Thompson (nc 5 at the Stockyards Stadium, Denver, Colorado on 30 November, the referee stopping the bout without giving a decision with Thompson on the floor looking for a foul) and Bill Tate (w pts 12 at the Stockyards Stadium, Denver, Colorado on 8 December).

Then, on 2 January 1922 (at the Milwaukie Arena), Wills seemingly lost his 'black title' by a first-round disqualification, having flattened Tate after the referee had called for the two men to break. This was a fight that was also considered to be a final eliminator for the world title. However, after much discussion the local commissioner refused to accept the result because it left a bad taste in the mouth. He then announced that it had been a no contest, withholding both fighters' pay while demanding the contest should be restarted in four days' time. The rematch, which duly took place at the same venue on 6 January, was declared a ten-round draw with Tate more than holding his own.

Regardless of all that had gone on Tate claimed the title despite Wills continuing to see himself as the rightful champion, and was supported by a fair percentage of the press. Putting his version of the 'black title' on the line, Tate took on Battling Owens (nd-w co 2 at Memphis, Tennessee on 6 February 1922), Rough House Ware (w rsc 2 at the Chamber of Commerce Auditorium, Columbus, Ohio on 20 March 1922), Sam Langford (nd-w pts 8 at Memphis on 27 March 1922) and the Boston Bearcat (nd-w co 1 at an open-air site in Porter, Indiana on 17 June 1922) before being outscored over 15 rounds by Jack Thompson at the Tulane Arena, New Orleans, Louisiana on 21 June 1922. While there was no support for Thompson, it is clear that Tate's 'black title' claim also disappeared on the result.

Meantime, Wills went on to defend the 'black title' against Langford (w pts 10 at the Milwaukie Arena on 17 January 1922), Kid Norfolk (w co 2 at Madison Square Garden, Manhattan, NYC, New York on 2 March 1922), Jeff Clark (nd-w rtd 2 at The Arena AA, Trenton, New Jersey on 20 June 1922), Clark again (w co 3 at the Amphitheatre Rink, Winnipeg, Canada on 17 July 1922), Buddy Jackson (nd-w co 2 at the Broad AC, Newark, New Jersey on 21 August 1922), Tut Jackson (w co 3 at Ebbets Field, Brooklyn, NYC on 29 August 1922) and Clem Johnson (w rsc 12 at Madison Square Garden on 29 September 1922). The *Chicago Tribune* reported Wills' contest against Norfolk as a battle of the champions of the 'black heavyweight and light heavyweight titles', the winner to meet Jack Dempsey.

Now rated the number one challenger by *The Ring* magazine and the NYSAC, and backed by Jimmy Walker, of 'Walker Law' fame, who had promised the black voters in New York, during his campaign for mayor, that he would support a Wills v Jack Dempsey fight, Wills and his manager, Paddy Mullins, demanded a fight against Dempsey. Bearing in mind that many former champions had avoided black fighters by putting up the 'Colour Bar', and ever since Jack Johnson had scandalised the sport, it was always going to be difficult to get a championship fight for Wills.

4 July 1923. Jack Dempsey w pts 15 Tommy Gibbons.
Venue: The Arena, Shelby, Montana, USA. **Recognition:** World. **Referee:** Jack Dougherty.
Fight Summary: This was famous for the fact that two banks in the town went bankrupt, having guaranteed the champion $300,000. The fight itself provided few thrills, with Gibbons (175½) proving to be very elusive for round after round, never staying in one place longer than he needed. By the fourth Dempsey (188) was cut over both eyes, and although he was landing some heavy blows, especially to the body, Gibbons was still light on his feet and able to box his way out of trouble. It was at close quarters where the fight was won, as Dempsey mauled and pounded Gibbons unmercifully to pile up points. The last five sessions saw Gibbons tiring rapidly, but his superb defensive skills and ability to make Dempsey miss enabled him to get to the final bell where the referee's decision went to the latter. There were no knockdowns.

After Tex Rickard matched Dempsey against Luis Angel Firpo, Harry Wills' manager, Paddy Mullins, obtained a court order directing Rickard to show why the proposed fight should not be halted because of a $25,000 forfeit he had posted with the NYSAC a year earlier. Somehow Rickard overcame that problem, the fight going ahead on the premise that Wills would have to wait. Later, a claim that the Governor of New York had not desired a mixed match was strongly refuted.

Firpo had arrived in America from Argentina in early 1922, but it had not been until he knocked out Bill Brennan, Jack McAuliffe II and Jess Willard that he sprung to notice; the contest with the former champion, who was knocked out inside eight rounds at Boyle's Thirty Acres, Jersey City, New Jersey on 12 July 1923, ensuring him a world title shot.

14 September 1923. Jack Dempsey w co 2 (15) Luis Angel Firpo.
Venue: Madison Square Garden, Manhattan, NYC, New York, USA. **Recognition:** World. **Referee:** Johnny Gallagher.
Fight Summary: Just three minutes and 57 seconds of fighting saw Firpo (216½) floored seven times in the first and twice in the second, before a left to the body and a short right uppercut ended his challenge. However, Dempsey (192½) himself was decked twice in the first round, including being knocked out of the ring by a tremendous right swing to the jaw. And if the champion had not been illegally helped back in again Firpo would surely have won. The contest was generally seen as the most thrilling of modern times as both men fought tooth and nail, giving everything they could muster. Following the fight, the referee was suspended for five weeks for failing to enforce his pre-fight instruction to both men that they go to a neutral corner in the event of a knockdown. Also weighing heavily against him was the fact that he had allowed Dempsey to fight on after he had been helped back into the ring. As far as the Argentine press were concerned, it had taken Dempsey 17 seconds to make it. Even Nat Fleischer, of *The Ring* magazine, reported that Firpo should have won the title by disqualification after Dempsey struck him while he was still technically on the floor.

Further to the 'black champion', Harry Wills, successfully defending his claim against Jack Thompson (nd-w rsc 4 at the 1st Regiment Armoury, Newark, New Jersey on 5 November), there were several moves made to match him with Dempsey, who merely contented himself in 1924 with exhibitions. Wills also did himself a power of good when outclassing Firpo at Boyles Thirty Acres, Jersey City, New Jersey on 11 September 1924 to land the 12-round press decision.

On 24 March 1925, the NYSAC named Wills as the mandatory challenger for Dempsey, and the man the champion must first meet if he wanted to don the gloves again in New York, thus suspending Dempsey indefinitely in that State. Meanwhile, a group of businessmen, fronted by Floyd Fitzsimmons, signed up Dempsey and Wills to meet somewhere in the mid-west during the year. Although Wills collected an advance of $50,000, when Dempsey failed to receive the $125,000 fee to bind the deal the prospective contest was called off. According to Wills, who kept the money, it was the racial issue that stopped the fight from taking place. For whatever reason, whether it was marriage, outside business interests, getting into films, or interference from Tex Rickard as suggested by Charley Rose, Dempsey remained inactive until September 1926.

Despite the stalling and ultimate three-year inactivity, Dempsey continued to have the support of the NBA. Towards the end of 1925, with Dempsey set on returning to the ring he was again pressed by the NYSAC to accept Wills as his first opponent in a heavyweight title defence. However, after much debate, Rickard stated that he wanted his man to first meet Gene Tunney, not Wills, but with NYC, New York and Chicago, Illinois made unavailable, Dempsey's first defence for over three years would take place in Philadelphia, Pennsylvania.

Tunney, a master boxer who mixed science with power, had well-earned the opportunity to face Dempsey, having beaten both Georges Carpentier (w rsc 15 at the Polo Grounds, Manhattan on 24 July 1924) and Tommy Gibbons (w co 12 at the same venue on 5 June 1925). The Gibbons' bout had been a final eliminator. He had earlier made his mark in the light heavyweight class before deciding to move up a division in order to obtain a match with Dempsey. Only one man, Harry Greb, the former middleweight champion, had ever beaten him in 80 contests, but having twice avenged that defeat as well as beating Chuck Wiggins, Charley Weinert and Erminio Spalla, he looked to pit his wits against Dempsey's all-out aggression.

23 September 1926. Gene Tunney w pts 10 Jack Dempsey.
Venue: Sesquicentennial Stadium, Philadelphia, Pennsylvania, USA. **Recognition:** World. **Referee:** Pop Riley.

Fight Summary: Fought in a rainstorm, Tunney (189½) adapted to the prevailing conditions far better than Dempsey (190), who was sorely ring-rusty. The fight was a promotional success with 120,757 fans turning out in anticipation of Tunney being put to sleep. Fighting on the back foot and stepping in when needed Tunney fought a brainy, technical battle over the whole ten rounds that left Dempsey shorn of his title. Moving well, while in the main evading Dempsey's wild swings, Tunney, who boxed on the counter, was only once in real trouble when he was caught in the sixth round by a solid left hook to the jaw that almost felled him. But sticking to his boxing the challenger continued to ram the left into Dempsey's face, with the occasional right thrown in for good measure, and at the end of the ninth it was the champion who was the one suffering most. By now Dempsey's left eye was almost closed, and into the tenth it was Tunney who was looking to finish matters as he smashed heavy rights in to the champion's head. At the final bell it was clear as to who had won in the eyes of the referee. Tunney's victory had not only turned the heavyweight division on its head, but had also proved that skill could overcome power.

It was announced on 29 September that Harry Wills would be meeting Jack Sharkey, who had recently outpointed George Godfrey over ten rounds at the Mechanics Building, Boston, Massachusetts on 21 September. Paddy Mullins, Wills' manager, criticised Dempsey for sidestepping his man for five years, and then Tunney for indicating that he too would also be drawing the 'Colour Line'. Although Wills had, up to a point remained active while all the hassles with Dempsey were going on, the damage had been done, and at the age of 37 he was beaten by the future champion, Sharkey, when suffering a 13th-round disqualification defeat at the Ebbets Field, Brooklyn, NYC, New York on 12 October.

Having overcome Wills, Sharkey next defeated Homer Smith and Mike McTigue, the former light heavyweight champion, before eliminating Jim Maloney (w rsc 5 at the Yankee Stadium, Bronx, NYC on 20 May 1927). The win over Maloney effectively took Sharkey to the top of the pile, but with Dempsey angling for a return with Tunney it was obvious that the pair should come together in a final eliminator. Matched by Tex Rickard and contested on 21 July 1927 at the Yankee Stadium, Dempsey earned the right to meet Tunney again when he knocked out Sharkey (who was complaining to the referee at the time) inside seven rounds, but not before the former champion had been badly hurt himself in the first session.

With black fighting men still feeling that they were not getting a fair crack of the whip, George Godfrey won the unofficial vacant 'black heavyweight title' when stopping Larry Gains inside six rounds (at the Broadway Auditorium, Buffalo, New York on 8 November), before successfully defending against Bearcat Wright (nc 10 at the Armoury, Portland, Oregon on 23 November), Cowboy Billy Owens (w rsc 8 at the Coliseum, Chicago, Illinois on 3 December), Leon Chevalier (w co 4 Wrigley Field, Los Angeles, California on 18 April 1927), Long Tom Hawkins (w co 7 at The Coliseum, San Diego, California on 13 May 1927), Jake Kilrain (w pts 10 at The Arena, Culver City, California on 23 June 1927) and Neal Clisby (w co 7 at the Olympic Auditorium, Los Angeles on 5 July 1927) prior to the second Tunney v Dempsey fight.

Beaten by Godfrey, Chevalier would later achieve notoriety when losing to Primo Carnera in the sixth round at the Oaks Ballpark, Emeryville, California on 14 April 1930. The fight came to an end when Bob Perry, one of Chevalier's seconds, threw the towel in after the latter had got up apparently unhurt, having slipped over. Reports stated that Chevalier was winning the fight at that stage. At a hearing afterwards Chevalier said that he had earlier been offered a considerable sum of money by an unknown party to throw the fight, but referred them to his manager. Chevalier went on to say that Perry had continually rubbed an irritant into his eyes between rounds when it was clear that he was not prepared to go down. While Chevalier was exonerated the handlers were not, being banned from working in the State again with the same conditions applying to Carnera's people.

22 September 1927. Gene Tunney w pts 10 Jack Dempsey.
Venue: Soldier Field, Chicago, Illinois, USA. **Recognition:** World. **Referee:** Dave Barry.
Fight Summary: This fight was made famous for 'the long count' after it was estimated that Tunney (189½) was on the canvas for at least 14 seconds during the seventh round, having taken four vicious blows to the head. However, with the referee refusing to take up the count until Dempsey (192½) went to a neutral corner the champion managed to struggle to his feet in time to continue. Having got himself in better condition for this one Dempsey went after Tunney from the opening bell, slamming in rights and lefts to head and body and occasionally going low

in his attempts to win inside the distance. In the fourth Tunney had Dempsey groggy at the end of the round, but was unable to follow it up in the next couple of sessions. After the well documented seventh, during which he managed to keep Dempsey at bay for the remainder of the round, Tunney came back strongly in the eighth. Dropped by a left to the jaw, Dempsey was up quickly, but now Tunney was beginning to force the fight, getting home with some good deliveries in the ninth. The final session saw Dempsey going all out for a kayo as Tunney countered and stayed out of trouble, but ended with the former champion being staggered by a succession of solid rights to the jaw. Although it had been a great effort by Dempsey, the majority of the press gave the fight to Tunney by six or seven rounds, with all three judges voting for him. As in their first contest, the fight took in a large gate with 104,943 in attendance.

In looking for Tunney's next opponent, and following the announcement that Dempsey was retiring due to eye trouble, the promoter, Tex Rickard, set up an eliminating series at Madison Square Garden, NYC, New York involving the former undefeated light heavyweight champion, Jack Delaney, Johnny Risko, Jack Sharkey and Tom Heeney, who had fought a 12-round draw at that venue on 13 January 1928. After Heeney beat Delaney (w pts 15 on 1 March 1928) and Sharkey lost to Risko (l pts 15 on 12 March 1928) the obvious match was Heeney v Risko, but with Tunney looking to retire in the immediate future and the fact that Heeney had already beaten Risko (w pts 10 at the Olympia Arena, Detroit, Michigan on 26 October 1927) Rickard circumvented the elimination route by matching the New Zealander with Tunney for the title. Since arriving in America, apart from the fights already mentioned, Heeney had drawn against Sharkey, drawn and lost against Paulino Uzcudun, and beaten Charley Anderson, Jack DeMave, Bud Gorman and Jim Maloney.

Meanwhile, further 'black heavyweight title' defences for George Godfrey in 1927, if you could call them that, came against Clem Johnson (nd-w co 1 at the Waltz Dream Arena, Atlantic City, New Jersey on 21 November) and Jack Townsend (w pts 4 at the Olympia BC, Manhattan, NYC, New York on 22 November).

26 July 1928. Gene Tunney w rsc 11 (15) Tom Heeney.
Venue: Yankee Stadium, Bronx, NYC, New York, USA. **Recognition:** World. **Referee:** Ed Forbes.
Fight Summary: Heeney (203½) made a fast start, catching the champion with good punches, and in the second round both men were rocked back on their heels. With Tunney (192) clearly the better boxer, once he had got the jab working he was able to gain the upper hand, countering with blows to head and body. The tough New Zealander was always dangerous, especially with the left hook, but by closing on the inside Tunney was able to negate its effect. By the eighth, with Heeney's left eye swollen, it was then that Tunney began to come off the back foot to spear home lefts that worsened the damage. At this stage all Heeney had left was his courage, and in the tenth he was dropped by a solid right to the head. Although saved by the bell the challenger had to be revived during the interval. Despite the brave Heeney coming out for the 11th he was ready to be taken as Tunney battered away at him, and with eight seconds of the session remaining the referee came to his rescue.

Almost immediately afterwards, on 31 July, Tunney announced his retirement, which then saw Johnny Risko, who had recently beaten Jack Sharkey (w pts 15 at Madison Square Garden, NYC on 12 March) in an eliminator, filing a claim on 3 August with the NYSAC to be recognised as the champion. He was then followed by the light heavyweight champion, Tommy Loughran, Young Stribling, Heeney and Sharkey and others, all trying to stake a claim. However, after an elimination tournament was ordered by both the NYSAC and NBA, the promoter, Humbert Fugazy, staged a bout between Risko and Roberto Roberti, won by the latter on a sixth-round disqualification at Ebbets Field, Brooklyn, NYC on 15 August, while his main promotional rival, Tex Rickard, looked to get busy. It was also reported that Tunney and the NYSAC Chairman, William Muldoon, would be putting up a trophy that would be inscribed with the names of future heavyweight champions.

While Rickard was banking on Jack Dempsey returning to the ring to meet the next best opponent, highly-rated men such as Pierre Charles (outpointed over ten rounds by Otto von Porat at the Mills Stadium, Chicago, Illinois on 9 August) and Knute Hansen (who was knocked out in the eighth round by KO Christner at the Public Hall, Cleveland, Ohio on 4 December) were effectively eliminated during 1928, prior to Rickard introducing his year-end ratings which had Dempsey, Sharkey, Stribling and Paulino Uzcudun as the leading men.

Unfortunately, while in Miami trying to set up an official eliminator between Sharkey and Stribling, Rickard was taken ill before dying on 6 January 1929 following an operation to remove an appendix. With the former champion, Dempsey, who announced his retirement a few weeks later, being drafted in to help the promotion along, the fight eventually took place, Sharkey winning on points over ten rounds at Flamingo Park, Miami Beach, Florida on 27 February 1929. Following his victory, the majority of the American press were reporting that Sharkey should now be recognised as the American champion.

Meantime, Max Schmeling, who had already beaten Joe Monte, Joe Sekyra and Pietro Corri since arriving in America, and had stopped Risko inside nine rounds at Madison Square Garden on 1 February 1929, was being lined up to meet Uzcudun in a semi-final eliminator, the winner to meet Sharkey for the vacant title. Since losing to Big Boy Peterson on a second-round disqualification at Ebbets Field on 19 October 1928, a result nobody took too seriously, Uzcudun had beaten von Porat and Jack Renault before pushing Christner (w pts 10 at Madison Square Garden on 22 February 1929) further down the queue. After Schmeling defeated Uzcudun over 15 sessions at the Yankee Stadium on 27 June 1929, plans for Schmeling v Sharkey in September were unfortunately scuppered due to a series of contractual disputes between Schmeling and his former manager, Arthur von Bulow.

Due to Schmeling being ultimately sidelined, in the interim the NYSAC set up contests between Phil Scott and Victorio Campolo (a first-series eliminator), the winner to meet Schmeling in a semi-final, and Sharkey and Loughran (the other semi-final leg being an American title fight). Sharkey beat Loughran (w rsc 3 at the Yankee Stadium on 26 September 1929), while Scott beat Campolo (w pts 10 at Ebbets Field on 23 September 1929) and looked forward to meeting Schmeling for the right to fight for the vacant title. However, with Schmeling still unavailable to fight and now temporarily suspended by the NYSAC, von Porat was drafted in as Scott's opponent, losing on a second-round disqualification at Madison Square Garden on 9 December 1929. When it was recognised that the German was not going to be available for some time yet, Scott and Sharkey signed to meet at the Madison Square Garden Stadium, Miami, Florida on 27 February 1930. Reported in some quarters as being a world title bout, Sharkey beat Scott (w rsc 3) and would go on to meet Schmeling in what would be generally recognised as a fight that would decide the championship.

By the time Schmeling v Sharkey was in place, Tuffy Griffiths had punched his way into a position to meet the winner after beating Risko (twice), Big Boy Peterson, Ludwig Haymann, George Cook and Uzcudun. Unfortunately for Griffiths he was then stopped by Jack Gagnon inside six rounds and although gaining revenge shortly after, his big chance had gone.

In the course of all of this going on the 'black heavyweight champion', George Godfrey, had lost his title after being disqualified in the third round against Larry Gains at the Maple Leaf Stadium, Toronto, Canada on 15 August 1928. Then, after Gains had been adjudged by the newspapers to have dropped a ten-round decision to Seal Harris at the Cadle Tabernacle Arena, Indianapolis, Indiana on 20 December 1928 in his first defence, the winner also laid claim to the 'black title'. This was confirmed in the February 1929 edition of *The Ring*.

A series of 'black title' fights in 1929 saw Harris beat Neal Clisby (w pts 10 at the Olympic Auditorium, Los Angeles, California on 7 May). Harris then drew over ten rounds against Long Tom Hawkins (at The Coliseum, San Diego, California on 17 May) prior to losing his 'black title' claim when Hawkins knocked him out in the seventh round at the same venue on 21 June. Hawkins then defended against Harris (w co 1 at the Dreamland Auditorium, San Francisco, California on 19 July) before taking on the former champion, Godfrey, and winning on a third-round disqualification at the Olympic Auditorium, Los Angeles on 13 August. After putting his version of the 'black title' on the line against Al Walker (w pts 10 at the Olympic Auditorium, Los Angeles on 1 October), Hawkins was stripped of it by Bearcat Wright, who stopped him in the ninth round at the Dreamland Auditorium, San Francisco on 25 October. Wright then made successful defences against Cowboy Billy Owens (w co 2 at The Coliseum, Des Moines, Iowa on 12 November) and Hawkins (w pts 10 at The Coliseum, San Diego on 10 January 1930).

Just to add to the 'black heavyweight title' confusion, Bob Lawson had beaten Walker twice in 1929 (w pts 10 on 2 April and w disq 4 on 7 June) in billed title fights at The Auditorium, Atlanta, Georgia, but as he had already been defeated by Godfrey he failed to gain much support. Lawson, who had been claiming the 'black title' since 1927, was yet another of his colour who failed to get proper recognition.

Having knocked out Leonard Dixon inside three rounds at The Auditorium, Roanoke, Virginia on 23 December 1929, and with Gains fighting in Europe, Godfrey reclaimed the 'black title', making defences against Roy Ace Clark (w co 7 at The Arena, Philadelphia, Pennsylvania on 24 March 1930) and Jack Rozier (w rsc 1 at The Ballpark, Baltimore, Maryland on 16 May 1930).

12 June 1930. Max Schmeling w disq 4 (15) Jack Sharkey.
Venue: Yankee Stadium, Bronx, NYC, New York, USA. **Recognition:** World. **Referee:** Jim Crowley.
Fight Summary: With the vacant title on the line, Schmeling (188) became the first man to win the heavyweight crown while sitting on the floor. The opening two rounds saw both men sorting themselves out until Sharkey (197) picked the pace up in the third and stepped in with heavy blows to head and body to have Schmeling wobbling at the bell. Although the German had landed heavily on occasion with short rights, Sharkey had come to no harm. In the fourth Sharkey looked like a man who meant business, ripping in punches from both hands before stunning Schmeling with a heavy right to the head, immediately prior to dropping him with a left to the body with just seconds of the session left. Unable to get up and fight on Schmeling had to be carried to his corner before the referee belatedly disqualified Sharkey for going low. Regardless of what was said about the punch being a fair one, Nat Fleischer of *The Ring* magazine, who was well placed to judge, stated that it was a wild swinging left hook that landed well below the belt. He went on to say that when the blow sank into Schmeling's groin with the full force of Sharkey's shoulder and body behind it an affair that was beginning to become one-sided ended. Following the contest, which left a bad taste in the mouth, the NYSAC only confirmed Schmeling's position as champion six days later on the proviso that he would have to give Sharkey a return, while the NBA went along with the verdict.

However, on 7 January 1931, Schmeling, inactive since winning the title, was suspended in New York for continually refusing to meet Sharkey. At virtually the same time he was also in danger of forfeiting NBA recognition in favour of Young Stribling, who the Association reasoned had been beaten on a debatable points decision over ten rounds by Sharkey in the elimination series and had since defeated several of the leading contenders. When common sense eventually prevailed the NBA's stance was soon forgotten once Schmeling signed to defend against Stribling.

Meanwhile, on the 'black title' front in 1930, Al Walker took over Bearcat Wright's claim when outpointing him over ten rounds at The Auditorium, Atlanta, Georgia on 17 June. Walker went on to risk his new title against Leonard Dixon (w pts 6 at Shibe Park, Philadelphia, Pennsylvania on 23 June) and Carl Carter (nc 6 at the Hurley Stadium, East Hartford, Connecticut on 5 September), but following a bad defeat at the hands of Walter Cobb at the Jamaica Arena, Queens, NYC, New York on 18 May 1931 any recognition he may have had was extinguished.

Still seen as the 'black heavyweight champion' by the great majority in 1928, George Godfrey defended his claim against Elijah Lee (w rsc 1 at Tomlinson Hall, Indianapolis, Indiana on 20 August), Seal Harris (w co 4 in Lansing, Michigan on 7 November), Harris again (w co 3 at The Auditorium, Milwaukee, Wisconsin on 8 December) and Wright (drew 10 at the City Auditorium, Atlanta, Georgia on 19 December)

3 July 1931. Max Schmeling w rsc 15 (15) Young Stribling.
Venue: Municipal Stadium, Cleveland, Ohio, USA. **Recognition:** NBA. **Referee:** George Blake.
Fight Summary: Despite being on the receiving end in four of the first five rounds, the champion eventually began to warm to the task as he weaved in beneath Stribling's left to fire in jabs of his own. He also mixed his punches up when going from head to body and Stribling (186½) was showing signs of wear and tear at the end of the sixth. By the tenth Schmeling (189) was sending in right hooks and uppercuts that would have finished off many an opponent, but somehow Stribling remained upright. In the final session Stribling was eventually dropped, a short right to the jaw sending him down for 'nine'. After rising on quivering legs and trying to fight on, just as Schmeling was lining him up for the 'coup de grace' the referee brought the contest to an end with just 22 seconds remaining. There were no complaints.

Nineteen days later, on 22 July, at Ebbets Field, Brooklyn, NYC, New York, Jack Sharkey put his American title up for grabs against Mickey Walker, the former welter and middleweight champion, but could only manage a 'political' draw over 15 rounds, the latter seeming a clear winner. Although not a good result for Sharkey, the NYSAC still matched him against Primo Carnera for their version of the world title at Ebbets Field on 12 October. It was thus no surprise that the Madison Square Garden promoters, who had Schmeling under contract to defend the title, applied for and won an injunction against the NYSAC on the grounds that Sharkey v Carnera could not be billed as a world championship fight. Although the fight went ahead as planned, with Sharkey winning on points over 15 rounds, it was seen to be nothing more than an eliminator despite the Commission recognising him as champion. Shortly afterwards, contracts were signed for a match with Schmeling.

While all of this was happening, on 24 August, at the Arena Gardens, Toronto, Canada, George Godfrey successfully defended his 'black title' claim when knocking out Seal Harris inside two rounds.

21 June 1932. Jack Sharkey w pts 15 Max Schmeling.
Venue: MSG Bowl, Queens, NYC, New York, USA. **Recognition:** World. **Referee:** Gunboat Smith.
Scorecards: 7-3-5, 8-7, 5-10.
Fight Summary: Keenly contested from start to finish, but with no exciting action to speak of, Sharkey (205) got revenge over the champion following their previous bout that had ended unsatisfactorily. Regardless of Sharkey's victory, with the majority of experts feeling that Schmeling (188) had retained the title they were upset that the championship should change hands in such a close affair. It was certainly a difficult fight to score. Starting every round on the back foot Sharkey used the left to good effect, countering consistently and keeping the hard-punching Schmeling off balance. It was a good tactic, especially when Sharkey was forced to fight on from the 11th with his left eye almost closed. The general feeling was that had Schmeling landed his powerful right, known as 'Big Bertha', with accuracy he would have retained his title.

After Sharkey had signed contracts with the Madison Square Garden promoters to defend the title in New York the following summer, the scramble was on to find the next challenger, with Schmeling, Ernie Schaaf, Mickey Walker (the former double champion), Larry Gains and Primo Carnera being the leading five contenders according to *The Ring* magazine.

Following his loss to Sharkey, Schmeling beat Walker (w rsc 8 at the MSG Bowl on 26 September) before falling out with the Madison Square Garden promoters and aligning himself to Jack Dempsey, while Gains, the British Empire champion from Canada, got himself beaten by the non-rated Walter Neusel (l pts 15 at the Sports Palace, Paris, France on 17 October).

As it had now become clear that the winner of a fight between Carnera and Schaaf would provide the opposition for Sharkey, the much derided Carnera beat Schaaf (w co 13 at the Yankee Stadium, Bronx, NYC on 10 February 1933) in what was a final eliminator scheduled for 15 rounds. Unfortunately, the contest had tragic consequences when Schaaf passed away in the aftermath. The Medical Examiner's report following the autopsy stated that Schaaf had entered the ring with a brain ailment that could not possibly have been detected prior to the contest, and with the amount of clubbing blows delivered to his head by Carnera the damage was exacerbated. It was also mentioned that Schaaf had suffered a bad bout of flu a month earlier before spending six days in hospital from its effects.

Max Baer gained the right to meet the winner of Carnera v Sharkey when he beat Schmeling (w rsc 10 at the Yankee Stadium on 8 June 1933) in a 15-round eliminator, but after continuing to play in vaudeville and partying he would be out of the ring for another year.

Earlier, George Godfrey knocked out Roy Ace Clark in the fifth round to retain his 'black title' on 5 September 1932, at The Tex Rickard Memorial Arena, Nuevo Laredo, Tamaulipas, Mexico. He then successfully defended it again against Tiger Jack Fox (w pts 10 at the Northside Armoury, Indianapolis, Indiana on 31 January 1933) and Bearcat Wright (nc 6 at the Convention Hall, Kansas City, Missouri on 10 February 1933).

29 June 1933. Primo Carnera w co 6 (15) Jack Sharkey.
Venue: MSG Bowl, Queens, NYC, New York, USA. **Recognition:** World. **Referee:** Arthur Donovan.
Fight Summary: In a fight made famous because of the 'Phantom Punch', a right uppercut that very few people witnessed clearly, Sharkey (201) became the first heavyweight champion to lose his title in his first defence. Having outscored Carnera (260½) in 1931, Sharkey made a solid start, his better boxing being too much for the clumsy Italian giant. It was in the sixth that the fight changed course, Carnera being told by his corner to get his big punches off. Driving in with both hands, Carnera was thumping Sharkey around the ring when the latter was caught off balance and slipped over. Up immediately, Sharkey charged into Carnera, slamming in a terrific blow to the temple that spun his man around but failed to halt him. According to Nat Fleischer, of *The Ring* magazine, Sharkey went to pieces when unable to halt Carnera's attack. It would have been better for Sharkey had he reverted to his earlier tactics but, in foolhardy fashion, when he persisted in rushing Carnera he was made to pay a heavy price. Holding Sharkey off with his left, Carnera ripped in four heavy rights to the body before a right uppercut to the jaw put the champion down for the full count, timed at 2.27 of the session. Regardless of rumours spreading to the effect that the fight had been rigged, Fleischer reported that the punch in question had crashed against Sharkey's chin with powerful force, while the referee remarked afterwards that it was one of the hardest delivered punches he had ever seen.

On 9 October, Obie Walker landed the 'black title' after outpointing George Godfrey over ten rounds at The Arena, Philadelphia, Pennsylvania. Apart from one more contest, the next two and a half years saw Walker campaigning in Europe.

22 October 1933. Primo Carnera w pts 15 Paulino Uzcudun.
Venue: Sports Palace, Rome, Italy. **Recognition:** World. **Referee:** Roger Nicod.
Fight Summary: Amidst boos and jeering Carnera (259½) was given the unanimous decision over the rugged challenger, who had been battered all over the ring without ever being decked. Uzcudun (229¼) had barely landed six or seven solid blows all night as Carnera used him as a human punch-bag, and at the finish he sported cuts over both eyes and damage to cheeks, nose and mouth. It was reported afterwards that, because Carnera had fractured his right hand in the ninth, it had severely hampered his performance, but the fact remained that he had kept it long all night. It had been similar to their previous fight in November 1930, which also went the distance, and in a career of 70 contests that started in 1923 and ended in 1935 Uzcudun was only ever floored once, against Joe Louis in his last fight.

1 March 1934. Primo Carnera w pts 15 Tommy Loughran.
Venue: MSG Stadium, Miami, Florida, USA. **Recognition:** World. **Referee:** Leo Shea.
Scorecards: 10-1-4, 10-1-4, 12-3.
Fight Summary: Outweighed by a massive 86 pounds, Loughran (184), who was unable to keep the champion off him, spent most of the time being crowded into corners where he took plenty of punishment. Using rough-house tactics Carnera (270) ploughed his way forward continuously, being also guilty of stepping on Loughran's feet at times, whether intentional or otherwise. Although Loughran won the odd round by a close margin, from the tenth onwards he failed to do so, finishing worn out after fighting the last few sessions in a fog. The unanimous decision in the 6'6" Carnera's favour was well deserved, but his biggest test was still to come when it was announced that Max Baer would be his next challenger.

14 June 1934. Max Baer w rsc 11 (15) Primo Carnera.
Venue: MSG Bowl, Queens, NYC, New York, USA. **Recognition:** World. **Referee:** Arthur Donovan.
Fight Summary: Floored three times from overarm punches to the jaw in the opening round the champion never recovered, and apart from his courage he had nothing to sustain him. Down again three more times in the second and again in the third the fight looked to be over, but because of Baer's antics and his lack of condition the contest lasted far longer than it should have done. Carnera (263¼) even won the fourth and seventh sessions before hurting Baer (209½) with a big right uppercut in the eighth. He then came under real pressure again as the latter picked it up. Somehow Carnera got through to the tenth, but after being floored three more times the referee decided to determine whether he was fit enough to carry on. In doing so he enabled Carnera to make it to the bell. The 11th started with a rush before a terrific right to the head had Carnera down for 'three'. Then, after Baer had

him down again, this time with blows to head and body, the referee rescued the giant on the 2.16 mark. A record for the number of knockdowns suffered by a fighter in a heavyweight title fight, several times Baer was dragged down at the same time. Clumsy and awkward with little skill, Carnera ultimately proved to be a poor champion. However, for sheer bravery he was on a par with anyone.

Inactive until December, Baer then began a series of four-round exhibition bouts around the country, knocking out the fifth-ranked King Levinsky on the way. With an agreement already in place for Baer to defend his title in New York during the summer of 1935, the NYSAC were rightly worried that he might be knocked out or stopped in one of these exhibitions, thus rendering the deal useless. Other than Levinsky, the men who had already or would be meeting Baer in exhibition bouts were Johnny Miler, Les Kennedy, Babe Hunt, Dick Madden, Tony Cancela, Jim Maloney, Stanley Poreda, Ed Wills, Harold Anderson, Hobo Little and Eddie Simms. On behalf of the NYSAC, Bill Brown's response was that Baer could defend his title in a 15-rounder in New York against either the top-rated Steve Hamas, Primo Carnera, Max Schmeling or Art Lasky, or he could clash with any of the four named in a four-round bout with the championship at stake. Despite the edict nothing changed for the champion, who carried on with the exhibition bouts.

Meanwhile, Hamas got himself beaten by Schmeling (l co 9 at the Hanseatic Hall, Hamburg, Germany on 10 March 1935) in what was seen by the NYSAC as an unofficial eliminator. On top of that, Schmeling's advisers had been negotiating with Baer with a view to him making a defence in Germany, something that went against the grain as far as the NYSAC were concerned. And when the German was asked to meet Jim Braddock, a former light heavyweight title challenger, in a final eliminator for the right to fight Baer, he refused, reasoning that as the number one contender he should not have to be involved in any eliminators.

In the event, the promoters, not wishing Carnera to be Baer's next opponent, went with Braddock who had been in virtual retirement and on the breadline due to the Great Depression prior to coming back to shock the up-and-coming Corn Griffin and the future light heavyweight champion, John Henry Lewis. He next eliminated Lasky (w pts 15 at Madison Square Garden, Manhattan, NYC, New York on 22 March 1935). Lasky was still highly ranked, but successive defeats at the hands of Ford Smith and Charley Retzlaff saw him drop out of *The Ring* magazine's top ten. Although Carnera beat Ray Impelletiere on a ninth-round stoppage at Madison Square Garden on 15 March 1935, the NYSAC argued that they would like to see him in action against the rising Joe Louis for the right to meet the winner of Baer v Braddock.

Throwing a spanner into the works, on 6 May 1935 the International Boxing Union (IBU) declared the world heavyweight title to be vacant. This came about due to Carnera earlier failing to defend against Belgian, Pierre Charles, following repeated challenges, and Baer apparently not being interested in fighting a man whom he had once used as a sparring partner. Naming Charles as the outstanding challenger and others such as Obie Walker, Don McCorkindale, Jack Petersen and Vincenz Hower, the IBU announced that they would be setting up a tournament to find a champion. Although Charles narrowly outpointed Hower over 15 rounds at the Sports Palace, Berlin, Germany on 21 June 1935 to win the vacant European championship, the IBU were unable to entice the above mentioned men to box-off in a tournament. At that point they were seriously thinking of handing their version of the title to the Belgian fighter until they were contacted by George Godfrey. Having been in Europe since the end of 1934 on a boxing and wrestling tour the 38-year-old Godfrey, a former 'black heavyweight champion', was eventually signed up to meet Charles in early October.

13 June 1935. Jim Braddock w pts 15 Max Baer.
Venue: MSG Bowl, Queens, NYC, New York, USA. **Recognition:** GB/NBA/NY. **Referee:** Jack McAvoy.
Scorecards: 9-5-1, 11-4, 7-7-1.
Fight Summary: Nicknamed the 'Cinderella Man', Braddock (193¾), in winning the title (recognised by all bar the IBU) provided one of the greatest upsets in the history of the division. Given no chance as an 8-to-1 shot, he shocked everybody in boxing when taking the points decision. Building up a solid lead in the opening four rounds as Baer (209½) clowned around, Braddock was then shaken up by a crashing right to the jaw in the seventh and was on the verge of going down before being let off the hook as the champion stood back to admire his work. Throughout, Braddock carried the fight to Baer, shooting out the left both up and down, while ripping his right into

the ribcage to cause maximum discomfort. The fact that Braddock was so aggressive surprised Baer, but it did not account for the latter's lack of ambition. Baer also lost three rounds when penalised twice for the use of a backhand punch and once for going low. Immediately following the contest Baer claimed that he had broken both hands in the fifth, an argument that failed to stand up on inspection. Having tried to take Braddock out from the fifth through to the seventh, landing well with lefts and rights, Baer continued to act the clown when a sustained attack could well have saved his title.

Two weeks after Braddock's victory, a young black heavyweight called Joe Louis, who had only been a pro since July 1934, hit the headlines when he stopped the former champion, Primo Carnera (w rsc 6 at the Yankee Stadium, Bronx, NYC on 25 June). Louis then went on to record further successes against King Levinsky, Baer, Paulino Uzcudun and Charley Retzlaff to take his record to 23 straight. Prior to beating Carnera, Louis had already recorded wins over Stanley Poreda, Charley Massera, Lee Ramage (twice), Patsy Perroni, Natie Brown and Roy Lazer, all good fighters in their own right.

Although the 'black title' had reverted back to Larry Gains when he outpointed Obie Walker over 15 rounds at the Tigers' Rugby Stadium, Leicester, England on 20 July, it would soon pass into history following the rise of Louis who almost single-handedly put black fighters back into heavyweight title contention following the dark days of Jack Johnson. Despite his seemingly unstoppable rise to the top there was to be a blip in Louis's fortunes when he met another former champion, Max Schmeling, who kayoed him inside 12 rounds at the Yankee Stadium on 19 June 1936.

On the same day a Philadelphian promotional team offered Braddock a large purse to defend his title against Leroy Haynes, a man who had twice stopped Carnera, but after he had been beaten by Al Ettore and Jack Trammell the offer was withdrawn. While all of this was going on the NYSAC ordered Braddock, who was contracted to make his first defence at Madison Square Garden, Manhattan, NYC, to defend his title against Schmeling in September 1936. However, on 18 August 1936 Braddock made a successful application to the NYSAC that the fight be postponed because he had developed arthritis in his right hand.

Meantime, on 18 August 1936, at the Yankee Stadium, Louis had got back on the winning trail with a three-round kayo win over Jack Sharkey, another former champion, and by February 1937, excluding exhibition bouts, he put victories over Ettore, Jorge Brescia, Eddie Simms, Bob Pastor and Natie Brown under his belt.

With the Braddock v Schmeling fight now pencilled in for the summer of 1937, to be held in an outdoor stadium, Braddock made the decision to break his contract with the Madison Square Garden promoters in order to fight Louis for promoter, Mike Jacobs, in Chicago. On hearing the news those running the Garden immediately filed a suit with the courts that Braddock's contract was binding, but were refused when the court ruled that the contract placed an unreasonable restraint upon the champion's liberty. The Garden promoters then appealed against the ruling, even having tickets printed and put on sale for Braddock v Schmeling to take place on 3 June 1937. Still, despite Schmeling weighing in successfully on the day it came as no surprise when Braddock failed to make the weigh-in that morning as everyone involved knew he was in training to defend against Louis in Chicago. Bearing in mind the earlier legal judgement, the NYSAC felt that the only remaining action left open to them was to suspend both Braddock and Louis from fighting in New York for an indefinite period rather than strip the former. With many secretly relieved that there was now no chance of the title passing into Nazi Germany's hands in the immediate future, a furious Schmeling, who was claiming the title by default, was left to ponder his next move.

Having been given an undertaking that he would be meeting the winner of Louis v Braddock in London, England on 30 July 1937, Tommy Farr, the British and British Empire champion, was understandably upset when Mike Jacobs, the promoter, representing both Braddock and Louis, then offered him ridiculous terms. However, calling Jacobs' bluff, on the afternoon of the Braddock v Louis fight taking place in Chicago Farr signed to meet Schmeling at the White City Stadium, Shepherds Bush, London on 30 September 1937 in a contest that would be recognised by the British Boxing Board of Control (BBBoC) as being for the vacant world title due to Braddock's earlier refusal to meet the German.

2 October 1935. George Godfrey w pts 15 Pierre Charles.
Venue: Sports Palace, Brussels, Belgium. **Recognition:** IBU. **Referee:** Rene Scheman.
Fight Summary: Billed for the IBU version of the vacant world title, Godfrey (264½) was far too strong for Charles (226¼), a man he had knocked out inside two rounds back in 1928. It was clear that Charles appeared to be intimidated early on as the American piled up the points with solid left leads. However, little by little Charles got himself into the fight, and following some violent exchanges by round six he was moving away from danger having got his left jab working well. There was no doubt that Godfrey's sheer weight advantage was gradually taking its toll on the Belgian man, but during the last three sessions Charles staged a grandstand finish, using his speed to score with jabs and countering blows. While Godfrey continued to throw heavy uppercuts from both hands many of them were missing, and at the final bell the majority of the partisan audience thought that Charles had just about won. When the announcement was made that Godfrey had won by two votes to one the crowd erupted in anger, the American being escorted to the dressing room for his own safety.

Godfrey gained nothing by his win after both he and his manager were suspended indefinitely by the IBU for what was classified as 'Irregular Conduct' and stripped of the title in May 1936. A little over a year later, Godfrey's career came to an end when he was halted inside eight rounds by Hank Hankinson at the Olympic Auditorium, Los Angeles, California on 10 August 1937.

Although Nat Fleischer, writing in *The Ring* magazine, reported that Charles had been handed the title by the IBU he had not, despite remaining the European champion. In their September 1936 ratings the IBU stated that they would recognise the winner of Jim Braddock v Max Schmeling as champion, but with that fight never taking place it was only after an international boxing convention held in Rome during April 1938 that the IBU agreed to stand by one universally recognised champion.

22 June 1937. Joe Louis w co 8 (15) Jim Braddock.
Venue: Comiskey Park, Chicago, Illinois, USA. **Recognition:** NBA/NY. **Referee:** Tommy Thomas.
Fight Summary: Out of the ring for almost two years was not the ideal way to prepare for a defence of his title, but Braddock (197) confounded many when taking the fight to the red-hot Louis (197¼) and even dropping him in the opening session. Up without a count, even though Louis came back strongly to cut Braddock over the left eye in the second, he still lost the round. Picking it up in the third Louis rammed home heavy blows as he looked to find openings, although Braddock would not be denied either. Boxing well, going forward with both hands, Braddock took the fourth and fifth before coming under fire in the sixth and being cut over the right eye. With Braddock now beginning to take a battering from the educated fists of the challenger, despite being badly wobbled he refused to give ground. Immediately under pressure in the eighth Braddock weakened badly, and following an exchange of lefts he walked into a crushing right to the jaw that sent him down to be counted out on the 1.10 mark. In victory, Louis became the first black champion since Jack Johnson, while Braddock gained much acclaim for his gritty performance.

With Tommy Farr and Max Schmeling due to contest the vacant world title, as recognised in Britain, on 30 September, a furious Mike Jacobs who was in danger of being upstaged turned his attentions to stop the fight taking place. Having been turned down by Schmeling, he next offered Farr the chance to meet Louis in America and got his man. In agreeing to take on Louis the Welshman risked substantial claims for damages on behalf of Schmeling, but, ultimately, the courts decided there was nothing contractually to stop him fighting in the meantime.

30 August 1937. Joe Louis w pts 15 Tommy Farr.
Venue: Yankee Stadium, Bronx, NYC, New York, USA. **Recognition:** NY/NBA/GB. **Referee:** Arthur Donovan.
Scorecards: 13-1-1, 9-6, 8-5-2.
Fight Summary: Going into the ring to end the fight as quickly as possible the champion met a man who would not succumb like some of his previous opponents. Fighting savagely throughout the contest, with Farr (204½) there for the sole purpose of winning, he took all Louis (197) could muster and dished out plenty of his own despite suffering a badly swollen thumb. Farr's long reach and bobbing-and-weaving style made him a difficult opponent for Louis, and although he was cut up badly he continued to go with the jab. Taking Louis's best shots unflinchingly,

especially in the seventh, he walked into the champion in the eighth as though nothing had happened bringing cheers from the crowd. By the end of the 11th, Nat Fleischer of *The Ring* magazine's card had the two men dead level, but the remainder of the bout saw Louis piling up points with the left as Farr, by now badly cut and bruised facially, tried hard to force matters but to no avail. Even though Louis claimed that he had damaged both hands prior to the fight it did not wear with the fans in the light of the pre-fight predictions that Farr would only last a few rounds at most.

Following the contest it became apparent that Max Schmeling would finally get his opportunity to meet Louis when he was contracted to meet the champion the following summer in New York. In the event of beating Louis and returning to Nazi Germany, Schmeling was also contracted to defend his title in America and fight for Mike Jacobs up to and through 1939.

Looking to get himself a crack at Louis, the former Olympic champion, Alberto Lovell, had been making good progress since arriving in America, beating Andre Lenglet, Maxie Rosenbloom, Hank Hankinson, Eddie Simms, Red Burman and Eddie Blunt among others before losing his top-ten rating after dropping a ten-round points decision to Gunnar Barlund at The Hippodrome, Manhattan, NYC on 29 December.

23 February 1938. Joe Louis w co 3 (15) Nathan Mann.
Venue: Madison Square Garden, Manhattan, NYC, New York, USA. **Recognition:** NY/NBA/GB. **Referee:** Arthur Donovan.
Fight Summary: Having won the opening round, staggering the champion with left hooks and rights to the jaw, Mann (193½) should have continued to attack the body and bide his time. Instead, he tore into Louis (200) in the second, feeling he was ready to be taken, and found himself on the floor from a left hook. Up at 'nine' Mann was now at the mercy of Louis, being dropped twice more in the third by solid lefts before a power-laden right smashed him down to be counted out on one knee at 1.56 of the session. Although it was now clear that Louis could be caught by right hands over the top, his all-round ability and destructive finishing power made him the stand-out heavyweight fighter of the day.

1 April 1938. Joe Louis w co 5 (15) Harry Thomas.
Venue: The Stadium, Chicago, Illinois, USA. **Recognition:** NY/NBA/GB. **Referee:** Dave Miller.
Fight Summary: After taking the first session with the left jab the champion was forced to endure an uncomfortable second round as Thomas (196) smashed in big rights and lefts to both head and body while looking anything but the mug he was supposed to be. Leaping out of his corner for the third Louis (202½) rammed in several solid blows on Thomas, but was forced to take a fair few himself before a left hook had the latter out on his feet grasping the ropes for support. At that point the referee had obviously made up his mind to stop the fight. Chaos ensued after Thomas's trainer assisted his man to his stool from outside the ring and by the time the referee had worked out what was going on the bell to end the round clanged. Following a discussion with the officials it was decided to let the bout continue rather than disqualify Thomas for his corner's misdemeanours. Thereafter, Thomas had no chance, being knocked down four times in the fourth before surprising the crowd when staggering Louis a few seconds prior to the bell. Coming out for the fifth, with the intention of finishing the contest, Louis dropped Thomas for 'eight' with a short left. Although Thomas bravely tried to fight his way back, another cracking left hook sent him down and out with ten seconds of the round remaining.

At the international boxing convention held in Rome during April 1938, Louis was now generally recognised as champion.

22 June 1938. Joe Louis w rsc 1 (15) Max Schmeling.
Venue: Yankee Stadium, Bronx, NYC, New York, USA. **Recognition:** World. **Referee:** Arthur Donovan.
Fight Summary: Avenging the only defeat on his record, Louis (198¾) destroyed the 'Black Uhlan of the Rhine' in just over two minutes (2.04) of a contest made famous by the fact that whether he liked it or not Schmeling (193) was being used for Nazi propaganda purposes by Adolph Hitler. After a quiet start the champion began to let the punches go, soon staggering Schmeling with a left to the jaw before dropping him for 'three' with a right to the same spot. Up again, Schmeling was immediately floored after taking two lefts and a right to the chin. Somehow

regaining his feet Schmeling was a sitting duck for Louis, and following a volley of rights and lefts to the head a terrific left hook-right cross put the challenger down for the third time. With Schmeling helpless and the referee starting the count it was all too much for the German corner, who threw the towel in so that they could tend to their man as quickly as possible. However, it was not until the timekeeper had reached the count of 'eight' that the referee called the fight off. Stretchered out of the ring with fractures to the vertebrae and with Schmeling spending several months back in Germany recovering from the beating it was almost a year before a return to the ring was possible.

In a bid to find future opponents for Louis, the NYSAC matched Gunnar Barlund and Lou Nova in an eliminating contest at Madison Square Garden on 3 October. Winning by a seventh-round stoppage in what was a surprise result Nova would eventually get a crack at Louis despite being stopped by Tony Galento in the 14th round of another eliminator at the Municipal Stadium, Philadelphia, Pennsylvania on 15 September 1939.

25 January 1939. Joe Louis w rsc 1 (15) John Henry Lewis.
Venue: Madison Square Garden, Manhattan, NYC, New York, USA. **Recognition:** World. **Referee:** Arthur Donovan.
Fight Summary: Forgetting Jack Johnson v Battling Jim Johnson in 1913, which was not recognised by some as a title fight, this meeting was the first occasion that the official championship was contested between two black opponents. Lewis (180¾), the light heavyweight champion, was already being scrutinised for failing eyesight and should never have been allowed in the ring with Louis (200¼), but with the latter quickly running out of opposition the fight went ahead. Even at the weigh-in Lewis looked a shot fighter, and after just 2.29 of the opening round he was rescued by the referee at the count of 'five' after being hit by several heavy rights and tumbling to the canvas a thoroughly beaten man. Prior to that, when Lewis had been dropped for 'three' by a right hand to the jaw, on getting up he had been put down again, this time for 'two', by another tremendous right to the head. Although the two men were pals outside the ring Louis treated Lewis just as he would any other challenger, being ferocious in the extreme and getting the job done as soon as he could manage it.

17 April 1939. Joe Louis w co 1 (10) Jack Roper.
Venue: Wrigley Field, Los Angeles, California, USA. **Recognition:** World. **Referee:** George Blake.
Fight Summary: Up against the veteran challenger, Louis (201¼) was expected to do the job quickly, something he achieved inside 140 seconds, but that alone did not tell the complete picture. Roper (204¾) had said prior to the fight that he would come out punching, and that is exactly what he did when the first punch of the fight, a cracking left hook, nearly lifted Louis off his feet. Angry that he had almost been dropped, Louis came roaring back as both men let their punches go. Despite being cut over the left eye, with Roper still dangerous, Louis was nearly caught again with a terrific left that just missed the target. Following that the champion quickly got on top with a barrage of blows before a right to the head, followed by a left to the body, sent Roper down for the full count.

28 June 1939. Joe Louis w rsc 4 (15) Tony Galento.
Venue: Yankee Stadium, Bronx, NYC, New York, USA. **Recognition:** World. **Referee:** Arthur Donovan.
Fight Summary: Galento (233¾), made famous by his "I'll moider der bum" comments, and called 'Two Ton Tony' because of his roly-poly appearance, got this shot against the champion following 11 straight wins inside the distance. In one of the most talked about contests for ages, Galento powered into Louis (200¾) from the opening bell, nearly taking him off his feet early on before being forced to taste the champion's punches. Cut over the left eye in the second, when Galento continued to charge in despite being visibly hurt, a terrific left hook to the jaw eventually dropped him for the first time in his career. Up at 'two', he made it to the end of the round but was still groggy. In the third Galento was under real pressure before smashing Louis down with a left hook to the jaw and a right to the body. The place was in uproar. Although Louis, up at 'two', came back strongly when hitting Galento with heavy blows to head and body the latter had won the round. Louis was now going to work, and at 2.29 of the fourth the referee rescued Galento when he was gradually sliding to the floor after being cornered and spun round by all manner of punches. It took more than five minutes to revive the battered and bruised Galento, but having inflicted the fourth knockdown on Louis he had done far better than hoped for.

The champion's next opponent would be Bob Pastor, who had lost just four of 46 bouts, one of them being a ten-round points defeat at the hands of Louis in January 1937. Since then, Pastor had beaten Al Ettore, Lee Ramage, Maurice Strickland, Al McCoy and Roscoe Toles, and held *The Ring* magazine's number two rating.

20 September 1939. Joe Louis w co 11 (20) Bob Pastor.
Venue: Briggs Stadium, Detroit, Michigan, USA. **Recognition:** World. **Referee:** Sam Hennessey.
Fight Summary: Down four times in the first and again in the second, few felt after two sessions that Pastor (183) would turn out to be a test for the champion despite him going ten rounds with Louis (200) early in 1937. Somehow getting through the next two rounds, Pastor started the fight back in the fifth when landing some heavy blows to Louis's jaw before he was again under pressure in the sixth. Cut badly over the left eye, Pastor stood his ground when staggered by powerful rights in the seventh before coming out firing in the eighth when taking Louis before him. If Pastor had carried a heavy blow, Louis would have been done for claimed Nat Fleischer of *The Ring* magazine. Again, in the ninth and tenth, Pastor took the fight to Louis, giving him all manner of problems, including a mouse under the left eye. Unfortunately, not listening to his corner, when Pastor came out for the 11th intent on fighting rather than boxing Louis, he was counted out inside 38 seconds, having been measured by a solid right to the head followed by two lefts and another right that took his legs away. It had been a tremendous effort that left many wondering what might have happened had Pastor carried dynamite in his gloves.

9 February 1940. Joe Louis w pts 15 Arturo Godoy.
Venue: Madison Square Garden, Manhattan, NYC, New York, USA. **Recognition:** World. **Referee:** Arthur Donovan.
Scorecards: 10-4-1, 10-5, 5-10.
Fight Summary: Bobbing and weaving in front of the champion, Godoy (202) breathed fresh life into the weight class when losing on a split decision. Louis (203), who had been unable to land effectively throughout the contest, was too often bundled into the ropes, and even when he cornered Godoy the Chilean fought back strongly. Breaking up Louis's rhythm with bulldozing tactics and the use of the head at times, Godoy also went down twice without being hit and crawled along the canvas to mock the champion. He even planted a kiss on Louis in the 14th. Afterwards, it was claimed that Louis had not been able to punch his hardest due to being afraid of damaging his hands on the Chilean's head.

29 March 1940. Joe Louis w rsc 2 (15) Johnny Paychek.
Venue: Madison Square Garden, Manhattan, NYC, New York, USA. **Recognition:** World. **Referee:** Arthur Donovan.
Fight Summary: At the mercy of the champion, and on the run from the opening bell, it was clear from the start that Paychek (187½) was not going to last. Thus it came as no surprise when he was dropped three times in the first round before being finished off after 0.44 of the second. It was a solid right to Paychek's jaw that began the rot, dropping the latter for 'nine'. Down again almost immediately from a left hook to the same spot, upon getting to his feet Paychek ran into another right to the jaw that enforced a further 'nine' count. Starting the second as if he needed to get home in a hurry, after Louis (201½) had rocked Paychek several times a tremendous right to the chin dumped the balding challenger on the deck out to the world. Having reached 'seven' the referee called the count off when he realised that Paychek was choking on his gumshield, care being administered to the beaten fighter before he could leave the ring.

20 June 1940. Joe Louis w rsc 8 (15) Arturo Godoy.
Venue: Yankee Stadium, Bronx, NYC, New York, USA. **Recognition:** World. **Referee:** Billy Cavanagh.
Fight Summary: A return battle saw Godoy (201¼) doing very much as he did last time for the opening six rounds, while the champion appeared more focused in trying to keep the Chilean at bay with right uppercuts and solid lefts to the body. In the sixth Godoy was at his best when catching Louis (199) with some heavy blows, but in the seventh the tide began to turn as the challenger tired. After chopping away at Godoy, Louis finally dropped his opponent for the first time in his career, having battered him with a barrage of rights and lefts. Coming out for the eighth Louis now had the bit between the teeth, and after rocking Godoy with a volley of blows to the head a right to the jaw decked the latter for 'eight' face down. Getting up in a dazed state, Godoy was eventually smashed down again and the referee halted proceedings at 1.24 of the session. It was not over as far as Godoy was concerned though as he leaped to his feet and tried to continue before being made aware that he had already lost.

16 December 1940. Joe Louis w rtd 5 (15) Al McCoy.
Venue: The Garden, Boston, Massachusetts, USA. **Recognition:** World. **Referee:** Johnny Martin.
Fight Summary: This fight heralded the beginning of Louis's 'Bum of the Month' campaign in which he took on a series of defences in double-quick time. Making his 12th defence, Louis (202¼) started in a rush and soon had McCoy (180¾) down on one knee from a smashing right to the kidneys. Up almost immediately, McCoy bobbed, weaved and sidestepped to keep out of further trouble during the next four rounds before being run down in the fifth. With McCoy jabbing his way out of danger once too often, Louis finally caught up with him and a crashing right to the head badly damaged his left eye. Back in the corner, when McCoy's handlers decided that the damage was too severe for their charge to continue he was pulled out of the contest during the interval. Yet again, Louis had failed to add to his prestige.

31 January 1941. Joe Louis w co 5 (15) Red Burman.
Venue: Madison Square Garden, Manhattan, NYC, New York, USA. **Recognition:** World. **Referee:** Frank Fullam.
Fight Summary: Surprising many in attendance the challenger took the fight to Louis from the opening bell, and when the latter was cut under the right eye there were strong feelings that an upset might be on the cards. But Louis (202½) remained alert, despite slipping badly in the third as Burman (188) charged into him. In the fourth Burman continued to go forward, taking all that Louis could muster while landing well himself at times, before coming unstuck in the fifth. Nailed by a heavy right to the head early in the session that damaged his left eye, Burman tried to take the fight to Louis prior to being badly weakened by a tremendous right to the stomach. Hurt again by another pile-driver to the body, Burman was dropped for the full count on the 2.49 mark after a further right had ripped into his solar plexus.

17 February 1941. Joe Louis w co 2 (15) Gus Dorazio.
Venue: Convention Hall, Philadelphia, Pennsylvania, USA. **Recognition:** World. **Referee:** Irvin Kutcher.
Fight Summary: Coming out in a crouch the challenger treated Louis (203½) to as much as he took himself in the opening session, especially body shots, while also proving to be difficult to hit. The game plan for Dorazio (193½) was to keep things much the same, but in the second round he began looking to land the left hook, believing that Louis was susceptible to the punch. That was his downfall. After being straightened up by solid lefts and rights to the head, Dorazio was counted out on the 1.30 mark having been smashed down face first by a tremendous right to the jaw. The punch that finished the fight, one of the hardest ever delivered by Louis, was said to have travelled less than six inches.

21 March 1941. Joe Louis w rsc 13 (20) Abe Simon.
Venue: Olympia Stadium, Detroit, Michigan, USA. **Recognition:** World. **Referee:** Sam Hennessey.
Fight Summary: Articled for 20 rounds, this would be the last world title bout contested over that distance. Running out of live opponents the champion probably figured that Simon (254½) would only last a round or so, especially after he knocked the latter down in the first with a solid right to the jaw. However, Simon was up at 'two' smiling, having suffered the first knockdown of his career, and was still walking into Louis (202) when he was put down for 'nine' in the third from a similar punch. Getting up, when the ponderous Simon began pumping out lefts regardless he started to outpoint and outpunch Louis in several sessions despite being staggered by one punch after another throughout. After the tenth Simon had shot his bolt, although still game to the core. The 12th saw Louis desperately trying to finish Simon off, but he had to wait until the 13th when a terrific right to the side of the head dropped the latter for 'nine'. Back on his feet Simon was ambushed as Louis landed punch after punch, and before long he was down again for 'nine' when felled by a right hand that landed spot on the jaw. Following a left hook to the jaw, with Simon looking totally dazed and holding on to the ropes for support, the referee halted the action on the 1.20 mark. At the end of the contest Louis was carrying a swollen left eye while Simon's face was a mask of blood from damage to both eyes. It was reported afterwards that Simon had actually broken his right hand in the days leading up to the fight.

8 April 1941. Joe Louis w rsc 9 (15) Tony Musto.
Venue: The Arena, St Louis, Missouri, USA. **Recognition:** World. **Referee:** Arthur Donovan.
Fight Summary: Fighting out of a crouch the compact 5'8" Musto (199½) made life difficult for the champion, who quickly decided that the best way to deal with his opponent was to concentrate on the left and not to risk the

right, having come to the ring with bruising to the knuckle. After opening up a cut over Musto's right eye in the opener Louis (203½) had his man over in the third when he cut loose with rights and lefts, but the challenger was quickly back in the fray when rushing to close quarters. Tossing in overarm rights, Musto had Louis more than worried in the fifth and sixth rounds when hitting the target on a regular basis. Into the seventh, Louis, using jabs, hooks and uppercuts, had Musto on the run, and in the eighth a series of left jabs further damaged the latter's right eye. With the injury worsening the referee had no alternative other than to stop the fight at 1.36 of the ninth when it was clear that Musto was having difficulty in focusing.

23 May 1941. Joe Louis w disq 7 (15) Buddy Baer.
Venue: Griffith Stadium, Washington DC, USA. **Recognition:** World. **Referee:** Arthur Donovan.
Fight Summary: Baer (237½), who became the first man to fight for the title that was once held by his brother, almost won it when tagging the champion with a tremendous left hook to the jaw in the first round. Although going over the ropes and landing on the ring apron, Louis (201½), got back into the ring at the count of 'four' but with the noise so great both men thought the round had ended, and with the referee holding Baer away from the dazed champion Louis had gained valuable recovery time. Gaining in confidence Baer charged into Louis in the second, doing well until taking more punches than were necessary in his anxiety to finish the latter off. By the third Louis was beginning to pick it up, and in the fourth he was hurting Baer with jolting lefts and rights to the head. Although Baer began the fifth well, by the end of the session he was being tagged by solid blows to head and body. The sixth saw Louis at his determined best, landing tremendous blows on the game Baer before rights to the chin sent the latter down for counts of 'six' and 'nine'. At that point, amidst the din of the crowd, Louis, who had not heard the bell, dropped Baer heavily before being made aware that the round was over. Advised by his handlers to stay on his stool when the bell rang to start the seventh, Baer was disqualified when his manager refused two calls from the referee to leave the ring. Adding to the heated discussions after the fight had ended it came to notice that the timer had already counted Baer out, but he had been allowed to fight on because he was on his feet when the referee had reached 'nine'.

18 June 1941. Joe Louis w co 13 (15) Billy Conn.
Venue: Polo Grounds, Manhattan, NYC, New York, USA. **Recognition:** World. **Referee:** Eddie Joseph.
Fight Summary: Having recently vacated the light heavyweight title, Conn (174) came closer to taking the champion's crown than any previous challenger in a contest that will go down in history as a near miss. Hurt in the second by body punches, after dropping the opening two rounds Conn picked it up in the third when belting Louis (199½) around the ring, with the latter looking a sucker for the left hook. Ripping in many telling blows, Conn was proving to be a difficult opponent, his speed making it hard for Louis to catch him. However, Louis came back strongly in the fourth through to the sixth to hurt Conn several times, the youngster being forced to take more blows to the stomach. By the eighth Conn was warming to the task, making great progress, and he continued the good work in the ninth before Louis shaded the tenth due to his infighting. Back came Conn in the 11th and 12th sessions as he smothered Louis and almost dropped him in a tremendous rally, but it was here that he lost the fight, his spirit getting the better of him. Coming out for the 13th, just about ahead on the cards of most scribes, Conn decided to go for broke, belting the champion to head and body before a terrific right to the jaw took all the fight out of him. Despite Conn making an effort to keep going, attempting to clinch after being forced to take a series of lefts and rights to head and body, Louis dropped him for the full count with a right to the jaw. There were just two seconds of the session remaining.

29 September 1941. Joe Louis w rsc 6 (15) Lou Nova.
Venue: Polo Grounds, Manhattan, NYC, New York, USA. **Recognition:** World. **Referee:** Arthur Donovan.
Fight Summary: A victim of ballyhoo, and nicknamed the 'Yoga Man' due to him being a student of that subject, although Nova (202½) had been backed to do well against the champion he failed to deliver. Despite having two wins over Max Baer on his record, right from the onset he spent most of his time on the back foot. For almost five rounds, with both men feeling each other out, even when Louis (202¼) occasionally landed a solid blow Nova merely backtracked. Finally, when Louis decided to go to work in the sixth a terrific right to the jaw dropped Nova in a heap. Nobody really expected Nova to get to his feet, but he did. Up at 'nine', Nova was battered from head to body by punch after punch as Louis laid into him, and when the referee eventually stopped the fight to rescue the challenger there was just one second of the round remaining. With his right eye bleeding profusely, and helpless

on the ropes, when the stoppage came Nova had to be helped back to his corner while still complaining that he should have been allowed to carry on.

Meanwhile, on 28 November, at the Olympic Stadium, Detroit, Michigan, Lee Savold outpointed Jack Marshall over ten rounds in the final of a 'White Hope' tournament that was organised to find a suitable opponent for Louis. The recipient of a split-decision verdict, with *The Ring* magazine rating Savold at number 16 it would be almost ten years before he stepped into a ring with Louis.

9 January 1942. Joe Louis w co 1 (15) Buddy Baer.
Venue: Madison Square Garden, Manhattan, NYC, New York, USA. **Recognition:** World. **Referee:** Fred Fullam.
Fight Summary: Following his previous crack at Louis (206¾) that ended in controversial circumstances Baer (250) was given a further opportunity at the title. This time round Louis was quickly into action, and although Baer got in the first blow, a right to the jaw, from there onwards it was only his gameness that caught the eye. Stepping up the pace, Louis floored Baer for 'nine' with crashing rights and lefts to the head doing the damage before sending in another heavy right to put the latter down for a second count of 'nine'. Back on his feet and trying to fight his way out of his dilemma, Baer was under enormous pressure as Louis went for the kill. With Louis hammering in lefts and rights, a terrific right uppercut to the jaw sent the challenger down to be counted out on the 2.56 mark.

27 March 1942. Joe Louis w co 6 (15) Abe Simon.
Venue: Madison Square Garden, Manhattan, NYC, New York, USA. **Recognition:** World. **Referee:** Eddie Joseph.
Fight Summary: After making a reasonable start Louis (207½) began stalking Simon (255½), and as the second round drew to a close two cracking rights to the jaw dropped the challenger who was saved by the bell at the count of 'two'. Surprisingly, Simon came out with rush in the third, charging Louis all over the ring and looking to attack the body but had the round deducted from him after going low with a blow to the thigh. It was much the same in the fourth before Louis went to work in the fifth, nailing Simon with at least two dozen blows from both hands until the latter was dropped by two cracking rights. Again the bell saved Simon, coming to his rescue when the count had reached 'six'. After Simon charged out for the sixth it was only a matter of moments before he was smashed to the floor by a left hook that was followed by a straight right to the jaw. The contest then came to an end controversially when Simon was deemed to have lost on rising at the count of 'ten', only for the timekeeper to claim that the count had reached 'nine' when the challenger was on his feet. Regardless of that the decision stood, the time of the kayo being announced as 16 seconds of the sixth.

With Louis joining the Army in June 1942, Maryland and then Ohio decided to set up a 'duration' championship. First into the arena came Alfred Big Boy Brown, a cousin of Louis, who outpointed Lou Brooks over 15 rounds at The Coliseum, Baltimore, Maryland on 23 November. Brown cemented that result with a ten-round points win at the same venue against Pat Comiskey on 21 December. Although that fight was probably not billed as such, *The Ring* correspondent claimed it to be a successful defence. Meanwhile, on 29 December, at the Auditorium, Columbus, Ohio, Harry Bobo, an Army corporal stationed at Camp Lee, outscored Buddy Walker over ten rounds to win the Ohio version of the title.

Matters came to a head when the two men met at The Coliseum, Baltimore on 25 January 1943, with Bobo winning on points over 15 rounds. The title then changed hands after Lee Q. Murray stopped Bobo in the eighth round at Oriole Park, Baltimore on 9 August 1943, but the winner ceased to be recognised after twice being outpointed over ten rounds at The Arena, Cleveland, Ohio by Jimmy Bivins on 1 December 1943 and 29 February 1944. Neither of the Murray v Bivins fights were billed as involving the 'duration' title, but were generally considered as such. Earlier, on 12 March 1943, at Madison Square Garden, Bivins had outpointed Tami Mauriello over ten rounds for what was thought at the time to be the NYSAC version of the title, although that billing never quite materialised. At this stage of his career, Bivins, rated the world's number one in two weight divisions, was inactive for over a year on military service after joining up on 1 March 1944, and with the 'duration' title getting such bad publicity the public quickly lost interest. Bivins eventually came back to run up an unbeaten sequence of 12, including a draw against the former NYSAC light heavyweight champion, Melio Bettina, but forfeited any title aspirations he may have had after losing three on the trot, to Jersey Joe Walcott, Murray and Ezzard Charles.

Towards the end of 1944, in an effort to help swell the Army Relief Fund Louis took on several unpaid exhibition bouts during a 15-month period. One of them was against one Johnny Davis at the Auditorium, Buffalo, New York on 14 November. Not many people realised at the time that exhibitions were banned by the State Athletic Commission, and this one went ahead as four-round contest to a decision. When asked if Louis's title was at risk, John Phelan, the NYSAC chairman, stated that it was not as 15 rounds was the stipulated distance for a championship fight. The *New York Evening Post* went on to say "What would happen if Louis was knocked out?" In the event it did not matter as Louis put Davis away inside 53 seconds with the first right hand he threw.

Once Billy Conn was released from the Army in September 1945, followed by Louis a month later, both men were quickly signed up for the long-awaited return that would gross $1,925,564, the second largest amount ever. With Conn reinstalled as *The Ring* magazine's number one challenger, the other men who made up the top ten were Mauriello, Bivins, Bruce Woodcock, Elmer Ray, Freddie Schott, Arturo Godoy, Walcott, O'Dell Riley and Lee Oma, while there was no room for Joe Baksi and Murray who had both held down the number one spot at some stage or another during the previous two years.

19 June 1946. Joe Louis w co 8 (15) Billy Conn.
Venue: Yankee Stadium, Bronx, NYC, New York, USA. **Recognition:** World. **Referee:** Eddie Joseph.
Fight Summary: In a contest that most fans were looking forward to it failed to reach the heights of their previous battle when the challenger failed to take the fight to Louis (207) as he had previously done. With Conn (187) continually on the back foot and not engaging Louis he was outscored in five of the seven completed rounds according to the referee's card. Conn only really showed in the second round when hurting Louis with a right to the jaw before going back on the retreat. Having decided to pick up the pace in the eighth Louis went after Conn with a purpose, crashing in a left-right to the jaw that had its desired effect. Quick as a flash Louis pounced again, and another left-right to the jaw sent Conn down in a heap. Although the challenger desperately tried to get to his feet he just failed to make it, being counted out at 2.19 of the session.

Louis's next opponent would be Tami Mauriello, who had risen through the ranks to become the number one contender after disposing of Bruce Woodcock (w co 5 at Madison Square Garden, Manhattan, NYC on 17 May).

18 September 1946. Joe Louis w co 1 (15) Tami Mauriello.
Venue: Yankee Stadium, Bronx, NYC, New York, USA. **Recognition:** World. **Referee:** Arthur Donovan.
Fight Summary: Making his 23rd defence, Louis (211) continued as world champion after knocking out Mauriello (198½) inside 129 seconds of what was an exciting fight while it lasted. Having almost dropped Louis with a cracking left hook that sent the champion clear across the ring, Mauriello continued to fire in punches. However, it was Louis who had the accuracy, and a left-right to Mauriello's jaw that was followed by a heavy right to the same spot sent the latter to his knees for 'nine'. Even after Mauriello had regained his feet he was hurting Louis, but following a bout of solid blows he found himself caught up in the corner with nowhere to go before two terrific rights, one that further damaged his left eye and the other to the jaw, sent him down to be counted out.

Strongly thought to be considering retirement due to a lack of challengers, Louis dispelled the rumours by stating that he would defend his title again before the end of 1946. Unfortunately, prospective championship opposition kept getting beaten. First it was Curtis Sheppard who was twice outpointed over ten rounds by Jimmy Bivins, at The Arena, Philadelphia, Pennsylvania on 17 February 1947 and at The Coliseum, Baltimore, Maryland on 21 April 1947. Then, on 15 April 1947, Bruce Woodcock was stopped by Joe Baksi inside seven rounds at The Arena, Harringay, London, England, which was followed by Baksi losing to a little-known Swede, Olle Tandberg (l pts 10 at the Rasunda Football Stadium, Stockholm, Sweden on 6 July 1947).

Earlier, Melio Bettina, the former light heavyweight titleholder, was knocked out in the first round by the light heavyweight champion, Gus Lesnevich, at Madison Square Garden, Manhattan, NYC on 23 May 1947, while another prospect for honours, Ezzard Charles, lost on points over ten rounds to Elmer Ray at the same venue on 25 July 1947.

The one man who remained in contention in 1947 was Jersey Joe Walcott, who reversed former defeats when gaining ten-round points verdicts over Joey Maxim (at the Convention Hall, Philadelphia, Pennsylvania on 6 January), Ray (at The Orange Bowl, Miami, Florida on 4 March) and Maxim again (at Gilmore Field, Los Angeles, California on 23 June) to become number one in the ratings. In the previous 18 months Walcott had also beaten Bivins, Lee Oma and Tommy Gomez. Following an offer by Frank Sinatra, the famous entertainer, to promote a non-title bout between the pair, Louis v Walcott was eventually made for December.

5 December 1947. Joe Louis w pts 15 Jersey Joe Walcott.
Venue: Madison Square Garden, Manhattan, NYC, New York, USA. **Recognition:** World. **Referee:** Ruby Goldstein.
Scorecards: 9-6, 8-6-1, 6-7-2.
Fight Summary: This was the first time Louis (211½) had successfully defended his title courtesy of a points decision since his meeting with Tommy Farr back in 1937, and it proved that at the age of 33 he was no longer the fighter he once was, especially bearing in mind that Walcott (194½) was a few months older. While it was true that Louis had done most of the leading, Walcott had scored two knockdowns following cracking rights to the jaw, the champion being put down for a count of 'two' in the first round and for 'seven' in the fourth. However, because Walcott decided that the best way to fight Louis was to circle around, jab with the left and sprint backwards whenever the latter got near him, only the first, fourth and ninth sessions were exciting. After the ninth, when both men mixed it for a time and Walcott came close to being put down, the latter continued to stay on his bike. In the 11th Walcott was hurt by a powerful left to the jaw, but came back well to outbox Louis in the next two rounds. Nat Fleischer, of *The Ring* magazine, stated that had Walcott continued to box in that fashion instead of backing off he would have undoubtedly won the title. After a contest which many thought Walcott had won, the two men were signed up for a rematch.

During May 1948, many papers in America were reporting that Henry Flakes was the man who could eventually replace Louis and Walcott. A pro since January 1947, Flakes had run up 24 wins, beating Pat Comiskey (twice), Bill Weinberg and Lee Oma (twice), while losing to Colion Chaney and Charles Lester and drawing with Chaney. Just as these pronouncements were being made Flakes was being told that he could never box again due to cataract problems. Away from boxing, Flakes was executed for murder in 1960.

25 June 1948. Joe Louis w co 11 (15) Jersey Joe Walcott.
Venue: Yankee Stadium, Bronx, NYC, New York, USA. **Recognition:** World. **Referee:** Frank Fullam.
Fight Summary: In what had been a boring contest, at the end of the tenth the two judges had Walcott (194¾) in front by 5-4 and 6-3 respectively, while the referee had it as 5-2 for Louis (213½). The opening two rounds saw little action before Louis was dropped in the third from a right to the face. More embarrassed than hurt, Louis got to his feet immediately. Again, in the fifth, Louis was hurt by a right hand to the jaw, but for the next few sessions the champion generally found a defence for such punches by ducking under them. However, by the end of the ninth Walcott was getting bolder, coming on to shake Louis up with heavy rights to the head, and in the tenth he served up more of the same. Louis, who was looking flustered and bothered in the tenth, suddenly turned loose in the 11th having been told that Walcott was tiring, and within half a minute he undid all that had gone before. Unleashing a tremendous attack, after Walcott had gone for him, Louis became the clinical fighter of previous years when finding the punches to win the fight by a kayo with just four seconds of the session remaining. It had been a massive turnaround, and before collapsing to the floor to be counted out Walcott had been hit with every conceivable blow Louis could muster.

With Louis having made a record 25 successful defences and pondering retirement, the NBA decided to set up eliminating contests between Ezzard Charles v Jimmy Bivins and Walcott v Gus Lesnevich, the recently deposed light heavyweight champion. While Charles outpointed Bivins over ten rounds at the Griffith Stadium, Washington DC on 13 September, with there being no takers for the other prospective contest Walcott remained inactive.

Another eliminating contest put together by the NYSAC saw Charles stop Joe Baksi in the 11th of a 15-rounder at Madison Square Garden, Manhattan, NYC on 10 December. At that moment it was still unclear as to what Louis intended, but on the same day of another NBA eliminator, which saw Charles defeat Joey Maxim (w pts 15 at The Gardens, Cincinnati, Ohio on 28 February 1949), Louis signified that he was retiring as the undefeated champion.

Having made the announcement through the auspices of the NBA Louis upset the men at the NYSAC, and when the NBA matched the foremost two challengers, Walcott and Charles, to decide the title in Cincinnati it would go ahead without their backing.

As the NYSAC felt the championship should only be decided after a series of eliminators they were prepared to keep their options open. Meanwhile, Louis became the matchmaker of the recently formed International Boxing Council (IBC), who would be promoting in Madison Square Garden, while the British, angry that the European champion, Bruce Woodcock, did not figure in America's plans, matched him against the future world light heavyweight champion, Freddie Mills, to decide who would take on the highly-ranked Lee Savold for the BBBoC version of the title. On 2 June 1949, Woodcock, defending his British, British Empire and European titles, duly knocked Mills out in the 14th round of their battle at the White City Stadium, Shepherds Bush, London, before being signed up to meet Savold the following year.

Savold had been a pro since 1933 with an in-and-out record, but had won and lost against Baksi prior to being disqualified in the fourth round of contest against Woodcock at The Arena, Harringay, London on 6 December 1948. Despite being beaten by Phil Muscato (twice) and Fitzie Fitzpatrick in his previous nine contests, Savold had victories over Ford Smith, Maurice Strickland, Eddie Simms, Solly Krieger, Lou Brooks, Buddy Knox, Lou Nova, Bill Poland, Tony Musto, Johnny Flynn, Nate Bolden, Lem Franklin, Eddie Blunt and Gus Dorazio, and had 70 inside-the-distance wins to his credit.

22 June 1949. Ezzard Charles w pts 15 Jersey Joe Walcott.
Venue: Comiskey Park, Chicago, Illinois, USA. **Recognition:** NBA. **Referee:** Dave Miller.
Scorecards: 78-72, 78-72, 77-73.
Fight Summary: Billed for the vacant title, despite Walcott (195½) making the early running and occasionally forcing Charles (181¾) on to the ropes he was unable to make it pay due to the latter's clever defence and his own poor timing. While Charles did well, especially with the left hand, both men missed with rights when a target presented itself. At least Charles pulled himself together in the seventh, shaking the older man with solid lefts and rights, but he was unable to follow up his advantage until having Walcott in further trouble in the tenth. Again Charles failed to grasp the opportunity, and while scoring more effectively with the left jab to claim the title he failed to light up the crowd as the clock ran down.

Despite Gus Lesnevich losing to Joey Maxim (l pts 15 at The Garden, Cincinnati, Ohio on 23 May) he had earlier been contracted to meet the winner within 60 days due to him being bypassed in the NBA eliminators.

10 August 1949. Ezzard Charles w rtd 7 (15) Gus Lesnevich.
Venue: Yankee Stadium, Bronx, NYC, New York, USA. **Recognition:** NBA. **Referee:** Ruby Goldstein.
Fight Summary: Promoted by the IBC, and with Joe Louis acting as the matchmaker, the fight took place in New York, a State where Charles (180) was not even recognised as world champion. However, regardless of the venue, the contest was supported by 47 States of America under the banner of the NBA. Charles, making his first defence of that title, was always going too well for the former light heavyweight champion, hitting his ageing opponent almost at will during the opening five sessions. As early as the first round Lesnevich (182) was wobbling under a barrage of lefts and rights to the jaw as Charles cast off the shackles of his title-winning fight. Lesnevich's best chances of victory came with the hope of him getting solid rights off, but every time he went with the punch he was effectively countered and as a consequence was soon carrying damage to his right eye. Giving it everything he had in the sixth Lesnevich went for broke, and although getting in solid rights that Charles seemed unable to avoid he had shot his bolt. In the seventh, with his left eye almost closed, Lesnevich was on the receiving end of almost everything that Charles threw at him. Having become patently obvious that Lesnevich could not continue for much longer, his corner sensibly retired him at the end of the session.

14 October 1949. Ezzard Charles w co 8 (15) Pat Valentino.
Venue: Cow Palace, San Francisco, California, USA. **Recognition:** NBA. **Referee:** Jack Downey.
Fight Summary: The sixth-rated Valentino (188½) was the next one up for Charles (182) in front of almost 20,000 fans, and although he had not been in the ring for close on ten months he was the Californian champion, having

drawn with Joey Maxim and beaten Freddie Beshore, Tony Bosnich and Turkey Thompson in his previous four contests. What he lacked in class Valentino more than made up with aggression, especially when fighting on the inside to work the body over, which he did to real effect in the second and third rounds. However, by the fifth, Charles was bouncing lefts and rights off every available target that Valentino had on offer. Even though Valentino came back strongly in the sixth it proved to be his last big effort. Mixing up jabs, hooks, uppercuts and crunching rights in the seventh, Charles almost finished Valentino off, but in the eighth a cracking right to the jaw sent the Californian crashing to the floor to be counted out with just 35 seconds on the clock.

Following a series of exhibition bouts in October, and an absence away from the ring for a further three months, Charles signed up to defend the NBA title against Beshore in New York on 28 February 1950. Put back until 29 March, after Charles was injured in training just four days before the fight was due to take place it was discovered that he had sustained severe damage to the left anterior chest in the region of the eighth rib at which point the apex of the heart was located. Charles was then told that he could not train for at least two months to allow the injury to repair itself. According to the specialist, Charles would be better than ever after taking time out and that there would be no recurring problems.

6 June 1950. Lee Savold w rtd 4 (15) Bruce Woodcock.
Venue: White City Stadium, Shepherd's Bush, London, England. **Recognition:** GB. **Referee:** Andrew Smythe.
Fight Summary: Contesting the British version of the world title in front of 50,000 fans, Woodcock (190½) made a fair start with the left jab and solid right hands to the head before Savold (192) began to get his left working well in the second round. Having just about shaded the opening two sessions Woodcock came out confidently in the third, again using his right to batter down Savold's defences, but it was now becoming clear that the latter could take whatever came his way without flinching. Early in the fourth Woodcock was cut over the left eye, and although he tried to keep Savold at bay the American continued to work on the damaged optic. At the end of the round, with blood pouring from a three-inch gash that would require several stitches, Woodcock's corner pulled him out of the contest, knowing full well that the task for their man had become nigh on impossible. There would be just one more contest for Woodcock, an 11th-round stoppage defeat at the hands of Jack Gardner that saw him shorn of his British and British Empire heavyweight titles.

Surprisingly Savold, who turned down an offer to meet Ezzard Charles in a contest that would be recognised throughout the world of boxing, was then out of the ring for over a year.

15 August 1950. Ezzard Charles w rsc 14 (15) Freddie Beshore.
Venue: Memorial Auditorium, Buffalo, New York, USA. **Recognition:** NBA. **Referee:** Barney Felix.
Fight Summary: Not even rated in the top ten, and beaten in his last two contests by Lee Oma, Beshore (184½) was given a shot at Charles (183¼) in a contest that failed to gain the support of the NYSAC despite it being held on their territory. Although Beshore, who was badly outclassed at times, was stopped at 2.53 of the 14th round, due to sustaining a seriously swollen ear in the tenth that worsened, Charles had been unable to floor him. Rushing in head down whenever he could to attack the body, Beshore was still in the fight up to the seventh but thereafter he never stood a chance as Charles began to open up more. In that session Charles punished Beshore at close range with hooks to the body and straight rights to the head before opening up again in the tenth and doing even more damage. Even though he had suffered cuts under the eyes in the 11th Beshore continued to come forward without let up but, with it becoming clear that he had no chance of winning, when Charles opened up again in the 14th the referee had seen enough. In the aftermath of the fight, Charles, who suffered a cut left eye in the 14th, said that his poor showing was down to the fear that he might not be able to go the full distance following his recent injury problems.

Prior to meeting Beshore, Charles had signed to fight Joe Louis after Lee Savold had been offered the opportunity but had declined. Louis, who was experiencing severe financial problems, decided to take a fight where the winner would be recognised by all the American authorities as the champion.

27 September 1950. Ezzard Charles w pts 15 Joe Louis.
Venue: Yankee Stadium, Bronx, NYC, New York, USA. **Recognition:** NBA/NY. **Referee:** Mark Conn.

Scorecards: 10-5, 13-2, 12-3.

Fight Summary: Coming back after being out of the ring for more than two years, Louis (218) was just a shell of the once great fighter that everyone recognised. By the fourth round Charles (184½) was outspeeding Louis, who was beginning to look ponderous, while continually proving to be too elusive for the older man to batter down with his bigger punches. At this stage of the fight both men were carrying damage to their left eyes and by the ninth Charles was having difficulty in focusing with Louis being too slow to take advantage. The tenth saw Louis at his best as he bored in with solid blows that shook Charles up, but by the end of the session the latter was fighting back strongly. Picking up the pace in the 11th, after Charles came out throwing big punches at Louis's head he continued to bang away during the remaining sessions in an effort to score a kayo. In the final round Louis was sold-out, being almost helpless on the ropes as Charles fired punches at him before the bell came to his rescue.

Due to his problems with the taxman Louis continued to fight on, defeating Cesar Brion, Freddie Beshore, Andy Walker and Omelio Agramonte before meeting up with Lee Savold on 15 June 1951 at Madison Square Garden, Manhattan, NYC. Still recognised in Britain as the champion, Savold was knocked out in the sixth of a 15-rounder contested under championship conditions. Initially not giving their consent to it being a championship fight as they did not recognise Louis as the leading challenger, on 19 June the BBBoC retrospectively recognised the winner as champion.

5 December 1950. Ezzard Charles w co 11 (15) Nick Barone.
Venue: The Gardens, Cincinnati, Ohio, USA. **Recognition:** NBA/NY. **Referee:** Tony Warndorf.

Fight Summary: Boxing with purpose the champion had little difficulty in dealing with Barone (178½) who, as the fourth-rated light heavyweight, really did not belong in the division. However, with Charles also considered too light for the weight class the fight was given official approval. Although Barone kept pressing Charles (185), tossing in short punches and aiming to stay at close quarters, he was nearly always fought off with jabs, hooks and uppercuts whenever the latter picked up the pace. By the ninth round, which Charles took by a wide margin, it was clear that Barone would be lucky to last the distance. Coming out fast in the 11th Charles set about Barone with all manner of blows, a jarring right uppercut sending the challenger almost into dreamland, such was the power of the punch. Cutting loose with everything he had Charles had Barone at his mercy, and following a battery of shots from both hands a crashing right sent the former marine down to be counted out on the 2.06 mark.

12 January 1951. Ezzard Charles w rsc 10 (15) Lee Oma.
Venue: Madison Square Garden, Manhattan, NYC, New York, USA. **Recognition:** NBA/NY. **Referee:** Ruby Goldstein.

Fight Summary: Charles (185) was a disappointment when taking on the fourth-rated Oma (193), the challenger standing up to whatever was thrown at him in the early rounds while being able to come back with plenty of his own. Charles' left eye was cut as early as the second, causing his timing to be off at times, especially when he strayed below the belt and had points deducted in the fifth and eighth. While stabbing his left into Charles' damaged features Oma also made life difficult for the champion, as well as making for an elusive target as he rode and slipped punches. However, despite the fight being mainly listless the finish will live on in the memories of those who were there. Eventually catching up with Oma in the tenth, Charles smashed in more than a dozen left hooks to the jaw and a few to the body for good measure to send his rival staggering around the ring in such a manner that *The Ring* magazine reported it as a walk on "queer street". The fight was as good as over, and with a now defenceless Oma forced into a neutral corner as Charles was raining in punches the referee halted proceedings at 1.19 of the session.

7 March 1951. Ezzard Charles w pts 15 Jersey Joe Walcott.
Venue: Olympia Stadium, Detroit, Michigan, USA. **Recognition:** NBA/NY. **Referee:** Clarence Rosen.
Scorecards: 80-70, 80-66, 83-62.

Fight Summary: Making his fourth attempt to win the title, Walcott (193) was once again seen off in a contest where he could never quite get to grips with the champion. Following an opening round that was marred by too much holding and negative tactics, having hurt Charles (186) in the fourth with an overarm right Walcott played second fiddle thereafter as the latter began to pick up points with the left lead. In the ninth, when Walcott walked on to a heavy right-hand counter he was dropped for 'nine', the only knockdown of the fight, before being forced to take plenty of rights and lefts until the bell ended the session. Although Walcott came back strongly in the tenth and 11th with left and right hooks it was Charles who took three of the last four sessions with his more effective punching, especially in the 14th when the challenger walked into smashing right hands that rocked him back on his heels. After sustaining a badly swollen left ear in the fourth Charles' prospective fight against Joe Louis, tentatively set for 18 April, was put on the backburner. It then failed to take place when negotiations broke down.

30 May 1951. Ezzard Charles w pts 15 Joey Maxim.
Venue: The Stadium, Chicago, Illinois, USA. **Recognition:** NBA/NY. **Referee:** Frank Gilmer.
Scorecards: 78-72, 85-65, 85-65.
Fight Summary: Defending his title against the current light heavyweight king, Charles (182) scored a relatively easy win that was made to look less than straightforward by the referee's card that gave the challenger four rounds with four even. According to Nat Fleischer, of *The Ring* magazine, the referee's decision was so wide of the mark it was almost laughable. It was Charles' body punching that took all the steam out of Maxim (181½), a man he had beaten three times previously and who at times was almost gasping for breath. What irked the fans was the ultra-cautious Charles' inability to drop Maxim, even when the latter was reeling around the ring exhausted from his exertions and carrying a swollen and cut face. In the fourth, when Charles was warned for a foul that nobody else in the crowd saw he actually stopped fighting in amazement, allowing Maxim a few free shots. It was in the frequent clinches that Charles excelled, getting off right-hand blows to head and body as Maxim, a past master at tying opponents up, tried desperately to contain him without success. From the 13th onwards Maxim was out on his feet, but Charles was unable to take advantage of the situation despite landing some heavy shots on his man.

18 July 1951. Jersey Joe Walcott w co 7 (15) Ezzard Charles.
Venue: Forbes Field, Pittsburgh, Pennsylvania, USA. **Recognition:** NBA/NY. **Referee:** Buck McTiernan.
Fight Summary: At the age of 37½ Walcott (194) became the oldest man to win a title at any weight for the first time. He also became the oldest heavyweight champion up to that time when knocking out Charles (182) inside 55 seconds of the seventh round. Walcott's main tactic was to throw right hands over the top of the left lead, followed by a left hook, and in the third he rocked Charles with a couple of cracking rights before having the latter bleeding from cuts around the face after left hooks had got home in the fourth. At this stage of the fight Walcott was getting on top, and in the seventh he exploded a left hook to Charles' jaw that sent him down flat on his face to be counted out. Although Charles desperately tried to get to his feet at the count of 'nine', on failing he tumbled on to his back in a neutral corner.

Despite Walcott's victory the British Boxing Board of Control still saw Joe Louis as the champion, but following wins over Cesar Brion and Jimmy Bivins and a defeat at the hands of Rocky Marciano (l rsc 8 at Madison Square Garden, Manhattan, NYC, New York on 26 October) the BBBoC fell into line with the rest of the world. For Louis it was the end of the line, thus bringing the curtain down on a wonderful 17-year career.

While all this was going on Clarence Henry had continued his rise up the rankings, being rated at the end of the year by *The Ring* magazine behind Charles and Marciano, having beaten John Holman, Rusty Payne, Turkey Thompson, Omelio Agramonte (twice), Jimmy Bivins and Bob Baker. In 33 contests Henry had lost just two before reversing them. However, after defeating Bob Satterfield he lost to Harold Johnson and then Archie Moore before taking a year away from boxing.

Instead of being a fighting champion Walcott was prepared to put the championship into cold storage while taking time out for a year. At the heart of the matter was the fact that Walcott had contractually agreed to give Charles a return within 60 days if he won, but was now saying that he would fight Charles in June 1952 and not before. Not sure whether Walcott's plans were to ignore Charles and take a fight against Marciano or Harry Matthews, the NYSAC issued him with an ultimatum that he either accepted the Charles return and file his acceptance by 15 February 1952 or face being stripped. Cocking a snook at the NBA and NYSAC, Walcott challenged them to strip him if they felt that strongly about it. Needless to say that did not happen, and at the end of March Walcott v Charles was made for Philadelphia at the beginning of June 1952.

5 June 1952. Jersey Joe Walcott w pts 15 Ezzard Charles.
Venue: Municipal Stadium, Philadelphia, Pennsylvania, USA. **Recognition:** World. **Referee:** Zack Clayton.
Scorecards: 9-6, 8-7, 8-7.
Fight Summary: Making his first defence against the man he won the title from Walcott (196) dominated the early stages of his fight against Charles (191½), using solid lefts and rights to keep the challenger at arm's length and hurting him with a right to the jaw in the third. In the early stages Charles concentrated on the body, but it was not until the latter part of the fight that Walcott began to come under heavy pressure when tiring. Cut over both eyes, Charles gave it everything he had over the last four rounds, hurting Walcott several times in the 14th before he ran out of time. There were no knockdowns, and at the age of 38 Walcott became the oldest man to successfully defend the world heavyweight title.

On 28 July, at the Yankee Stadium, Bronx, NYC, New York, Rocky Marciano earned the right to be Walcott's next opponent when he knocked out Harry Matthews in the second session of their 15-round eliminator. Although unbeaten in 42 contests, the power-punching 28-year old Marciano was still seen as wild-swinging and somewhat clumsy opponent for the skilful veteran.

23 September 1952. Rocky Marciano w co 13 (15) Jersey Joe Walcott.
Venue: Municipal Stadium, Philadelphia, Pennsylvania, USA. **Recognition:** World. **Referee:** Charley Daggert.
Fight Summary: For the best part of 12 rounds the champion, boxing a cagey fight, kept the younger Marciano (184) chasing shadows after dropping him for 'four' with a solid left hook in the opening session. Standing up to Marciano and countering well Walcott (196) continued to pick up points despite being cut badly over the left eye in the sixth. Riding the punches well, by the ninth Walcott was landing the heavier shots, and in the 11th he almost dropped Marciano, now cut over both eyes, with a terrific left hook. Boxing more defensively in the 12th Walcott was still landing the better punches, but 43 seconds into the 13th he was counted out after momentarily dropping his guard and taking a tremendous right to the chin.

Following the contest Walcott relished the opportunity that the return clause would bring, hoping for an early meeting in 1953. Meanwhile, Al Weill, Marciano's manager, was holding out for a June date in New York. All the wrangling ended at the end of February when, after six weeks of negotiations, the International Boxing Club announced that the fight would take place at the Chicago Stadium on 10 April. Unfortunately, a few days before it was due to take place Marciano suffered a series of heavy nose bleeds which caused a postponement until 15 May.

15 May 1953. Rocky Marciano w co 1 (15) Jersey Joe Walcott.
Venue: The Stadium, Chicago, Illinois, USA. **Recognition:** World. **Referee:** Frank Sikora.
Fight Summary: Concentrating on his defence, blocking and moving, Walcott (197¾) kept the champion at arm's length for two thirds of the opening round. Then, as Marciano (184½) continued pressing forward he suddenly found a right to the jaw that sent Walcott crashing. The din was so intense that it was a good couple of seconds before Marciano realised that he had to go to a neutral corner, but it made no difference as Walcott was counted out on the 2.25 mark in the act of rising. It came as no surprise when Walcott, who had complained that the count was too quick, retired in the aftermath of the contest.

24 September 1953. Rocky Marciano w rsc 11 (15) Roland LaStarza.
Venue: Polo Grounds, Manhattan, NYC, New York, USA. **Recognition:** World. **Referee:** Ruby Goldstein.
Fight Summary: Having gone the distance with Marciano in March 1950, losing controversially by a split decision over ten rounds, LaStarza (184¾) felt that he had a reasonable chance of dethroning the champion. Even though he was cut over the right eye in the second round LaStarza boxed well on the retreat against the wild, clumsy Marciano (185), being still in the fight up to the eighth. He was never going to win though, and once Marciano's heavy wallops began to take effect LaStarza was fighting a losing battle. Brushing aside his challenger, who was now cut over both eyes, Marciano went for the finish in the 11th, dropping LaStarza with a right to the jaw. Although getting up, LaStarza was an open target. With punches coming in from all angles and with LaStarza looking as though he could suffer serious injury the referee rescued him with 89 seconds of the session remaining. This was the first heavyweight title fight between white men for 18 years.

Although it was earlier felt that the International Boxing Club would like Marciano to make his next defence against Nino Valdes in February 1954, possibly in Miami and well inside the 'every six-month defence' ruling, Al Weill, his manager, seemed adverse to the idea. Having recently beaten Ezzard Charles and the European champion, Heinz Neuhaus, Valdes was the number one challenger as far as *The Ring* magazine ratings were concerned. He seemed to be the obvious choice, but after coming back to beat Coley Wallace and Bob Satterfield it was Charles who was selected as Marciano's next opponent during the coming summer. Valdes never did get to fight Marciano despite being his leading challenger on and off for 18 months, and while there were many who felt that the big Cuban was being blatantly avoided others argued that he was not box office.

17 June 1954. Rocky Marciano w pts 15 Ezzard Charles.
Venue: Yankee Stadium, Bronx, NYC, New York, USA. **Recognition:** World. **Referee:** Ruby Goldstein.
Scorecards: 8-5-2, 9-5-1, 8-6-1.
Fight Summary: Putting on a great display of pure guts, Charles (185½) became to first man to take the champion the distance over 15 rounds. After winning three of the opening four rounds Charles then came under more and more pressure as Marciano (187½), cut over the left eye, began to find the range, and he was badly rocked in the sixth. Boxing calmly, Charles came back well to take the eighth but in the ninth, after Marciano had crashed home several tremendous punches, the challenger's right eye began to swell badly. By the 12th Charles started to stand his ground more, managing to remain upright following some fierce exchanges right through to the final bell. Both men needed medical attention after the fight, Marciano having ten stitches inserted over his left eye.

17 September 1954. Rocky Marciano w co 8 (15) Ezzard Charles.
Venue: Yankee Stadium, Bronx, NYC, New York, USA. **Recognition:** World. **Referee:** Al Berl.
Fight Summary: Twice postponed due to heavy rain, the contest eventually took place two days later than originally planned. Constantly charging in to put Charles (192½) under pressure Marciano (187) was well on top by the fifth round, having handed out a lot of punishment to head and body. By the sixth though, Charles seemed to have a second wind, and by the end of the session the champion's nose was split badly and blood was pouring down his face. Sticking with it in the seventh, when Charles cut the champion over the left eye early in the eighth thinking the fight might be halted Marciano tore in with both hands to drop his man with a right to the jaw. Back on his feet at 'four' Charles was now in real trouble, and following a barrage of blows to the head he was sent down to be counted out with 24 seconds of the session remaining.

After suffering severe damage to his nose and eyes, Marciano was out of the ring for quite a time to allow for plastic surgery to take, only getting back into sparring sessions during mid-February 1955. At the same time it was announced that he would be defending his title against Don Cockell in May. Cockell had earned the right to meet Marciano, in that he had beaten Harry Matthews three times and also eliminated Roland LaStarza, but hopes of the fight taking place in England were dashed the following week when it was announced that it would take place in America.

16 May 1955. Rocky Marciano w rsc 9 (15) Don Cockell.
Venue: Kezar Stadium, San Francisco, California, USA. **Recognition:** World. **Referee:** Frankie Brown.
Fight Summary: Not given much of a chance Cockell (205) proved his critics wrong when putting up a wonderful display of courage in the face of heavy odds. The challenger even took the opening two rounds before Marciano (189) came on strong. Even then Cockell was still fighting back hard. In the sixth, Cockell, now badly cut on the forehead, actually halted Marciano momentarily with a vicious right cross, but by the eighth he was gradually beginning to be ground down before being dropped on the bell. Soon after the start of the ninth, with Marciano on the rampage, Cockell was put down from a battery of punches to head and body. Struggling up at 'nine' Cockell was at the mercy of Marciano, and following another count, of 'five', the referee called it off 59 seconds into the session when the Englishman was all over the place. After the contest the British press complained about the foul tactics that would have seen Marciano tossed out of a British ring, but as far as Cockell was concerned the fight was in America and he knew what he was letting himself in for.

21 September 1955. Rocky Marciano w co 9 (15) Archie Moore.
Venue: Yankee Stadium, Bronx, NYC, New York, USA. **Recognition:** World. **Referee:** Harry Kessler.

Fight Summary: Looking to become the first light heavyweight champion to take the heavyweight title Moore (188) gave it a real go, flooring Marciano (188¼) for a count of 'four' in the second with a right to the jaw. Boxing with great verve and a brilliant defence Moore made life extremely difficult for Marciano, but once the champion began to batter him against the ropes the end was in sight. Put down twice in the sixth, Moore tried to clear his head. However, by the end of the seventh his right eye was almost closed, and in the eighth he was floored by a right to the jaw before being saved by the bell. Coming into the ninth Marciano rolled all over Moore, who was eventually counted out on the 1.19 mark after taking a well-timed left hook to the jaw that smashed him to the floor and left him in a heap in his own corner.

Marciano retired as undefeated champion in April 1956 and with Moore recognised by both the NBA and EBU as the leading challenger, having already eliminated Cuba's Nino Valdes on points over 15 rounds at Cashman Field, Las Vegas, Nevada on 2 May 1955, in order to find his opponent the NYSAC set up another eliminator between Floyd Patterson and Tommy Jackson, won on points by the former over 12 rounds at Madison Square Garden, Manhattan, NYC on 8 June 1956.

Another contest of some significance saw Moore beat James J. Parker (w rsc 9 at the Maple Leaf Stadium, Toronto, Canada on 25 July 1956) in a fight the promoter had sought world title billing for but had been denied by the Canadian Boxing Federation. In his previous five contests Parker had lost to Valdes, drawn with Earl Walls and the 7'2" Ewart Potgieter, and beaten Johnny Arthur and Heinz Neuhaus, hardly the form of an aspiring world champion. Incidentally, at 94", South Africa's Potgieter would appear to have one of the longest reaches ever seen in a boxing ring.

Patterson, with the peek-a-boo style and fast hands, was an Olympic middleweight champion at the age of 17 in 1952. He had already participated in 31 pro contests, losing just once, to Joey Maxim. Prior to meeting Jackson, Patterson had beaten Dick Wagner (twice), Gordon Wallace, Wes Bascom, Yvon Durelle (twice), Jacques Royer-Crecy, Tommy Harrison, Jimmy Slade (twice), Willie Troy, Archie McBride, Dave Whitlock and Jimmy Walls, all seasoned fighters.

30 November 1956. Floyd Patterson w co 5 (15) Archie Moore.
Venue: The Stadium, Chicago, Illinois, USA. **Recognition:** World. **Referee:** Frank Sikora.
Fight Summary: In a battle for the title vacated by Marciano, although Moore (187¾) started brightly enough after being hurt by speedy left hooks and a heavy right under the heart towards the end of the first round he was under a lot of pressure. Cut over the left eye in the third and hurt again, Moore rallied in the fourth before going for broke in the fifth. However, unable to deal with the speed of Patterson (182¼), Moore was now having difficulty in locating the younger man. Deposited on the canvas by a whistling left hook, on getting up Moore ran into a two-fisted attack that dropped him for the full count, timed at 1.19.

On winning, Patterson, at 21 years and ten months of age, became the division's youngest ever champion. Having let Patterson drop out of the public eye, at a press conference in mid-May 1957 Cus D'Amato, the champion's manager, stated that he had broken from the International Boxing Club (IBC) and was planning a title defence against Tommy Jackson in the summer. Accepting there were no great fights out there for Patterson was one thing, but using him for political ends was another. The majority of people in boxing thought that Patterson should be an active champion, fighting every two or three months against whoever was put in front of him. Instead, he remained inactive.

However, Jackson, who was the leading challenger according to *The Ring* magazine, was certainly talking a good fight, having recently beaten Bob Baker (w pts 12 at Forbes Field, Pittsburgh, Pennsylvania on 26 September) in what was effectively an eliminator, and Julio Mederos. The wild swinging Jackson had run up 30 fights since turning pro in 1952, beating Rex Layne (twice), Clarence Henry, Dan Bucceroni, Charley Norkus, Jimmy Slade, Ezzard Charles (twice), Baker (twice) and Johnny Williams, the former British and British Empire champion. Apart from losing to Patterson in a 1956 eliminator, Jackson's porous defence also let him down against Bert Whitehurst, Slade (twice) and Nino Valdes.

29 July 1957. Floyd Patterson w rsc 10 (15) Tommy Jackson.
Venue: Polo Grounds, Manhattan, NYC, New York, USA. **Recognition:** World. **Referee:** Ruby Goldstein.
Fight Summary: Unable to cope with the speed of the champion's punches, Jackson (192½) was put down by a combination of rights and lefts to the head just as the bell rang to end the opening session. It did not get any better for Jackson in the second round, Patterson (184) having him over again from a right to the jaw. Named 'The Hurricane' due to his fighting style, even though Jackson bravely punched away it was Patterson who was doing all the scoring. By the sixth it was apparent that the end was drawing near, but Jackson, his right eye almost closed, would not hear of it. Although he was dropped by body blows in the ninth and took a terrific left to the jaw immediately prior to the bell he came out fighting in the tenth. It had now become totally one-way traffic, and with the brave Jackson walking into punches and refusing to go down the referee stopped the contest to save him from taking further punishment. The finish was timed at 1.52.

22 August 1957. Floyd Patterson w co 6 (15) Pete Rademacher.
Venue: Sick's Stadium, Seattle, Washington, USA. **Recognition:** World. **Referee:** Tommy Loughran.
Fight Summary: Rademacher, the 1956 Olympic champion, made history by becoming the first man to contest a world heavyweight title when making his professional debut. A big outsider as you would expect, Rademacher (202) did reasonably well for two rounds, but was downed for 'nine' in the third before somehow holding Patterson (187¼) off in the fourth. Although the fifth round was a disaster for Rademacher, being dropped four times in all, he came out for the sixth as though nothing had happened. After Rademacher was decked when coming out of a clinch upon rising he was soon down again, courtesy of a left hook. Almost up and ready to go again, Rademacher was counted out with just three seconds of the session remaining.

Paterson remained inactive for almost a year due to his manager, Cus D'Amato, being unprepared to allow fighters associated with the IBC, whom he considered to hold an unfair monopoly, to challenge for the title. The two men most affected by this state of affairs were Eddie Machen and Willie Pastrano, the future light heavyweight champion. Despite pressure being brought to bear by the NBA, the NYSAC, the World Championship Committee and other powerful bodies, the fact that prospective rivals for the title failed to take advantage of the situation, such as Machen and Zora Folley, who drew over 12 rounds at the Cow Palace, San Francisco, California in an unofficial eliminator on 9 April 1958, merely helped D'Amato's stance.

The situation changed when Roy Harris returned to boxing after finishing a reserve hitch in the Army, a match being made for the autumn. This followed an ultimatum by the World Championship Committee, which stated that Patterson had to meet either one of Machen, Folley, Pastrano or Harris by the end of September. With good reason, there were many in boxing who thought that D'Amato used his arguments with the IBC as a tool to get Patterson easier options. *The Ring* magazine certainly thought this to be the case when Harris was selected for the champion's next defence. In January 1959 the US Supreme Court confirmed the decision of the Federal Tribunal, made on 24 June 1957, to dissolve the IBC in New York and Chicago.

18 August 1958. Floyd Patterson w rtd 12 (15) Roy Harris.
Venue: Wrigley Field, Los Angeles, California, USA. **Recognition:** World. **Referee:** Mushy Callahan.
Fight Summary: Following an uneventful first round and being knocked down for 'four' by a right uppercut in the second, the champion got up as if nothing had happened. With Patterson (184½) finding his feet by the end of the fourth, Harris, cut over both eyes, was staring defeat in the face. Getting well on top without exerting himself, Patterson (184½) dropped Harris for 'eight' in the seventh and twice in the eighth, and although there were no further knockdowns in the next three sessions the finish was in sight. Towards the end of the 12th the badly outclassed Harris was put down for the fourth time before being retired by his corner during the interval.

After Patterson had made no apparent moves to defend his title, his manager, Cus D'Amato, was invited to appear before the NBA Executive Committee in early January 1959 to explain what the champion's plans were as he was getting close to his six-monthly defence limit. D'Amato told the Committee that because Patterson was in the 90% tax bracket his accountants were advising that he should take just one fight a year. Most sympathetic (the Committee said that it would be seeking government legislation to ease the problem), they accepted D'Amato's word that contracts for a Patterson v Ingemar Johansson fight in June were due to be signed that week on the proviso they be kept better informed in future.

Johansson had arrived at the top of the rankings due his first-round kayo win over Eddie Machen at the Nya Ullevi Stadium, Gothenburg, Sweden on 14 September, his famed 'Hammer of Thor' fairly exploding on the latter's jaw. With D'Amato looking for a warm-up fight for Patterson prior to him meeting Johansson, Brian London was selected. London, who had recently lost his British and British Empire titles to Henry Cooper, asked the BBBoC for permission to meet Patterson but had his application turned down as the Board did not consider it to be in the best interests of British boxing. Despite the threats, London still went ahead.

1 May 1959. Floyd Patterson w co 11 (15) Brian London.
Venue: Fairgrounds Coliseum, Indianapolis, Indiana, USA. **Recognition:** World. **Referee:** Frank Sikora.
Fight Summary: Not given much of a chance, London (206) surprised many by his ability to absorb a steady battering as the champion powered into him from the first round. Maintaining a high defence, and set on coming through the contest unscathed, it was this tactic that got London a bad press as he rarely took the fight to Patterson (182½). By the ninth London had slowed considerably, having taken many of Patterson's blows to the body while guarding his head. Although Patterson had been content to make his openings at long range before punching away with both hands, that all changed in the tenth when he dropped London with a long right to the jaw. Despite London being saved by the bell there would be no let-up in the 11th. With the end now in sight Patterson raced into London, hitting him with all the punches in the book, a left hook eventually seeing the Englishman crash to the floor to be counted out with 51 seconds on the clock. On his return to England, London, who was heavily fined by the BBBoC, had his licence suspended for six months.

26 June 1959. Ingemar Johansson w rsc 3 (15) Floyd Patterson.
Venue: Yankee Stadium, Bronx, NYC, New York, USA. **Recognition:** World. **Referee:** Ruby Goldstein.
Fight Summary: In one of the biggest shocks in the history of the heavyweights, Johansson (196) upset the formbook to become the first European to win the title since Primo Carnera. The opening two rounds were not indicative of what was to follow, Johansson using a jarring left jab to keep the champion at bay while having a good look at his opponent. With the third round only 30 seconds old a right to the jaw had Patterson (182) down. Bravely getting up, almost instinctively, Patterson was hammered to the canvas six more times in quick succession before the referee ended the carnage on the 2.03 mark when calling a halt. It came as a complete surprise to many Americans, who had been unaware of Johansson's punching power as he had cleverly disguised it in training.

Johansson stated in December that he would obviously abide by the contracted return clause but would not be doing any further business with Patterson's manager, Cus D'Amato, who by then had lost his licence to work in New York due to various breaches of the rules. Having moved his tax base to Switzerland to avoid heavy taxes in Sweden, Johansson also stated that he had only recently got himself sorted financially, hence his inability to prepare any earlier for the Patterson fight. Once all objections had been cast aside the fight was made for June 1960.

20 June 1960. Floyd Patterson w co 5 (15) Ingemar Johansson.
Venue: Polo Grounds, Manhattan, NYC, New York, USA. **Recognition:** World. **Referee:** Arthur Mercante.
Fight Summary: Planning the fight carefully Patterson (190) made a fast start, keeping well away from the champion's right hand while darting in and scoring before getting on the move. With Johansson (194¾) looking to jab with the left and cross with the right he was being outmanoeuvred and made to look clumsy by the American. By the fourth it was clear that Patterson's tactics were working as Johansson, cut over the left eye, was being hit by hooks and combinations without response. And in the fifth a left hook to the jaw saw the Swede floored. Although Johansson was up at 'nine' when another left hook found its mark he crashed down to be counted out, the time of the knockout being 1.51. In winning, Patterson became the first man to regain the heavyweight title, but by now it was becoming clear that title fights were taking a lot longer to organise, for whatever reason, than the regular six-month defence programme allowed.

With a return clause yet again in place it was obvious that there would be a rubber match, an announcement coming in November that it would take place sometime between January and March 1961 depending on the venue. At the end of December the Miami Beach Convention Hall was confirmed as the venue and 13 March the date.

Earlier, Sonny Liston had secured the number one rating by his 12-round elimination wins over Zora Folley (w co 3 at The Coliseum, Denver, Colorado on 18 July) and Eddie Machen (w pts 12 at Sick's Stadium, Seattle, Washington on 7 September), but would have to wait. A fearsome puncher who intimidated his opponents, Liston had taken up boxing while in prison, and even when he was up and running as a pro he served another sentence that saw him out of the ring for close on two years.

13 March 1961. Floyd Patterson w co 6 (15) Ingemar Johansson.
Venue: Convention Hall, Miami Beach, Florida, USA. **Recognition:** World. **Referee:** Billy Regan.
Fight Summary: In a sensational opening round the champion was decked twice before Johansson (206½) was sent down. That was followed by both men deciding to take a breather by clinching. Apart from Patterson (194¾) missing with a big punch and falling over, the second round was anti-climactic as there was little action. At the end of the third it was seen that both men were cut, Johansson over the right eye and Patterson over the left, and the next two sessions were hardly awe inspiring as both men bided their time. By the sixth, Johansson, who was now cut over both eyes, decided to pick up the action. However, after forcing Patterson against the ropes he was caught by a fearsome left hook and two rights before crashing down to be counted out on the 2.10 mark. Afterwards, Patterson claimed that he was not happy with his own performance, mainly because he did not quite know whether to box or fight.

The NBA announced in September that they had changed the every six-month defence ruling to that of every 12 months for the heavyweight division. That would stand as long as the champion met whoever the Association rated as the number one contender during that period.

4 December 1961. Floyd Patterson w rsc 4 (15) Tom McNeeley.
Venue: Maple Leaf Gardens, Toronto, Canada. **Recognition:** World. **Referee:** Jersey Joe Walcott.
Fight Summary: Not in the same class as the champion the rough, tough McNeeley (197) tried to make a fight of it, but before he could get going he was dropped by a left hook halfway through the opening round. Thereafter, it would be just a matter of time, and when the fight was stopped with just nine seconds of the fourth session remaining the hapless McNeeley had been decked a further nine times. It seemed as though Patterson (188½) could have ended this one as and when he wanted, McNeeley proving to be more dangerous with his head than his fists.

Finally, with the fight public doubting whether Paterson would ever defend his title against the long-time outstanding challenger, Sonny Liston, the match was made. The NBA had called upon Patterson to defend by 13 March 1962 but, as that was not realistic, the Association was forced to accept that the fight everyone wanted to see would take a little longer to come to fruition. When the NYSAC refused to give Liston a licence to box in the State due to his past criminal record the fight was booked for Chicago, Illinois.

Prior to meeting Patterson, Liston had posted 33 wins (23 inside the distance) and suffered one defeat to Marty Marshall, which he twice avenged. He had also defeated Johnny Summerlin (twice), Billy Hunter, Bert Whitehurst (twice), Wayne Bethea, Frankie Daniels, Mike DeJohn, Cleveland Williams (twice), Nino Valdes and Roy Harris, and Zora Folley and Eddie Machen in eliminating contests.

25 September 1962. Sonny Liston w co 1 (15) Floyd Patterson.
Venue: Comiskey Park, Chicago, Illinois, USA. **Recognition:** World. **Referee:** Frank Sikora.
Fight Summary: Clearly a fight the champion did not want, after a slow start followed by some fairly heavy punches that saw him backing off fast, he caught Liston (214) with a right-hander to the head that had no effect on the 'Bad Man' of boxing whatsoever. Before Patterson (189) had time to think, Liston had slammed in a left hook

that was followed by a terrific right and another left, and he was down with no way of getting up. The referee completed the count with 54 seconds still left of the opening session.

22 July 1963. Sonny Liston w co 1 (15) Floyd Patterson.
Venue: Convention Centre, Las Vegas, Nevada, USA. **Recognition:** World. **Referee:** Harry Krause.
Fight Summary: Once again Liston (215) wasted little time, walking into the former champion and dropping him with three heavy rights to the head after the pair had clinched. Given the compulsory 'eight' count, with Patterson (194½) still befuddled it was not long before Liston had him over again from a long right to the head. Again Patterson failed to take proper advantage of the count, and he was immediately backed up against the ropes and sent to the canvas after taking three clubbing rights to the head followed by a left hook. This time there was no reprieve, Patterson being counted out on the 2.10 mark in a fight that lasted just four seconds longer than their first meeting.

By now the former Olympic champion, Cassius Clay, who would eventually be known as Muhammad Ali (due to him becoming a Muslim in mid-1964), was coming along fast, making predictions on which round he would win and generally causing a stir wherever he went. His brashness also won him the soubriquet of the 'Louisville Lip'. Following 18 straight, including wins over men such as Argentina's Alex Miteff, Sonny Banks, who dropped him, the ill-fated Alejandro Lavorante (who died in 1964 from injuries sustained when knocked out by John Riggins), Archie Moore and Doug Jones, he then defeated Henry Cooper (w rsc 5 at Wembley Stadium, London, England on 18 June 1963) in what was a world title eliminator. This was a fight made famous by Cooper's left hook that almost destroyed Clay in the fourth round; the American being saved by the alertness of his corner-man, Angelo Dundee, who cut his gloves during the interval and brought valuable time for his charge. Having made the number one slot the young fighter would be next in line for Liston.

25 February 1964. Cassius Clay (Muhammad Ali) w rtd 6 (15) Sonny Liston.
Venue: Convention Hall, Miami Beach, Florida, USA. **Recognition:** World. **Referee:** Barney Felix.
Fight Summary: Clay (210½), on beating the 7-1 on favourite, Liston (218), amidst stories of the latter taking a dive, backed up his pre-fight comments in what was in all probability the biggest upset in the division's history. Circling the ring at speed from the opening bell Clay made it difficult for the champion to catch up with him before trading blows and going on his bike again. That was the pattern of the fight. In the fifth round Clay began blinking his eyes as if there was a real problem as he scurried around the ring with Liston in pursuit, later inferring that he thought there was a substance on the champion's gloves, something that was never proved. After that, with Clay making the head his target and Liston going for the body, the two men traded more punches in the sixth than in the previous sessions before the latter retired on his stool prior to the seventh getting underway. Liston, who had six stitches inserted in a cut under his left eye that was almost shut, claimed to have dislocated his left shoulder in the opening round. Although his purse was initially held his story was later accepted. What could not be disputed was the fact that Clay had taken Liston's best punches and also given him a boxing lesson.

When Ali, having recently changed his name from that of Cassius Clay, was stripped by the WBA in September due to his decision to go ahead with a return fight with Liston, plans were made to set up an elimination tournament. Following a fight between Doug Jones and George Chuvalo at Madison Square Garden, Manhattan, NYC, New York on 2 October, which produced an 11th-round stoppage win for the latter, four men - Chuvalo, Ernie Terrell, Cleveland Williams and Floyd Patterson - were named for the semi-final legs. However, Patterson had already been matched against Chuvalo, which broke a WBA regulation, and although the winner (Patterson outpointed Chuvalo over 12 rounds at Madison Square Garden on 1 February 1965) was promised first crack at the new champion it was Williams and Terrell who were selected to contest the vacant title. Unfortunately for Williams, after he was put out of action when suffering bullet wounds during a scuffle with a policeman he was replaced by the next logical contender, Eddie Machen.

Both men had met the cream of the division and deserved their opportunity. With just five defeats in 54 contests, the 6'6" Terrell had already outpointed Machen, and had also beaten Frankie Daniels, Amos Lincoln, Young Jack Johnson (twice), Williams, Zora Folley and Bob Foster among a good many others. Despite being effective he was not box-office, his long left jab and holding routine not going down well with the punters. His opponent, Machen, was a box-fighter with a good jab, fast hands and punching ability. Having recovered from a first-round defeat at the hands of Ingemar Johansson, Machen had notched up wins over Julio Mederos (twice), Nino Valdes (twice), John Holman, Johnny Summerlin, Joey Maxim (twice), Bob Baker, Tommy Jackson, Alex Miteff, Brian London and Jones. He had also shown his mettle when going 12 rounds with Liston.

5 March 1965. Ernie Terrell w pts 15 Eddie Machen.
Venue: International Amphitheatre, Chicago, Illinois, USA. **Recognition:** WBA. **Referee:** Bernard Weissman.
Scorecards: 72-67, 70-67, 72-66.
Fight Summary: Contesting the vacant WBA title, Terrell (199) scored an unpopular points win over Machen (192) when taking four of the last five rounds after it had been a fairly even affair up to that point. A solid left jab was Terrell's best weapon, but eventually Machen found a way of blocking the punch while scoring well with effective right-hand counters to head and body. Despite both men visiting the canvas there were no knockdowns recognised, the referee feeling that they had more to do with wrestling than punching.

Disappointingly, the Ali v Liston contest set for 13 November was postponed indefinitely after Ali underwent a hernia operation, having complained of severe pains during a meal. Examined by specialists at the beginning of February 1965 to see how well he had recovered from his recent surgery, Ali was given the all clear. A few weeks later it was announced that he would be meeting Liston in Boston, Massachusetts, which was later changed to Lewiston, Maine.

25 May 1965. Muhammad Ali w co 1 (15) Sonny Liston.
Venue: St Dominic's Youth Centre, Lewiston, Maine, USA. **Recognition:** WBC. **Referee:** Jersey Joe Walcott.
Fight Summary: In a fight shrouded in mystery, Ali (206) retained the WBC version of the title when knocking Liston (215¼) out in the opening round. According to Nat Fleischer, of *The Ring* magazine, the short right-hand punch that knocked Liston out clearly landed, the referee counting to ten before continuing to let the time run a further 12 seconds. Called the 'Phantom Punch', Fleischer went on to say "How hard a blow? Only Liston knows." The fiasco of the finish rumbled on after the fight was over, with the official timer saying it lasted 60 seconds, while the camera men and Fleischer had it at 1.48 and 1.42 respectively.

Having picked up his career, losing just once more in a further 16 contests and still active, Liston was found dead at his home on 30 December 1970. To say he died in mysterious circumstances would be an understatement, and the question as to whether or not he threw the two Ali fights he took to the grave.

1 November 1965. Ernie Terrell w pts 15 George Chuvalo.
Venue: Maple Leaf Gardens, Toronto, Canada. **Recognition:** WBA. **Referee:** Sammy Luftspring.
Scorecards: 72-65, 73-65, 69-65.
Fight Summary: After building up a good points lead, his reach advantage enabling him to score with solid left jabs to head and body, the WBA champion spent the last few rounds fighting to hold on to what he had as Chuvalo (206) surged forward. At the end of the fight Chuvalo complained bitterly about the decision, while Terrell (206) accused the Canadian of intentionally butting him, opening up a bad cut under his left eye in the 14th and continually treading on his feet. There were no knockdowns.

22 November 1965. Muhammad Ali w rsc 12 (15) Floyd Patterson.
Venue: Convention Centre, Las Vegas, Nevada, USA. **Recognition:** WBC. **Referee:** Harry Krause.
Fight Summary: Right from the start the champion controlled the fight, maintaining a good lead before knocking Patterson (196¾) down with a left to the jaw in the sixth. After taking the mandatory 'eight' count, Patterson was soon back in the action until round seven saw his left eye swelling up as he tired. From the eighth onwards Ali (210) seemed to be landing at will, sending in lefts and rights to Patterson's head while taunting the latter continually. Following an inspection by the doctor at the end of the 11th Patterson was allowed out for the 12th, but after Ali set up a strong attack, driving the former champion before him, the referee called the fight off at 2.18 of the session. Although Patterson had struggled with back trouble in the 11th, in reality he could not cope with Ali's extra reach, winning only the first round on the cards.

29 March 1966. Muhammad Ali w pts 15 George Chuvalo.
Venue: Maple Leaf Gardens, Toronto, Canada. **Recognition:** WBC. **Referee:** Jackie Silvers.
Scorecards: 73-65, 74-64, 74-63.
Fight Summary: Although Chuvalo (216) put up a courageous show in forcing Ali (214½) to travel the distance he won only one round at best, the second. Lacking in defensive skills, from the third onwards the challenger seemed to be on the end of anything thrown his way. Having been cut over the left eye in the sixth Chuvalo's right eye was also damaged by the 14th, and at the final bell both eyes were almost closed shut. It was testament to Chuvalo's strength and courage that he remained on his feet throughout the contest despite being hit with lefts and rights at will on occasions, while his best shots barely made Ali blink.

21 May 1966. Muhammad Ali w rsc 6 (15) Henry Cooper.
Venue: Highbury Stadium, Finsbury Park, London, England. **Recognition:** WBC. **Referee:** George Smith.
Fight Summary: Taking the fight to the champion during the first two rounds of their return match, it was only in the third that Cooper (188) started to come under any pressure. Round four saw Cooper continuing to attack, but at the end of the session he was shaken up by lefts and rights to the head and unable to retaliate as Ali (201½) danced away from him. Still playing a waiting game, Ali allowed Cooper to take the fight to him before slamming into him in the sixth with slashing blows that opened up a bad cut on the Englishman's left eye. Cooper was allowed to fight on after an inspection, but with Ali firing in sturdy punches to his challenger's head, with the eye damage an obvious target, the referee stopped the fight on the 1.38 mark.

28 June 1966. Ernie Terrell w pts 15 Doug Jones.
Venue: Sam Houston Coliseum, Houston, Texas, USA. **Recognition:** WBA. **Referee:** Ernie Taylor.
Scorecards: 145-140, 146-141, 146-140.
Fight Summary: Making his second defence of the WBA title, Terrell (209½) proved yet again that his reach advantage, coupled to a solid left jab, made him a difficult man to contend with as the brave Jones (187½) found out to his cost. Even with two rounds, the second and 14th, taken away from him for low blows Terrell continued to march on, dropping Jones in the 14th with a hard right to the body that was thought by many to be low but was not given. After the fight Terrell claimed that he had damaged both hands on Jones' head, while the cut on his right eye had been caused by a butt in the sixth. Although Jones had given his all he was unable to overcome the left hand stabbed into his face and body with regular monotony.

6 August 1966. Muhammad Ali w co 3 (15) Brian London.
Venue: Exhibition Centre, Earls Court, London, England. **Recognition:** WBC. **Referee:** Harry Gibbs.
Fight Summary: Expected to give the champion a bit of a tousle in the earlier rounds, London (201½) proved a big disappointment when unable to go beyond the third. Not noted for making a fast start Ali (209½) surprised all when he began shooting out solid lefts and rights from the opening bell. With punches coming at him from all angles London's only way of avoiding them was to put up his guard to protect himself. Unfortunately, that was the story of the contest and at 1.40 of the third London was counted out after being dropped from a cluster of lefts and rights followed by a short right to the head. As an experienced fighter it had been expected that London might try to force the fight, but on backing away from Ali he played right into the champion's hands.

The next man up for Ali was the European champion, Karl Mildenberger, a solid and workmanlike southpaw who had put together 49 wins in 54 bouts, defeating Jimmy Slade, Franco Cavicchi, Harold Carter, Frankie Daniels, Young Jack Johnson, Wayne Bethea (twice), Pete Rademacher, Alonzo Johnson, Joe Bygraves, Von Clay, Joe Erskine, Archie McBride, Eddie Machen and Ivan Prebeg in the process. He had also drawn with Zora Folley and Amos Johnson.

10 September 1966. Muhammad Ali w rsc 12 (15) Karl Mildenberger.
Venue: Frankfurt Walk Stadium, Frankfurt, Germany. **Recognition:** WBC. **Referee:** Teddy Waltham.
Fight Summary: In what was Ali's fourth defence of the WBC title during the year, the German southpaw put up a courageous show before being stopped at 1.30 of the 12th round. It was clear that Mildenberger (194¼) had decided that attack was the best form of defence, and for five rounds that is what he did when chasing Ali (203½) down at every opportunity. However, once Mildenberger had been cut by the left eye in the fifth he was forced to

change tactics. At that point he started to fall behind before being dropped in the eighth by a flurry of lefts and rights and forced to take the mandatory count. Saved by the bell, Mildenberger decided it was time to take the fight to Ali again, but in the tenth he was dropped by a hard right cross to the jaw before coming back hard on his own account. In the 12th, after Mildenberger, who was bleeding badly and tiring, was caught by a tremendous right uppercut the referee stepped in when it was clear that he was in a helpless position.

14 November 1966. Muhammad Ali w rsc 3 (15) Cleveland Williams.
Venue: The Astrodome, Houston, Texas, USA. **Recognition:** WBC. **Referee:** Harry Kessler.
Fight Summary: Defending his title against the dangerous, hard-punching Williams (210½), Ali (212¾) made a careful start before hurting the latter with body punches towards the end of the first session. Ali was more aggressive in the second, dropping Williams three times before the bell rescued the forlorn challenger, who was now bleeding badly from the mouth and nose. Despite being hurt, Williams made an aggressive start to the third, charging in to Ali before a terrific right cross dropped him in a heap. Somehow, Williams made it to his feet before the count was completed, but after stumbling about under a hail of lefts and rights he was rescued by the referee with 112 seconds of the session remaining.

6 February 1967. Muhammad Ali w pts 15 Ernie Terrell.
Venue: The Astrodome, Houston, Texas, USA. **Recognition:** World. **Referee:** Harry Kessler.
Scorecards: 148-138, 148-133, 148-137.
Fight Summary: This was a battle to create one heavyweight champion, the WBC titleholder, Ali (212¼), having an easy time of it despite being unable to stop the WBA representative, Terrell (212½). Terrell won just two rounds, the second and fifth, but although always trying to match Ali with the jab on finding the latter a difficult target he was forced to concede ground. Cut over the left eye in round three and the right eye in the seventh, Terrell began to look a sorry sight, and during the last third of the contest he was barely able to see as both eyes were badly swollen. At that stage Ali was in total control, but instead of trying to knock Terrell out he seemed happy to continue berating him right through to the final bell.

Having disposed of Terrell, Zora Folley was next in line for Ali. With just seven losses in 85 contests, Folley was a skilful, hard-punching boxer who had beaten Roger Rischer, Nino Valdes, Wayne Bethea (twice), Pete Rademacher, Alex Miteff, Eddie Machen, Henry Cooper, Bob Cleroux (twice), Doug Jones, George Chuvalo, Oscar Bonavena, Bob Foster and a host of other top men in a career stretching back to 1953.

22 March 1967. Muhammad Ali w co 7 (15) Zora Folley.
Venue: Madison Square Garden, Manhattan, NYC, New York, USA. **Recognition:** World. **Referee:** John LoBianco.
Fight Summary: Making a good start, Folley (202½) took the opening two rounds while Ali (211½) appeared content to see what his challenger had to offer. By the third, Ali, warming to the task, was beating Folley to the punch. The fourth round saw Ali go up a gear, and after a left-right to Folley's head dropped the latter for the mandatory 'eight' count many believed he would end the contest quickly. However, it was Folley who was throwing the harder punches in the fifth and sixth sessions despite being outscored. Although Folley continued in the same vein into the seventh, with Ali beginning to pick up the pace a right to the jaw put the former down to be counted out at 1.48 of the round.

Ali forfeited his title in the eyes of the WBA and NYSAC, who suspended him in April, after he refused to serve in the US Army, fighting in Vietnam, due to his religious beliefs as a Muslim. While the WBC said they would continue to support Ali on the grounds that he had not violated any boxing rules, the WBA and the NYSAC both inferred that Ali's refusal to enter the army was detrimental to the best interests of boxing.

While Ali faced a possible conviction which could bring a five-year prison sentence and a large fine or both, a series of eliminators got underway to determine a new champion. The WBA eventually announced that eight men - Thad Spencer, Jimmy Ellis, Oscar Bonavena, Jerry Quarry, Ernie Terrell, Leotis Martin, Karl Mildenberger and Floyd Patterson - would compete despite the WBC continuing to support Ali until 6 March 1968.

Although the WBA had earlier named Joe Frazier for their tournament he decided not to enter, being supported by the NYSAC who failed to recognise what the WBA were doing as the best means of finding the champion. Frazier then met George Chuvalo (w rsc 4 at Madison Square Garden on 19 July) in a 12-round eliminator sanctioned by the NYSAC.

The WBA quarter-finals got underway with Spencer (w pts 12 Terrell at the Astrodome, Houston, Texas on 5 August), Ellis (w rsc 9 Martin on 5 August at the Astrodome, Houston), Bonavena (w pts 12 Mildenberger at the Bicycle Stadium, Frankfurt, Germany on 16 September) and Quarry (w pts 12 Patterson at the Olympic Auditorium, Los Angeles, California on 28 October) qualifying. The semi-final stage saw Ellis (w pts 12 Bonavena at the Freedom Hall, Louisville, Kentucky on 2 December) and Quarry (w rsc 12 Spencer at The Arena, Oakland, California on 3 February 1968) winning their way through to the final.

Meanwhile, Frazier was matched to contest the NYSAC version of the title against another former amateur star, Buster Mathis, who had run up 23 victories against no one of any significance since turning pro. Regardless of this apparent lack of substance, other States who joined forces with the NYSAC to recognise the winner of Frazier v Mathis as the world champion were Massachusetts, Maine and Illinois, the last two breaking ranks with the WBA in doing so.

4 March 1968. Joe Frazier w rsc 11 (15) Buster Mathis.
Venue: Madison Square Garden, Manhattan, NYC, New York, USA. **Recognition:** NY. **Referee:** Arthur Mercante.
Fight Summary: Fighting for the vacant NYSAC version of the title Frazier (204½) picked it up in the sixth after sharing the earlier rounds, and while Mathis (243½) was looking for a winning punch he was by far the busier of the pair. Why Mathis adopted this tactic beggared belief as Frazier took full advantage of the situation when popping away with left hands before a left hook sent the bigger man crashing in the 11th. Although making a supreme effort to rise, with Mathis in no condition to fight on the referee wisely stopped the contest with 27 seconds of the session remaining. Following the fight, Frazier, the first Olympic heavyweight champion to win the heavyweight title, stated that he knew he had Mathis going in the tenth having worked his body continuously.

A little later the WBC announced that they would recognise Frazier as champion if a match-up with Muhammad Ali became impossible to make. The next State to recognise Frazier as champion was Pennsylvania, which was hardly surprising as Philadelphia was his hometown. They were followed by Illinois, Massachusetts and Maine.

27 April 1968. Jimmy Ellis w pts 15 Jerry Quarry.
Venue: The Coliseum, Oakland, California, USA. **Recognition:** WBA. **Referee:** Elmer Costa.
Scorecards: 7-6, 10-5, 6-6.
Fight Summary: In a contest to decide the vacant WBA title, as early as the second round both Ellis (197) and Quarry (195) were cut above their eyes, on the left and right respectively. However, neither cut became a factor in a fight that saw Ellis boxing on the back foot and using his extra reach to counter Quarry as he came forward. With Ellis happy to box on the outside there were no heavy exchanges until Quarry was caught by a smashing right to the head in the seventh, the pair trading blows until the end of the session. Thereafter, Ellis was content to score with heavy right hands to the head whenever in range, but in the main he boxed in a safety-first fashion without Quarry being able to influence the fight. At the final bell the scorecards showed that had the judges credited Quarry with one more round he would have won the contest.

24 June 1968. Joe Frazier w rtd 2 (15) Manuel Ramos.
Venue: Madison Square Garden, Manhattan, NYC, New York, USA. **Recognition:** NY. **Referee:** Arthur Mercante.
Fight Summary: Making his first defence of the New York version of the title, Frazier (203½) had too much power for Ramos (208) despite the latter landing heavily with two cracking rights about a minute into the fight. Having weathered the storm Frazier became the aggressor, banging in four heavy left hooks to the head of Ramos to knock the Mexican over for the first time in his career. The second round was all Frazier as he smashed in left hook after left hook to the face of the hapless Ramos, who was eventually dropped near the end of the session. After beating the count and being saved by the bell, Ramos indicated that he was through for the night before slumping on to his stool.

14 September 1968. Jimmy Ellis w pts 15 Floyd Patterson.
Venue: Rasunda Stadium, Stockholm, Sweden. **Recognition:** WBA. **Referee:** Harold Valan.
Scorecard: 9-6.
Fight Summary: According to many of the ringsiders it seemed incredible that the WBA champion retained his title after being so ineffective, and it was no real surprise that *Boxing News* had Patterson (188) winning 6-3. Throughout the fight there was nothing of note, but it was Patterson who made the running. In the 14th Ellis (198) seemed to have been floored by a left hook, although the referee called it a slip. Afterwards, Ellis, having had seven stitches inserted over his damaged right eye, said that his nose had been broken by an unintentional butt in the opening round and that his left thumb had gone in the third.

Despite remaining inactive, at the end of May 1969 the WBA confirmed that Ellis was still their champion and that they had been authorised by his management that he would fight Joe Frazier to unify the title but had received no indication from Frazier whether he welcomed the challenge or not. Interestingly, the British, British Empire and European champion, Henry Cooper, was lined up to challenge Ellis for the WBA title but failed to gain support from the BBBoC due to the fact that they were affiliated to the WBC who regarded the championship as being vacant. After much argument, when Cooper relinquished his British title the match against Ellis was eventually made by the promoter, Harry Levene, to take place at Wembley Stadium, London England on 27 September 1969. To get around the BBBoC rules the match would be billed as Jimmy Ellis (WBA champion) v Henry Cooper (British Empire and European champion) over 15 rounds under championship conditions and would be recognised by the WBA as a title fight. Two weeks before the fight, when Cooper picked up a knee injury the bout was put back until 25 October 1969 before being moved on again. Just when things could not get much worse the fight was called off completely when it was learnt that Cooper would have to enter hospital to have a cartilage operation.

For Ellis, however, it was back to the drawing board and into negotiations regarding a Frazier fight. At the end of November 1969, talks broke down for the second time when the promoter of Madison Square Garden said that Ellis wanted the fight to be held in Miami and had decided to defend the WBA title against Gregorio Peralta on 3 January 1970. With insurmountable problems in the way of the fight actually happening, Ellis pulled out of the Peralta fight on 27 December 1969 and headed for New York after the WBA had warned him that he would be shorn of the title if he had not negotiated a fight with Frazier to unify the championship by 1 January. Finally, with common sense prevailing, both were men signed up to meet on 16 February 1970.

10 December 1968. Joe Frazier w pts 15 Oscar Bonavena.
Venue: The Spectrum, Philadelphia, Pennsylvania, USA. **Recognition:** NY. **Referee:** Joe Sweeney.
Scorecards: 72-64, 74-64, 70-67.
Fight Summary: Right from the opening bell neither man budged, but it was the champion's better work that earned him the decision while Bonavena (207) tended to throw single shots. Although there were no knockdowns it was a vicious battle, made worse by the fact that Bonavena was unable to keep his punches up, Frazier (203) being forced to complain on several occasions. After the referee deducted a point from the Argentine in the eighth it failed to make the slightest difference, Bonavena continuing to punch wildly despite the referee warning him again and again. All the better blows came from Frazier, especially in the fourth when he rocked the tough Bonavena with several terrific left hooks that would have seen off most opponents. At the end of the contest both of Bonavena's eyes were almost closed.

22 April 1969. Joe Frazier w co 1 (15) Dave Zyglewicz.
Venue: Sam Houston Coliseum, Houston, Texas, USA. **Recognition:** NY. **Referee:** Jimmy Webb.
Fight Summary: A bad mismatch saw the wild swinging Zyglewicz (190½) challenge for the title without having any kind of name on his record, and within 20 seconds he was over from a Frazier (204½) left hook. Back on his feet, Zyglewicz was a sitting target. Then, after Frazier had softened Zyglewicz up further with blows to head and body, a smashing left hook to the jaw saw the latter crash to the floor to be counted out on the 1.36 mark.

23 June 1969. Joe Frazier w rsc 7 (15) Jerry Quarry.
Venue: Madison Square Garden, Manhattan, NYC, New York, USA. **Recognition:** NY. **Referee:** Arthur Mercante.

Fight Summary: Although beating the New York champion to the punch in the opening session that was about it as far as Quarry (198½) was concerned. Gashed under the right eye Quarry almost became a punch-bag as Frazier (203½) began to take him apart, but he still would not go down as hard as the latter tried. Continually stunned, Quarry could barely make it to his corner on a couple of occasions, and at the end of the seventh the doctor advised the referee to stop the fight.

Towards the end of the year Muhammad Ali tried to make a fight with Frazier, but too many States refused to even allow him to box exhibitions due to his legal tangles with the government. In the wake of that, in February 1970 Ali announced his retirement from the ring. However, as support for the Vietnam War abated, Georgia held out an olive branch, allowing him to box exhibitions in the State prior to licensing him for a 15-round comeback fight against Quarry (w rsc 3 at the City Auditorium, Atlanta, Georgia on 26 October 1970). Although the Governor of Georgia had second thoughts immediately prior to the contest it had been too late. This was followed by a Federal Court decision which saw the NYSAC agree to re-license Ali to box in New York, thus paving the way for an Ali v Frazier contest. There was still the matter of Ali's legal appeal, and on that subject his lawyers were basing his defence on the High Court's new guidelines for cases involving conscientious objectors. Their submissions to the Supreme Court made clear that Ali should have been exempted from the Draft as a minister for the 'Lost Found Nation of Islam'.

16 February 1970. Joe Frazier w rtd 4 (15) Jimmy Ellis.
Venue: Madison Square Garden, Manhattan, NYC, New York, USA. **Recognition:** World. **Referee:** Tony Perez.
Fight Summary: In a fight to unify the title, the New York champion, Frazier (205), ultimately proved too strong for Ellis (201), the WBA titleholder. Earlier in the day the WBC and the BBBoC, who had both regarded the title as being vacant up to that point in time, agreed to support the winner as champion. By the second round Frazier was beginning to surprise Ellis with his non-stop attacking, and in the third the latter was staggered by massive left hooks to the jaw before gingerly making his way back to his corner. In the fourth it was all one-way traffic as Frazier went for the kill, twice dropping Ellis for long counts with cracking left hooks. Saved by the bell on the second occasion, Ellis was pulled out of the fight by his corner before the bell to start the fifth had rung.

18 November 1970. Joe Frazier w co 2 (15) Bob Foster.
Venue: Cobo Hall, Detroit, Michigan, USA. **Recognition:** World. **Referee:** Tom Briscoe.
Fight Summary: Defending his title against the world light heavyweight champion, Frazier (209) proved far too strong for Foster (188) despite the latter giving a good account of himself in the opening session. Starting fast in the second, Frazier soon had Foster over from a left hook to the jaw, and when the challenger was back on his feet he was felled for the full count, timed at 49 seconds, after a double left hook to body and head had smashed him down.

With Muhammad Ali now licensed to box in New York, after he beat Oscar Bonavena (w rsc 15 at Madison Square Garden, Manhattan, NYC, New York on 7 December) in what was effectively an eliminating contest to find Frazier's next opponent, the match that all boxing fans had been waiting for was set for 8 March 1971.

8 March 1971. Joe Frazier w pts 15 Muhammad Ali.
Venue: Madison Square Garden, Manhattan, NYC, New York, USA. **Recognition:** World. **Referee:** Arthur Mercante.
Scorecards: 8-6-1, 9-6, 11-4.
Fight Summary: Recognised as one of the greatest fights in the history of the division, and one where neither man would ever be the same again, Ali (215) proved himself a real fighting man despite losing by a unanimous decision. The fight was fairly even right up until the latter stages, with Ali jabbing and moving as was expected while Frazier (205½) continually looked to work on the inside. By the tenth Frazier's right eye was beginning to swell, but in the 11th he almost had Ali over from a crashing left hook to the head. It was at this point that Frazier began to forge ahead. And in the 12th he staggered Ali badly, although the latter came back well with jabs to even the round up according to the referee. The 13th was a big round for Frazier, who was landing all the solid punches and crowding Ali non-stop as he went for the kayo. By the 14th Frazier's left eye was beginning to swell up, but he was the one throwing the more solid punches, flooring Ali with a smashing left hook to the jaw in the final session. Taking the 'eight' count, Ali was almost spent, his jaw badly swollen and just sheer guts keeping him going. Somehow Ali kept

his feet to last out until the final bell, having earlier refused to quit at the end of the 11th after the doctor had asked him if he was fit to continue.

Following the fight, Ali vowed to get his title back. Meanwhile, at the end of June there was good news when Ali finally won his four-year legal battle with the US Government after the Supreme Court overturned his suspended jail sentence for refusing to serve in the Army. The Court went on to say that the process in which Ali was denied conscientious objector status was flawed and should be dismissed.

Looking to make up for lost time, Ali won the North American Boxing Federation (NABF) title when beating his old sparring partner, Jimmy Ellis, and defended it against Buster Mathis, George Chuvalo, Jerry Quarry, Floyd Patterson and Bob Foster before losing to Ken Norton. Regaining the NABF title in his next contest, beating Norton (w pts 12 at the Inglewood Forum, Los Angeles, California on 10 September 1973), he went on to also turn the tables on Frazier (w pts 12 at Madison Square Garden on 28 January 1974) in what was a final eliminator for the world title.

15 January 1972. Joe Frazier w rsc 4 (15) Terry Daniels.
Venue: Rivergate Auditorium, New Orleans, Louisiana, USA. **Recognition:** World. **Referee:** Herman Dutreix.
Fight Summary: Admittedly Daniels (195) was not the greatest of challengers, but after Frazier (215½) had given the millionaire's son a sound beating, having staggered him with the first blow of the fight, it was clear that it would take a very good man to relieve him of his title. Punching away viciously, Frazier had Daniels down from a left hook to the head just as the bell rang to end the first session, and although the latter escaped being dropped again in the second he was twice smashed to the floor in the third. After bravely coming out for the fourth, Daniels was soon floored by a whole battery of punches. Taking a count of 'seven', on getting up and being belted non-stop on the ropes the referee stopped the fight at 1.45 of the round.

26 May 1972. Joe Frazier w rsc 4 (15) Ron Stander.
Venue: Civic Auditorium, Omaha, Nebraska, USA. **Recognition:** World. **Referee:** Zack Clayton.
Fight Summary: Right from the first bell Stander (218) was under attack from Frazier (217½), who crowded in throwing big punches, and while the challenger held his own in the opening round it was all one-way traffic from there onwards. By the third Frazier was ripping Stander to pieces, sending in blows to head and body that would have downed a less courageous fighter. Coming out for the fourth, Stander, his face soon covered in blood from cuts over both eyes, was immediately put under attack. Even though Frazier was unable to drop him he was staggering about like a drunk for the most part. At the end of session when it was quite clear that Stander could not continue the referee stopped the fight.

Frazier's next opponent would be George Foreman, the 1968 Olympic champion, who had blasted his way to 37 straight wins, 34 of them coming inside the distance.

22 January 1973. George Foreman w rsc 2 (15) Joe Frazier.
Venue: National Stadium, Kingston, Jamaica. **Recognition:** World. **Referee:** Arthur Mercante.
Fight Summary: Contested between two big punchers, both being former Olympic champions, Frazier (214) lost his title at 1.35 of the second round when the referee stopped the fight to save him from taking further punishment. Towering over the squat champion Foreman (217½) was happy to wait for him to come into him, and after clearly hurting Frazier with solid long rights to the head he proceeded to drop him three times in the opening round. Coming out for the second still on shaky legs Frazier tried to bob and weave to get a breather but Foreman was only intent on finishing him off. Three more times Frazier was deposited on the floor in the second, a crashing right to the head, a big left hook and a thunderous right uppercut that lifted him off the ground being the key punches. Following the sixth knockdown, with Frazier in a kneeling position and trying to get up the referee finally acted.

1 September 1973. George Foreman w co 1 (15) Jose Roman.
Venue: Martial Arts Hall, Tokyo, Japan. **Recognition:** World. **Referee:** Jay Edson.
Fight Summary: In what was a fight that should never have taken place, Roman (196½) lasted just two minutes and failed to land a punch. Dropping to the floor under the first serious attack Roman was then cuffed by Foreman (219½) while in a sitting position, and although the Puerto Rican's manager wanted a disqualification rendered or

at the very least a five-minute rest for his charge he was overruled. Having knocked Roman down again with a right uppercut, Foreman finished the job with a tremendous right to the body that put the challenger down for the full count.

26 March 1974. George Foreman w rsc 2 (15) Ken Norton.
Venue: The Polyhedron, Caracas, Venezuela. **Recognition:** World. **Referee:** Jimmy Rondeau.
Fight Summary: Having been wobbled a couple of times and seen his best punches bounce off the champion things looked ominous for Norton (212¾) as he returned to his corner at the end of the first round. Coming out with steely intent in the second Foreman (224¾) soon got his big punches off and, after dropping Norton for 'eight' following three crashing right uppercuts, he pushed the latter over. Not counted as a knockdown, Norton was quickly on his feet before being bowled over by a right-left to the jaw, his head striking the floor heavily. Although he made it up at 'nine' he was stopped on the two-minute mark when reeling helplessly against the ropes.

30 October 1974. Muhammad Ali w co 8 (15) George Foreman.
Venue: Twentieth of May Stadium, Kinshasa, Zaire. **Recognition:** World. **Referee:** Zack Clayton.
Fight Summary: Billed as the 'Super Fight' it was all of that and more as Ali (216½) regained his old title against all the odds when knocking Foreman (220) out with just two seconds of the eighth remaining. After seven completed rounds the two fighters were probably level. Even though Foreman had made all the running he had been unable to knock out Ali, who coined the phrase 'Rope a Dope' as he laid on the ropes for long periods while allowing the champion to burn himself out after throwing so many big punches that failed to have the desired effect. By the fifth Ali had begun to take over as Foreman tired, repeatedly shaking the champion up with heavy rights to the head. Although still coming forward in the eighth Foreman was making no impression on Ali, and when the latter suddenly cut loose with a whole batch of blows, mainly to the head, a big right sent him crashing down to be counted out.

24 March 1975. Muhammad Ali w rsc 15 (15) Chuck Wepner.
Venue: The Coliseum, Cleveland, Ohio, USA. **Recognition:** World. **Referee:** Tony Perez.
Fight Summary: Making his first defence, Ali (223½) took on the unranked Wepner (225), a man not even rated in the top ten, and toyed with him for much of the time while just fighting in short bursts. Tired and out of ideas by the eighth, Wepner actually knocked Ali down for 'three' in the ninth with a right to the ribs. Clearly embarrassed, Ali pounded away at Wepner, who was now cut over the left eye, and for a while it looked as though the latter would be taken out. By the end of the 11th both of Wepner's eyes were badly swollen and bleeding but he managed to continue despite taking much punishment. Wepner was always trying to fight back, even connecting solidly with Ali's jaw in the 15th, but after being blasted by four big punches the man who would come to be known as the 'Bayonne Bleeder' was sent down heavily. Although getting to his feet, when it was clear to the referee that Wepner was in no position to defend himself properly he stopped the fight with just 19 seconds remaining.

Ali's next challenger would be the dangerous, hard-hitting Ron Lyle, who had been outpointed over ten rounds by Jimmy Young on 11 February, a few weeks after signing on the dotted line. That loss cost Lyle his number three rating. Lyle had only lost to Jerry Quarry prior to that, and among his 30 wins were victories over Manuel Ramos, Vicente Rondon, Buster Mathis, Gregorio Peralta (twice), Jose Luis Garcia, Jurgen Blin and Jimmy Ellis.

16 May 1975. Muhammad Ali w rsc 11 (15) Ron Lyle.
Venue: Convention Centre, Las Vegas, Nevada, USA. **Recognition:** World. **Referee:** Ferd Hernandez.
Fight Summary: By Ali's standards this was a poor performance when allowing Lyle (219) to dominate many of the rounds prior to the tenth, a session in which the latter looked to be well on his way to victory as he plastered the champion without return. Coming into the 11th two judges had Lyle ahead and the other had him even but, realising that his title could be slipping away, Ali (224½) stepped up the tempo right from the bell. After catching Lyle with a big right to the jaw, Ali forced him to the ropes, and eventually a corner, where he pounded away at his now defenceless opponent. To his credit Lyle refused to go down, but at 1.08 of the round the referee stopped the fight after a cracking left uppercut landed heavily.

Having gone 12 rounds with both Ali and Joe Frazier in 1973 non-title fights, the fourth-rated 6'4" Joe Bugner was selected for the champion's next defence. While there was no doubting Bugner's strength, toughness and excellent jab he was viewed as being too mechanical. However, he had only lost six out of 58 contests and had beaten Manuel Ramos, Ray Patterson, Brian London, Chuck Wepner, Eduardo Corletti, Henry Cooper, Mac Foster and Jimmy Ellis.

1 July 1975. Muhammad Ali w pts 15 Joe Bugner.
Venue: Independence Stadium, Kuala Lumpur, Malaysia. **Recognition:** World. **Referee:** Takeo Ugo.
Scorecards: 73-67, 72-65, 73-65.
Fight Summary: Turning back the clock to dance his way through the fight the champion had far too much for the game Bugner (230), who was almost pedestrian at times. Although Bugner was never on the floor he was not fast enough to catch Ali (224½), being forced to absorb everything thrown at him, especially in the opening five rounds. Bugner's best round was the tenth when he forced Ali to retreat, but unable to keep the pressure up when he did close down the space the latter cleverly boxed his way out of trouble. It was not until the 13th that Ali managed to shake Bugner up with punches from both hands to head and body, but the European champion took them in his stride to make it to the final bell.

1 October 1975. Muhammad Ali w rtd 14 (15) Joe Frazier.
Venue: Araneta Coliseum, Manila, Philippines. **Recognition:** World. **Referee:** Carlos Padilla.
Fight Summary: Recognised as 'The Thrilla in Manila', the champion was forced to take all that Frazier (214½) could throw at him in the opening ten rounds before coming on strong himself in the latter stages. Every round was exciting, but from the 11th onwards Ali (224½) upped the pace as Frazier weakened, knocking the latter's gumshield out in the 13th with a crunching right hand. It now appeared to be only a matter of time and, after a torrid 14th for Frazier, who was almost taking punches for fun as Ali continually hit the target, he was pulled out by his corner at the end of the session.

20 February 1976. Muhammad Ali w co 5 (15) Jean-Pierre Coopman.
Venue: Roberto Clemente Coliseum, San Juan, Puerto Rico. **Recognition:** World. **Referee:** Ismael Quinones Falu.
Fight Summary: Even though the WBC failed to recognise this contest as involving the title they continued to see Ali as the champion, while the EBU banned Coopman from fighting for the European title for two years after going against their wishes. Following a fairly quiet opening round the next session saw the champion began to toy with Coopman (206), who was badly hurt by fast combinations to the head. At this stage it could be seen that Coopman's left eye was beginning to swell. Having taken a breather in the third and fourth rounds Ali (226) picked it up again in the fifth, and after striking with a burst of solid blows from both hands he put Coopman down for the full count, timed at 2.46, with a right uppercut.

30 April 1976. Muhammad Ali w pts 15 Jimmy Young.
Venue: Capital Centre, Landover, Maryland, USA. **Recognition:** World. **Referee:** Tom Kelly.
Scorecards: 72-65, 71-64, 70-68.
Fight Summary: Giving one of his worst ever displays, seeming almost lethargic at times, the champion later revealed that his right eardrum had been burst. That, as well as underestimating Young (211), had made it a difficult night for him. Young, who was in good condition and boxed an intelligent fight, was never in any real trouble despite being given a standing count when leaning out of the ring in the twelfth. By the end of the 13th Ali (230) appeared to have shot his bolt after trying to take Young out, the latter coming on strongly in the 14th when sending in solid lefts and rights while making his man miss. Afterwards, Young felt that his ploy of ducking, swaying and leaning so far out of the ring between the ropes had frustrated Ali and deserved more.

Although Ali already had a defence lined up against Ken Norton, the unrated awkward southpaw, Richard Dunn, was given an earlier date. As the reigning British, Commonwealth and European champion, Dunn had improved since losing his first pro contest and eight others, and had beaten Bunny Johnson (twice), Ray Patterson and Danny McAlinden.

25 May 1976. Muhammad Ali w rsc 5 (15) Richard Dunn.
Venue: Olympic Hall, Munich, Germany. **Recognition:** World. **Referee:** Herbert Thomser.
Fight Summary: As the British, Commonwealth and European champion Dunn (206½) deserved a title crack, and for the opening three rounds he was right in the fight as he chased Ali (220) down, going forward all the time. He even sent the champion reeling across the ring at one point in the third. In the fourth, however, Ali finally began to crank up the pressure on his southpaw opponent, having him over three times in the session from cracking right hands over the top. Regardless of what had happened in the fourth Dunn came out for the fifth as though he meant business, but after two further knockdowns from similar punches the referee called it off on the 2.05 mark.

28 September 1976. Muhammad Ali w pts 15 Ken Norton.
Venue: Yankee Stadium, Bronx, NYC, New York, USA. **Recognition:** World. **Referee:** Arthur Mercante.
Scorecards: 8-7, 8-7, 8-6-1.
Fight Summary: Putting his title on the line against a man who he had already won and lost to was always going to be a gamble for Ali (221) but it was one he was prepared to take. There was never much between them, both being caught by jarring blows to the head, but after ten rounds it looked as though Norton (217½) was out in front due to him getting off more punches and coming forward for much of the time. With his title now well and truly at risk Ali made his run for home during the last five rounds, and while he did most of the better work during that period it did not look like he had done enough to save his crown as far as the ringsiders were concerned.

16 May 1977. Muhammad Ali w pts 15 Alfredo Evangelista.
Venue: Capital Centre, Landover, Maryland, USA. **Recognition:** World. **Referee:** Harry Cecchini.
Scorecards: 71-65, 72-64, 72-64.
Fight Summary: In a fast-paced bout, the champion was happy to get back to his boxing, moving well on the back foot and scoring with solid jabs as Evangelista (209½) tried to walk him down in a straight line. Occasionally Evangelista scored with good right hands while mixing his punches up well, but Ali (221¼) was never at risk as he sauntered to a fairly comfortable points win.

29 September 1977. Muhammad Ali w pts 15 Earnie Shavers.
Venue: Madison Square Garden, Manhattan, NYC, New York, USA. **Recognition:** World. **Referee:** John LoBianco.
Scorecards: 9-6, 9-6, 9-5-1.
Fight Summary: Having hurt the champion in the second round and staggered him at various stages of the fight, the big-hitting Shavers (211¼) forced Ali (224½) to fight every step of the way. *Boxing News* had the men level after eight rounds, with Ali pulling ahead when winning rounds nine to 12. But with Shavers coming on strong in the 13th and 14th rounds, banging away with solid blows to head and body, Ali was forced to call upon all his resources for the final session. Countering solidly and picking his punches well it was probably Ali's best round, and in the final minute he had Shavers under tremendous pressure.

Ali's next challenger would be Leon Spinks, who had won the same Olympic title that he had, only 16 years later. Held to a draw by Scott LeDoux in his eighth fight, Spinks had been a pro for just 13 months and had little experience to count on.

15 February 1978. Leon Spinks w pts 15 Muhammad Ali.
Venue: Hilton Sports Pavilion, Las Vegas, Nevada, USA. **Recognition:** World. **Referee:** Davy Pearl.
Scorecards: 145-140, 144-141, 142-143.
Fight Summary: This was the biggest upset in the heavyweight division since Ali beat Sonny Liston, the 10-1 outsider, Spinks (197¼), winning the title on a split decision over the ageing champion. Pressing forward for much of the fight Spinks would not allow Ali (224½) the space to do his best work, and every time the latter got through with good punches he would retaliate immediately. From the seventh onwards Ali was trying to turn the fight his way, but even when he backed Spinks up in the tenth with some heavy shots the challenger would not be put off, coming back with good punches of his own. By the 13th Ali looked extremely weary and dispirited. However, in the 15th he came right back to slug it out with Spinks in what would be one of the 'Rounds of the Year', despite being almost out on his feet. It had been a great effort but it was not enough.

Spinks forfeited WBC recognition in March for not being prepared to defend against their leading contender, Ken Norton, who had been promised first crack at the winner. Norton, having won a final eliminator when outscoring Jimmy Young over 15 rounds at Caesar's Palace, Las Vegas on 5 November 1977, was immediately proclaimed champion on the basis of that victory. To qualify as his first challenger, Larry Holmes outscored Earnie Shavers over 12 rounds of a WBC final eliminator at the same venue on 25 March 1978.

9 June 1978. Larry Holmes w pts 15 Ken Norton.
Venue: Caesar's Palace, Las Vegas, Nevada, USA. **Recognition:** WBC. **Referee:** Mills Lane.
Scorecards: 143-142, 143-142, 142-143.
Fight Summary: Making his first defence of the title awarded to him by the WBC when Leon Spinks was stripped, Norton (220) was narrowly outpointed by Holmes (209). Holmes had started well, winning the first six rounds by means of an accurate left jab, but in the seventh Norton came back strongly with heavy blows to the head. At this stage of the fight, although the challenger was still boxing well, the heavier punches were now coming from Norton. At the end of the 14th the judges had them dead level, and while Norton continued to throw big shots almost in desperation it was Holmes, having landed several rights to the jaw without reply immediately prior to the final bell, who was given the split decision.

15 September 1978. Muhammad Ali w pts 15 Leon Spinks.
Venue: The Superdome, New Orleans, Louisiana, USA. **Recognition:** WBA. **Referee:** Lucien Joubert.
Scorecards: 11-4, 10-4-1, 10-4-1.
Fight Summary: Winning the title for a record three times, the 37-year-old Ali (221) danced his way to victory over the much younger Spinks (201), even though he conserved his energy by fighting for less than a minute in each round. While Spinks occasionally landed heavy punches that unsettled the challenger he failed to follow up any advantage he might have gained. As the fight wore on it became repetitive, with Ali popping in the jab before moving on, and with Spinks failing to work out what to do next he was steadily outboxed from start to finish. Even though he had the fifth round taken away for holding and hitting, Ali was allowed to get away with that tactic throughout. It clearly formed an important part of his strategy to stop Spinks from working at close quarters.

When Ali, having remained inactive, relinquished the WBA version of the title on announcing his retirement in June 1979 an eliminating series was set up to find the next champion. In the first semi-final leg, John Tate knocked out Kallie Knoetze inside eight rounds at the Independence Stadium, Mmabatho, South Africa on 2 June 1979, while the second leg, held at the Fontvieille Big Top, Monte Carlo on 24 June 1979, saw Gerrie Coetzee force the referee to come to the rescue of Spinks in the first.

Prior to meeting Coetzee the hard-punching Tate was unbeaten in 19 contests, with only three going the distance. He had also demolished Bernardo Mercado and Duane Bobick. With the ability to take a good punch as well as being a big hitter Coetzee was unbeaten on 22, scoring good wins over Jimmy Richards (twice), Ron Stander, Mike Schutte (twice), Knoetze, Pierre Fourie and Randy Stephens.

10 November 1978. Larry Holmes w co 7 (15) Alfredo Evangelista.
Venue: Caesar's Palace, Las Vegas, Nevada, USA. **Recognition:** WBC. **Referee:** Richard Greene.
Fight Summary: In his first defence, Holmes (214) was far too good for the European champion, Evangelista (208¼), dominating each round with the left jab while picking the angles and smashing in solid rights whenever there was an opening. By round seven Evangelista looked a sorry mess, and after being set up by rights to the ribs and head another heavy right to the head sent him crashing to the floor to be counted out on the 2.14 mark.

23 March 1979. Larry Holmes w rsc 7 (15) Ossie Ocasio.
Venue: Hilton Pavilion, Las Vegas, Nevada, USA. **Recognition:** WBC. **Referee:** Carlos Padilla.
Fight Summary: Although the awkward Ocasio (207) set the champion a few problems early on, by the fourth round he was out of ideas after stinging left jabs began to set him up for solid rights. For the next couple of sessions Ocasio somehow weathered the storm, but in the seventh Holmes (214) picked it up, having the Puerto Rican over from a right uppercut followed by a left hook after just 30 seconds. On his feet following the mandatory

'eight' count, when Ocasio was quickly set upon the referee stopped the contest on the 2.38 mark after three further knockdowns.

22 June 1979. Larry Holmes w rsc 12 (15) Mike Weaver.
Venue: Madison Square Garden, Manhattan, NYC, New York, USA. **Recognition:** WBC. **Referee:** Harold Valan.
Fight Summary: With reach advantage the champion was soon into his stride, spearing Weaver (202) with lefts and rights, but in the fourth he was embarrassed when sent down by a left-right. Although it was deemed by the referee to be a slip, to most it appeared to be a knockdown. For the next few sessions Weaver came right back into contention as he took the fight to Holmes (215) and in the ninth and tenth the latter was forced to cover up under a hail of heavy blows. In the 11th Holmes finally reasserted himself, having Weaver over from a cracking right uppercut that all but won the fight. Saved by the bell, after Weaver came out for the 12th looking very shaky, when a battery of lefts and rights had him all over the place the referee stopped the contest 44 seconds into the session

28 September 1979. Larry Holmes w rsc 11 (12) Earnie Shavers.
Venue: Caesar's Palace, Las Vegas, Nevada, USA. **Recognition:** WBC. **Referee:** Davy Pearl.
Fight Summary: Unable to relax against the hard-hitting Shavers (211), despite outboxing him for much of the time, the champion almost became a cropper in the seventh when a tremendous overarm right to the head dropped him heavily for the first time in his career. After getting up in a weakened condition, Holmes (210) had to sustain a pounding for the rest of the session before coming back strongly in the eighth. Subsequently, it was all one-way traffic as Holmes unleashed solid rights and lefts at his rapidly tiring opponent. Clearly wilting, after two minutes of the 11th the referee stopped the fight to save Shavers, cut over both eyes, from taking further punishment.

20 October 1979. John Tate w pts 15 Gerrie Coetzee.
Venue: Loftus Versfeld Stadium, Pretoria, South Africa. **Recognition:** WBA. **Referee:** Carlos Berrocal.
Scorecards: 147-144, 148-145, 147-142.
Fight Summary: Fighting for the title vacated on Muhammad Ali's retirement, although badly stunned in the third round Tate (240) had got into his stride by the fifth after a slow start and was working the body well with rights over the top against a strangely subdued Coetzee (222). By the tenth Coetzee was visibly tiring, having taken plenty of leather to the body, and although Tate was also tired he had enough left to box his way to victory despite being occasionally hurt by vicious rights and lefts to the head.

3 February 1980. Larry Holmes w co 6 (15) Lorenzo Zanon.
Venue: Caesar's Palace, Las Vegas, Nevada, USA. **Recognition:** WBC. **Referee:** Raymundo Solis.
Fight Summary: Even though he boxed in an unimpressive fashion the champion had far too much for Zanon (215), especially in the opening three rounds when the latter was extremely negative. However, the fourth saw Holmes (213½) pull himself together when battering Zanon down for three counts, including one of the standing variety. Surprisingly, Zanon came back well in the fifth before Holmes opened up in the sixth, and following a series of left jabs followed by a right to the head the Italian went over to be counted out on one knee at 2.39 of the round.

31 March 1980. Larry Holmes w rsc 8 (15) Leroy Jones.
Venue: Caesar's Palace, Las Vegas, Nevada, USA. **Recognition:** WBC. **Referee:** Richard Greene.
Fight Summary: Coming to the ring unbeaten after 24 starts the bulked-up Jones (254½) proved to be not of championship class, being battered by Holmes (211) for round after round before the referee had seen enough and stopped the fight with just four seconds of the eighth remaining. Although Jones had not been off his feet, with his left eye almost shut and unable to fight back the referee's decision was a humane one.

31 March 1980. Mike Weaver w co 15 (15) John Tate.
Venue: Stokely AC, Knoxville, Tennessee, USA. **Recognition:** WBA. **Referee:** Ernesto Magana.
Fight Summary: The opening four rounds saw the champion dominating when working well to the body, but after he was cut over the right eye Weaver (207½) pushed on strongly in the fifth and sixth, banging in rights and lefts to push his man back. However, Tate (232) came right back in the seventh when beginning to take over again,

Weaver being under a lot of pressure against the ropes in the tenth. Yet again the fight turned when Weaver nailed Tate with a left hook to the jaw, and although the latter was hurt again by a similar punch in the 14th he somehow made it to the end of the session. Behind on points, Weaver came out firing in the 15th, throwing punch after punch at the visibly wobbling Tate. On nearing the end of the session a tremendous left hook to the jaw sent Tate down as if hit with a poleaxe to be counted out with just 45 seconds remaining on the clock.

7 July 1980. Larry Holmes w rsc 7 (15) Scott LeDoux.
Venue: Metro Centre, Minneapolis, Minnesota, USA. **Recognition:** WBC. **Referee:** Davy Pearl.
Fight Summary: Although LeDoux (226) did his best he was no match for the champion, who fired in left jabs followed by stiff rights and left hooks with monotonous regularity. Finally, the tough LeDoux was dropped in the sixth, complaining that he had been thumbed in the eye. Back on his feet LeDoux managed to get through the round, but in the seventh, his left eye now swollen shut and with Holmes (214¼) almost using him a punch-bag, the referee brought matters to a halt on the 2.05 mark.

2 October 1980. Larry Holmes w rtd 10 (15) Muhammad Ali.
Venue: Caesar's Palace, Las Vegas, Nevada, USA. **Recognition:** WBC. **Referee:** Richard Greene.
Fight Summary: Making an ill-advised comeback two years after retiring and 20 years after winning an Olympic gold medal, Ali (217½) was on the end of a steady beating from his former sparring partner in every round before being retired by his corner at the end of the tenth. In the ninth Ali was in real trouble several times as Holmes (211½) landed with a whole range of heavy rights, punctuated with solid lefts, and in the tenth he just could not miss the former champion, even backing off at times. At the end of the session after a brief scuffle between his cornermen, his trainer, Angelo Dundee, retired Ali, who was badly swollen under both eyes, thus bringing to an end his charge's championship career.

Ali would have just one more fight, a losing ten-rounder against Trevor Berbick in December 1981, before retiring for good and becoming a victim of 'Parkinson's Syndrome' in 1984.

25 October 1980. Mike Weaver w co 13 (15) Gerrie Coetzee.
Venue: Super Bowl, Sun City, South Africa. **Recognition:** WBA. **Referee:** Jesus Celis.
Fight Summary: Having made a poor start, being caught by heavy rights to the head early on and badly cut by the side of the nose in the fifth, the champion had come back into contention by the eighth before running into blistering rights to the head. Several times it seemed in that session that Coetzee (226½) was just one punch from the title, but inexplicably he failed to take full advantage. By the tenth Coetzee was in full retreat, and in the 11th after the cut worsened he looked spent as Weaver (210) closed him down and worked him over. Following a mauling 12th round in which he was drained of energy it was clear that Coetzee was almost finished. With Weaver bombing on in the 13th, after being dropped by a left hook and a right to the head Coetzee was counted out on the 1.49 mark.

Inactive since beating Coetzee, Weaver was ordered by the WBA to defend against James Tillis, who he was committed to meet, or risk being stripped after he had agreed to fight Gerry Cooney for $3,000,000. Taking the threat seriously, Weaver put the Cooney fight on the back burner.

11 April 1981. Larry Holmes w pts 15 Trevor Berbick.
Venue: Caesar's Palace, Las Vegas, Nevada, USA. **Recognition:** WBC. **Referee:** Mills Lane.
Scorecards: 150-135, 146-139, 146-140.
Fight Summary: Try as he might the champion was unable to drop the muscular and awkward Berbick (215½) before recognising that he could control the fight from the middle of the ring where he could use his extra reach to advantage. Berbick's best round was the fifth when he pinned Holmes (215) in a corner and banged away at him, but it was only in the last four rounds that he was able to catch the latter more frequently when lunging in. Although the final session was the hardest of the fight as Berbick tried to finish strongly, it was Holmes who landed the more accurately.

12 June 1981. Larry Holmes w rsc 3 (15) Leon Spinks.
Venue: Joe Louis Arena, Detroit, Michigan, USA. **Recognition:** WBC. **Referee:** Richard Steele.
Fight Summary: Holmes (212¼), assuming the ascendancy right from the opening bell, was soon planting the left jab into the challenger's face. It was only when the bell was rung by mistake 20 seconds from the end of the second round and Holmes stopped fighting that Spinks (200¼) was able to get some good shots in. Still angry, Holmes came out for the third and began to rock Spinks with both hands, eventually putting the latter down with a left hook followed by a solid right to the head. Although Spinks was up on his feet well before the mandatory count was completed he seemed to have lost his bearings, and with Holmes picking his punches without return the referee stopped the contest on the 2.34 mark after the challenger's corner threw the towel in.

3 October 1981. Mike Weaver w pts 15 James Tillis.
Venue: Horizon Arena, Rosemont, Illinois, USA. **Recognition:** WBA. **Referee:** Stan Christodoulou.
Scorecards: 147-142, 145-143, 146-142.
Fight Summary: Making a good start, using the jab well, Tillis (209) appeared to be on the way to becoming champion early on as Weaver (215) found it difficult to get going, often looking slow and lethargic. However, by the sixth when Tillis began to slow and Weaver came more into it, nailing his challenger with hard left-rights. It was clear that Tillis was fast tiring, and in the tenth he was backing off as Weaver began to let the punches go. Tillis was still in the fight though, having Weaver on the verge of being knocked out after bombing him with a short right in the 12th. Both men were staggered in the 14th, but from thereon in it was all Weaver while Tillis appeared lucky to make it to the final bell.

Once again inactive, this time it was not entirely Weaver's fault when a scheduled defence against Randall Cobb was twice postponed due to first Weaver and then Cobb being injured. The fight was eventually cancelled when Weaver was ordered by the WBA to make a defence against the number one challenger, Michael Dokes.

6 November 1981. Larry Holmes w rsc 11 (15) Renaldo Snipes.
Venue: Civic Arena, Pittsburgh, Pennsylvania, USA. **Recognition:** WBC. **Referee:** Rudy Ortega.
Fight Summary: After dominating the first six rounds, when the champion got careless in the seventh he was dropped on the seat of his pants after Snipes (215¾), cut over the left eye in the fifth, had caught him heavily with an overarm right to the jaw. Back on his feet in a dazed state Holmes (213¼) looked to be there for the taking, but Snipes, throwing punches wildly, was unable to take advantage. From the eighth onwards Holmes had fully recovered, and although Snipes was still taking the fight to him he was having little success in finding the target. With the damage to Snipes' eye worsening and spitting blood the referee stopped the fight at 1.05 of the 11th after the latter had been pinned in a corner taking heavy shots to the head without reply.

11 June 1982. Larry Holmes w rsc 13 (15) Gerry Cooney.
Venue: Caesar's Palace, Las Vegas, Nevada, USA. **Recognition:** WBC. **Referee:** Mills Lane.
Fight Summary: Although he had been floored by a countering right in the second round the challenger had fought his way back into the contest with dogged determination, and if he had not been deducted three points for low blows he would have been on level terms with Holmes (212½) going in to the 13th. Despite being badly cut over the left eye and on the bridge of the nose early on Cooney (225½) went toe-to-toe with Holmes in the tenth in what was the best round of the fight, both men giving it everything. The end was in sight for Cooney in the 12th when he had virtually stopped punching back, and in the 13th the referee was forced to pull the big Irish-American out when his second jumped into the ring to save his charge from taking further punishment after he had shipped ten solid blows without return. By rights Cooney should have been disqualified, but he had put up such a great battle that it would have made a mockery of the sport had that been the official decision.

26 November 1982. Larry Holmes w pts 15 Randall Cobb.
Venue: The Astrodome, Houston, Texas, USA. **Recognition:** WBC. **Referee:** Steve Crosson.
Scorecards: 150-135, 149-136, 150-135.
Fight Summary: Despite being outclassed by Holmes (217½) the challenger, who finished with cuts and swellings around both eyes, was always looking to fight back. It was soon clear that if Cobb (234¼) wanted to get to grips with the smooth-boxing Holmes he would have to take the fight to him, and that is just what he did regardless of

walking on to punches throughout. Several times in the fight Cobb was wobbled when hammered by both hands, but he was still there at the final bell to receive the plaudits for his great display of courage in becoming only the second challenger to stay the distance with Holmes.

Towards the end of the year the WBC announced that as from 1 January 1983 all world title bouts held under their banner would be contested over 12 rounds.

10 December 1982. Michael Dokes w rsc 1 (15) Mike Weaver.
Venue: Caesar's Palace, Las Vegas, Nevada, USA. **Recognition:** WBA. **Referee:** Joey Curtis.
Fight Summary: In what was a hugely controversial affair Dokes (216) won the title when beating Weaver (209¾) after just 63 seconds, the referee stepping in to rescue the latter. Both men had come out fast, hurting each other with heavy punches, before Dokes put the champion down following two cracking left hooks. Getting up quickly, Weaver was forced to take the mandatory 'eight' count before being allowed to box on. It was when he was immediately backed against the ropes taking punches to head and body that the referee stepped in. With the crowd calling it a 'fix', the referee said that he stopped the contest because Weaver was not fighting back. He went on to say "I was not going to have another Duk-Koo Kim on my hands", a reference to the South Korean lightweight who died after being beaten by Ray Mancini in a recent title fight.

27 March 1983. Larry Holmes w pts 12 Lucien Rodriguez.
Venue: Watres Armoury, Scranton, Pennsylvania, USA. **Recognition:** WBC. **Referee:** Carlos Padilla.
Scorecards: 120-109, 120-108, 120-108.
Fight Summary: An extremely poor fight saw Holmes (221) successfully defend his title for the 14th time when easily beating the European champion, Lucien Rodriguez (209). By keeping on the move the Frenchman made for a difficult target, but Holmes did not help himself when plodding after Rodriguez. Even though Holmes knocked Rodriguez down in the sixth with a big right uppercut and hurt him several times with rights to the head he was unable to force an early finish.

20 May 1983. Larry Holmes w pts 12 Tim Witherspoon.
Venue: Dunes Hotel, Las Vegas, Nevada, USA. **Recognition:** WBC. **Referee:** Mills Lane.
Scorecards: 118-111, 115-113, 114-115.
Fight Summary: Being out of the ring for almost a year was not the best way to prepare for a title challenge. However, in running Holmes (213) close Witherspoon (219½) proved he was definitely one for the future. Holmes had started with good left hands before Witherspoon began to match him, and with the latter banging in big punches to head and body it looked as the though the championship might be changing hands. The ninth round was a big one for Witherspoon, and Holmes, who was badly hurt on several occasions, was forced to call upon all his experience to weather the storm. At this stage of the fight it was Witherspoon's to lose, but when allowing Holmes to outwork him during the last three sessions it proved to be a costly mistake.

20 May 1983. Michael Dokes drew 15 Mike Weaver.
Venue: Dunes Hotel, Las Vegas, Nevada, USA. **Recognition:** WBA. **Referee:** Richard Steele.
Scorecards: 145-141, 144-144, 143-143.
Fight Summary: Having previously won the title from Weaver (218½) under controversial circumstances Dokes (223) had been ordered give the former champion this rematch. And once again there was so little between them that it left the door open for a third meeting between them. It started with both men tearing into each other from the opening bell and throwing big punches, but at the end of the session although each had been rocked they were still standing. Thereafter, Weaver took the best that Dokes had on offer, often blazing back, and in the ninth he had the champion badly hurt from a right to the jaw. The fight continued in its intensity with Dokes getting back to his boxing while Weaver continued to look for the finisher, but the last three rounds saw the latter blasting away at his man before the 15th became an out-and-out slugging match. Weaver, who finished the contest with cuts and swellings under both eyes, thought his work to the body and general aggression had won the day for him, while Dokes stated that even though his left hand had gone early on he felt he had done the better work.

10 September 1983. Larry Holmes w rsc 5 (12) Scott Frank.
Venue: Harrah's Casino Hotel, Atlantic City, New Jersey, USA. **Recognition:** WBC. **Referee:** Tony Perez.
Fight Summary: After coming through a tough defence against Tim Witherspoon, when Holmes (223) took on the plodding Frank (211¼) he was in total control from the opening bell when jabbing and belting the inept challenger as and where he liked throughout. The only time Holmes was hurt came in the second round when two heavy rights to the head got through, and by the fifth, Frank, having soaked up a systematic beating, had nowhere to go. Dropped by a countering right uppercut, Frank claimed that he had been thumbed in the right eye. Ignoring the protest the referee completed the mandatory 'eight' count before sending Frank on his way, only to stop the fight moments later when the latter was covering up on the ropes and making no attempt to fight back. At the time of the stoppage, recorded at 1.28, Frank was virtually unable to see out of either eye as well as carrying damage to his right ear.

23 September 1983. Gerrie Coetzee w co 10 (15) Michael Dokes.
Venue: The Coliseum, Richfield, Ohio, USA. **Recognition:** WBA. **Referee:** Tony Perez.
Fight Summary: Boxing with control and efficiency, and following two earlier attempts to become a champion, Coetzee (215) ripped the title away from Dokes (217) in the tenth round after a slow start. Being cut over the right eye in the second made Coetzee cautious, but in the fifth he dropped Dokes with a cracking right to the jaw. Despite the latter fighting back well he was hurt again in the seventh. Although Dokes stunned Coetzee in the ninth with a big left hook, with the South African soon back on the attack he was battering the champion around the ring by the end of the session. Coming out for the tenth Coetzee continued where he had left off, and eventually two crunching rights to the head sent Dokes crashing to the floor to be counted out eight seconds after the bell rang to end the round.

When Coetzee's right hand was found to be broken for the second time in his career he was forced to have another operation, which put him out of action for several months. Then, after signing for a unification fight against Larry Holmes more bad luck followed when he broke his hand for the third time. Now known as 'The Bionic Man' due to the corrective items built in to his right hand, Coetzee would be ready to defend his title against Greg Page in December 1984 after the number one challenger, David Bey, refused to fight in South Africa.

25 November 1983. Larry Holmes w rsc 1 (12) Marvis Frazier.
Venue: Caesar's Palace, Las Vegas, Nevada, USA. **Recognition:** WBC. **Referee:** Mills Lane.
Fight Summary: Up against the unbeaten 23-year-old son of Joe Frazier the champion made a much quicker start than normal, being completely dominant as he went about dismantling his rival. Officially this was not recognised as a title fight by the WBC as they considered that the ten-fight Frazier (200) was not of championship standard. However, as far as Holmes (219) was concerned he was defending his title. Firing on all cylinders it wasn't too long before Holmes had put Frazier down with a solid right to the head after measuring him with the left. Although Frazier made it up at 'nine', after Holmes had slammed in at least nine or ten heavy rights the referee stopped the fight with three seconds of the round remaining.

Holmes relinquished the WBC version of the title at their convention on 11 December, having rejected an offer to defend against his number one challenger, Greg Page, who had outpointed Renaldo Snipes over 12 rounds at the Dunes Hotel, Las Vegas on 20 May in a final eliminator, stating that he had not been offered enough money for the fight and would be negotiating his own fights in future. The WBC's immediate response was that Page would meet Tim Witherspoon, who had stopped James Tillis in one round on 23 September at The Coliseum, Richfield, Ohio, to contest the vacancy.

Earlier, in late October, at their first convention, the newly formed International Boxing Federation (IBF) had announced that they would be supporting Tim Witherspoon as the champion. The new body had come about when the member States of the United States Boxing Association (USBA) had voted to set up an international body named United States Boxing Association/International (USBA/I) back in April before being reformed as the International Boxing Federation (IBF). Following that, it was announced that Holmes had accepted recognition from the IBF with immediate effect.

9 March 1984. Tim Witherspoon w pts 12 Greg Page.
Venue: Convention Centre, Las Vegas, Nevada, USA. **Recognition:** WBC. **Referee:** Mills Lane.
Scorecards: 117-111, 117-111, 114-114.
Fight Summary: In a contest for the vacant title it was Witherspoon (220¼) who made the better start when rocking Page (239½) in the opening session, his punches appearing to carry more weight than the flicking left jabs from the latter. Page was the better boxer of the two but he was unable to keep Witherspoon at distance and, although he began to wrest control from the latter in the eighth and ninth, once he was hurt by a cracking left hook in the tenth his chances receded. Coming on strong in the last two sessions, having upped his work-rate, Witherspoon belted Page with rights and lefts throughout the final six minutes to fully deserve the win.

31 August 1984. Pinklon Thomas w pts 12 Tim Witherspoon.
Venue: Riviera Hotel, Las Vegas, Nevada, USA. **Recognition:** WBC. **Referee:** Richard Steele.
Scorecards: 116-112, 115-112, 114-114.
Fight Summary: Piling up points with a solid left jab from round two, having been the recipient of some lusty punching in the opening session, Thomas (216) stuck to his game plan even when the champion tried to find his way back into the fight from the seventh onwards. Up until then Witherspoon (217) had been strangely lethargic, not helping himself when having a point deducted for back-handing in the fifth. Fighting with some urgency in the eighth and ninth Witherspoon hurt Thomas with solid blows, but the latter refused to buckle and got back to his boxing to run out a deserved winner.

9 November 1984. Larry Holmes w rsc 12 (15) James Bonecrusher Smith.
Venue: Riviera Hotel, Las Vegas, Nevada, USA. **Recognition:** IBF. **Referee:** Davy Pearl.
Fight Summary: Defending the IBF title for the first time, Holmes (221½) made a winning start when stopping Smith (227) with just 50 seconds of the 12th round remaining. Having been out of the ring for just under a year Holmes was a bit rusty, but his use of the trusty left jab kept him in front against a difficult opponent who stayed with him all the way. Being cut over the left eye in round seven bothered Holmes with Smith coming right back into the fight with heavy rights to head and body before the champion reasserted himself fully in the tenth. In the 11th Smith was in real trouble when blood began to flow freely from the swelling over his left eye, and with Holmes battering away at him and the injury worsening the referee called it off in the following round.

1 December 1984. Greg Page w co 8 (15) Gerrie Coetzee.
Venue: Super Bowl, Sun City, South Africa. **Recognition:** WBA. **Referee:** Isidro Rodriguez.
Fight Summary: Making his first defence after being out of action for 14 months, Coetzee (218) never really got going. He was not helped by the fact that he was struck several times by Page (236½) at the start of round two before the ring had been cleared and then floored by a right to the head well after the bell to end the sixth. Still not fully recovered Coetzee was back on the canvas from another right to the head in the seventh, and although fighting back strongly he was then counted out at the end of the eighth after being caught by left-right combinations. The official time of the knockout was given as 3.03, but unofficial observers, including South African Broadcasting Corporation Television, recorded the round as being 3.50 at the time of the finish; the discrepancy thought to have been due to a malfunction of the electric clock.

15 March 1985. Larry Holmes w rsc 10 (15) David Bey.
Venue: Riviera Hotel, Las Vegas, Nevada, USA. **Recognition:** IBF. **Referee:** Carlos Padilla.
Fight Summary: Taking the champion out of his stride during the opening four rounds, landing well with left hooks and long right hands, Bey (233¼) looked like he might go all the way before he made the mistake of sitting back in the fifth. Thereafter, the fight belonged to Holmes (223½), and in the eighth Bey was put down by a big right to the head. Getting up but disorganised, Bey was then sent down again from a left hook-right uppercut before being saved by the bell. Although the challenger came back well in the ninth he was taken apart in the tenth as Holmes ripped into him throwing punches from both hands, and with just two seconds of the session remaining the referee stopped the fight when Bey was not hitting back.

29 April 1985. Tony Tubbs w pts 15 Greg Page.
Venue: Memorial Auditorium, Buffalo, New York, USA. **Recognition:** WBA. **Referee:** Vincent Rainone.

Scorecards: 145-140, 147-140, 145-142.

Fight Summary: Although the champion started reasonably well, with his work-rate already dropping by the second round Tubbs (229) began to gradually impose himself even though he hardly got out of first gear. Boxing cautiously, Tubbs continued to pick up points with the left jab and occasional rights to the head as Page (239½) continually ambled along with no sense of urgency. The last third of the fight saw Tubbs landing the better blows and, while Page threw the odd solid left hook, when he failed to up the pace the contest degenerated into a sloppy affair with far too much holding.

20 May 1985. Larry Holmes w pts 15 Carl Williams.
Venue: Lawlor Events Centre, Reno, Nevada, USA. **Recognition:** IBF. **Referee:** Mills Lane.
Scorecards: 143-142, 146-139, 146-139.

Fight Summary: Showing the champion no respect the unbeaten Williams (215) got away well. He was even outjabbing Holmes (222¼) before the latter gradually turned things around when scoring with solid left jabs and rights to head and body. The fight had been relatively level up unto the 12th, although from thereon in Holmes showed his experience when outworking Williams. There were no knockdowns, but at the final bell Holmes' left eye was closed while Williams carried a cut over the same eye.

15 June 1985. Pinklon Thomas w co 8 (12) Mike Weaver.
Venue: Riviera Hotel, Las Vegas, Nevada, USA. **Recognition:** WBC. **Referee:** Carlos Padilla.

Fight Summary: Defending his title for the first time, having been out of action following an operation to repair a detached retina, Thomas (220¼) ultimately proved too good for Weaver (221¼). However, he had to weather a few storms on the way. Having been dropped in the first round Weaver came back strongly to take the next few sessions with big rights and lefts paving the way, but by the sixth he was clearly tiring. At this stage of the fight Thomas took over with stiff left jabs, and after catching Weaver with some heavy blows in the seventh he sent the latter crashing to the floor in the eighth to be counted out on the 1.42 mark following a tremendous right over the top.

21 September 1985. Michael Spinks w pts 15 Larry Holmes.
Venue: Riviera Hotel, Las Vegas, Nevada, USA. **Recognition:** IBF. **Referee:** Carlos Padilla.
Scorecards: 143-142, 143-142, 145-142.

Fight Summary: Looking to equal Rocky Marciano's record of consecutive wins in his 49th contest, Holmes (221½) not only lost his unbeaten record but also lost his title to the former Olympic middleweight champion, Spinks (200). Still holding three versions of the light heavyweight title, Spinks boxed intelligently, slipping and ducking away from punches before coming back with two-fisted attacks that kept Holmes guessing all night. Coming into the 15th round it was still extremely tight, both men being level on the cards, but taking the bull by the horns and landing lefts and rights throughout the session Spinks was given the win over an extremely disappointed Holmes. After the fight, Holmes, his eyes badly swollen, stated that although he had found Spinks too slippery to catch with the right he would be better prepared next time.

17 January 1986. Tim Witherspoon w pts 15 Tony Tubbs.
Venue: The Omni, Atlanta, Georgia, USA. **Recognition:** WBA. **Referee:** Nate Morgan.
Scorecards: 144-143, 144-141, 143-143.

Fight Summary: In what was a very close fight it was the challenger's extra determination and stamina that ultimately won him the title. There were no knockdowns, although the bulky Tubbs (244) almost went over in the eighth after a terrific left hook sent him staggering into the ropes. Boxing well at times, especially with left hand, Tubbs often failed to follow up his good work. And in the last round with the result depending on who wanted it most it was Witherspoon (227), punching away with both hands, who edged it.

22 March 1986. Trevor Berbick w pts 12 Pinklon Thomas.
Venue: Riviera Hotel, Las Vegas, Nevada, USA. **Recognition:** WBC. **Referee:** Richard Steele.
Scorecards: 115-113, 115-113, 115-114.

Fight Summary: Making his second attempt to win a title, Berbick (218½), boxing in determined fashion, upset the odds stacked against him when outpointing Thomas (222¾). Unable to dictate the fight as Berbick moved out of range and blocked jabs while getting his own on target, Thomas often appeared listless and out of ideas. Even though Berbick was swollen under the left eye as early as the second round Thomas failed to take advantage. By the eighth it was clear that Thomas was tiring, and when he was cut over the left eye it inspired Berbick to come on stronger, repeatedly taking the fight to the champion with solid left hooks and rights to head and body. Although there were no knockdowns it was the better quality of Berbick's blows that won him the fight, Thomas being warned on several occasions for punching with the open glove.

19 April 1986. Michael Spinks w pts 15 Larry Holmes.
Venue: Hilton Hotel, Las Vegas, Nevada, USA. **Recognition:** IBF. **Referee:** Mills Lane.
Scorecards: 144-141, 144-142, 141-144.
Fight Summary: Putting his title on the line against the man he won it from, Spinks (205) just about got home in a gruelling affair that saw the champion landing the greater number of blows while Holmes (223), responsible for the heavier shots, almost had his man over on at least three occasions. Holmes had made the better start, hurting his man badly in the second, but by the fifth Spinks was coming more and more into it, scoring well with stiff jabs and rights. Almost over from a tremendous right to the head in the ninth, Spinks again boxed his way back from the brink before nearly hitting the floor again as Holmes measured him with the right in the 14th. With both men putting in a strong finish it was Spinks' better work that had him winning the last round on all three judges' scorecards. Following the fight it was claimed that Holmes had broken his right thumb in the third, but no excuses were given.

19 July 1986. Tim Witherspoon w rsc 11 (15) Frank Bruno.
Venue: The Stadium, Wembley, London, England. **Recognition:** WBA. **Referee:** Isidro Rodriguez.
Fight Summary: Having started well, especially with the left jab, it was only in the sixth that the challenger began to be caught heavily. And in the eighth Witherspoon (234¾) was letting right swings go with a vengeance. Although Bruno (228) was now hanging on he came back well in the eighth as Witherspoon's left eye began to close, but from there onwards he tired rapidly, the American virtually walking through him in the 11th. A big left hook followed by heavy rights to the head had Bruno staggering backwards and, following a blitz of right hands from Witherspoon that ended with the Englishman slipping to the floor, the referee finally stopped the fight with just three seconds of the round remaining. With the right side of Bruno's face badly swollen it was first feared that he had suffered a broken jaw, but X-rays showed no fracture.

6 September 1986. Michael Spinks w rsc 4 (15) Steffen Tangstad.
Venue: Hilton Hotel, Las Vegas, Nevada, USA. **Recognition:** IBF. **Referee:** Richard Steele.
Fight Summary: Despite being the European champion Tangstad (214¾) was no match for Spinks (201), who had worked out his weaknesses by the second round before sending him to his knees with a right to the head in the third. The end was now in sight. Coming out strongly in the fourth Spinks quickly got down to business, putting Tangstad down twice more with big left hooks, and after the Norwegian got up from the second knockdown looking shaken and cut over the right eye the referee called the fight off on the 58 second mark.

Spinks forfeited his IBF version of the title in February 1987 when refusing to defend against Tony Tucker and signing to meet Gerry Cooney instead. Billed as 'The People's World Heavyweight Championship', but not supported by any of the commissions, Spinks stopped Cooney in the fifth round at the Convention Centre, Atlantic City, New Jersey on 15 June 1987. He then remained inactive until taking on Mike Tyson for the undisputed title.

Meantime, the IBF matched Tony Tucker, who had outpointed James Broad over 12 rounds to win the vacant USBA title on 26 September, with James Buster Douglas to decide their vacancy.

22 November 1986. Mike Tyson w rsc 2 (12) Trevor Berbick.
Venue: Hilton Hotel, Las Vegas, Nevada, USA. **Recognition:** WBC. **Referee:** Mills Lane.
Fight Summary: Tyson (221¼) was the new kid on the block, having blasted 25 of his 27 opponents into early submission, and he made a tremendous start when tearing into the champion right from the opening bell and then wobbling him with clubbing rights to the head before the round ended. Picking it up where he left off Tyson soon had Berbick (218½) under pressure in the second and, after staggering the latter with heavy rights that sent him

reeling across the ring, he dropped him with a short right to the jaw. On his feet at 'three', but taking the mandatory count before getting back in action, Berbick was still on unsteady legs. With Tyson looking to finish, although taking a couple of hard shots to the head, the moment he connected with a short left hook Berbick was down again. Up at 'nine', the referee waved the fight off on the 2.35 mark when it was clear that Berbick was unable to control his legs.

12 December 1986. James Bonecrusher Smith w rsc 1 (15) Tim Witherspoon.
Venue: Madison Square Garden, Manhattan, NYC, New York, USA. **Recognition:** WBA. **Referee:** Luis Rivera.
Fight Summary: Challenging Witherspoon (233½) for the title, Smith (228½) made a great start when racing across the ring to have the champion in trouble with the very first punch of the fight, a crashing right to the head. Throwing 59 punches, of which 28 landed, Smith had Witherspoon on the floor three times in the opening round before the fight was automatically stopped after 2.12 of the session when the WBA's 'three knockdowns in a round' ruling came into play. Witherspoon should have been counted upon when he touched down earlier but was allowed to continue. Smith's next outing would be a WBA/WBC unification contest against Mike Tyson.

With the WBA's scheduled distance for championship fights being 15 rounds, an agreement was brokered to go along with the WBC's stipulated 12 while having their own 'three-knockdown' ruling in place. This deal remained in situ up until the WBA announced at their convention in October 1987 that all championship contests would be scheduled for 12 rounds forthwith.

7 March 1987. Mike Tyson w pts 12 James Bonecrusher Smith.
Venue: Hilton Hotel, Las Vegas, Nevada, USA. **Recognition:** WBA/WBC. **Referee:** Mills Lane.
Scorecards: 120-106, 119-107, 119-107.
Fight Summary: In a contest with two titles on the line the WBC champion outscored Smith (233) by a long chalk, and despite the prediction of it being an exciting contest it failed to live up to the ballyhoo. In a boring affair it was noticeable almost from the start that the slow and awkward looking Smith, cut over the left eye in the second, was intent on stopping Tyson (219) from working by tying him up again and again. Even though he was deducted two points for those infringements he carried on regardless. Although Tyson tried to make a fight of it he showed his limitations when unable to close Smith down and allowing him far too much room.

30 May 1987. Mike Tyson w rsc 6 (12) Pinklon Thomas.
Venue: Hilton Hotel, Las Vegas, Nevada, USA. **Recognition:** WBA/WBC. **Referee:** Carlos Padilla.
Fight Summary: Making up for his poor performance against James Bonecrusher Smith last time out the champion quickly dispelled the doubts when he tore into Thomas (217¾) from the opening bell, hitting his man with everything bar the kitchen sink. Amazingly, Thomas remained upright, even coming back during the next four rounds to make a fight of it despite being hurt again on several occasions. Just when the crowd thought Thomas might get back into it in the sixth Tyson (218¾) struck when a tremendous right uppercut almost lifted the challenger off his feet. Throwing punch after punch at the hapless Thomas, eventually Tyson found another big left hook that floored him. It was clear that Thomas was through for the night, and even though he was in the process of getting up the referee stopped the contest on the two-minute mark.

30 May 1987. Tony Tucker w rsc 10 (15) James Buster Douglas.
Venue: Hilton Hotel, Las Vegas, Nevada, USA. **Recognition:** IBF. **Referee:** Mills Lane.
Fight Summary: Contesting the vacant title, even though both Tucker (222¼) and Douglas (228¼) had promised much, the fight never really got going. By the seventh Douglas seemed to be in front with his better boxing, but thereafter he began to tire. Following that, it was Tucker, despite having pulled a muscle in his right arm in the second, who picked up the pace with good body punches. In the tenth, after being badly hurt by a big right to the jaw and not fighting back, Douglas was rescued by the referee at 1.36 of the session.

1 August 1987. Mike Tyson w pts 12 Tony Tucker.
Venue: Hilton Hotel, Las Vegas, Nevada, USA. **Recognition:** World. **Referee:** Mills Lane.
Scorecards: 118-113, 119-111, 117-112.

Fight Summary: Cut from 15 to 12 rounds a day earlier in order to satisfy the WBC, and fighting to finally unify the title, Tyson (221) was always working that little bit harder than the IBF champion. Tucker (221), who staggered Tyson with a left uppercut in the opening round, failed to build on his early success, appearing happy to jab and move while the WBA/WBC champion looked to land heavy shots. The fight was always competitive, and Tucker, who had held the IBF title for just 63 days, claimed afterwards that having hurt his right hand in the sixth he was unable to find the punches to put Tyson away with. On winning, Tyson became the youngest fully recognised heavyweight champion in history at 21 years and one month of age, nine months younger than Floyd Patterson was when he defeated Archie Moore back in 1956.

16 October 1987. Mike Tyson w rsc 7 (15) Tyrell Biggs.
Venue: Convention Centre, Atlantic City, New Jersey, USA. **Recognition:** World. **Referee:** Tony Orlando.
Fight Summary: Although Biggs (228¾) towered above the champion and began the fight well when firing in jabs, by the end of the first round he had been hurt by solid blows to head and body. Before too long it had become one-sided, Biggs reduced to holding just in order to survive as Tyson (216) looked to unload at every opportunity. By the seventh Biggs was only offering token resistance, and after getting up at 'nine', having been sent through the ropes from a left hook, he was battered by a series of mean looking blows before another left hook sent him reeling across the ring. When Biggs dropped down in his own corner the referee did not even bother to count, calling the fight off with one second of the session remaining. Despite being contested over the IBF's recognised distance of 15 rounds, it carried WBA/WBC support.

22 January 1988. Mike Tyson w rsc 4 (12) Larry Holmes.
Venue: Convention Centre, Atlantic City, New Jersey, USA. **Recognition:** World. **Referee:** Joe Cortez.
Fight Summary: Having been out of action for 21 months since losing for the second time to Michael Spinks, Holmes (225¾) came back to the ring looking to regain the title he once held. At the age of 38 Holmes was up against a man who had no time for past reputations. With Tyson (215¾) piling in from the opening bell the once famous Holmes' jab was used purely for defence, and although he got through with several right uppercuts in the third by the end of the session he was badly hurt by a right to the jaw. Tyson needed no more excuses, quickly having Holmes over from a series of blows to head and body. Getting up at 'four', but having to take the mandatory 'eight' count, Holmes tried to fiddle his way back before another right soon had him down again. Back on his feet, Holmes was quickly under attack prior to being rescued by the referee after Tyson had sent him crashing again from a right to the head with five seconds of the fourth remaining. According to the *Boxing News*, the WBA and WBC both approved the fight because of Holmes' past greatness while the IBF, despite recognising Tyson, did not give it their full backing as it was being contested over 12 rounds and not 15.

21 March 1988. Mike Tyson w rsc 2 Tony Tubbs.
Venue: The Dome, Tokyo, Japan. **Recognition:** World. **Referee:** Arthur Mercante.
Fight Summary: Despite doing well in the opening round, scoring with good jabs and claiming his man on the inside, before the end of the session was over Tubbs (238¼) knew what he was up against when the champion landed heavily to the body and head just as the bell rang. Picking the pace up in the second Tyson (216¼) applied constant pressure, throwing punches from both hands, and just when it looked as though Tubbs would make it to the end of the round a tremendous left hook to the head ripped open a cut on his right eye and sent him down heavily. Even before the referee could take up the count Tubbs' second rushed into the ring to give the stricken fighter aid; the fight being stopped with six seconds of the round remaining. Although the second's action should have bought Tubbs a disqualification the result was announced as a technical knockout win for Tyson. Regardless of the fact that the IBF saw Tyson as the champion, they were not involved in the promotion due to them not being recognised by the Japanese Boxing Commission.

27 June 1988. Mike Tyson w co 1 Michael Spinks.
Venue: Convention Centre, Atlantic City, New Jersey, USA. **Recognition:** World. **Referee:** Frank Cappuccino.
Fight Summary: Prior to the fight the unbeaten Spinks (212¼) had been seen by many as the man to stop the champion's incessant march, but he too ultimately went the way of all the others. Right from the start Spinks was under pressure as Tyson (218¼) tore into him, lashing in lefts and rights, and a left uppercut soon had the challenger over. Although Spinks made it to his feet at 'two' before taking the rest of the mandatory count, after

trying to fight back a big left uppercut to the jaw followed by a right to the body sent him down to be counted out flat on his back at 1.31 of the session. Despite being contested over 12 rounds, it was recognised by the IBF as a world title bout.

During the summer of 1988, at their convention, the IBF announced that as from 1 September all world title bouts held under their banner would be contested over 12 rounds, thus bringing them into line with the WBC and the WBA.

Following the setting up of the World Boxing Organisation (WBO), which came about after 27 delegates walked out of the WBA convention in October, in their wisdom the new organisation decided to support the winner of the Francesco Damiani v Johnny du Plooy bout as their first heavyweight champion rather than recognising Tyson.

25 February 1989. Mike Tyson w rsc 5 Frank Bruno.
Venue: Hilton Hotel, Las Vegas, Nevada, USA. **Recognition:** World. **Referee:** Richard Steele.
Fight Summary: Out of the ring for 16 months, waiting for his title crack at the champion, Bruno kept himself in condition while Tyson was suffering from managerial and domestic problems that almost threatened to sink him. When the fight finally went ahead Bruno (228) was on the floor almost immediately after taking a right to the temple. On his feet at 'three' despite being hit while on one knee, Bruno eventually got back in action, having Tyson (218) badly hurt from a cracking left hook to the jaw before the session ended. Unfortunately for Bruno he was unable to take full advantage of the situation, letting his opponent off the hook and ultimately paying the price. By the third Tyson was in full swing after an erratic start, and at the start of the fourth he had hurt Bruno with a huge right to the head. Tyson was also weakening Bruno with body blows that were sapping all the strength out of him. With just five seconds of the fifth remaining it was all over, the referee stopping the contest with Bruno not hitting back and floundering on the ropes under a barrage of punches to head and body.

6 May 1989. Francesco Damiani w co 3 Johnny du Plooy.
Venue: The Stadium, Syracuse, Sicilia, Italy. **Recognition:** WBO. **Referee:** Tony Perez.
Fight Summary: Fighting to decide the inaugural WBO title Damiani (234) took his time to get going, but by the third round he was beginning to find the range with big lefts and rights. With Du Plooy (210) now under a fair amount of pressure from heavy right hands, he was eventually counted out at 1.24 of the session after being laid low by a left hook that was followed by a right cross.

21 July 1989. Mike Tyson w rsc 1 Carl Williams.
Venue: Convention Centre, Atlantic City, New Jersey, USA. **Recognition:** IBF/WBA/WBC. **Referee:** Randy Neumann.
Fight Summary: Boxing well from the opening bell, his 14-inch reach advantage allowing him to keep the champion on the end of the jab, it looked like Williams (218) might be the man to give Tyson (219¼) a fair test. However, in leaving his right hand low he paid the price when caught by a crashing left hook to the jaw. Dropped heavily, after making two attempts to get off the floor the referee called the fight off with only 93 seconds on the clock, stating that Williams had looked to be concussed and was unable to respond to a simple question.

16 December 1989. Francesco Damiani w rsc 2 Daniel Neto.
Venue: Sports Palace, Cesena, Italy. **Recognition:** WBO. **Referee:** Bernie Soto.
Fight Summary: In what was clearly a mismatch Damiani (229) soon had the South American cruiserweight champion in trouble, dropping him with a left hook towards the end of the first round. Up at the count of 'five' Neto (198¼) was saved by the bell, only to be put under immediate pressure again at the start of the second. Following up several solid combination punches with a right uppercut that drove Neto into a corner, the latter was floored for the second time when Damiani sent in two short rights to the head. Although Neto beat the count, when his corner threw in the towel the referee stopped the fight. The finish was timed at 1.57 of the session.

11 February 1990. James Buster Douglas w co 10 Mike Tyson.
Venue: The Dome, Tokyo, Japan. **Recognition:** IBF/WBA/WBC. **Referee:** Octavio Meyran.
Fight Summary: Given no chance against the champion, Douglas (231½) pulled off one of the biggest upsets in the history of boxing when knocking out Tyson (220½) at 1.22 of the tenth round. Using his 12-inch reach advantage to

maximum benefit, Douglas stabbed the left jab in and followed it up with good, solid right uppercuts to leave Tyson unable to get through his guard. In the fifth Tyson was shaken by a left-right to the head, and with his left eye swelling he began to become disheartened. The next two rounds were slow, but in the eighth just after Douglas had hurt Tyson with a left-right-left combination he was himself put down by a right uppercut to the jaw. Despite the so-called long count that could have been 12 or 13 seconds due to poor liaison between the timekeeper and the referee, Douglas, who was up at 'nine', somehow got through the rest of the session. Having survived an early blitz in the ninth, as Tyson went all out, Douglas had the champion in big trouble when blasting away at him, finishing the round in total control. The tenth saw Tyson trying to take the fight to Douglas, but it seemed to be mission impossible at that point. Opening up with the left jab and with the champion all at sea, Douglas sent Tyson crashing down on his back to be counted out after a right uppercut following by several combinations and a left to the temple parted the champion from his senses.

With Tyson's big money fight against Evander Holyfield out of the window, the WBC, egged on by Don King, decided five hours afterwards that they would not accept the verdict due to the long count, while the WBA stated that it would give its verdict within a week. With public opinion against them, within a few days the WBA, followed quickly by the WBC, had joined the IBF in recognising Douglas as the new champion as long as he took on Holyfield.

25 October 1990. Evander Holyfield w co 3 James Buster Douglas.
Venue: Mirage Hotel & Casino, Las Vegas, Nevada, USA. **Recognition:** IBF/WBA/WBC. **Referee:** Mills Lane.
Fight Summary: Right from the start it was clear that Douglas (246) had failed to prepare himself properly when barely landing on Holyfield (208) during the seven minutes and ten seconds of action. Although sprightly enough, Douglas was nearly always out of distance with the jab while Holyfield made his punches count, and in the third round, having moved away from an uppercut, he slammed in a short right-hand counter that put the champion down and out. To most onlookers it appeared that Douglas could have beaten the count, while Ferdie Pacheco, who was doing the inter-round analysis for TV, felt that the former champion had the personality traits of a loser.

When it was announced at the beginning of November that Holyfield's first defence would be against George Foreman, the WBC threatened to strip Holyfield and bill the forthcoming Mike Tyson versus Donovan Ruddock fight for the vacant title. Firstly, an injunction stopped that from happening, and then the Supreme Court stated that Holyfield was the champion and his contest against Foreman was a legitimate world title bout. Ultimately, Tyson beat Ruddock (w rsc 7 at the Mirage Hotel & Casino, Las Vegas, Nevada on 18 March 1991) in what would be recognised as a WBC eliminating contest only.

Having returned to the ring in 1987 after a ten-year absence, George Foreman had won all 24 fights, 23 of them inside the distance, and even at the age of 43 had a puncher's chance. Foreman had beaten Dwight Muhammad Qawi, J. B. Williamson, Bert Cooper, Gerry Cooney and Adilson Rodrigues inside the distance, along with 18 other opponents, and only Everett Martin had reached the final bell.

11 January 1991. Ray Mercer w co 9 Francesco Damiani.
Venue: Trump Taj Mahal, Atlantic City, New Jersey, USA. **Recognition:** WBO. **Referee:** Rudy Battle.
Fight Summary: Using the ring well the champion began piling up points with the jab and counters almost from the start as Mercer (215) lunged in and found himself hitting fresh air more often than not. At the start of the ninth Damiani (229½) was well clear and looked to be a sure winner, but towards the end of the round Mercer suddenly found a swinging left uppercut from below the waist that put the Italian down. Well ahead on the scorecards, although Damiani made a desperate attempt to get up he just failed to make it to his feet, being counted out with just three seconds of the session remaining.

19 April 1991. Evander Holyfield w pts 12 George Foreman.
Venue: Convention Centre, Atlantic City, New Jersey, USA. **Recognition:** IBF/WBA/WBC. **Referee:** Rudy Battle.
Scorecards: 116-111, 117-110, 115-112.
Fight Summary: Outspeeded over the first half of the contest as Holyfield (208) whipped in punches and moved, in the seventh Foreman (257) came alive when shaking the champion up with two thumping right hands. After the eighth round passed him by Foreman came again in the ninth when it was clear that Holyfield was also tiring, and

in the tenth he hurt the latter with another big right. During the fight Foreman had occasionally landed low with just a warning given, but in the 11th after going downstairs yet again he finally had a point deducted. The last session saw both men extremely tired, and while Holyfield was doing most of the work it was Foreman, his face by now badly swollen, who received a standing ovation for making it to the final bell.

Further to Mike Tyson's win over Donovan Ruddock (w pts 12 at the Mirage Hotel & Casino, Las Vegas, Nevada on 28 June) in another WBC eliminator, it was announced in mid-July that Holyfield would be defending his title against him on 8 November. This followed an earlier announcement that Holyfield would be meeting Foreman in a rematch on the same date. With Don King, Tyson's promoter, trying to get support for his fighter to meet Foreman for the vacant title if a match between Holyfield could not be made, when the latter agreed to defend against 'Iron Mike' all thoughts of Foreman's involvement were discarded. However, after Tyson was injured in sparring at the end of October, when a rescheduled date could not be agreed upon Holyfield was booked to meet Francesco Damiani on 23 November. When the WBC failed to support the fight due to Damiani not being a top-ten rated fighter, after an ankle injury put the Italian out of the contest and Bert Cooper stepped in as a late substitute their stance remained the same.

18 October 1991. Ray Mercer w rsc 5 Tommy Morrison.
Venue: Convention Centre, Atlantic City, New Jersey, USA. **Recognition:** WBO. **Referee:** Tony Perez.
Fight Summary: Making a good start against the champion Morrison (221¾) got away well, banging in punches and having it almost all his own way until the last few seconds of the third round saw the tide beginning to turn. The fourth round saw Mercer (225) getting a foothold in the contest as he began to belt Morrison with solid right hands, and pushing on in the fifth it suddenly became one-way traffic. At this stage of the fight Morrison was out of it as Mercer smashed in punch after punch against his defenceless opponent. Somewhat belatedly, Morrison was rescued by the referee on the 25-second mark when he finally went to the floor after taking a fearful hammering.

Mercer forfeited the WBO version of the title in January 1992 when signing up for a fight against Larry Holmes instead of making a defence against Michael Moorer. Although Mercer versus Holmes was intended to be a title bout it did not wear with the WBO, who then matched Moorer and Bert Cooper to decide the vacancy.

23 November 1991. Evander Holyfield w rsc 7 Bert Cooper.
Venue: The Omni, Atlanta, Georgia, USA. **Recognition:** IBF/WBA/WBC. **Referee:** Mills Lane.
Fight Summary: After looking likely to finish early when putting Cooper (215) down with a left hook to the body, the champion soon realised that his opponent was no patsy when he came roaring back before the end of the opening session. With Cooper continuing to throw dangerous shots he had Holyfield (210) in such trouble on the ropes in the third that a standing count was enforced. The pace was terrific as Cooper went for broke, and with Holyfield hitting back hard it left both men almost exhausted. The next three sessions saw Cooper trying to force matters but coming off worse as Holyfield picked his punches. And in the sixth the challenger was cut over the right eye. Although under the cosh Cooper was still giving it everything but he was gradually falling apart. Then, with two seconds left of the seventh the referee came to Cooper's rescue when he was backed up on the ropes being hit with all manner of shots and not fighting back.

Although the WBC refused to sanction the contest on the grounds that Cooper was not a top-ranked fighter they still recognised Holyfield as the champion, and while there were those who felt that the WBC would only recognise a Holyfield title fight when he defended against Mike Tyson, that would have all changed after the latter received a jail sentence at the end of March 1992.

15 May 1992. Michael Moorer w rsc 5 Bert Cooper.
Venue: Trump Taj Mahal, Atlantic City, New Jersey, USA. **Recognition:** WBO. **Referee:** Joe O'Neil.
Fight Summary: Contesting the vacant title, boxing went out of the window as both men brawled their way through the fight as if it was their last. The action had barely got underway when Cooper (224½) had Moorer (217) in difficulty on the ropes prior to dropping him with lefts and rights. On getting up and being battered on the ropes the latter found a southpaw right hook that put Cooper over. Up at about 'six', Cooper lasted out the round before

immediately going on the rampage in the second. It was blow for blow in the third, Moorer being put down again from six unanswered heavy shots. Although forced to take the mandatory 'eight' Moorer came right back with solid blows of his own. And in the fifth he began to outfight the courageous Cooper, now cut over the left eye. Following another fierce bout of fighting the referee rescued a groggy Cooper on the 2.21 mark when he had just about made it to his feet at 'nine' after a left hook-right uppercut had downed him.

When Moorer relinquished the WBO version of the title in February 1993, in order to be available to challenge either Riddick Bowe or Lennox Lewis, the 44-year-old George Foreman and Tommy Morrison were matched to find a new champion.

19 June 1992. Evander Holyfield w pts 12 Larry Holmes.
Venue: Caesar's Palace, Las Vegas, Nevada, USA. **Recognition:** IBF/WBA/WBC. **Referee:** Mills Lane.
Scorecards: 116-112, 116-112, 117-111.
Fight Summary: Having outpointed Ray Mercer in his previous fight the former champion was given a crack at Holyfield (210), and although he gave it his best shot he was well beaten. By now, Holmes (233), hardly a patch on the great fighter he once was, never really looked like winning. His main tactic to conserve energy was to stay on the ropes and come on strong in the final two sessions, which he did. Holyfield, cut over the right eye by Holmes' elbow in the sixth, was hardly inspiring. Even though Holyfield was always ahead on points he never looked likely to win inside the distance, the best two punches of the fight, both heavy right hands, coming from Holmes in the 11th.

Holyfield's next title defence would be against Riddick Bowe, who beat South Africa's Pierre Coetzer (w rsc 7 at the Mirage Hotel & Casino, Las Vegas on 18 July) in a final eliminator for the WBA title.

13 November 1992. Riddick Bowe w pts 12 Evander Holyfield.
Venue: Thomas & Mack Centre, Las Vegas, Nevada, USA. **Recognition:** IBF/WBA/WBC. **Referee:** Joe Cortez.
Scorecards: 115-112, 117-110, 117-110.
Fight Summary: Even though Holyfield (205) fought gallantly, Bowe (235) was always ahead of him, and when he opened up in the seventh with big punches from both hands it looked ominous for the champion. Holyfield, who already had a swollen right eye, was also cut over the left eye from a head clash in the eighth, but with Bowe tiring he came on strongly until a crushing right hand to the head in the tenth virtually finished him. How Holyfield stayed on his feet was almost miraculous as Bowe hit him with every punch in the book and some that were not. Holyfield even fought back towards the end of the session before being dropped by a left hook in the 11th. That was the end for Holyfield in terms of keeping his title, but Bowe could not finish him.

Bowe forfeited his WBC version of the title in December when failing to sign for a defence against their leading contender, Lennox Lewis. Lewis, who had stopped Donovan Ruddock inside two rounds at the Exhibition Centre, Earls Court, London on 31 October in a final eliminator, was immediately proclaimed WBC champion.

6 February 1993. Riddick Bowe w rsc 1 Michael Dokes.
Venue: Madison Square Garden, Manhattan, NYC, New York, USA. **Recognition:** IBF/WBA. **Referee:** Joe Santarpia.
Fight Summary: There was no way on current form that the ageing Dokes (244) should have been given a crack at the champion, and when the referee stopped the fight at 2.19 of the first round to save him from taking further punishment the critics were proved right. Bowe (243) opened up with four left jabs before a left-right had Dokes sliding down the ropes to take a standing count that was not even completed before he was allowed back into action. By now it was just a matter of time. After Bowe connected with the left hook and another couple of crunching rights, that had Dokes reeling into the ropes, the fight came to an end before the champion could do any further damage.

8 May 1993. Lennox Lewis w pts 12 Tony Tucker.
Venue: Thomas & Mack Centre, Las Vegas, Nevada, USA. **Recognition:** WBC. **Referee:** Joe Cortez.
Scorecards: 117-111, 116-112, 118-111.

Fight Summary: Making his first defence, and unbeaten in 22 fights, Lewis (235) showed his class when outboxing and hurting his man several times. Lewis almost had Tucker (235) over in the second round, and in the third a long right put the latter down for the first knockdown of his career. Although Lewis failed to finish it there and then he continued to walk Tucker down, nearly having him over in the seventh before doing the trick again with a big right early in the ninth. Up at 'three', after taking the mandatory count Tucker came back with some big punches of his own to win the next two sessions as Lewis went on the back foot with the jab, being happy to box his way to the decision.

22 May 1993. Riddick Bowe w rsc 2 Jesse Ferguson.
Venue: RFK Stadium, Washington DC, USA. **Recognition:** IBF/WBA. **Referee:** Larry Hazzard.
Fight Summary: Outgunned right from the start Ferguson (224) was wide open to the champion's punches, being made to eat left jabs before heavy shots, followed by a big left hook, sent him to the floor. There looked to be no way back for Ferguson and, although he just about got up before the 'ten', the bell to end the opening round came to his aid. Surprisingly allowed out for the second, Ferguson was immediately at the mercy of Bowe (244). When Ferguson was floored following a big right to the head that preceded several solid blows the referee stopped the fight 17 seconds into the session.

7 June 1993. Tommy Morrison w pts 12 George Foreman.
Venue: Thomas & Mack Centre, Las Vegas, Nevada, USA. **Recognition:** WBO. **Referee:** Mills Lane.
Scorecards: 117-110, 117-110, 118-109.
Fight Summary: In a fight for the vacant title, Morrison (226) boxed a clever, tactical battle when using his speed to score points before moving away from real trouble against the much older Foreman (256). Even then Morrison was forced to endure some heavy hits when the men came together. Both Foreman and Morrison were tiring from their exertions by the eighth, and when the latter was hit low he was allowed to take time out. The remainder of the fight saw Foreman plodding after Morrison, who would occasionally jump in with fast blows before getting away. Although Foreman was deducted two points for low blows and lost the fight it was he who received the plaudits for his determined efforts to track Morrison down.

30 August 1993. Tommy Morrison w rtd 4 Tim Tomashek.
Venue: Kemper Arena, Kansas City, Missouri, USA. **Recognition:** WBO. **Referee:** Danny Campbell.
Fight Summary: Having been on reserve duty, Tomashek (205) became a last-minute replacement when the challenger, Mike Williams, left the venue after being asked to supply a pre-fight drugs test. At that point the beer-barrelled Tomashek (alias Doughboy), a mere club fighter, had won 30 contests against no one of note in 46 outings. After letting his opponent stay in the fight for three rounds, when Morrison (226) began to open up in the fourth four heavy blows dropped the shaken Tomashek towards the end of the session. Back on his feet and allowed to stay the remaining few seconds, Tomashek, now badly swollen around both eyes, was ruled out of the fight by his seconds during the interval on the advice of the ringside doctor. Badly embarrassed, the WBO eventually overruled their supervisor in withdrawing title status on the grounds that, despite paying the sanction fee, Tomashek was not of championship standard.

1 October 1993. Lennox Lewis w rsc 7 Frank Bruno.
Venue: Arms Park, Cardiff, Wales. **Recognition:** WBC. **Referee:** Mickey Vann.
Fight Summary: Boxing at his best Bruno (238) made life extremely difficult for Lewis (229), especially in the third round when smashing in heavy punches that wobbled the champion, and at the end of the sixth he was on level terms despite being hurt moments earlier. At the start of the seventh both men were carrying swellings around their left eyes. Then Bruno, as he clubbed away at Lewis, was badly hurt by a wide left hook to the head. Retreating to the ropes in a defenceless state, with Bruno looking in a bad way and with Lewis piling in heavy punches, the referee stepped in to save the brave challenger on the 1.12 mark.

29 October 1993. Michael Bentt w rsc 1 Tommy Morrison.
Venue: Civic Centre, Tulsa, Oklahoma, USA. **Recognition:** WBO. **Referee:** Danny Campbell.
Fight Summary: Catching Bentt (226) heavily with a terrific left hook, with what was virtually the first punch of the fight, Morrison (226¾) walked in to the challenger looking to take him out. Unfortunately for Morrison, having left

himself wide open, Bentt was not slow to take advantage, knocking him down three times with solid rights before the contest was ended after just 93 seconds under the 'three knockdowns in a round' ruling. Following just ten more fights, Morrison, the grandnephew of the famous actor, John Wayne, tested HIV positive in Nevada, leaving his career in tatters.

6 November 1993. Evander Holyfield w pts 12 Riddick Bowe.
Venue: Caesar's Palace, Las Vegas, Nevada, USA. **Recognition:** IBF/WBA. **Referee:** Mills Lane.
Scorecards: 115-113, 115-114, 114-114.
Fight Summary: On a night when a paraglider crashed into the ring from out of the sky in the seventh round, causing a 22-minute delay, Holyfield (217) became only the third man in history to regain the heavyweight title. Although Bowe (246) had the power, Holyfield, boxing in a smart fashion, was looking good by the fifth, having taken the champion's best blows and cut him over the right eye. Prior to the enforced delay Holyfield seemed to be getting on top as Bowe, now cut between the eyes, was beginning to look ragged. Afterwards, Holyfield carried on where he left off, but in the ninth Bowe had his best round to date despite being unable to drop the challenger. As at the end of the eighth Bowe landed punches after the bell, one of which hurt Holyfield, but there was no warning. Holyfield sealed his victory when taking the fight to Bowe in the tenth and 11th, and even though the latter came back strongly in the final session he was unable to influence the result

19 March 1994. Herbie Hide w co 7 Michael Bentt.
Venue: New Den Football Ground, Bermondsey, London, England. **Recognition:** WBO. **Referee:** Paul Thomas.
Fight Summary: Looking overweight, the champion made his first defence in the country of his birth and proved to be a big disappointment when going down to defeat ten seconds from the end of the seventh. Right from the start Bentt (230) had trouble with the speed and movement of Hide (216), who made for a difficult target, and in the third round he was dropped and hurt by heavy right hands. Thereafter, the fight belonged to Hide. Although Bentt came back well in the seventh, towards the end of the round the challenger finally caught up with him when two solid rights sent him down to be counted out. The aftermath saw Bentt detained in hospital for several days after suffering cumulative concussive damage to the brain and being retired forthwith.

22 April 1994. Michael Moorer w pts 12 Evander Holyfield.
Venue: Caesar's Palace, Las Vegas, Nevada, USA. **Recognition:** IBF/WBA. **Referee:** Mills Lane.
Scorecards: 115-114, 116-112, 114-114.
Fight Summary: Sticking to the southpaw jab that Holyfield, the champion, was unable to find a way through, Moorer (214) did what he had to in order to win the title, apart from when he was put down in the second round by a couple of heavy right hooks. Up at 'five' but forced to take the mandatory 'eight' count, after Moorer got himself back in the fight he had Holyfield (214) cut over the left eye in the fifth and in trouble. At the end of the contest Moorer looked a good winner, but had one of the judges marked the second round correctly the result would have been a draw. Afterwards Holyfield claimed damage to his left shoulder, that necessitated a trip to the hospital, had hindered him badly.

6 May 1994. Lennox Lewis w rsc 8 Phil Jackson.
Venue: Boardwalk Convention Centre, Atlantic City, New Jersey, USA. **Recognition:** WBC. **Referee:** Arthur Mercante.
Fight Summary: After putting Jackson (218) down inside the opening 20 seconds with a left jab followed by a right cross, the champion continued to wear his rival down with the jab before striking again in the fifth. Having been knocked over by a heavy right to the head, Jackson got up at 'nine' only to be floored again by two more heavy blows after the bell had sounded. Despite no one apparently hearing the bell, Lewis (235) was deducted a point. From then on Lewis merely bided his time before ripping into Jackson in the eighth, dropping his man with a right uppercut-left hook-right hook, whereupon the referee stopped the fight on the 1.35 mark.

24 September 1994. Oliver McCall w rsc 2 Lennox Lewis.
Venue: The Arena, Wembley, London, England. **Recognition:** WBC. **Referee:** Lupe Garcia.
Fight Summary: Lewis (238) lost his title when stopped by McCall (231¼) 31 seconds into round two, in what was a big surprise in Britain. Despite being a big favourite to win, after Lewis was hurt in the first session when the pair

exchanged heavy rights he ended up with a swelling under the right eye prior to the bell. In the second, having just connected with a long right-left jab, Lewis walked in to McCall with his chin exposed, and after missing with a right he was smashed to the floor by a crunching left hook. Although Lewis got his feet, when he was stumbling around at the end of the mandatory 'eight' count the referee rightly concluded the action.

Coming back strongly, Lewis would eventually get another crack at his old title after beating Lionel Butler, Justin Fortune, Tommy Morrison and Ray Mercer. The Butler contest, which Lewis won by a fifth-round stoppage at the Arco Arena, Sacramento, California on 13 May 1995, was an official WBC title eliminator.

5 November 1994. George Foreman w co 10 Michael Moorer.
Venue: MGM Grand, Las Vegas, Nevada, USA. **Recognition:** IBF/WBA. **Referee:** Joe Cortez.
Fight Summary: Twenty years after losing the title to Muhammad Ali, Foreman (250), a 46-year-old grandfather, became the oldest man to win the heavyweight crown when he knocked out Moorer (222) at 2.03 of the tenth round. After nine almost one-sided rounds, with Moorer using the southpaw jab to knock Foreman's head back in virtually every round, and with the latter's face beginning to swell the end seemed imminent. However, most good judges thought it would be Moorer who would have his arm raised, but with the fight continuing in his favour in the tenth he was taken out by a crunching right to the jaw that gave him no chance of beating the count.

When Foreman was stripped of the WBA version of the championship in March 1995 for failing to take on the organisation's leading challenger, Tony Tucker and Bruce Seldon were selected to contest the vacancy.

11 March 1995. Riddick Bowe w co 6 Herbie Hide.
Venue: MGM Grand, Las Vegas, Nevada, USA. **Recognition:** WBO. **Referee:** Richard Steele.
Fight Summary: Having started brightly, winning the opening two rounds, the champion was dropped twice in the third, twice in the fourth, once in the fifth and twice more in the sixth, the final time seeing him counted out with 35 seconds of the session remaining. With a two stone advantage Bowe (241) made his power count from the third onwards, but Hide (214) was never disgraced and was always trying to fight back whenever he could.

8 April 1995. Bruce Seldon w rsc 7 Tony Tucker.
Venue: Caesar's Palace, Las Vegas, Nevada, USA. **Recognition:** WBA. **Referee:** Mills Lane.
Fight Summary: Contesting the vacant title, Seldon (236) produced his best-ever form against the favoured Tucker (243) despite carrying a bicep injury that affected his lead-up to the fight. Both men opened fast with solid punches and, although Seldon was badly hurt in the second round, by the third Tucker's face was becoming a mess, his left eye having been damaged earlier. With Seldon's work now the snappier, he took the next two sessions with accurate jabs paving the way for long rights to the body. Although Tucker won the sixth, after Seldon stormed through to take the seventh the former was pulled out of the contest during the interval by the referee on the advice of the doctor. Tucker, whose left eye was closed, had also suffered a broken nose.

8 April 1995. Oliver McCall w pts 12 Larry Holmes.
Venue: Caesar's Palace, Las Vegas, Nevada, USA. **Recognition:** WBC. **Referee:** Richard Steele.
Scorecards: 115-112, 114-113, 115-114.
Fight Summary: Trying to become a champion again at the age of 45 Holmes (236) gave it his best shot, but it was ultimately not enough as McCall (231), while showing his limitations, just about scraped home. With many of the rounds evenly contested up until the ninth the scores were about even, but in that session Holmes almost came apart at the seams when he was backed up for long periods and ended up with a cut left cheek. That was really the turning point, and although Holmes came back well to win the tenth on all of the cards it was not enough.

22 April 1995. George Foreman w pts 12 Axel Schulz.
Venue: MGM Grand, Las Vegas, Nevada, USA. **Recognition:** IBF. **Referee:** Joe Cortez.
Scorecards: 115-113, 115-113, 114-114.
Fight Summary: Making his first defence Foreman (256) appeared lucky to have got the decision over Schulz (221), having been often outboxed and outpunched by the lowly regarded German, who stuck to his game plan of jabbing

and moving. Extremely ragged at times, Foreman, who finished exhausted with a large swelling over the left eye, really showed his age in this one while Schulz appeared to be an improving fighter.

After refusing Schulz a rematch, Foreman relinquished his IBF version of the title in July, having just three more fights before retiring at the end of 1997 on being outpointed by Shannon Briggs. Following that, Schulz was signed up to meet Frans Botha to contest the vacancy.

17 June 1995. Riddick Bowe w co 6 Jorge Luis Gonzalez.
Venue: MGM Grand, Las Vegas, Nevada, USA. **Recognition:** WBO. **Referee:** Mills Lane.
Fight Summary: In what was his first defence, Bowe (243) dominated the fight from the opening bell, getting close to the 6' 7" Gonzalez (237) where he could measure him with heavy punches from both hands while giving him no room to work. The fourth round was so one-sided that one of the judges scored it as though there had been a knockdown. At the end of the fifth Gonzalez walked back to his corner with the air of a beaten man and when he was sent out for the sixth everyone watching could see that it was a pointless exercise. It came as no surprise when Gonzalez was counted out at 1.50 of the session after Bowe had toppled him with a crunching right immediately followed by a left hook and another right.

Bowe relinquished the title in late July to take a fight against Evander Holyfield for what was loosely termed the 'People's Championship'. Contested at Caesar's Palace, Las Vegas on 4 November, Holyfield, who had not wanted to fight under the jurisdiction of the WBO, was stopped by Bowe in round eight after both men had been on the floor. Following the fight Bowe reclaimed the WBO title as if by agreement but after a dispute with HBO, the television company, he relinquished it again in May 1996.

To decide the vacancy the WBO organised a contest between Henry Akinwande, the former undefeated Commonwealth and European champion, and Alexander Zolkin, the NABF champion, who would eventually be replaced by Jeremy Williams.

19 August 1995. Bruce Seldon w rsc 10 Joe Hipp.
Venue: MGM Grand, Las Vegas, Nevada, USA. **Recognition:** WBA. **Referee:** Richard Steele.
Fight Summary: Starting with the left jab, after Seldon (234) found Hipp (233) easy to hit with the punch he rarely moved up the gears. With both eyes closing fast from the middle stages of the fight, due to Seldon paying specific attention to them, it was just a matter of time before the southpaw challenger was pulled out. It came as no great shock when Hipp, having turned away from his opponent, was stopped at 1.47 of the tenth. As the first 'native American' to fight for the heavyweight title, Hipp, with both his eyes almost closed tight and a gash on his left cheek pouring blood at the finish, had tried his best but lacked the calibre to win the title.

2 September 1995. Frank Bruno w pts 12 Oliver McCall.
Venue: The Stadium, Wembley, London, England. **Recognition:** WBC. **Referee:** Tony Perez.
Scorecards: 117-111, 117-111, 115-113.
Fight Summary: Defending the title he had won from Britain's Lennox Lewis the American was expected to have too much for Bruno (247¾), and if he had fought with the same impetus as he showed in the last three rounds it might have been different. Stabbing out the left jab and following through with solid rights took Bruno into an early lead before he began to tire. However, McCall (234¾), not working hard enough, failed to take advantage of the situation when allowing Bruno to tie him up and fight his fight. All that changed in the tenth as McCall rallied desperately, but it was too little and too late.

9 December 1995. Frans Botha w pts 12 Axel Schulz.
Venue: Hanns Martin Schleyer Hall, Stuttgart, Germany. **Recognition:** IBF. **Referee:** Rudy Battle.
Scorecards: 116-112, 118-111, 113-115.
Fight Summary: Fighting for the title relinquished by George Foreman, although Schulz (222¾) was expected to win in front of his home fans it was Botha (227) who initially got the nod in what was a poor advert for a championship contest. There were no knockdowns and few highlights, and with both men fighting wildly at times Schulz finished with both eyes almost closed.

Having failed a post-fight drugs test Botha was eventually stripped of the IBF version of the championship by the courts in March 1996, the fight result being reclassified as a no contest. Following that, Schulz and Michael Moorer were selected to contest the vacant title.

16 March 1996. Mike Tyson w rsc 3 Frank Bruno.
Venue: MGM Grand, Las Vegas, Nevada, USA. **Recognition:** WBC. **Referee:** Mills Lane.
Fight Summary: Making his first defence Bruno (247) was looking for a better result than the one rendered in their previous contest, but he was to be disappointed once again. Being docked a point for holding and hitting in the second round, as Tyson (220) drove in blows to the body, summed up Bruno's performance. When he was badly cut over the left eye in the opener it merely added to Bruno's woes, and after 50 seconds of the third the referee stepped in to rescue the champion after several heavy punches followed by a left hook had deposited him on the bottom rope.

Tyson forfeited the WBC version of the championship in early September for failing to defend against the leading challenger, Lennox Lewis, and taking a fight against Bruce Seldon for the WBA title. Following that, Lewis was matched against Oliver McCall to contest the vacancy.

22 June 1996. Michael Moorer w pts 12 Axel Schulz.
Venue: Westphalia Stadium, Dortmund, Germany. **Recognition:** IBF. **Referee:** Bill Connors.
Scorecards: 116-113, 115-113, 113-115.
Fight Summary: Contesting the vacant title, and having his third crack at it, once again Schulz (222¾) failed to make the most of his opportunity when allowing Moorer (222¼) to control the fight at times with his southpaw jab. Schulz simply lacked the power to hurt Moorer, who had gained momentum by the fourth, and although the latter went off the boil he had plenty left when it mattered. Most of the best action took place in the final session, but it was not enough to get Schulz the win he wanted.

29 June 1996. Henry Akinwande w co 3 Jeremy Williams.
Venue: Fantasy Springs Casino, Indio, California, USA. **Recognition:** WBO. **Referee:** Raul Caiz.
Fight Summary: In a battle for the vacant title, once Akinwande (232) had got into his rhythm with the left jab and cross routine he began to pick Williams (216½) apart. Having come in at short notice for Alexander Zolkin, who withdrew five days earlier after suffering a cut in training, Williams gave it his best shot before he was counted out after 43 seconds of the third round. Leading up to the knockout Williams had hurt Akinwande with an overarm right, but on charging in to capitalise he was straightened up with a left jab before being dropped heavily by a short right to the jaw.

7 September 1996. Mike Tyson w rsc 1 Bruce Seldon.
Venue: MGM Grand, Las Vegas, Nevada, USA. **Recognition:** WBA. **Referee:** Richard Steele.
Fight Summary: Coming out fast, Tyson (219) stayed on the front foot as Seldon (229) retreated before having the champion over from a blow that barely landed. The referee, initially ruling it a slip, was forced to start the count when Seldon stayed down. Up again after taking the mandatory 'eight', Seldon was immediately sent down again from a left hook to the jaw, and although it seemed he would make it to his feet without too much difficulty the fight was stopped on the 1.49 mark when he fell back into the ropes.

9 November 1996. Evander Holyfield w rsc 11 Mike Tyson.
Venue: MGM Grand, Las Vegas, Nevada, USA. **Recognition:** WBA. **Referee:** Mitch Halpern.
Fight Summary: Relatively even at the end of the fifth round with Holyfield (215) beginning to pick up the pace, the fight changed dramatically in the sixth when the champion, cut over the left eye, was smashed to the floor by a crashing left hook immediately after an inspection. Although recovering, Tyson (222), now resorting to holding, was doing less and less as Holyfield seemed to make every punch count. In the tenth, following a tremendous right to the jaw, Holyfield rammed in over 20 unanswered blows, and although Tyson somehow managed to stay on his feet to get to the end of the session the next would be his last. Tearing into Holyfield at the start of the 11th, with Tyson soon being set up with jabs and hooks, when he was smashed up against the ropes by another big right the referee rescued him after just 37 seconds of the round had elapsed.

9 November 1996. Henry Akinwande w rsc 10 Alexander Zolkin.
Venue: MGM Grand, Las Vegas, Nevada, USA. **Recognition:** WBO. **Referee:** Richard Steele.
Fight Summary: Although missing more often than not with his left jab, reported to be a massive 86 inches, Akinwande (238) had too much power in his right for the southpaw Zolkin (235), knocking his challenger down in the fourth round before inflicting an inch-long cut over his right eye in the sixth. Zolkin, who had already been cut over the left eye in the third, was always running second best. And with the cuts worsening round after round the referee halted the contest with 28 seconds remaining of the tenth.

9 November 1996. Michael Moorer w rsc 12 Frans Botha.
Venue: MGM Grand, Las Vegas, Nevada, USA. **Recognition:** IBF. **Referee:** Mills Lane.
Fight Summary: Defending his title against the former undefeated IBF champion, Botha (224), Moorer (219) was soon on top, his southpaw jab leading the way. Picking up the pace in the third round Moorer staggered the South African, pouring in punches right through to the bell. Although Botha scored well with rights to head and body in the fifth and seventh, from there onwards he was second best, and after being floored twice in the 11th and being put under terrific pressure in the 12th the referee pulled him out 16 seconds into the final session.

11 January 1997. Henry Akinwande w pts 12 Scott Welch.
Venue: The Arena, Nashville, Tennessee, USA. **Recognition:** WBO. **Referee:** Bill Connors.
Scorecards: 120-108, 120-108, 119-110.
Fight Summary: An extremely poor fight saw Akinwande (232½) winning as he pleased against a challenger almost incapable of getting to him. Badly hurt in the sixth and again in the seventh, thereafter Welch (229) was only interested in survival. However, he nearly got lucky in the ninth when nailing Akinwande with a big left hook. Using his reach advantage to good effect Akinwande was winning easily, but lacking the power to finish Welch off the contest degenerated into one long maul right through to the final bell.

When Akinwande relinquished the WBO version of the title in February in order to obtain a crack at the WBC champion, Lennox Lewis, Herbie Hide was selected to meet Tony Tucker to decide the vacancy.

7 February 1997. Lennox Lewis w rsc 5 Oliver McCall.
Venue: Hilton Hotel, Las Vegas, Nevada, USA. **Recognition:** WBC. **Referee:** Mills Lane.
Fight Summary: Fighting for the title taken away from Mike Tyson, Lewis (251), out to avenge the defeat McCall (237) inflicted on him back in September 1994, was soon placing the left jab into the latter's face without any real response. After the third round McCall began circling around the ring, either clinching or walking away from Lewis. By the fourth he was openly crying, and after Lewis had driven him into a corner in the fifth the referee stopped the fight 55 seconds into the session. The general consensus was that McCall had suffered some kind of breakdown, but his trainer, Emanuel Steward, explained afterwards that he was completely rattled when unable to get inside due to Lewis's great strength and wanted to defuse his emotion.

29 March 1997. Michael Moorer w pts 12 Vaughn Bean.
Venue: Hilton Hotel, Las Vegas, Nevada, USA. **Recognition:** IBF. **Referee:** Mitch Halpern.
Scorecards: 116-113, 115-113, 114-114.
Fight Summary: Coming to the ring in a seemingly poor condition the southpaw champion should have beaten Bean (212) out of sight, but he only did what was needed to win against a man who spoiled his way through the fight. For much of the time Moorer (212) merely followed Bean around without doing too much, and although he opened up to some degree in the eighth it was back to plodding around the ring for the remainder of the contest. Afterwards, on an inspection of the scorecards, Bean said that he should have worked that little harder, while Teddy Atlas, Moorer's trainer, said that it would be the last time he worked with the champion.

28 June 1997. Evander Holyfield w disq 3 Mike Tyson.
Venue: MGM Grand, Las Vegas, Nevada, USA. **Recognition:** WBA. **Referee:** Mills Lane.
Fight Summary: After dominating the first two rounds with his better boxing, neither the champion nor the rest of the world for that matter would have expected Tyson (218) to have twice bitten him in the following session to get himself disqualified. Having started the third so well Tyson was still in the fight, but after a fierce struggle in a

clinch he bit a lump out of Holyfield's right ear. With Holyfield (218) jumping up and down in rage the referee took four minutes out to decide what to do next, eventually deducting two points from Tyson before sending them back to work for the final minute. At the end of the round following another bite, this time on Holyfield's left ear, Tyson was thrown out of the fight. The following day Tyson admitted that he had lost control after Holyfield had been allowed to butt him without getting a point's deduction, and that he had taken the law into his own hands. While Holyfield had an unsuccessful operation to stitch his piece of missing ear back, the Nevada State Boxing Commission revoked Tyson's licence indefinitely and fined him three million dollars.

28 June 1997. Herbie Hide w rsc 2 Tony Tucker.
Venue: Sports Village, Norwich, England. **Recognition:** WBO. **Referee:** Raul Caiz.
Fight Summary: In a contest for the vacant title it was Hide (214¾), overcoming a nervous start, who made all the running, and having knocked Tucker (243¼) down three times in the second round he enforced the stoppage win on the 'three knockdowns in a round' ruling with 15 seconds of the session remaining. Although being badly beaten by Riddick Bowe, Hide showed in this fight that he had recovered from that. It was also clear that, with added speed and power, Hide was now a force to be reckoned with.

12 July 1997. Lennox Lewis w disq 5 Henry Akinwande.
Venue: Caesar's Maximus Theatre, Lake Tahoe, California, USA. **Recognition:** WBC. **Referee:** Mills Lane.
Fight Summary: Outboxed in every round and deducted a point for repeated holding in the second, Akinwande (237½) was eventually disqualified at 2.34 of the fifth when clutching the champion like a limpet. Apart from putting Lewis (242) down on one knee in the third after a short burst of punching, which was missed by the referee for some reason or another, Akinwande had no appetite for the fight.

4 October 1997. Lennox Lewis w rsc 1 Andrew Golota.
Venue: Convention Centre, Atlantic City, New Jersey, USA. **Recognition:** WBC. **Referee:** Joe Cortez.
Fight Summary: Moving in quickly with the jab the champion immediately put pressure on Golota (244), two heavy rights to the head soon having him over for 'eight'. Golota, with no defence to speak of, was immediately in trouble again as Lewis (244) raked him with at least ten solid blows that sent him down, slumped in a corner. There was no way Golota could fight on even if he had managed to rise in time, the referee calling a halt after just 95 seconds. Afterwards, Lewis, whose game plan had been to get the fight over with quickly in case of fouling, felt that the referee had given Golota at least 20 seconds to recover from the first knockdown in order to keep the fight alive.

8 November 1997. Evander Holyfield w rtd 8 Michael Moorer.
Venue: Thomas & Mack Centre, Las Vegas, Nevada, USA. **Recognition:** IBF/WBA. **Referee:** Mitch Halpern.
Fight Summary: With both men putting up their titles there was much expectancy that the heavyweight division was not far away from being unified. Moorer (223), the IBF champion, made the better start when taking the opening two rounds and staggering Holyfield (214) on one occasion at least. However, the WBA champion turned things around in the third, despite being cut over the right eye from a clash of heads, and although Moorer remained a danger he was the one carrying the extra firepower. That became clear in the fifth when heavy combination punches had Moorer over for 'eight'. Following a less hectic sixth round, Holyfield then had his southpaw opponent down twice more before he was saved by the bell. The eighth round turned out to be the last. Slow to get going, Holyfield eventually put Moorer down twice more with heavy combinations doing the damage before the latter was retired by his corner at the end of the session.

28 March 1998. Lennox Lewis w rsc 5 Shannon Briggs.
Venue: Convention Centre, Atlantic City, New Jersey, USA. **Recognition:** WBC. **Referee:** Frank Cappuccino.
Fight Summary: Starting the better of the two, Briggs (228) had Lewis (243) badly hurt the opening round, a left hook and big right hands doing the damage, but with the ropes holding him up the champion was able to clear his head until the bell. Thereafter, the fight belonged to Lewis, who despite being hurt again in the third started to put his boxing together before having Briggs over from several rights to the head in the fourth. On getting up Briggs stormed back into the fray and, although being dropped again by a massive right to the head, he almost had Lewis going with a left hook that had him hanging on. By the fifth, with Lewis back in charge, a thumping right cross had

Briggs over again. Showing plenty of spirit Briggs got himself up, but after throwing himself to the floor following a wild swing the referee pulled him out of the contest on the 1.45 mark.

18 April 1998. Herbie Hide w rsc 1 Damon Reed.
Venue: Nynex Arena, Manchester, England. **Recognition:** WBO. **Referee:** Rudy Battle.
Fight Summary: One of the fastest ever finishes for the weight division saw the champion put Reed (199) down from a left hook almost before the fight had started, and the majority watching may well have thought that was it for the night. Getting up at 'seven' and given more time than normally allowed by a benevolent referee, Reed was immediately caught by a right-left combination before hanging on to Hide (219) as if his life depended on it. At that point, when it was seen that Reed had a terrible horizontal cut under his left eye, the referee stopped the fight with just 55 seconds on the clock.

19 September 1998. Evander Holyfield w pts 12 Vaughn Bean.
Venue: The Dome, Atlanta, Georgia, USA. **Recognition:** IBF/WBA. **Referee:** Brian Garry.
Scorecards: 117-110, 117-110, 116-111.
Fight Summary: After cruising through the opening four rounds Holyfield (217) found that he had a real live challenger in Bean (231), who came on strong in the next two sessions when nailing his man several times with big rights. The seventh saw Holyfield back in control, landing cleanly with solid shots to head and body, and although he dropped Bean with a left hook in the tenth he was unable to repeat the trick before having to settle for the points win.

26 September 1998. Herbie Hide w rsc 2 Willi Fischer.
Venue: Sports Village, Norwich, England. **Recognition:** WBO. **Referee:** Joe Cortez.
Fight Summary: Having allowed the challenger to make the early running, by the end of the opening round Hide (220) was picking his shots with precision. Not wasting much time in the second Hide ripped into Fischer (231), dropping him after a battery of blurring punches had got home inside the first 20 seconds. Although Fischer made it to his feet, still dazed he went down again. When Fischer went down for the third time the referee had seen enough, stopping the contest 64 seconds into the session with the German still on his knees.

26 September 1998. Lennox Lewis w pts 12 Zeljko Mavrovic.
Venue: Mohegan Sun Casino, Uncasville, Connecticut, USA. **Recognition:** WBC. **Referee:** Frank Cappuccino.
Scorecards: 117-111, 119-109, 117-112.
Fight Summary: Boxing in a laboured fashion the champion found himself unable to stow away the tough Mavrovic (214¼), a former European titleholder, who finished the contest with a cut over the right eye but still standing. Occasionally Lewis (243) would let the punches go but unable to move the tough Croatian he often ran out of steam. Lewis's best punch was the right uppercut, a fact admitted by Mavrovic, and he opened up a cut under the challenger's chin that would require five stitches. Finishing the fight with both eyes swollen, it was not one of Lewis's better nights.

13 March 1999. Evander Holyfield drew 12 Lennox Lewis.
Venue: Madison Square Garden, Manhattan, NYC, New York, USA. **Recognition:** IBF/WBA/WBC. **Referee:** Arthur Mercante Jnr.
Scorecards: 115-113, 113-116, 115-115.
Fight Summary: In a battle to decide three titles, Lewis (246), the WBC champion, made the brighter start when taking the first two rounds and, although the contest never reached the heights, to most of the qualified onlookers it appeared that his use of the left jab had won him the decision by at least nine rounds to three according to *Boxing News*. Even though Lewis never totally dominated Holyfield (215), the latter rarely looked convincing. And when the pair fell to the floor together at the start of the seventh it appeared that the American was there for the taking. Both men finished the fight with damage to their left eyes and, while there had been no knockdowns and exciting action for most of the fight, there was a stunned silence when the decision was announced. According to the judges it was a fight of two halves, with Holyfield finishing the stronger. Afterwards, Larry O'Connell, the English judge who scored it 115-115, conceded that Lewis might have done enough in hindsight, but the American

woman judge, Eugenia Williams, actually had Holyfield winning 115-113. Further to an investigation into all aspects of the fight, the people involved were told that a return was not an option but a must.

26 June 1999. Vitali Klitschko w co 2 Herbie Hide.
Venue: London Arena, Millwall, London, England. **Recognition:** WBO. **Referee:** Genaro Rodriguez.
Fight Summary: Although Hide (221) took the opening session against the 6'8" Klitschko (245¾) by dint of speedy boxing, the warning signs were already there at the end of the round. Taking the middle of the ring in the second, Klitschko merely waited for the champion to make a mistake, and after jumping in and missing the target a couple of times a chopping right put Hide down. Forced to take the mandatory 'eight' Hide was soon back in the fray, but having faltered when in position to throw a punch he was dropped heavily for the full count on the 1.14 mark after taking a smashing right to the left ear.

9 October 1999. Vitali Klitschko w rsc 3 Ed Mahone.
Venue: The Arena, Oberhausen, Germany. **Recognition:** WBO. **Referee:** Rudy Battle.
Fight Summary: Controlling the fight from the start with stabbing left jabs and left hooks, the champion was merely biding his time before laying into Mahone (229¼) with a vengeance in the third round. With the crowd looking for more action, Klitschko (246) floored Mahone, having belted him with a mixture of hooks, uppercuts and right crosses. Despite taking advantage of the mandatory count on getting up at 'five', Mahone was soon put down again after Klitschko opened up with hooks and uppercuts from both hands. And at 1.45 of the session the referee stopped the fight when it was clear that Mahone was through for the night.

13 November 1999. Lennox Lewis w pts 12 Evander Holyfield.
Venue: Thomas & Mack Centre, Las Vegas, Nevada, USA. **Recognition:** IBF/WBA/WBC. **Referee:** Mitch Halpern.
Scorecards: 116-112, 117-111, 115-113.
Fight Summary: This time round there were no mistakes made by the judges, all three of them voting for Lewis (242). There were no knockdowns but Lewis's jab was again the deciding factor and, although Holyfield (217) did well when outfighting the WBC champion on the inside in the middle rounds and banged in the occasional hooks to the head, he was unable to sustain it. Most of the press felt that the contest was not as one-sided as their previous one and even though the IBF declared their title to be vacant following a row over licensing fees the matter was soon sorted out.

Lewis forfeited the WBA version of the title on 13 April 2000 when deciding to meet Michael Grant rather than their leading contender, John Ruiz, who was then selected to meet Holyfield to decide the vacancy.

11 December 1999. Vitali Klitschko w rtd 9 Obed Sullivan.
Venue: Alsterdorfer Sports Hall, Hamburg, Germany. **Recognition:** WBO. **Referee:** Joe Cortez.
Fight Summary: Retaining his title for the second time, Klitschko (244¾) dominated the punch stats when it was revealed that Sullivan (227¾) landed only 11 of the 283 thrown. Klitschko found Sullivan an easy target, his stabbing left leads followed by crashing rights taking a lot out of the latter. However, Sullivan, with his right eye closed, made it into the seventh and boxed on for three more rounds before being retired by his corner at the end of the ninth. This was the first time that Klitschko had gone beyond six rounds.

1 April 2000. Chris Byrd w rtd 9 Vitali Klitschko.
Venue: Estrel Convention Centre, Berlin, Germany. **Recognition:** WBO. **Referee:** Genaro Rodriguez.
Fight Summary: While Byrd (210¾) was a difficult target to hit and made Klitschko (244¼) miss repeatedly, the crowd were amazed when the champion was retired on his stool with the tenth almost ready to get underway. Although Klitschko had not been at his best he was well ahead at that stage of the fight, having won seven of the nine rounds contested, but had failed to shift his southpaw opponent with the occasional heavy right. Afterwards, the reason given for Klitschko's retirement was that he had suffered a rotator cuff injury to his left shoulder, something that probably occurred in the third round.

29 April 2000. Lennox Lewis w co 2 Michael Grant.
Venue: Madison Square Garden, Manhattan, NYC, New York, USA. **Recognition:** IBF/WBC. **Referee:** Arthur Mercante Jnr.
Fight Summary: In what was reckoned to be the heaviest fight in the history of the sport, Lewis (247) dropped Grant (260) with a crunching right uppercut to the jaw inside the first couple of minutes. Back on his feet but in a daze, the challenger was given a standing count after he had been smashed into the ropes by four more solid blows. And before the round ended he was flattened by another terrific right. Saved by the bell, Grant should have been pulled out of the fight there and then, but having come out for the second round and been swamped by one uppercut after another he was finally put down for the full count with 21 seconds of the session remaining.

15 July 2000. Lennox Lewis w rsc 2 Frans Botha.
Venue: London Arena, Millwall, London, England. **Recognition:** IBF/WBC. **Referee:** Larry O'Connell.
Fight Summary: The champion immediately went on the attack at the start of the fight, using the jab to set Botha (236) up for right hands, and before the session was over the latter had somehow survived a couple of terrific shots that threatened to take him out. Still working with a spearing left jab Lewis (250) picked up the pace in the second, having Botha down and through the ropes after two or three heavy punches got home. The finishing blows were not long in coming. When they did arrive the final right almost lifted Botha off the ground, and at 2.39 of the session the referee stopped the fight without taking up the count.

12 August 2000. Evander Holyfield w pts 12 John Ruiz.
Venue: Paris Hotel, Las Vegas, Nevada, USA. **Recognition:** WBA. **Referee:** Richard Steele.
Scorecards: 116-112, 114-113, 114-113.
Fight Summary: Contesting the vacant title Holyfield (221) appeared to be lucky to get the decision despite hurting Ruiz (224) several times, especially when the latter was left-hooked to the floor in the 12th round without a count being administered. After Ruiz went to the floor in the tenth, complaining that he had been hit low he was allowed a few seconds rest, but when the video was revisited it seemed that the punch had been perfectly legal. According to the scorecards, two judges gave Holyfield a 10-8 round in the third when he had Ruiz in trouble from a big right to the head, and if they had each correctly scored it 10-9 the result would have been a draw. It came as no surprise when the WBA ordered a rematch.

14 October 2000. Wladimir Klitschko w pts 12 Chris Byrd.
Venue: The Arena, Cologne, Germany. **Recognition:** WBO. **Referee:** Lou Moret.
Scorecards: 120-106, 118-108, 119-107.
Fight Summary: Up against the man who beat his brother to take the title, Klitschko (238) gained revenge for the family when dethroning Byrd (213½) by a wide margin. Following a nervous start Klitschko began to use his height and reach advantage to good effect, keeping his southpaw opponent at bay with long left jabs while occasionally sending over heavy right hands. For most of the fight Byrd seemed at a loss as how to deal with Klitschko, and the contest could easily have been halted after he was dropped in the ninth and 11th, his father wanting the fight to be stopped. However, Klitschko missed the opportunity of a stoppage win by not forcing the action in the last two rounds, Byrd, cut over the right eye, keeping out of danger to make it to the final bell.

11 November 2000. Lennox Lewis w pts 12 David Tua.
Venue: Mandalay Bay Resort & Casino, Las Vegas, Nevada, USA. **Recognition:** IBF/WBC. **Referee:** Joe Cortez.
Scorecards: 117-111, 119-109, 118-110.
Fight Summary: Towering above Tua (245), who had boasted that he would take the title, Lewis (249) spent all night smacking his left hand into the challenger's face to make it one of the easiest wins of his career. Although the crowd called for more action, Lewis just got on with the job of retaining his title while taking no risks. There were no knockdowns, and Tua, having hardly laid a glove on Lewis, finished the contest with his left eye badly swollen and bleeding.

3 March 2001. John Ruiz w pts 12 Evander Holyfield.
Venue: Mandalay Bay Resort & Casino, Las Vegas, Nevada, USA. **Recognition:** WBA. **Referee:** Joe Cortez.
Scorecards: 116-110, 115-111, 114-111.

Fight Summary: Ruiz (227) made a better start than the champion, scoring well with the jab, and he appeared to be clear at the end of the fifth despite having a bad cut over the left eye that was caused by an accidental butt in the fourth. With Holyfield (217) not yet out of it, by the end of the ninth he had begun to close the gap. The fight effectively ended for Holyfield, though, in the tenth when he had a point deducted for going low, which allowed Ruiz to take time out. Refreshed, Ruiz came on strongly in the 11th, a left-right putting Holyfield down for 'five', and although the champion, now cut on the left eye, somehow lasted the round out and made it to the final bell the victory would not be his.

24 March 2001. Wladimir Klitschko w rsc 2 Derrick Jefferson.
Venue: Rudi Sedlmayer Hall, Munich, Germany. **Recognition:** WBO. **Referee:** Genaro Rodriguez.
Fight Summary: Showing impressive hand-speed and control, the champion soon had Jefferson (260) in trouble and on the floor from a left-right to the head. The American might have made it to the bell to end the opening round but it was clear even at that stage he would not last much longer. Down for the second time from a crashing right to the jaw in the second, Jefferson got up only to be bludgeoned to the floor again by Klitschko (246), whereupon the referee called a halt, timed at 2.09.

22 April 2001. Hasim Rahman w co 5 Lennox Lewis.
Venue: Big Top Arena, Carnival City, Brakpan, South Africa. **Recognition:** IBF/WBC. **Referee:** Daniel Van de Wiele.
Fight Summary: Despite Lewis (253½) scoring well with the left hand, the warning signs were there for him early on as Rahman (238) kept low to avoid right hands and jabbed well to the body. When Lewis crashed in a terrific body shot at the end of the third it seemed as though all was well, but in the fourth Rahman picked up the pace to win the round, and at times ominously backed up the champion with rights through the middle. In the fifth, when Lewis came out firing after Rahman appeared to be having difficulty with his left eye, which was now swollen and cut, it looked as though the latter was in real trouble. However, Lewis seemed to switch off, his left held low. Inexplicably, Lewis allowed the 20-1 underdog to jab him across the ring, and with his back to the ropes, a tremendous right to the jaw sent him down to be counted out on the 2.32 mark. In suffering a loss of credibility it was clear that Lewis had not been in the best of condition, either mentally or physically, and had taken Rahman far too lightly.

4 August 2001. Wladimir Klitschko w rsc 6 Charles Shufford.
Venue: Mandalay Bay Resort & Casino, Las Vegas, Nevada, USA. **Recognition:** WBO. **Referee:** Kenny Bayless.
Fight Summary: Having knocked Shufford (234) down in the second and third rounds with solid rights to the head after setting him up with left jabs, the champion was in total control at the start of the fourth. From then on it ceased to be a fight as Shufford went on the back foot while Klitschko (241) followed him around. The contest followed the same pattern in the sixth before coming to life when Klitschko caught Shufford, trapped in a corner, with a big left hook that sent him down, his back against the ring post. Surprisingly, Shufford was up at 'eight', but on closer inspection the referee stopped the fight with five seconds of the session remaining.

17 November 2001. Lennox Lewis w co 4 Hasim Rahman.
Venue: Mandalay Bay Resort & Casino, Las Vegas, Nevada, USA. **Recognition:** IBF/WBC. **Referee:** Joe Cortez.
Fight Summary: After blasting his man to defeat in South Africa to win the title Rahman (238) was expected to do more of the same, but with Lewis (253½) well prepared this time he was unable to exact any kind of superiority, being completely outboxed while the fight lasted. The master of cutting down the distance and getting his punches off Lewis was content to outbox Hasim (or 'Has-Been' as Lewis continually referred to him as), and when the opportunity presented itself he took it. Having landed a solid right hand in the third, that had a marked effect on the champion, it was merely a matter of time before Lewis caught up with Rahman. Sure enough, early in the fourth after the left had done its job, when another long right landed flush on the jaw Rahman crashed to the floor to be counted out at 1.29 of the round.

15 December 2001. John Ruiz drew 12 Evander Holyfield.
Venue: Foxwoods Resort Casino, Mashantucket, Connecticut, USA. **Recognition:** WBA. **Referee:** Steve Smoger.
Scorecards: 115-113, 112-116, 114-114.

Fight Summary: In what was the third meeting between the pair, because they knew each other so well it rarely hit the heights. Still, it was the 39-year-old Holyfield (219) who appeared to do the better work, landing more quality blows at least, while the champion plodded along as if there was no championship belt at stake. How one of the judges had Ruiz (232) ahead by seven rounds to five beggared belief, but it allowed him to retain his title if nothing else.

16 March 2002. Wladimir Klitschko w rsc 8 Frans Botha.
Venue: Hanns Martin Schleyer Hall or Hall, Stuttgart, Germany. **Recognition:** WBO. **Referee:** Genaro Rodriguez.
Fight Summary: Although Botha (241½) tried hard to get through the defences of the 6'6" champion he was up against it right from the opening bell as jabs rained in on him. By the fifth both of Botha's eyes were beginning to close, and prior to the end of the seventh he had been staggered several times by heavy blows from both hands. The end was in sight. After Botha had been smashed to the floor by a Klitschko (242) left hook, which came on the back of a cracking right that had sent him stumbling around the ring, the referee concluded the contest after just 48 seconds of the eighth despite the South African being back on his feet.

8 June 2002. Lennox Lewis w co 8 Mike Tyson.
Venue: The Pyramid, Memphis, Tennessee, USA. **Recognition:** IBF/WBC/The Ring. **Referee:** Eddie Cotton.
Fight Summary: This was the one everybody had been waiting for; the defining fight in Lewis's career and the one that would tell us whether Tyson (234½) was a spent force. Once the fight was underway it was clear that all the questions were going to be answered, Tyson being unable to respond to the Lewis (249¼) left jab. Then, with his right eye cut in the third Tyson was beginning to be gradually taken apart. Pushed over in the fourth the former 'great' was becoming desperate as he was being completely outboxed with no idea of how to handle it. Nearly taken out in the seventh, with the bell coming to his rescue, a left uppercut smashed all remaining resistance out of him in the eighth. After taking a count of 'eight' a tremendous right hand from Lewis landed on Tyson's jaw, smashing him to the canvas where he was counted out at the 2.25 mark. Lewis was also defending *The Ring* Championship Belt he had been awarded at the end of 2001.

Lewis gave up the IBF Championship Belt on 5 September rather than defend against Chris Byrd, who was then selected to meet Evander Holyfield to decide the vacancy. On 1 June, Holyfield had won a WBA eliminating contest when beating Hasim Rahman, thanks to an eighth-round technical decision.

29 June 2002. Wladimir Klitschko w rsc 6 Ray Mercer.
Venue: Trump Taj Mahal, Atlantic City, New Jersey, USA. **Recognition:** WBO. **Referee:** Randy Neumann.
Fight Summary: At 41 years of age Mercer (228) had obviously seen better days, and after testing the champion's jabs, hooks and right hands in the opening session a double left hook put him down for just the second time in his career. Although he got up Mercer was in real trouble as Klitschko (243) hit him with all manner of blows, including a supposed 81 scoring shots in the second round. In the third Mercer began to get his own jab going, but he was soon under pressure again. With his eyes beginning to swell up, Mercer was badly wobbled by left-rights in both the fourth and fifth before a bad cut opened up over his right eye. Having sensed that the end might not be far away, Klitschko ripped into Mercer in the sixth, and after sending the latter crashing into the ropes from a big right to the head the referee stopped the fight in his favour on the 1.08 mark.

27 July 2002. John Ruiz w disq 10 Kirk Johnson.
Venue: Mandalay Bay Resort & Casino, Las Vegas, Nevada, USA. **Recognition:** WBA. **Referee:** Joe Cortez.
Fight Summary: A poor fight with far too much holding and lack of control, when Johnson (238) was docked a point for going low as early as the opening round the pattern was set. Both men went with the left jab, but by the end of the third it seemed that Ruiz (233) was getting on top. When Johnson had Ruiz over in the fourth from another low blow and was allowed to get away with it, the latter, on being told to get on with it butted the Canadian. In the seventh Johnson again went low with the left hook, dropping Ruiz for the third time before being deducted another point. Taking a four-minute break to recover, much against the referee's better judgement, Ruiz got going again, almost having Johnson over in the ninth only to be pulled down himself. Then, at the end of the session the challenger was chopped down by a rabbit punch, but no count was taken up. The tenth started with

Ruiz well on top before coming to an end on the 2.17 mark when Johnson was disqualified after going low again with another left hook.

7 December 2002. Wladimir Klitschko w rtd 10 Jameel McCline.
Venue: Mandalay Bay Resort & Casino, Las Vegas, Nevada, USA. **Recognition:** WBO. **Referee:** Jay Nady.
Fight Summary: With Klitschko (240) dictating the fight from the third round onwards, his left jab landing at will, the champion had started to take McCline (263) apart by the seventh before finally stepping up the pace in the tenth. Wobbling McCline with several lefts and rights Klitschko put him down with a big left, and although the challenger made it to his feet and was saved by the bell his corner retired him at the end of the session. McCline had given it his best shot, but had been outclassed.

14 December 2002. Chris Byrd w pts 12 Evander Holyfield.
Venue: Boardwalk Hall, Atlantic City, New Jersey, USA. **Recognition:** IBF. **Referee:** Randy Neumann.
Scorecards: 116-112, 117-111, 117-111.
Fight Summary: Fighting for the title that Lennox Lewis gave up, the southpaw Byrd (214) was the first into action when stabbing in right jabs. Although Holyfield (220) was never really hurt he admitted to being constantly kept off balance by the punch and struggled to get close. Occasionally Holyfield got past the right hand to bang in punches of his own, notably in the fourth and fifth, but with it being a rarity Byrd was soon back to flicking in jabs and following up with solid rights to head and body. Stepping up the pace in the tenth Byrd seemed to be punching harder, while the 40-year-old Holyfield was finding it difficult to close his rival down. Even when he did it had no effect. The punch stats told the story of the fight, Byrd landing 154 jabs to Holyfield's three.

1 March 2003. Roy Jones w pts 12 John Ruiz.
Venue: Thomas & Mack Centre, Las Vegas, Nevada, USA. **Recognition:** WBA. **Referee:** Jay Nady.
Scorecards: 117-111, 116-112, 118-110.
Fight Summary: Moving up from the light heavyweight division, where he was still the WBA/WBC champion, Jones (193) was looking to add the WBA heavyweight title to his collection when taking on the champion, Ruiz (226). There were no knockdowns, but the much lighter Jones simply outclassed Ruiz in at least eight of the rounds, snapping in left jabs and left-rights to head and body before moving away. It was only when he took a breather that Ruiz did his best work but never able to pin Jones down to do any damage he finished the fight minus his title, his pride dented and carrying a broken nose.

Following this, after Ruiz won the 'interim' title when beating Hasim Rahman on points over 12 rounds at the Boardwalk Hall, Atlantic City, New Jersey on 13 December, he was appointed champion in February 2004 on Jones deciding to go back to the light heavyweights.

8 March 2003. Corrie Sanders w rsc 2 Wladimir Klitschko.
Venue: Preussag Arena, Hannover, Germany. **Recognition:** WBO. **Referee:** Genaro Rodriguez.
Fight Summary: At the age of 37 no one saw Sanders (225) as a future champion, but after knocking Klitschko (242½) down twice in the opening round and twice more in the second for a stoppage win inside three minutes and 20 seconds the WBO title was his. Klitschko never really recovered from the first knockdown, a thudding southpaw left to the jaw, and after he had been floored for the fourth time, with blood pouring from a cut over his left eye, the referee called a halt without bothering to pick up the count.

Sanders was next due to make a defence against Lamon Brewster on 18 October but instead handed his belt back early in October unhappy with the demands the WBO placed on him. As a consequence, Brewster was matched to meet Klitschko in a fight for the vacant title.

21 June 2003. Lennox Lewis w rsc 6 Vitali Klitschko.
Venue: Staples Centre, Los Angeles, California, USA. **Recognition:** WBC/The Ring. **Referee:** Lou Moret.
Fight Summary: Looking overweight and sluggish, Lewis (256½), turning in one of his worst championship performances, would surely have lost his two championship belts had it not been for Klitschko (248) suffering from an horrendous cut around his left eye from the third round, an injury which eventually necessitated 60 stitches. At

the end of the sixth the ringside doctor failed to let the challenger continue, the fight being called off without going to the scorecards because the initial punch that did the damage was deemed to be legal.

When Lewis announced his retirement on 6 February 2004, Corrie Sanders was nominated to meet Klitschko for the vacant WBC title and *The Ring* Championship Belt.

20 September 2003. Chris Byrd w pts 12 Fres Oquendo.
Venue: Mohegan Sun Arena, Uncasville, Connecticut, USA. **Recognition:** IBF. **Referee:** Eddie Cotton.
Scorecards: 115-113, 116-112, 117-111.
Fight Summary: Making his first defence Byrd (211¾) looked extremely lucky to have retained the title after Oquendo (224) had worked out how to deal with his slippery southpaw style as early as the fourth round. There was never a great deal between them, but by the seventh HBO's unofficial judge, Harold Lederman, had Oquendo four points ahead. Although Byrd improved a bit from thereon in he continued to get caught far too often by the right hand and fast combinations, and Oquendo had him over with a left-right at the start of the 12th only for the referee to call it a trip. With this being the fourth time in the contest that Byrd had been down without a count administered, it merely added to the general anger of the crowd when the decision was announced.

10 April 2004. Lamon Brewster w rsc 5 Wladimir Klitschko.
Venue: Mandalay Bay Resort & Casino, Las Vegas, Nevada, USA. **Recognition:** WBO. **Referee:** Robert Byrd.
Fight Summary: Contesting the vacant title, Brewster (226) came back from the brink of defeat to beat the former champion. For the opening four rounds Klitschko (243) found Brewster an easy target for the left jab and straight rights, and in the fourth he had the latter over from a solid right to the head. Although the referee saw it as a slip, moments later when Klitschko hammered in another terrific right to the head Brewster was counted upon. Up at 'seven' Brewster came right back at Klitschko in the fifth. And with the big man now running out of wind he was given a standing count after taking a left hook that knocked him into the ropes. When Klitschko, who could barely stand up at this stage of the fight, fell to his knees virtually drained of energy, the referee stopped the contest just after the bell rang to end the session.

17 April 2004. Chris Byrd drew 12 Andrew Golota.
Venue: Madison Square Garden, Manhattan, NYC, New York, USA. **Recognition:** IBF. **Referee:** Randy Neumann.
Scorecards: 113-115, 115-113, 114-114.
Fight Summary: Weighing in at his lightest for quite a while the southpaw champion scored well at times with the jab, but spent too much time allowing Golota (237½) to back him up on the ropes in an effort to tire him out. As there was never much between them at any stage a draw appeared to be a fair reflection. Only in the last two rounds did the action warm up, with punches going back and forth, and with Byrd (210½) taking a few hefty wallops he ended the contest nursing a badly swollen left eye.

17 April 2004. John Ruiz w rsc 11 Fres Oquendo.
Venue: Madison Square Garden, Manhattan, NYC, New York, USA. **Recognition:** WBA. **Referee:** Wayne Kelly.
Fight Summary: Ruiz (240) failed to impress when making his first defence after being appointed champion, and although he was just about ahead at the time of the stoppage there was not much in it. Just when it looked as though Ruiz might get the job done in the ninth when he hurt his challenger with a cracking left hook to the body, Oquendo (222½) came back well in the tenth, picking up points with single jabs. Carrying on where he left off Oquendo threatened to take the last two sessions and the decision in the 11th, but after Ruiz had unleashed a sustained attack of blows to the head that were unanswered the referee stopped the fight on the 2.33 mark.

24 April 2004. Vitali Klitschko w rsc 8 Corrie Sanders.
Venue: Staples Centre, Los Angeles, California, USA. **Recognition:** WBC/The Ring. **Referee:** Jon Schorle.
Fight Summary: With the vacant WBC title and *The Ring* Championship Belt up for grabs, and aiming to beat the man who defeated his brother, Klitschko (245) made a sloppy start when caught by some good punches as Sanders (235) looked to end early. From there onwards though Klitschko took control, and although he had a few shaky moments along the way he was gradually wearing his southpaw opponent down, so much so in the fifth round that the South African seemed lucky to remain on his feet. In the sixth and seventh Sanders barely showed as Klitschko

continued to grind him down. And in the eighth with just four seconds of the session remaining the referee stopped the fight. At that point, Sanders, cut over the left eye, was on the ropes taking a pounding and unable to fight back.

4 September 2004. Lamon Brewster w pts 12 Kali Meehan.
Venue: Mandalay Bay Resort & Casino, Las Vegas, Nevada, USA. **Recognition:** WBO. **Referee:** Jay Nady.
Scorecards: 115-113, 114-113, 113-114.
Fight Summary: Having been the champion's sparring partner a short while earlier, Meehan (236), not expected to win the title, was rated a 10-1 outsider prior to the fight. Struggling with a damaged nose from the second round, at the start of the eighth Brewster (227) was only marginally ahead, both men having landed with some heavy shots. With Meehan attacking non-stop in that session, Brewster was forced to take a beating, coming close to being stopped. It was clear in the ninth that Meehan had almost punched himself out, but he was still dangerous. However, having conserved some energy Brewster rallied to win three of the last four sessions, a late surge that allowed him to squeeze in front of the tough Australian.

13 November 2004. Chris Byrd w pts 12 Jameel McCline.
Venue: Madison Square Garden, Manhattan, NYC, New York, USA. **Recognition:** IBF. **Referee:** Wayne Kelly.
Scorecards: 115-112, 114-113, 112-114.
Fight Summary: In a battle between friends, McCline (270) got away the better, dropping the southpaw champion in the second round with a solid right to the head and winning at least four of the opening six rounds. Things began to go better for Byrd (214), who was outweighed by 56 pounds, from the sixth onwards as McCline tired. With Byrd clawing back the deficit, even though McCline had an excellent tenth there was little between them at the final bell.

13 November 2004. John Ruiz w pts 12 Andrew Golota.
Venue: Madison Square Garden, Manhattan, NYC, New York, USA. **Recognition:** WBA. **Referee:** Randy Neumann.
Scorecards: 114-111, 113-112, 114-111.
Fight Summary: Following a scrappy opening round, when the champion walked into Golota (238) in the second he was promptly floored by a countering right. Quickly on his feet, moments later Ruiz (239) was pulled down by Golota, being punched while he was still on the floor, and adding insult to injury it counted as a knockdown. Coming back well when taking the third Ruiz was then docked a point in the fourth for rabbit punching prior to picking up the pace to take the next four sessions in what had become a boring spectacle. By the ninth, still landing the better blows, even though Ruiz was exhausted Golota was unable to take advantage until he dropped the champion after both men had carried on punching following the bell to end the tenth. Obviously not counted as a knockdown, Golota, now cut over the right eye, took the 11th before Ruiz came on strongly in the final session with solid combinations to make sure of retaining his title.

11 December 2004. Vitali Klitschko w rsc 8 Danny Williams.
Venue: Mandalay Bay Resort & Casino, Las Vegas, Nevada, USA. **Recognition:** WBC/The Ring. **Referee:** Jay Nady.
Fight Summary: Although he showed great bravery in the face of a one-way thrashing the challenger had no answers to the hard-punching Klitschko (250), being put down four times before the referee had seen enough and brought matters to a halt at 1.26 of the eighth round. If nothing else, Williams (270), who strangely came in at a weight that hindered his speed, certainly disproved the British 'horizontal' heavyweight theory prevalent in America over the years. However, courage itself does not win contests and the man famous for beating Mike Tyson a few months earlier had to be rescued, almost from himself. Both of Klitschko's championship belts were on the line in this one.

Due to defend *The Ring* Championship Belt and WBC titles on 12 November 2005 against Hasim Rahman, who had outpointed Monte Barrett over 12 rounds at the United Centre, Chicago, Illinois on 13 August 2005 to win the vacant WBC 'interim' title, Klitschko announced his retirement on 8 November 2005, having pulled out of the fight on suffering an injury to his right knee. Just days later it was announced that Rahman was the new WBC champion.

30 April 2005. James Toney w pts 12 John Ruiz.
Venue: Madison Square Garden, Manhattan, NYC, New York, USA. **Recognition:** WBA. **Referee:** Steve Smoger.
Scorecards: 115-112, 116-111, 116-111.
Fight Summary: Controlling the pace of the fight for the opening six rounds, despite being rocked by a left hook in the fifth, the champion came under more pressure from Toney (231) in the seventh when dropped by a similar blow. Complaining, to no avail, that he had been tripped, Ruiz (244) was edged out in most of the remaining rounds as Toney, having conserved his energy, scored nearly all the punches that mattered from then on. In the ninth Ruiz was forced to take several heavy rights to the jaw before suffering the same again in the 11th, and although trying to pull the coals out of the fire in the 12th it was clear that Toney had done more than enough.

When the result was accorded no contest status by the NYSAC on 11 May after Toney failed the post-fight drugs test, Ruiz was reinstated as champion on 17 May in line with WBA rules.

21 May 2005. Lamon Brewster w rsc 1 Andrew Golota.
Venue: United Centre, Chicago, Illinois, USA. **Recognition:** WBO. **Referee:** Genaro Rodriguez.
Fight Summary: The champion came out fast, throwing big punches, and within ten seconds he had Golota (248) down with a cracking left hook. And although the Pole got up at 'five', moments later he was dropped again by a similar punch. Again, Golota was up at 'five', but looking in poor condition another solid left hook to the temple from Brewster (224) sent him crashing to the floor. Getting up groggily, when it was obvious that Golota could not continue the referee stopped the fight with just 53 seconds on the clock.

28 September 2005. Lamon Brewster w rsc 9 Luan Krasniqi.
Venue: Color Line Arena, Hamburg, Germany. **Recognition:** WBO. **Referee:** Jose Rivera.
Fight Summary: Having won virtually every round by the end of the seventh, using the left-right effectively, Krasniqi (224¾) came unstuck in the eighth when the champion dropped him with a battery of solid hooks. To catch up with his rival Brewster (228¼) had been forced to take plenty of leather on the way in, but it proved to be worth it. Amazingly, despite failing to beat the count immediately prior to the bell, Krasniqi was allowed to return to his corner to continue the fight. Although the challenger came out for the ninth defiantly, even landing a solid right uppercut, Brewster now had him in his sights. Nothing was going to stop Brewster now, and having decked Krasniqi with a crashing right to the head the fight was over on the 2.48 mark after the referee reacted to the towel being thrown in by the latter's corner.

1 October 2005. Chris Byrd w pts 12 DaVarryl Williamson.
Venue: The Events Centre, Reno, Nevada, USA. **Recognition:** IBF. **Referee:** Vic Drakulich.
Scorecards: 115-113, 116-112, 116-112.
Fight Summary: Defending his title for the fourth time Byrd (213) was up against a former sparring partner in Williamson (225), the pair being constantly booed for providing so little action. There were few good points, the southpaw champion prepared to go along with the pace of the fight while Williamson, who possessed a good left jab, was only interested in using it occasionally. Never properly challenged, with Byrd always having points in the bank he did as little as possible in order to preserve his title.

17 December 2005. Nikolay Valuev w pts 12 John Ruiz.
Venue: Max Schmeling Arena, Berlin, Germany. **Recognition:** WBA. **Referee:** Stan Christodoulou.
Scorecards: 116-114, 116-113, 114-114.
Fight Summary: Using his huge reach to good advantage with the jab, Valuev (324¼) made life tough for the champion, who found it difficult to get his punches off. Occasionally Ruiz (237¾) got inside, but unable to do any damage it was only in the latter stages when there was a hint of desperation that he did his best work. Ruiz, who finished with a swollen right eye, failed to work hard enough in the middle rounds while the Russian did just enough to make sure of the decision. On winning, Valuev, at seven foot plus, became the tallest champion of all time.

18 March 2006. Hasim Rahman drew 12 James Toney.
Venue: Boardwalk Hall, Atlantic City, New Jersey, USA. **Recognition:** WBC. **Referee:** Eddie Cotton.

Scorecards: 117-111, 114-114, 114-114.
Fight Summary: After being handed the title following Vitali Klitschko's decision to retire, this was Rahman's first defence. With height advantage over the 37-year-old Toney (237) it was Rahman (238) who made the better start, a heavy right to the jaw early on concentrating the challenger's mind. By the fourth Toney was having success with short lefts to the body and overarm rights to the head, while Rahman, who was cut over the left eye in the fourth, was happy to throw single shots. First one man would have a good session and then the other, and at the end of the 11th two of the judges had Toney a round up. Although Toney began the 12th well Rahman finished the stronger, sending his man to the ropes with solid punches to win the round and earn a majority draw.

1 April 2006. Siarhei Liakhovich w pts 12 Lamon Brewster.
Venue: Wolstein Centre, Cleveland, Ohio, USA. **Recognition:** WBO. **Referee:** Ernie Sharif.
Scorecards: 115-112, 115-113, 117-110.
Fight Summary: Despite being floored in the seventh, having been forced to take several solid blows to the body, Liakhovich (238½) did enough to convince all three judges that he was a worthy new champion. The taller man, Liakhovich made a positive start when winning the opening three rounds before being hurt in the fifth as Brewster (232) loaded up. He then came back well to batter Brewster against the ropes before the bell rang six seconds early to save the latter. Both men had put a lot into the fight, but following the knockdown Liakhovich picked up the pace to win the last five sessions, Brewster finishing the contest with a badly swollen left eye and bereft of his title.

22 April 2006. Wladimir Klitschko w rsc 7 Chris Byrd.
Venue: SAP Arena, Mannheim, Germany. **Recognition:** IBF. **Referee:** Wayne Kelly.
Fight Summary: Almost three years after losing his WBO title, Klitschko (241) came back to win another version of the championship when beating the southpaw Byrd (213½), a former victim and the current IBF champion. Following a slow start, Klitschko dominated every round, his left paving the way for solid right hands to the head, and in the fifth Byrd was sent crashing by a left-right that almost saw him counted out. It was now just a matter of time. In the seventh, with Klitschko totally on top, Byrd was floored heavily again from a hard right to the head. With Byrd's left eye pouring blood, the referee stepped in immediately to stop the fight after just 41 seconds had elapsed.

3 June 2006. Nikolay Valuev w rsc 3 Owen Beck.
Venue: TUI Arena, Hannover, Germany. **Recognition:** WBA. **Referee:** Luis Pabon.
Fight Summary: Making his first defence, although the 78lbs heavier Valuev (320¾) took his time, by the second round he was up and running before sending in a hard right to the jaw that sent the challenger down. Up after the mandatory count, Beck (242½) was saved by the bell when in a dazed condition. Having come out for the third Beck was soon floored by a right uppercut, and despite making it to his feet the referee stopped the contest on the 1.44 mark when he was badly hurt by a three-punch combination.

12 August 2006. Oleg Maskaev w rsc 12 Hasim Rahman.
Venue: Thomas & Mack Centre, Las Vegas, Nevada, USA. **Recognition:** WBC. **Referee:** Jay Nady.
Fight Summary: Having survived a scare against James Toney this time round the champion came unstuck against the 37-year-old Maskaev (238), a man who had already knocked him out almost seven years earlier. Fairly even throughout, Rahman (235) jabbing well on occasion while Maskaev tried to work inside, in the eighth it looked as though the latter was flagging before coming back strongly in the ninth. In the tenth through to the 11th Maskaev made his run for home, landing heavy rights as Rahman looked to hold and in the 12th, following two knockdowns, the referee rescued the American at 2.17 of the session as he lay defenceless on the ropes.

7 October 2006. Nikolay Valuev w rsc 11 Monte Barrett.
Venue: Allstate Arena, Rosemont, Illinois, USA. **Recognition:** WBA. **Referee:** John O'Brien.
Fight Summary: At seven foot and almost 100lbs the heavier of the pair the champion was giant-like compared to Barrett (222½), the shorter man by seven inches, in what was a messy affair. The pattern of the fight was similar throughout as Barrett slung in wild rights while Valuev (328) laid on his man whether he landed or missed. Several times Barrett was down in what were ruled as slips, although one in the eighth counted, but in the 11th after

another stumble he was clearly groggy. Further to that two more heavy knockdowns saw the referee halt the contest at 2.12 of the session on the advice of the 35-year-old Barrett's corner.

4 November 2006. Shannon Briggs w rsc 12 Siarhei Liakhovich.
Venue: Chase Field Baseball Stadium, Phoenix, Arizona, USA. **Recognition:** WBO. **Referee:** Bobby Ferrara.
Fight Summary: In what was described as a terrible contest to watch by most of the scribes present, Liakhovich (238) lost his title at the first time of asking when Briggs (268), behind on all three scorecards, forced the referee to intervene in his favour with just one second of the fight remaining. Although he made a reasonable start Briggs failed to sustain it, allowing Liakhovich to box him off with the jab for round after round before coming to life in the 11th. Both men let the punches go in the final session, but despite being tired Briggs found the strength to drop Liakhovich twice, the last knockdown enforcing the stoppage. Had Liakhovich lasted out the round he would have retained his title by a majority draw.

11 November 2006. Wladimir Klitschko w rsc 7 Calvin Brock.
Venue: Madison Square Garden, Manhattan, NYC, New York, USA. **Recognition:** IBF. **Referee:** Wayne Kelly.
Fight Summary: Defending the IBF title for the first time, Klitschko (241), with a six-inch reach advantage, failed to find the range and held too much in the opening four rounds as Brock (224½) took the fight to him. In the fifth both men were cut on their left eyes, Brock from a left jab and Klitschko from an accidental head butt. Although Brock was having some success it could be seen by the sixth that Klitschko was finding the range for straight rights, and after the challenger was stunned by solid lefts and rights in the seventh he was dropped heavily by a crashing right to the jaw. Up at 'seven' looking extremely dazed, Brock was stopped on the 2.10 mark when the referee recognised that it would be foolhardy to let him continue.

10 December 2006. Oleg Maskaev w pts 12 Okello Peter.
Venue: Olympic Sports Arena, Moscow, Russia. **Recognition:** WBC. **Referee:** Lupe Garcia.
Scorecards: 120-107, 118-109, 120-107.
Fight Summary: Always in control, the champion took virtually every round on his way to a straightforward points win. Right from the start the ambling Peter (254½) was on the back foot as he looked to survive, Maskaev (240) pressuring him with solid jabs but unable to find a finisher. Eventually, in the tenth, Maskaev dropped Peter with a right uppercut having set him up with short jabs to the head. Although Maskaev moved in on his man following the knockdown he failed to find a similar punch and was forced to go the distance.

With Maskaev pulling out of an October 2007 defence against Samuel Peter after suffering a multiple disc herniation, the latter was named as the WBC 'interim' champion on 24 September 2007, and later held on to his honours against Jameel McCline (w pts 12 on 6 October 2007 at Madison Square Garden, Manhattan, NYC, New York, USA) despite being floored three times in the bout. Maskaev v Peter was eventually scheduled for Cancun, Mexico on 8 March 2008.

20 January 2007. Nikolay Valuev w rtd 3 Jameel McCline.
Venue: St Jacob Hall, Basel, Switzerland. **Recognition:** WBA. **Referee:** John Coyle.
Fight Summary: Full of energy, McCline (268½) made a good start against the lumbering champion, banging in lefts and rights before moving on. While Valuev (322½) picked it up in the second when getting his left-right working, McCline was still going well when winning the third before suffering an injury to his left knee after missing with a left-right and crashing to the floor at the end of the session. Unable to get off the floor without assistance, McCline was dragged back to his stool before being retired by his corner.

10 March 2007. Wladimir Klitschko w rsc 2 Ray Austin.
Venue: SAP Arena, Mannheim, Germany. **Recognition:** IBF. **Referee:** Eddie Cotton.
Fight Summary: Predicted to be an early night for the champion, that is how it turned out. Following a slow opening session with Austin (247) carrying a low guard and looking far too casual, Klitschko (246½) opened up in the second. After Klitschko caught Austin with a long left hook and backed that up with several more solid blows the latter crashed to the floor before being rescued by the referee at 1.23 of the session. Austin had looked likely to continue until realising the third man had deemed his challenge was over.

14 April 2007. Ruslan Chagaev w pts 12 Nikolay Valuev.
Venue: Porsche Arena, Stuttgart, Germany. **Recognition:** WBA. **Referee:** Luis Pabon.
Scorecards: 117-111, 115-113, 114-114.
Fight Summary: Despite the champion, who was on 46 straight wins, pressing continuously it was Chagaev (228¼) who picked up the majority of the points that his cleaner work merited. By keeping on the move Chagaev not only made for a difficult target, but gave himself the room to get hard southpaw lefts off as Valuev (319) came on to him, especially in the sixth when two exploded on the latter's chin. However, by the eighth Valuev was back in the fight as uppercuts to the body began to slow Chagaev down, his extra strength also noticeable at this stage of the fight. It was still close, and had Valuev won the last two sessions he would have retained his title.

2 June 2007. Sultan Ibragimov w pts 12 Shannon Briggs.
Venue: Boardwalk Hall, Atlantic City, New Jersey, USA. **Recognition:** WBO. **Referee:** Eddie Cotton.
Scorecards: 117-111, 119-109, 115-113.
Fight Summary: Although Briggs (273) took the opening session Ibragimov (221) soon got on top, moving around his man while sending in solid southpaw jabs. Unfortunately for Briggs he did not have an answer to the challenger's hand-speed and movement, being unable to fire off heavy right hands that had gained him 42 quick wins in the past. Following the fight, Briggs, who lost the title in his first defence, claimed that he had wanted to call the fight off due to suffering asthma attacks.

7 July 2007. Wladimir Klitschko w rtd 6 Lamon Brewster.
Venue: The Arena, Cologne, Germany. **Recognition:** IBF. **Referee:** Sam Williams.
Fight Summary: Having beaten the champion previously inside the distance Brewster (228¼) must have been confident he could do it for the second time. Unfortunately for him, however, the Klitschko (243½) who turned up this time handed him a steady beating before he was retired by his corner at the end of the sixth round, his eyes badly swollen. Having got his left jab going from the start Klitschko dominated throughout as he looked to set Brewster up for the right hand, and in the fifth and sixth it was clear to the latter's corner that it was just a matter of time when their man kept getting caught in the headlights.

13 October 2007. Sultan Ibragimov w pts 12 Evander Holyfield.
Venue: Khodynka Ice Palace, Moscow, Russia. **Recognition:** WBO. **Referee:** Raul Caiz.
Scorecards: 117-111, 117-111, 118-110.
Fight Summary: Still fighting at 44 years of age, the former champion was unable to draw Ibragimov (219) into a fight where he could work at close quarters. Instead, Ibragimov was happy to box at long range where he picked his man off with southpaw jabs before moving on. Occasionally, he dug in blows to the body, and in the tenth such a punch almost doubled Holyfield (211½) up. In sheer desperation Holyfield charged at Ibragimov in the 11th, only to miss with a right hand and go crashing to the floor. Ruled a slip by the referee, Holyfield came back hard to hurt the champion at the end of the session with a cracking right to the jaw prior to giving it a real go in the 12th. Having taken a couple of heavy rights, Ibragimov held on before cantering through the rest of the session with Holyfield, on tired legs, unable to chase him down.

19 January 2008. Ruslan Chagaev w pts 12 Matt Skelton.
Venue: Castello Castle-Keeper Arena, Dusseldorf, Germany. **Recognition:** WBA. **Referee:** Guillermo Pineda Perez.
Scorecards: 117-110, 117-112, 117-111.
Fight Summary: Defending his title after nine months out of the ring, Chagaev (229¼) came back to face the 40-year-old Skelton (254¾), a man who only took to boxing in 2002, and was forced to travel the full route. Skelton certainly made the southpaw champion work when giving him little room to manoeuvre, but lacked the finesse and power required to take the title. Deducted a point for excessive holding in the eighth, Skelton was falling behind on the cards as Chagaev picked up the pace. Having taken Chagaev's big punches without flinching, Skelton came back well in the 11th before being forced to hang on in the 12th after a body shot took all the wind out of his sails and was followed up with a non-stop battering.

Whilst preparing for a defence against Nikolay Valuev on 5 July, the fight was cancelled when Chagaev suffered a complete tear of an Achilles tendon in the final week of training. With Chagaev given the title of 'champion in recess', the two leading contenders, Valuev and John Ruiz, were selected to meet for the vacant title.

After returning from injury with a sixth-round technical decision win over Carl Davis Drumond at the Stadium Hall, Rostock, Germany on 7 February 2009, Chagaev was lined up to meet Valuev in Finland on 30 May 2009. Although Chagaev failed the Finnish medical tests, allegedly due to hepatitis, it did not stop him from stepping in at short notice to take on Wladimir Klitschko for the IBF/WBO versions of the title on 20 June after David Haye had picked up a late injury. Thus it was no surprise that he lost his 'champion in recess' status with the WBA on losing to Klitschko.

23 February 2008. Wladimir Klitschko w pts 12 Sultan Ibragimov.
Venue: Madison Square Garden, Manhattan, NYC, New York, USA. **Recognition:** IBF/WBO. **Referee:** Wayne Kelly.
Scorecards: 119-110, 117-111, 118-110.
Fight Summary: In a unification battle, Klitschko (238), the IBF champion, outpointed by some margin the WBO titleholder, Ibragimov (219). Many felt that Klitschko should have opened up more instead of relying on a solid left jab that was occasionally followed by hooks and straight rights, but the Ukranian had a battle plan and stuck to it. Always in control, Klitschko was content to outbox his dangerous unbeaten southpaw opponent, who had decided early on to fight out of a crouch. Although there were no official knockdowns recorded, when Klitschko sent Ibragimov on to the lower ropes in the ninth from a right-left-right combination the referee was possibly lenient when not calling one, especially as the latter would have been floored had the support not been there. Both fell down together in the tenth, and while Klitschko felt the effects more than Ibragimov it did not stop him continuing his march.

8 March 2008. Samuel Peter w rsc 6 Oleg Maskaev.
Venue: The Bullring, Cancun, Mexico. **Recognition:** WBC. **Referee:** Lupe Garcia.
Fight Summary: Starting fast, Peter (250) quickly showed that he was a man to be reckoned with, and in the third he stepped inside the champion's southpaw stance to land two cracking right hands prior to following up with a battery of blows. Coming back hard, Maskaev (243) laid into Peter with no great damage being done right through to the sixth before being caught heavily by a solid right towards the end of the session. Stepping it up, Peter piled on the pressure when winging in blows from both hands until the referee jumped in between them on the 2.56 mark to rescue Maskaev after he had been trapped in a corner.

12 July 2008. Wladimir Klitschko w co 11 Tony Thompson.
Venue: Color Line Arena, Hamburg, Germany. **Recognition:** IBF/WBO. **Referee:** Joe Cortez.
Fight Summary: Putting his two titles on the line against an awkward southpaw challenger, Klitschko (241) was forced to go 11 rounds before finding a tremendous right that landed flush on the jaw and dropped Thompson (247½) heavily to be counted out at 1.38 of the session. Winning all rounds bar the fifth, Klitschko gradually wore Thompson down. Both men were cut following an accidental headbutt in the second and in the tenth, after Klitschko pushed Thompson to the floor, the latter was given time to recover by the referee. *Boxing News* summed it up as a vintage Klitschko performance with no exchanges, rather ugly pushing and much holding.

30 August 2008. Nikolay Valuev w pts 12 John Ruiz.
Venue: Max Schmeling Hall, Berlin, Germany. **Recognition:** WBA. **Referee:** Derek Milham.
Scorecards: 114-113, 116-113, 116-111.
Fight Summary: Contested for the vacant title after Ruslan Chagaev had been classified as a 'champion in recess' due to injury, Valuev (317¾) came back to regain his old title when outpointing the much smaller Ruiz (239). Starting well with the left jab, Valuev soon began to have difficulty with Ruiz's speed that gave him problems for several rounds before his strength began to wear the latter down. By the seventh Ruiz was holding on without throwing enough punches, and in the eighth he was forced to take a heavy right to the head which did not help his cause. Despite both men tiring it was Valuev who produced the better work in the last few sessions.

11 October 2008. Vitali Klitschko w rtd 8 Samuel Peter.
Venue: O2 World Arena, Berlin, Germany. **Recognition:** WBC. **Referee:** Massimo Barrovecchio.
Fight Summary: Coming back after almost four years away from the ring following a serious knee injury, Klitschko (247) started strongly and soon had a grip on the fight as the champion was pushed back, seemingly unable to take up the attack. Although Peter (253½) picked it up somewhat in the seventh when he began throw more punches, in the eighth he was in dire straits as Klitschko ripped in cracking right hooks and followed up with more solid blows from either hand. Having realised that this was a fight that Peter, his right eye badly swollen, was not going to win, his corner pulled him out at the end of the session.

13 December 2008. Wladimir Klitschko w rsc 7 Hasim Rahman.
Venue: SAP Arena, Mannheim, Germany. **Recognition:** IBF/WBO. **Referee:** Tony Weeks.
Fight Summary: With both of his titles on the line, Klitschko (244¾) was quickly down to business with the left jab pounding into the challenger's face. Within no time at all it was realised that Rahman (253½) was not the fighter of old. With the fight continuing at Klitschko's pace, in the sixth Rahman was battered down following left hooks that landed solidly and took an 'eight' count before being forced to take more heavy shots. Having asked Rahman if he wanted to continue, the referee eventually halted the action after 44 seconds of the seventh when the latter was in trouble as Klitschko opened up with both hands.

20 December 2008. Nikolay Valuev w pts 12 Evander Holyfield.
Venue: Stadium Hall, Zurich, Switzerland. **Recognition:** WBA. **Referee:** Luis Pabon.
Scorecards: 116-112, 115-114, 114-114.
Fight Summary: In what was a very close fight that many thought the 46-year-old Holyfield (214¼) deserved to draw at the very least, it was the champion who came out on top according to two of the judges. With Holyfield's plan of campaign based on countering the ponderous Valuev (310¾) his work-rate suffered as the latter kept him on the end of left jabs in many rounds. However, by the ninth Holyfield was making progress inside, and in the 11th he was the more dominant with solid hooks to head and body. Whether it was tiredness or not, Holyfield was unable to push on in the 12th and was outworked as Valuev let go with both hands to make sure of the verdict.

21 March 2009. Vitali Klitschko w rsc 9 Juan Carlos Gomez.
Venue: Hanns Martin Schleyer Hall, Stuttgart, Germany. **Recognition:** WBC. **Referee:** Daniel Van de Wiele.
Fight Summary: Despite taking the fight to the champion from the opening bell, Gomez (230½), a southpaw, was soon under pressure when being speared by left jabs and solid rights, punches that would produce a swelling on his right eye by the fourth. Although Gomez, now cut on the right eye, tried to pick it up in the fifth when landing some good shots he was still being held up by the jab, and in the seventh he was forced to take a knee after a three-punch combination badly hurt him. With both men on the floor in the same round after Gomez, who was again hurt, pulled Klitschko (249¼) down with him, the challenger looked a spent force. Allowed to continue, a clash of heads in the ninth, for which Klitschko was deducted a point, saw Gomez in further trouble, and following 'time out' he took another count before being battered into a corner and rescued by the referee at 1.49 of the session.

20 June 2009. Wladimir Klitschko w rtd 9 Ruslan Chagaev.
Venue: Veltins Arena, Gelsenkirchen, Germany. **Recognition:** IBF/WBO/The Ring. **Referee:** Eddie Cotton.
Fight Summary: As well as successfully defending his IBF and WBO titles, Klitschko (240½) also won the vacant *Ring* Championship Belt when forcing Chagaev (225) out of the contest at the end of the ninth round. Replacing the injured David Haye at just two weeks' notice, Chagaev was soon being held up by the left jab before being dropped by a left-right in the second. Back in the fight the unbeaten southpaw, who was recognised by the WBA as a 'champion in recess', had no answer to the Klitschko jab, and after he was cut on the left eye in the seventh his spirit diminished further. Having taken some heavy rights in the ninth when not fighting back, his eye damage worsening, Chagaev was retired on his stool at the end of the session.

26 September 2009. Vitali Klitschko w rtd 10 Chris Arreola.
Venue: Staples Centre, Los Angeles, California, USA. **Recognition:** WBC. **Referee:** Jon Schorle.

Fight Summary: Winning one round at most, the challenger, as game as they come, took the fight to Klitschko (252) for the opening five rounds despite being pounded by jabs and follow-up rights. It seemed that Klitschko could not miss Arreola (251), who was far too pedestrian and unable to cut the ring down. As the sessions progressed Arreola's features became more swollen and, rapidly tiring having tried everything within his compass, he was pulled out of the contest by his corner at the end of the tenth.

7 November 2009. David Haye w pts 12 Nikolay Valuev.
Venue: Insurance Arena, Nuremberg, Germany. **Recognition:** WBA. **Referee:** Luis Pabon.
Scorecards: 116-112, 116-112, 114-114
Fight Summary: Massively outweighed by close on 100lbs, the challenger stuck to his game plan when using his advantage of speed and movement to outscore Valuev (314¾), who found it difficult get any serious punches off against a man that just was not there for much of the time. Having damaged his right hand in the second when trying for an early night, Haye (216¾) settled down to hand out a boxing lesson. Despite tiring as the fight wore on Haye still finished the rounds strongly, and in the final session he went for Valuev in pursuit of a stoppage, hurting the latter with left hook to the head before the bell. Although one of the judges made that a 10-8 round, the scores were much closer than it seemed with one of the officials even giving it as a draw.

12 December 2009. Vitali Klitschko w pts 12 Kevin Johnson.
Venue: Post Finance Arena, Bern, Switzerland. **Recognition:** WBC. **Referee:** Kenny Bayless.
Scorecards: 119-109, 120-108, 120-108. .
Fight Summary: Spending most of the contest ducking out of the way as the champion loaded up was hardly the right tactic for someone who wanted to pick up a title, and although Johnson (242½) lasted the full course it was a shut-out win for Klitschko (247) as far as two judges were concerned, with the other judge giving him the fourth. In that session Johnson scored well with the jab, but once Klitschko began to counter him with the right that was as far as it went. In the aftermath, *Boxing News* reported Klitschko as saying "I prepared to knock Johnson out, but it was not easy to hit him. He was always defensive."

20 March 2010. Wladimir Klitschko w co 12 Eddie Chambers.
Venue: Esprit Arena, Dusseldorf, Germany. **Recognition:** IBF/WBO/The Ring. **Referee:** Genaro Rodriguez.
Fight Summary: With his three championship belts on the line, Klitschko (244¾) began as normal with solid left jabs that were followed by right crosses, and twice in the opening two sessions Chambers (209½), six inches the shorter man, ducked down and lifted the champion on to his shoulders. The second time he did this he threw Klitschko to the floor before the latter almost fell when hurt by a countering right. Even at this stage it was clear that Chambers did not have an answer. Still proving elusive, more so when cut over the left eye in the fifth, Chambers continued to avoid Klitschko right up until the final session when a wide left smashed him to the floor where he was counted out with five seconds of the fight remaining.

3 April 2010. David Haye w rsc 9 John Ruiz.
Venue: MEN Arena, Manchester, England. **Recognition:** WBA. **Referee:** Guillermo Perez Pineda.
Fight Summary: Making an electric start the champion had Ruiz (231) on the floor within 30 seconds from a cracking left-right to the head before dropping him again and being docked two points for hitting behind the head. Having sustained a battering in the next two sessions as Haye (222) unloaded, Ruiz came back well to win the fourth. It did not last, however, and in the fifth and sixth Ruiz took two more counts after being battered by hard shots from both hands. Although Ruiz managed to get through the seventh and eighth rounds, his days were numbered. With the third man close to stopping the fight on several occasions his mind was finally made up for him at 2.01 of the ninth when Ruiz's corner tossed in the towel, the official decision being announced as a referee's stoppage.

29 May 2010. Vitali Klitschko w rsc 10 Albert Sosnowski.
Venue: Veltins Arena, Gelsenkirchen, Germany. **Recognition:** WBC. **Referee:** Jay Nady.
Fight Summary: After winning the opening nine rounds the champion finally found what he was looking for when a hard right to the body followed by a left-right saw Sosnowski (224½) out of the fight at 2.30 of the tenth after the referee called it off. Having been outboxed in the opening two sessions Sosnowski came back well in the third, but

failing to unsettle Klitschko (247) he slipped further and further behind as the fight progressed. His best punch was a hard right to Klitschko's jaw in the eighth, but when that had little effect it was clear that his chances of winning the contest were limited, especially when the scores showing him not to have won a single round were announced at the end of the session. From there it was all downhill.

11 September 2010. Wladimir Klitschko w rsc 10 Samuel Peter.
Venue: Commercial Bank Arena, Frankfurt, Germany. **Recognition:** IBF/WBO/The Ring. **Referee:** Robert Byrd.
Fight Summary: Having lost his WBC title to Vitali Klitschko and been outpointed by Wladimir five years earlier, this was a big ask for Peter (241½). Although the holder of three championship belts was staggered by a left hook in the opening session he soon had Peter eating the left jab, and by the end of the fourth the latter's left eye was swelling fast. For round after round Peter was forced to suffer hard one-twos that broke through his porous guard before the tenth saw him come apart as Klitschko (247) unloaded. At 2.55 of the session the referee rescued Peter after he had been sent crashing on to his back by a murderous left uppercut. Immediately prior to that, Peter had been unhinged by left and right hooks.

16 October 2010. Vitali Klitschko w pts 12 Shannon Briggs.
Venue: O2 World Arena, Hamburg, Germany. **Recognition:** WBC. **Referee:** Ian John-Lewis.
Scorecards: 120-107, 120-105, 120-106.
Fight Summary: Showing tremendous spirit to last the distance against a dominant champion, Briggs (262½) suffered a broken nose, a broken left orbital bone and torn left biceps in his vain pursuit of the title. He had been widely outscored and hurt by solid lefts and rights in virtually every session, and in the tenth all three judges made it a 10-8 round, such was the punishment he took without being decked. Klitschko (251½) paid Briggs the ultimate compliment when stating that he had never seen anything like his courage before, while the latter felt that he would have done a lot better had his left arm not been damaged so early in the contest.

13 November 2010. David Haye w rsc 3 Audley Harrison.
Venue: MEN Arena, Manchester, England. **Recognition:** WBA. **Referee:** Luis Pabon.
Fight Summary: In what was a bad mismatch, the 39-year-old Harrison (253½), a former Olympic champion, was rescued by the referee after 1.53 of the third. With very little happening in the opening two sessions as both men sized each other up, it was the champion who made the running in the third when moving forward with solid rights, hooks and uppercuts. Caught in the headlights Harrison appeared unable to defend himself before toppling over and taking a count of 'nine', and after Haye (120½) jumped on him with some venom the referee called it off.

17 March 2011. Vitali Klitschko w rsc 1 Odlanier Solis.
Venue: Lanxess Arena, Cologne, Germany. **Recognition:** WBC. **Referee:** Lupe Garcia.
Fight Summary: Expected to give the champion a run for his money, Solis (247) was stopped at 2.59 of the opening session when a ruptured cruciate ligament in his right knee saw his title opportunity come to a grinding halt. The fight had started well enough with Solis, showing good speed, sending in scoring blows and beating Klitschko (249½) to the punch before it all changed. With both men still sizing each other up, the final piece of action came when Solis, having missed with a left hook and being pushed back by a Klitschko left jab, lost his balance and toppled over. Afterwards, Klitschko claimed that despite his speed Solis did not have the power to go with it and he had expected to win in the second half of the contest.

2 July 2011. Wladimir Klitschko w pts 12 David Haye.
Venue: Imtech Arena, Hamburg, Germany. **Recognition:** IBF/WBA/WBO/The Ring. **Referee:** Genaro Rodriguez.
Scorecards: 118-108, 117-109, 116-110.
Fight Summary: A disappointing fight after all the hype, Haye (212¾), the WBA champion, went down widely on points, claiming that a broken toe suffered three weeks earlier was the reason for his poor performance. Even though Klitschko (242½), who came into the contest with three championship belts of his own, was deducted a point in the seventh round for pushing Haye down it barely mattered, such was his margin of victory. The real problem for Haye was that he could not get through Klitschko's guard, and even though the latter transgressed several times when pushing down on his challenger without warnings he was simply too big and strong. An example of this came in the 11th when Haye was counted over after being pushed down. Even when Haye got

through with heavy punches to the head Klitschko remained unmoved, his solid left hands keeping the former at bay throughout.

On 27 August, at the Fair Hall, Erfurt, Germany, Alexander Povetkin outpointed Ruslan Chagaev over 12 rounds to win the vacant WBA 'second tier' title. Povetkin went on to retain the belt when knocking out Cedric Boswell in the eighth round of their contest at the Hartwall Arena, Helsinki, Finland, on 3 December. Another successful defence of the WBA 'second tier' title for Povetkin came on 25 February 2012 at the Porsche Arena, Stuttgart, Germany, when he outpointed Marco Huck over 12 rounds.

10 September 2011. Vitali Klitschko w rsc 10 Tomasz Adamek.
Venue: Miejski Stadium, Wroclaw, Poland. **Recognition:** WBC. **Referee:** Massimo Barrovecchio.
Fight Summary: By successfully defending his title against Adamek (216¼), a former champion at light heavy and cruiser, the 40-year-old Klitschko (243) once again proved that he and his brother could control the heavyweight division for as long as they were fit enough, such was their dominance. Adamek came into the contest knowing that he had to keep away from Klitschko's big punches, but he was systematically battered throughout and failed to win a round. In the sixth after a heavy right to the head forced Adamek against the ropes the referee gave him an 'eight' count having decided that the strands had saved him from going down. By the tenth Adamek had nothing left to offer, and following three heavy blows to the head the referee called the fight off at 2.20 of the session.

18 February 2012. Vitali Klitschko w pts 12 Dereck Chisora.
Venue: Olympic Hall, Munich, Germany. **Recognition:** WBC. **Referee:** Guido Cavalleri.
Scorecards: 118-110, 118-110, 119-111.
Fight Summary: Even though the champion was in control for the majority of the fight, Chisora (241¼) gamely stuck to the task at hand and was never floored or embarrassed. Showing a good mentality regardless of all that had gone on prior to the bout, and despite lacking the power to finish Klitschko (243¾) off, Chicora's work-rate kept him in the fight for the full 12 rounds. At best Chisora won two rounds, but he never let Klitschko relax even after he tired in the latter stages. Following the fight Klitschko claimed that a torn ligament in his left shoulder had made it difficult for him to use the left jab.

3 March 2012. Wladimir Klitschko w rsc 4 Jean-Marc Mormeck.
Venue: Esprit Arena, Düsseldorf, Germany. **Recognition:** IBF/WBA/WBO/The Ring. **Referee:** Luis Pabon.
Fight Summary: Putting all four championship belts on the line against Mormeck (217½) after the original date was cancelled due to Klitschko (246¾) having a kidney stone problem, the latter saw his opponent off quickly. Unable to find his range in the opener due to Mormeck's ducking and diving, Klitschko got to his man in the second when a right-left floored him. Having battered Mormeck for the remainder of the session, Klitschko again had difficulty getting to Mormeck in the third before dropping him with a three-punch combination in the fourth. Although Mormeck was up at 'nine' the referee considered that he was in no fit state to continue and stopped the fight on 1.12 mark.

7 July 2012. Wladimir Klitschko w rsc 6 Tony Thompson.
Venue: National Stadium, Bern, Switzerland. **Recognition:** IBF/WBA/WBO/The Ring. **Referee:** Sam Williams.
Fight Summary: Getting another crack at Klitschko (246¼), whose four championship belts were up for grabs, Thompson (244¾) had hoped to do better this time around but was again found wanting. Down twice in the second from hard rights and pushes the southpaw challenger was right up against, and in the fifth he was again on the floor after taking another heavy right to the head. Although Thompson beat the count and was able to make it to the end of the session, he was stopped at 2.56 of the sixth having being battered to the floor and showing no interest in continuing when back on his feet.

Alexander Povetkin successfully defended the WBA 'second tier' title when knocking out Hasim Rahman in the second round at the Sports Hall, Alsterdorf, Germany on 29 September.

8 September 2012. Vitali Klitschko w rsc 4 Manuel Charr.
Venue: Olympic Sports Complex, Moscow, Russia. **Recognition:** WBC. **Referee:** Guido Cavalleri.
Fight Summary: Although an undefeated fighter, Charr (241½) was up against it right from the opening bell as the champion jabbed him off with ease. In the second round things got worse for Charr when he was hurt by a body shot before being sent crashing following a heavy right to the head. Saved by the bell, Charr, outjabbed in the third, was badly cut over the right eye in the fourth, an injury that saw him being rescued by the referee at 2.04 of the session following advice from the ringside doctor.

Inactive for 15 months, Klitschko relinquished the WBC title on 16 December 2013 in order to concentrate on his political career in Ukraine and the coming elections in 2015. Following the announcement, the WBC appointed him an 'emeritus champion'.

At the end of December 2013, the WBC ordered a match between Bermane Stiverne and Chris Arreola to decide the vacant title. This followed a contest for the WBC 'silver' title on 27 April 2013 at the Citizens Business Bank Arena, Ontario, California, in which Stiverne had received a unanimous 12-round points win. The WBC went on to say that if the pair had failed to agree a match by 17 January 2014 the fight would go to purse bids.

11 November 2012. Wladimir Klitschko w pts 12 Mariusz Wach.
Venue: 02 World Arena, Hamburg, Germany. **Recognition:** IBF/WBA/WBO/The Ring. **Referee:** Eddie Cotton.
Scorecards: 120-107, 120-107, 119-109.
Fight Summary: Defending his four championship belts for the first time since the death of his trainer, Emanuel Steward, Klitschko (247) was up against a man who was even taller and heavier than him in Wach (251). Boxing well within himself Klitschko took every round, bar the fifth on one of the judges' cards when he was rocked by a cracking right hand. Apart from that Klitschko handed Wach quite a beating, his left-rights finding their mark on a regular basis, and in the eighth two of the judges made it a 10-8 round after he had badly battered the latter. Although Wach tired in the later rounds he was still there at the final bell, having proved his toughness.

4 May 2013. Wladimir Klitschko w rsc 6 Francesco Pianeta.
Venue: SAP Arena, Mannheim, Germany. **Recognition:** IBF/WBA/WBO/The Ring. **Referee:** Ernie Sharif.
Fight Summary: With his four championship belts once again on the line, Klitschko (249) powered to victory over the outgunned Pianeta (240), an Italian southpaw. Dropped in the fourth by a left-right, having been pushed down earlier, although Pianeta tried hard enough it was all downhill. Another punch-push from Klitschko in the fifth saw Pianeta counted over, but two of the judges decided that it was not a knockdown. However, in the sixth after a left-right-left had Pianeta on the floor again, the last two blows doing the damage, the referee called the fight off at 2.52 of the session despite the challenger being on his feet at 'nine'.

On 17 May, Alexander Povetkin made a successful defence of the WBA 'second tier' title when stopping Andrzej Wawrzyk inside three rounds at the Crocus City Hall, Moscow, Russia.

5 October 2013. Wladimir Klitschko w pts 12 Alexander Povetkin.
Venue: Olympic Stadium, Moscow, Russia. **Recognition:** IBF/WBA/WBO/The Ring. **Referee:** Luis Pabon.
Scorecards: 119-104, 119-104, 119-104.
Fight Summary: Once again putting his four championship belts on the line, Klitschko (241¾) had to defend himself from swarming, swinging attacks in the opening session as Povetkin (225¾) tried to confuse him before being pushed down almost in anger. From the second round onwards Klitschko, who put Povetkin down in this session from a left hook, took over with hard lefts and rights making their mark. By the seventh, it already seemed mission impossible for Povetkin, and that was before he was counted over three times, all three judges marking it as a 10-6 round. When Povetkin was pushed to the floor heavily in the ninth and finished the session with a cut right eye one might have thought he'd had enough, but he was still there in the tenth. Continuing to take stiff lefts and rights in the tenth, Povetkin was again thrown to the floor in the 11th, a transgression that saw Klitschko deducted a point. After being wrestled to the canvas once again, this time in the 12th, Povetkin tore into Klitschko immediately prior to receiving a rousing ovation for his brave stand at the final bell. On the result, Povetkin lost his WBA 'second tier' title.

26 April 2014. Wladimir Klitschko w rsc 5 Alex Leapai.
Venue: Konig Pilsener Arena, Oberhausen, Germany. **Recognition:** IBF/WBA/WBO/The Ring. **Referee:** Eddie Cotton.
Fight Summary: Challenging Klitschko (247½) for the latter's four championship belts Leapai (248) made a poor start when being dropped by a left jab in the opening session. From there onwards it was never much of a contest as Leapai took punch after punch without any lateral movement while only throwing wild shots in the hope of catching his man. Having been floored by a left-right in the fifth after taking some hard rights to the head, on getting to his feet Leapai was quickly hammered to the deck again by another one-two. At that point the referee called it off at 2.05 of the session without taking up the count.

Ruslan Chagaev won the vacant WBA 'second tier' title when outpointing Fres Oquendo over 12 rounds at the Akhmat Arena, Grozny, Russia on 6 July.

In a battle for the vacant WBA 'interim' title, Luis Ortiz stopped Lateef Kayode in the opening session of their contest at the Hard Rock Hotel & Casino, Las Vegas, Nevada, USA on 11 September. Ortiz was stripped of his title in January 2015 when testing positive for Nandrolone.

10 May 2014. Bermane Stiverne w rsc 6 Chris Arreola.
Venue: USC Galen Centre, Los Angeles, California, USA. **Recognition:** WBC. **Referee:** Jack Reiss.
Fight Summary: Contesting the vacant title following the abdication of Vitali Klitschko, it was Stiverne (239½) who took over the latter's mantle when stopping Arreola (239), a former victim, at 2.02 of the sixth round. For five rounds the contest was fairly even, both men having their success, but in the sixth it all changed when Arreola was dropped by a bunch of shots that followed a heavy right to the temple. Although Arreola made it up he was quickly sent down again from another bombardment, and after being allowed to continue the referee called it off when he was immediately put under fire.

15 November 2014. Wladimir Klitschko w rsc 5 Kubrat Pulev.
Venue: 02 World Arena, Hamburg, Germany. **Recognition:** IBF/WBA/WBO/The Ring. **Referee:** Tony Weeks.
Fight Summary: Being the IBF's mandatory contender allowed the unbeaten Pulev (246¾) to challenge Klitschko (245¾) for that title, but like many others before him he was found wanting. Strangely, Pulev's management team only paid the IBF sanctioning fee, so had he won the WBA and WBO titles would have become vacant. As far as Klitschko was concerned all four belts were on the line and he made a very fast start to drop Pulev twice in the opening session, the first time from a left hook, the second appearing to be more of a push than a punch. Despite somehow finding his way back into the fight, Pulev was smashed to the canvas via the ropes in the third following another left hook. Although Pulev bothered Klitschko in the fifth with a few blows of his own he was rescued by the referee, who abandoned the count at 'six', on the 2.11 mark, having taken a tremendous left hook to the jaw that left him prostrate on the floor. Klitschko's *Ring* Championship Belt was also up for grabs in this one.

17 January 2015. Deontay Wilder w pts 12 Bermane Stiverne.
Venue: MGM Grand, Las Vegas, Nevada, USA. **Recognition:** WBC. **Referee:** Tony Weeks.
Scorecards: 118-109, 119-108, 120-107.
Fight Summary: Defending the title he won in May 2014, Stiverne (239) lost it by a wide points margin at the first time of asking when outpointed by Wilder (219). Getting away well Wilder hurt Stiverne badly in the second, and having been hammered non-stop throughout the session the latter went down dragging the challenger with him. There was no count from the referee, who stated that both men were on the floor after the bell had ended the round. With Wilder capturing the rounds, Stiverne was again hurt by a hard right in the fifth before coming under fire in the seventh. Although there were no knockdowns it was such an emphatic round for Wilder that all three judges marked it as 10-8. From thereon in, with Stiverne unable to cut the ring down, Wilder cruised to victory.

25 April 2015. Wladimir Klitschko w pts 12 Bryant Jennings.
Venue: Madison Square Garden, Manhattan, NYC, New York, USA. **Recognition:** IBF/WBA/WBO/The Ring. **Referee:** Michael Griffin.
Scorecards: 118-109, 116-111, 116-111.

Fight Summary: With his four championship belts on the line, Klitschko (241½) was back in America to fight Jennings (226¾), a man on 19 straight but lacking the vast amateur experience of the champion. Despite Klitschko doing well with his commanding left jab to rack up the points it was noticeable that he had less luck with his normally potent right, which had to be down to Jennings' good movement and defence. Although Klitschko cruised through many of the rounds, he was not at his best in the third, sixth and ninth when Jennings got several punches off, and being continuously forced to hold on the inside in the later rounds he was docked a point in the tenth.

Ruslan Chagaev knocked out Francesco Pianeta inside a round to retain his WBO 'second tier' title at the GETEC Arena, Magdeburg, Germany on 11 July.

The vacant WBA 'interim' title was won by Luis Ortiz when he knocked out Matias Ariel Vidondo inside three rounds at Madison Square Garden on 17 October.

13 June 2015. Deontay Wilder w rsc 9 Eric Molina.
Venue: Bartow Arena, Birmingham, Alabama, USA. **Recognition:** WBC. **Referee:** Jack Reiss
Fight Summary: Defending his title for the first time the champion was expected to have little difficulty turning back Molina (239¼), but although he ultimately retained his belt he was forced to overcome some difficult moments en route. Having skated through the opening two sessions Wilder (229) was badly hurt in the third when Molina connected with a three-punch combination, but the latter was unable to follow up. Wilder's response came in the following session when he dropped Molina with a cracking left hook, and in the fifth he had his man down twice before the bell came to his rescue. In the sixth through to the eighth Molina found another gear to have Wilder gasping at times from assaults to the body, but at 1.03 of the ninth it was all over when the referee pulled the challenger out of the contest after a crunching right to the jaw had left him spread-eagled on the deck.

26 September 2015. Deontay Wilder w rsc 11 Johann Duhaupas.
Venue: Legacy Arena, Birmingham, Alabama, USA. **Recognition:** WBC. **Referee:** Jack Reiss.
Fight Summary: This was a contest that was supposed to have an early ending as far as the bookies were concerned, but it did not work out that way as the tough challenger held up Wilder (228½) for more than ten rounds. Wilder, who was badly swollen under the left eye by third, was always in control but could not find the punches to floor the tough Duhaupas (236) who carried a cut left eye into the latter rounds. With both men tiring Wilder stunned Duhaupas with some heavy hooks to the head in the tenth, but was unable to extricate himself from the ensuing clinch. The fight was halted by the referee after 55 seconds of the 11th when Duhaupas was badly hurt by solid head shots, much to the disgust of the latter.

28 November 2015. Tyson Fury w pts 12 Wladimir Klitschko.
Venue: ESPRIT Arena, Dusseldorf, Germany. **Recognition:** IBF/WBA/WBO/The Ring. **Referee:** Tony Weeks.
Scorecards: 115-112, 115-112, 116-111.
Fight Summary: There was no doubt that it was a massive shock to many fight fans when the 6'9" Fury (247) outpointed Klitschko (245¾), thus picking up four championship belts and achieving what he said he would do beforehand. Switching from orthodox to southpaw and back again, standing sideways on to Klitschko with his hands down created problems in the latter's mind, and with Fury's movement making it hard for the champion to throw left-rights the fight was turned on its head. The sheer size and strength of Fury, allied to his excellent movement, also bothered Klitschko. Although many of the rounds were close it was Fury's punch stats of 86 from 371 as opposed Klitschko's 52 of 231 and his better work-rate that ultimately counted, even though so few punches landing was said to be unheard of in a distance fight of such magnitude. By the seventh Klitschko was cut under the left eye, and in the tenth he was cut over the right eye following a clash of heads before Fury was docked a point in the 11th for punching behind the head. The final session saw Fury out of the blocks fast just to make sure that there were no doubts in the judges' minds, holding his arms aloft at the bell.

Just a week or so later, after agreeing to a contractual return against Klitschko, the IBF stripped Fury for not meeting their mandatory challenger, Vyacheslav Glazkov, instead.

On 19 December, Luis Ortiz retained his WBA 'interim' title when stopping Bryant Jennings inside seven rounds at the Turning Stone Casino Resort, Verona, New York, USA. Having taken on Tony Thompson (w co 6 at The Armoury, Washington DC, USA on 5 March 2016), Ortiz failed to be given WBA approval as an 'interim' defence as his opponent was not rated in the top 15.

Ruslan Chagaev lost his WBA 'second tier' title on 5 March 2016 when he was stopped in ten rounds by Lucas Browne at the Coliseum Sports Hall, Drozd, Russia. When Browne forfeited the title on 15 May 2016 after testing positive for Clenbuterol, a banned drug, Chagaev was reinstated. Stripped on 25 July 2016 for not paying his sanctioning fee, Chagaev announced his retirement from boxing due to ongoing eye problems.

Fury relinquished his WBA and WBO titles on 12 October 2016 in order to give himself time to recover from depression away from the public eye. This was followed by the BBBoC suspending his licence pending further investigation into anti-doping and medical matters.

Luis Ortiz was stripped of the WBA 'interim' belt on 30 October 2016 after failing to agree to a defence against Alexander Ustinov.

16 January 2016. Charles Martin w rsc 3 Vyacheslav Glazkov.
Venue: Barclays Centre, Brooklyn, NYC, New York, USA. **Recognition:** IBF. **Referee:** Albert Earl Brown.
Fight Summary: Fighting for the vacant IBF title forfeited by Tyson Fury, it was Martin (249½), a southpaw, who came out the winner at 1.50 of the third after the unfortunate Glazkov (218) tore the anterior cruciate ligament in his right knee and was unable to fight on. Up until then it had not been much of a contest, with little action forthcoming. The injury came about in the third after Glazkov went down without being hit and although getting up when he went over again the referee brought matters to a halt.

16 January 2016. Deontay Wilder w rsc 9 Artur Szpilka.
Venue: Barclays Centre, Brooklyn, NYC, New York, USA. **Recognition:** WBC. **Referee:** Michael Griffin.
Fight Summary: Remaining elusive right up until the end, the southpaw challenger gave Wilder (228¾) a run for his money as he moved in and out with the jab to frustrate his man before getting away. There was never much between them but by the fifth Wilder was beginning to have some success with the right hand, Szpilka (239) being forced to take a cracking uppercut in that session. Gradually Wilder was cutting the ring down and several times he went close before eventually catching Szpilka in the ninth with a cracking short right to the jaw. With the count being a formality, the referee called it off at 'five' when it became apparent that Szpilka required immediate treatment.

9 April 2016. Anthony Joshua w co 2 Charles Martin.
Venue: O2 Arena, Greenwich, London, England. **Recognition:** IBF. **Referee:** Jean-Pierre Van Imschoot.
Fight Summary: After just 15 pro contests the 2012 Olympic champion, Joshua (244), was clearly ready to be unleashed in the eyes of his management. With Joshua moving in on the southpaw champion from the opening bell there was an air of expectancy as he started to unload solid shots. Having hurt Martin (245) towards the end of the first Joshua was soon at work in the second, and after being belted to the body the American moved straight into a cracking right hand that left him on the floor. At first it looked as though Martin would not make it, but when he did he was there for the taking as far as Joshua was concerned. Getting up, wide open defensively, Martin again walked into a smashing right that deposited him on the floor. This time it was curtains for Martin as the referee continued counting him out, the finish being timed at 1.32.

25 June 2016. Anthony Joshua w rsc 7 Dominic Breazeale.
Venue: O2 Arena, Greenwich, London, England. **Recognition:** IBF. **Referee:** Howard Foster.
Fight Summary: Boxing patiently against a determined challenger who mainly resided behind a high guard, Joshua (243¼) showed that he could box as well as punch when gradually walking his man down. Winning every round against the slightly taller Breazeale (255), using jabs, hooks and an occasional solid right, Joshua was ready to get going by the seventh. Finally catching up with Breazeale after a hard left had shaken him, Joshua took his man to the ropes where he proceeded to thump him down with punches from both hands. On getting up there was no

respite for Breazeale, and following vicious blows from both hands he fell to the floor where he was immediately rescued by the referee on the 1.01 mark.

16 July 2016. Deontay Wilder w rtd 8 Chris Arreola.
Venue: Legacy Arena, Birmingham, Alabama, USA. **Recognition:** WBC. **Referee:** Jack Reiss.
Fight Summary: Winning every round contested, Wilder (226¼) maintained his undefeated record when forcing the challenger's corner to retire their man at the end of the eighth round despite damaging his right hand in the fourth. There was no doubting that Arreola (246¼) was always dangerous, but in the fourth he was rescued by the bell after being battered to the floor by a volley of solid shots from both hands. Although Arreola continued it was obvious that he was taking too much punishment from Wilder's thudding fists and it was no surprise when the end came.

Heavyweight Boxers' Index:
(Country of birth where known/Domicile - birthplace and domicile are the same unless stated)

A
Tomasz Adamek (Poland/USA)
Omelio Agramonte (Cuba)
Henry Akinwande (England/USA)
Muhammad Ali (USA)
Tom Allen (England)
Charley Anderson (USA)
Harold Anderson (USA)
Bob Armstrong (USA)
Chris Arreola (USA)
Johnny Arthur (South Africa)
Fred Atwater (USA)
Ray Austin (USA)

B
Buddy Baer (USA)
Max Baer (USA)
Bob Baker (USA)
Joe Baksi (USA)
Sonny Banks (USA)
Gunnar Barlund (Finland/USA)
Nick Barone (USA)
Monte Barrett (USA)
Dave Barry (Ireland/England)
Jim Barry (USA)
Wes Bascom (USA)
Vaughn Bean (USA)
Boston Bearcat (USA)
Owen Beck (Jamaica/USA)
Woolf Bendoff (England)
Ray Bennett (USA)
Michael Bentt (England/USA)
Trevor Berbick (Jamaica/Canada)
Freddie Beshore (USA)
Wayne Bethea (USA)
Melio Bettina (USA)
David Bey (USA)
Tyrell Biggs (USA)
Black Bill (USA)
Jimmy Bivins (USA)
Jurgen Blin (Germany)
Eddie Blunt (USA)
Duane Bobick (USA)
Harry Bobo (USA)
Nate Bolden (USA)
Oscar Bonavena (Argentina/USA)
Tony Bosnich (USA)
Cedric Boswell (USA)
Frans Botha (South Africa/USA)
Riddick Bowe (USA)
Jim Braddock (USA)
Fred Bradley (USA)

Dominic Breazeale (USA)
Bill Brennan (USA)
Jorge Brescia (Argentina/USA)
Lamon Brewster (USA)
Shannon Briggs (USA)
Cesar Brion (Argentina)
James Broad (USA)
Calvin Brock (USA)
Battling Brooks (USA)
Lou Brooks (USA)
Alfred Big Boy Brown (USA)
Natie Brown (USA)
Lucas Browne (Australia)
Frank Bruno (England)
Dan Bucceroni (USA)
Joe Bugner (Hungary/England & Australia)
Dick Burge (England)
Jack Burke (Ireland/England)
Red Burman (USA)
Tommy Burns (Canada)
Joe Butler (USA)
Lionel Butler (USA)
George Byers (Canada/USA)
Joe Bygraves (Jamaica/England)
Chris Byrd (USA)

C
Ralph Calloway (USA)
Marvin Camel (USA)
Jim Cameron (USA)
Victorio Campolo (Italy/Argentina)
Tony Cancela (USA)
Patsy Cardiff (Canada/USA)
Primo Carnera (Italy)
Georges Carpentier (France)
Carl Carter (Cuba/USA)
Harold Carter (USA)
Jim Casey (Ireland/USA)
Franco Cavicchi (Italy)
Ruslan Chagaev (Uzbekistan/Germany)
Arthur Chambers (England)
Eddie Chambers (USA)
Colion Chaney (USA)
Ezzard Charles (USA)
Pierre Charles (Belgium)
Manuel Charr (Lebanon/Germany)
Leon Chevalier (USA)
Frank Childs (USA)
Dereck Chisora (Zimbabwe/England)
Joe Choynski (USA)
George Chrisp (England)
KO Christner (USA)

Heavyweight Division

George Chuvalo (Canada)
Jeff Clark
Roy Ace Clark
Cassius Clay-Muhammad Ali (USA)
Von Clay (USA)
Bob Cleroux (Canada)
Neal Clisby (USA)
Randall Cobb (USA)
Walter Cobb (USA)
Don Cockell (England)
Gerrie Coetzee (South Africa)
Pierre Coetzer (South Africa)
Pat Comiskey (USA)
Billy Conn (USA)
George Cook (Australia/England)
Gerry Cooney (USA)
Bert Cooper (USA)
Henry Cooper (England)
Jean-Pierre Coopman (Belgium)
James J. Corbett (USA)
Eduardo Corletti (Argentina)
Pietro Corri (USA)
Josh Coshett (England)
George Kid Cotton (USA)
Frank Craig (USA)
Joe Craig (Ireland)
Dan Creedon (New Zealand/Australia)
PO Curran (Ireland/England)

D
Pat Daly (Ireland/England)
Francesco Damiani (Italy)
Frankie Daniels (USA)
Terry Daniels (USA)
Jimmy Darcy (Romania/USA)
Carl Davis Drumond (Costa Rica)
Charley Davis (England)
Jack Davis (England)
Johnny Davis (USA)
Mike DeJohn (USA)
Jack Delaney (Canada/USA)
Jack DeMave (Netherlands/USA)
Jack Dempsey (USA)
Harry Slounch Dixon (England)
Leonard Dixon (USA)
Michael Dokes (USA)
Gus Dorazio (USA)
James Buster Douglas (USA)
Jack Douglass (USA)
Johnny Du Plooy (South Africa)
Johann Duhaupas (France)
Richard Dunn (England)

E
Jimmy Ellis (USA)

Joe Erskine (Wales)
Al Ettore (USA)
Alfredo Evangelista (Uruguay/Spain)

F
Tommy Farr (Wales)
Peter Felix (Virgin Islands/Australia)
Jesse Ferguson (USA)
Sandy Ferguson (Canada/USA)
Jack Finnegan (USA)
Luis Angel Firpo (Argentina)
Willi Fischer (Germany)
Fitzie Fitzpatrick (USA)
Bob Fitzsimmons (England/USA)
Henry Flakes (USA)
Fireman Jim Flynn (USA)
Johnny Flynn (USA)
Zora Folley (USA)
George Foreman (USA)
Justin Fortune (Australia/USA)
Bob Foster (USA)
Mac Foster (USA)
Pierre Fourie (South Africa)
Tiger Jack Fox (USA)
Scott Frank (USA)
Lem Franklin (USA)
Joe Frazier (USA)
Marvis Frazier (USA)
Fred Fulton (USA)
Tyson Fury (England)

G
Jack Gagnon (Canada/USA)
Larry Gains (Canada/England)
Tony Galento (USA)
Jose Luis Garcia (Venezuela)
Jack Gardner (England)
Tommy Gibbons (USA)
Tompkin Gilbert (England)
Vyacheslav Glazkov (Ukraine/USA)
Joe Goddard (Australia)
George Godfrey (Canada/USA 1878-1896)
George Godfrey (USA 1919-1937)
Arturo Godoy (Chile)
Andrew Golota (Poland/USA)
Juan Carlos Gomez (Cuba/Germany)
Tommy Gomez (USA)
Jorge Luis Gonzalez (Cuba/USA)
Bud Gorman (USA)
George Grant (USA)
Michael Grant (USA)
Morris Grant (USA)
Harry Greb (USA)
Silas Green (Canada/USA)
Alf Greenfield (England)

Corn Griffin (USA)
Tuffy Griffiths (USA)
Joe Grim (Italy/USA)

H
Charles Hadley (USA)
Iron Hague (England)
Steve Hamas (USA)
Hank Hankinson (USA)
Knute Hansen (Denmark)
Morris Harris (USA)
Roy Harris (USA)
Seal Harris (USA)
Audley Harrison (England)
Tommy Harrison (USA)
Marvin Hart (USA)
Cleve Hawkins (USA)
Long Tom Hawkins (USA)
David Haye (England)
Ludwig Haymann (Germany)
Leroy Haynes (USA)
Tom Heeney (New Zealand)
Clarence Henry (USA)
Gunner Hewitt (England)
Herbie Hide (Nigeria/England)
Joe Hipp (USA)
John Holman (USA)
Larry Holmes (USA)
Evander Holyfield (USA)
Vincenz Hower (Germany)
Marco Huck (Serbia/Germany)
Babe Hunt (USA)
Billy Hunter (USA)

I
Sultan Ibragimov (Russia)
Ray Impelletiere (USA)

J
Buddy Jackson (Panama/USA)
John Jackson (England)
Peter Jackson (Virgin Islands/Australia)
Phil Jackson (USA)
Tommy Jackson (USA)
Tut Jackson (USA)
Young Peter Jackson (USA)
Joe Jeannette (USA)
Derrick Jefferson (USA)
James J. Jeffries (USA)
Bryant Jennings (USA)
Ingemar Johansson (Sweden)
Alonzo Johnson (USA)
Amos Johnson (USA)
Andy Johnson (USA)
Battling Johnson (Denmark/USA)

Battling Jim Johnson (USA)
Bunny Johnson (Jamaica/England)
Clem Johnson (Guyana/USA)
Harold Johnson (USA)
Jack Johnson (USA)
John Lester Johnson (USA)
Kevin Johnson (USA)
Kirk Johnson (Canada)
McHenry Johnson (USA)
Walter Johnson (USA)
Young Jack Johnson (USA)
Doug Jones (USA)
Leroy Jones (USA)
Roy Jones (USA)
Anthony Joshua (England)

K
Al Kaufman (USA)
Lateef Kayode (Nigeria/USA)
Soldier Kearns (USA)
Les Kennedy (USA)
Tom Kennedy (USA)
Yank Kenney (USA)
Stanley Ketchel (USA)
Dixie Kid (USA)
Jake Kilrain (USA 1879-1899)
Jake Kilrain (USA 1924-1928)
Vitali Klitschko (Kyrgyzstan/Ukraine)
Wladimir Klitschko (Kyrgyzstan/Ukraine)
Klondike (USA)
Jack Knifton (Scotland)
Kallie Knoetze (South Africa)
Buddy Knox (USA)
Luan Krasniqi (Kosovo/Germany)
Solly Krieger (USA)

L
Bill Lang (Australia)
Sam Langford (Canada/USA)
Art Lasky (USA)
Roland LaStarza (USA)
Bob Lawson (USA)
Rex Layne (USA)
Roy Lazer (USA)
Alex Leapai (Samoa/Australia)
Scott LeDoux (USA)
Elijah Lee (USA)
Andre Lenglet (France)
Gus Lesnevich (USA)
Charles Lester (USA)
Battling Levinsky (USA)
King Levinsky (USA)
John Henry Lewis (USA)
Lennox Lewis (England)
Siarhei Liakhovich (Belarus/USA)

Heavyweight Division

Amos Lincoln (USA)
Sonny Liston (USA)
Brian London (England)
Tom Longer (England)
Tommy Loughran (USA)
Joe Louis (USA)
Alberto Lovell (Argentina)
Ron Lyle (USA)

M
Jem Mace (England)
Eddie Machen (USA)
Dick Madden (USA)
Peter Maher (Ireland/USA)
Ed Mahone (USA
Jim Maloney (USA)
Nathan Mann (USA)
Rocky Marciano (USA)
Jack Marshall (USA)
Marty Marshall (USA)
Charles Martin (USA)
Denver Ed Martin (USA)
Everett Martin (USA)
Leotis Martin (USA)
Oleg Maskaev (Kazakhstan/Russia)
Charley Massera (USA)
Buster Mathis (USA)
Harry Matthews (USA)
Tami Mauriello (USA)
Zeljko Mavrovic (Croatia)
Joey Maxim (USA)
Danny McAlinden (Northern Ireland)
Jack McAuliffe 11 (Canada/USA)
Joe McAuliffe (USA)
Archie McBride (USA)
Dominick McCaffrey (USA)
Oliver McCall (USA)
Luther McCarty (USA)
Jameel McCline (USA)
Don McCorkindale (South Africa/England)
Jack McCormick (USA)
Pat McCourt (Northern Ireland)
Al McCoy (USA)
Charles Kid McCoy (USA)
Battling Jim McCreary (USA)
Victor McLaglen (England)
Tom McNeeley (USA)
Mike McTigue (Ireland/USA)
Sam McVea (USA)
Julio Mederos (Cuba/USA)
Kali Meehan (New Zealand/Australia)
Bernardo Mercado (Colombia)
Ray Mercer (USA)
William Coddy Middings (England)
Karl Mildenberger (Germany)

Johnny Miler (USA)
Dave Mills (USA)
Freddie Mills (England)
Billy Miske (USA)
Charlie Mitchell (England)
Alex Miteff (Argentina/USA)
Gunner Moir (England)
Eric Molina (USA)
Joe Monte (Brazil/USA)
Archie Moore (USA)
Michael Moorer (USA)
Frank Moran (USA)
Jean-Marc Mormeck (Guadeloupe/France)
Carl Morris (USA)
Tommy Morrison (USA)
Jack Mullen (England)
Jack Munroe (Canada)
Lee Q. Murray (USA)
Phil Muscato (USA)
Terry Mustain (USA)
Tony Musto (USA)

N
Daniel Neto (Argentina)
Heinz Neuhaus (Germany)
Harry Neumier (England)
Walter Neusel (Germany)
Kid Norfolk (USA)
Charley Norkus (USA)
Ken Norton (USA)
Lou Nova (USA)

O
Jim O'Brien (USA)
Philadelphia Jack O'Brien (USA)
Steve O'Donnell (Australia)
Ossie Ocasio (Puerto Rico)
Lee Oma (USA)
Fres Oquendo (Puerto Rico/USA)
Luis Ortiz (Cuba/USA)
Battling Owens (USA)
Cowboy Billy Owens (USA)

P
Greg Page (USA)
Jack Palmer (England)
Al Palzer (USA)
James J. Parker (Canada)
Tom Parks (Ireland)
Mate Parlov (Croatia)
Bob Pastor (USA)
Willie Pastrano (USA)
Floyd Patterson (USA)
Ray Patterson (USA)
Johnny Paychek (USA)

Rusty Payne (USA)
Arthur Pelkey (Canada)
Gregorio Peralta (Argentina)
Patsy Perroni (USA)
Okello Peter (Uganda/Japan)
Samuel Peter (Nigeria/USA)
George Peters (USA)
Jack Petersen (Wales)
Big Boy Peterson (USA)
Billy Peyton (USA)
Francesco Pianeta (Italy/Germany)
Bill Poland (USA)
Stanley Poreda (USA)
Ewart Potgieter (South Africa)
Alexander Povetkin (Russia)
Ivan Prebeg (Croatia)
Ted Pritchard (Wales/England)
Sam Pruitt (USA)
Kubrat Pulev (Bulgaria)

Q
Dwight Muhammad Qawi (USA)
Jerry Quarry (USA)
Scaldy Bill Quinn (USA)

R
Pete Rademacher (USA)
Hasim Rahman (USA)
Lee Ramage (USA)
Manuel Ramos (Mexico)
Elmer Ray (USA)
Damon Reed (USA)
Jack Renault (Canada)
Charley Retzlaff (USA)
Jimmy Richards (South Africa)
John Riggins (USA)
O'Dell Riley (USA)
Roger Rischer (USA)
Johnny Risko (Austria/USA)
Roberto Roberti (Italy)
Dick Roberts (England)
Jem Roche (Ireland)
George Rodel (South Africa/USA)
Adilson Rodrigues (Brazil)
Lucien Rodriguez (Morocco/France)
Jose Roman (Puerto Rico/USA)
Vicente Rondon (Venezuela)
Jack Root (Czech Republic/USA)
Jack Roper (USA)
Tony Ross (Italy/USA)
Jacques Royer-Crecy (France)
Jack Rozier (USA)
Donovan Ruddock (Jamaica/Canada)
Gus Ruhlin (USA)
John Ruiz (USA)

Australian Jim Ryan (Australia)

S
Corrie Sanders (South Africa)
Bob Satterfield (USA)
Cloggy Saunders (England)
Lee Savold (USA)
Jack Scales (England)
Ernie Schaaf (USA)
Max Schmeling (Germany)
Freddie Schott (USA)
Mike Schreck (USA)
Axel Schulz (Germany)
Mike Schutte (South Africa)
Phil Scott (England)
Tom Scrutton (England)
Joe Sekyra (USA)
Bruce Seldon (USA)
Mike Shallow (Canada)
Jack Sharkey (USA)
Tom Sharkey (Ireland/USA)
Earnie Shavers (USA)
Curtis Sheppard (USA)
Charles Shufford (USA)
Eddie Simms (USA)
Abe Simon (USA)
Matt Skelton (England)
Jimmy Slade (USA)
Frank Slavin (Australia)
C. C. Smith (USA)
Denver Ed Smith (England/USA)
Ford Smith (USA)
Gunboat Smith (USA)
Harry Smith (England)
Homer Smith (USA)
James Bonecrusher Smith (USA)
James Tiger Smith (Wales)
Jem Smith (England)
Jewey Smith (England)
Renaldo Snipes (USA)
Odlanier Solis (Cuba/USA)
Albert Sosnowski (Poland)
Erminio Spalla (Italy)
Thad Spencer (USA)
Leon Spinks (USA)
Michael Spinks (USA)
Bill Squires (Australia)
Ron Stander (USA)
Randy Stephens (USA)
Jem Stewart (Scotland)
Bermane Stiverne (Haiti/USA)
Young Stribling (USA)
Maurice Strickland (New Zealand)
Charley Strong (USA)
Jim Styles (England)

Heavyweight Division

Jack Twin Sullivan (USA)
John L. Sullivan (USA)
Obed Sullivan (USA)
Johnny Summerlin (USA)
Sergeant Sunshine (England)
Artur Szpilka (Poland)

T
Olle Tandberg (Sweden)
Steffen Tangstad (Norway)
Bill Tate (USA)
John Tate (USA)
Ben Taylor (England)
George Taylor (USA)
Ernie Terrell (USA)
Harry Thomas (USA)
Pinklon Thomas (USA)
Cyclone Johnny Thompson (USA)
Jack Thompson (USA0
Tony Thompson (USA)
Turkey Thompson (USA)
Geoff Thorne (England)
James Tillis (USA)
Roscoe Toles (USA)
Tim Tomashek (USA)
James Toney (USA)
Jack Townsend (USA)
Jack Trammell (USA)
Willie Troy (USA)
David Tua (Samoa/New Zealand)
Tony Tubbs (USA)
Tony Tucker (USA)
Gene Tunney (USA)
Mike Tyson (USA)

U
Alexander Ustinov (Russia/Belarus)
Paulino Uzcudun (Spain)

V
Nino Valdes (Cuba)
Pat Valentino (USA)
Nikolay Valuev (Russia)
Punch Vaughn (England)
Matias Ariel Vidondo (Argentina)
Otto Von Porat (Sweden/USA)

W
Mariusz Wach (Poland/USA)
Dick Wagner (USA)
Jersey Joe Walcott (USA)
Joe Walcott (Guyana/USA)
Al Walker (USA)

Andy Walker (USA)
Buddy Walker (USA)
James J. Walker (USA)
Mickey Walker (USA)
Obie Walker (USA)
Toff Wall (England)
Coley Wallace (USA)
Gordon Wallace (Canada)
Earl Walls (Canada)
Jimmy Walls (Bermuda/USA)
Jack Wannop (England)
Rough House Ware (USA)
Cyclone Billy Warren (USA/Ireland)
Bill Watkins (USA)
Andrzej Wawrzyk (Poland)
Mike Weaver (USA)
Bill Weinberg (USA)
Charley Weinert (Hungary/USA)
Scott Welch (England)
Bombardier Billy Wells (England)
Chuck Wepner (USA)
Bert Whitehurst (USA)
Dave Whitlock (USA)
Chuck Wiggins (USA)
Deontay Wilder (USA)
Jess Willard (USA)
John Wille (USA)
Carl Williams (USA)
Cleveland Williams (USA)
Danny Williams (England)
Jeremy Williams (USA)
Jim Williams (England/USA)
Johnny Williams (Wales)
Mike Williams (USA)
DaVarryl Williamson (USA)
J. B. Williamson (USA)
Ed Wills (USA)
Harry Wills (USA)
Billy Wilson (USA)
Charlie Wilson (England)
Tug Wilson (England)
Tim Witherspoon (USA)
Bruce Woodcock (England)
Harry Woodson (USA)
Bearcat Wright (USA)

Y
Jimmy Young (USA)

Z
Lorenzo Zanon (Italy)
Alexander Zolkin (Russia/USA)
Dave Zyglewicz (USA)

Printed in Great Britain
by Amazon